European Conference of Ministers of Transport

12TH INTERNATIONAL SYMPOSIUM
ON THEORY AND PRACTICE IN TRANSPORT ECONOMICS

Transport Growth in Question

CEMT 1953 1993 ECMT

THE EUROPEAN CONFERENCE OF MINISTERS OF TRANSPORT (ECMT)

The European Conference of Ministers of Transport (ECMT) is an inter-governmental organisation established by a Protocol signed in Brussels on 17th October 1953. The Council of the Conference comprises the Ministers of Transport of 28 European countries[1]. The work of the Council of Ministers is prepared by a Committee of Deputies.

The purposes of the Conference are:

a) to take whatever measures may be necessary to achieve, at general or regional level, the most efficient use and rational development of European inland transport of international importance;

b) to co-ordinate and promote the activities of international organisations concerned with European inland transport, taking into account the work of supranational authorities in this field.

The matters generally studied by ECMT - and on which the Ministers take decisions - include: the general lines of transport policy; investment in the sector; infrastructural needs; specific aspects of the development of rail, road and inland waterways transport; combined transport issues; urban travel; road safety and traffic rules, signs and signals; access to transport for people with mobility problems. Other subjects now being examined in depth are: the future applications of new technologies, protection of the environment, and the integration of the Central and Eastern European countries in the European transport market. Statistical analyses of trends in traffic and investment are published each year, thus throwing light on the prevailing economic situation.

The ECMT organises Round Tables and Symposia. Their conclusions are considered by the competent organs of the Conference, under the authority of the Committee of Deputies, so that the latter may formulate proposals for policy decisions to be submitted to the Ministers.

The ECMT Documentation Centre maintains the TRANSDOC database, which can be accessed on-line via the telecommunications network.

For administrative purposes, the ECMT Secretariat is attached to the Secretariat of the Organisation for Economic Co-operation and Development (OECD).

1. Austria, Belgium, Bulgaria, Croatia, Czech and Slovak Federal Republic, Denmark, Estonia, Finland, France, Germany, Greece, Hungary, Ireland, Italy, Latvia, Lithuania, Luxembourg, Netherlands, Norway, Poland, Portugal, Rumania, Slovenia, Spain, Sweden, Switzerland, Turkey and United Kingdom. (Associate Member countries: Australia, Canada, Japan, New Zealand, the United States. Observer countries: Morocco, Russia.)

Publié en français sous le titre :

12ème SYMPOSIUM INTERNATIONAL
SUR LA THÉORIE ET LA PRATIQUE DANS L'ÉCONOMIE DES TRANSPORTS
LA CROISSANCE DU TRANSPORT EN QUESTION

ECMT publications are distributed by the OECD Publications Service,
2, rue André-Pascal, 75775 PARIS CEDEX 16, France

TABLE OF CONTENTS

OPENING SESSION

Adresses by:

N. GELESTATHIS
Minister for Transports and Communications
of Greece

Chairman of the ECMT Council of Ministers

G. AURBACH
Acting Secretary-General of the ECMT

N. Gelestathis

As president of the European Conference of Ministers of Transport during the year 1992, it is a great pleasure for me to address you today, at our opening session of this twelfth ECMT Symposium.

For more than twenty years now the Conference has been organising these meetings, centred on scientific research in the sphere of transport economics, the aim being to enable specialists to examine the specific aspects of the subject in greater depth. In this respect, the main topic for the present symposium is particularly appropriate since growth in the transport sector is indeed in question. We need only briefly examine the problem of congestion in urban areas to see at once that it is practically impossible to cope with further increases in traffic.

How have we reached that point? The one single factor with the greatest influence on the structure of urban travel over the past thirty years has been the five-fold increase in the rate of car ownership and use. Even the economic recession has had little effect on use of the private car. Moreover, user costs have tended to diminish in the course of these recent decades, rising only slightly during the oil crises.

Given its flexibility and convenience, the private car does, of course, have qualities that seem beyond the means of public transport services, and it has in fact also helped to shape the geographical layout of urban areas. The dispersal of housing around the outskirts of towns took place as a result of the more general use of the car. Even in cities with well-established traditions, the population has tended to move away from the inner city to enjoy the advantages of more residential space, a trend that may also reduce the importance of central areas and lead to the development of towns with a number of centres of activity.

These trends do not, as a whole, encourage the use of public transport which cannot really provide fine-meshed services covering an entire area. Some specialists therefore consider that greater use will continue to be made of the car in the coming years despite the risk of congestion becoming even more widespread, a problem that certainly has to be dealt with since congestion in and around towns is already at unacceptable levels and we cannot ignore the consequences in terms of deterioration of the quality of life, disamenities, pollution and energy wastage. The public is, moreover, extremely sensitive to these problems, as is quite evident from the advances made by our ecological movements.

Furthermore, by making places less accessible, congestion is detrimental to the development of our economies, since traffic has to be facilitated if transport is to fulfil its function as a link between economic activities.

Accordingly, policymakers have realised what they have to do, and different approaches to the restriction of traffic are now to be found in a number of countries, the aim being to reduce car traffic in town centres and promote the use of public transport. In Athens, for example, cars whose registration plates end in an even number are allowed on the roads on certain days, cars with odd-numbered plates on other days. In some countries a financial instrument is used in the form of charging for road use. Pedestrian zones have been introduced in city centres almost everywhere.

If these measures are to be effective, the discouragement of car use must be accompanied by improvements in public transport services. For instance, to cater for people travelling in from the suburbs, park-and-ride facilities have to be provided at peripheral metro stations which give access to the centre of the city.

A whole range of such measures taken together will certainly be called for in order to reduce congestion and damage to the environment.

From a more general standpoint, it can be said that the awareness of the need to protect the environment is not a particularly recent development, since the ECMT's last symposium in Athens in 1973 had as one of its topics: "The impact of transport on the quality of life". We have gradually realised that our environment has to be protected against the threat of pollution. Transport is one source of many disamenities that spoil the quality of life and interfere with the ecological balance of our planet. To begin with, the growth of transport would seem inevitable since it accompanies the economic growth that we want to achieve. An increase in personal mobility is also synonymous with freedom and cannot easily be curbed by any measures that would be well received.

It is an established fact, however, that uncontrolled growth of transport can be destructive. Energy sources are not inexhaustible, while air pollution from emissions creates ecological imbalances and damages everybody's health.

Transport is also one of the main sources of noise. All these factors suggest that our practices have to be reappraised. In this respect we are certainly confronted with a dilemma since, while we all agree that the opening of European markets and freedom of trade throughout the Continent must not be called into question, at the same time we know that we cannot continue to treat the environment in the same way as we have done in the past.

These problems are of immediate concern to Ministers of Transport and, in this sense, ECMT has already taken action in that the Ministers devoted a special session of one whole day to the question of transport and the environment. The Resolution adopted at that time laid down the principles of a transport policy that would give greater consideration to environmental issues, specifying in particular that:

1. As far as possible in practice, vehicles should make use of the best available technology to reduce pollution;

2. Traffic should be managed in such a way as to ensure that users pay the full costs they generate, including those of damage to the environment;

3. Infrastructure should be constructed and used in such a way as to reduce environmental damage to the strict minimum.

Since this Resolution was adopted in November 1989, the ECMT Council of Ministers has consulted with representatives of motor vehicle manufacturers with a view to the production of cleaner, quieter and more fuel-efficient vehicles.

Another significant development was the Council's recent decision to introduce the concept of the "green" lorry in the context of the ECMT multilateral quota for the international transport of goods by road. Such a vehicle must comply with more stringent standards than a conventional vehicle as regards emissions of noise and other pollution. On the basis of this concept it has been possible to increase the multilateral quota while at the same time curbing the impact on the environment. This is a very important point insofar as it is to be feared that the technical advances achieved by means of these vehicles may in future be negated by the growth in traffic, thus showing how important it is to have the most advanced vehicles in terms of environmental protection and energy consumption.

Where energy consumption is concerned, progress has been made with respect to every type of road vehicle, whether passenger or freight. However, vigilance is now called for with respect to another trend, namely that of constructing and marketing increasingly powerful vehicles which in turn can negate all the progress made in terms of fuel efficiency. The road vehicle of the future should be cleaner, safer and more fuel efficient in order to comply with the requirements for a better quality environment and greater safety on the roads, thus providing for a more harmonious relationship between economic development and protection of the environment.

As we all know, each of these issues is of current concern and calls for responses by researchers. That is clearly the *raison d'être* of a symposium, and I am quite sure that our work here will help to provide these responses. I am sure that everybody will appreciate at its true dimension, as I do, the effort made by our hosts in this respect.

G. Aurbach

For the twelfth time since 1964, the ECMT has organised an International Symposium on Theory and Practice in Transport Economics. For the twelfth time it has opened its institutional framework to bring together those who are professionally concerned with the transport sector -- scientists and researchers, policymakers, representatives of the various modes, transport workers and users, and of government departments and international organisations -- with a view to examining together a current topic of the utmost importance. The City of Lisbon is today carrying on a tradition that has now existed for nearly thirty years.

The Lisbon Symposium does, in fact, represent an opening in two respects so far as the Conference is concerned: a traditional opening, as I have said, in terms of the diversity of backgrounds of participants from the transport sector, but also a new opening from a geographical standpoint, since we are welcoming here for the first time our colleagues from the European countries in transition; and, if I may, I should like to extend to them our special greetings, in that three countries of central and eastern Europe -- the Czech and Slovak Federal Republic, Hungary and Poland -- are now full Members of the Conference, while Russia is attending in the place of the former USSR as an observer, and five other countries -- the three Baltic States, Bulgaria and Rumania -- have, likewise, recently acquired observer status.

The Symposiums, which are held once every three years, are among the activities undertaken by the ECMT in the sphere of scientific research, activities which -- as most of you already know -- include the more frequent Round Tables reserved for a smaller group of specialists who examine a highly specific problem in depth, as well as Seminars which can be said to occupy an intermediate position.

I should like to stress the fact that Symposiums are an essential link in the ECMT's chain of operation, since they not only back up the Organisation's other research activities by providing fresh impetus and broadening their scope but also enable the Conference to become better equipped to fulfil its policymaking function.

What, then, is the place of research in a policymaking body like the ECMT, which is primarily a forum for consultation and concerted action among Ministers of Transport?

I think I can say that our Conference was among the first intergovernmental organisations to recognise the need to set up a European system for co-operation in the sphere of research to serve as a source of reference for policy decision-making.

The topics for research, including those of Symposiums, are accordingly selected by a Committee of government representatives so as to ensure that they relate as closely as possible to matters of concern to policymakers while, at the same time, those involved enjoy the complete independence of spirit that is essential to ensure that the research can indeed be called "scientific".

This free expression of scientific opinion is consistent with the ECMT's aim to base its action on a whole range of considerations, some of which may sometimes be taken to be early warning signs and so, by definition, are not always conventional.

The subsequent course of events has in no way detracted from the importance of the system set up by the ECMT for this purpose during the 1960s. Quite the contrary, since what might at first have been regarded as some as a kind of intellectual luxury, has over the years proved to be a precious, an extremely precious, instrument for shaping policy. Even if the contribution made by economic research cannot always be incorporated as such in policy decisions, the line of approach that it indicates is real enough and corresponds more than ever to the demands of our time and to the need for decision-makers to make the most rational choices possible.

Why was the topic "Transport Growth in Question" selected for the Twelfth Symposium?

As matters now stand, I really do not believe there is any need to establish either the importance or the current relevance of the topic. It is enough to look at recent trends in traffic in Europe, especially in the road sector which, on the strength of its inherent qualities, has shown such strong growth. And, may I say, has at the same time become the victim of its own success in becoming a focus for the major problems experienced in the transport sector today.

The fact is that, for many years, the rates of growth for road freight traffic, especially on international routes, have been significantly higher than those for the increase in economic activity as a whole, largely as a result of specialisation in our economies and, accordingly, an increasingly marked international division of labour -- itself the source of our standard of living and well-being.

That is precisely what we wanted, otherwise we would not have created the European Communities or EFTA. We would not have concluded the agreement on the European Economic Area, nor would we have established all the other facilities for international trade.

However, in the light of these developments with respect to flows of trade and tourism and the consequences in terms of transport, the populations of sensitive regions such as the Alps in particular -- but also regions with high density populations around conurbations and major traffic arteries -- are increasingly voicing their protest against the damage to their environment.

The ecological movement has, over the years, become a movement that must be taken seriously from both the political and technical standpoints, a fact that we have too often seen confirmed by the refusal to allow the construction of new infrastructure, whether it be for roads, railways or airports.

There is, however, a severe shortfall of land transport capacity in Europe, especially in those parts of our continent where the major flows of traffic are concentrated and cross. This pattern, already established in western Europe with its preponderantly north-south flows, is now being compounded by the east-west flows.

As we know -- and as ECMT studies have clearly shown -- for quite some time now, the overall pattern of investment in infrastructure has been lagging a long way behind the increase in traffic.

While the situation has clearly improved somewhat over the past few years, the fundamental question today is not one of trends or carefully balanced proportions but is, in fact, an existential question: how can we continue to ensure the future development of mobility and trade flows? How can we prevent the total asphyxiation of land transport at particularly critical locations? How can we prudently assume the responsibility for the sector *vis-à-vis* society as a whole? How can we take the earliest possible advantage of the most advanced technologies in the process of developing our transport systems? How can we involve the railways, inland waterways and, where appropriate, short-sea shipping in this question of growth, as a means of achieving a more balanced modal split?

While it is true that the present recession, which is lasting longer than might originally have been thought, has to some extent made these questions less pressing, in the normal course of events economic growth can be expected to resume in a Europe in which a large part will have completed the establishment of its Single Market and another equally large part can look forward to tangible results from the current reforms in the process of transition towards the market economy -- in short, in a Europe that has closed one chapter in its history and is now very gradually moving into a period of co-operation with more intensive flows of trade and closer relations.

In such a context, still fragile in many respects, it would be disastrous to find a state of paralysis at points where mobility is most crucial, to see congestion on the increase everywhere, together with damage to the environment and the subsequent rejection by the public of particular patterns of development that are in any case inevitable, such as transit traffic. We must certainly bear in mind that our economies, based on the division of labour, must be able to rely on a fluid and efficient transport system, otherwise the inadequacy of the system may very well promptly bring about a recession, especially as there is no possibility of finding short-term solutions in such circumstances.

We are therefore confronted with a profound difficulty which calls for the urgent attention of policymakers, all those engaged in a professional capacity in the transport sector, researchers, etc. -- in short, all of you here today.

The difficulty has, in fact, already led some people to call into question one of the basic principles of transport policy which has hitherto been inviolable, namely, freedom of modal choice. Many others have started to ask whether there are limits to personal mobility -- a subject absolutely taboo up to now, to examine the *raison d'être* of certain freight traffic accordingly termed "irrational", in other words, to ask whether supply is to continue to be geared to demand or whether, on the contrary, action should now be taken directly on the formation of demand so as to ensure that it is compatible with what we have come to call "sustainable development". This concept is difficult to define precisely but it essentially means that any development catering for today's requirements must not compromise the capacity of future generations to meet their own requirements. In the last analysis, the aim is to reconcile short-term interests with what are clearly advantages in the longer term, it being understood that both the short and long term do, of course, begin right now. However, there seems to be a very broadly shared feeling that the present growth of transport is really not in harmony with this idea of sustainable development.

Briefly, therefore, ladies and gentlemen, as far as I can see in the light of the policy issues raised in our Conference, that just about describes the overall problem area that you will be dealing with, analysing and discussing in the next three days in Lisbon.

The Symposium approaches this general topic by means of five sub-topics, the first concerning demographic structures and social behaviour. Sociological and demographic changes, including the effects of the slow but continuous transformation of the age pyramid, will be central to the debate since they largely determine the pattern of mobility in the years to come. These changes may well give rise to increasing use of the car. It should be borne in mind that our grandparents were hardly ever car drivers and our parents only occasionally, whereas we now have a generation reaching retirement age which has experienced in full the development of car ownership and expects to enjoy the advantages of the car for as long as possible.

The second sub-topic relates to economic trends and transport specialisation. As elsewhere throughout the world, economic change in Europe is based on increasing specialisation of activities, a context in which the transport sector relies increasingly on logistics to the extent that some people are already complaining, moreover, that the community at large is covering costs that should normally be borne by producers and distributors.

The third sub-topic concerns infrastructure capacity and network access. We shall here see that, while some areas are subject to congestion, others still have inadequate access to communications networks and, accordingly, to major centres of economic activity, so the situation of regions at a disadvantage in this fundamental respect will be examined.

The fourth sub-topic focuses on the impact of new technologies on efficiency and safety, areas in which information technologies play a major role, as we all know, and offer a very broad and promising range of subjects for research, a sector that the ECMT is already monitoring essentially with a view to ensuring compatibility of the systems now being developed.

The fifth and last sub-topic covers the environment, global and local effects. One of the major challenges with which we are now faced is that of protecting the environment, that is to say, not simply preserving standards in the areas in which we live but also taking increasingly effective steps to prevent any deterioration in the ecological equilibrium on which we depend. As the Chairman of the ECMT has just stressed, this subject has become one of the major matters of concern to our Conference over the past few years.

As you can see, ladies and gentlemen, you will be discussing during your three days in Lisbon some issues of the utmost importance to the organisation of inland transport in Europe in the coming years. Given the quality of the background reports and the diversity of professional interests and skills represented here, your debate will be rich, stimulating and productive.

This debate is, in fact, being held at an extremely opportune moment in the life of our Conference since we are at present preparing a new three-year programme of work for ECMT and, within this context, it would seem highly desirable to establish closer links between our research activities and the work to be carried out in the policy sphere.

It has been suggested that the ECMT has not always made the most of the findings of economic research carried out on its own initiative. Indeed, some may even have the impression that such research has eventually had greater impact outside the Conference than within. I can promise you that this time I shall be very careful to ensure that the key ideas in your discussions will be reflected in the ECMT's new programme of work and that the current of thought emerging from this Symposium will accordingly give rise to specific proposals for action to be submitted for the attention of our Ministers.

That current of thought will, moreover, be given immediate expression in the form of the full publication that the Secretariat's team will be preparing after the Symposium, a publication that will include, as usual, the background reports and the general summary report to be drawn up by Mrs. Cristina Paulino.

I now come to the most agreeable part of this address, that of thanking you: first, for the fact that so many of you accepted our invitation, since by your presence here you not only showed your interest in the Conference's Symposium but you give it vitality and broaden its approach at the same time. My thanks go in particular to all those who accepted to play an active part in the Symposium: session chairmen, rapporteurs, panel members, the general rapporteur and, of course, all of you attending the sessions. I am quite sure that the contribution made by all concerned will enable each one of us, on our return from Lisbon, to say -- to use a phrase from a well-known guidebook -- that "Lisbon was well worth the journey".

I should also like to convey my warmest thanks to my colleagues in the Secretariat, Mr. De Waele and his team, for their commitment and their painstaking and dedicated work in preparing and holding this Symposium.

Arthur De Waele has taken part in all twelve ECMT Symposiums and, as many of you know, he is one of the principal architects of our system of co-operation in the sphere of economic research. From the very start of the current preparations, he has worked assiduously with the members of his division and our Portuguese colleagues to ensure that our meeting here today would be held in the best possible conditions and meet with success in both the research and social contexts.

Last, but not least, I should like to say how pleased I am, both personally and on behalf of the ECMT Secretariat in particular, to endorse the words of our Chairman in paying sincere tribute to our hosts. I say this last of all, not through lack of courtesy but rather to ensure that this part of my address will be kept in mind by all of you at the end of this opening session. May I extend to you, Minister, and to Mr. Silva Rodrigues, Mrs. Sequeira and every member of their team, our warmest and most sincere thanks for having carried out the preparatory work here so efficiently and, especially, for the generous welcome that you have reserved for us in the capital of your country, where hospitality is a long-standing tradition. As I understand, there are some agreeable surprises in store for us during our stay here, and in a country like Portugal, surprises are always something quite out of the ordinary.

Ladies and gentlemen, thank you for your attention.

INTRODUCTORY REPORTS

Sub-topic 1

DEMOGRAPHIC STRUCTURES AND SOCIAL BEHAVIOUR

A. BONNAFOUS
Laboratoire d'Économie des Transports
Lyons
France

SUMMARY

Lyons, January 1992

1. SITUATING THE PROBLEM

It is not by accident that the general theme of the 12th Symposium, "Transport Growth in Question" should be tackled first from the standpoint of demographics and social behaviour. Transport is nothing more than a response to human and human behavioural development, in particular the need for mobility. This paper will attempt to chart future transport growth by investigating the changing patterns of mobility that transport will probably be called upon to cater for. To do so, the demographic and social factors determining mobility will have to be pinpointed.

Anyone who has tried to understand mobility and its evolution knows how complex the subject and the factors determining it are. If we are to avoid becoming entangled in its complexity, we need to be clear on three points before we start: what we mean by mobility; methodological discipline as to determinants and factors; and the implications for transport of our thinking, since transport considerations have governed the choice of material in this paper.

1.1. What sort of mobility?

Mobility can mean many things, not all of them involving change of place. Social mobility, for example, refers to a change of status or condition by an individual or a generation. But we shall restrict ourselves to the term as it is used in transport economics: narrowly speaking, it means the movement of people -- except for house moving, which has more to do with "residential mobility". The latter will be borne in mind, but only as a factor affecting day-to-day mobility.

The idea of mobility as movement from place to place is, however, broader than that of travel -- as research in the 1970s and 1980s demonstrated (P. Jones *et al.,* 1983, O. Andan *et al.*, 1988). True, travel is what causes transport system problems, and it is therefore important to understand its characteristics -- temporal and spatial distribution, modal split, etc. But we cannot understand trends in travel unless we go beyond the simple act of going from one place to another and examine the reasons for travelling, the nature of those who travel and of the places where travel occurs, and indeed everything liable to contribute to explaining travel. Overall, then, travel is to be seen as a necessary element in people's activity as performed within a given space. This broader focus distinguishes the study of mobility from a mere statistical analysis of travel.

The investigation of mobility in this broader sense unfortunately raises a number of problems, beginning with problems of methodology.

1.2. From explanation to predicting the future

The following sentence is, it so happens, taken from a study of mobility based on an analysis of personal activity: "Men do less housework as they grow older". On the face of it, this has little to do with mobility, yet the sentence provides a good illustration of the difficulty of going from an established relation (age and man's propensity to do housework) to a prediction (e.g. that men will do more or less work in the house in fifteen years' time).

The difficulty is that the answer depends entirely on how the relation is interpreted. One can treat it is a symptom of age -- as a man gets older, he does less work in the house, so that, given the predictable ageing of the population, it may be inferred that in fifteen years' time men will do less work in the house than they do today. But one can also consider that the statistical link has to do with a social and cultural cleavage which is evidenced so far only by the younger generations. As time goes by, future generations of men will on average have a greater propensity to do housework. We end up with two conflicting forecasts.

Trends in mobility will confront us with precisely the same kind of problem. Where statistical links exist between mobility and a particular factor, such as age, future developments can be predicted only by interpreting cause and effect, and these can be substantiated only by observation over time.

Accordingly, reliable statistics can only be obtained by establishing series of data on the basis of surveys taken over a period of time. This leads us to another difficulty, since data from different periods must be comparable, that is, they must correspond to the same statistical definitions. Statistics on the number of trips may be compared only if the unit of travel is always defined in the same way.

A trip can, in theory, be defined by simple criteria:

-- A starting and a stopping point;
-- A departure and an arrival time;
-- A reason;
-- A mode of transport.

In practice, the number of trips connected with the same activity may vary greatly according to the conventions adopted. Should two or four trips be counted for someone who goes out to buy something, then goes to the hairdresser, stops afterwards to buy something else and finally returns home? Do we count the same number of trips if the journey is made on foot or by car?

The answer is purely a matter of convention, but such conventions have never been standardized, at least not internationally. So mobility indicators are not very comparable, just as not very much is known about certain kinds of mobility, such as walking.

1.3. Mobility factors and transport issues

What we have just said explains why we cannot make much use here of cross-classified statistics from different sources. Yet, taken individually, a number of sources tell us enough about mobility for us to deduce major trends which have important implications for transport. What are these implications?

One goal has been assigned to transport policy everywhere, and that is to satisfy travel needs at the lowest economic and social cost to the community. Any discussion of transport policy thus requires a sound knowledge of travel needs and trends.

Two major series of problems have then to be addressed -- one concerns the determination of mobility requirements that are currently or potentially inadequately catered for, the other the determination of the best means of meeting those requirements while keeping costs under control. In both cases, the essential problems relate more specifically to those parts of the transport system subject to congestion. It is there that needs are not met adequately, the cost of increasing services is usually high and marginal social costs may also become quite substantial.

This paper will therefore concentrate on those aspects of mobility whose continued development would be likely to aggravate such difficulties and, since the difficulties are in many cases related to car use, mobility will be considered more particularly from the standpoint of modal choice.

In the following three sections, we shall be looking at the main socio-economic and demographic trends (2.), the particular problem of urban development (3.) and, lastly, the relevant challenges arising for transport systems in all those respects (4.).

2. SOCIO-ECONOMIC AND DEMOGRAPHIC TRENDS

Richer but older. That, in a nutshell, sums up the main socio-economic trends in the industrialised countries over the past twenty or thirty years. Let us see how these trends have affected mobility.

2.1. More!

Notwithstanding a series of deepening recessions over these past decades, the trend is towards higher purchasing power among households, a trend fuelled by growth in production over the longer term. In the developed capitalist countries such growth averaged 3.1 per cent per year in the 1970s and 2.9 per cent in the 1980s, while the overall figures for western Europe were only slightly lower.

Table 1 shows that overall mobility in terms of surface transport traffic in passenger/kms has kept pace with this growth [G. Dobias (1989)] in a selection of seven major European countries where the elasticity of such mobility in relation to the growth in the longer term has remained around 1.

Statistics of this kind should be treated with caution, since they cover all trips of whatever distance, lumping together urban travel and travel over much longer distances. They do, however, confirm that in both cross-section series and time series there is an "income effect" on mobility. The countries where mobility was lower in the 1980s (France, Germany, Belgium, Italy, the Netherlands) were those that experienced slower economic growth, whereas those with higher mobility in the 1980s (United Kingdom, Denmark) also had better growth rates in the 1980s than the 1970s.

The table is also useful in showing that, in all the countries concerned, while public transport by rail and road accounted for a substantial proportion of the increase in mobility in the early 1970s, the increase in the 1980s was largely attributable to the private car.

Another conclusion is that public road transport out-performs rail and, overall, stands up slightly better to the private car in all countries except Belgium and France. Growth in surface passenger transport is therefore attributable to road traffic and, primarily, the use of the car.

The big question is whether this trend will continue or will reach its limits. The answer is perhaps essentially to be found in trends in car ownership by households.

2.2. Car ownership rates and mobility

The relationship between the car ownership rates and mobility might seem obvious but the situation has to be examined in the light of more precise data. Urban travel has to be separated from inter-city road travel, partly because the two types of travel differ in character but also because different statistical sources are used.

Where urban transport is concerned, the effects of car ownership rates are well known and fully concordant. The findings of the household survey conducted in Lyons in 1986 confirm the relationship (see Figure 1).

The number of motorised trips (car and public transport) per person per day more than doubles according to whether the household lacks a car or has two cars. As the number of cars in the household increases, public transport gives way to the car for the purpose of mobility, as would be expected (see Figure 2, same source).

The figures clearly show that, the more vehicles a household has at its disposal the less use it makes of public transport, despite the overall increase in motorised mobility. The car ownership rate therefore acts as a "key variable" in mobility; it accompanies and provides the means for an overall increase in mobility and enables the private car to account for a larger proportion in the modal split. It is thus important to determine the most likely changes in this variable.

2.3. Is the household car ownership rate reaching its limits?

It is often claimed that, since the increase in car ownership rates is closely bound up with household purchases of a second, third or even fourth car, the uptrend will be curbed at a certain level of saturation as determined by the number of driver's licence-holders in the household. While the theoretical existence of such an asymptote is hard to deny, it is not quite so easy to say where it lies and even more difficult to know whether, in the early 1990s, it is still some distance away.

We can provide some sort of answer to the last question by looking at the comparative trends in car ownership possession rates in different countries. The curves in Figure 3 are particularly eloquent in this regard.

The first thing that comes to mind when looking at the figure is that very few of the curves give the impression of reaching an asymptotic limit. However that may be, the position of the curves with respect to the United States suggests that any such asymptotic limit must lie far higher than anything reached by the European countries. The singular situation in the United States also needs qualifying since the car ownership rate includes large numbers of specialty vehicles (campers, four-wheel drives, etc.).

Secondly, Figure 3 shows that the car ownership rate is strongly correlated with per capita income, as may be seen from the relative positions of the United States', German, French, Spanish, Greek and other curves. The only significant exceptions concern densely populated countries with plentiful public transport such as the Netherlands and Japan.

These conclusions suggest that the trend in household car ownership is linked to rising incomes. This is clearly demonstrable if income is viewed not in terms of mean levels but in terms of distribution. J.L. Madre and T. Lambert (1989), who drew up Figure 4, have made a study of this relationship.

The income effect on car ownership -- both over time and in comparisons across quartiles -- can be seen quite clearly in this figure. Starting from 1972, the third quartile reaches the level of the fourth (the richest) with an eight-year lag. The same is true of the second quartile with respect to the third. There is a twelve-year lag between the poorest and the second quartile. This "catching up" effect explains why average car ownership, starting in 1972, grew by a third in ten or so years. If a similar catching up effect were to continue from 1987 on, the average increase over a ten-year period would be slightly over twenty per cent.

The lesson to be drawn from the income variable is that, while car ownership may increase at a slower rate, it will continue to grow for as long as household incomes continue to rise. Viewed from the income effect angle, saturation will come only gradually and in a somewhat distant future.

This conclusion could, however, be modified by demographic factors, such as the ageing of the population.

2.4. Effect of an ageing population

Population forecasts over a twenty-five year period are reasonably reliable. A study conducted by the Forward Studies Unit of the European Commission outlines a number of trends that may be taken as next-to-certain. Present demographic patterns already contain what needs to be known about the ageing of Europe's population. Today the proportion of over-65s to those aged 15-65 is 20 per cent; in 2020 it will have reached 29 per cent in the European Community.

The normal result of this ageing, on the basis of a simple age-mobility relation, should be a general decline in mobility. But, as we said earlier (see 1.2), behavioural changes from one generation to another can significantly affect such trends.

Work by J.L. Madre (1989) on household surveys carried out by INSEE (*Institut National de la Statistique et des Etudes Economiques*) sheds some interesting light on this subject. The author was able to track "generations" of households (heads of household born in the same decade) over the period 1962-1986 with regard to car ownership rates, and 1977-1986 with regard to the kilometres clocked per vehicle. The latter is shown in Figure 5.

The authors note that the curves for succeeding generations, except for a break between those born before and after the 1930s, nearly all join up, thus establishing that the age effect is more powerful than any generation effect and confirming the axiom that mobility declines as from about thirty years of age. This holds for car-driven mobility, but the result is very different when we look at motorisation rates.

Here, the age effect appears to be in sharp contrast with a generation effect. As Figure 5 shows, vehicle-kms decline by nearly twenty per cent from age 40 to age 60; but we see from Figure 6 that car ownership of the 60 year-olds in the 1923-1932 generation is 125 per cent higher than it was twenty years earlier for the corresponding generation, that of 1902-1912. It follows that, while the age effect causes a decrease in vehicle/kms, the generation effect produces an increase in the number of vehicles, and therefore the ageing of the population does not necessarily imply a decline in private car mobility.

These findings are probably not valid over the very long term. As shown by Figure 6, there is less variation in the car ownership rates of the younger generations than in those of the older ones. In other words, the generation effect should gradually disappear.

J.L. Madre (1989) has calculated the combined effect of the main private car mobility factors. Without discussing the calculations in detail, we may note the elasticities obtained between national road or motorway traffic and the more relevant explanatory variables (Table 2).

Table 2 shows that rising private car mobility, like the generation effect, is essentially prompted by economic growth. But it is also attributable to household customs (which are handed on), the ongoing development of road infrastructure and, probably, the inadequacy of public transport services. There is every reason to think, moreover, that it is not unconnected with another basic demographic trend, namely urban growth.

3. URBAN GROWTH OR URBAN SPRAWL?

Five centuries ago there were only thirty-two cities in the world with over 100 000 inhabitants. Now there are more than two thousand, although problems of definition make the exact number difficult to determine. Over the same span of time, the number of cities with over 500 000 inhabitants has gone up from two to more than four hundred. In spite of this centuries-old trend, the notion of urban growth has been disputed.

3.1. Urban growth in question

One very cursory analysis, which nevertheless deserves mention, is based on census returns from communes. These show that for several decades the inner communes of large cities have been barely maintaining or have even been losing their populations. Built-up areas themselves have sometimes been growing at a very slow rate.

The evidence supporting this view is, in fact, misleading. New forms of urban development require that the growth of "rural" communes, as observed in France from 1975 to 1982, should be interpreted with care. This growth has been the subject of ill-considered comment which overlooked what later came to be known as "rurbanisation".

In correcting this misconception, one could hardly do better than quote P. Aydalot (1985):

> "*...the rural areas taken as a whole (according to the 1982 definition) grew much faster (5.6 per cent) from 1975 to 1982 than the urban entities (2.2 per cent from the standpoint of the pre-existing definition; 3.8 per cent if one includes the total population of the rural communes incorporated in the urban entities during this period). Despite this, the rate of urban growth was high (because, when the total population of the communes considered as rural in 1975 and as urban in 1982 is subtracted, the apparent growth rate of the rural areas falls to 1.5 per cent).*"

This ambiguous interpretation of the population figures is, of course, a problem of definition. The urban-rural distinction was based on over-simple criteria, too simple to cope with modern changes in land occupation. The old yardstick of population size within an administrative district was soon seen to be unsatisfactory. The concept of urban entities was introduced to cover the grouping of several communes on the basis of contiguous residential occupation. The entities were thus defined by the morphological continuity of the urban fabric, but they left out of account areas which, although isolated when seen from the air, were extremely dependent on the city for jobs, services, consumption and so forth. Accordingly, France introduced the term Industrial and Urban Population Areas (IUPA) (French abbreviation: ZPIU). These areas took account of commuting, the proportion of non-agricultural inhabitants, the size and number of industrial, commercial or administrative premises. "Rural-dormitory" communes were included with the ZPIU in which the commuter-related jobs were located. The remaining communes outside the ZPIUs were regarded as "rural proper".

Every industrialised country has had to find an answer to this kind of statistical problem, with each one trying to match its definitions to the changing realities of land occupation. In the United States, for example, where the "mega-city" is a fact of life, the working definition has been changed a number of times. The "Statistical Metropolitan Area", based on the notion of urban continuity, gave way in 1986 to the "Metropolitan Consolidated Area", a more broadly-based concept. The upshot of the quest for realistic definitions has been to make international comparisons more difficult. P. Cheshire *et al.* (1983), in a study of the EEC, felt obliged to come up with a new definition, "Functional Urban Regions" (FUR) -- based, like the ZPIUs, on functional considerations but comprising a minimum size requirement (20 000 jobs) for the urban region centre.

Coming after the work of L. Klaassen *et al.* (1981), this study relied on a theory of "disurbanisation" that was much less primitive than the one mentioned at the start of this section. The essential points of the theory may be summed up as follows:

-- All cities go through a process whereby population growth shifts towards the outskirts;

-- The result is inner city decline followed later by decline of the outskirts;

-- The largest cities, those with the most advanced economies, are the first to be affected, but all cities are affected in the long run;

-- A cyclical process then sets in, decline being followed by renewal, beginning with that of the inner city;

-- External costs explain both this process and the fact that large cities are the first to be affected.

Although this is a beguiling model of urban change, in that it explains the population losses of the 1970s and certain urban crises, it poses problems of interpretation, as P. Aydalot (1985) pointed out. He noted in particular that in the general context of a declining population, there must certainly be some regional shortfalls, that the economic crisis had accelerated the decline of the first industrial revolution's activities along with the cities that had prospered from them, and that during the period of the study the big city crisis had primarily affected British towns whose own economic base had failed, like the ports associated with the heyday of the British Empire.

However detailed they may be, the studies offer no clear definition of urban entities. While urban growth is clearly beginning to wane and some cities are undoubtedly losing population, we need to know whether the long-term trend towards concentration is likely to taper off.

3.2. Spatial concentration

Any study of spatial concentration, identified on the basis of urban statistics, runs up against the problem that the statistics relate to areas based on definitions which are no longer consistent with the realities of the urban situation. In order to have an overall view, population trends over the whole country must be analysed. In France, the trend concerning "rural" communes is highly revealing.

In "rural" communes with a population of under two thousand, annual population growth was 0.87 per cent from 1975 to 1982 and 0.84 per cent from 1982 to 1990. Over the same periods, growth in "urban" communes (over two thousand inhabitants) was only 0.31 and 0.39 per cent respectively. Figure 7 shows what underlies these trends by distinguishing between four types of rural commune.

Regardless of the size of the rural communes, which is not a decisive factor, concentration is clearly evident. The population growth rate of communes which are not part of a ZPIU, i.e. "rural proper", is nearly flat. The annual rate of variation in the others is distinctly positive and all the more so the larger the ZPIU. In ZPIUs with a population of over 200 000, the rate is nearly 2 per cent.

Concentration on these urban, or rather "rurban", areas is thus clearly proven notwithstanding the low growth of urban communes (in the narrow sense). Sprawl and concentration, far from being contradictory, appear to go hand in hand and even to feed one another -- as H. Le Bras (1991) found in his study, illustrated by the figures in Table 3.

The slow and steady population drift from the least populated part of the country helps to swell the other half but, at the same time, the small area where half the population is concentrated is "spreading" to an appreciable extent. All this confirms the trends in Figure 7, i.e. the stagnation of "rural proper" and the dynamism of the communes in the ZPIUs, where most of the spatial concentration and urban sprawl are taking place, both of the latter being characterised by the development of detached housing.

3.3. A century-old spread/concentration model

It is fair to say that these deep-seated trends correspond to an urban development model that goes back a long way in time and appears to be working well still. It is the exponential density distribution model imagined a century ago by H. Bleicher (1892) and often attributed to Colin Clark (1951 and 1967). There was no way of empirically verifying the model until the arrival of computer science. This was done by R. Bussière (1972), who first pointed out that the model was founded on the principle of maximum entropy, in other words, that it corresponded to the most probable forms of location as defined by A.G. Wilson (1969) when applied to continuous space. The main interest of R. Bussière's work, where we are concerned, is that he was able to make the model function by using particularly convincing statistics.

The formal expression of the model is simple. It can be expressed by either an equation involving the density D of an urban area contained within a distance r from the centre:

$$D(r) = A\exp(-br)$$

or an equivalent equation (see Figure 8) relating the population P contained within a distance r from the centre, to distance r. In this static form, the model has two variables and two parameters, A and b. Parameter A is the (extrapolated) density at the centre of the urban area; b is the rate of decrease in density according to the distance from the centre. The expression of P(r) in the case of the Paris area in 1962 is shown in Figure 8.

There are two comments to be made on this example. First, the chart shows the remarkable quality of the fit between the theoretical curve and the dots obtained from the actual census figures. It should be mentioned that equally good fits, involving the same relation, were obtained by the author for Bordeaux (1962), Montreal (1964), Toronto (1961) and Zurich (1968) -- the values of A and b being, of course, different in each case.

Second, the model holds up equally well in both time series and cross-section series. R. Bussière's fundamental contribution was to explain the phenomenon of spread, which he attributed solely to changes in the parameters A and b. *"The growth of modern cities, at their present stage of development, is consistently associated with a gradual decrease in density at the centre, and a decrease in the rate of density fall-off depending on distance from the centre."* The author is careful to talk of the "present stage of development" of cities, since the model works beautifully for the parameters of Paris from 1911 to 1968, but fails to match the earlier development of Paris from 1876 to 1911. It is as though the spread model in question applies only to the motor-car era.

The model has been tested on Paris, Montreal, Toronto, Stockholm, Winnipeg, Malmö and Helsingborg. We shall confine ourselves to the case of

Paris, the development of whose spread is charted in Figure 9. The development parameter used is not time but total population N.

Given the consistency and durability of the trends it describes, the model enables us to define simple indicators. Their variation gives a very fair picture of urban change from one period to another. These indicators are shown in Figure 10, which reproduces the previously found curves for two situations in periods 1 and 2.

The outer limits of the urban area (taken as the distance from the centre beyond which population shows little further tendency to grow) are shown respectively as L_1 and L_2 for the two periods. Hence,:

-- L_1C represents urban growth in the usual sense of increased population;

-- CL_2 represents the additional urban spread.

Point M is useful in interpreting successive census figures. If we look at the population trend closer to the centre than M, at a radius of 4 km, for example, we shall find a decrease, whereas further out than M there will be an increase. M tends with time to shift away from the centre. Figure 9 shows that at the start of the century it was located about 6 km from the centre; between the 1962 and 1968 censuses it was located 12 km from the centre. If the model is correct, it could move as far out as 25 km. The situation here is familiar to town planners: inner city dwellers seem to move towards the outskirts under the combined effect of "social eviction", due to mounting inner city property prices, and strong demand for detached housing.

The real question is whether these long-term trends will continue to follow the model or whether they will take another direction. The validity of the model is not called into question by data later than those used by R. Bussière, far from it. In the Paris region, the central urban population decreased from 1975 to 1982 (from -- 16 per cent in the inner city to -- 2 per cent in the immediately surrounding or "first belt" suburbs), whereas the population of the furthest outskirts grew (from + 7.7 per cent in the contiguous "second belt" suburbs to + 16.7 per cent in the non-contiguous satellite areas beyond). The more recent, but as yet little studied, findings of the 1990 census confirm these trends, as Figure 7 and Table 3 show.

To conclude on the subject of urban sprawl, three remarks are in order. The first is that calculations of population within a given distance from the centre take no account of differences of form which may develop in certain sectors of the urban area. R. Bussière has, however, checked the validity of his model for a few sectors (from 45 to 60 degrees) and obtained specific factor values, an approach that may pave the way towards the construction of a differentiated spread model.

The second remark is that the spread model attains its limits where several urban areas meet to form a conurbation. The urban space so formed changes in character, as do the transport problems associated with it. A special section will be devoted to this subject in Chapter 4.

The third remark concerns the fact that spread-concentration cannot continue in ageing European countries if it is fed solely by the natural surpluses of urban populations. It also needs the migratory surpluses produced by either domestic or international migration. The former depend on population reserves that will gradually become exhausted and eventually slow down the process. The latter are a source of particular problems, which are already acute in the major cities.

3.4. Urban concentration and immigration

Any review of major population trends would be incomplete if it did not include immigration, which is a fact of urban life in most European countries.

In overall terms, the foreign population of the EEC totals only eight million immigrants from countries outside the Community, a mere 2.4 per cent of the whole population, according to a recent study by the Giovanni Agnelli Foundation (1991). The proportion obviously varies in the different countries -- less than one per cent in Spain, Greece and Portugal; less than two per cent in Denmark and Italy; less than three per cent in the Netherlands and the United Kingdom; almost four per cent in Belgium and France; over five per cent in what was formerly West Germany. But the real difference in distribution lies in the fact that immigrants are heavily concentrated in urban areas, as may be seen from Figure 11.

Moreover, the concentration is usually heaviest in the largest cities. In the United Kingdom, for example, over forty per cent of immigrants live in Greater London, just as in France, where over forty per cent of migrants live in the Paris region.

Within the urban area, immigrants are further concentrated in particular communes or neighbourhoods. As the original residents leave, these neighbourhoods tend to become outright ghettos characterised by high unemployment, insecurity and educational difficulties -- all of which work against integration into the host society. This residential segregation is viewed as an important factor in social exclusion.

The mobility and mobility-related problems of migrant populations are not well documented, as very few special studies have so far been devoted to them. It may be inferred from household surveys that their mobility is not high. Surveys conducted in Lyons for SYTRAL (1990) revealed that the mobility of people who had not received any schooling (a condition found normally only among immigrants) was lower than that of every other category of the population. Walking not being included among the types of travel recorded, other mobility was half that of inhabitants who had received post-secondary education and, for private car travel only, it was eight times less.

A study of a number of suburban areas carried out in France by the *Conseil National des Transports* (1991) showed that low car use can be only partially offset by public transport owing to the low level of provision in these areas.

Accordingly, a policy problem arises: should more transport be provided in these areas so that the inhabitants can have better access to other parts of the city, at the risk of detracting from local shopping and recreational activities which contribute to the life of these neighbourhoods? A policy of easier access would seem to be fully warranted by the needs of schoolchildren for whom transport would offer a wider range of schools. Measures along these lines would, however, have to form part of a general local development policy, regardless of any other steps taken to remedy geographic segregation.

4. CHALLENGES FACING TRANSPORT

The large-scale trends discussed above pose transport problems which, while not new, may well grow more acute, especially as the factors favouring transport growth could combine to produce a cumulative effect.

4.1. Combination of factors

In seeking to read the future of transport, we need only to look at the salient points of the major trends dealt with in the two preceding parts of this paper. Population is slowly accumulating at the outer edges of urban areas; although it is ageing, its everyday mobility continues to increase and, to the extent that economic growth allows, private cars are being increasingly used.

The probability of growth therefore is of immediate concern to urban transport, since it is already confronted with twin crises -- that of traffic congestion and that of public transport finance. We need to know whether these crises will deepen or become less acute.

Part of the answer is suggested by the case of Lyons, where we have simulations for the year 2000 describing the effects of the above-mentioned major trends on the urban transport system as a whole. The simulations use the QUINQUIN model devised by A. Bonnafous (1985), D. Bouf (1985 & 1989), C. Raux (1991) and E. Tabourin (1988, 1989 & 1991), who carried out the simulations referred to below.

The simulated situations shown in Figures 12 and 13 are determined with respect to two axes representing the twin crises facing urban transport: motor vehicle traffic (base 100 in 1991) is on the x-axis and the amount of public finance needed to operate public transport (FF 360 million in 1991) on the y-axis.

The four situations simulated in Figure 12 give an indication of the course of future events in theory. The "no special factor effects" situation shows in particular the consequences of an increase in car ownership, which is itself linked to changes in the age structure of a population remaining the same size; the income effect is fairly small since the growth in household income is assumed not to exceed 1.5 per cent per annum. In this situation, it is primarily the congestion crisis that grows worse, car travel rising by almost 10 per cent. While appreciable, the effect on the financing crisis remains moderate; the external productivity of the public transport surface network suffers owing to heavier road congestion; the extra public finance expenditure corresponds with practically unchanged taxation in proportion to household income.

The "population growth effect" situation is along the same lines. It differs from the "no special factor effects" situation by the assumption of annual population growth of 0.5 per cent until the year 2000. This is the maximum assumption for the urban area served by the local public transport network. The traffic situation becomes even more critical -- private car travel increases by nearly 13 per cent. This illustrates the basic incompatibility between urban growth and transport system efficiency: the system must carry heavier traffic in central areas where road space cannot be greatly extended.

The "economic growth effect" supposes a 3 per cent increase in real household income as compared with the 1.5 per cent increase in the "no special factor effects" scenario. It has an even more drastic impact on both the traffic and public transport finance situations than the "population growth effect", owing to the combined effects of income on the general level of mobility and on car ownership and use.

A fourth situation was simulated. Determined by the "investment effect" point, it corresponds to an effort to remedy congestion by massive investment in dedicated right-of-way public transport (FF 6 billion for the 1990s). While this policy has the advantage of appreciably improving mobility by means of public transport, it has little effect on car traffic (which declines by less than 1 per cent compared with the "no special factor effects" scenario), and considerably increases the need for public transport financing. As was argued in an OECD-ECMT paper (A. Bonnafous, 1991), a policy of massive investment in public transport, however necessary it may be, will not alone suffice to prevent the perverse effects of growth and solve the twin crises of urban transport.

This is all the more true in that the effects considered separately above are likely to combine, thus leading the urban transport system into situations of the kind shown in Figure 13.

The effects of factor change are here combined and the consequences should surprise no one. It is worth emphasizing that a combination of the urban growth and rising income factors is not at all improbable. The latter favours housing construction which, in turn, is a major factor in the increase of urban population. On the assumption of a return to sustained growth, therefore, the trend will probably be towards the "Inc+Pop" situation shown in Figure 13. However, traffic density and the accompanying congestion would be so great that the situation would probably never be reached since, one way or another, the city would have to be saved from asphyxiation.

Taking the case of Lyons, where the population served totals 1.1 million, it may be asked whether the findings are universally applicable and whether comparable developments are to be expected in other cities. Some light may be thrown on this matter by examining the effect of size on public transport.

4.2. Urban concentration and public transport

Transport systems do not necessarily vary homothetically with the size of the city. Moreover, the effect of size is not always comparable with the effect of urban growth discussed in the previous section. The broad lines of the latter were established by means of a chronological approach using a model based on past developments which gave some idea of future trends. But to determine a size effect, cross-section series of data on cities of various sizes have to be used. An analysis of this kind was carried out by A. Chausse *et al.* (1991) on a group of 48 public transport networks in French towns, including the Paris region. The main findings relevant to our subject are shown in Figures 14 and 15.

In both charts, the two dots furthest to the right correspond to Paris, one representing the area served by the RATP (Paris transport authority), the other the more extensive area served by the SNCF (French railways). The charts have logarithmic co-ordinates, so that the linearity of the dot clusters expresses constant elasticity between the variables.

Public transport capacity is measured by units of Passenger-Kilometre-Capacity (PKC). The fitted line through the logarithms shows an elasticity of capacity to city size of 1.20, thus indicating a rising need for public transport capacity as the size of the town increases: between two urban areas in a size ratio of 1 to 10, to each other, the capacity is in a ratio of 1 to 16. Like the urban growth effect, the size effect here may be explained by the incompatibility between a fixed-size receptacle, i.e. the road system of the high-density parts of the city, and traffic which keeps increasing as the city grows. The more acute this incompatibility, the more public transport -- which uses road space economically -- can be expected to develop.

Variation in public transport demand corroborates this theoretical adjustment. In terms of the number of trips, the elasticity of demand to city size is 1.28, which gives a patronage ratio of 1 to 19 for a size ratio of 1 to 10. This seems to show that urban concentration promotes not only the need for but also the efficiency of public transport, a conclusion that must however be qualified, since a number of connecting "trips" may go to make up a single "journey", especially in the case of large public transport systems which provide interconnected services. In terms of the number of journeys, elasticity of demand to city size is only 1.12.

The reason is that large cities tend to have more suburbs, and public transport cannot easily secure a strong share of the market in suburban areas, as will be seen in Section 4.3. This is another of the problems related to urban sprawl. Such problems are all the harder to solve in that public transport costs are, as Figure 15 suggests, also extremely sensitive to the size effect.

The effect of size on network operating costs is considerable. The elasticity of these costs in respect to city size is 1.33, giving a cost ratio of 1 to 21 for a size ratio of 1 to 10. This is not much more than the effect of size on capacity. What these figures clearly show is that large public transport networks are not economically more efficient than smaller ones. It may be concluded that returns to scale are offset by traffic difficulties in large built-up areas.

Economies of scale are likewise offset by heavier investment requirements. The elasticity of investment expenditure in relation to size is 1.53, giving an expenditure ratio of 1 to 34 for a size ratio of 1 to 10. This confirms that urban concentration leads to rising unit costs for public transport. The higher capital needs are related, among other things, to spending on the dedicated transport routes required by cities of over 400 000 inhabitants. The bigger the population served, the more ambitious the transport systems have to be.

The problem is that, in addition to these heavy duty services capable of moving thousands of passengers at peak hours -- and which usually have the best rates of coverage of operating costs -- public transport must also be provided in places where patronage is much lighter, and especially in outlying districts.

4.3. Urban spread and suburban transport

As P. Bovy (1987) noted in a study of urban area transport in Switzerland, *"patronage in Swiss cities, while still higher than in most European cities of comparable size, is far from growing as fast as personal mobility. The tendency is towards a relative decline in the proportion of urban area travel accounted for by public transport."* The author illustrates his assertion with a chart by P. Güller, reproduced here as Figure 16. It is particularly revealing since it applies to Bern, which is one of Europe's best-served cities in terms of public transport.

Of the fifteen routes shown, only on the five innermost was there an increase in the market share of public transport over the period 1970-80. On these central routes, public patronage is sufficiently massed to warrant service of a quality that can compete with the private car. As from band 5, market share is flat at best, and it declines markedly on the five routes that begin in the outermost band, thus clearly indicating evidence that urban sprawl is a formidable challenge for urban transport.

Recent work by O. Andan *et al.* (1991) helps to explain why public transport meets with little success in outlying communes made up of detached housing.

The study is based on a survey of 297 families living in the outskirts of Lyons; they all own detached houses in which they have been living for less than fifteen years. Previously, they had all been settled in the Lyons city area. Of the 450 working people surveyed, 92 per cent use only private cars to go to work. Figure 17 provides an explanation for this modal choice that is so much to the detriment of public transport.

Even though one working person out of five was objectively in a position to choose his or her mode of transport, that person gave preference to the private car, particularly in places of residence where public transport services run infrequently. This is obviously so in the case of rural communes with a small population. While the potential clientele for public transport shown on the chart theoretically includes half the trips made, it could not be attracted to any large extent without considerably stepping up the transport supply. In sparsely inhabited areas, this would result in a great deal of excess capacity and consequently a high cost/revenues ratio. The spread of the city into these outlying areas can thus only add to the congestion crisis, even as the financial crisis becomes worse.

The areas overrun by urban sprawl thus provide a very favourable terrain for private car use. Against this, public transport can usually offer little but skeleton services. To do better, public transport would have to increase its market share. From this standpoint, the more central routes or those serving heavily populated districts are a much more promising field for prospection.

The alliance between urban spread and the private car thus seems practically indissoluble. Does this also have to be the case for giant conurbations?

4.4. Mega-cities and city regions

A recent study undertaken by F. Moriconi-Ebrard, in collaboration with the PARIS team from the *Centre National de Recherche Scientifique*, provides some insight into the large city phenomenon. Working from a database containing all the world's cities of over 10 000 people (GEOPOLIS), which he himself built on the basis of a standard definition of an urban area, he extracted a list of the hundred largest urban concentrations in the world. The population threshold was 2.5 million. Fifteen European conurbations fell into this category in 1990 as against only six in 1950.

Alongside the great urban complexes that have grown up around city nuclei -- these often being capital cities -- we find among the "top 100" such polycentric ensembles as Essen-Duisburg-Dortmund or Düsseldorf-Wüppertal-München-Gladbach. Since the standard definition used tended to exclude non-contiguous complexes, urban regions such as the *Randstad* do not appear in the list. By and large, however, there is evidence in Europe of the build-up of mega-cities. They may not be comparable to the "megalopolis" of the United States' East Coast, but they do form "city regions", stretching over tens of kilometres and containing several million inhabitants.

These city regions pose a specific problem for transport, which has already been identified in the largest regions. In the case of the Paris region, P. Merlin (1991) has conducted an analysis which is clearly illustrated in two maps. The first (Figure 18) shows the percentage of the working population who work in the commune where they live (or, if they live in Paris proper, who work in their own *arrondissement*). Here and there, the proportion is higher than 40 per cent but, for the most part, it is lower than 30 per cent. For a good percentage of the working population, therefore, home-to-work travel is intercommunal. In suburban communes, this has nothing out of the ordinary -- there has always been a severe imbalance in these communes between housing and employment, characterised by daily commuting to the central city area.

The modern development, even if it is not entirely new, is that radial (suburb-to-Paris) travel no longer accounts for most trips, as may be seen in Figure 19.

The percentage of daily travellers to Paris rarely exceeds 40 per cent and, in most areas, it is less than 30 per cent. This means that radial travel is a minority phenomenon, despite the fact that it corresponds to routes normally well served by public transport. As in the large city regions, the geographical distribution of work has become more varied, with the result that suburb-to-suburb travel has taken on greater importance. This is indeed the type of travel that has grown most, as all the household surveys conducted over the last twenty years testify.

The problem is that this suburb-to-suburb travel is highly dispersed and does not lend itself to mass streaming. It is therefore not a market where public transport can provide efficient enough service to rival the private car. It is not surprising that traffic delays, measured in km/hrs, have increased by over 10 per cent in the Paris region over the past few years, despite an economic situation that has not been particularly favourable.

The remedy often suggested for these back-and-forth migrations is to redesign urban areas so that residential and working areas coincide better. This is obviously a good idea but it can be carried only so far. As P. Merlin has remarked, daily migration is driven by powerful factors: increasing job specialisation, lack of transparency of the labour market, job mobility (which does not always reduce the distance from home to work) and the presence of more than one working member in a family.

Serious congestion problems thus pose a threat to city regions, especially as interregional flows also pass through them.

4.5. Major interregional corridors

It is often said that interregional passenger transport today needs to be considered on a European scale. This is true, but doing so reveals, above all, that this transport is still for mostly intra-national, as shown by the map in Figure 20 [G. Dobias (1989)]. This is in spite of the fact that the unit used is the passenger/kilometre, which reflects the longer distances involved in international travel.

This traffic, once again, is dominated by the private car. The modal share of all the flows shown has been calculated by INRETS, *et al.* (1986) as 73 per cent for private cars, 14.3 per cent for rail, 5.5 per cent for air and 6.9 per cent for motor coaches. Even when taken as approximations, in view of the uncertainty surrounding the data, the figures tell their own story and tally with those in Table 1 concerning travel over all distances.

The dominant position of the private car appears to be reinforced by a strong upsurge centred on the motorway networks. Motorway traffic in France, for example, grew by 50 per cent from 1985 to 1989. The increase each year has been nearly twice that forecast. These unexpected increases, confined to motorway traffic, may be due to certain factors having been underestimated -- such as geographical concentrations boosting trunk road traffic or the public's preference for fast travel, also reflected in the growth of air traffic and the success of high-speed trains.

Developments in international traffic have, perhaps, been similarly underestimated. Even though its proportional volume is still fairly modest, it has quite certainly grown faster than that of national traffic. Despite the statistical difficulties involved, all those who have studied international passenger traffic agree that there is a strong tendency for the so-called "frontier effect" to be less apparent.

On the basis of German traffic figures, H.G. Nüsser (1989) was able to show that international passenger traffic from 1960 to 1980 increased by 200 per cent whereas national traffic grew by only 50 per cent over the same period. Both types of traffic then levelled off, suggesting that their growth is very sensitive to that of the economy. The elasticity of international flows in relation to economic growth is far higher than that of national flows.

These trends teach us that, if there is any return to sustained economic growth, congestion problems will not be confined to urban areas. The major corridors, especially those handling international flows, are already prone to saturation, even outside of seasonal rush periods, and we have every reason to believe that investment will lag behind newly developing needs.

It is an understatement to say that transport faces formidable challenges in the future. The ECMT, which in 1975 was already predicting probable traffic bottlenecks in Europe, has good cause in 1992 to call "transport growth into question".

TABLES

Table 1. **Trend in passenger traffic**

	Passengers (billion)						Modal split (%)		
	1970	1975	1980	1984	1985	1986	1975	1980	1986
Private cars	1 306.9	1 542.3	1 828.0	1 972.1	2 005.7	2 109.4	78.7	81.1	82.7
France	304.7	374.8	452.5	491.7	494.4	517.3	80.8	81.9	82.8
Germany	350.6	405.4	470.3	483.1	481.6	510.3	78.6	80.4	82.9
Belgium	49.2	57.5	65.4	67.8	67.4	68.1	82.3	86.7	87.8
Italy	230	279.3	324	355.3	373.7	394.4	76.7	76.9	78
United Kingdom	267	294	365	410.3	424.8	448	77.1	83.5	86.1
Netherlands	72.1	93.5	112.5	122.8	120.8	126.2	80.1	84.2	85.7
Denmark	33.3	37.8	38.3	41.1	43	45.1	80.7	76.6	77.1
Rail	166.3	179.9	192.8	196.7	196	200.1	10	8.5	7.8
France	47.1	57.2	62.2	69.1	71.2	68.4	12.5	11.3	10.9
Germany	37.3	36.9	40.5	39	37.4	40.5	8.4	6.9	6.6
Belgium	7.6	7.5	7	6.4	6.6	6.5	12.7	9.2	8.4
Italy	32.5	36.3	39.6	39.1	37.4	40.5	10.8	9.4	8
United Kingdom	30.4	30.3	30.3	29.7	29.7	30.8	8.8	6.9	5.9
Netherlands	8	8.5	8.9	9	9.2	8.9	8.9	6.7	6
Denmark	3.4	3.2	4.3	4.4	4.5	4.5	8.1	8.6	7.7
Bus and coach	187.5	203.1	234.4	238.9	236	240	11.3	10.4	9.4
France	25.2	28.9	38	40.3	38.4	39	6.7	6.9	6.2
Germany	58.4	67.7	73.9	70.5	65	64.6	13.1	12.6	10.5
Belgium	3.0	3.2	3.1	2.9	3.1	3.0	5.0	4.1	3.9
Italy	37.4	42.3	57.8	63.0	66.6	70.6	12.5	13.7	14.0
United Kingdom	49.0	45.0	42.0	42.0	42.0	41.8	14.1	9.6	8.0
Netherlands	9.9	10.3	12.2	11.8	12.2	12.1	11.0	9.1	8.2
Denmark	4.6	5.7	7.4	8.4	8.7	8.9	11.2	14.8	15.2
	Passenger/kms (billion)						% change		
	1970	1975	1980	1984	1985	1986	1975	1980	1986
All modes	1 660.6	1 925.3	2 255.2	2 407.6	2 437.7	2 549.5	15.9	35.8	53.5
France	377.0	460.9	552.7	601.1	604.0	624.7	22.3	46.6	65.7
Germany	446.3	510.0	584.7	592.6	584.0	615.4	14.3	31.0	37.9
Belgium	59.8	68.2	75.5	77.1	77.1	77.6	14.1	26.2	29.8
Italy	299.9	357.9	421.4	457.4	477.7	505.5	19.3	40.5	68.6
United Kingdom	346.4	369.3	437.3	482.0	496.5	520.6	6.6	26.2	50.3
Netherlands	90.0	112.3	133.6	143.6	142.2	147.2	24.8	48.4	63.6
Denmark	41.3	46.7	50	53.9	56.2	58.5	13.1	21.2	41.8

Source: G. Dobias (1989).

Table 2

Elasticity of national road or motorway car traffic in relation to:	
Size of car population =	+ 0.65[1] ou + 0.57[2]
Real mean household income =	+ 0.45[1] ou + 0.46[2]
Motor fuel prices =	- 0.21[1] ou - 0.23[2]
Total length of motorways =	+ 0.15[1] ou + 0.21[2]

1. Model showing yearly changes.
2. Logarithmic model.

Source: J.L. Madre and T. Lambert (1989).

Table 3. **Spatial concentration and urban sprawl**

PROPORTION OF POPULATION LIVING IN THE LEAST DENSELY POPULATED HALF OF COUNTRY:

7.5 % in 1975	7 % in 1982	6 % in 1990

PROPORTION OF COUNTRY INHABITED BY THE MOST DENSELY CONCENTRATED HALF OF POPULATION:

2 % in 1975	2.3 % in 1982	2.5 % in 1990

Source: H. Le Bras (1991).

FIGURES

Figure 1. **Extent to which mobility is influenced by the number of cars in a household**

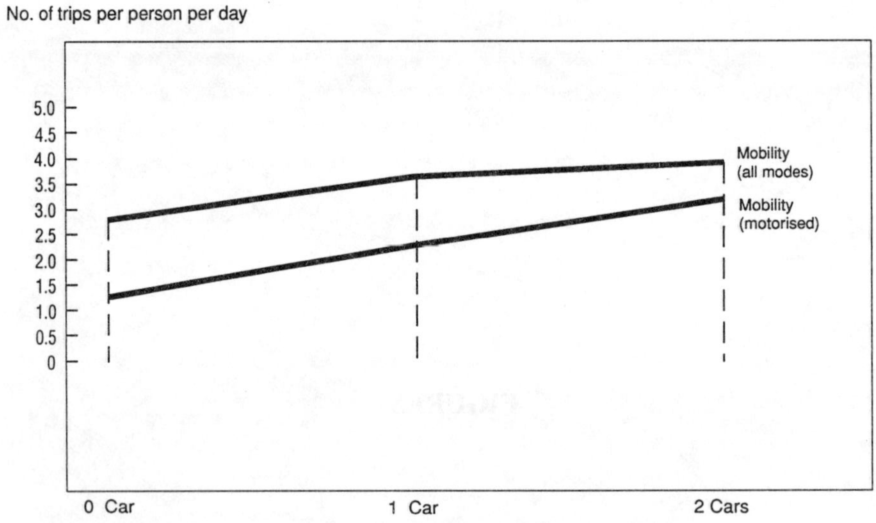

Source: SYTRAL (1990).

Figure 2. **Mobility based on public transport, with a breakdown by size of household and number of cars**

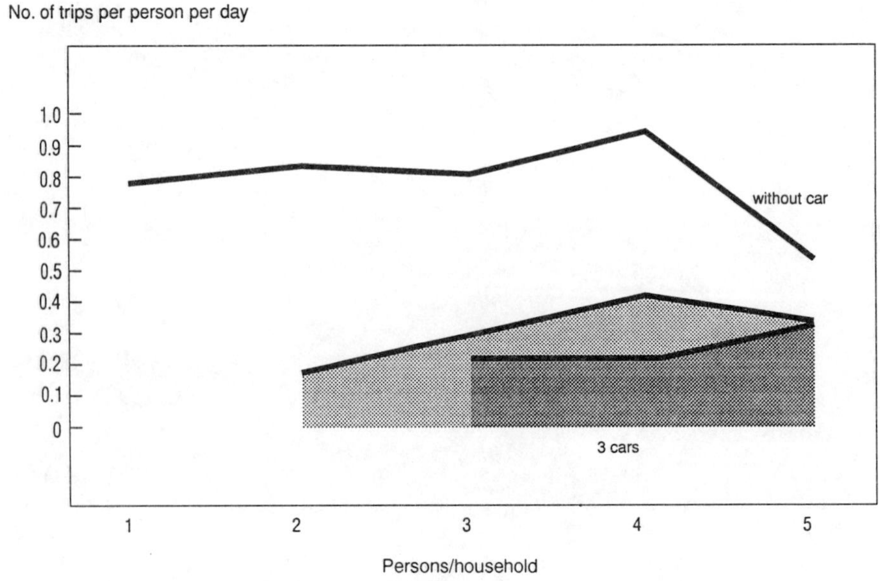

Source: SYTRAL (1990).

Figure 3. **Number of cars per 100 population**

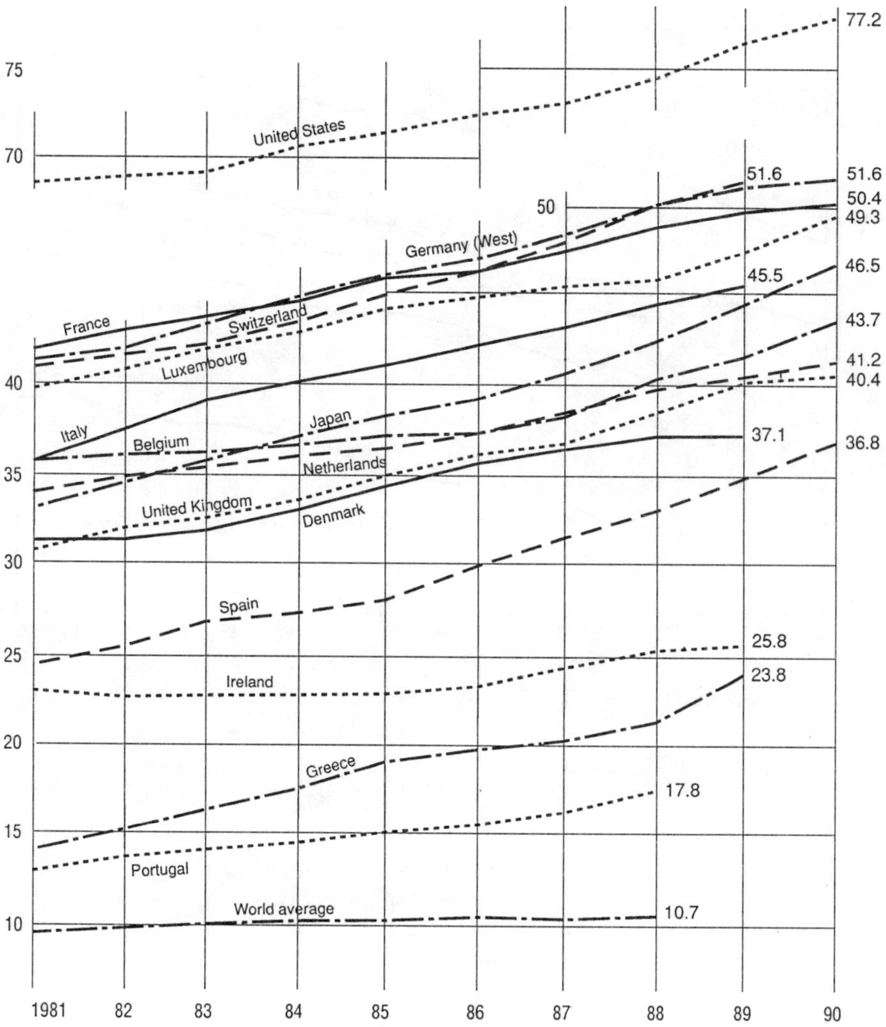

Source: Union Routière de France (1991).

Figure 4. **Trends in car ownership rates among adults by level of income**

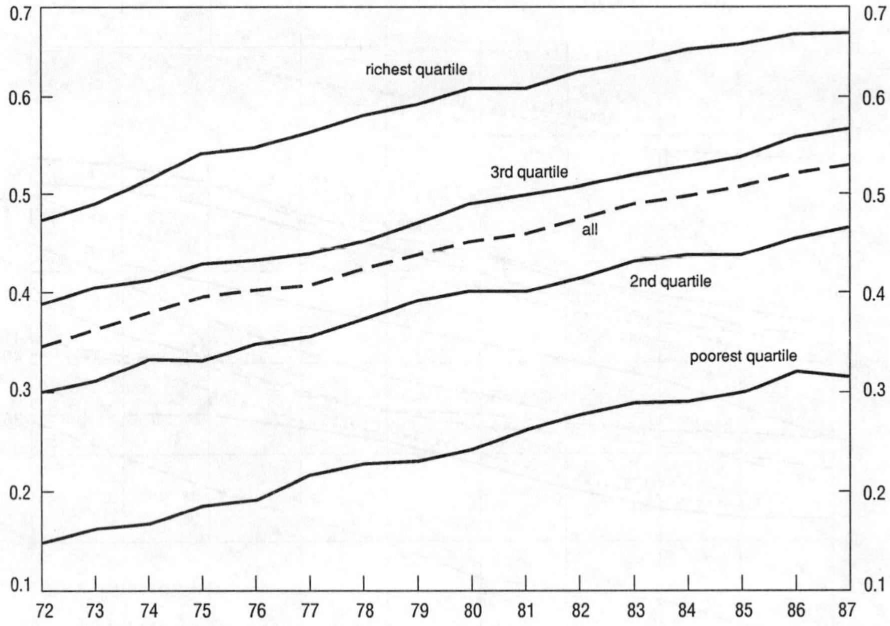

Source: J.L. Madre and T.Lambert.

Figure 5. **Trend in average vehicle/kms travelled per year by different generations**

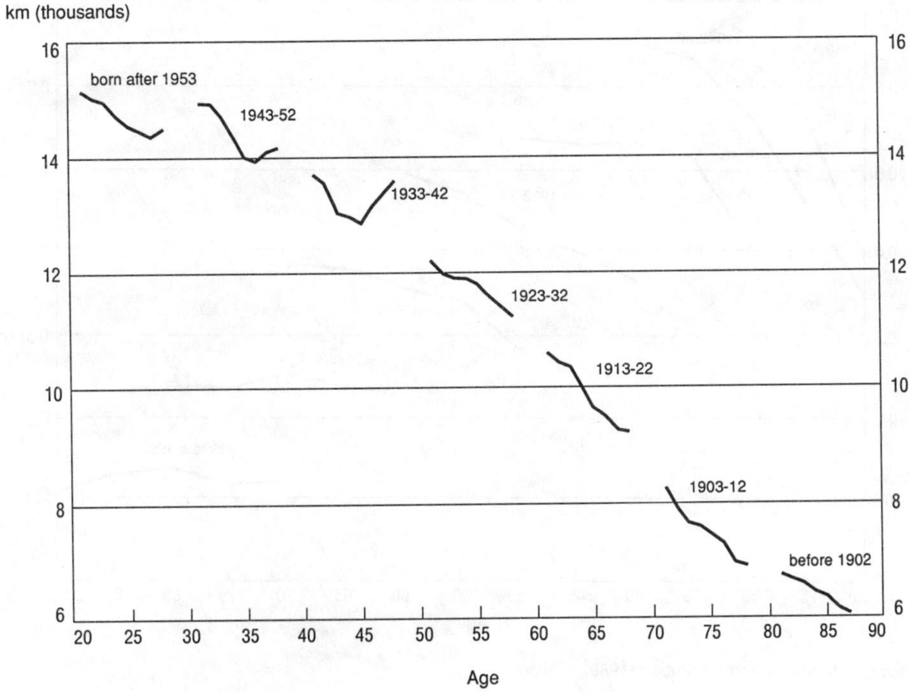

Source: J.L. Madre and T. Lambert (1989).

Figure 6. **Trend in average car ownership rates among adults of different generations**

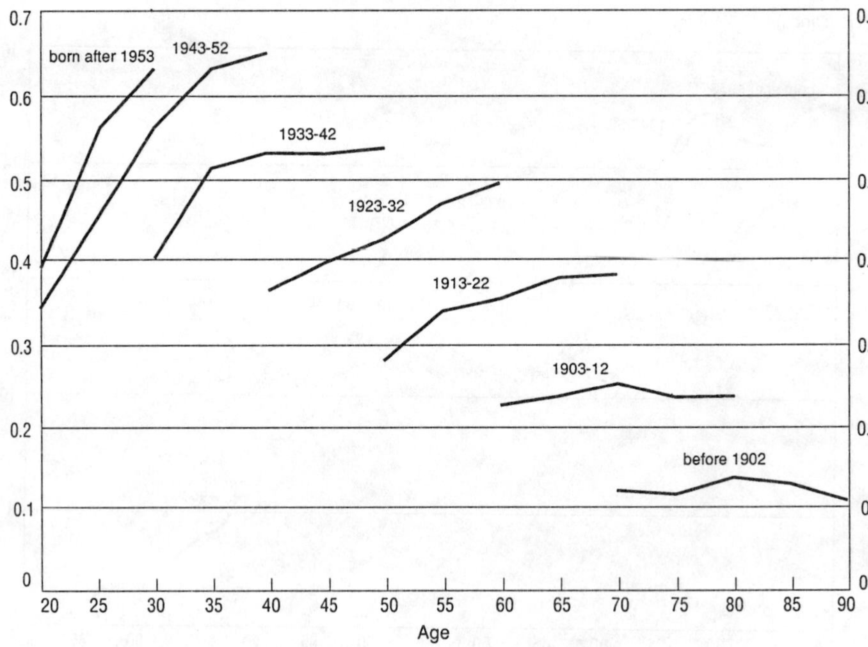

Source: J.L. Madre and T. Lambert (1989).

Figure 7. **Trend in growth of rural communes in France (1982-1990)**

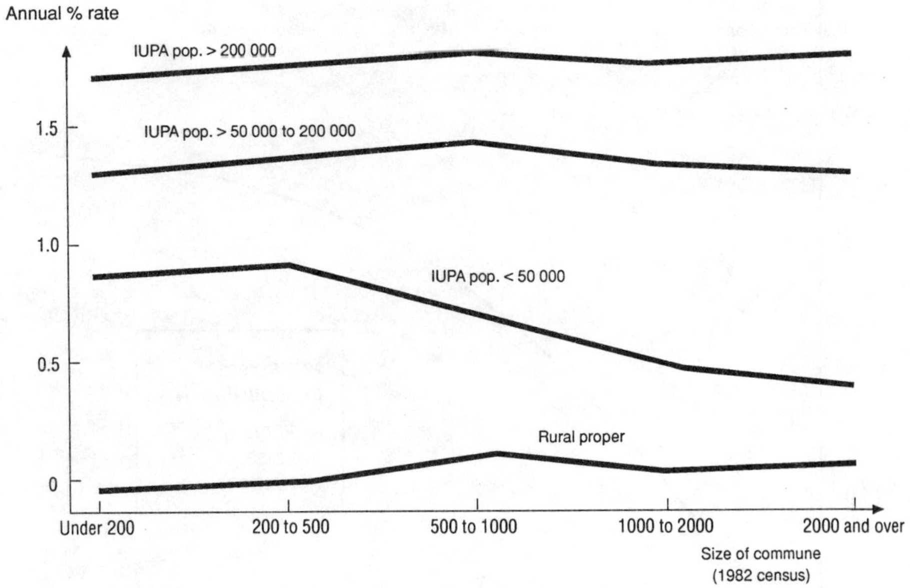

Source : S. Wachter (1991).

Figure 8. **Adaptation of R. Bussière's model**
Case of Paris (1962)

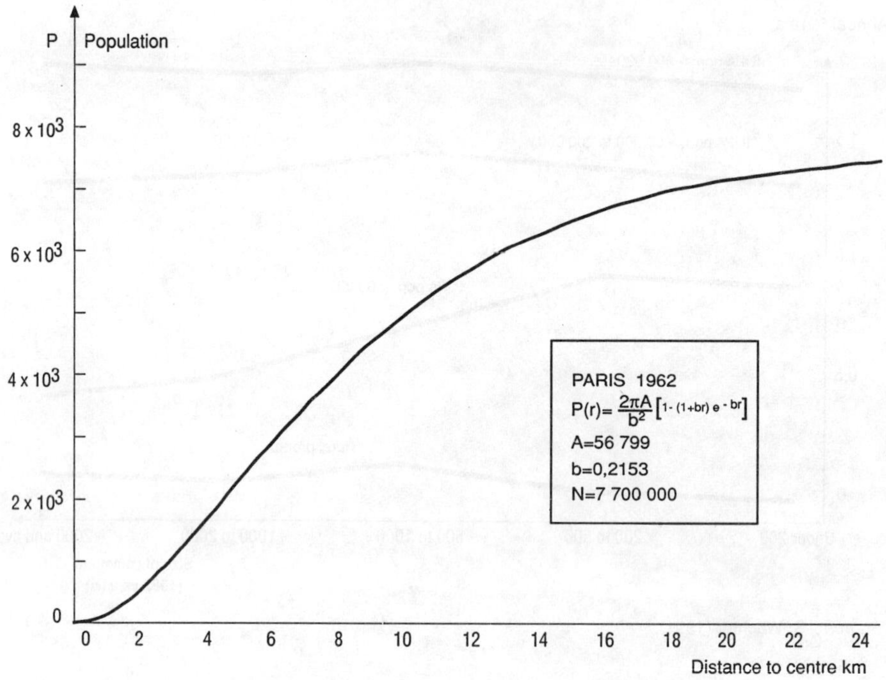

Source: R. Buissière (1972)

Figure 9. **Paris growth/spread tendency**
(1911-1968, fitted curves; after 1968, simulated curves)

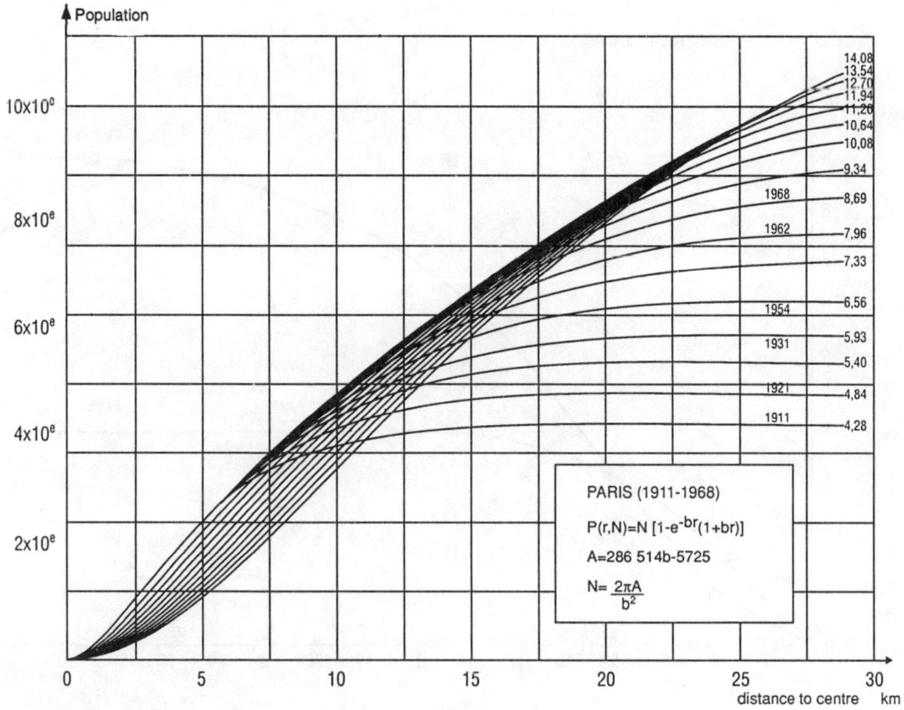

Source: R. Bussière (1972).

Figure 10. **Determination of growth/spread between two periods**

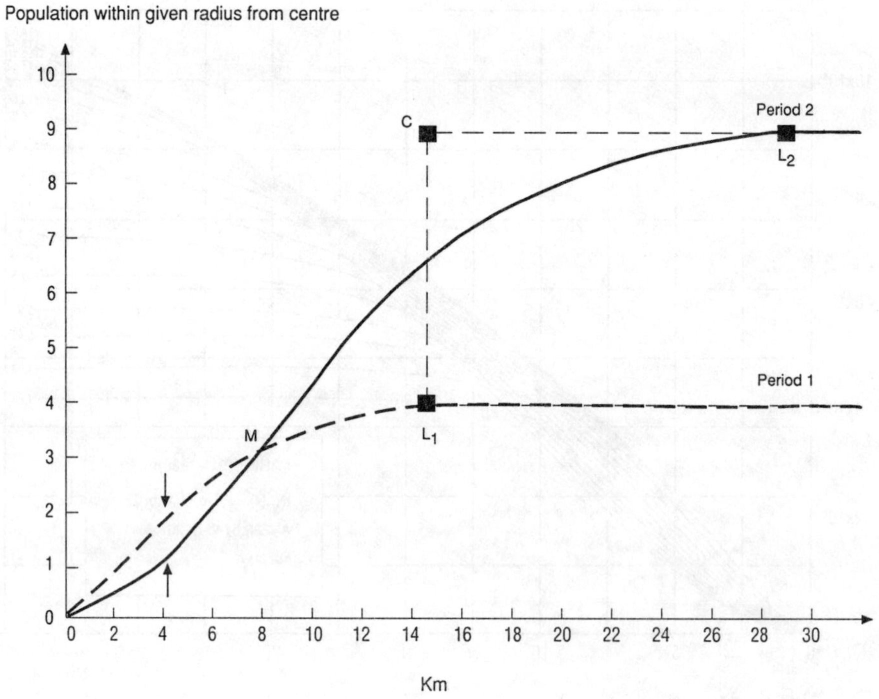

Source: A. Bonnafous, H. Puel (1983).

Figure 11. **Concentration of immigrants in urban areas**

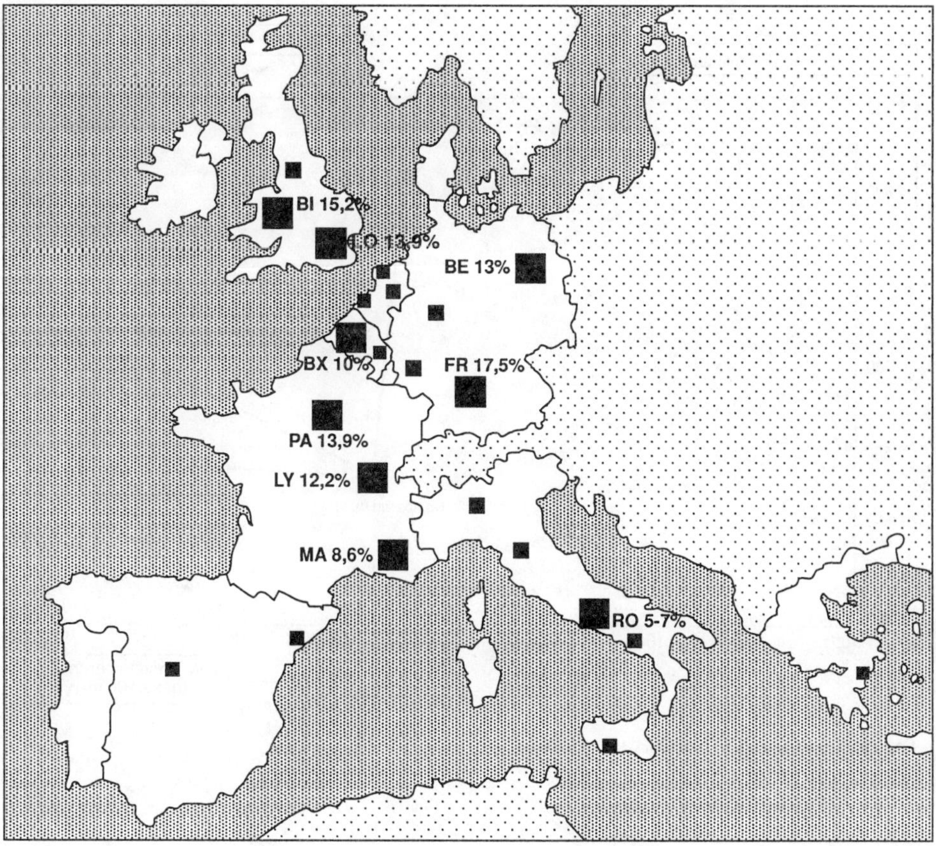

Source: Giovanni Agnelli Foundation (1991).

Figure 12. **Effects of major factors on the twofold crisis in urban transport**

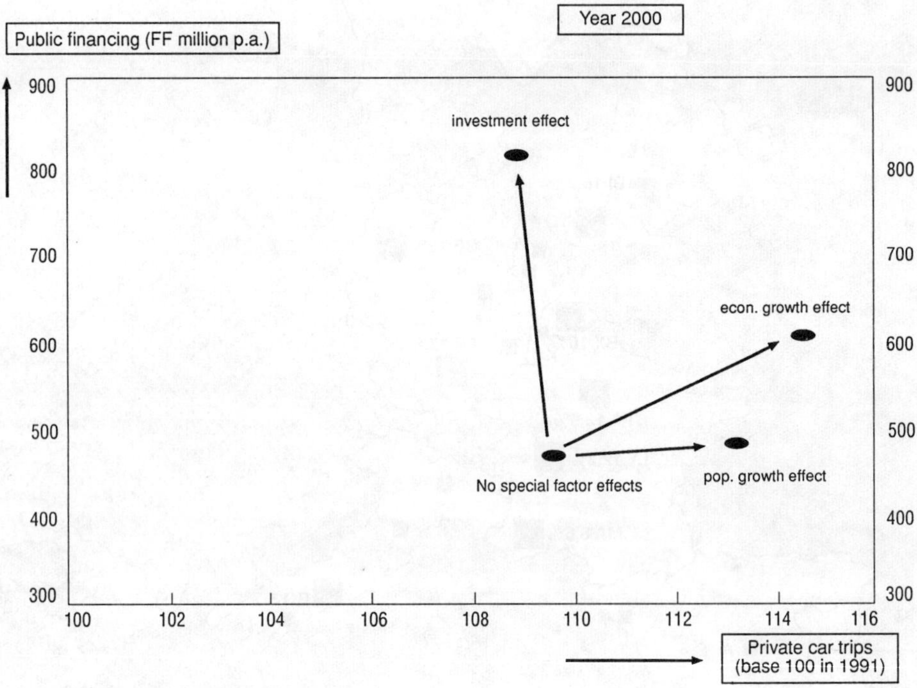

Source: **QUINQUIN (LET) model, case of Lyons.**

Figure 13. **Combined effects of major factors**

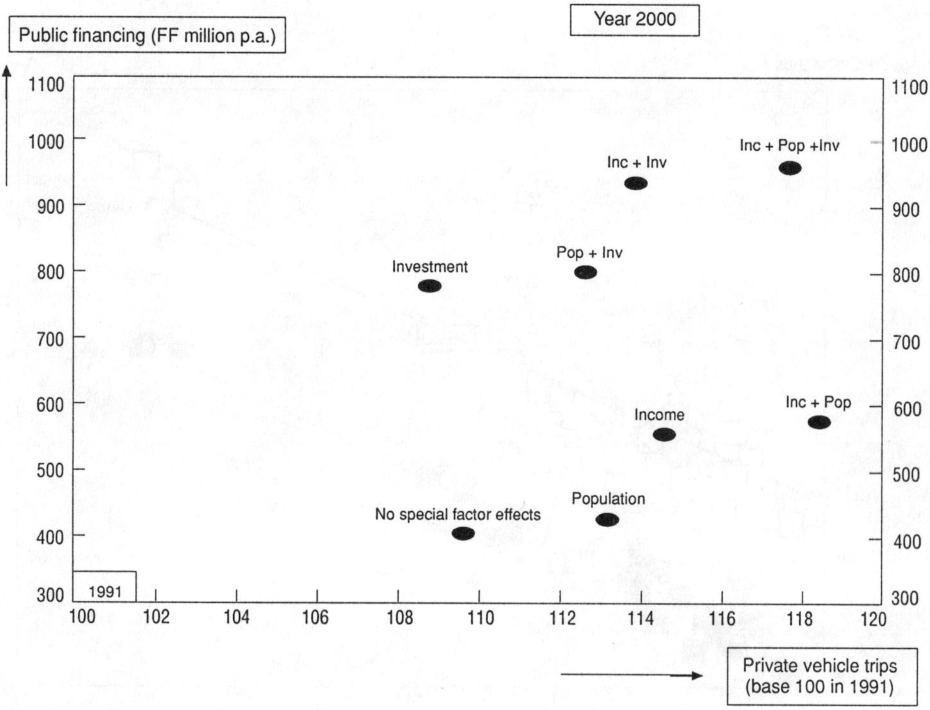

Source: QUINQUIN (LET) model, case of Lyons.

Figure 14. **Effect of size on public transport capicity and demand**
LOG-LOG chart

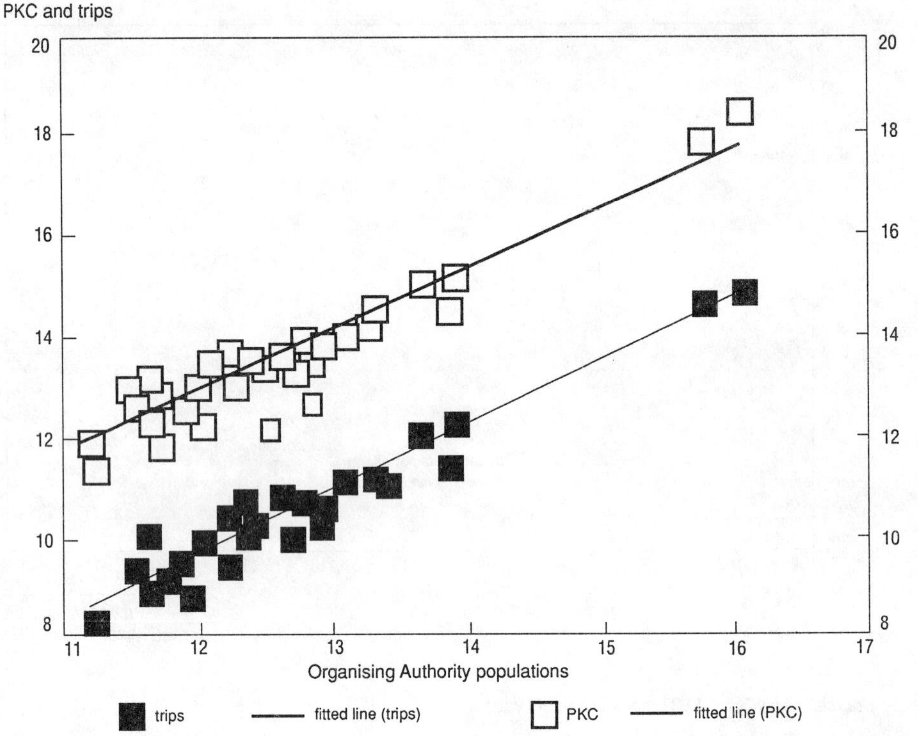

Source: A. Chausse *et al.* (1991).

Figure 15. **Effect of size on public transport capicity and operating costs**
LOG-LOG chart

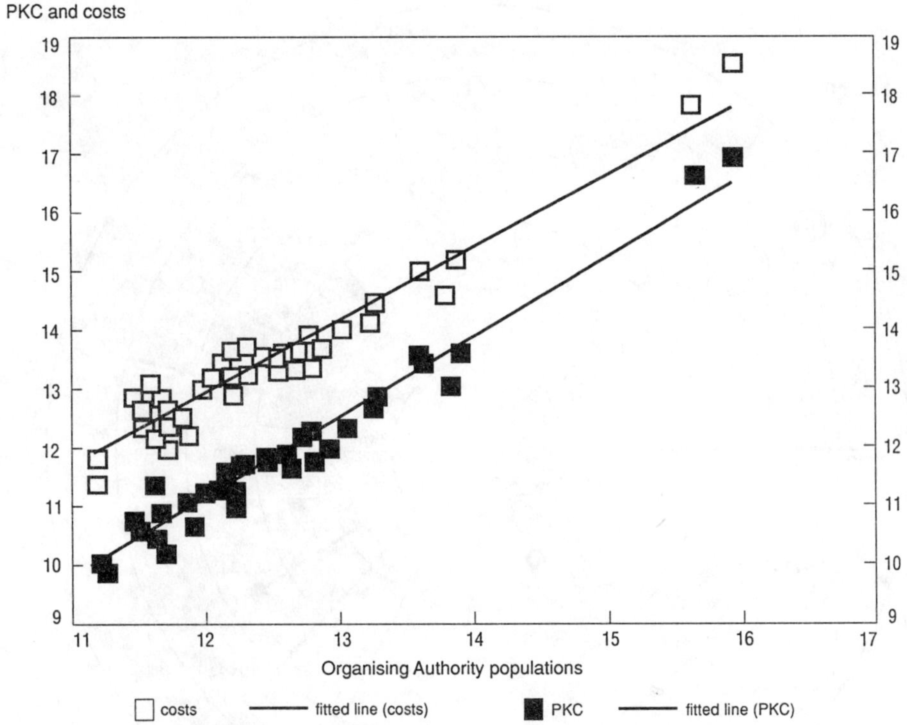

Source: A. Chausse *et al.* (1991).

Figure 16. **Trends in the proportion of total traffic, accounted for by public transport, 1970-1980 - Case of Bern**

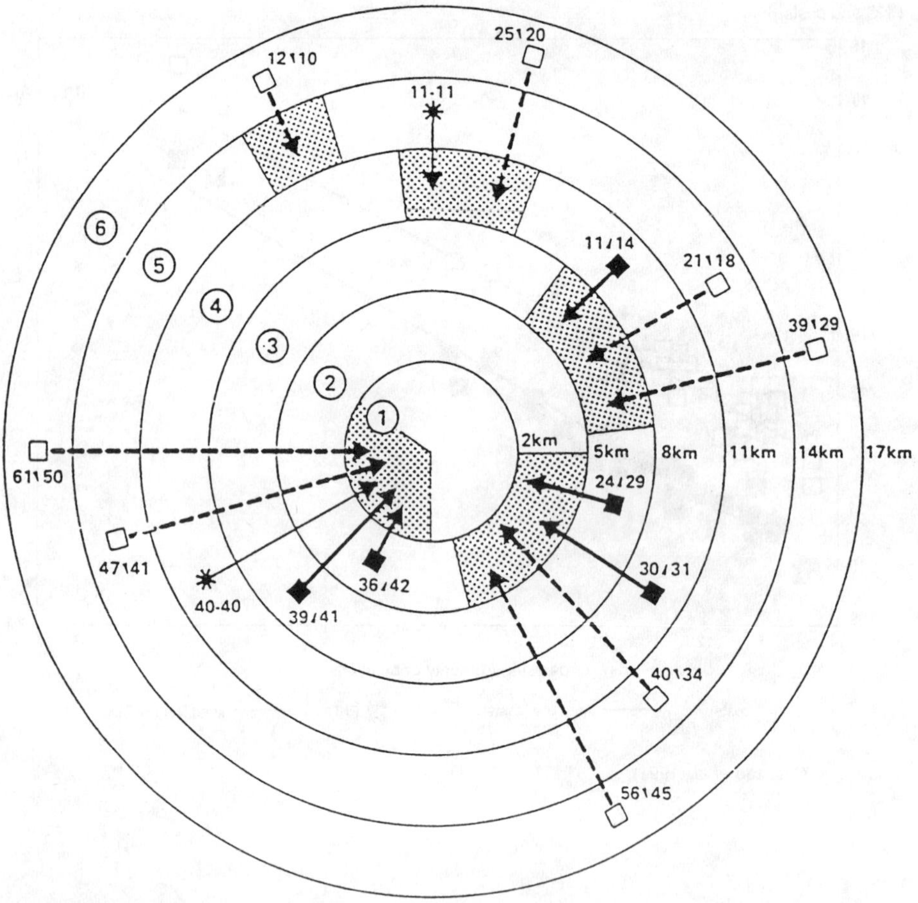

Key: 36/42 ■ Uptrend '70-'80 (5 routes)
40/40 ✳ Flat '70-'80 (2 routes)
47/41 □ Downtrend '70-'80 (8 routes)

Source: P. Güller (1987), quoted by Ph. Bovy (1987).

Figure 17. **Influence of constraints on modal choice in residential suburbs**

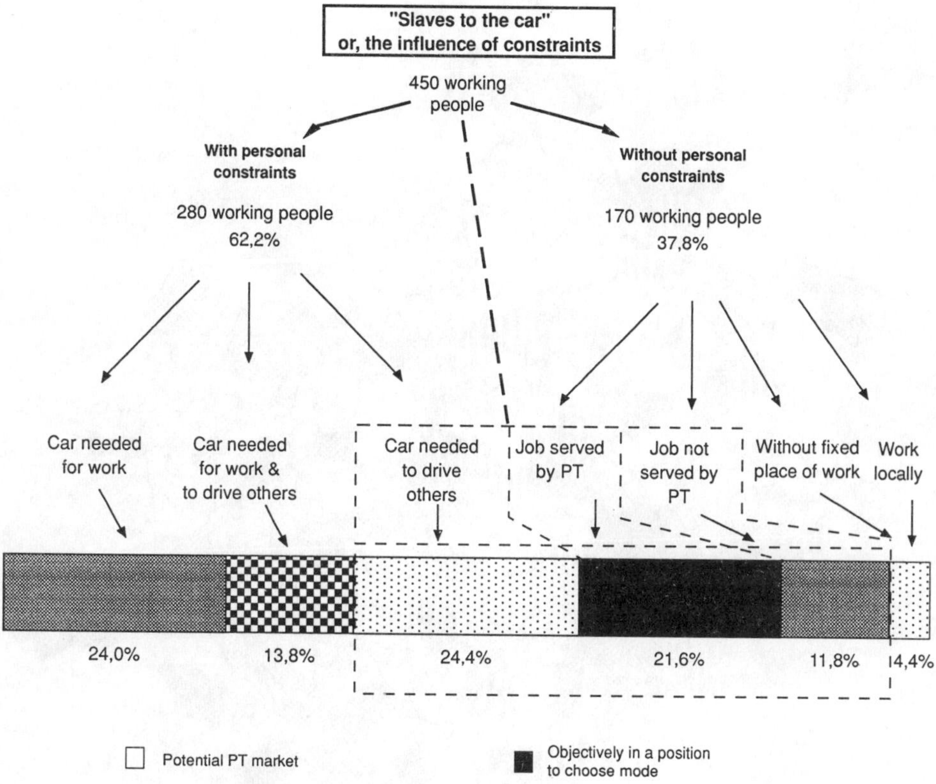

Source: O. Andan *et al.* (1991).

Figure 18. **Percentage of working population in the Paris region who work in the commune(*) where they live**

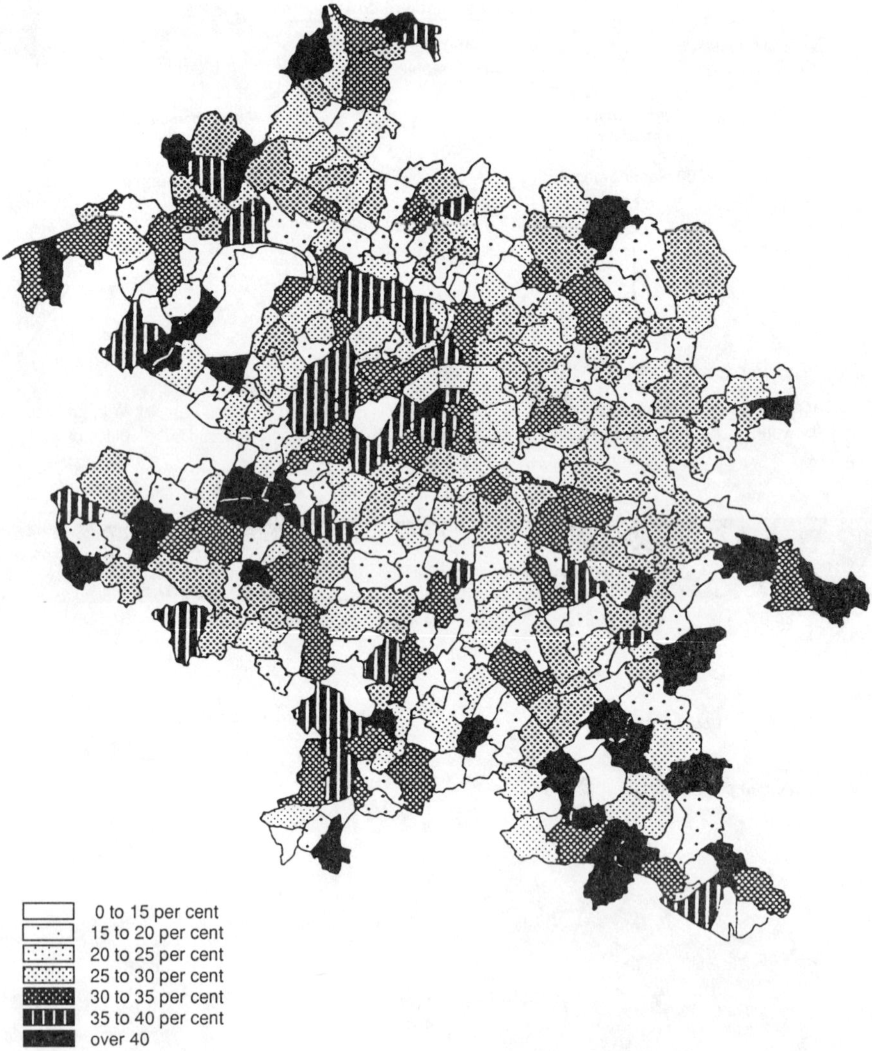

* Or Paris arrondissement.
Source: P. Merlin (1991.)

Figure 19. **Percentage of working population who work in Paris (*)**

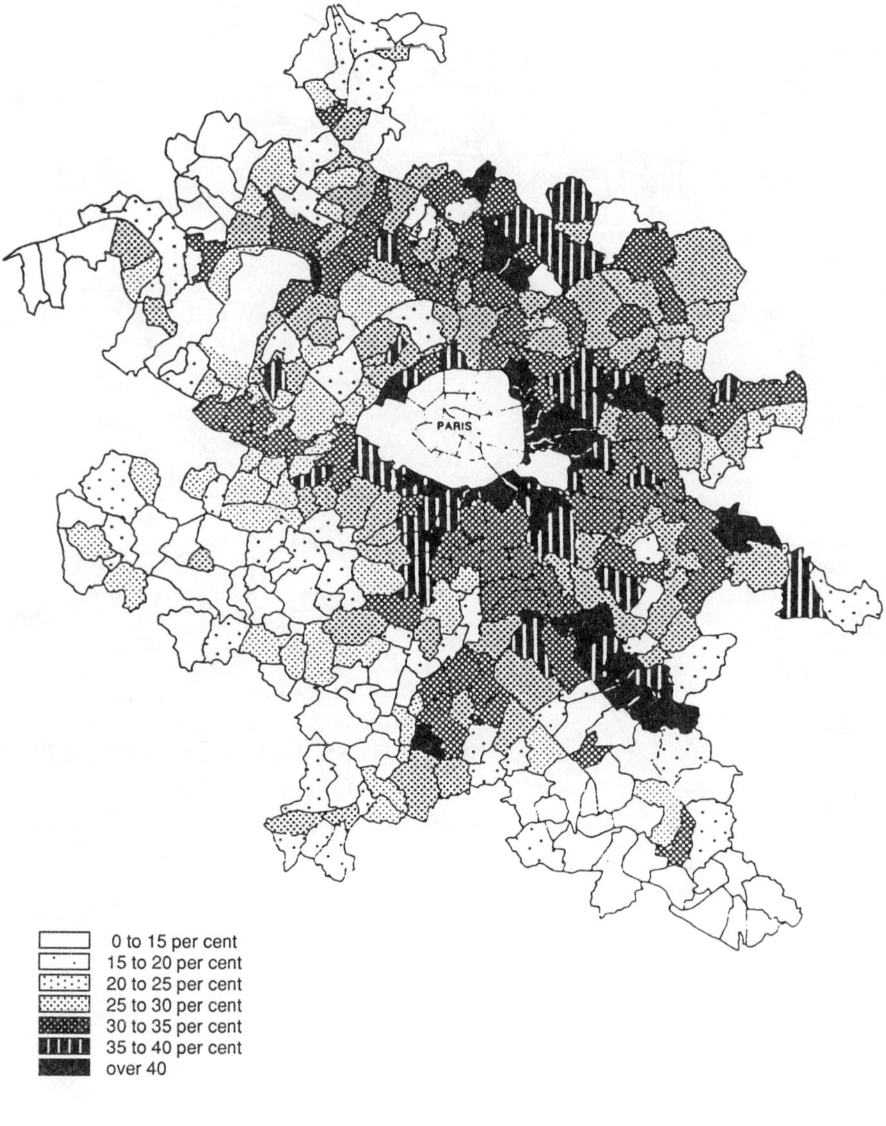

* Paris arrondissements: over 75 %.
Source: P. Merlin (1991.)

Figure 20. **Interregional flows in Europe in 1982**
(All modes of transport)

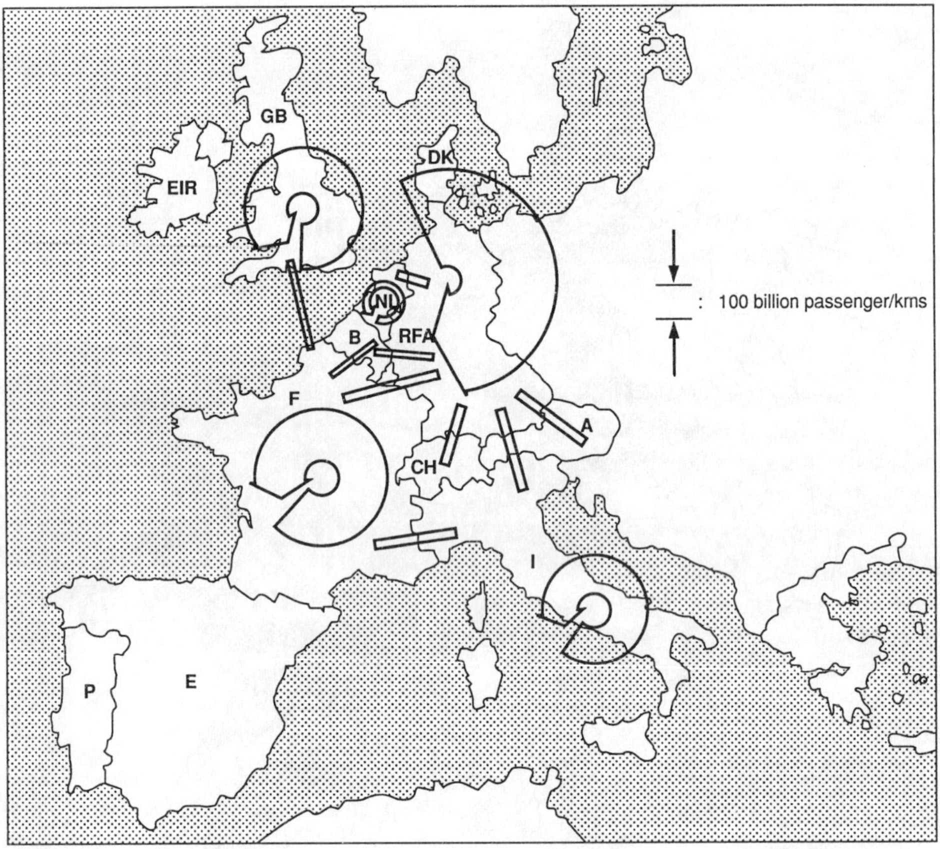

Source: G. Dobias (1989).

BIBLIOGRAPHY

Andan, O., Bonnel, P., Raux, C.: Les analyses des comportements de mobilité individuelle quotidienne -- Une synthèse bibliographique, Laboratoire d'Économie des Transports, Lyons, 1988.

Andan, O., Faivre d'Arcier, B., Raux, C., Cusset, J.M.: Transport et mode de vie des ménages périurbains, Summary Note, LET and INRETS, Lyons, 1991.

Aydalot, Ph.: Économie régionale et urbaine, Economica, Paris, 1985.

Bleicher, H.: Statistische Beschreibung der Stadt Frankfurt am Main und ihrer Bevölkerung, Frankfurt am Main, 1892.

Bonnafous, A., Puel, H.: Physionomies de la ville, Ed. Économie et Humanisme, les Éditions Ouvrières, Paris, 1983.

Bonnafous, A.: Simulation du financement du transport urbain: le modèle QUINQUIN, Transports Urbains No. 54, GETUM, Paris, 1985.

Bonnafous, A.: Comparison of the Effects of Urban Transport Investment, OECD-ECMT Report, Paris, 1991.

Bouf, D., Gargaillo, L.: Les modèles QUINQUIN, in "Villes déplacements et transports: quelles évolutions?", Transport Urbanisme Planification Vol. 7, Paris, 1985.

Bouf, D.: Un nouvel instrument pour le dialogue stratégique entre la RATP et ses partenaires: le modèle GROS QUINQUIN, thesis, University Lumière-Lyon 2, Lyons, 1989.

Bovy, Ph.: Réflexions sur les transports d'agglomération de l'an 2000, Route et trafic No. 12-87, Solothurn, 1987.

Bussière, R., Modèle urbain de localisation résidentielle, Centre de Recherche d'Urbanisme, Paris, 1972.

Chausse, A., Denant-Boemont, L., Hammiche, S.: Coûts de transport collectif en fonction de la taille des villes, Progress Report, Laboratoire d'Économie des Transports, Lyons, 1991.

Cheshire, P., Hay, D., Carbonaro, G.: Regional Policy and Urban Decline, University of Reading, 1983.

Clark, C.: Urban Population Densities, Journal of the Royal Statistical Society, Vol. CXIV, Part IV, 1951.

Clark, C.: Population Growth and Land Use, Macmillan, London, 1967.

Clark, C.: Transports urbains et exclusion sociale, Conseil National des Transports, Paris, 1991.

Dobias, G.: Les transports interrégionaux de personnes, Presse de l'École Nationale des Ponts et Chaussées, Paris, 1989.

Dobias, G.: Immigration Policies for Italy and Europe, Giovanni Agnelli Foundation, XXI Seculo No. 3, Turin, 1991.

Dobias, G.: Population Trends and Europe, Forward Studies Unit, Commission of the European Communities, Brussels, 1991.

Güller, P.: Agglomerationsverkehrsstudie Bern, Interim Report, Zurich, 1987.

Güller, P.: Étude du développement d'un réseau ferroviaire à grande vitesse dans la Communauté Européenne, INRETS, NVI, DFVLR, Study for the EEC, Brussels, 1986.

Jones, P.M., Dix, M.C., Clarke, M.I., Heggie, I.G.: Understanding Travel Behaviour, Oxford Studies of Transport, Gower, 1983.

Klaassen, L., Molle, W.T.M., Paelink, J.H.P.: Dynamics of Urban Development, St. Martin's Press, 1981.

Le Bras, H.: La concentration de la population française, Classeur DATAR -- Prospective et territoire, Paris, 1991.

Madre, J.-L., Lambert, T.: Prévisions à long terme du trafic automobile, Collection of Reports by the CREDOC, Paris, 1989.

Merlin, P.: Géographie, économie et planification des transports, Presses Universitaires de France, 1991.

Moriconi-Ebrard, F.: Les 100 plus grandes villes du monde, Économie et Statistique No. 245, INSEE, Paris, 1991.

Nüsser, H.G.: Effects of "Frontier Impedance Factors", Proceedings of the symposium "Les couloirs Rhin-Rhône dans l'espace européen", LET, Lyons, 1989.

Raux, C., Tabourin, E.: Les investissements en transports collectifs dans l'agglomération lyonnaise: simulation des effets et risques financiers, Laboratoire d'Économie des Transports -- Communauté Urbaine de Lyon, Lyons, 1991.

Raux, C., Tabourin, E.: Comment se déplacent les Lyonnais? SYTRAL *et al.*, (Syndicat Mixte des Transports pour le Rhône et l'Agglomération Lyonnaise), Lyons, 1990.

Tabourin, E.: Un modèle de simulation du financement public des transports collectifs urbains à l'horizon 2000: le modèle QUINQUIN, Transport Environnement Circulation No. 87, Paris, 1988.

Tabourin, E.: Un modèle de financement des transports collectifs à l'horizon 2000. Le modèle QUINQUIN. Application à l'agglomération lyonnaise, thesis, Université Lumière-Lyon 2, Lyons, 1989.

Tabourin, E.: La circulation routière, faits et chiffres, Union Routière de France, Paris, 1991.

Wachter, S.: Recensement 1990: Évolutions démographiques et enjeux pour l'aménagement du territoire, Classeur DATAR -- Prospective et territoire, Paris, 1991.

Wilson, A.G.: Development of Some Elementary Location Models, Journal of Regional Science No. 9, 1969.

Sub-topic 1

DEMOGRAPHIC STRUCTURES AND SOCIAL BEHAVIOUR

A. VAN DEN BROECKE
Social Research BV
Amsterdam
The Netherlands

SUMMARY

Amsterdam, January 1992

1. INTRODUCTION

The subject "Demographic Structure and Social Behaviour" covers a very broad field. This paper will deal with a subgroup of domains of social behaviour: only those domains of social behaviour which lead to mobility and to the acquisition of means for private transportation.

1.1. Definitions

Social behaviour is, for this purpose, defined as including every behaviour which is connected to or dependent on the society in which the behaviour takes place; excluded, however, is behaviour that has no connection with personal mobility (sitting at home, receiving guests or visitors, working at home, sleeping, etc.). Thus we include in "social behaviour": working outdoors, travelling for work, attending education, shopping, spending free time outside the house (visiting friends and relatives, going out, making leisure trips, spending vacations), other personal business.

Demographic structure can be regarded from many viewpoints: in this paper, demographic structure will be restricted to those aspects which have a significant relationship to the development of future mobility. For this purpose, demographic structure will be defined as the composition of the population as to age groups, decision units, and positions of persons with regard to the economic process (working versus not working in the economy).

1.2. A new approach

This paper will deal with a new approach in long-term forecasting of future mobility and future car ownership, based on the concept of demographic change and its impact on changes in the social behaviour which generates mobility.

In this new approach, mobility-generating social behaviour is linked to the demographic structure of the society in which this behaviour takes place.

Based on this linkage, the resulting development of mobility and acquisition of means for private transportation is then calculated. This new model for forecasting the development of mobility in a society is a disaggregated model with two special features:

-- It is based on developments in **birth year cohorts** instead of on developments in **age groups**;

-- **Consumption units** are used as mobility units instead of **total households.**

1.3. The choice of cohorts

As structures of present societies are undergoing dramatic changes as a result of demographic processes and as changes in mobility behaviour in societies depend heavily on these demographic processes, it is incomprehensible that many transport researchers who are working on forecasting still do not use the methods which are commonly used by demographers to forecast future developments in their field: analysis of developments in birth year cohorts and making forecasts on the basis of these developments.

1.4. The choice of decision units

It is also very striking that transport economists still regard the household as the unit for mobility production in this society. In a household-oriented society this is an adequate method, but it is a well-known fact that in modern western societies older children, even when they are still living with their parents, make their own decisions with regard to their behaviour which creates mobility.

As most children of 18 years and older are more or less financially independent from their parents, they will make their own decisions with regard to their social activities and with regard to buying mopeds, motor bicycles and cars. As the main concern for governments is the rapid growth of car ownership and use, I think it is better to abandon, for forecasts in this transport segment, the concept of households and use the concept of **consumer units**. Persons who share life together as "couples" -- married or unmarried -- will tend to make important decisions as to their "life style" together, whereas older children (over 18), as long as they do not have a permanent "living together" relationship, will take these decisions by themselves, just as "singles" will do (including the heads of one-parent families).

As **consumer units**, will be regarded "couples" on the one hand and "singles" on the other hand, with for "couples" their average age as the "age" of the couple.

2. DEMOGRAPHIC STRUCTURE AND THE SOCIAL BEHAVIOUR PATTERN

The pattern of (social) activities involving mobility and the use of means of transport of the population in a country or region depends, for an important part, on its demographic structure as defined in the previous chapter.

Populations of the same size with different social structures will have different activity patterns with subsequent different mobility patterns, even when all other factors are equal.

Among others are the following important variables:

-- The number of households, which is partly linked with the distribution of the population over age groups, but also with the ratio singles/couples in the adult part of the population.

   The latter depends also on the age distribution of adults because a high proportion of old people creates many singles as a result of widowing.

-- The age distribution itself: a high proportion of population in the occupational age group gives a higher proportion of mobility connected with work; a high proportion of children creates much mobility for school attending.

Every age group has a somewhat different pattern of mobility, with a large shift when entering adulthood and a large shift when retiring from participation in the production process.

For these reasons it is important, when linking demographic structure and the social behaviour pattern with its subsequent mobility pattern, and when trying to make forecasts for future developments in these patterns, to use a disaggregated model which takes into account at least the following variables:

-- Age and gender;

-- Household position: partner of couple, single, child;

-- Position in the economic process: attending education, working, not working.

3. SOCIAL BEHAVIOUR PATTERN AS GENERATOR OF THE MOBILITY PATTERN

This subject has already been touched upon before. We already restricted the social behaviour being the subject of this study to the social behaviour which generates mobility. It is obvious that with a disaggregation as mentioned in the previous section, the following parts of the mobility pattern are exclusively restricted to certain subgroups:

-- Commuting to work;
-- Travel connected with work;
-- Commuting to school or college.

Highly linked with certain subgroups is:

-- Household shopping;

whereas free time mobility is spread over all the groups, but with the amount of mobility, the distribution of travel modes and the composition of motives being different for different subgroups.

4. THE EFFECT OF DEMOGRAPHIC CHANGES ON THE MOBILITY PATTERN

It is clear that when the demographic structure is changing over time, this change as such can bring changes in the total mobility pattern as the proportions of the different subgroups in the population then change. As is well known, the populations in most European countries will change dramatically in the next decades as to age composition and the ratio couples/singles. Especially, the rapid increase of the proportion of elderly people in the next decades, being accustomed to a high degree of mobility by car and having a much larger spending budget than the previous generations of elderly people, will cause a large shift in the mobility pattern. Also the increasing proportion of singles and the lower birth rate can cause a shift in the mobility pattern, as cars will become more and more "personal cars" instead of "family cars".

5. ADVANTAGES OF THE COHORT MODEL FOR FORECASTING

To study changes over time in mobility pattern, caused by slow but dramatic demographic changes, needs a special approach. Whereas it is common for demographers to use cohort models to make their forecasts for demographic changes over time, in forecasting studies for mobility the cohort approach is new. The reason is that the model builders in transport research have mainly been economists and mathematicians, in which disciplines the concept of cohorts is not current.

The cohort approach can, however, significantly improve the understanding of changes to be expected in the mobility pattern of a population in a country or region which are caused by demographic processes as such.

Expanding a cohort model to also include external factors, such as economic growth, development of costs of car owning and car use, development of service level and prices for public transport, governmental policies with regard to the development of infrastructure and car use restriction measures, is a promising way to improve further understanding of the dynamics in the development of the mobility pattern over time.

External factors can be introduced as "future scenarios". Effects of scenario variations on the resulting mobility pattern can be studied to enable researchers to provide policymakers with information on possible outcomes of different external developments and different governmental policies. The application of scenarios will be discussed in Chapter 7.

There are many advantages of a cohort model over traditional non-cohort models. One of the main features is that a cohort model is a dynamical model.

Further, the cohort model is more accessible and comprehensible in contrast to many forecast models which make forecasts on an aggregated level using models which do not show the intermediate steps but only the end result and which are often mathematically rather complicated. Thus, the three main advantages of the cohort model are:

-- The model is dynamical: history is preserved as developments in each cohort depend upon the developments in the **same** cohort in previous periods; non-cohort models either neglect the fact that the composition of the population is drastically changing over a long period by the process of the continuous birth of new cohorts, ageing of all present cohorts and the dying of people, or these models are not dynamical when disaggregating into and working with age groups.

-- The model output shows all the intermediate steps and can easily be checked by others; the effects of all the calculations on cohorts remain visible or can easily be made visible when implemented on a spreadsheet program. There is no "black box".

-- The model is comprehensible as there is a close linkage with the input scenarios which can also be shown as output, as every link remains stored in the spreadsheet.

6. THE METHOD OF LONG-TERM FORECASTING WITH THE COHORT MODEL

In the long-term cohort forecasting model, the development of mobility over time of birth year cohorts is studied instead of the development of mobility over time within the same age groups. For this purpose, the first step is to extract mobility data and mobility-related data for birth year cohorts from past surveys and to relate these to the development of relevant factors in the covered (historical) time.

6.1. Two categories of variables

These (independent) relevant factors for cohorts consist of two categories of variables:

-- *External variables*: relevant historical developments in time (e.g. economic growth, the development of costs of car ownership and use, development of service level and prices for public transport).

-- *Internal variables for cohorts*: as birth year cohorts grow older they pass through specific life stages in which their composition as to household positions (single, part of a couple) and positions in participation in the economic process (study, work, retirement) as well as their incomes and disposable budgets, are changing.

Some internal variables within a birth year cohort remain fairly constant during life: the composition of the cohort as to educational and socio-economic level. But in this aspect different birth year cohorts differ: the later the birth year, the higher the percentages of higher educational levels.

For unravelling the effects of external versus the effects of internal variables, a procedure of analysis is necessary with which equations with two unknown independent variables can be solved.

The trick is to compare the values of the dependent variables in cohort X in year Y which has then the age A, with both the values of the dependent variables of the same cohort X in year Y-T and the values in the cohort X-T which had the age A in the year Y-T. With this procedure one can distinguish between the effect of ageing (with the change in values of its internal variables) and of the passing of time (with the change in values of its external variables).

In practice, this comparison is not as simple as described because of necessary corrections for the composition of both cohorts. What is described is the general procedure.

6.2. Five-year cohorts and five-year leaps

Even if we use large past surveys of tens of thousands of persons, disaggregation into single birth years, which for analysis purposes have to be disaggregated into further subgroups, gives results with a high degree of statistical inaccuracy. On the other hand, economic and demographic developments are slow and significant changes can only be found when a much longer period than one year is taken into account. Also for long-term forecasting into an uncertain future, leaps of five years make the forecast model simpler. For these reasons, but mainly for the first two reasons, it is practical not to disaggregate into birth year cohorts, but into cohort groups of five birth years (quinquennium cohorts) and to make the historical analysis also for periods of five years instead of for one-year periods. By grouping birth year cohorts into five-year cohorts, one can, of course, take every group boundary, but one has to consider that the choice of these boundaries determines the choice of the years of measurement and forecast. Because the years 2000, 2010 and 2015 are favoured by politicians as forecast years, it is practical to choose the birth year periods for five-year cohorts ending in 9 or 4. As an example: persons born in the years 1960, 1961, 1962, 1963 and 1964 will be in the age group 50-54 on 1st January 2015.

6.3. Data collection

In the Netherlands, the Dutch Central Bureau of Statistics started with very large surveys on mobility and car ownership in the late seventies, carried out every year; so, by averaging data derived from the surveys 1979-80, 1984-85 and 1989-90 for five-year age groups and converting these age groups into the related five-year cohorts, the dependent variables (average levels of mobility and car ownership per five-year cohort) are known for 1/1/1980, 1985 and 1990, respectively. It is obvious that the total mobility and car ownership of the total population can be found by simply aggregating the cohorts. From other Dutch Central Bureau of Statistics surveys and counts, we can derive demographic data on the composition of these five-year cohorts as to household position, position in the economic process, educational level, income level (internal variables for cohorts). From statistics of the Dutch Central Planning Bureau and other sources, levels of and changes in external variables can be derived for the mentioned years and yearly intervals.

6.4. Finding the mathematical functions in the model

The next step is to find the mathematical relationships between the changes of the mobility and car ownership pattern within each cohort with changes in internal variables, on the one hand and changes in external variables, on the other hand. The basic method with which this is done has been mentioned before: comparing values at T with values at T-5 for both same cohort and previous cohort. This analysis will result in mathematical functions and estimated parameters which can describe as closely as possible the changes in mobility pattern and car ownership within a cohort as functions of changes in internal variables, on the one hand and changes in external variables, on the other hand. Part of these parameters are elasticities.

6.5. Forecasting

The final step is to make the long-term forecasts. In this model, forecasts necessarily have to be made in five-yearly steps: from 1990 to 1995, from 1995 to 2000, from 2000 to 2005, from 2005 to 2010, from 2010 to 2015. For every five-year step we need for each five-year cohort the expected changes in internal variables, the expected changes in external variables and estimates for all the parameters in the functions.

7. THE USE OF FUTURE SCENARIOS

For forecasting the independent variables in future years, data for the future input variables and values for future parameters are needed.

This means that scenarios are needed about future developments of both external and internal variables and that assumptions have to be made about expected future developments in the values of parameters and elasticities.

This has to be done per five-year period.

Once the forecasting model has been made, the variables to be forecasted -- mobility pattern and car ownership -- can be recalculated for each scenario simply by changing the input variables and input parameters.

In the Netherlands, scenarios for the future development of input variables are made by the Dutch Central Bureau of Statistics (demographic developments per cohort) and by the Dutch Central Planning Bureau (economic and socio-economic developments at macro level, some developments at educational level and labour participation per cohort).

Future developments are, in fact, unpredictable and the only way to find out what is likely to happen under certain circumstances is to create scenarios about possible circumstances. Developments in elasticities have to be estimated from the elasticities found in the analysis of the past developments. This should be done by a panel of experts in transportation research. As values of some elasticities, e.g. for car ownership and use with economic growth, can be influenced by governmental policies other than price setting (e.g. parking restrictions), it is important also to include scenarios for possible future governmental policies when estimating future developments in these elasticities.

8. THE CONSTRUCTION OF THE LONG-TERM COHORT FORECASTING MODEL

The long-term forecasting model can be constructed and used on a personal computer (PC) with a normal spreadsheet program. The basic standard format for the input data, calculations and output, is a table consisting of columns for each target year (1995, 2000, 2005, 2010, 2015), preceded by columns for the measurement years (1980, 1985, 1990 and, if data available, 1975). Including 1975 and up to 2015, we have nine columns. On the rows we have the five-year age groups starting with 15-19, up to 80-84 and then 85+, altogether fifteen rows. (Mobility of persons <15 years old is neglected.)

One set of fifteen rows for singles, one set of fifteen rows for couples, the age for couples being defined as the average age of the partners. Thus the basic spreadsheet table format consists of a table with 9 x 30 = 270 cells. A first preceding column contains the age group labels. An additional row is added for the sums of the columns. This gives the figures for the total population of fifteen years and older.

The total cohort computer model consists of a large set of these basic tables, divided over a number of interlinked spreadsheet files. Part of the files contain tables with input data and input parameters, another part contains tables with the functions or formulas which make use of the input data and input parameters, to calculate the results.

Every cell in the 1995 column -- except those in the first two rows for the 15-19 and 20-24 year group which are calculated otherwise -- is a function of the value in the cell of the same cohort in 1990 (then five years younger), with parameters and other input data found in the identical corresponding cells on other spreadsheet tables. Immediately after 1995 has been calculated, the program calculates 2000 and so on. It is a matter of minutes with a fast PC. A macro program is made to control the necessary linkages and transfers between different spreadsheets and to control the calculation process. It is clear that in practice when constructing the model many partial problems have to be solved. What is described here in short is the general line of construction.

8.1. Side programs

The tables contain, as mentioned, only singles and couples. The main program is constructed in such a way that some tables are fed by calculations made in side programs. There are side programs containing, for instance, spreadsheets with tables of the singles divided into males and females, as these have different proportions of car ownership and different mobility patterns. The number of side programs can be expanded within the total program, with each side program feeding its results into the main program. For example, side programs can be made to calculate average car ownership and average mobility patterns for age groups of couples, starting from couples disaggregated into couples with 0, 1 and 2 workers.

The only purpose of the description in this chapter is to give a general idea about the implementation possibilities of the cohort model approach for forecasting.

9. THE INDEPENDENT VARIABLES

As mentioned before, these consist of two categories:

-- External variables such as economic growth and socio-economic developments (employment), developments in costs of car ownership and use, changes in service level and cost of public transport, governmental policies;

-- Internal variables for cohorts such as distributions over household positions (single, part of a couple) and positions in participation in the economic process (study, work, retirement), incomes and disposable budgets.

9.1. The internal variables

For the demographic variables in the Netherlands very detailed scenarios are being made and constantly updated by the Dutch Central Bureau of Statistics, from which data a detailed household forecast is derived by a private organisation TNO. So all the demographic input data are available for all the cells up to 2015. The Dutch Central Planning Bureau makes forecasts on the five-year age group level for participation in labour. For the development of incomes and disposable budgets no detailed database exists, so these have to be derived from past developments as measured by the Central Bureau of Statistics and macro estimates by the Central Planning Bureau. The estimates for future developments are made as well as possible within the context of the chosen scenario for the external variables.

9.2. The external variables

The external variables are macro variables and as the model needs input for each five-year age group separately, it is needed to derive from these macro variables the effects on each age group. This needs careful judgement, taking other data and known developments into account, looking also at the previous history of every cohort. The decisions about the best estimates within the context of the specific scenario have to be made with a team of experts on the subject.

10. APPLICATION OF THE COHORT MODEL FOR LONG-TERM FORECASTING OF CAR OWNERSHIP IN THE NETHERLANDS

The cohort model was introduced in the Netherlands in 1986 for forecasting car ownership in 2010. This was a first version of the cohort model, described in a paper presented at the Tenth International Symposium on Transportation and Traffic Theory. The report on this study was published in the Netherlands early in 1987 and had a great impact.

At present, the construction of a second version of the cohort forecasting model, as described in this paper, will start for updating the forecasts up to 2015. New future scenarios, at present being developed by the Dutch Central Planning Bureau, will be used. The results of the study will be available in the summer of 1992.

The demographic changes which can be expected in the Netherlands between 1990 and 2015 are given in Figures 1 and 2 on the following pages. Figures 3 and 4 give a possible scenario of growth of car ownership between 1990 and 2015 from 5.1 to 7.5 million cars, calculated with an input scenario that leads to this growth of 2 million cars.

Following the figures, the tables underlying the figures are presented. These tables give more details; the figures in the tables are, however, not yet final because not all the data for 1990 are already exactly known and the scenarios are not yet final. For the moment, however, these tables give the best estimates for 1990 and a reasonable scenario for 2015.

FIGURES

Figure 1. **The Netherlands: Population 15+ 1990 and 2015.**
Population Structure Age Groups Males / Females
Per age group: Sizes of sub-populations of males and females.

1990

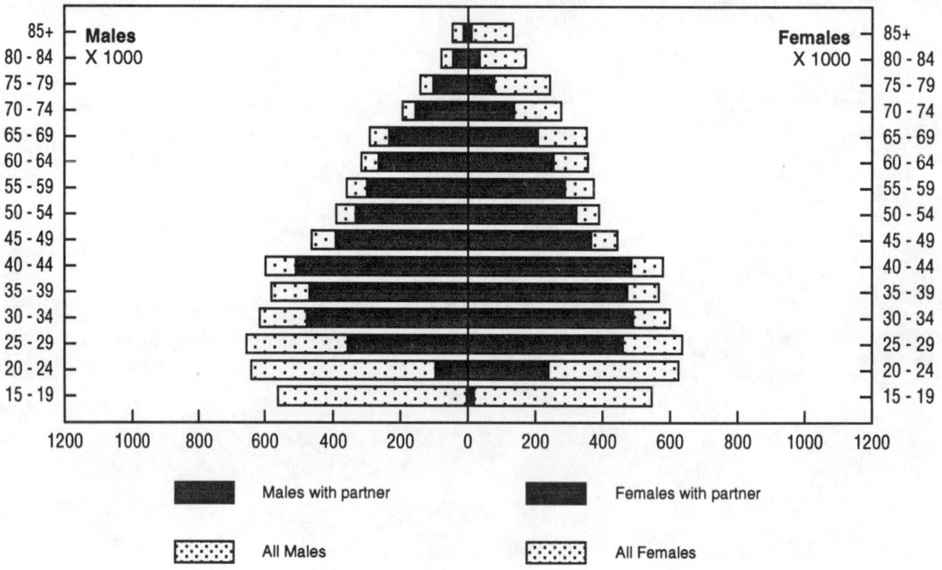

2015

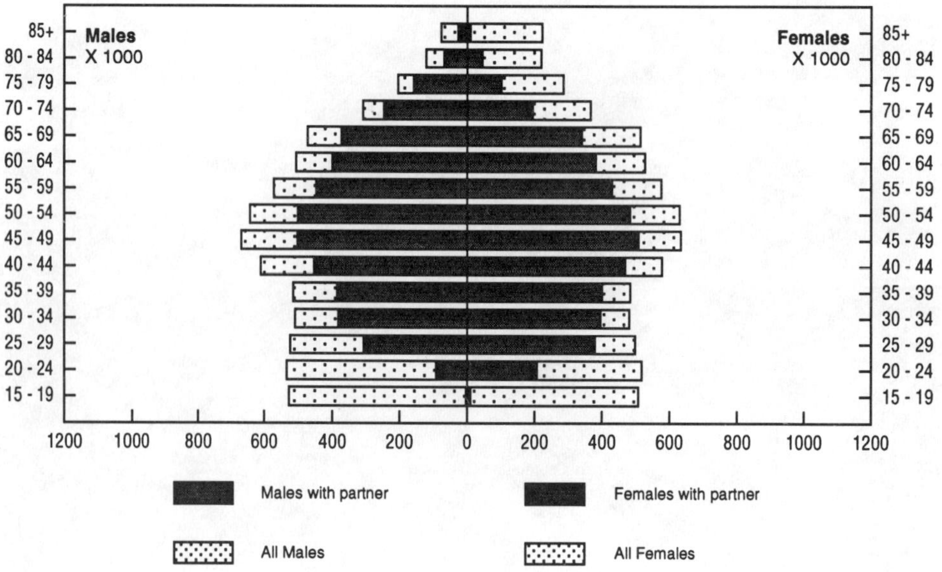

Figure 2. **The Netherlands: Population 15+ 1990 and 2015.**
Population Structure Singles and "Coupled" Persons
Per age group: Singles and "coupled" persons (= with partners).

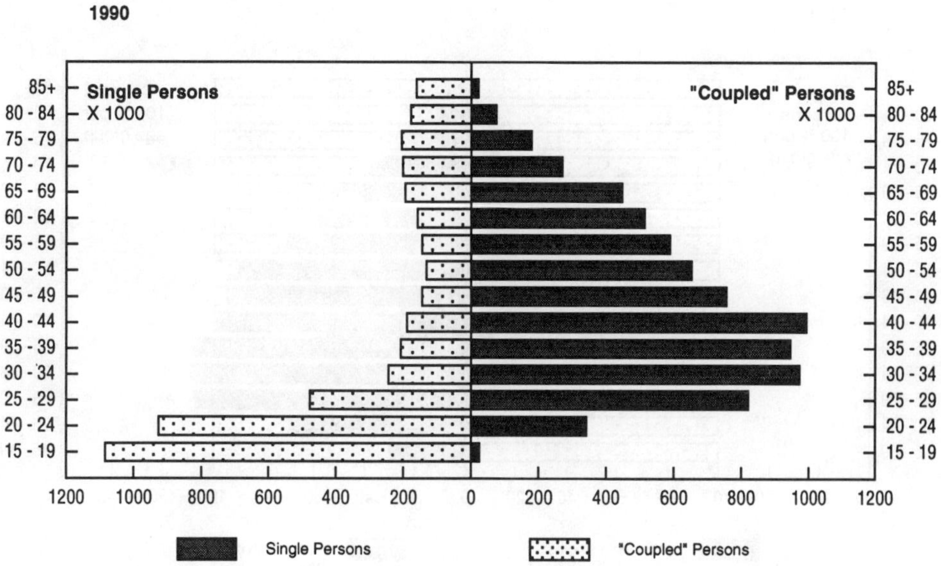

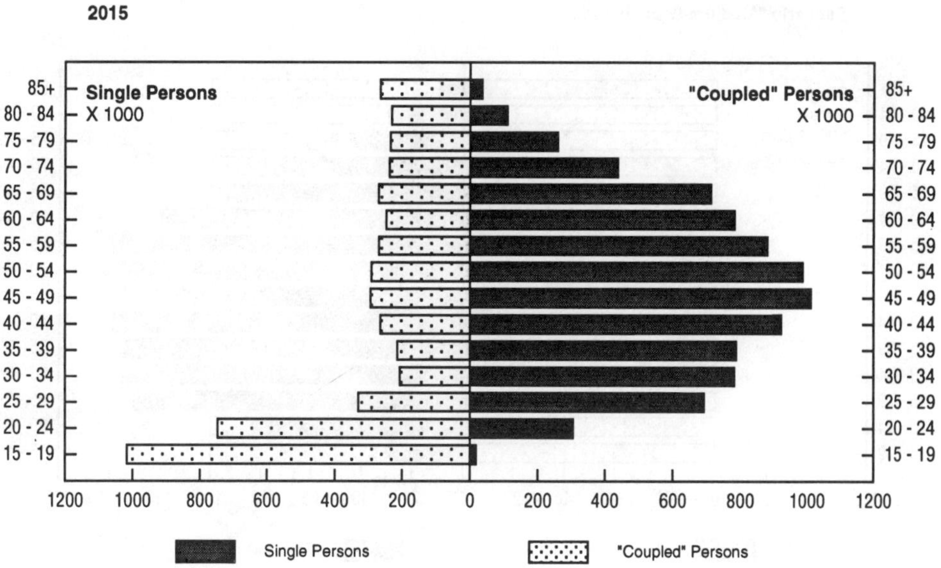

Figure 3. **The Netherlands: Cars 1990 and Scenario 2015.**
Car Ownership Densities with Singles and Couples
Per age group: Numbers of cars per100 singles / couples.

1990

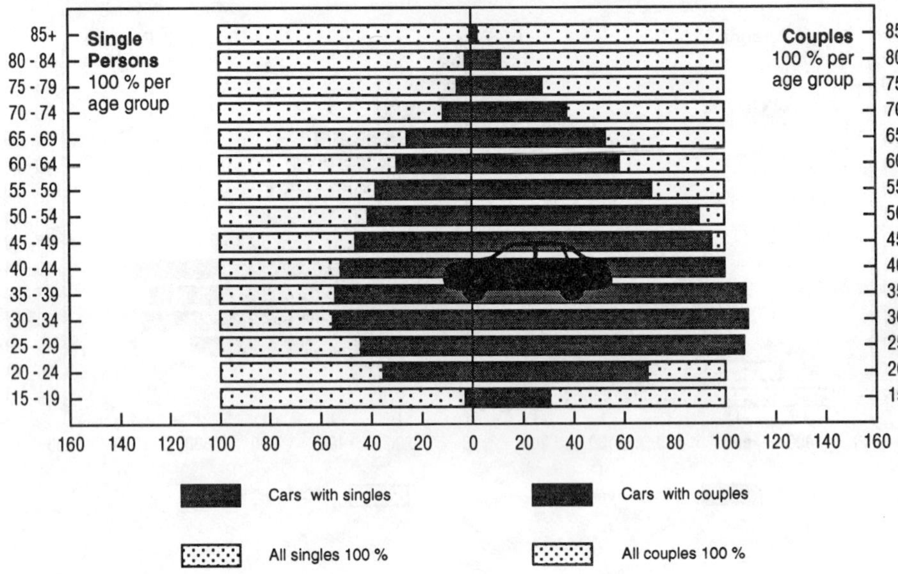

Scenario "Medium Growth": 2015

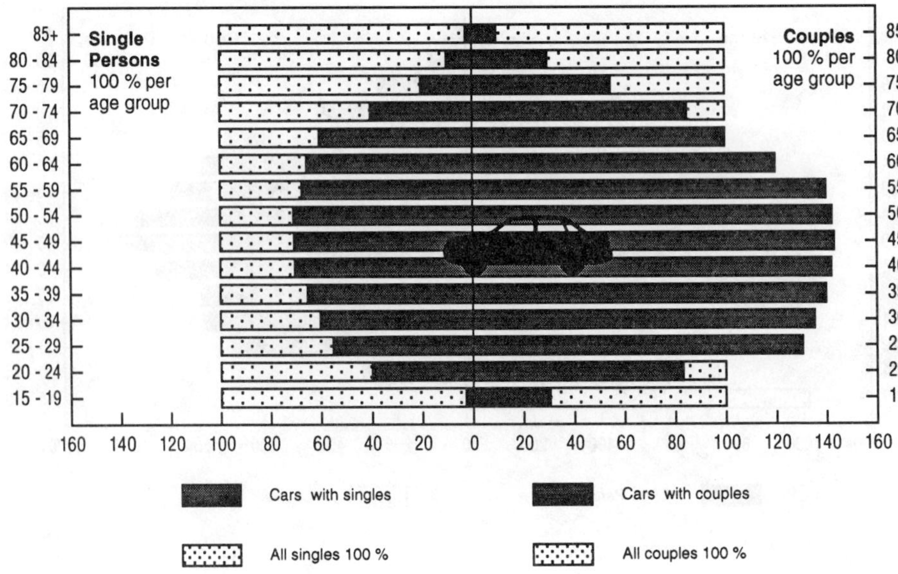

Figure 4. **The Netherlands: Cars 1990 and Scenario 2015.**
Numbers of Passenger Cars with Singles and Couples
Per age group: numbers of cars (x 1000) with singles and couples.

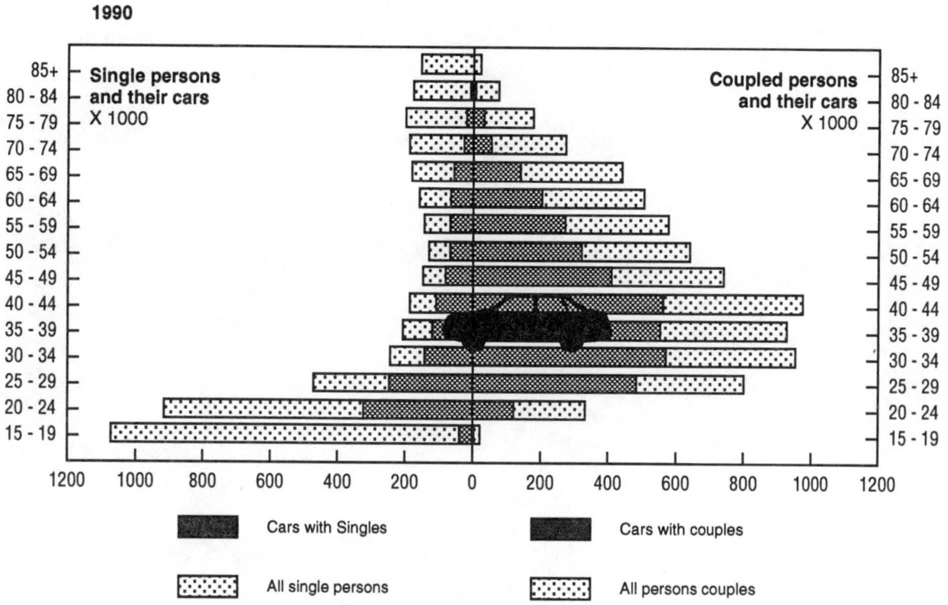

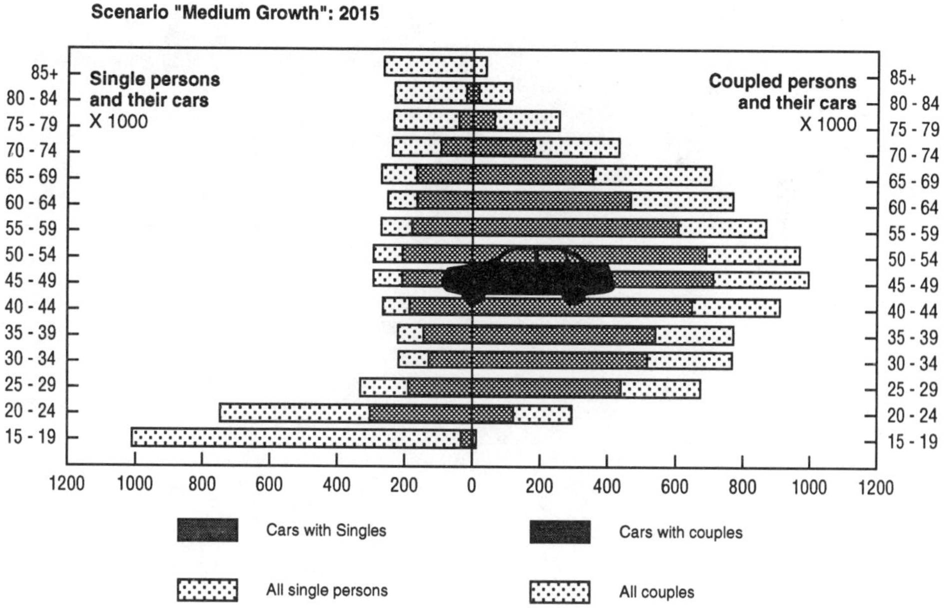

TABLES

Table 1. **POPULATION 1990**

Demographic structure of population: decision units disaggregated into age groups and participation in labour (The Netherlands 1990) (Labour participation: estimates)

Age Group	DECISION UNITS (x1 000)							
	All Persons	All Singles	All Couples	Singles		Couples		
				0 work	1 works	0 work	1 works	2 work
15-19	1 108	1 088	10	878	210	1	5	4
20-24	1 264	928	168	318	610	7	81	80
25-29	1 290	476	407	118	358	7	258	142
30-34	1 211	245	483	38	207	6	348	129
35-39	1 146	208	469	35	173	3	349	117
40-44	1 176	186	495	31	155	5	366	124
45-49	899	143	378	31	112	5	281	92
50-54	780	128	326	31	97	10	231	85
55-59	727	141	293	45	96	45	172	76
60-64	669	155	257	88	67	110	121	26
65-69	629	181	224	176	5	222	2	0
70-74	469	187	141	187	0	141	0	0
75-79	381	199	91	199	0	91	0	0
80+	430	326	52	326	0	52	0	0
AGE GROUPS AGGREGATED								
15-19	1 108	1 088	10	878	210	1	5	4
20-34	3 765	1 649	1 058	474	1 175	20	687	351
35-59	4 728	806	1 961	173	633	68	1 399	494
60-74	1 767	523	622	451	72	473	123	26
75+	811	525	143	525	0	143	0	0
Totals	12 179	4 591	3 794	2 501	2 090	705	2 214	875

Table 2. **PASSENGER CARS 1990**

Number of passenger cars (x 1 000) with decision units disaggregated into age groups and participation in labour (The Netherlands 1990) (Disaggregation figures: estimates)

Age Group	DECISION UNITS (x1 000)							
	All Persons	All Singles	All Couples	Singles		Couples		
				0 work	1 works	0 work	1 works	2 work
15-19	35	33	2	10	23	0	2	0
20-24	442	325	117	30	295	2	41	74
25-29	737	248	489	15	233	3	289	197
30-34	720	140	580	5	135	2	399	179
35-39	682	119	563	5	114	1	406	156
40-44	675	106	569	5	101	2	415	152
45-49	495	79	416	5	74	2	308	106
50-54	390	64	326	5	59	4	229	93
55-59	343	64	279	10	54	20	176	83
60-64	268	62	206	25	37	60	119	27
65-69	199	54	145	52	2	144	1	0
70-74	83	27	56	27	0	56	0	0
75-79	46	14	32	14	0	32	0	0
80+	15	7	8	7	0	8	0	0
AGE GROUPS AGGREGATED								
15-19	35	33	2	10	23	0	2	0
20-34	1 899	713	1 186	50	663	7	729	450
35-59	2 585	432	2 153	30	402	29	1 534	590
60-74	550	143	407	104	39	260	120	27
75+	61	21	40	21	0	40	0	0
Totals	5 130	1 342	3 788	215	1 127	336	2 385	1067

Table 3. CAR DENSITIES 1990

Densities passenger cars (cars/unit) with decision units disaggregated into age groups and participation in labour (The Netherlands 1990) (Disaggregation figures: estimates)

Age Group	DECISION UNITS (x1 000)							
	All Persons	All Singles	All Couples	Singles		Couples		
				0 work	1 works	0 work	1 works	2 work
15-19	0.03	0.03	0.20	0.01	0.11	0.00	0.40	0.00
20-24	0.35	0.35	0.70	0.09	0.48	0.29	0.51	0.93
25-29	0.57	0.52	1.20	0.13	0.65	0.43	1.12	1.39
30-34	0.59	0.57	1.20	0.13	0.65	0.33	1.15	1.39
35-39	0.60	0.57	1.20	0.14	0.66	0.33	1.16	1.33
40-44	0.57	0.57	1.15	0.16	0.65	0.40	1.13	1.23
45-49	0.55	0.55	1.10	0.16	0.66	0.40	1.10	1.15
50-54	0.50	0.50	1.00	0.16	0.61	0.40	0.99	1.09
55-59	0.47	0.45	0.95	0.22	0.56	0.44	1.02	1.09
60-64	0.40	0.40	0.80	0.28	0.55	0.55	0.98	1.04
65-69	0.32	0.30	0.65	0.30	0.40	0.65	0.50	
70-74	0.18	0.14	0.40	0.14	0.00	0.40		
75-79	0.12	0.07	0.35	0.07	0.00	0.35		
80+	0.03	0.02	0.15	0.02	0.00	0.15		
AGE GROUPS AGGREGATED								
15-19	0.03	0.03	0.20	0.01	0.11	0.00	0.40	0.00
20-34	0.50	0.43	1.12	0.11	0.56	0.35	1.06	1.28
35-59	0.55	0.54	1.10	0.17	0.64	0.43	1.10	1.19
60-74	0.31	0.27	0.65	0.23	0.54	0.55	0.98	1.04
75+	0.08	0.04	0.28	0.04		0.28		
Totals	0.42	0.29	1.00	0.09	0.54	0.48	1.08	1.22

Table 4. **POPULATION 2015**

Demographic structure of population with decision units disaggregated into age groups and participation in labour (The Netherlands: Forecast 2015) (Disaggregation figures: estimates)

Age Group	DECISION UNITS (x1 000)							
	All Persons	All Singles	All Couples	Singles		Couples		
				0 work	1 works	0 work	1 works	2 work
15-19	1 035	1 021	7	920	101	2	2	3
20-24	1 053	755	149	500	255	10	64	75
25-29	1 021	335	343	180	155	10	213	120
30-34	989	211	389	50	161	10	184	195
35-39	1 000	216	392	50	166	10	209	173
40-44	1 191	267	462	50	217	10	336	116
45-49	1 306	298	504	50	248	10	326	168
50-54	1 278	294	492	60	234	10	337	145
55-59	1 149	271	439	90	181	70	244	125
60-64	1 033	249	392	160	89	150	203	39
65-69	988	272	358	262	10	290	58	10
70-74	675	237	219	237	0	219	0	0
75-79	492	232	130	232	0	130	0	0
80+	643	491	76	491	0	76	0	0
AGE GROUPS AGGREGATED								
15-19	1 035	1 021	7	920	101	2	2	3
20-34	3 063	1 301	881	730	571	30	461	390
35-59	5 924	1 346	2 289	300	1 046	110	1 452	727
60-74	2 696	758	969	659	99	659	261	49
75+	1 135	723	206	723	0	206	0	0
Totals	13 853	5 149	4 352	3 332	1 817	1 007	2 176	1 169

Table 5. **PASSENGER CARS 2015**

Number of passenger cars (x 1 000) with decision units disaggregated into age groups and participation in labour (The Netherlands: 2015, Scenario "Medium")

Age Group	DECISION UNITS (x1 000)							
	All Persons	All Singles	All Couples	Singles		Couples		
				0 work	1 works	0 work	1 works	2 work
15-19	33	31	2	10	21	0	1	1
20-24	425	302	123	100	202	3	36	84
25-29	625	179	446	40	139	3	254	189
30-34	660	135	525	10	125	3	197	325
35-39	689	140	549	12	128	3	246	300
40-44	844	187	657	20	167	3	453	201
45-49	930	209	721	20	189	3	424	294
50-54	905	206	699	25	181	4	438	257
55-59	790	176	614	40	136	63	325	226
60-64	632	162	470	92	70	140	268	62
65-69	521	163	358	155	8	275	68	15
70-74	281	95	186	95	0	186	0	0
75-79	117	46	71	46	0	71	0	0
80+	48	29	19	29	0	19	0	0
AGE GROUPS AGGREGATED								
15-19	33	31	2	10	21	0	1	1
20-34	1 710	616	1 094	150	466	9	487	598
35-59	4 158	918	3 240	117	801	76	1 886	1 278
60-74	1 434	420	1 014	342	78	601	336	77
75+	165	75	90	75	0	90	0	0
Totals	7 500	2 060	5 440	694	1 366	776	2 710	1 954

Table 6. **CAR DENSITIES 2015**

Densities passenger cars (cars/unit) with decision units disaggregated into age groups and participation in labour (The Netherlands: 2015, Scenario "Medium")

Age Group	DECISION UNITS (x1 000)							
	All Persons	All Singles	All Couples	Singles		Couples		
				0 work	1 works	0 work	1 works	2 work
15-19	0.03	0.03	0.29	0.01	0.21	0.00	0.50	0.33
20-24	0.40	0.40	0.83	0.20	0.79	0.30	0.56	1.12
25-29	0.61	0.53	1.30	0.22	0.90	0.30	1.19	1.58
30-34	0.67	0.64	1.35	0.20	0.78	0.30	1.07	1.67
35-39	0.69	0.65	1.40	0.24	0.77	0.30	1.18	1.73
40-44	0.71	0.70	1.42	0.40	0.77	0.30	1.35	1.73
45-49	0.71	0.70	1.43	0.40	0.76	0.30	1.30	1.75
50-54	0.71	0.70	1.42	0.42	0.77	0.40	1.30	1.77
55-59	0.69	0.65	1.40	0.44	0.75	0.90	1.33	1.81
60-64	0.61	0.65	1.20	0.58	0.79	0.93	1.32	1.59
65-69	0.53	0.60	1.00	0.59	0.80	0.95	1.17	1.50
70-74	0.42	0.40	0.85	0.40		0.85		
75-79	0.24	0.20	0.55	0.20		0.55		
80+	0.07	0.06	0.25	0.06		0.25		
AGE GROUPS AGGREGATED								
15-19	0.03	0.03	0.29	0.01	0.21	0.00	0.50	0.33
20-34	0.56	0.47	1.24	0.21	0.82	0.30	1.06	1.53
35-59	0.70	0.68	1.42	0.39	0.77	0.69	1.30	1.76
60-74	0.53	0.55	1.05	0.52	0.79	0.91	1.29	1.57
75+	0.15	0.10	0.44	0.10		0.44		
Totals	0.54	0.40	1.25	0.21	0.75	0.77	1.25	1.67

Sub-topic 1

DEMOGRAPHIC STRUCTURES AND SOCIAL BEHAVIOUR

D. BANISTER
University College London
London
United Kingdom

SUMMARY

London, July 1991

ABSTRACT

This paper traces the changes in lifestyle brought about by changing demographic structure in Europe. The last two decades have seen unprecedented growth in travel distances, increases in affluence and the move to the post industrial society. Much of this growth has resulted from the motorisation revolution and it is argued that patterns and habits created in the 1980s are likely to continue into the next century. With the aging population, continued growth in wealth, increased life expectancy and leisure time, this new mobility will expand and the newly retired population will form a major new travel market. Their travel patterns will be car oriented, involving much leisure travel, and this in turn may result in a significant decline in the demand for public transport from the group which has in the past been the major user of public transport. Public transport operators must respond now to these changes through the provision and promotion of new quality services which would have priority in urban areas. Positive action is required to counter the motorisation effect and prevent total gridlock in Europe.

1. THE DECADES OF MOBILITY GROWTH

The car has revolutionised the way in which we look at travel and communications. Before the advent of mass car ownership in the 1960s, people travelled short distances by foot or bicycle with the longer journeys being made by bus and occasionally rail. Life was centred on the locality in which one lived with work, schools, shops and other facilities all being available locally. Travel outside the community was only undertaken for special reasons to visit relatives or to go on holiday. In 1960 each person in Britain travelled on average some 3 000 miles. By 1989 that figure had increased to 7 300 miles. In the 1990s no-one thinks twice about using the car to travel to work, to do the shopping, or to take the children to school. It is used as a form of transport, as a local bus service, as a goods vehicle and as a statement of status. It is often the second largest single item of family expenditure after the home and it is treated with respect and affection. It is generally believed to be the most desirable form of transport and will always be used as the preferred form of transport, no matter how attractive the alternative might be. The user can always think of a reason why the car is necessary for that particular journey.

In real terms the costs of motoring have never been cheaper and some two thirds of households now have a car. To the user the car offers real advantages which alternative forms of transport can never expect to match except in congested urban areas and over long distances. The car has a unique flexibility in that it is always available, it offers door-to-door transport and it effectively acts as a detached extension to the home. This freedom is entirely consistent with the emergence of ideologies of the New Right in the 1980s. In all countries significant growth has taken place and much of that growth can be explained by increased levels of car ownership, increased trip lengths and increases in the number of trips made. However, the picture is not so simple as considerable variation occurs between OECD countries. In thirteen countries the growth in car traffic is greater than the growth in all traffic, but in the other three countries (Italy, Denmark and Sweden) the reverse is true (Table 1). Similarly, in nine countries the growth in car ownership is greater than the growth in private road traffic, but in the other seven the reverse is true (Table 1). Across all EC countries both car traffic and car ownership have increased at the same rate, namely 29 per cent.

Great Britain is above the EC average for both car traffic and car ownership growth, and it seems to be an example of a country where all three parameters of increase have worked in the same direction (Table 2). Car ownership, the number of journeys and journey lengths have all increased over the last twenty years by 83 per cent, by 18 per cent and by 19 per cent respectively. This growth in demand for travel is likely to continue as the more advanced OECD countries move towards the post industrial society. National statistics show the increase in living standards, the increase in owner occupation in the housing market, the rise in leisure time, the increase in the number of women at work and the growth in the service sector and technologically based industries (Banister, Cullen and Mackett, 1990; Banister and Bayliss, 1991). However, in addition to these aggregate changes, there are other important factors which mean that not all changes are distributed equally and there is a dynamic element as people move homes and as businesses change location. Demographic change should be assessed within the context of the three other main developments which are taking place in society today.

Firstly, the changes in lifestyle, with the shortening of the working week and increased levels of affluence, have led to growth in the range and frequency of social and leisure traffic. Secondly, structural changes have taken place in the economy with the progressive decentralisation of people and jobs from city centres. The availability of a skilled labour force, together with affordable housing and a pleasant environment, are often key factors in determining where businesses locate. Modern industry can locate almost anywhere and cheap greenfield sites often seem to be the most attractive. Finally, the impact of technology is likely to be as significant as the car was thirty years ago in determining where people live and what they do. Technology allows many inventory, financial and communication transactions to be carried out remotely. The effects of physical distance are eliminated.

All of these structural changes, together with demographic changes, are affecting the demand for travel and they are likely to continue to do so over the next decade. Post industrial society is leading to the development of a more complex society. Before discussing the likely impact of demographic change, it would be useful to briefly outline the current situation. Table 3 summarises the travel patterns of each person over a week (1985-86) and shows the high mobility levels for men (16-59 years) who make more and longer journeys than all other groups.

The elderly and the young have the lowest journey rate, journey length and total distance travelled. As will be demonstrated in Chapter 3, much of this variation can be explained by work-related activities which account for 35 per cent of the distance travelled and 33 per cent of the journeys. The travel patterns for men and women for non work-related activities are very similar, and, if one disaggregates the elderly age group into those who have a car available as the main or second driver, this continuity remains. It even continues if all elderly people in car-owning households are included (Table 4).

Taking the empirical evidence from the last twenty years it seems that certain conclusions can be drawn concerning the changing travel patterns:

i) There has been a steady growth in travel with journeys made increasing by 18 per cent [from 11.2 (1965) to 13.2 (1985-86) journeys per person per week];

ii) Within these totals the journeys made for work related activities (i.e. work journeys, journeys made in course of work and education journeys) have declined marginally [from 4.4 (1975-76) to 4.2 (1985-86) journeys per person per week];

iii) The greatest increase in activities has been in the leisure activities which include social and entertainment purposes as well as holidays and day-trips [from 3.8 (1975-76) to 4.3 (1985-86) journeys per person per week]. These activities now account for more travel than work-related activities;

iv) There are great similarities between the aggregate journey patterns of men and women (16-59 years) and the elderly in car- owning households for non work-related activities (Table 4);

v) There have been significant increases in travel distances from 1965 to 1985-86 (+41.5 per cent) and this increase is apparent across all activities and all sectors of the population. The greatest increase seems to be in the elderly age group (about +76 per cent, but it should be noted that the age groupings are slightly different between the two travel surveys). The only below average increase has come in men between 16 and 64 years (+37 per cent). These percentages distort the absolute increases in mileage where the male dominance is still apparent and increasing (Table 5).

Much of this growth in mobility has been made possible by the growth in car ownership, which is apparent in all OECD countries where the close link between car ownership and GDP per head can be observed (Table 6). Britain falls around the centre of the distribution and even now may have considerable further potential for growth in car ownership levels. Mobility patterns are strongly correlated with car ownership patterns (Table 7). The distances travelled by people in non car-owning households has remained stable over the last twenty years at about 40 miles per person per week. In households with one car there has been a small increase of about 10 per cent, but in households with more than one car the increase is over 23 per cent with each person on average travelling some 160 miles per week. These changes in distances have been compounded by the growth in car ownership with non car-owning households declining from 59 per cent to 38 per cent and single car-owning households stabilizing at 45 per cent. The growth is in households with more than one car and these households also have had the greatest increases in weekly travel distances.

In conclusion, it seems that the summary points made on changes in travel patterns for the different demographic groups are compounded by car ownership changes. These two themes are developed in the remainder of this paper. Chapter 2 examines the influence of car ownership on travel and the likely effects of increasing levels of motorisation on social behaviour, and Chapter 3 focuses on the elderly as the demographic group which is likely to both grow in size in the next decades and to form a major growth point for travel demand. Most of the data used will be taken from Great Britain, and in the conclusions comparisons will be drawn with other OECD countries to see whether the evidence from Britain is typical of these other countries or not. The argument leads to the conclusion that public transport must respond now to the changes in social behaviour brought about by an aging yet highly motorised population (Chapter 4). The concluding chapter recapitulates on some of the main issues which should be discussed in the context of the changes that are taking place in society over the last decade of the twentieth century.

2. THE "MOTORISATION" REVOLUTION

Traditional analysis assumes that trip rates for particular age cohorts remain stable over time and that as population ages it adopts the travel characteristics currently undertaken by that group. For example, a person in an age group 40-50 today will adopt the current travel characteristics of the age group 60-70 in twenty years' time. The counter argument put forward here is that all age groups, but particularly the elderly, have experienced a motorisation effect which will fundamentally affect their habits and expectations. The 1990s is the first decade where the elderly (>60) have experienced full motorisation as they were the first generation of mass car ownership. They were in their thirties in the 1960s. Consequently, it is unrealistic to expect these people to take on the travel characteristics of those individuals who have never experienced full motorisation. These issues as they relate to the elderly are covered fully in Chapter 3, but in this chapter the related issue of car ownership is discussed. The corollary to the argument for dynamic approaches to analysis is that individuals will try to maintain the ability to drive and the car as long as possible. Hence it becomes important to discuss car ownership and car use, and the likely effects that these two critical factors will have on social behaviour.

A demographic analysis of car ownership and use patterns takes as its starting point the growth in licence holdership and car ownership for the different age groups for men and women. Evidence is taken from the USA, Norway and Britain on growth trends over the recent past and the likely saturation levels. As such, it differs to most car ownership forecasts where growth is considered to relate closely to increases in real incomes or GDP and the real changes in the costs of using the car (Department of Transport, 1989). These econometric forecasts complement demographic trends which examine the propensity of different cohorts to have a driving licence, to own and to use a car. As Goodwin comments, we are now (1990) about half-way from zero car ownership to saturation in 2025. But most of this growth has taken place in one working life (Goodwin, 1990).

In the USA, 59 per cent of households had at least one car in 1950 and by 1987 this figure had risen to 87 per cent. The number of households with two or more cars increased from 7 per cent to 52 per cent over the same period. The current number of cars per 1 000 population is 565 (Table 6), rapidly approaching the assumed saturation level of 650. The saturation level is based on the assumption that 90 per cent of those between 17 and 74 years of age will want to have a driving licence and a car. There does seem to be empirical evidence in the USA to support this argument (Greene, 1987). All men in the 25-69 age group now have a driving licence and there has been little change between 1969 and 1983. In the under 25-year age group about 80 per cent of those eligible to have a driving licence do have one, and it is only in the elderly age group (>70) that there is some fall-off in licence holdership. But even here, over 83 per cent of all men over 70 years of age still have a driving licence (1983). For women the picture is somewhat different and there has been a huge catching up process between 1969 and 1983. In the 25-40 age group over 90 per cent of women have a driving licence, and this level falls in the 41-60 age group to 85 per cent. In the under 25 age group the level is 70 per cent. Of the women over 70 years of age only 40 per cent have driving licences (FHWA, 1984). There does seem to be some convergence between men and women on driving licences, but the miles driven by each do not converge as they are both increasing by about two per cent per annum (Greene, 1987). This growth means a strong divergence as men have historically driven more than twice the distance that women have in the USA. In 1983, the average number of annual kilometres driven per licensed male driver in the USA was 22 350 kilometres, whilst the corresponding figure for females was 10 200 kilometres (US Department of Transportation, 1986). Estimates can be obtained of travel demand given the growth in travel distance and the increase in licensed drivers. It would seem that in the USA, saturation levels of drivers and cars should be reached by the year 2000, some twenty-five years before Europe. However, it also seems true that the desire to own a car will not end here. There is a strong trend towards multiple car ownership with the greatest growth occurring in households owning three or more vehicles. Prevedouros and Schofer (1989) put forward an argument that the value of owning and using cars exceeds the value of the transport produced -- "the automobile may be viewed as an office, a storage unit, a home away from home, a means and place of recreation, and a social instrument of increasing significance; people increasingly define themselves by the number and types of automobiles they own. As a result, automobile mobility may have social status value beyond that reflected in travel forecasting models."

In Europe the picture is somewhat different. In a recent paper, Vibe (1991) takes data from three surveys in the Oslo region for men and women with driving licences and their own car. He concludes that the level of licence holdership and car ownership for men is stabilizing across all age groups at about 85 per cent with a lower figure for the 25-34 age group of 80 per cent, and for the youngest age group (18-24) a level of about 55 per cent (Table 8). For women, a completely different conclusion is drawn. Here he suggests that there is still considerable potential for growth with a saturation level of between 65-70 per cent. Licence holdership for all women in all age groups has increased by about 20 per cent over the three surveys. For all people the level of 75 per cent is suggested as being realistic for the population between 18-80 years by the year 2000. The present day level of 64 per cent and nearly 400 cars per 1 000 population will increase to 470 cars per 1 000 population which Vibe (1991) suggests is a saturation level higher than the former FR of Germany (461 per 1 000 in 1988) but still far below the US level (565 per 1 000). The crucial unknown factor in these calculations is the saturation level of licence holdership for women, but even if it reached the 85 per cent level assumed for men, this would still only give an upper limit of 531 cars per 1 000 population.

In Britain, the numbers of men and women with driving licences is summarised in Table 9. The figures (1978-89) are remarkably similar to those for Oslo in 1977 for both men and women. This similarity is continued to 1985-86 for men, where some 86 per cent in the 30-50 age group have licences and over 80 per cent in the 50-60 age group are still drivers. The two age groups (20-29 and 60-69) have over 70 per cent licence holdership. If that comparability extends to 1990 then one would expect that 85 per cent of British men between 30-75 years would have driving licences. There are no figures in Britain to corroborate this. For women there are differences between Oslo and Britain (Tables 8 and 9) with higher licence holdership figures in Norway in the youngest and eldest age groups, but less across the middle age groups where British women have licence holdership levels of 62 per cent. This might suggest that the saturation level for women in Britain is higher than that for women in Oslo.

If the same types of assumptions are used in Britain, with 85 per cent of men 20-70 and 55 per cent of the youngest and eldest age groups having driving licences and with the corresponding figures for women being 75 and 50 per cent, the levels of car ownership will reach 436 cars per 1 000 persons shortly after the turn of the century. If the 85 per cent figure across all age groups for both men and women (17-80 years) is used, the resulting figure is 494 cars per 1 000 persons, well below the lowest figure in the official forecasts for 2025 [1].

The National Road Traffic Forecasts (Department of Transport, 1989) suggest that traffic in Britain will double between 1988 and 2025 with car ownership levels increasing from 331 cars per 1 000 population to between 529 and 608 cars per 1 000 population. About 46 per cent of the population between 17 and 74 years have a car (1988) and this proportion will increase to between 73 and 84 per cent. This means that the saturation level, given the assumptions stated previously, will very nearly be reached by 2025, and the levels of car ownership in Britain will be close to those found at present in the USA and significantly higher than those suggested in Oslo. It also means that women are just as likely to drive and own a car as men and that the elderly will retain the use of the car as long as possible.

The conclusions reached concerning car ownership and demographic factors are the following:

i) Over the next thirty years there will be significant increases in car drivers and in the numbers of cars (averaging between 60 and 80 per cent) in many European countries to around 550 cars per 1 000 population or similar to the current USA levels of car ownership.

ii) Much of this growth will take place in households where there is already one car.

iii) Men already have high rates of licence holdership and this will remain stable at between 85-90 per cent of those aged 20-70. The greatest growth in licence holdership among men will be in the youngest age group (17-20) and those in the elderly age group (>70).

iv) For women the growth in licence holdership is likely to be significant across all age groups to between 70-80 per cent. The greater access of women to cars as drivers is likely to be a major source of new travel. Although some of these new activities will be work related as women increase their participation in the labour force, much will reflect their multivariate and complex pattern of activities which involve escorting, personal business, shopping activities as well as social and recreational activities.

v) The expectations of young people will be raised with many aspiring to car ownership. Again, given rises in income levels, it is likely that as soon as they can drive, young people will want to drive and here again one can expect a significant increase in travel demand.

vi) The elderly age group are the third and perhaps the most important growth area for travel demand. This group has traditionally had low levels of car ownership and licence holdership, but over the next thirty years one can anticipate that this will change dramatically. Many of those who will be elderly in 2025 are at present among the highest car ownership and licence holdership groups, and they are also the most mobile. This is the "grey" revolution to which we now turn.

3. THE "GREY" REVOLUTION

The 1990s could be the decade when "grey" power becomes a major factor in determining levels of travel demand. It is widely assumed that the elderly have low levels of mobility and this can be illustrated in Table 10 where the elderly have low levels of mobility and a high dependence on the bus. However, it is important to realise that the elderly may not have the same travel demand patterns in the future as the corresponding group has at present. A systematic study carried out in the USA (Kostyniuk and Kitamura, 1987) has found that a "motorisation effect" has to be linked with an aging effect. Increases in mobility have taken place across all age groups, but the increases have been much greater for men than for women (1963-1974). Both cohort and time effects, at given levels of motorisation, influence travel patterns and so future elderly cohorts will behave differently to those of today. Studies of the elderly as transport disadvantaged have often assumed that they have low income, low car availability and some physical disability. But these assumptions are increasingly being violated and it is essential to include a dynamic element for the changing experiences and expectations of the elderly.

In addition to this increasing tendency to keep the car as long as possible, there are also other factors which lead to the conclusion that one major growth sector in travel demand will be from the elderly. Over the next thirty years significant growth will occur in the numbers of elderly. This growth is partly due to demographic factors and the increase in life expectancy, and partly due to definitional factors with the tendency to retire earlier. It is estimated that in western Europe the proportion of persons over 65 years will increase from 13 per cent in 1985 to more than 20 per cent in 2020. For OECD countries the number will increase by 50 per cent from 98 million in 1990 to 147 million in 2020, and peaking in 2040 with 175 million people over the age of 65. The growth is particularly significant in the age group >80 which is projected to triple in the next fifty years. Taking the decline in fertility rates and the growth in the elderly population means that not only does the absolute number of elderly double, but the proportion of the elderly increases due to the relative decline in the younger population (OECD, 1989).

Within the elderly population there will be considerable variation between those who are affluent and highly mobile car drivers, and those who are disabled, on low or fixed levels of income. It may be appropriate to subdivide the elderly age group into the mobile age of personal fulfilment (60-80 years: Laslett's 3rd Age or 55-80 years if early retirement continues) which is likely to remain stable over the next decade, and those who are fully retired and dependent (over 80 years: Laslett's 4th Age) which is the major growth sector in the next thirty years. Within each of these two groups there is also likely to be considerable variation in travel demand patterns, as it seems that age is a key determinant of mobility. As senility and age-related disabilities occur, significant changes in activities and lifestyles do take place.

The personal fulfilment group have ended the complex responsibilities of earning a living and raising a family, they are reasonably affluent, and so have both money and time to spend on leisure-based activities. Many of these activities will involve travel, and their purpose may be to visit friends or relatives or to achieve a life long ambition. Alternatively, the mobile, early retired groups may also be involved in a wide range of social and voluntary activities where their time, skill and knowledge can be given to an activity and where no payment is received. In Britain there has been a steady growth in real incomes over the last decade and this has been augmented by increased levels of inherited wealth. As a result of unprecedented increases in levels of house prices, large amounts of capital are now available for spending or passing onto ones children. Levels of home ownership have been traditionally high in Britain, and with the right to buy the council house in which one was living at lower than market prices, some 70 per cent of people now own their homes. As there is no tax to pay on the sale of one's own home, housing forms the main capital asset of many families. With retirement, people often decide to move to a smaller house or to an area where housing is cheaper. In 1990 the inherited wealth from the sale of property amounted to £8 billion. Tax free capital is released so that more consumer expenditure can take place. Similarly, people are borrowing against actual or expected rises in house prices, and this wealth together with income growth and available credit has fuelled the increases in consumer spending which has been a feature of the late 1980s. It is estimated by the Mortgage Corporation (1990) that the amount of capital that will be released over the next ten years by this mechanism will be a massive £29 billion. Although house prices are at present falling (1989-1991) as the gearing between prices and wages is gradually readjusted, the underlying increases in value are likely to continue.

It will only be when people reach the age of 80 that full retirement and dependency take place. This group of people, which accounts for about 21 per cent of the elderly, will require special facilities and transport services which can accommodate their particular requirements, for example, to be wheel-chair accessible or to have a person to accompany them. This group will not be able to drive a conventional car and so will require public transport services or taxis or chauffeur-driven private cars. The voluntary sector organisations provide many of these services.

One possible development might be to design a vehicle specifically for the elderly to give them some degree of independence, perhaps similar to the battery-operated tricycles which are already available with voice-activated controls to ease the physical requirements of driving. Special routes could be provided for these low-performance vehicles which could be used by the elderly and perhaps children.

An examination of data from the last four National Travel Surveys in Great Britain illustrates some of the changes which are taking place and the implications for travel demand among the elderly. Due to slight differences in definitions and the way in which the data have been aggregated, exact comparisons are not possible but the trends are still apparent. Overall, the elderly (>60) travel some 58.2 miles per person per week for 8.6 journeys exceeding one mile in length (1985-86). About 55 per cent of this distance is for leisure activities which account for 38 per cent of journeys. Within this elderly group, some 84 per cent of single person households have no car access and a further 40 per cent of two adult households (one or both >60 years) have no car access. These two groups account for 33 per cent of all households. Other elderly households have a much higher level of car access with 73 per cent being in car-owning households. This variation in the existing travel patterns within the different types of elderly households can be clearly illustrated (Table 11) where the different journey and distance patterns are presented for the four levels of car availability.

The most interesting conclusion here is that main drivers in elderly households have similar driving patterns to other drivers, both male and female in the 16-59 year age group (Table 11: see definitions of main driver and other driver). They make 87 per cent of their journeys by car (65 per cent for other male drivers 16-59 years and 90 per cent for other female drivers 16-59 years), and travel 110.3 miles per week as compared with 141.4 miles and 112.5 miles for the other two groups respectively. Other drivers in elderly households are also heavily car dependent for their travel (77 per cent), and even elderly non-drivers in car-owning households make 69 per cent of their journeys by car. It is only in the elderly non car-owning households that both journey frequencies and use of car are substantially reduced. These non car-owning households make only 5.5 journeys per person per week with some 20 per cent being made by car. These households make most use of public transport of anyone within elderly households (40 per cent).

A second conclusion is that if work and education trips are excluded the travel patterns of all adults are very similar in the four car availability groups both for journeys made and for distances travelled (Table 12). Both women and elderly people who are main drivers make more journeys than their male counterparts, but the men travel further than the elderly. A very similar pattern can be observed for other drivers in car-owning households for the three groups, and it is only in the non-driver and the non car-owning households that the elderly have fewer journeys than those people in the younger aged categories. It seems that it is the higher mobility levels of working age adults for work-related activities (often by car) which seems to give the higher journey and distance levels observed in Chapter 1 (Table 3).

The empirical evidence seems to indicate that for given car availability conditions there is a certain stability in non-work trip-making by age. If this simplifying assumption holds for the next decade, calculations for the number of journeys made and distances travelled for the elderly can be made (Appendix 1 and Table 13). Depending on the strength of the assumptions used, the growth in journeys made by the elderly will increase between 23-34 per cent with journey distances per person per week increasing by between 30-50 per cent. The modal split will also change, with an increase in trips as car driver and car passenger from 60.5 per cent (1985-86) to about 75 per cent (2001). The elderly will no longer be seen as a disadvantaged group in terms of their travel patterns as these will now fully reflect non-work activities of those currently in the 45-60 year age group. Use of public transport by the elderly, principally bus services, will also decline by between 14-24 per cent over the fifteen year period. The implications for public transport operators are severe as one of the major user groups for bus services has traditionally been the elderly, and their loyalty has been assumed captive. This assumption may no longer hold.

Public transport operators may need to start planning for an elderly population which will want a much greater quality of service provision with convenient and comfortable services that are easy to get on and off. Other users may require door-to-door services with an escort facility. The disadvantaged and physically frail are one group who will continue to be dependent on public transport. Their quality of life needs careful consideration as the effects of aging seem to progress rapidly after the age of 80, and these people are often living on their own. As noted earlier, some 84 per cent of those living on their own, who are over 60 years, have no car and these account for 16 per cent of all households. It will not be cheap to provide a quality service for these people who have traditionally had low levels of mobility, and much has depended on the voluntary sector to provide backup to the statutory sector (Banister and Norton, 1988). These services are unlikely to be cost-effective or to make a profit, and so the allocation of subsidy and the opportunity costs of that subsidy will have to be considered. Evaluation will have to take on social and equity criteria as well as conventional efficiency criteria.

It seems that two types of public transport services are required for the elderly. On the one hand, there would be a quality service provided by the operator at a premium price with no subsidy. This service would accommodate the day-to-day requirements of the mobile elderly without access to a car, and would also be a leisure mode to take them on day trips and to visit friends and relatives. On the other hand, there would be a special service for those with low levels of mobility which would provide door-to-door access with wheel chair and escort facilities. This subsidised service would enable the physically frail and elderly to travel to shops, to day-care centres, to the local hospital and to friends. This is the crisis facing public transport. Traditional captive markets are diminishing and new types of services are required for the elderly, but also for the young and for women. People will choose to travel by public transport and not because they have no other alternative.

4. THE CRISIS FOR PUBLIC TRANSPORT

Although this paper has focused on car ownership and the elderly as two of the main changes which are taking place in demographic structure, the evidence leads to the same conclusion, namely that the traditional markets for public transport are likely to decline significantly over the next twenty years. In Britain, the most comprehensive survey has been carried out by Hill and Rickard (1990). For business travel by rail they conclude that "population shifts alone would have led to an increase in the trip rate for each segment but a decrease in trip rates overall, as the infrequent users increased at the expense of the high wage groups". The business market is relatively price inelastic and influenced by other factors apart from population change. They suggest that the long-distance business rail market seems fairly robust, but that the non-business market is likely to decline as is the demand for local bus travel. Similar analysis carried out by Goulcher and Kearns (1989) on the demand for London Underground confirm these findings, namely that population change between 1988-1996 is likely to reduce travel demand across all time periods and that the loss is likely to be greatest for education trips. Over a longer period (1988-2001) a decline of 2.4 per cent is expected due to population change, and this decline will be concentrated in the education and social markets. Other changes such as increases in incomes and car ownership levels would add to this decline.

This pessimistic view of the demand for rail travel in Britain contrasts with the expected growth in demand for rail travel in Europe, principally as a result of the completion of the international high-speed rail network (e.g. Roundtable of European Industrialists, 1991 and Group Transport 2000 Plus, 1990). Apart from generating new traffic, the high-speed rail network would attract intercity traffic from road and air. Technological change and major infrastructure investment decisions may reinforce or frustrate structural demographic and economic trends, and so projected losses from demographic change may be more than compensated for by growth brought about by other factors.

For bus demand the picture is much bleaker because all the traditional "captive" markets are being eroded as more young people, women and elderly people acquire cars. Hill and Rickard (1990) suggest that women's use of buses follows that of men but with a time lag of ten years. The impact of this effect, together with young people learning to drive earlier and elderly people keeping their cars longer means that bus operators will have a market which divides itself into a declining but persistent "captive" sector, who do not have the choice of going by car, and a growing "optional" sector, who require a high quality service which they are prepared to pay for. Satisfying the requirements of both groups may be difficult as a standard service would satisfy neither group and two separate services might be politically unacceptable.

In addition to the changing demographic structure of the population, other factors are also likely to affect behaviour and the demand for public transport.

i) **Returning Young Adults** usually result in an increase in the number of cars available in a household and an increase in the trip generation rates. These highly mobile young people are returning home after a period of education and training before they get a permanent job and set up home. This phenomenon may increase in times of high unemployment or high property prices, both of which make independence uncertain and expensive.

ii) **Female Participation Rates** in the labour force have increased, particularly for part-time work and for those returning to work after raising a family. In Britain it is expected that 90 per cent of the one million increase in the labour force (1988-2000) will be women. The activity rates for men have remained constant at 73 per cent, whilst that for women has increased by 12 per cent over the last ten years to nearly 50 per cent. The greatest growth in female participation rates has been and is likely to continue to take place in the sunbelt countries of the Mediterranean.

iii) The decline in average **Household Size** across all developed countries by about 20 per cent over the last thirty years reflects lower fertility rates, but also the breakdown of the conventional family unit. Many children live in single parent families, divorce rates have increased, more people now cohabit, and there are a larger number of births outside marriage. These trends have an impact on the housing market with an increase in demand for smaller units, which would either be located in the city centres through subdivision of existing properties or in the suburbs in purpose built units. In each case the ratio of car parking spaces to homes will be near unity and this may create parking problems, particularly in the city centre location. If the location is in the suburbs, then the numbers of trips generated and the length of those trips is likely to be greater.

iv) With increased **Suburbanisation and Greater Complexity of Work Journeys,** the pattern of daily movements is becoming more varied both spatially and temporally. Commuting patterns have become more complex with cross commuting becoming more important than commuting to city centres. Households with an established residential base are likely to meet their career needs by longer distance commuting. In a tight labour market (such as that in the South of England), there is often more than one person employed in the household and these complicated travel patterns emerge as the transport system has to accommodate to this change. With high interest rates and low levels of residential mobility, it is again the transport system that has to respond as people cannot move home.

v) Increased **Leisure Time** and the shortening of the working week may also affect the demand for travel. Trips taken for social and recreational activities have increased by over 28 per cent between 1975-76 and 1985-86, and leisure now accounts for 16 per cent of all household expenditure in Britain (1989). Most of this increase can be explained by the growth in social activities as holidays and day-trips have remained constant over time. Shorter local trips by walking and bicycle have been replaced by longer trips overseas and by car-based trips.

vi) Increased **Affluence** brought about by increases in real income levels and growing levels of inherited wealth, particularly from the capital value of property, has also led to more travel demand (Chapter 3). This increase will continue until saturation levels of car ownership, licence holdership and car use are reached.

vii) The greatest unknown factor is **Migration** patterns in Europe with the opening up of the Single European Market and the breaking down of barriers between East and West. Although natural population growth may be very low, significant changes in population could be brought about by internal migration as labour seeks employment and as industry moves to locations where labour is available, and where other factors such as land availability, environment and communications are positive.

All these factors suggest that the demand for travel will continue to increase and that the present pattern of longer journeys will also be maintained. This means that walking, bicycle and bus trips may continue to decline as these journeys are replaced by the car. Superimposed on all these demographic factors is an underlying change in society brought about by the car, namely the "motorisation" effect or what the French have called "irreversible behaviour". Low motorisation is not an inherent characteristic of particular groups within the population, but they have been impacted by it because of the cohort effect (Kostyniuk and Kitamura, 1987). The elderly are one such group, but women and young people are the other two main groups. As has been demonstrated in Chapter 3, car drivers in the elderly age group have very similar non-work journey patterns by modes as other drivers in younger car-owning households. Motorisation may have permanent impacts on people's attitudes towards trip-making, expectations for mobility and for the formation of habitual trip patterns. However, as Kostyniuk and Kitamura (1987) point out, one must differentiate between motorisation at the societal level, and the longitudinal profile of car acquisition and pattern development at the individual level. All the evidence presented here is at the aggregate level with data taken at repeated cross sections following individual cohorts. A different methodology is required for examination of the dynamics of individual behaviour using panel and other survey methods (Goodwin and Layzell, 1985).

This process of motorisation seems to be nearing completion in the USA (Lave, 1990). Over the last ten years there has been a phenomenal growth in both vehicle ownership and use, but Lave claims that this atypical period is coming to an end as saturation levels are reached, both in vehicle ownership and licence holdership. This growth is explained by more young people with driving licences, more women drivers, more women in the labour force and income growth. Lave (1990) does not suggest that the elderly may be subject to the motorisation effect. Once this phase has passed then stability returns as vehicle growth and use per vehicle declines. Similar trends can be found in Britain, but as argued in Chapter 2 the car ownership and licence holdership levels are much lower than those in the USA, and are likely to remain so for the next thirty years. This conclusion can be illustrated through licence holdership levels for different cohorts of people born at different times (Table 14).

The dilemma facing public transport operators is that although the increase in travel demand is likely to continue, the demand for their services is likely to decline. Public transport will account for a smaller proportion of an expanding market. The decline of public transport is a result of demographic change and the motorisation effect which is now affecting the traditional markets for these services. It is no longer sufficient to provide the same services as innovation and new markets must be sought.

The assumption underlying this discussion is that there may be a continued desire to travel, but there may also be a limit to that desire. With the increased levels of congestion on all transport modes, and with delays at termini and interchanges, people's appetite for travel may decline, particularly where they have a choice. Quality of life factors become more important with increasing affluence and leisure time, and travel may not provide an attractive alternative. However, this limit may only be apparent with particular groups in affluent post-industrial western economies. It is likely that any reduction in one group's appetite for travel will be more than compensated for by another group's increased propensity to travel.

It seems that the demand for travel will continue to increase but that the nature of that demand may change as a result of demographic factors. Although the changes in population structure are important, other changes (such as the industrial structure, technological innovation, levels of affluence and leisure time) will also influence travel demand. The difficulty is unravelling this complexity so that the effects of one group of factors can be isolated. Similarly, there are a range of policy instruments which can be used to influence the levels of demand and mediate between the different interests. The basic question is whether and how that increase in demand can be accommodated given the economic, social and environmental costs which will be incurred in developed nations if these mobility trends are allowed to continue unchecked. The alternative must be some form of planning in the allocation of resources and priority to the more efficient modes. The implications for transport operators are considerable if both the demand for public transport is uncertain and the stability of traditional public transport markets is being eroded. Certain conclusions can be drawn and an agenda for action suggested.

i) Public transport must be given priority, particularly in urban areas, through the extensive use of bus priority schemes and a network of bus-only streets. This will make public transport more attractive and increase the total capacity of the system with increasing road capacity. Priority for public transport should be coupled with increasing the price for the use of the private car in congested urban areas, principally through market pricing of parking space. It could be argued that subsidy policy has helped both car and public transport as it has enabled people to switch from walking to motorised forms of transport. Low fares and cheap tickets (e.g. travelcards and the *Carte Orange*), together with the subsidy to the company sector for cars, have enabled people to travel further and may have assisted the decentralisation of both cities and employment. Even the road tolls in Oslo have often been paid by companies as employees have been refunded the cost. The toll is paid in full by the elderly residents of Oslo who fear that their children will visit them less often (Orfeuil, 1991). Priority for public transport together with an extensive review of subsidy policy for both public and private transport must form an essential part of the agenda.

ii) Quality of public transport is important if it is to be attractive as an alternative to the car. The new affluence means that price becomes less important. However, "captive" public transport users may have to be subsidised as they often come from low income groups and may have difficulty in affording the new premium fares on the quality public transport. Integration of rail and bus services would form part of the quality service as would the increased use of parkway stations. This integration would cover interchanges, marketing and information. More imaginative use of demand responsive transport services and hotel type airport services with flexible routing, hub and spoke operations and employer based services would all feature in the quality public transport.

iii) Design in public transport should be an integral part of the service provided, particularly for their main users such as those with small children or with the shopping, and for the elderly and the disabled. At present, most public transport services are not "user friendly" and many minibuses were not even designed to carry people. The bus should be as well designed for the user as the car is. An attractive, quality public transport service with priority will compete with the car and the evidence for this is apparent in many European cities.

iv) The potential for public transport as a leisure mode should be explored as this is one rapidly expanding travel market. In France the elderly have had the highest growth rate in holiday demand over the last fifteen years averaging about 2 per cent per annum for summer holidays and over 5 per cent for winter holidays (Orfeuil, 1991). Organised tours, day-trips and visits to cultural events are all possible growth markets for coach operations. With the completion of the high-speed rail network and the Channel Tunnel, long-distance, leisure-related travel can also be marketed, particularly when there is spare capacity in the transport system.

In short, the future for public transport is bleak if current and future demographic and behavioural changes are analysed. But the new quality public transport must be debated and invested in now to ensure its survival and growth into the next century.

5. THE FUTURE

This paper has focused on the demand for transport and the impact that changing demographic factors will have on that demand. The individual's right to use their car wherever and whenever desired has to be modified when the broader societal objectives are matched against the more narrowly focused individual desires. Public attitudes have to change and the "love affair" with the car may have to be modified as the road capacity and unrestricted parking will never be available to meet the expected growth in demand. However, the car also contributes to people's happiness and individualism and for the elderly it may be the main means by which self-fulfilment can be achieved.

With the growing number of drivers it is likely that societal pressures will be brought to bear on people deemed to be antisocial in their driving behaviour. Excessive speed will not be acceptable as the majority of new drivers may favour lower speeds. Safety and environmental concerns over the use of resources and increasing levels of pollution may result in pressure being exerted on manufacturers to produce "green" cars. These vehicles would only be capable of being driven at low speeds and so would prove attractive to the elderly and women, and the age of acquisition of a driving licence could be reduced to allow the young to acquire this type of vehicle. In Japan 90 per cent of elderly drivers (60-69) want to continue driving, and 80 per cent of those over 70 feel the same way even though 30 per cent are under family pressure to stop driving (Orfeuil, 1991). There must be a market for a safe, low-speed, environmentally benign vehicle which would form an intermediate stage before the acquisition of one's first car (for the 13-16 age group) and before the complete loss of personal mobility by the elderly (for the 70-80 age group). These two groups account for nearly 13 per cent of the population. Concerns that individuals have over driving at night and their own security are increasingly important factors for all modes of transport, and often forms the main reason why some people will not go out or drive at certain times, even if the car is available. Safety and security in travel are two important deterrents to road users and non road users. By responding to these concerns through better training and management schemes to reduce traffic speeds in towns, further increases in demand for travel may be released.

The alternative to providing more or different forms of transport to accommodate the expected changes in demographic structure must be through positive planning policies which allow mixed development and the provision of local facilities to minimise the need for car travel. Car dependence can be reduced by the use of the new quality public transport for local travel together with the "green" car and the bicycle. At present life cycle changes influence both the mobility patterns and the location decisions of households (Table 15).

The question here is: what is the most appropriate use in residential terms of the city centre? Often it is too expensive for young couples or workers with children to locate, and it is the institutions, families of adults and the elderly who have city centre property. The other life cycle groups are forced to live in the suburbs or out of the cities and to undertake long-distance commuting. The work journey is accepted as a cost to be paid. Allowing workers to live near their workplace would reduce travel distances, but this simplifies the reality of the location decision.

The last two decades of mobility growth seem likely to continue for the next two decades as important groups within the population acquire driving licences and cars. Unprecedented growth in car use by the elderly and women seems certain. If the car manufacturers can produce a vehicle that is environmentally attractive and efficient to use at low speed in towns, then the young teenagers and the more dependent elderly will also join the motorised culture. The future for public transport is less clear and positive action is required to increase its attractiveness to all potential users as it can no longer depend on the diminishing captive user group. Demographic factors, together with economic, social and technological changes, mean that the relentless increase in demand for travel will continue. With the breaking down of political boundaries, the increase in international travel and the expected real growth in income levels all suggest that we may be close to the final gridlock when not only do our cities come to a standstill, but when the whole of Europe grinds to a halt.

NOTES AND REFERENCES

1. It should be noted that there is a fundamental difference in the assumptions made between the USA calculations and those in Europe. In the USA it is assumed that saturation is reached when 90 per cent of those between 17-74 years have a car -- 650 cars per 1 000 population. In Europe it has been assumed that the present ratio between licences held and cars owned will remain constant. In Oslo, as 64 per cent licence holdership results in 400 cars per 1 000 population (1990), then 85 per cent licence holdership results in 531 cars per 1 000 population. In Britain the difference between 494 cars per 1 000 population calculated here and the official forecasts can be explained in this way. If all drivers have their own car (the US assumption) then the numbers of cars per 1 000 population increases to 608. It is likely that the actual levels will lie between the two figures as not all people will want or need the exclusive use of a car.

TABLES

Table 1: **Growth in Passenger Traffic 1978-1988**

Country	All Traffic	Private Road Traffic	Increase in Car Ownership
Great Britain	30.0	37.8	34.4
German FR	15.6	20.2	36.8
France	28.5	28.8	21.0
Italy	47.8	37.6	51.6
Japan	31.3	59.6	35.7
USA	15.8	16.2	18.2
Spain	9.1	11.6	55.9
Belgium	13.5	17.0	20.5
Denmark	22.8	19.7	16.2
Netherlands	35.8	40.1	21.5
Portugal	54.9	67.6	74.8
Austria	24.8	33.8	34.9
Finland	26.6	33.4	55.1
Norway	33.9	41.8	35.7
Sweden	22.1	21.2	20.1
Switzerland	12.8	15.0	27.9
Greece	-	-	81.3
Ireland	-	-	5.5

Source: Based on data from Transport Statistics.

Notes: Figures give percentage increase in passenger kilometres travelled over the decade (1978-1988). Figures for Italy, FR of Germany, Belgium, Japan, USA, Norway, Switzerland are all estimated in the private road traffic column.

Figures on car ownership increases are the percentage increase in cars owned per 1 000 population (1978-1988).

Table 2: **Increases in Travel in Great Britain (1965-1985/86)**

	Travel distance per person per week (miles)	Number of journeys per person per week	Average journey length (miles)	Cars per household
1965	70.1	11.2	6.3	0.46
1972-73	82.0	11.4	7.2	0.63
1975-76	85.9	12.4	6.9	0.68
1978-79	92.6	14.1	6.6	0.73
1985-86	99.5	13.2	7.5	0.84

Source: Various National Travel Surveys.

Table 3: **Travel per Person per Week in Great Britain (1985-86)**

	Distance travelled (miles)	Journeys	Journey length (miles)
Children	56.6	9.8	5.78
Men 16-59	163.2	18.0	9.07
Women 16-59	100.2	14.5	6.91
Elderly >60	58.2	8.6	6.77
All people	99.5	13.2	7.54

Table 4: **Non-work Travel per Person per Week in Great Britain (1985-86)**

	Distance travelled (miles)	Journeys	Journey length (miles)
Children	47.6	7.0	6.84
Men 16-59	78.4	10.0	7.84
Women 16-59	74.9	10.3	7.27
Elderly >60	51.4	7.7	6.68
Elderly drivers	87.4	11.4	7.64
Elderly in car-owning households	75.8	10.5	7.23
All people	65.0	9.0	7.22

Source: National Travel Survey 1985-86.

Note: Elderly drivers account for 32 per cent of all people in the elderly category and include main drivers and other drivers in car-owning households. These figures are the weighted average for the two-car-driver groups. If non-drivers in car-owning households are included, this covers 48 per cent of all people in the elderly category and the weighted figures for all elderly in car-owning households can be calculated.

Table 5: **Changes in Distance Travelled per Person per Week in Great Britain (1965-1985/86)**

	1965 Mileage	1985-86 Mileage	Absolute Increase	Percentage Increase
Children	39.2	56.6	+17.4	+44.3
Men 16-59	118.2	163.2	+44.7	+37.7
Women 16-59	64.1	100.2	+36.1	+56.3
Elderly	33.0	58.2	+25.2	+76.4
All People	70.3	99.5	+29.2	+41.5

Source: National Travel Surveys

Note: Some of the age groups have changed and they are not strictly comparable -- the figures are only indicative.

Table 6: **Rates of Car Ownership, GDP per Head and Car Use in 1988**

	Cars per 1 000 population	GDP per head in $ US	Kilometres per car per year
USA	565	19 600	14 200
German FR	461	14 200	13 000
Canada	459	18 500	-
Australia	429	13 500	-
Switzerland	410	16 700	12 000
Sweden	398	14 700	14 800
France	394	13 700	13 300
Italy	392	13 000	9 600
Norway	388	16 400	14 800
Austria	353	12 600	10 900
Belgium	350	12 800	12 300
Netherlands	348	13 000	14 500
Finland	344	13 900	17 000
United Kingdom	343	13 500	15 100
Denmark	310	13 700	17 000
Spain	250	9 500	6 800
Japan	240	14 400	10 000
Ireland	202	8 300	-
Greece	144	7 000	-
Portugal	125	6 400	12 000

Sources: House of Commons (1990) and Transport Statistics.

Table 7: **Travel Distance per Person per Week by Car Ownership in Great Britain**
(Distances in miles and percentage of households in brackets)

	People in Households with			All People
	No Cars	One Car	Two or More Cars	
1965	42.0 (59)	96.0 (36)	132.0 (5)	70.1
1972-73	40.6 (48)	103.8 (44)	134.5 (8)	82.0
1975-76	40.8 (44)	101.8 (45)	144.2 (11)	85.9
1978-79	48.6 (42)	110.0 (45)	150.5 (13)	92.6
1985-86	40.6 (38)	104.5 (45)	162.7 (17)	99.5

Source: National Travel Survey 1985-86.

Table 8: **Percentage of People with Driving Licences and their Own Car in the Oslo Region**

Age	Men			Age	Women		
	1977	1985	1990		1977	1985	1990
18-24	37	56	54	18-24	15	35	40
25-34	79	79	76	25-34	44	51	61
35-44	82	83	84	35-44	45	54	62
45-54	81	82	85	45-54	27	43	59
55-66	70	75	83	55-66	15	34	48
67-74	45	65	84	67-74	4	19	25

Source: Vibe (1991).

Table 9: **Individuals in Great Britain Holding a Full Car Driving Licence by Age and Sex**

Age	Men			Women		
	1972-73	1978-79	1985-86	1972-73	1978-89	1985-86
17-19	31	29	31	12	11	25
20-29	70	70	72	31	41	53
30-39	79	84	86	34	49	62
40-49	74	81	87	27	38	56
50-59	68	72	81	19	26	41
60-69	52	59	72	9	16	24
>69	21	33	51	2	7	11
Total	63	68	74	21	30	41

Source: Transport Statistics Great Britain 1978-88.

Table 10: **Journeys per Week by Age 1985-86 in Great Britain**

	Car Journeys	Bus Journeys	All Journeys
Children	5.6	1.8	9.8
Men (16-59)	13.7	1.3	18.0
Women (16-59)	10.1	1.9	14.5
Elderly	5.4	1.8	8.6

Source: National Travel Survey 1985-86.

Table 11: **Travel Characteristics of the Elderly by Car Availability**

Journeys and distances (miles) per person per week

Purpose	Overall		Main Drivers	
	Journeys	Distance	Journeys	Distance
Work	0.8	4.5	1.9	12.5
Shopping	2.9	11.5	4.1	18.3
Social/Entertain	2.5	19.2	4.3	36.3
Personal Business	1.4	7.5	2.4	14.3
Holidays/Day-trips	0.8	12.5	1.3	18.8
Total	8.6	58.2	15.0	110.3

Purpose	Other Drivers		Non Drivers	
	Journeys	Distance	Journeys	Distance
Work	0.8	2.9	0.4	1.6
Shopping	3.2	15.8	3.0	12.8
Social/Entertain	3.1	28.8	2.1	18.0
Personal Business	2.0	14.0	1.1	6.6
Holidays/Day-trips	1.2	14.7	0.8	15.2
Total	10.5	78.4	7.5	54.7

Table 11 (continued): **Travel Characteristics of the Elderly by Car Availability**

Journeys and distances (miles) per person per week

Purpose	Non car-owning households	
	Journeys	Distance
Work	0.3	1.5
Shopping	2.1	7.2
Social/Entertain	1.6	9.8
Personal Business	0.9	3.5
Holidays/Day-trips	0.5	8.5
Total	5.5	30.6

Notes: *Main driver*: Drivers who had a car in which they did most of the mileage in the course of a year.

Other driver: Those in car-owning households with occasional use of the car.

Non drivers: Others in car-owning households.

Non car-owning households: All people in households without cars. All trips under one mile in length are excluded.

Table 12: **Non-work Journeys and Distances per Person per Week in Great Britain -- 1985-86**
(Distances in miles in brackets)

Car-owning households								
Main Driver	Men	16-59	Women	16-59	Elderly	>60	Overall	
Car Driver	10.0	(81.7)	10.7	(60.9)	10.3	(70.1)	10.3	(74.0)
Car Passenger	0.8	(8.5)	3.1	(39.9)	0.8	(10.1)	1.4	(17.4)
Other	0.9	(7.4)	0.9	(10.1)	1.6	(9.6)	1.0	(8.4)
TOTAL	11.7	(97.6)	14.7	(110.9)	12.7	(89.8)	12.7	(99.8)
Other Drivers								
Car Driver	5.7	(44.7)	3.9	(21.2)	1.8	(9.4)	4.1	(25.9)
Car Passenger	1.7	(17.1)	5.3	(52.3)	5.8	(55.2)	4.4	(43.2)
Other	2.1	(17.0)	1.9	(13.6)	2.1	(9.9)	2.0	(14.1)
TOTAL	9.5	(78.8)	11.1	(87.1)	9.7	(74.5)	10.5	(83.2)
Non Drivers								
Car Passenger	2.8	(23.8)	5.2	(47.1)	4.9	(43.2)	1.1	(45.7)
Other	5.5	(30.7)	3.1	(15.7)	2.1	(9.5)	4.4	(12.5)
TOTAL	8.3	(54.5)	8.3	(62.8)	7.0	(52.7)	5.5	(58.2)
Non car-owning households								
Car Passengers	1.0	(8.2)	1.5	(12.2)	1.0	(8.4)	1.1	(8.8)
Other	5.2	(25.2)	5.1	(24.1)	4.2	(20.5)	4.4	(21.0)
TOTAL	6.2	(33.4)	6.6	(36.3)	5.2	(28.9)	5.5	(29.8)

Source: National Travel Survey 1985-88.

Note: Overall includes children.

Table 13: **Calculations of Journeys and Distances for the Elderly Age Group in 2001**

	1985-86	2001	
		No change in journeys	Dynamic element in journeys
Journeys per Person per Week	7.74	9.52	10.35
Miles per Person per Week	51.43	66.99	77.09

Note: Assumptions and calculations are shown in Appendix.

Table 14: **The Motorisation Effect -- Licence Holdership as a Percentage in Each Age Cohort in Great Britain**

Year of Birth	Age				Car Ownership Levels
	20	40	60	70+	
1910	9	20	30	33	Very few cars
1920	20	40	46	50	Some cars
1930	30	53	70	60	Extensive car ownership
1940	37	71	75	70	Mass car ownership
1950	51	78	80	75	Multiple car ownership
1960	62	80	90	80	Saturation of car ownership

Note: Some interpolation has been used to fill the missing cells and some of the figures are approximate due to lack of data.

Table 15: **Life Cycle Effects on Travel and Location**

Life Cycle Group	Travel Patterns	Location
Individuals or couples without children, often all working	High level of mobility with maximum levels of car ownership	City centre
Families with young children	Age of youngest child influences adults' travel patterns. Wage earner keeps former pattern but other partner develops short day time trips and complex escort trips with older children	Suburbs
Families of adults	Children independent and separate patterns develop for all households with maximum car ownership	City centre
Elderly and retired	Substantial opportunities for non work travel. Mobility decreasing with age	Some stay in city centre and others move to suburbs or rural areas

APPENDIX

Calculations of Journeys and Distances for the Elderly Age Group in 2001

Current Level of Journeys and Distances 1985-86			
Car Availability Category	1985-86	Journeys	Distance (miles)
Main driver in car-owning household	27	12.7	89.8
Other driver in car-owning household	5	9.7	74.5
Non-driver in car-owning household	16	7.0	52.7
Non-car-owning household	52	5.2	28.9

The levels are taken from the National Travel Survey 1985-86 and are for non-work journeys. The figures in the first column show the percentage distribution of the elderly (>60) between the four car availability categories.

The weighted total for all the elderly population (>60 years):

7.738 journeys per person per week

51.43 miles per person per week

If it is assumed that in 2001 the distribution of the elderly will reflect the current distribution of households in the 45-60 year age group, but with the same journey rates as the current elderly, the weighted total for all the elderly population becomes:

9.52 journeys per person per week

66.99 miles per person per week

Over this period of time (1986-2001) there will be little increase in the total elderly population (+2.3 per cent) and most of this increase will occur in the over 80 year age group. However, given the assumptions stated, there may be an increase of 23 per cent in the journeys made by the elderly and some 30 per cent increase in the distances travelled as many of the elderly retain the use of the car as long as possible.

If it is also assumed that there is a dynamic element to the demand for travel and the elderly retain the activity patterns for non work journeys of the 1985-86 cohort in the year 2001, then the weighted total for all the elderly population becomes:

10.35 journeys per person per week
77.09 miles per person per week

The increase in the journeys made is now 34 per cent and 50 per cent for the distances travelled.

If it is now assumed that the elderly will also use the same mode to make the increased travel, the figures are as follows (percentages). It should be noted that all this analysis is based on the demand for travel given the assumptions stated. It takes no account of changes in supply, new forms of transport or in any of the other factors (e.g. price) which influence the demand for transport.

Percentages	1985-86	2001 - Static Assumptions	2001 - Dynamic Assumptions
Car Driver	37.1	51.1	50.6
Car Passenger	23.4	24.3	23.9
Other Modes	39.5	24.5	25.5

Note that short walk trips are not included (under 1 mile).

BIBLIOGRAPHY

Banister, D. and Bayliss, D. (1991): Structural Changes in Population and Impact on Passenger Transport Demand, Paper presented at the European Conference of Ministers of Transport Round Table 88, Paris, June 1991.

Banister, D. and Norton, F. (1988): The role of the voluntary sector in the provision of rural services -- the case of transport, Journal of Rural Studies 4(1), pp. 57-71.

Banister, D., Cullen, I. and Mackett, R. (1990): The Impacts of Land Use on Travel Demand, University College London, Planning and Development Research Centre, Working Paper 3, July 1990.

Department of Transport (1989): National Road Traffic Forecasts (Great Britain) 1989, London, HMSO.

Department of Transport (1990): Transport Statistics Great Britain 1979-1989, London, HMSO.

Department of Transport: (Various) National Travel Surveys, 1965, 1972-73, 1975-76, 1978-79 and 1985-86, London, HMSO.

European Roundtable of Industrialists (1991): Missing Networks: A European Challenge, ERTI, Brussels.

FHWA (1984): Highway Statistics, US Department of Transportation.

Goodwin, P. (1990): Demographic impacts, social consequences and the transport policy debate, Oxford Review of Economic Policy 6(2), pp. 76-90.

Goodwin, P. and Layzell, A. (1985): Longitudinal analysis for public transport policy issues, in Jansen, G.R.M., Nijkamp, P. and Ruijgrok, C.J. (eds): Transportation and Mobility in an Era of Transition, North Holland, Elsevier, pp. 185-200.

Greene, D.L. (1987): Long run vehicle travel prediction from demographic trends, Transportation Research Record 1135, pp. 1-9.

Group Transport 2000 Plus (1990): Transport in a Fast Changing Europe, CEC Report, December 1990.

Goulcher, A. and Kearns, W. (1989): Demographic change in London and its impact on London Underground travel patterns, Paper produced by the LUL Strategic Planning Unit, November 1989.

Hill, E. and Rickard, J. (1990): Forecasting public transport demand; The demographic dimension, Rees Jeffreys Road Fund, Transport and Society Discussion Paper 16, April 1990.

House of Commons (1990): Roads for the Future, Report of the Transport Committee, HC 198-I, London, HMSO.

Kostyniuk, L.P. and Kitamura, R. (1987): Effects of aging and motorization on travel behavior: An Exploration, Transportation Research Record 1135, pp. 31-36.

Laslett, P. (1990): A Fresh Map of Life: The Emergence of the Third Age, Weidenfeld and Nicholson, London.

Lave, C. (1990): Things won't get a lot worse: The future of US traffic congestion, University of California, Irvine, Economics Department, Mimeo.

OECD (1989): Comparative socio-demographic trends: Initial data on ageing populations, OECD Group on Urban Affairs, UP/TSDA(89)1, April 1989.

Orfeuil, J.-P. (1991): Structural Changes in Population and Impact on Passenger Transport Demand, Paper presented at the European Conference of Ministers of Transport Round Table 88, Paris, June 1991.

Prevedouros, P.D. and Schofer, J.L. (1989): Suburban transport behaviour as a factor in congestion, Transportation Research Record 1237, pp. 47-58.

Vibe, N. (1991): Are there limits to growth in car ownership? Some recent figures from the Oslo region, Preliminary paper presented at the ECMT Round Table 88, June 1991, TP/0371/1991.

US Department of Transportation (1986): Personal Travel in the US, In the Nationwide Personal Transportation Study, Vol 2, November 1986.

Sub-topic 2

ECONOMIC TRENDS AND TRANSPORT SPECIALISATION

M. TURRO
Universitait Politècnica de Catalunya
European Investment Bank
Luxembourg-Kirchberg
Luxembourg

The points of view reflected in this paper are exclusively the owner's responsibility. They do not represent the opinion of either the EIB or the UPC.

SUMMARY

Luxembourg, October 1991

INTRODUCTION

Some might consider long-term prospecting to be a futile exercise. In fact the probability of taking a correct picture of the future depends very much on how far away the focus is placed. If, as suggested, economic development is to be considered a "chaotic phenomenon", long-term outcomes could diverge widely. However, even under this assumption, evolution would be quite predictable in the first cycles (short/medium term). Therefore, a "continuous" look into the future, introducing periodically the appropriate corrections, could provide a quite solid approximation to the actual development of the economy.

In any case, if correctly done, prospective exercises have the undeniable virtue of setting bounds to the range of probable scenarios. They should allow the detection of those elements of the present system that are incompatible with reasonable future options and drive the policies needed to transform the system in a suitable way. The proper detection of such hindrances and policies is, in fact, the challenge of the Symposium. This comes not too soon, because, as stated by a high level group put together by the European Commission (1): "*the European Community and the Member States have failed to anticipate the consequences of transport development*." The same comment is applicable to the other members of the ECMT.

The reflections that follow pretend only to sketch a plausible outcome for the future of the European land-use/transport system in order to outline the aspects where major changes are needed if sound economic development is to be pursued. This is no more than a working hypothesis directed at opening the mind and, eventually, the imagination of the reader. The goal is to put into perspective some of the "major" concerns we face now (notably the challenges of the Single European Market) and to realise how "minor" they may be in a long-term approach.

Many books and articles have appeared lately, devoted to the expected revolution of specific aspects of our society. Some of them are even loaded with quantitative analyses. There are also global approaches, sometimes with a strong political bias (2). In the transport field, however, only relatively few prospective exercises have been carried out (3).

This presentation has drawn from some of these sources and on the author's experience in planning and evaluation. It cannot be considered a scientific exercise, but it is hoped it will constitute an acceptable base for the discussions of the Symposium.

In any case forecasting is a most difficult task and, as I could not count on Nostradamus' help, I can only beg the eventual twentieth-century reader (4) to be understanding.

1. A "GROWTH" FRAMEWORK

The countries of the European Community and those of the EFTA (Sweden, Norway, Austria and Switzerland) have been developing since the Second World War at an unprecedented pace. Among the characteristic cycles around a steady upward trend, the past five to six years mark a most noticeable growth period, with the slight slump created by the Gulf War. As EC countries get ready for a single market and head towards political and monetary union, as EFTA countries seem prone to join the Community and as eastern and central European countries start recovering from decades of inefficient command economy, most macroeconomic indicators appear to be giving positive signals.

Transport is a derived activity and future scenarios for the system can only be established under adequate economic and social development frameworks. Therefore, although "global" forecasts are extremely complex, some assumptions on the evolution of the factors with the strongest influence on the transport system have to be assumed.

1.1. Political issues

European development cannot be analysed without considering its position in the world. In fact, of the three economic megapowers (USA, Japan and EC), the European Community is probably the most engaged in the political issues raised by the present trend towards worldwide co-operation. As economic and social issues overcome ideological dissent, following the abandonment of communist experiments all over the planet, geographical disparities (at the regional, national and "continental" levels) will become the major source of political conflict. Spatial redistribution of wealth, which underlies most inter-ethnical problems and is the core of north-south relations, will become the key factor in the so-called "new world order".

As stated before, industrialised countries seem to be heading for a period of sustained economic growth. At the same time, the perspectives for the majority of less developed countries appear rather narrow. Burdened with heavy foreign debt, with their income from raw materials severely curtailed by stable or decreasing world prices, and unable to cope with their endemic mismanagement problems, they will probably see their gap with the rich countries widen. In fact it seems that only a kind of world government would be able to reverse the situation. The provision of adequate living conditions to the entire world would become its main objective. Even without such global consensus, the rich countries will be forced either to share some of their wealth or to face migrations that will be intolerable for the preservation of the system. Keeping a "fortress" is both impossible in the long run and unacceptable under the panorama of freedom and human rights that has led to their economic superiority.

The efficiency of aid requires, in any case, a global approach (involving social and political aspects as well as economic ones) that has seldom been applied. This makes the challenge not only extremely pressing but also very complex and it will be the centre of political debate for the next decades. The European Community has already been facing a similar problem with the poorer regions of Europe. The experience, not always positive, demonstrates both the difficulties and the possibilities of a global approach to development.

In fact, a much stronger view than in the past will be adopted at the European level, where east-west and centre-periphery relations will also acquire a prevalent role in the political arena. Assistance to eastern and central European countries and regional development efforts will increase as balanced growth all over the Continent is recognised as the only path to uphold development in Europe.

The decisions on these key issues will have enormous impacts on present land use and transport patterns. In the process of establishing a world economy, new trade dependencies, implying new transport flows in much wider areas, will be created. Central European countries will recover their natural position and face their "destiny" as transit regions, peripheral development will swell transport needs, etc.

These broad issues, requiring a global approach and substantial planning, seem bound to be handled by political systems prone to reduce public intervention, to decentralise and to sustain greater citizen involvement in decision-making. As ideological barriers fade, a political system more adapted to the new context should appear where consensus mechanisms among national, regional and local authorities make political action possible. A redistribution of responsibilities and functions and the creation of communication channels between hierarchical levels seem the only way to cope with the challenge.

Transport infrastructure decisions will be especially affected by this political evolution. A minimum "waiting period" of some ten years is presently needed between conception and inauguration of any major transport project, mostly due to the inefficiency of present decision procedures, which tend to be more complex with the growing concerns about social and environmental issues. In an ever faster evolving society, facing urgent transport needs, such delays are illogical and adequate mechanisms must appear to avoid collapse.

1.2. Economic issues

In the envisaged framework of sustained and more balanced economic growth, activity location patterns are bound to change. The relative weight in location decisions of human resources, capital, proximity to raw materials and energy sources, accessibility, environmental concerns, etc., will change substantially in the next decades, following developments in products and services demand, in production technology and management and in transport and telecommunications. The strategies adopted to foster development will also have an influence on where new activities will take place.

The final "economic map" of the world and, particularly, that of Europe will reflect the equilibrium between centripetal and centrifugal forces. Technological developments such as automation and telecommunications improvements favour concentration of capital intensive production units and high value added services in central areas where skilled labour is available. On the other hand, politically driven environmental and "balancing" constraints will be deterring this tendency, which is not sustainable in the long run.

Transport is a key factor in the materialisation of location patterns. Proximity to specific sites is ever less determinant of site choice, as suggested by the increase in mobile employment from 30 per cent in 1950 to more than 50 per cent in 1990 (Group Transport 2000 Plus, 1991), but adequate accessibility is now a basic requirement for the creation of new economic activities. Efficient transport is fundamental for trade, which is widely accepted as one of the determinant factors to induce competition, productivity and, finally, growth to less developed regions. The protection of local markets via high transport costs, as through import taxation, has proved to be a recipe for failure.

On the other hand, the location patterns of multinational companies are increasingly based on logistic parameters. Enterprises tend to become bigger, but new management techniques lean towards smaller, flexible production units. As products become increasingly specialised and consumer oriented, economies of scale will have to be found, more in organisation and in financial and marketing services than in production. Reliable and efficient telecommunications and transport become, then, a necessity for such dispersed industrial conglomerates.

The new economies of scale will also have implications for transport. A few financial centres located all over the world (New York, London, Tokyo, Frankfurt, Paris, Hong Kong) and some emerging ones (Moscow, Singapore, Johannesburg, etc.) will control most capital flows. This should provide an integration of the world's economy and contribute to a stabilization of the markets and to a mitigation of the fluctuations in development cycles. Events such as the energy crisis of the seventies will become unlikely. As a consequence, a consolidation of trade-related flows (transport, information), especially at the international level, can be expected.

All in all, the evolution of the economy will induce expanding and well-established transport and communication flows. This trend should be especially observable in Europe, where internationalisation of the economy under the Single Market and monetary union will multiply the percentage of transnational traffic in total freight transport (it was only 5.2 per cent of the 8.6 billion tons moved in the EC countries in 1987). This increase will be even more impressive in absolute terms because total transport will grow along with GDP (5) and trade. The European Parliament (Romera, 1991) forecasts for the Community an increase in land transport of 34 per cent between the years 1988 and 2000. A yearly growth of 3.5 per cent has been forecast in a study for the ECMT (ECMT, 1991) that would lead to much higher traffic volumes. This growth will be basically due to the augmentation of average travel distance, as tonnage moved remains stable or even decreases.

There are, however, three main factors which could deter this expected expansion: capacity constraints, transport costs and environmental concerns. They will be frequently outlined in this paper. Here, only general developments affecting the sector are given some comment.

The kind of economic development observed during the past century is based on declining transport costs which, in turn, following the "dispersion" model mentioned before, tend to take a higher percentage of total production costs. Reductions in the cost of consumed energy per transport unit explain a great deal of the decline in costs. Nonetheless the sector, which eats up approximately 30 per cent of the EC's energy budgets (mostly from petrol) and has the highest consumption growth, has become very dependent on energy cost fluctuations. The Gulf crisis has shown that a repetition of the harsh energy crisis of the seventies is not likely to happen. The envisaged world situation should prevent major crises and, on the other hand, alternative fuels seem to be becoming practical alternatives to petrol. In fact, in the longer term, if nuclear fusion fulfils its expectations as a cheap, clean source of energy, the present incidence of energy on the cost structure of the sector might be substantially reduced. As vehicle production costs should also continue a declining trend, major changes in future transport costs will come from quality requirements or from external factors.

These are, in fact, key elements in the development of the sector and, consequently, of future logistic patterns and the location of economic activity. Goods to be transported will continue their trend to higher value per unit of weight. Primary treatment of raw materials will be carried out increasingly at the source, notably in less developed regions where this is an obvious industrialisation option. Downsizing will continue to be a compelling design trend. Lighter materials (plastics, composites) will be replacing metals.

Higher unit values imply better transport services. Reliability and speed will become the key elements for many trades following the widespread use of just-in-time processes. These will grow along with the financial constraints of the industrial sector. Smaller load units and specialised transport will be required. Safety and security aspects will be given greater importance (6). The application of logistic strategies will be necessary to cope with this ever more complex system, which will have to attract competent managers.

In general, the quality enhancement will lead to a "tailor-made" system with low utilisation of rolling stock and an impressive growth in investment in facilities and material. Specialised handling facilities in increasingly sophisticated and automated terminals, purpose-built ships and rolling stock (such as the TransManche wagons) and containers to suit all needs, will continuously push back the limits on standards and regulations.

Among private users a similar trend is to be expected: land vehicles for infrequent use (sports and mountain cars, caravans, snowmobiles) will raise currently accepted ceilings for motorisation levels, while a wider utilisation of "spaces" not accessible to most individuals (7), for example, through the expansion of general aviation, might develop markets that are presently very selective.

Along these lines the amount of assets devoted to transport will increase considerably. As a consequence, in spite of the envisaged decrease in unit transport costs, quality requirements might more than compensate for this. Therefore, the sector's participation in macroeconomic indicators (especially if non-commercial aspects are included) might surge.

This evolution will certainly have special developments in central and eastern European countries. As cost-based pricing of transport services is applied, a radical transformation of flows and of modal split should appear. Heavy transport (mostly by rail and barge), which was the core of traffic in these countries, will be strongly reduced with industrial rationalisation and give way to more sophisticated, national and international services responding to the restructuring of trade patterns.

The economic development scenario which has been presented, suggesting an important expansion of freight transport, will also have implications for passenger travel. As international trade develops and the need for personal contact remains, an increase in the number and length of business trips is to be expected. Tourism and social travel should also become more frequent, especially at the international level. This subject is analysed further on.

1.3. Technological issues

No dramatic technological changes in the transport sector are likely to occur in the next ten to twenty years. Changes in the present system will come mostly from applications of information technology. Probably the only major breakthrough to be witnessed in the next two decades will be hypersonic aviation, which could become a tangible factor in the creation of a true "world economy".

The process of the expansion of the size of vehicles which has been quite apparent for many decades, has probably reached a ceiling in most transport modes. Only in aviation the need for massive transport of passengers and high value freight between the main economic areas of the world (North America, Far East and Europe) will foster a growth in the size of aircraft (8). In the other modes most efforts will be directed to uphold performance: more efficient design and operation, reduction or elimination of emissions (which might have a strong effect on present energy consumption patterns), speed increases, standardization and specialisation (not necessarily contradictory) and safety improvements. The most impressive changes will probably occur in the intermodal connections. Automated terminals and adapted mobile material are necessary if combined transport has to reach the expected levels.

The transformation of the system will come mostly from applications of telematics and computer-based techniques. Management of the system will be greatly enhanced through EDI (electronic data interchange), mobile communications, satellite-based localisation devices and other information facilities. Automatic conduction will provide the most apparent changes and they seem the most obvious candidate to provide substantial capacity improvements to congested networks. Guided public transport vehicles, offering efficient high frequency services in urban areas, will be followed by the implementation of dual-mode technologies (allowing automatic or manual conduction) on lorries and private cars in the most dense corridors.

Some of the available applications of road transport informatics (RTI) such as dynamic tolling will help to increase capacity but others, like those supplying dynamic route information, will probably have only substantial benefits for users as long as they remain a small proportion of total traffic. They will certainly contribute to reduce congestion, but even under a full coverage situation their effect might not be impressive. Present RTI applications will be, in any case, very positive for the future of transport as, besides improvements to safety and driver's information, they will pioneer developments like dual-mode technologies which will transform road usage.

1.4. Social issues

European society has undergone an impressive transformation in the past decades, but what lays ahead may well minimise what has happened to date. Television and mobility (in particular, tourism) have been key factors in the recent evolution of social behaviour. Along with telecommunications and automation, they will probably continue to be major determinants of the future course of European society.

The fall of the Iron Curtain is a new factor that will profoundly mark the years ahead. Differences in social patterns between eastern and western countries will persist for a long time, though. In the EC countries, affected by the single market, life will necessarily become more standardized and cultural barriers (being raised mostly by language difficulties) will falter. Travel will continue to increase although at a slower pace due to time-budget constraints, but leisure trips and especially culture-oriented tourism should expand considerably. Eastern countries, in the meantime, will undergo an accelerated passage to a consumer society involving much higher car ownership and mobility ratios. As time becomes increasingly the key factor in the private perception of the quality of life, delays caused by congestion will be increasingly hard to accept by the population (9).

Growing concern for the environment will also contribute to modify present attitudes. A "return to nature" philosophy will be spreading, affecting present urbanisation patterns and reducing the appeal of the present megalopolises, because most of their advantages (anonymity, access to specialised facilities, job opportunities, etc.) will be found in other surroundings with a better quality of life. In a context of cheap and adequate telecommunications, the major concerns in the location of residential and working activities will be adequate environment (natural and social) and accessibility. This process, which will run in parallel with the retreat of the "welfare state", could aggravate some of the social problems already observed in many European urban areas. Socially segregated "zoning", increasingly under racial lines, could endanger an already difficult equilibrium in major cities.

In Europe, demographic forecasts indicate a stabilization of the population and consequently its overall ageing. Only a limited population growth is expected in the southern countries (10). Although several governments are fighting this trend with fertility programmes, it will not be easily reversed.

As demography stabilization is compensated in the labour market by immigration, the increasing participation of women in the work force and perhaps by late retirement and as working time is reduced and becomes more flexible, mobility patterns will change. Present peak-hour demands following working schedules might be diluted, but new capacity constraints will appear. In particular, additional leisure time will induce (as already observed in the Alps' accesses on certain days during the ski season) massive non-recurrent travel with specific needs. All in all, household consumption of transport (which already takes around 13 per cent of the total) will probably maintain a growing trend.

1.5. Environmental issues

The environment is taking the political weight that welfare issues used to have in past decades. Environment preservation is, however, a rather undefined expression that is often used demagogically. The amount of quantitative analysis being carried out on the subject should soon allow, however, for it to be treated along more objective lines than at present. There are no doubts, in any case, of the increasing awareness of the public, and therefore politicians, of the difficult balance between economic growth and nature conservation.

Air pollution, especially in urban settings (11), noise, visual obstruction and transport-related land occupation (sometimes affecting the ecological equilibrium) are resented by the population, which considers the sector to have, along with nuclear energy, the most negative impact on the environment. This is an overstatement, but such considerations will have an obvious effect on decisionmaking. In fact, unless precise guidelines or standards are set, environmental concerns can be expected to be used (often without any substantial base) to endorse policies and investment options that would not resist a proper socioeconomic analysis.

Environmental constraints will become increasingly a key factor in the development of the transport sector. They will affect regional and urban planning, transport infrastructure layouts, traffic management and, of course, the amount of investment required for a certain level of efficiency. It is obvious that additional construction costs will be incurred due to increased lengths to avoid sensitive zones, more expensive designs (especially through a growing utilisation of tunnels), the installation of sonic barriers, landscaping, etc. Automobiles will also be forced to comply with more compelling emission and noise standards, with corresponding effects on their production costs. In a related field -- as the fifty thousand deaths resulting from road accidents reported annually in the EC represent an obvious ecological problem -- safety aspects will also require important investments.

Thus, environmental constraints can be seen as a main factor in the reversal of the past trend that provided for a continuous reduction in transport costs.

2. A LOOK INTO THE CRYSTAL BALL

The different issues just evoked suggest a continuous growth for the European transport sector at even higher levels than overall economic growth. Most probably neither the rather pessimistic views of the early eighties (Bessay, 1988) nor the extrapolation of the sector's expansion in the last years of the decade taken by some lobbies in their reports (12) will prove right in the long run. The author's look into his "crystal ball" shows a sustained growth of the sector well above GDP, but subject to important qualitative changes, especially in its geographic projection. In this sense, two major factors could severely alter the present European transport system: migrations of unprecedented size and the decline of the megalopolis. The final impact of these factors will depend on how demography and urban and regional planning will be affected by political decisions.

2.1. Migrations

The fall of command economy in the USSR and in the central and eastern countries of Europe will induce migration flows that might minimise the "military invasion threat" that has been a major concern for decades in western Europe. As our political system, because of its democratic base calling for human rights, is intrinsically incapable of creating a new "reverse" iron curtain, even massive aid will not prevent a multitude of impoverished but quite educated people, eager for access to a "consumer's paradise", to move south. Western propaganda has been a major element in the political turnaround of the USSR, but the expectations it has created -- which the country, even under optimum circumstances, cannot fulfil -- will push millions of emigrants to the rich but already crowded countries of the EC and EFTA (suffering, in some cases, from high unemployment levels). Looking at the migrations of the southern countries of Europe during the fifties, sixties and seventies (13) and taking into account that communication means have improved enormously since then, it is easy to imagine that permanent expatriation for tens of millions of people could take place in Europe in the next decade.

A similar but probably slower population shift from Third World countries, especially from the Maghreb and the poorer regions of sub-Saharan Africa, will also take place. Race and cultural differences will make this flow less pressing in the short term but, as integration is more difficult, its social impact could be of similar intensity.

Political and administrative barriers, under our system, will be unable to prevent these migrations (14). The only alternative -- fast economic development for the countries of origin -- would require extremely hard political decisions in the wealthier countries. Measures such as the limitation of growth in order to transfer resources to poorer countries or the application of a much stronger interventionism to ensure the efficiency of aid programmes (which could be taken as a new form of colonialism) will only be taken if the pressure can no longer be sustained. A new, bolder approach to external migrations and unemployment -- two of the key political issues of the near future -- is urgently required at the national and European levels.

An internal rearrangement of the western populations can also be expected. As administrative and cultural barriers fade and good communications become available globally, location patterns will continue their present evolution at a much faster pace. Climate, availability of open space and a pleasant natural environment, when complemented with adequate social facilities, are attracting more and more residents. Retired people in particular are eager to take advantage of this possibility. Regarding productive activities, the trend towards a better working environment is also conspicuous. High-tech industries and research centres are, however, tied to other constraints like adequate access to transport and telecom facilities, or appropriate cultural and technical contexts (availability of qualified service suppliers, research facilities, etc.). They will be using their location to attract limited numbers of highly qualified personnel. The American experience on the subject is quite impressive, but in Europe, in spite of the single market, the trend might be much less dramatic due to language barriers and national inertia.

Regarding seasonal migrations, it is to be expected that, in the present context of cheap transport, tourism and leisure-related travel will continue to grow steadily. However, wealthier people will tend to substitute cultural tourism for traditional sun-based holidays. The ceiling of acceptability of visitors will be reached in some places and this will create severe problems with local populations (compelling the appearance of new formulae of accessibility restrictions). A resumption of the mass tourism of the seventies, brought by the proliferation of tour operators, will start in the eastern countries where low income populations are eager to travel. Reduced working periods will also contribute to an enormous development of seasonal mobility which will be developing along increasingly longer distances.

2.2. Urban development

Most megalopolises, which have been the nuclei of economic development in the last century, have probably reached their ceiling of performance. Changes in social attitudes and a decline in the role of central governments which have been supporting their capitals, on the one hand and developments in telecommunications on the other, will be responsible for this evolution. Big cities have been able to cope with increasing diseconomies of scale (mainly due to lack of infrastructures) thanks to direct or indirect subsidies from other minor urban areas. Congestion, environmental distress and security problems, characteristic of the centres of major cities have been reaching their periphery (15). Thus, a situation is appearing where inefficiency in most sectors (transport, public utilities, etc.) is erasing the benefits of urban concentration.

Good transport and new telecommunication developments will be able to provide such concentration benefits for most sectors in medium-sized cities. Service efficiency and quality of life will end up being much better there than in the megalopolis. In fact, most of the opportunities being offered by the big cities are rarely used. Therefore a good access from outside to their centre, even if it is expensive (i.e. high-speed rail), would eliminate the need of proximity to enjoy its facilities. Only highly specialised sectors (public administration, finance, sophisticated health services, elite cultural centres, international exhibitions, etc.), attracting people from wide areas, will find an economic justification for their location in the central areas of the megalopolis.

There are image factors and, for some businesses, important benefits arising from the nearness of competitors, that will continue to justify the important additional expenditure arising from locating in major towns, but probably most of the work which is not related to "image" -- manufacturing, administration, etc. -- will eventually be transferred where employees can enjoy better living and working conditions. The new tendencies in management towards decentralisation and especially the improvement in voice, data and image telecommunications will make geographic dispersion of production units less of a constraint.

The transfer of activity (and population growth) from major capitals to medium-sized cities can only be effective if the latter are given the required infrastructure. Regarding external connections, high-speed links to the centre of a major city, good access to the other transport networks (motorways, freight transport system, airports) and adequate telecom services are inescapable requirements.

Aggressive urban planning, on the other hand, will be necessary to allow for a balanced growth of these cities. Access to the exterior should be a most important design constraint. The role of private cars and public transport should be well defined in order to provide for the needed "reserve" capacity that should allow for future growth.

The development of medium-sized cities with functional dependencies to megalopolises should produce a "mesh" of cities with the linkages between major areas taking place in some of the smaller towns. This dispersed urban structure will act as the new motor of economic development. A primary network, relaying megalopolises, embedded in a more or less quadrangular basic network drawn along medium-sized cities, will be developed from present infrastructure (16). This "extensive grid" will meet the transport needs of the "mesh" of cities and, at the same time, provide accessibility to the overall territory in a more homogeneous way.

The primary network will include some high-speed lines, which will carry an important share of the traffic. The basic network, constituted of motorways and, for some sections, of conventional railways, will have good direct connections to the interior of the grid, where basic activities (industrial, agricultural, tourism), not requiring a transport system of the same quality, will be able to develop, thanks to the adequate accessibility levels provided with such a structure. Intermodal platforms located at the nodes of the grid will become key points in the flows of freight and information.

3. PRESENT SITUATION. THE TRANSPORT SYSTEM'S CONSTRAINTS

If the expected growth of the European transport system and these qualitative changes are to occur, important modifications of the present situation are unavoidable. It seems an interesting exercise, therefore, to analyse such conditions in the light of the projected picture for the future. Of course, here only a rough review of the most relevant issues is possible.

3.1. Infrastructure

The analysis of transport infrastructure is simpler if split in two parts, the interurban level (including the European and regional networks) and the urban level.

3.1.1. Interurban transport

Present interurban networks reflect the weight of history. Curiously enough, it is the most ancient, the Roman, that has a conception closest to what is now considered as a European system. Centralism prevailing during the construction of the "modern" networks and a follow-the-demand approach have been major contributors to the development of the present situation, which is poorly adapted to the objectives of an integrated Europe-wide operation and the provision of accessibility to all its territory. The feed-back effect between transport and development, the emission of "wrong signals" by the existing biased system (17), and, often, lack of adequate planning explain why, in spite of the awareness of the deficiencies of the model, the inherited unbalanced situation has been consolidated.

Only adequate planning can produce, however, the investment programmes required to adapt the European transport system to tomorrow's needs. Technical and administrative mechanisms exist for the elaboration of plans at the national and, in most European countries, at the regional levels, even though problems at the information-gathering, decisionmaking and implementation stages are still appalling in most settings. At the European level, however, almost everything is to be done. The ECMT has not even been able to establish a comprehensive set of standards. Present transport infrastructure policy in the EC countries consists of the general objective definition by the European Parliament, a marginal (118 million ECU in 1991) contribution of the Commission's budget to projects of "European interest" presented by the Member countries (18) and the loans of the European Investment Bank (2.8 billion ECU on transport infrastructure, including aircraft acquisition, in 1990). Actions undertaken until now, like air transport liberalisation, have been more the result of the application of other Community policies, such as the opening of competition, than the consequence of sector planning.

In the meantime the need for action is obvious. A rather prudent forecast issued by the ECMT for its nineteen countries gives a 51 per cent global increase in land goods traffic by the year 2010, with road transport growing by 74 per cent, though with rail ton/km decreasing by 4 per cent.

In the face of a situation approaching collapse, and observing the minor effect of past policies on modal choice, much more decisive action is required to transform the European transport system into one responding to the social, economic and environmental concerns of the future.

Indeed, road congestion is growing, but where flows are most massive (in the "banana" enclosing the London area, Flanders, the Netherlands and the Rhine Valley in Germany) motorway capacity expansion is extremely difficult. Besides, and in spite of rail taking a decreasing share of total traffic, their best services, usually in the densest corridors, are highly used. As the majority of interurban transport takes places over short distances, where road transport is most competitive, this trend will be difficult to stop. In freight transport, even the absorption of total traffic growth would represent an absolute increase in traffic that railways would not be able to cope with. Railways could, however, do much better in share of long-distance shipments, especially if combined transport develops (19). Waterways, on the other hand, represent an acceptable option for bulk products and containers only along the "banana" (the Rhine takes more than 50 per cent of all EC fluvial traffic) thanks to the leading role of the Rotterdam and Antwerp harbours, but cannot be expected to keep a strong position outside the few major routes (20).

Similarly in passenger intercity services, the share of rail could improve substantially only if the present offer of capacity is enhanced (through improved signalling, automatic conduction, etc.) and commercial speeds become more competitive. In fact, under the present circumstances (congestion concentrated in a relatively small number of interurban corridors), only high-speed lines would be able to substantially modify the current modal split. It has been suggested (21), however, that even under a complete high-speed network, interregional travel by automobile would not be reduced further than 10 per cent. This would mean doubling the railway's share, but a relatively minor effect on major corridors with high-speed lines and a negligible impact on roads elsewhere.

High-speed trains will be the only challenge to the domination that aviation has exercised on long-distance travel for decades now. Air transport, which has been thriving in a non-competitive environment, will keep its position almost untouched for the longest distances market, but high-speed trains will get a substantial share of intermediate distances and may pick small parts of their specific markets.

The privileged position of aviation may be blamed for most of the problems facing air transport. Lack of overall planning, especially apparent in air traffic control, slow adaptation to technological developments and military interference explain present congestion in air space. Similar planning problems and a nationalistic (and often centralistic) approach by the responsible authorities also explain the saturation of many airports.

Maritime transport, which carries ninety per cent of the external exchanges and thirty per cent of the internal exchanges of Member countries, is the subsector where the free market has been largely in place and seems the best positioned to respond to important demand growth. Ports, following a tradition of infrastructure-prone management (not always justified, in fact), have more spare capacity than the other parts of the system. Problems might appear mostly in the provision of adequate equipment, specialised terminals and in the land accesses. The world fleet has always been subject to characteristic market cycles. Leaving aside the question of flags, it can be assumed that it will be able to respond to any expected demand growth.

Taken globally, therefore, present infrastructural assets in Europe do not seem capable of responding to the demand forecasts that have been proposed before. Indeed, they can hardly cope with existing requirements. A study carried out for the European Parliament (22) estimates that the present transport infrastructure deficit costs ECU 3.75 billion annually to the EC (23), but this amount could reach almost ECU 20 billion by 2010 if strong action is not taken (24).

Curiously enough, problems will probably be harsher where the system is more developed. Western Germany, for example, has an impressive motorway network, but it is already very stressed by an extremely high mobility level. The country has suddenly seen its position switched from one of a "European dead end", with an almost impermeable bottom due to the Iron Curtain, to that of a transit country. Because planning has followed the typical demand-lead approach, east-west links are much scarcer than north-south. When trade between the former Comecon countries and the EC acquire the level envisaged and overall mobility levels for the new *Ländern* surge, the situation could become untenable.

A similar situation will be faced by other countries of central Europe. The increase in east-west traffic [a process that most conservative estimates put at 50 per cent for the next decade, but others (Seidenfus, 1990) put at 450 million tons by 2010, ten times more than the 1995 level] will develop much faster than eventual transport infrastructure construction. As investment and environmental constraints will make it difficult to find suitable solutions on time, transit countries in central Europe will suffer terrible pressure.

3.1.2. Urban transport

Transport problems are one of the major worries of local authorities all over Europe. They reflect the steady growth in mobility undergone by the cities in spite of modifications to working schedules and other actions to reduce traffic conflicts. The increase in the number of trips per person is associated with a growing demand for the usage of private cars, which often remains unsatisfied due to congestion and lack of parking space. Capacity restraint, either regulatory (bus lanes, pedestrian zones, etc.) or by saturation (of traffic flows, parking places), is presently the only policy widely used to refrain a demand that is ready to appear as soon as conditions improve. No alternative solutions seem technically ready or politically acceptable (25), and local decisionmakers feel overwhelmed by a problem that affects the very development potential of their towns.

Public transport is not the miracle solution for the transport problems of major cities, at least if it is required to fully cover investment, maintenance and operation costs and externalities. The provision of quality levels comparable to those of the private vehicle in consolidated urban areas entails either enormous investments (i.e. automated guided underground systems) or very expensive services (i.e. bus fleets that would have overall costs eventually higher than those of automobile usage).

Information technology does not seem able to contribute to solve this problem in a substantial way. It can certainly improve public transport performance, reduce trip length or duration (directing the cars to the best path or to available parking facilities) and in a more general way through working at home and shopping, reduce mobility needs especially at peak hours, but its effects will probably be compensated with more free time devoted, in part, to travel.

There is no cheap, politically acceptable solution for the transport problems of big cities. This leads to a situation where either major financial transfers from other (often poorer) zones occur or the additional costs of major towns will offset their advantages and they will be bound to stagnate.

Inertia and lack of suitable alternatives explain the endurance of the megalopolis. As stated before, if well-planned, high quality of life urban environments were developed in medium-sized cities and a correct assignment of transport and other utility costs were applied, important shifts of population (26) would probably occur.

The experience shows that location trends responding to natural reasons are, eventually, unstoppable. To handle the situation it is necessary to prepare for it ahead of time. A new framework for regional planning is needed where, besides people's immediate requirements, other considerations such as a global European design, adequate resource allocation (27), environment preservation and workable implementation procedures are considered.

3.2. Services

The quality of transport services shows important differences depending on the mode. While maritime, fluvial and road transport are subject to strong internal competition and, as a consequence, provide high flexibility, specialisation, etc., rail and aviation, still controlled mostly by national public companies, tend to look at the market in a monopolistic way and to serve customers with quality levels well below their technical capability.

The market, in the meantime, is becoming more sophisticated and demanding. Passengers require lower door-to-door times, on-board facilities, convenient schedules, precise information, etc. Goods transport is also increasingly demanding. Special treatment is sought for more and more shipments (dangerous goods, perishable stuff). New management techniques require position control (to fulfil the information needs of logistic chains), destination flexibility (to follow market fluctuations) and, more than anything else, high reliability, the most difficult attribute to obtain in a congested network. All in all, an integrated approach to obtain the advantages of separate modes is becoming ever more important.

The integration of transport services might be facilitated by the extension of logistic techniques in manufacturing and the increasing size and reach of transport operators. Economies of scale and scope are the justification for hub-and-spoke strategies used by airlines, notably in the USA. These have allowed substantial cost reductions, although not necessarily in the best interests of passengers. Express and door-to-door parcel delivery services are offered by operators using all modes available in the most efficient way in order to provide guaranteed delivery times. Similarly, travellers also expect comprehensive services, meaning easy and quick access to the system (a reduction of out-of-vehicle times), freedom to adapt travel to their needs and, increasingly, "package" deals to avoid uncertainties in accommodation and transfers.

Both the growing requirements of customers and the logistic chains need a much improved operation of the system. Reliability and speed -- two basic aspects for passengers with high time value and for some goods -- become endangered in a congested environment. The driver and the transport operator can only improve them through information. Data transmissions running in parallel with actual transport are becoming, therefore, increasingly important. In fact, information flows are growing much faster than actual physical flows.

Some integrated and also some information-based strategies are already applied. Magnetic cards to provide direct access to planes and to land services (limousines, car rental, etc.), accommodation and luggage delivery services for air travellers, intermodal co-ordination (28) are just a few examples of practical applications. A substantial part of the benefits of such developments is presently being lost, however, by the inefficient management of security problems (customs, drugs, terrorism, etc.).

In freight transport, some shippers already provide fast door-to-door integrated services. As an example, the case of an operator located on an island can be mentioned. This operator uses local truckers for the collection and distribution of containers between customers and one of his intermodal terminals, where block trains carry them to his port terminal. There his scheduled maritime cabotage line takes the containers to a continental logistic centre, from where the containers are delivered by barge, rail or road depending on the location of the receiver, or treated for groupage, repackaging, etc. into a new shipment unit. The management skills and the efficient use of telematics are fundamental to the operation's success.

However, the possibilities of the present system to respond to the demand for flexibility, reliability, speed, together with safety, security and comfort, in a high productivity context, depend not only on infrastructure capacity and on adequate management but on the possibilities of competitive forces to progress towards improved performance. The present treatment of the different transport modes in the various European countries is unequal and does not respond to the needs of the market.

3.3. The market

The European transport market is still a superposition of national markets, most of them suffering from a high intervention by the public sector. This intervention has produced corresponding price distortions inside the national boundaries which, added to the differences in competitiveness among the Member countries, have prevented the creation of a common transport market in spite of the fact that it was specifically contemplated in the Treaty of Rome.

Liberalisation and harmonization, meaning the reduction of public sector intervention and the establishment of equal treatment for the carriers of all Member countries, have advanced slowly. Lately, more action has been undertaken, however (elimination of contingents and cabotage restrictions, separation of infrastructure and operation accounts in railways, liberalisation of air transport, standardization of technical parameters), following the recognition that, if left aside, the sector could become one of the critical aspects that could hinder the development of the single market.

Although strong differences exist among countries (in technical standards, working conditions, professional requirements, tariff controls, etc.), some policies generating market distortions are easy to observe in most of them:

a) Infrastructure costs are assigned to vehicles in a way completely unrelated to wear-and-tear and to investment;

b) Transport taxation follows only a logic of revenue maximisation for the national budget, which is exclusively restrained by macroeconomic constraints (notably the inflation index);

c) External factors such as the interests of national industry, public service obligations, regional development or environment considerations are often determinant factors in decisions on transport infrastructure and services.

Operators which were rather mode-specific are in a transformation process, following the need to adapt to the new market conditions in Europe and the growing application of complex logistic strategies. Multimodal operators are taking a larger share of the trade and tend to become transport management enterprises supported by small, technically or geographically specialised operators, efficient but unable to obtain the market penetration, organisation advantages and stability they enjoy through the big firms. The high disaggregation of road carriers (especially in the southern countries) and barge companies makes such a transformation almost unavoidable. Medium-sized companies are probably the most affected by the changes and are being increasingly absorbed by large conglomerates. In fact, it seems that in the transport sector the single market is being fostered more by the financial moves than by deregulation.

Rail companies and airlines are also following a transformation process. Railways are finally recognising the need to overcome their nationalistic approach, improving their co-ordination with the other rail operators, and to adapt to the requirements of the present market. As land transport of bulk products, which was the core business of railways, is declining in Europe along with heavy industry, a flexible and adaptable tariff policy, increased service quality and co-operation with the other modes (i.e. in combined transport development) are fundamental conditions for the preservation of their weight in the sector.

In the air transport field, changes started by deregulation in the USA have been producing enormous transformations on the international scene, but the repercussions in Europe have been minor until now. Well-protected national companies, often achieving very poor results, are just beginning to face the liberalisation measures adopted by the EC. The sector, with practically no competition from other modes, with the national airlines protected from outside operators by bilateral agreements and public sector security, has been losing most of the stamina it had when it was created. It is appalling to observe the inefficiencies built into the system over the years in all its elements (airlines, airports, air traffic control). They provide the sole explanation as to why European airlines are often losing money in a growing, protected market. Radical transformations are needed. In this sense some of the experiences of the last few years (29) are reassuring. The third "package" of measures issued by the Commission should break the last administrative constraints to a free market, but the internal problems (labour relations, bureaucratic practices, etc.) and those related to the sector's ties to the State (affecting management practices, tariff setting, selection of suppliers, financial deals, etc.) will not be easily solved. Privatisation, concentration to compete with the American megacarriers, development of complementary companies (regional) and specialised services, etc. are the most observable trends at this time.

Undoubtedly, under the present situation road transport provides the most competitive supply option unless distance or other constraints (e.g. sea crossings) make it unreasonable. It offers convenience (door-to-door, non-scheduled, flexible service) and for the passenger, privacy and "status". Only congestion can reduce its performance enough to make people give up on their cars. And it is questionable that businesses would discard trucking even under heavy saturation. In any case, congestion has such negative effects that it is a dangerous way to reach objectives. People will not accept restrictions on movement unless they are provided with an acceptable justification. As already mentioned, air transport for long-distance travel has a similar preponderance. In this case, however, capacity problems could be solved much more easily.

The present transport market faces a difficult equilibrium between the requirements of the economy, public intervention and capacity constraints. Price mechanisms are not sufficient to produce an efficient sector under such circumstances. The context of the Single European Market will undoubtedly induce substantial transformations which will lead to a much more efficient system, but liberalisation policies will only be fully realised when a harmonized context exists. The challenges of the future are so impressive that any further delay in progress towards such a context due, finally, to shortsighted and counterproductive protection policies, will be paid for dearly.

3.4. Taxation and pricing

The investment needs of the European transport sector have been estimated to be some 300 to 400 billion ECU for the next ten years. This means a twofold increase with respect to recent investment practice. To fulfil such a requirement demands that new financing mechanisms are studied. On the other hand, taxes and tolls constitute the key issues in the harmonization negotiations in the Community. It is obvious that important decisions should be taken in the short term regarding the financial aspects of the sector.

The present situation varies considerably among countries and shows strong distortions but, in general, it can be said that revenues (basically from fuel taxes, vehicle taxes and tolls) outweigh expenditure. In 1986, for the ten Member countries, the imbalance was estimated at 24 per cent. Very often transport taxes (notably those on petrol) are used as a handy resource to cover budget deficits.

Even though the countries with specific funds for road construction and maintenance levied directly from taxes (Germany, Austria) tend to show better infrastructure provision levels, most governments are reluctant to establish a separate fiscal policy for the sector. On the other hand, transport produces extremely important externalities (air and noise pollution, property value modifications, etc.) that must have an appropriate fiscal framework. Indeed, both a global quantification of the positive and negative impacts of the sector and a clear procedure to redistribute them among the different users and between users and non-users are necessary to bring economic rationality to the system. The market motivated exclusively by direct costs would not lead to an economic optimum.

In spite of its being an important source of revenue for the treasury, it might be said that, in general, transport is cheap. This fact is producing an excess of demand, especially in some areas where marginal costs are high (i.e. the congested parts of the system). Probably some of the present logistic strategies (where vehicles become "moving warehouses") would not be adopted if the users were to pay their full costs (direct, indirect and external). As congestion develops the correct "pricing" policy and its application to all the modes will increasingly become a matter of concern all over Europe. The advantages and inconveniences of tolls, road-pricing schemes, new taxes such as those proposed in relation to carbon dioxide emissions (30) or the 0.01 ECU per litre of oil equivalent proposed to finance a European Infrastructure Fund (EIF), which will collect an estimated one billion ECU per year, will certainly be the centre of much future debate.

It seems logical to expect the transport system to pay for the damage it causes (especially if funds were devoted to revert such damage, which is not the case) but if transport is to pay its social costs it does not seem appropriate that the profits generated by transport investments outside the system be excluded from the "accounts". In the case of some political objectives -- regional development, public service obligations, etc. -- they might be difficult to estimate but some simpler cases, such as the increase in real estate values produced by projects like TGV stations, motorways, etc. (which constitute one of the few attractions for private capital to intervene in transport infrastructure projects) should be systematically included.

3.5. Planning

Planning is not in fashion now. This also applies for transport, in spite of the fact that even the most liberal-minded governments have kept a strong hand on the sector. It is somehow surprising, because most of the severe problems being faced by the European transport system are due to a lack of serious and adapted planning.

Indeed, past planning experience is not very encouraging. Many factors, mostly technical and political, can be blamed for the failures. There is, however, an intrinsic factor that makes long-term planning especially difficult and provides an explanation for the present saturation problems. It is the "erroneous" position of medium- and long-term planning in growth cycles. Overambitious investment plans are produced in high growth periods but they are scratched as soon as recession appears. They are subsequently substituted by "rationalisation" plans, better adapted to stagnant situations. Optimisation leads, then, to the use of most of the buffer capacity left on the system and, therefore, when the economy expands again serious congestion problems cannot be avoided. The only solution to reduce the effects of cycles is continuous planning, but this involves a long-term perspective that is rarely adopted. The low profile and the little practical success of transport planning are a direct consequence of this. The rather poor results obtained in the past by planning are not, however, the only explanation for the present situation. The lack of long-term vision among most of the politicians with executive responsibilities in the sector has favoured a decisionmaking practice based almost exclusively on political grounds (31). Failures have been blamed on plans that have never been followed through. In fact, continuous planning, the only way of keeping an adaptable and efficient process, is still a rare species in Europe.

Planners, on the other hand, have also proved unable to build the necessary bridges of co-operation between themselves and the politicians, and to present their work in a simple way, easy to understand and to "sell" to the public. The transport planning process, in general, lacks equilibrium. Sophisticated models are calibrated from and applied to poor data bases, integration with land use and even among different transport modes is often non-existent, evaluation procedures and the values of key parameters are extremely rough compared to demand modelling, the financial and even the operational aspects are systematically left aside, etc. On top of that, administrative constraints, basically a political issue, tend to distort the planning process in scope, extension and horizon.

It is amazing, in any case, to observe that the resources devoted to analysing the sector, including data gathering and R & D activities (which have a more profit-oriented profile), are ridiculous compared to the investments involved (32). Very often the lightest benefit derived from these decision-making supports would more than justify the additional expenditure they represent. The funds for planning, information and research do not come, however, from investment budgets (as does, for example, design) and present administrative practices make it rather difficult to obtain the required increase in such funds.

4. TRANSPORT IN THE FUTURE

The framework wherein the European transport system will develop is that of sustained economic growth, an impressive expansion of trade due to the progressive integration of the former COMECON countries into the Community and very strong tensions, internal and external, that will induce important changes in the social and political arenas. It can be expected that such pressures (migrations from poorer countries, the fading role of the states, increased competition from emerging economies, etc.) will be adequately handled and that the opportunities and risks they offer will be combined to maintain or improve the present long-term growth trend.

By its very nature (geographic market expansion) this scenario will produce an even higher increase in transport demand. Business trips will augment and become longer, reduced working periods will induce more and longer leisure travel. As living conditions improve, people will become increasingly time-conscious and this will affect their travel (and location) behaviour and the quality they expect from the transport system. The continuing reduction of direct costs (energy, vehicles) will be compensated by an increase in infrastructure costs (due to limited space availability and environmental concerns) and in taxes to pay for the externalities incurred by the specific mode in the area where they are produced. The application of strict pricing policies, where each transport user will pay in relation to the total costs involved in order to establish a socially efficient competition, will make unit transport costs differ dramatically depending on the geographic location. This will foster a restructuring of the system.

The very concept of urban and regional development could change following this restructuring. As unit transport costs, including transfers to pay for externalities, increase their range, the most socially efficient modes for every kind of transport service will dominate the scene.

Such a demanding scenario, full of practical implementation difficulties, lies far away from present distorted modal relationships. New concepts, most of them multimodal in order to obtain better utilisation of each mode within a logistic strategy, will develop. Also the symbiosis between transport and telecommunications will have important effects both on mobility (reducing unnecessary trips but expanding the range of relationships and of travel requirements) and on the performance of the different modes. Even then, however, road transport (probably under new forms) should keep the key role in the sector. People will not renounce the freedom, privacy and convenience that the automobile provides and similar considerations can be applied to freight transport.

Road transport will take new forms, more friendly to the environment, safer and requiring less space. A grid of motorways, reinforced with direct links between the major urban centres and complementary "feeding" roads, will spread over all European territory providing adequate access to allow for the economic development of most inhabited land. In the principal axes and along the densest zones, dual-mode motorways will provide the additional capacity required. New engines and mechanical improvements will reduce pollutants and noise emissions by cars. Alternative modes will be used in preference only when they clearly out-perform road: aviation will keep the very long-distance passenger market and take a higher share of freight transport as products become lighter and more valuable. Rail will maintain its role in major urban areas and for certain massive flows (high-speed lines, block trains). Maritime cabotage and fluvial transport will develop where waterways can provide a cheap and efficient option for low-value commodities over congested axes.

Rail networks will be substantially reduced and reshaped in order to adapt the new integrated European rail system to the tasks where it is competitive: heavy flows and medium/long-distance transport. It is probably the mode that will undergo the most severe transformation, both in its scope (with the closure of thousands of kilometres of uncompetitive regional lines), in its operating techniques and its organisation. Most remarkable will be the role of the network of high-speed lines, conceived at the European level. High-speed service will transform the relations among cities and create new kinds of dependencies inside a wider "neuronal" network of urban areas that will be the motor of economic growth in the Europe of the first quarter of the twenty-first century.

The megalopolises and medium-sized cities constituting this network will face a development strongly related to their capacity to cope with their internal transport problems. Rail, and public transport in general, is extremely expensive if it is to provide an adequate level of service, but it is the only solution for the congestion problems of the megalopolis. However, well-planned smaller towns, connected by high-speed rail to the major cities, but still able to provide adequate private transport to their inhabitants, will have an enormous expansion that will induce growth in surrounding areas (33).

Following its deep transformation, the transport sector will become much more complex and integrated with other sectors with strong influence over its development. Complex transport chains, interwoven with telecommunications networks, will allow some modes like rail and waterways to stabilize their market share in the transport of goods, but only on privileged axes (i.e. the Rhine-Danube for fluvial transport). Combined transport will develop under automatised procedures. It will be the first "new" network conceived at the European level, and planners will have the opportunity to define the intermodal platforms where traffic will concentrate: along heavy rail axes, maritime and fluvial ports, airports, etc. Road transport will still provide the most efficient distribution and give the system the needed flexibility through terminal choice. The information system running side by side with combined transport will allow on-line management of the fleet of trucks. These will carry unitised loads to terminals where fast, automatic loading and unloading operations will have them placed in previously reserved slots in trains and ships, running on reliable scheduled services between terminals. Dual-mode operation of trucks, which will allow a continuous "train" of heavy vehicles along equipped corridors, might become a most serious threat to combined transport in the future.

The development foreseen for the transport sector will be made possible by the increasing role of European and regional authorities in the sector and the declining influence of the State. The "three-level" administration will add complexity to the planning and implementation processes but, on the other hand, the initiative needed to transform the system and the concertation required to earn acceptability for increasingly contested projects can only develop from this kind of political framework.

The growing integration of transport with urban and regional planning, telecommunications and logistically driven industrial ventures, will also produce a horizontal co-ordination to enhance cross-fertilization. In spite of this, the intervention of the public sector will be reduced and concentrated on infrastructure provision and on the establishment of market rules in such a way that competition can lead to a socially efficient system. Users will therefore be expected to pay for the costs they generate (direct, indirect and external) plus the normal indirect taxes (like VAT). Subsidies will come under specific funds (regional development might be the most conspicuous) with ear-marked budgets. They will be carefully weighted to avoid competition distortion. Public funds will be devoted, in any case, mostly to investment and maintenance and they will waive the present widespread practice of covering operating deficits. Tolls will only be applied in places where true alternatives are non-existent (major tunnels and bridges), to induce proper competition (urban road pricing) or to pay for special services (i.e. in dual-mode operation) but then such services will be charged over the whole system, according to the principle that all alternatives must be charged their global costs.

The development of this future, more efficient transport system will only be possible under a new approach to planning to overcome the present stalemate in decisionmaking at all levels. This will be comprehensive (involving connected sectors, such as regional and urban planning and telecommunications), integrated (as the system becomes more and more multimodal), implementation oriented (with much more emphasis on the evaluation phase and on financial and administrative aspects, in order to facilitate decisionmaking), continuous and feeding back from actual implementation experience. Planning will also be carried out at interconnected levels, from European to local, with co-ordination at all levels (objective setting, data bases, evaluation and programming), to provide coherence and applicability. As transport infrastructures and, in some cases, services (i.e. railway closures) become increasingly politically sensitive, citizen participation in the planning process will be extended and improved to retain the majority's points of view and not only those of the most vociferous.

Important changes are necessary to reconvert the present system to this more appealing future. Some of them are apparent already:

-- The urgent definition of pan-European transport policies based on the new political context. The EC and EFTA countries must have the leading role in their implementation. This implies co-operation with and technical and financial assistance to eastern and central European countries.

-- The establishment of appropriate planning strategies that under such policies would define, at the European, national and regional levels, the networks to be created from existing infrastructure. The co-ordination mechanisms should be clearly laid down.

-- The acceleration of a harmonization process allowing for the correct deployment of liberalisation measures. This includes technical, fiscal and administrative matters and should lead to pricing schemes reflecting the real costs (including the externalities) involved. The process should also produce a set of mechanisms for the transfer of network effects, for compensations or charges due to externalities and the determination of fair allocations for public service obligations. A complete restructuring of the financial mechanisms of the system seems unavoidable to avert present inefficiencies and to cope with the enormous investments required to avoid its collapse.

-- An increase of at least the equivalent of the resources allocated to the follow-up and research and development of the sector.

Others must already make their way inside the social conscience, and on the agenda for decisionmakers especially should appear:

-- The definition of a coherent regional planning for Europe, where the role of megalopolises, medium-sized cities, transport networks and environment conservation are well specified in order to provide the best quality of life to the whole population. Transport planning will be integrated in this wider framework.

-- The implementation of a grid of adequate transport infrastructure covering the whole of Europe, in order to provide all the territory with the minimum accessibility conditions required for economic development. These should be, nevertheless, accompanied by other vital elements to spark growth.

-- The adaptation of the transport sector to the "information age", supporting technological developments (mostly in automation) that will make the system workable in the long run.

All in all, there is an urgency to define the planning framework, the evaluation criteria, the role to be played by the different administrations and the co-ordination mechanisms, to develop in the shortest time lag an integrated, coherent and efficient transport system for Europe.

NOTES

1. Group Transport 2000 Plus (1991).

2. Megatrends 2000.

3. Reynaud C. (1991) gives a most interesting discussion on the lack of such exercises and its implications on decision-making.

4. Fortunately, hardly anybody enjoys reading old forecasts which allow many "erudite" people to continue writing shamelessly.

5. Although transport has been growing in Europe at 2.5 per cent for freight and 3.1 per cent for passengers, at an annual rate similar to GDP, some experts suggest that transport could grow as much as 50 per cent more than GDP. Bernadet (1990) has shown that a very strong long-term correlation exists between both indexes, but that transport cycles are more marked.

6. To adequately reflect the importance of quality, new measurement units for freight transport flows will have to be adopted. The ton/km indicator presently being used does not reflect the service provided and, therefore, the relative importance of the various modes or the overall sector.

7. Due to military, legal or technical constraints.

8. Ultra-capacity aircraft, able to carry up to 700-800 passengers, are in the initial stages of development (Boeing and Airbus). The transformation of heavy cargo aircraft (Antonov) to even larger passenger loads, including private cabins and large common-use spaces (bars, fitness centres, etc.) is also being analysed. Some prototypes should be ready by the late nineties.

9. Although the number of trips and the time devoted to transport per person seem to remain rather stable they are bound to longer distances.

10. De Jouvenel (1989) and NEI (1988).

11. Transport is assumed to produce 60 per cent of the NO_x and 25 per cent of the CO_2 emitted in Europe.

12. RTEI, AIMPE, CCFE, European Airline Association.

13. And at the present experience of the Russian Jews moving massively to Israel, even though that country is facing a tough situation.

14. Hébrand & Trenner (1991) propose a suspension of migrations until strategies have been developed, but recent experiences (Albanians, North-Africans) show how difficult and expensive it is to apply controls. An interesting document by the Commission of the EC (SEC/90 1813 final) presents a more comprehensive view of migration issues.

15. This is becoming a major issue in the urban areas of the USA, where it has been estimated that delays caused the loss of 2 billion hours in 1990 (US DoT, 1990).

16. See Serratosa (1988) for a proposal of a European grid.

17. For example, the congestion on the Rhône axis is due, in part, to the absorption of parallel demand not served by appropriate alternatives.

18. The financing of transport infrastructure via ERDF has a "regional development" objective and, in principle, no "trans-European" purpose.

19. The Kearney report forecasts a volume of 43 million tons/year of international combined transport (three times the present figure) if adequate investments are carried out (estimated at 2.6 to 2.9 billion ECU in the next five to ten years).

20. The opening of the Rhine-Main-Danube connection in 1993 will reinforce the dominance of this major axis.

21. The AIMSE Report (IRF, 1990).

22. DHV & Colquhoun (1991).

23. The value of transport in the EC, including that of time, has been estimated at 500 billion ECU/year (Carpentier).

24. A figure of US$40 billion for the cost of highway congestion in the USA in 2005 has been given by AASHTO.

25. Road pricing schemes do not seem to attract popular support. They have been rejected in Hong Kong and in the Netherlands. They only appear feasible in very particular contexts (Singapore, Bergem).

26. Among them, some of the 55 per cent of Paris' inhabitants eager to leave the city, according to a recent "Time" magazine survey.

27. The basic alternative being enormous investments in infrastructure or equivalent operation deficits in the megalopolis, or unknown but possibly lower investments in MSC and in the "extensive grid".

28. Lufthansa trains serving Frankfurt airport or some dial-a-bus operations.

29. The privatisation of British Airways is probably the most spectacular.

30. It is curious to see that even before knowing with certainty the effects of CO_2 on nature, some legislators are already thinking of taxing transport. Of course, no effect on demand can be expected unless the tax is very high. On the other hand, its use in ways to reduce the unknown impacts of the effect is hard to imagine...

31. This explains the proliferation of lobbies, especially at the European level, because their impact is strong when no proper planning is being carried out (Turró, 1991).

32. On top of that, "market driven" research (such as the programme DRIVE for RTI) is providing funds unavailable for more basic analyses of the sector and draining the already scarce human resources devoted to them.

33. That will depend on the planning and managerial skills of local decisionmakers who will often face controversial options. Environmental issues will be widely used, in these cases, to foster individual interests.

BIBLIOGRAPHY

American Association of State Highway and Transportation Officials (AASHTO) (1989), "New Transportation Concepts for a New Century", *Transportation 2020*, Washington.

Bendixson, T. (1989), "Transport in the Nineties. The Shaping of Europe", The Royal Institution of Chartered Surveyors, London.

Bernadet, M. (1990), "Le transport de marchandises en Europe, dans vingt ans", *Transports*, January-February.

Bessay, G. (1988), "Perspectives Transports 2005", OEST, Paris.

Bourdillon, J. *et al.* (1991), "Les réseaux de transport français face à l'Europe", Ministère de l'Équipement, des Transports et de la Mer, Paris.

Commission of the European Communities (1990), "Europe 2000: Les perspectives de développement du territoire communautaire", COM(90) 544, Brussels.

Commission of the European Communities (1990), "Towards Trans-European Networks. For a Community Action Programme", COM(90) 585, Brussels.

Commission of the European Communities (1990), "The European Highspeed Train Network", General Directorate of Transport, Brussels.

de Jouvenel, H. (1989), "Le vieillissement démographique en Europe. Tendances et enjeux à l'horizon 2025", *Futuribles*, February-March.

De Waele, A. (1990), "Consequences of Closer East-West Relations", in *Prospects for East-West European Transport*, ECMT, International Seminar, December 1990, OECD, Paris, 1991, p. 9.

DHV & Colquhoun (1991), "Le coût de l'inadaptation des infrastructures de transport en Europe", Direction Générale des Études, European Parliament.

European Roundtable of Industrialists (1991), "Missing Networks. A European Challenge", ERTI, Brussels.

Frybourg, M. (1990), "L'innovation dans les transports", *Futuribles*, July-August.

Garrison, W.L. (1989), "Using Technology to Improve Transportation Services", in Batten, D.F. and R. Thord, *Transportation for the Future*, Springer Verlag, Berlin.

Group Transport 2000 Plus (1990), "Transport in a Fast Changing Europe", Report of a Working Group set up by the European Commission.

Hébrand, J. and P. Treuner (1991), "Perspectives de l'aménagement du territoire européen", Franco-German Working Group ARL-DATAR.

IRF (1990), "AIMSE. The Motorway Project for the Europe of Tomorrow", International Road Federation, Geneva.

Johnston, W.B. (1989), "Transportation for the Next Century", in *Moving America. A Look Ahead to the 21st Century*, US Department of Transportation, Washington.

Kearney, A.T. (1989), "A Strategic Study into a European Combined Transport Network", Community of European Railways.

Marchetti, C. (1987), "The Dynamic Nature of European Transport During the Past 50 Years and the Next 20 Years", First Forum on European Transport in the Future, Munich, September 1987.

Quinet, E. and C. Reynaud (1990), "Les flux de transport en Europe: continuités et mutations", *Futuribles*, July-August.

Reynaud, C. (1990), "Infrastructures: une reprise des investissements nécessite la définition du cadre d'évaluation", *Transports*, May-June.

Reynaud, C. (1991), "Recréer une dynamique d'arbitrage et de décision". La tribune de transport et société. *Transports*, March-April.

Romera i Alcázar, D. (1991), "Rapport sur la politique communautaire en matière d'infrastructures de transport", Commission des Transports et du Tourisme, European Parliament.

Rothengatter, W. (1989), *Private and Public Investment in Transport, ECMT* Round Table 81, OECD, Paris, 1990, p. 49.

Sabriá, F., M. Turró, *et al.* (1987), "Catalunya en el context mundial del Transport", Institut Català per el Desenvolupament du Transport, Barcelona.

Seidenfus, H. (1990), "Prospects for Railway Transport", in *Prospects for East-West European Transport*, ECMT, International Seminar, December 1990, OECD, Paris, 1991, p. 263.

Serratosa, A. (1988), "La difficile vertébration de l'Europe: Trafic et réseau routier", Centre Européen du Développement Régional (CEDRE), Strasbourg.

Turró, M. (1989), "La financiación de los grandes proyectos de infraestructura del transporte en la Europa del año 2000", in *Horizonte 2000: El gran desafío para el ferrocarril europeo*, Fundación de los Ferrocarriles Españoles, Madrid.

Turró, M. (1991), "Parlem d'infrastructures. Unes reflexions per a polítics", *Revista Espais*, Generalitat de Catalunya, Barcelona.

US Department of Transportation (1990), "Moving America. New Directions. New Opportunities", Washington.

Sub-topic 2

ECONOMIC TRENDS AND TRANSPORT SPECIALISATION

L. NORDSTRÖM
Gothenburg University
Gothenburg
Sweden

SUMMARY

Gothenburg, November 1991

1. ECONOMIC EVOLUTION

The history of humankind has always been characterised by an effort to improve its material circumstances, to cope with the obstacles imposed on human life and aspirations by refractory Nature. From the time of the earliest settlements, groups of people have sought to create living conditions that would guarantee the security of coming generations. This has occurred through the gradual improvement in the store of available knowledge, and thus there has been an accumulation of experience down through the ages. What we may refer to as economic evolution is therefore a slow process with gradual stages, in which rapid changes have transpired during isolated periods over time.

In a historical perspective, the ancient Chinese culture is one example of a well-functioning economy which also secured the well-being of the contemporary population. Later, the Roman Empire can be regarded as a very well-developed economy that sustained millions of people. It also managed to attain superpower status both militarily and culturally. Structures from that period impress us still, and testify to a highly advanced social order that guaranteed the supply of both labour and material.

However, what is generally perceived as the true dawn of economic expansion is the process begun with the birth of industrialism in Europe towards the end of the 18th century. Industrialism was based on utilising other sources of power than the muscles of human beings and domestic animals, by mechanising the production process and introducing automatic controls. The production of large units was made possible by the expansion of factories and by an extreme division of labour, involving both different social groups and the individuals employed in the same production unit.

At the basis of the theory of industrialism and, later, the theory of the development of international commerce, is the so-called theory of comparative economics. This is founded on the maxim that every unit of production should concentrate on what it is best qualified to do as compared with other production units. Consequently, industrialism and the subsequent development of industrial enterprises is a function of an intense specialisation that matured through the gradual refinement of insights into how the prerequisites of production can be improved. Another precondition for the birth and growth of industrialism, i.e. the exploitation of comparative advantages, was the improvement of communications that facilitated the expansion of the market for industrial products. Industrialisation has entailed the reallocation of labour within the production process and, naturally, mass movements of population, primarily from the countryside to urban areas. Both socially and politically, industrialism and economic development have had enormous consequences. One of them is the emergence of a large working class; that development created differences in living conditions as well as in economic circumstances. In the political sphere, industrialism and the economic growth associated with it led to the conception of different political ideologies and the formation of different political parties.

Industrialism and its associated economic growth began in England in the late 18th century. Those factors which contributed primarily to the emergence of industry in England at that time were rich deposits of coal, rapid technical development, good communications and a tolerant political climate. In addition, there was a large and comparatively affluent domestic market. England's well-developed contacts with her neighbours also facilitated foreign trade. Hence it was easy to sell industrial products and acquire new capital. The earliest industrialism primarily affected the textile business. In some cases, production rose by a hundredfold. This increase was the result of new inventions, improvements in spinning machinery and the introduction of mechanical looms and steam engines.

One crucial element in the nurture of industrialism in its infancy was the appearance and expansion of the railroads, which indelibly stamped the history of the entire 19th century. Mechanisation and the building of railroads required enormous amounts of steel and iron. The development of the iron and other metal industries through new and improved processes, as well as the mechanisation and concentration of the steel industry, resulted in a vast increase in steel production. All of this, in combination with the expansion of the engineering industry, which facilitated the rapid growth of rail service, created favorable conditions for further industrialisation in other parts of Europe. The industrialisation of western European countries began early in the 19th century, following the conclusion of the Napoleonic wars and by mid-century France, Belgium, Holland and certain parts of Germany were able to begin competing with England in several areas. In the United States, industrialisation accelerated at the end of the Civil War in the 1860s. There was no similar development to speak of in the Nordic countries before the middle of the 19th century, with the exception of the iron industry. Here, industrial methods were primarily used first in the wood products business, while the pioneer mechanical industries were just beginning to appear.

Hence, the birth and development of industrialism can be schematically divided into three periods. The first industrial revolution is characterised by steam engines, the building of railroads, the emergence of factory towns replete with enormous social problems and dizzying business fluctuations and the genesis of socialist ideology. This period stretches from the mid-18th century to the outbreak of World War I in western and northern Europe.

The second period, extending from the outbreak of World War I in 1914 to the end of World War II in 1945, is characterised by the replacement of coal by oil as the most important source of energy. Furthermore, electricity became increasingly important in the production of energy. It contributed to broadening the horizons of industrialisation and also encompassed agriculture, among other areas. Progress in the communications sector, such as the telephone and radio, also played an important role in this period. In many countries, governments began to intervene to regulate business conditions and societal developments. At the same time, industrialisation began to include other parts of the world in addition to Europe and North America.

The third period, beginning in 1945 and including our own times is, above all, characterised by the development of electronics, i.e. mechanisation, process control, nuclear power, rapid communications, efficient transport systems and the emergence of global conglomerates. In addition, we have witnessed a high degree of governmental regulation of economic developments, and the gradual involvement of formerly underdeveloped areas in industrialisation. Perhaps most notably, it is the industrialisation of the Far East that has come to characterise the industrial process during the past few decades. These countries, especially Japan, have in many respects succeeded to the positions of the older industrial nations.

Viewed from a geographical perspective, industrialisation can thus be said both to have proceeded for a very long time, implying that there was favourable economic growth for a very long time, and to have carried with it continuous benefits for those who were affected by it. At the same time, there are still large numbers of the world's population who are excluded from the industrial marketplace and the industrial system of production. In the historical context, it is usually estimated that the economically powerful countries have enjoyed an annual economic growth of around 2.5 per cent throughout the industrial era. This does not mean that there has been a high annual rate of growth, but rather that the cumulative effect during the past two hundred years of industrialism has been gigantic. Accordingly, even though we are dealing with a long-term process, it is nevertheless possible to note significant differences during this phase of development. As indicated above, in purely economic terms industrialism can be divided into three periods. It is also possible to divide it into a number of phases geographically. From having initially been a European phenomenon -- bound together not least by the North Sea and launched in England, and later with the northern European countries as additional important ingredients -- in a second phase industrialism became an Atlantic Ocean enterprise, with Europe on one side and the east coast of the United States on the other side constituting the poles.

In recent times, especially after World War II and most dramatically since 1980, industrialism has acquired an additional arena of operations in the Pacific Ocean, connecting the west coast of the United States and the Far East. In several respects, this is the most dynamic element in the history of industrialism. In this context, it may not be irrelevant to point to the rapid growth of industrial production systems in old Russia and later in the Soviet Union during the first seven decades of the twentieth century. Over the past decade, however, the position of eastern Europe as one of the industrial superpowers has weakened drastically. Today, eastern Europe can be regarded more as an area requiring industrial development assistance than as an engine of industry.

As should be clear from the foregoing, the economic expansion in the classical industrial countries is of a very long-term and comprehensive character. Virtually no part of the social system has remained unaffected. It is perfectly obvious that economic expansion influences both industrial production and other sectors of a nation's economy. Economic growth has made it possible to transfer the constituents of productivity from unalloyed industrial production to the service sector, and to what is today referred to as the public sector. In most industrial countries today, only about thirty to forty per cent of the workforce are employed in the production of goods; the rest are engaged in the production of various kinds of services. It is, above all, in the production of services that the greatest changes have occurred during the past several years, and also where problems have been observed in many countries. It is relatively easy to measure industrial production and to quantify its results. On the other hand, it is considerably more difficult to correctly estimate production results in the service sector, and also to evaluate them qualitatively. Particularly because such a large share of the service sector falls within the public sector in so many countries, it has to some extent landed outside the traditional market-oriented production systems where the industrial sector has always been.

The decade of the eighties has in many ways proven to be a period of worldwide renaissance for updating the market economy even in this part of the production system. There are today far-reaching ambitions to change the qualitative and quantitative makeup of the service sector. This also implies that the service sector is increasingly becoming part of a competitive system. It will take on a more international stamp, whereas industrial production had an international market from the outset. Large parts of the service sector are oligopolistic or monopolistic. They are often protected by government ownership, or in other ways shielded from international competition by regulations. The deregulation now going on in some parts of the production of services will change its methods of operation and also open up new markets for more efficient service companies. Hence here, too, the geographical factor is interesting. Local markets suddenly become regional, national or international. It has been pointed out earlier that the full emergence of industrialism depended heavily on the development of the transport sector. A corresponding demand is now being placed, and will continue to be placed, on the service sector.

It is through improvements in transportation and communications systems, in personal transport systems and in telecommunications systems that this huge sector can develop and merge into a larger, market-oriented production system. The service sector revolution that can be expected during the nineties is thus in character no different from what we have observed of the industrial revolution, but it will undoubtedly have a number of different effects, which will be considered below. It is, however, perfectly clear that an expansion of the service sector will presuppose significant achievements in the field of transportation and place great demands on new investments in that area. At the same time, the shortfall in investments in the transportation and communications sector so apparent in many parts of the industrialised world today has a braking effect on the full utilisation of the knowledge resources that are available.

2. INTERNATIONAL COMMERCE AND ECONOMIC DEVELOPMENT

The rapid industrial development and the concomitant economic expansion in the industrial countries during the 19th and 20th centuries have resulted in making international commerce one of the most important functions of society. It is through trading across both large and small distances that it is possible to make use of the advantages created by industrial development. It is often the ability to transport people and information over great distances that enables the service sector to exploit the advantages of specialisation, and to open new markets. Consequently, international commerce has grown faster than economic development itself, as measured by traditional productivity yardsticks. Thus, if industrial production has enjoyed an annual increase of 2 to 2.5 per cent over the years, international commerce has gone up by at least 4 per cent as viewed in the long historical perspective. That this should be so is a consequence of several circumstances that are important for commerce. The first of these is that if trade is measured by some such productivity criterion as shipments/kilometres, the volume is immediately affected as transport distances are gradually extended. Local trade has become national and international without implying an increase in the production of goods. Hence the marketplace has expanded.

Another factor that explains the transport sector's increased share of overall industrial and economic activities is that advances in transportation technology have facilitated the movement of products that formerly could not be transported. Well into the 20th century, it was virtually impossible to transport bulk goods long distances because the transport technology resources were not yet available. There were no ore shipments across the Atlantic and Pacific Oceans. Nor were petroleum products shipped except for very short distances. Now, thanks to new types of vessels and modern handling techniques, goods that could previously be transported only locally can be shipped practically anywhere. This means that the economic value of goods has increased, and, accordingly, it has become possible to exchange products throughout the entire global system.

It is perfectly obvious that this development of transportation technology has meant significant benefits both for the expansion of the global economy and for many countries who were formerly unable to market their raw materials. Furthermore, many products have appeared for which there simply was no market before. It goes without saying that this applies to the entire range of high-tech products that have emerged, especially since World War II. Similarly, commodities for which there was once a limited market have become household items, at least in the industrialised world.

One example of this is the trade in automobiles, which constitutes one of the major items of commerce. At the end of World War II, it was thought to be quite unlikely that the automobile trade would acquire anything more than a very modest volume across the great oceans. Today a large number of the cars sold in Europe were produced in Japan. Similarly, a significant number of cars sold in the USA have been produced in Europe or Japan. International commerce in automobiles is hence one explanation for the expansion of the automobile industry, and its strong international position. What makes it at all feasible to trade in automobiles and other comparatively low-value products, is that transport technology has greatly lowered the relative costs. Consequently, a car manufactured in Europe costs little more in the USA than what the same car sells for in Europe. Another explanation, closely connected with that just mentioned, is that new transport systems have been developed that have solved a number of the earlier difficulties on the transport market in terms of organisation. This means not least that it is possible today, thanks to transportation and information technologies, to manage shipments in such a manner as to maintain a high degree of certainty. Previously, all shipping was risky: wind and weather often made the delivery of goods uncertain. Now, however, modern technology has progressed so far that obstructions in shipping operations are rare. Even if there is sometimes considerable damage and losses do occur, the normally functioning shipping link is the most common element in the entire transport chain.

Accordingly, this technological and organisational development in the transport sector has meant that we now have access to global markets. Ore produced anywhere in the world has the world as a market; cars manufactured anywhere in the world have the world as a market, and so on. Hence the tyranny of distance is a thing of the past. However, there are still many regulations that obstruct the effective utilisation of the comparative advantages of the service sector between countries and regions.

3. PARALLELS BETWEEN DEVELOPMENTS IN TRANSPORT AND INDUSTRIAL TECHNOLOGIES

As has been pointed out in the previous sections, industrial development has been characterised by a high degree of specialisation, in which each production unit seeks to guarantee the economic well-being of long production runs and, through refining its techniques, maintain superiority over potential competitors. Developments in the transportation sector resemble this process in many respects. It, too, has become specialised, and specialist operations have become increasingly common. Today there is no one single conveyor; every element involved in the transport sector is a small cog in an increasingly more sophisticated system. Not only has every task become specialised; the operations have also been divided into different obligatory divisions and firms. The specialist function in the transport chain means that more and more companies concentrate on submarkets, competing among themselves and trying to develop their respective submarkets.

The characteristics of the transport sector, then, are nearly identical with those of industrial production, although there are differences in some respects.

The resemblance is that, in addition to specialisation, there is also an ambition to exploit the advantages of large-scale operations in a broader international perspective. While it may be profitable for an industrial enterprise to have a large, integrated production facility in a large factory, the situation is different in the transport sector. Even if it is possible to aggregate certain functions, its large-scale operations are of such a character that it is important to be spread out over a large part of the marketing area. Thus, a large-scale transport firm is dispersed over a large, geographically varied area and tries to be available in as many markets as possible. In many cases, it is important to be an expert in one specific aspect of each market.

The transport sector is also characterised by a certain national organisation, in the sense that in many parts of the transport sector there is a close ownership connection between many individual firms and national institutions. Airlines are a good example of this; national companies have their own nations as their home base, but try to have a route network that services the largest possible share of the international market. Every such airline thus has a unique national base, but structurally they are all similarly organised. This observation includes Lufthansa, Air France, Sabena, SAS, etc. The competition that arises involves offering services that are largely similar, even though it is to a certain extent strongly linked to a more locally protected domestic market. In the long run, it will probably not be possible to sustain this form of international specialisation when a large number of operators offer similar services. The development of industrialism has shown that, eventually, either large oligopolistic systems will crystallise, or individual services must acquire different qualitative characteristics that distinguish them from others in the field. When there are too many firms offering exactly the same services, the usual result is poor profitability and increasingly formidable competition.

Now that we have observed how the character of the transport sector resembles that of the industrial sector by utilising specialisation and large-scale operations, it is possible to detect a further dimension of similarity, namely that transportation operations are becoming increasingly integrated with industrial activity. That is one of the reasons why these systems are similar. In the early stages of industrialism, a well-functioning transport system was a prerequisite for industrial expansion. Yet there was a clear distinction between the systems. Industrial firms ran their enterprises, shipping companies developed their route systems, railroad companies operated railroads, etc. Now, the transport operations are integrated into industrial production within the scope of a long list of modern guidance systems like just-in-time, lean production, etc. This does not imply that the owner of an industrial firm must own a transport company, but that there must be co-ordination in terms of planning. A specialised industrial firm, therefore, requires a specialised, customised transportation operation in order to sustain the optimal overall productive apparatus. This co-ordination, in turn, means that in many cases it is impossible to distinguish where the transport operation begins and industrial production ends. Everything has to be seen as a part of a total flow of goods and services, whose objective is to connect producer and consumer as effectively as possible. One important part of this integration has been the development of modern information technology and its adroitness in supervising the flow of goods and services.

As a consequence of the continual development of information technology, soon there will scarcely be any reason to talk about special functions for transportation. Rather, there will be an overall production pattern in which production, transport and consumption will merge in a carefully managed and predetermined fashion. As it becomes further refined, this predetermined fashion must be so flexible that the end-user has the experience of being in charge of both production and transport activities. One example is what today's modern auto manufacturers are trying to achieve when they encourage a customer to order a car which is then customised to the buyer's specifications and, in just a few days' time, appears in the driveway, exactly as envisioned and replete with the desired accessories. Obviously, this extreme refinement of planning and flexibility is not possible in all realms of our economic system, but a tendency in this direction can be detected in an increasing number of areas.

Specialisation in the transport sector has also led to a boosting of the level of competence and today's transportation suppliers are highly qualified professionals with a great amount of expert knowledge and experience. Previously, there was a rather low level of academic qualifications in the average transport company and most decisions were based on knowledge gained solely from experience. Today, education in transportation and communication is an important component in the curricula of all universities. The employees in leading positions in transport companies are generally well-educated people who can hold their own academically with their colleagues in industrial enterprises.

4. GEOGRAPHICAL DISPERSION AND CONCENTRATION

In many parts of the transportation business, there are discernible and conspicuous examples of the specialisation of the transport function that has been identified here as one consequence of the general specialisation throughout our entire economic system. Harbours, airports and railroad stations are symbols of extreme specialisation. Within such geographical spaces are performed many of the tasks which make it possible to curtail expenses in large-scale operations. A modern airport is a marvel of modern production efficiency where everything revolves around one basic business concept -- to distribute goods and passengers as rapidly as possible at the lowest possible cost. This applies to all parts of the transportation business. Specialisation also implies, however, that it is difficult to accommodate complementary transport systems within one and the same geographical space. Hence it is unusual, and geographically often impossible, to locate a harbour and an airport on the same site, even though in some respects it would be advantageous. Nor is it common that rail junctions and airports are sited together; each transport system selects its geographical location in its own unique way. However, there is obviously a need for integrated communications between the different systems, whether involving highway networks or railroads.

This geographical specialisation creates a troublesome problem for the purchasers of transportation services. Whereas customers strive to delegate as much of their transport investment as possible to one single transport company, there is often no one central location to which they can turn. That is why special transportation regions are being developed in several places, both in Europe and in the USA. The motivation is to be able to co-ordinate as many transport systems as possible in one relatively limited space. Simply in terms of space, this is difficult in Europe, whereas it is easier to develop special transport centres in the USA. Today, there are corresponding tendencies in the area of personal transportation. One example is the integration of high-speed railroads and highway systems currently going on in France as part of the extension of the TGV system. Accordingly, we can expect that in the future there will continue to be well-dispersed and often highly specialised transport operations even as a few large junctions are constructed in which all transport systems are co-ordinated and where co-ordination itself is the key concept. Being specialised to handle everything is somewhat of a paradox.

5. THE WORLD OF THE NINETIES

Given the connection we find today between economic development and specialisation, to which this essay has been devoted, it may be useful to consider some of the more interesting development tendencies of the 1990s.

For the past two hundred years, economic development in general has paralleled that of the market economy and free enterprise. In all probability this will also characterise the nineties. All over the world there is a move towards deregulation and the removal of trade restrictions and protected markets. This is true, for example, of the entire internal design of the European Community, which is aimed at creating a domestic market with as few barriers between countries as possible. Whether this will lead to some form of protectionism *vis-à-vis* other countries outside the EC remains to be seen. Regardless of whether that turns out to be the case, deregulation will nevertheless be the working method of the EC, the USA, Japan and the world economy as a whole. The most efficient production systems are achieved by allowing many players to compete freely. Not least, the collapse of the communist system in eastern Europe has clearly demonstrated the advantages of the market economy. There is keener competition in a deregulated market as well as a simultaneous expansion of the respective geographical markets of the companies that make up the system, whether they be industrial concerns or service enterprises.

As the entire history of industrialism has demonstrated, well-functioning transportation operations are required in order to exploit the advantages implied by this deregulation. Accordingly, if it is to have a meaningful effect, the deregulation now going on presupposes the existence of a transport capacity that will facilitate the movement of goods and people over large areas. The EC has clearly taken this into consideration. Parallel with the deregulation of trade and, perhaps eventually, agriculture, the service sector, governmental purchasing, etc., the EC is engaged in the construction of rapid-rail networks, improvements in the highway system, rehabilitation of inland waterways and in making it easier for new airlines to establish themselves. As a result, the EC will come to exemplify both a large domestic market and an enormous expansion of the transport sector. This represents a challenge. The extent to which this expansion will also be environmentally acceptable remains to be seen. Even in this respect, however, the question comes down to what regulations will apply. We will probably witness the paradox that even as transport operations themselves, together with other sectors of the economy, are being deregulated, a large number of new regulations will be put in place to dampen the less desirable environmental effects of the ongoing deregulation. Challenging, indeed.

Another challenge during the nineties is the reconstruction of the economies of eastern Europe. Here too, just as the West was being industrialised during the 19th century, it will be necessary to establish both specialised production for an international market and a well-functioning transport system. It is, perhaps, especially in the area of transport systems that the greatest advantage can be made of the low wages that still obtain in eastern Europe. If eastern Europe can forge a well-functioning transport market in relation to the West, then its industrial production can become very extensive and support the increase in prosperity that so many of its people are demanding today. On the other hand, if there is no improvement in the infrastructure of eastern Europe, any recuperation of its economy over the next twenty to thirty years will be problematic. The fact that there is relative proximity to the western European market will mean nothing unless goods produced can be transported to it, and unless western products can be made easily available to the consumers in eastern Europe. The challenge for eastern Europe is thus in many respects a matter of investments in transport capacity. This is also something of a global challenge, in the sense that investments in transport capacity rarely pay off during the first ten to twenty years. Such investments prove profitable only in the very long run. Hence the question that presents itself is: who is going to accept the long-term risk-taking represented by investments in the infrastructure of eastern Europe?

A third challenge for the future is the rapid development of information technology. This development has many consequences for the transport sector. There can sometimes be substitutions among transport services thanks to the development of this technology. The amount of private travelling, for example, can be reduced by using telephone and telefax communications. It can be taken for granted that travelling will also be affected when picture 'phones have been perfected. At the same time, however, the development of information technology should be more likely to stimulate, rather than retard, both travelling and the exchange of goods. One corollary of the advances in the field of information technology will be superior management of the flow of goods: products can be shipped faster and, consequently, there will be more stimulation of economic development and specialisation. Some of the problems brought about by modern information technology should also be pointed out. One of the central theses of this paper is that specialisation has been the key to economic development and to realising the advantages of different systems. However, somewhat different conditions apply in the field of information technology. The really appreciable advantages are achieved when its resources are co-ordinated. It is when you can use the same computer language, the same telephone network and the same basic system for the transfer of information that you optimise the benefits of being able to transfer information.

Therefore, one important issue will be how far information technology development can be pushed before the disadvantages associated with extreme co-ordination preclude the necessary technical development. Co-ordinated production systems, for example, the one constructed by the Soviet Union, illustrate the risk of stagnation. Hence modern information technology may depend on a fresh supply of new, specialised techniques in order to avoid being submerged in the disadvantages implied by excessive co-ordination. In this connection, it is obvious that the EC's various attempts to co-ordinate standards, by devising a system of regulations, must be monitored and sometimes questioned and discussed.

A fourth interesting challenge within the transport sector concerns the consequences of deregulation in areas traditionally regarded as natural monopolies. Railroad, telephone and electric companies, all of which are essential for economic development, have classically been owned by governments. Protected by special legislation, they have been able to set prices and run their enterprises without any bothersome competition. There are ambitions in the EC, as well as in large sectors of the American and Japanese economies, to find combinations of open competition while still maintaining natural monopolies. One method for accomplishing this is to separate the infrastructure from those who utilise the infrastructure. For example, the railroad network in a country is owned by a special authority, and different railroad companies compete for the right to use it. The same system could be applied to the ownership and utilisation of the electricity supply network, and so on. This is an unusually interesting way to introduce tension among specialisation, competition and co-ordination. While the ownership in an infrastructure strives to co-ordinate much of the infrastructure in a production system, it can yet be possible to allow different specialist companies to make use of the co-ordinated capacity.

There is a well-functioning example of this in Sweden, namely, that the government owns the railroad network through a separate authority and then lets SJ (Swedish State Railways) and other railroad companies purchase services on the network. This is, thus, an example of both specialisation and co-ordination, i.e. a combination of market economy and planned economy. To what extent this combination may prove to be generally applicable in the future remains to be seen.

6. CONCLUSION

The purpose of this essay has been to point out that all economic development occurs slowly, over a relatively long period of time, but that sudden changes sometimes occur during shorter periods. A pervasive feature of the economic development in the West is to make use of long production runs and industrial specialisation while employing trade to make the most of the comparative advantages of local, regional and national markets. The general increase in prosperity has been promoted by commerce and the exchange of services. Nothing suggests that this basic pattern will change in the future.

The specialisation that has thus occurred in the production system has its exact counterpart in the transportation sector, although there may be differences in some respects. The transport business has by no means been exposed to the same kind of competition as the industrial sector, nor has it been the object of the same kind of geographical and functional specialisation. In the period of market orientation and deregulation now ahead of us, the similarities between industrial production and the production of transportation will become increasingly noticeable. We will have competing transport companies specialising in different links in the transport chain, and they will be closely associated with producers of goods and services. The uniqueness of the transport sector's position will largely disappear. The natural monopolies will steadily decline in importance. To the extent that there are virtual natural monopolies, they will be separated from the transport companies, and there will be a division between the monopolistic and the competitive spheres. Consequently, the transport sector will increasingly become one more of the many businesses that are subjected to global development and global competition.

Sub-topic 2

ECONOMIC TRENDS AND TRANSPORT SPECIALISATION

C. KASPAR
Institut de Tourisme et d'Économie des Transports
Saint-Gall
Switzerland

SUMMARY

St. Gallen, August 1991

1. DEVELOPMENT OF THE ECONOMY AND OF TRANSPORT AS MUTUALLY DEPENDENT PROCESSES

The historical development of trade and industry is closely associated with that of the transport modes and a transport system is the essential precondition for an economy based on the division of labour. Even in ancient times, the natural transport infrastructures and the utilisation rate of a transport system to a large extent determined the economic structure. The transport system was often the starting point for economic and social but also political development, as we see in the expansion of the Greek and Roman Empires and the conquest of the oceans in more modern times.

The development of transport, seen from the very long-term standpoint, has been extraordinarily uneven and has progressed in sudden leaps. For thousands of years transport on land and water scarcely changed at all. Only the discovery of steam power, engines and machines introduced the modern era in transport as in industry. Predöhl (1) sees the development of transport, together with that of the world economy, in terms of three phases: integration, expansion and intensification.

The modern transport era, brought in by the railway and the steam ship, caused not only a revolutionary increase in the performance of land and water transport but also, in particular, much lower cost for the transport of both passengers and goods. This meant, in Predöhl's terms, that craft and agrarian activities could be integrated into the industrial world economy. The integration effects of the development of transport in the 19th and 20th centuries in the economic and social fields (rapid growth of centres) was significantly amplified by the advent of new transport modes such as the automobile (invention of the internal combustion engine in the 1860s) and the aircraft (development since the beginning of the century). At the same time, the new transport system of land and water modes brought a great expansion of the world economy with the two major population and economic poles of Europe and North America (migration from Europe).

According to Predöhl, intensification is to be seen, on the one hand, in the construction of new, and the further development of old, industrial centres and, on the other, in the technical development of existing (railways) and new transport modes (automobiles, aircraft, pipelines). Through improvements in transport speed, safety and performance, it has been possible to achieve continuing adjustment to the growing transport tasks. In terms of the system, there has been a great extension of transport coverage, as revealed by a description of the qualities of the different modes. However, these developments have brought far-reaching structural change in the transport systems of the industrialised countries, in which the railways played a dominant role until the 1920s. The economic and spatial flexibility of the motor truck, free from any public service obligations, rapidly undermined the railways' position as the backbone of the transport system, despite many attempts to regulate and distribute the traffic.

After the Second World War, the position of the railways as the main form of public transport deteriorated because of growing car ownership, while the expanding modes of air and pipeline transport took more traffic away from the railways.

To the three properties named by Predöhl, we should add that of increasing specialisation in view of recent trends in the development of transport modes, to some extent matched by growing division of labour in the world economy.

Increasing competition and the spectacular successes of technical progress have led to significant improvements in transport service supply, associated with increasing capital intensity of the individual transport modes. Specialisation is connected, above all, with the rationalisation of transport operations (rational packaging of goods, automatic coupling systems), improvements in transport safety (signalling and communications systems), higher transport speeds (Trans-Europe Express, high-speed trains, supersonic aircraft, etc.), together with bigger transport capacities (block trains, supertankers, push-towing, wide-bodied aircraft) and qualitative improvements in transport supply (comfort, new vehicles). Many organisational measures by individual transport undertakings (national and international co-operation in the fields of operations, tariffs, finance and law) or between modes (container traffic, price formation) and a differentiated organisation (liner services, tramp or charter services) have no doubt favoured this specialisation (2).

2. PROCESSES RESULTING FROM IMPROVEMENTS IN THE TRANSPORT SYSTEM

In his four-volume work, "Verkehr" (Transport), Fritz Voigt (3) traces the processes resulting from improvements in the transport system. Great importance is attributed to the introduction of the railways in this historical analysis:

"The railways first of all brought for the entrepreneur who could take advantage of them substantial savings in freight costs, improved safety and greater reliability of delivery. The further a firm was away from a railway station, the higher its costs, because it had to use the more expensive road mode and bear the additional time and money costs of transhipment between road and rail."

According to Voigt, the introduction of the railways had the following consequences:

a) Along the railway lines -- or more precisely, in the immediate vicinity of the stations -- advantaged locations developed. To this extent new enterprises were able to achieve a higher marginal productivity of capital here if they were looking for places for new investment;

b) The railways destroyed the protection provided by high transport costs for entrepreneurs who produced at higher costs or turned out inferior quality goods; hitherto it had not been possible for more efficient producers to demonstrate their superiority because of the poor transport system. The elimination of this "protection" happened insofar as the new transport mode made it possible to improve the current market value dimension;

c) Particularly favoured from the outset were the nodal points of different lines and, above all, connecting points with sea transport (ports) and inland waterway transport. The avoidance of transhipment always saves time and money and thus gives the entrepreneur in such a location a cost advantage and therefore, among other things, a competitive edge;

d) Railway construction entailed relatively high costs. It considerably increased the investment activity of the economy as a whole and resulted in significantly higher incomes. Again, it had a stimulating effect on the places where construction was going on, with particular advantage for nodal points, as the railway builders had their headquarters here and the additional workers were housed here.

The higher incomes meant increased solvent demand, notably where investment projects were being implemented. This led to increased sales mainly of goods for which the income elasticity of demand was the highest, thus benefiting mainly the food and textiles industries. Bigger sales led to further investment which, in turn, led to additional incomes and further increases in sales for the industries located in these places and, again, further investment.

The power of the railways and the inland waterways to shape economic activity began to decline when new transport modes such as motor vehicles and, since the Second World War, aircraft, took over important transport functions.

3. NEW, TRANSPORT-INDEPENDENT LOCATIONAL FACTORS

Even the once-compelling function of the transport system as a location-determining or shaping factor has now declined in importance, however. In the context of industrial location, the cost advantages of good transport links were long attributed the greatest importance. Today, we look at transport in quite a different light, and it is considerations such as the economic, political and ecological impacts that largely determine the value of the transport system, even if only in the negative sense: we only have to think of the ecological disadvantages of a transit axis through the environmentally sensitive Alpine region.

The future economic development of the European Community countries will be more influenced by the liberalisation of the movement of goods, services and capital than by the future transport system. On the contrary, this transport system will limit and restrict economic development through the bottlenecks that already exist.

The constant improvement of the transport supply, through new modes (road, air), new transport technologies and, above all, through new and better organisation of the transport process, has significantly influenced the division of labour and the specialisation of the economy.

Before we discuss in detail the just-in-time concept as a prime example of an improved transport service, we must examine the two, no doubt, most important elements of the freight transport market today: technology and organisation.

4. TECHNIQUE AND ORGANISATION MUST SATISFY THE DEMAND SIDE REQUIREMENT PROFILE

In the study of the European freight transport market carried out by Prognos (Basel) (4), the technology and organisation of freight transport are designated as qualitative framework conditions, alongside energy and the environment:

> *"In our opinion, transport technology and organisation are the decisive elements in establishing a synchronous relationship between transport supply and demand.*
>
> *These two elements also make it possible to exploit all the advantages of specialised transport."*

In view of the thorough study by Prognos, all it remains for us to do is to summarise the most important findings.

The second volume of the report establishes that the use of new technologies and new forms of organisation are closely linked with the freight transport requirements that emerge on the demand side on the part of shippers, the state and society. The following criteria were used to determine the demand side requirement profile:

- Adequate network density and infrastructure capacity;
- Transport speed;
- Adequate supply of information;
- Respect of deadlines/flexibility;
- No loss of value of the freight;
- Security of the transport process;
- Large volume containers;
- High payload;
- Attractive transport price.

On the basis of this requirement profile, the Prognos team evaluated the development potential and the resulting quality profile for the individual transport modes.

"The demand/supply comparison led to the following findings with regard to the competitiveness of the different transport modes for individual freight categories:

-- *Inland waterways will continue in the future to be the typical mode for 'traditional bulk goods';*

-- *Rail transport can be competitive not only for bulk goods but also for higher value goods such as iron, steel and non-ferrous metals (including intermediates), which as inputs require not only a high payload but also speed and respect of deadlines/flexibility;*

-- *The future road freight will be 'consumption related, high value piece goods'. The road haulage qualities of information supply, respect of deadlines/flexibility and network density are the main factors here."*

The team concludes that the freight transport requirement criteria of industry, the state and society will continue in future to be fulfilled to very differing degrees by the individual transport modes. All modes will in future do their utmost to exploit the possibilities offered by the information and communications technologies for improving their competitive position. The use of the new information and communications technologies will not be limited to the preparation of the information required to prepare for and accompany the transport operation, but will also contribute to meeting other requirements such as speed or respect of deadlines/flexibility. Information and communications technologies will therefore be increasingly used at all stages of the transport process.

The exploitation by the transport industry of the possibilities offered by the information and communications technologies is also in the interest of the State and of society as a whole because of the associated economic, ecological and safety advantages. Through political support for the establishment of Europe-wide communications technology infrastructures, the State, in co-operation with industry, can improve the conditions for the use of these technologies (e.g. satellite technology, freight exchanges, databases on the legal regulations for the transport of dangerous goods).

The efforts by all modes to enhance their technical and organisational efficiency lead us to expect that in the future a high technical and organisational level of the transport services offered will be an increasingly necessary, but on its own an increasingly inadequate, precondition for success in competition between carriers. The example of other fiercely competitive branches leads us to expect that, on the basis of a technically and organisationally high quality supply profile, increasing supply-side competition will develop in the provision of many kinds of additional services, guarantees and differentiated pricing structures.

In competition between modes, the railways in particular are competing on two fronts: with the inland waterways in bulk goods and with road haulage in piece goods. This means that the railways will have to develop and maintain a comprehensive supply profile if they are not to go on slipping back on traditional markets and are to participate in new ones. At the same time, this two-front competition situation shows how vital it is for the railways to be involved in developing efficient combined transport supplies. Combined transport represents an opportunity for the railways to turn competition on two fronts into partnerships on two sides, one with the waterways and the other with road transport, and thus ease the overall competitive pressure.

In addition to the systematic introduction of technical and organisational innovations to adjust transport services to the goods-specific requirement profile, the future growth of frontier-crossing transport will require new forms of international organisation and co-operation. This applies to all transport modes. Through appropriate adjustment of the legal and administrative framework conditions, national and international government organisations will have to create the necessary preconditions for a unified European freight transport market.

According to the Prognos study, comparing the requirement profile of trade and industry with the supply profiles of the transport modes leads to the following conclusions regarding the main thrust of transport enterprise market strategies for road, rail and inland waterways:

"-- ***Road**: The organisational separation of the forwarding and carrying functions supports the further rationalisation of transport processes. For forwarding, the emphasis should be on the development of new services that complement the transport service proper, the development of supply concepts that extend over different modes, the analysis of goods-specific requirement profiles and link-specific supply alternatives, and the consolidation and further development of progressive transport organisational know-how.*

Carriers should orient their enterprises mainly towards meeting the requirements involving technical elements (speed, safety, information supply, preserving the value of the goods, packaging, payload), vehicles, superstructures and communications with vehicles. For high value consignments more qualified staff are required.

-- ***Rail:*** *The railway undertakings need to go on eliminating any remaining bureaucratic elements in their organisation. Unlike the road hauliers, railway undertakings have to fulfil the functions of both forwarder and carrier if they are to assert themselves as market economy enterprises. Also of strategic importance are the development of international (bilateral and multilateral) forms of organisation and co-operation and the expansion of the combined transport supply.*

-- ***Inland waterways:*** *With a continuing clear orientation to the transport of bulk goods, it seems that inland waterway enterprises can improve their market position above all through co-operation with the other surface modes."* (4)

5. HIGHER TRANSPORT QUALITY REQUIREMENTS DUE TO THE STRUCTURAL CHANGE IN FREIGHT TRAFFIC

The comparison of the requirement profile of trade and industry with the supply profile of the different transport modes has already shown that higher transport quality requirements are to be expected. Quite apart from the general development of trade and industry in the direction of quality rather than quantity, this trend is due to structural change in the goods market.

In the field of private consumer demand, the proportion of expenditure on individual categories of goods decreases with increasing income. Thus, for example, in the period 1961 to 1985 the food, drink and tobacco proportion of gross value added fell sharply, while that for transport and information purposes rose somewhat. We would refer in particular to the "Maslov needs pyramid" which indicates a certain priority needs structure leading from essential needs through social to self-fulfilment needs.

Product innovations can certainly extend the saturation limits for utility goods, for example, but the demand for higher value goods goes on increasing at the same time.

As Puf (5) demonstrates, "service functions" within industrial enterprises are growing -- research and development, organisation, logistics, marketing, engineering and service, for example -- much more than proportionally and are accounting for an ever greater proportion of the end product value added. Conversely, the actual manufacturing process represents an ever-decreasing proportion of value added. It is thus possible to see strong growth in internal, i.e. production-related, services.

Between 1980 and 1988 the FRG recorded absolute growth in gross value added of DM 191 billion (at 1980 prices). Of this total increase, DM 167 billion was in the private services sector alone and only DM 24 billion in manufacturing industry.

Puf points out that for some time it has been clear that the transport of high value-added goods, in small quantities but frequently, is increasing, while material-intensive consignments are falling due to technical and economic developments and specialities. While the technical reasons are to be seen in more efficient use of energy and growth of the service components, the economic reasons for the falling trend in material-intensive consignments are due above all to the fact that bulk goods are, for the most part, highly subsidised goods. This applies, for example, to coal and steel production. The progressive removal of subsidies on these goods all over Europe will mean that national purchasing or production sources will decline while, at the same time, purchases from non-European sources will increase.

The transport quality requirements will therefore increase overall, while the transport cost as a percentage of the price of lower value goods will be sharply reduced: the incentive for greater specialisation in transport is growing, in particular in view of the increasing economic integration of Europe.

6. EXTENSION OF COMBINED TRANSPORT AS A TECHNICAL SOLUTION

We have already pointed out the importance of combined transport in connection with the rail transport supply profile. The development of modern industrial society has given a strong impetus to the development of an optimal transport chain in the form of combined transport using containers and piggy-back transport, largely thanks to the following (6):

-- Growing demand for specialised transport possibilities;

-- General decline in domestic demand for raw materials in favour of end products that require better protection during transport;

-- Inclusion of the loading unit in the production process;

-- General trend towards a more or less drastic reduction in inventories in favour of the introduction of the just-in-time concept.

Since 1st April 1991, the European Agreement on Important International Combined Transport Lines and Related Installations (AGTC), negotiated in the context of the UN Economic Commission for Europe (ECE) in Geneva, has been ready for signature.

According to the preamble of the ECE Agreement, the aim of combined transport is to relieve European roads -- notably on transalpine routes -- and reduce environmental damage. The multilaterally agreed guidelines are intended to lead, through improved co-ordination, to the concrete result of reduced rail transport times and hence to greater user friendliness. A coherent European transport system of this type requires more through freight trains over the longest possible distances. The first annex to the Agreement proper lists all the railway lines from the Iberian Peninsula to Scandinavia and from Ireland to the Soviet Union or Turkey that are suitable for combined transport and should be appropriately upgraded in the future. The second annex sets out the most important loading or transhipment terminals, the main frontier crossing points, ferry ports and track gauge-changing stations.

The last two annexes are mainly concerned with technical specifications for existing and new railway lines from the standpoint of combined transport requirements. The target year for the unified Europe-wide compliance with these guidelines is the year 2000. The minimum speed over the designated lines with an axle loading of 20 tonnes is to be 120 km/h for existing and new stretches; the lower speed of 100 km/h is admissible only if the axle loading is increased to 22.5 tonnes. Train lengths of 750 metres should be achievable, with the rail-bound vehicles and units carried (complete trucks, trailers, containers, etc.) corresponding to certain standard dimensions. Lastly, specific performance parameters for rail-bound transport are laid down or recommended, such as time requirements for loading, unloading or transhipment, reliable and punctual transport times, night-time operation for rail transport and the minimisation of control and administrative work through organisational efficiency.

The ECE Agreement is a first multilaterally agreed legal framework for international combined transport. Its aim is to achieve a service improvement above all in long-distance rail transport through the greatest possible optimisation of the transport process. This should create a true competitive alternative to road transport over long distances. It thus also constitutes a basis for transport policy investment planning for the future, with the central component of promoting combined transport in Europe. The slogan is: long distances by rail, local distribution by road. To this end, the annexes to the Agreement record the most important railway lines, the related installations (e.g. loading and transhipment stations), the technical characteristics and the main performance parameters.

7. ENHANCED TRANSPORT LOGISTICS AS AN ORGANISATION SOLUTION

We shall not consider the technical side of future dependencies between trade and industry and the transport system or transport specialisation any further, but would now like to turn, in particular, to the requirements concerning transport system organisation and management.

From the Prognos study, we see the growing importance of the organisation of the transport process and with it the information and communications technologies on the one hand, and of international organisation and co-operation on the other.

Transport logistics, because all-encompassing and intermeshed, offers itself as a solution.

The logistics function embraces all processes within and between social systems (organisations, enterprises) that serve to cover distance, bridge time, control and regulate.

Transport logistics is thus systems- and decision-oriented and is the idea behind the full service approach. The basic idea is the realisation that the complexity of systems is the determining characteristic of their behaviour and not, for example, the characteristics of individual system components, for these are only activated through the relations of the components with one another.

The all-embracing coverage of all processes triggered by the moving of people, goods and information is in line with practice, because the demand is less and less for individual transport, storage and transhipment services, but rather for problem-solving approaches that cover the processes involved both before and after the transport operation itself.

This should lead, in particular, to time and cost savings. Function fulfilment or meeting the required standard of service should be achieved with the lowest stocks and the smallest possible storage or buffer capacities (*cf.* the just-in-time concept). As Kuhn, *et al.* (7) point out, smaller buffers with the same service times promote significantly more efficient transport systems, because security of supply can be guaranteed only by means of the system components buffer capacity (shipper or consignee side) and transport service. Better transport service in road transport, for example, means more vehicles. If the transport contracts are differentiated, then transport frequencies will be increased over a link, which again leads to increased vehicle numbers because smaller loading areas are used. Because this development -- smallest stocks, intensification of goods exchange relationships, differentiation of transport requirements -- must not result in higher procurement or distribution costs, "intelligent logistics solutions" are being sought and found. Here, a new form of logistics service will be established.

Demand from trade and industry will increasingly be met by the transport industry and carriers with the supply of logistical solutions containing a full service package. Transport undertakings will therefore be able to open up new market potential thanks to innovative logistical solutions -- and this all over Europe.

Stabenau (8) describes the impacts of enterprise-related logistics systems on the requirements of the transport function as follows:

- The coupling effect between the different operators in a logistical chain is achieved through transport. About sixty per cent of all logistical activities consist, in principle, of transport. This means the movement of materials and goods before, during and after production, within, between and beyond enterprises.

- Because of the logistical tasks described, the demand for transport services is becoming further individualised which, at the same time, leads to a demand for specialised transport installations and processes.

- The spatial division of labour in the production and distribution of goods is becoming more marked on the international level, too. This is one of the main reasons for the growth of transport demand as a whole.

-- Because of the continuing goods structure effect, the average value of goods to be carried will go on rising. The qualitative transport requirements thus grow accordingly.

-- Since transport costs have fallen relative to other logistical costs, such as storage, transhipment, etc., these logistical functions will be increasingly replaced by greater use of transport. This will lead, at the same time, to a change in the forms of transport.

This qualitative change in transport demand places different requirements concerning the service performance of the transport system, which Stabenau describes as follows:

-- **Versatility**: This means that as far as possible in every place several types and forms of transport may be used. The transformation of the transport function is leading to an extraordinarily differentiated technical and organisational need for individualised transport services.

-- **Reliability**: Here, the time dimension plays an extremely important role. The transport time here means the door-to-door time including all customs clearance and transhipment times and the precision of arrival (punctuality). The greater the degree of reliability of a given form of transport, the more realistic the implementation of the just-in-time concept in the supply of inputs and the distribution of products. By this means, giving up carrying stocks becomes a calculable parameter corresponding to the degree of reliability of the possible types of transport.

-- **Specialisation**: The degree of specialisation, notably of transport packaging, will be further developed against the background of future transport system requirements. Tailor-made transport will be developed to suit the transport properties of different goods. From the standpoint of increased transport security in particular, the risks involved in transhipment and storage will be reduced. The optimal solution is to design the transport unit in such a way that it is, at the same time, the transhipment and storage unit, as in container traffic.

Specialisation is not, of course, just a matter of the appropriate transport packaging and handling equipment, but also of the vehicle itself. Thus the same effect is achieved, for example, when the vehicle is fitted for the requirements of a given link or type of good.

-- **Availability**: The concept of availability is concerned with both the supply of an appropriate capacity, where necessary, specialised capacity within the transport system, i.e. the forms of transport required in each case and availability at a given time. Availability thus has a static (capacity) and a dynamic (time) aspect. Precisely the availability factor, with respect to specialised transport containers and vehicles, has been a criterion for the extension of own-account transport in the past.

-- **Ease of integration**: This refers to the technical and organisational combination of transport containers with carriers (e.g. rail/road), storage and transhipment facilities and the information system. A precondition for ease of integration is national and international standardization and harmonization and the construction of the corresponding terminals for combined transport.

As Kuhn, *et al.* point out, competition-oriented goods distribution systems meet macro- and micro-economic targets better than the former "goods distribution centres". This means that information is promoted to the status of a true factor of production.

In establishing the information required to prepare for and accompany a freight transport operation, the use of computer-based information and communications technologies is becoming increasingly important. In the ideal case, there would be on-line links between shipper, forwarder, carrier, vehicle driver and consignee. The use of information and communications technologies for on-line transmission of transport information will go on expanding in the future.

While these technologies have been introduced in road haulage (on-board computer), the corresponding measures in European rail transport are not yet sufficiently widespread (*cf.* the HERMES information project).

In future, the information and communications systems will become all the more important as, for example, international and national freight exchanges -- electronic systems to improve transport capacity utilisation and vehicle load factors -- can substantially reduce empty hauls, notably on the roads and thus significantly reduce the environmental pollution caused by heavy vehicles.

8. THE JUST-IN-TIME CONCEPT AS MODEL OF SPECIALISATION

Just-in-time transport is a basic precondition for flexible production while maintaining minimum stocks. This type of precisely calculable transport process requires a high degree of dispatching flexibility on the part of the carrier. Precisely-timed transport can be achieved only if there are adequate capacities and reliable information networks.

Wildenmann (9) defines the just-in-time concept as an effective instrument for exploiting the existing potential for rationalisation. This is necessary in view of growing competition, increasing costs and the market requirement of flexibility.

The target criteria for introducing the just-in-time concept, according to a survey cited by Wildenmann, are shown in Figure 1.

In addition to the cost aspects, the time, flexibility and quality factors seem to be equally important.

The just-in-time concept stems from the aim of producing the smallest possible quantity at the latest possible moment. Specialisation, automation and optimisation are achieved through improving the assembly-line principle.

The potential impacts of the just-in-time concept are shown by Wildenmann in the form of an IS and SHOULD BE diagram (Figure 2).

Among European enterprises, the just-in-time concept is used mainly in the automobile and components industry (66 per cent), electrical and electronics (33 per cent), household appliances (25 per cent), chemicals and pharmaceuticals (15 per cent) and mechanical engineering (15 per cent).

As Wildenmann says, the basic idea of transport optimisation is that the usual individual consignments for a limited area should be handed over to a single forwarder, who combines them and transports them to the destination. In accordance with the production programme, the smallest necessary quantities can then still be economically transported to where they are needed. An area forwarder is responsible for this. Criteria for the delimitation of the area are:

-- The transport volume and weight involved;

-- Distance to the individual destinations;

-- Delivery frequency;

-- Infrastructures;

-- Climatic conditions.

The area forwarder delivers either according to a fixed timetable or on demand. Consignments are then gathered together centrally and delivered to the consignees. On the return haul, the shipper carries the reusable empty containers or pallets in which the goods were delivered. Through concentrating several individual consignments on a single vehicle, bottlenecks in the delivery of goods are eased. The unloading process is simplified so that labour requirements as well as transport costs are reduced.

The advantages of the area forwarder concept are optimal for carrier, consignee and supplier. They again emphasize the trend towards transport specialisation. (See the following table)

Area forwarder	Consignee	Supplier
Stable plans • Frequency • Transport volume	Small number of forwarders	Reduced expenditure on logistics
Close contact between consignees and suppliers	Regulated return of empty containers	Proximity to forwarder
Route optimisation	Less transport problems with deliveries	Simpler cost calculations
Long-term co-operation	Simplified reception of goods	Simpler agreement of shipment availability times for the forwarder
Secure payment procedures	Automatic data processing	Greater punctuality for deliveries
Reduced acquisition expenditure	Simplified control of delivery dates	Regulated return of empty containers
Well-defined tasks	More rapid availability of special deliveries	Transfer of the transport risk
Takeover of additional functions	Transfer of routine functions	
High capacity utilisation	Reduced transport costs	
	Limited field of responsibility	
	Reduced expenditure on logistics	

9. CONCLUSIONS

The development of transport has accompanied that of the economy in four phases that can be summed up under the headings: integration, expansion, intensification and specialisation.

Increasingly fierce competition and the spectacular successes of technical progress have led to great improvements in transport service supply. At the same time, the capital-intensity of the individual transport modes has increased.

Specialisation is associated, above all, with an advantageous rationalisation of the transport process (rational packaging, automatic coupling systems), improved transport safety (signalling and communications technology), higher transport speeds (Trans-Europe Express, high-speed trains, supersonic aircraft, etc.) together with bigger transport capacities (block trains, supertankers, push-towing, wide-bodied aircraft) and qualitative improvements in transport supply (comfort, new vehicles). Many organisational measures by individual transport undertakings (national and international co-operation in the fields of operations, tariffs, finance and law) or between modes (container traffic, price formation) and a differentiated organisation (liner services, tramp or charter services) have, no doubt, favoured this specialisation.

The constant improvement of the transport supply through new modes (road, air), new transport technologies and, in particular, new and better organisation of the transport process has significantly influenced the division of labour and the specialisation of trade and industry. A perfect example is that of the just-in-time concept, which provides substantial rationalisation possibilities for the future. The result is, however, a sharp increase of relatively small, time-sensitive and high-value consignments.

The demands on transport organisation and the quality of transport supply are increasing, to a large extent due to structural change in the goods market, and require corresponding technical and organisational measures on the part of transport enterprises.

The transport logistics function, which embraces all processes within and between social systems (organisations, enterprises) that serve to cover distance, bridge time, control and regulate, offers itself as a solution. As a comprehensive systems approach it enables transport and forwarding enterprises to meet the demand on the part of trade and industry with logistical solutions that contain a full service package.

Through providing an innovative logistical supply, transport enterprises can, on the one hand, open up new market potential and, on the other, optimise their supply. A precondition for the full exploitation of the advantages of transport logistics is the improvement of computer-based information and communications systems.

REFERENCES

1. Predöhl, Andreas (1964): Verkehrspolitik, 2. Aufl., Göttingen.

2. Kaspar, Claude (1977): Verkehrswirtschaftslehre im Grundriss, Bern und Stuttgart.

3. Voigt, Fritz (1965): Verkehr, 2. Band, 2. Hälfte, S. 1122 *ff.*, Berlin.

4. Prognos (1988): Gemeinschaftsuntersuchung Güterverkehrsmarkt Europa, Arbeitsheft 2: Technik und Organisation des Güterverkehrs.

5. Puf, Peter (1991): Veränderungen der Güterstruktur. In: Innovationspotentiale im Güterverkehr, Schriftenreihe der Deutschen Verkehrswissenschftl. Gesellschaft, B 130, Bergisch Gladbach.

6. Dente, Giulio (1990): Zum kombinierten Verkehr aus der Sicht der Wirtschaftskommission der Vereinigten Nationen für Europa. In: Euro Modal 1/90, Basel.

7. Kuhn, A., *et al.* (1991): Innovationen im Produktions- und Distributionsbereich. In: Innovationspotentiale im Güterverkehr, a.a.O.

8. Stabenau, Hanspeter (1987): Transportfunktion im Wandel -- Die Anforderungen der Logistik an den Transport und an die Verkehrspolitik. In: Jahrbuch der Schweiz. Verkehrswirtschaft 1986/87. Herausgeber: Prof. Dr. C. Kaspar, St. Gallen.

9. Wildenmann, Horst (1990): Das Just-In-Time Konzept, 2. Aufl., Zurich.

FIGURES

Figure 1. **Just-in-time concept**

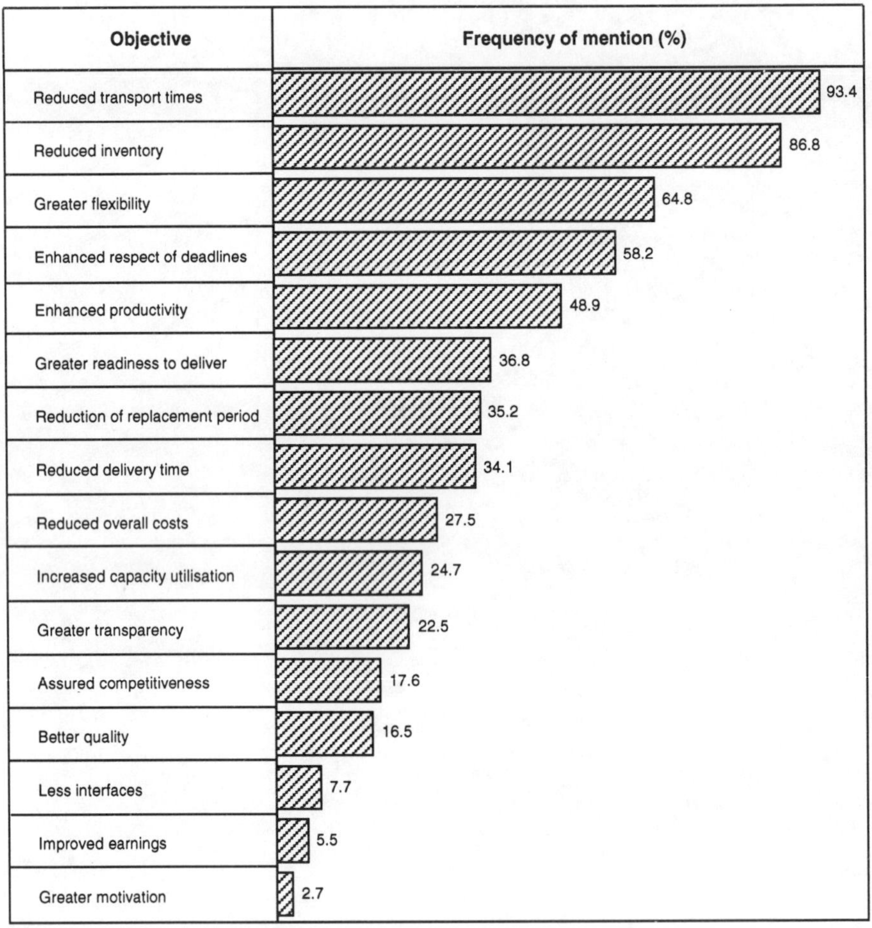
Objective
Frequency of mention (%)
Reduced transport times
93.4
Reduced inventory
86.8
Greater flexibility
64.8
Enhanced respect of deadlines
58.2
Enhanced productivity
48.9
Greater readiness to deliver
36.8
Reduction of replacement period
35.2
Reduced delivery time
34.1
Reduced overall costs
27.5
Increased capacity utilisation
24.7
Greater transparency
22.5
Assured competitiveness
17.6
Better quality
16.5
Less interfaces
7.7
Improved earnings
5.5
Greater motivation
2.7

Figure 2. **Potential of just-in-time**

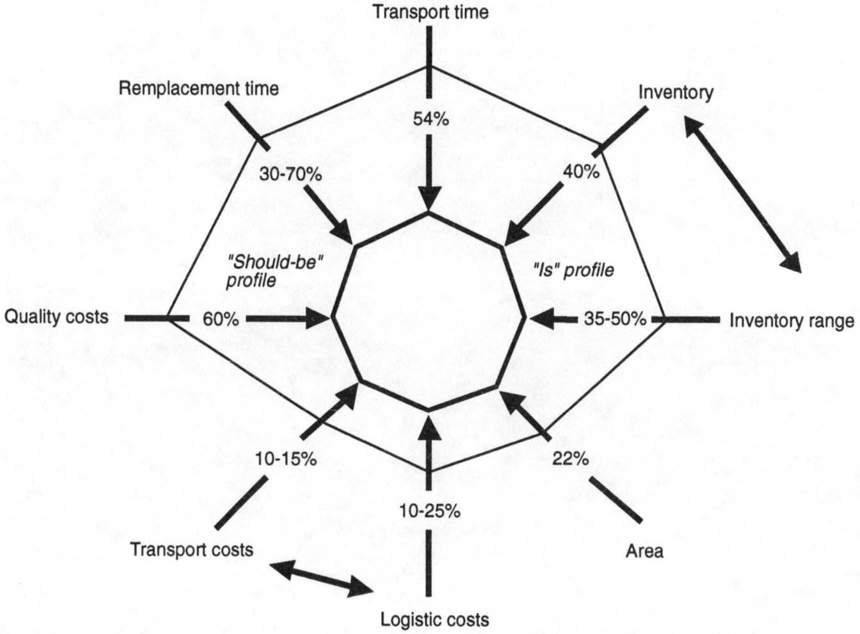

Sub-topic 3

INFRASTRUCTURE CAPACITY AND NETWORK ACCESS

R. IZQUIERDO
A. MONZON
Universidad Politècnica de Madrid
Madrid
Spain

SUMMARY

Madrid, December 1991

1. ACCESSIBILITY AS A PLANNING AND REGIONAL DEVELOPMENT OBJECTIVE

1.1. Accessibility as an objective in infrastructure planning

The main changes marking the 1970s were the slowdown in economic growth as a result of the economic crisis; the trend in the behaviour patterns of society whereby people were showing greater concern about social and environmental issues and, more generally, about anything that improved the quality of life; the surge in regionalism promoted movements; greater concern for regional imbalances and physical and land use planning; and the form of the Community framework. As a result of this process, planning techniques started to provide a more coherent approach in response to current requirements. This situation coincided with progress in the statistical and analytical techniques used to evaluate regional systems and with the development of new methods of assessment based on multicriteria analysis.

It is therefore not surprising that considerable changes have been seen in transport planning since that period. The fact that transport is considered part of a regional system, the interactions between transport and land use, the possibilities for integration it provides, the external effects it produces, its role as a factor in economic and social progress, etc., are all now the subject of studies and have gradually made it possible to bring new criteria into decision-making processes and even to modify the processes in general use.

In this context, the problems of regions or areas with poor access to communications networks and to economic centres have gradually taken such a significant place in regional planning processes that, as already stated by Morris (1) in 1978, the aim of providing good accessibility in a region is to a large extent replacing the aim of avoiding congestion. This obviously requires a new, more selective approach to infrastructure programmes which, as a rule, were almost exclusively intended to develop and improve existing communications infrastructure without making provision for new, more homogeneous and balanced regional structure. Myrdal's so-called "cumulative process" was being introduced and resulted in a greater concentration of traffic on the improved infrastructure which, in its turn, required further extensions, thereby contributing to greater regional imbalances, and gave rise to a centre-periphery pattern.

That is not to say that the gearing of the level of service to meet transport demand is not a major objective in any infrastructure plan, but simply that action to improve the accessibility of the least well-equipped zones must also be taken into account.

On this subject we can refer to Spain's 1984-91 General Road Plan and to the Regional Plans implemented by the various autonomous communities which, for the first time, included among their basic objectives the contributions of roads to a better regional and social balance and to improving accessibility in zones where its inadequacy was a brake on development. It was for this reason that a series of admittedly very simple, but quite significant accessibility indicators were drawn up. By using them on maps, it has been possible to define the least well-equipped zones and to implement measures compatible with regional policy (see Annex).

Within this process marking the 1970s and the first half of the 1980s, it can thus be seen that the new concept of "accessibility" has emerged and developed in the transport sector, and has become a transport planning and policy instrument. Although this concept is not used to any great extent at present, the changes which have occurred since the second half of the 1980s and which are giving a new form to Europe may, however, turn it into an instrument for economic and social cohesion, not only at the national but also at the Community and even European level.

However, so far, efforts have mainly focused on developing a concept and indicators for social accessibility in towns, in rural areas, in mountainous zones, etc., with emphasis on ease of access for various sections of the population to various amenities, including public transport.

It was not until the European Community realised the serious problems caused by regional imbalances for the new Community structure that the accessibility concept was extended to the regional, national and transnational level.

1.2. Accessibility as an objective in regional policy and in economic and social cohesion

As already pointed out, accessibility is one of the objectives in transport infrastructure planning which usually addresses specific, practical problems. However, owing to the development of the European Community and the serious regional imbalances at the present time, accessibility is one of the objectives in the process of economic and social cohesion which the Community has set since the second half of the 1980s, at a time when, as will be explained later, the basis for the new framework for the year 2000 is starting to be organised in connection with the future internal market.

Article 2 of the Treaty of Rome stated that the objectives to be promoted by the Community included "*a harmonious development of economic activities, a continuous and balanced expansion, an increase in stability, an accelerated raising of the standard of living and closer relations between the States belonging to it*" and, for this purpose, proposed a series of measures specifically including the adoption of a common transport policy.

There is no need to stress that there is still no real Community transport policy -- despite all the efforts made in recent years to start 1993 on a sound footing -- and that not only has a regional balance not been achieved but, as the Community concedes, the situation has even deteriorated.

The lack of an overall infrastructure policy from both the Community and regional viewpoint, which would have contributed to the integration of the various geographical areas is, in my opinion, partly responsible for this situation. The aid granted by the Community through DG VII (Directorate-General for Transport) and DG XVI (Directorate-General for Regional Policy) via the ERDF has not helped to achieve a regional balance and Community cohesion.

Firstly, infrastructure as a common transport policy instrument is the main factor in the integration of Member States since it undoubtedly improves communications between the centre and the periphery of the Community. However, Community policy is exclusively centred on the major European routes which take the bulk of international traffic and act as a basis for transport policy. This implies that, although Community measures are intended to eliminate bottlenecks, improve traffic conditions, reduce congestion, cut transport costs and provide very good connections between the main urban centres (high-speed rail network), they do not in themselves contribute to more balanced regional development. Quite the contrary, since it is precisely the regions which attract the most traffic and which are the best equipped that benefit, the measures tend to increase imbalances and consolidate the centre-periphery structure.

Secondly, transport infrastructure is an important component in regional policy since it helps to achieve such objectives as the correction of the various regional imbalances, a more balanced geographical distribution of economic activities, growth in economic potential, the promotion of development and the structural adjustment of under-developed zones.

The European Community itself proposed to reduce differences between the regions and enable the most disadvantaged regions to catch up by using the new policy of strengthening economic and social cohesion set up by the Single European Act and the reform of structural funds in 1988. The considerable increase in the funds allocated to the ERDF to help adjust the main imbalances within the Community is a tangible sign of this concern.

Very large sums have been allocated to transport and telecommunications infrastructure. In the specific case of Spain, they exceeded 70 per cent of the ERDF funds for the period 1986-89, while the sums for the period 1989-93 amount to almost 52 per cent of the funds allocated to Objective 1.

Although this new regional Community policy is a marked improvement as far as regional or local transport networks are concerned, it is still inadequate, since the Community support arrangements, which determine structural intervention by the Community, are based exclusively on national plans for regional development which are worked out from the corresponding regional plans.

As stated by the Commission "Europe 2000" (2), Community Regional policy should not be concerned solely with providing financial assistance to a limited number of regions, but must also address issues reflecting the use and development of Community territory as a whole.

As regional imbalances were a source of concern, the Community took the studies by Keeble (3) as the basis for a series of analyses to show the centrality or peripherality of Community regions in relation to centres of economic activity, the aim being to classify them and establish a correlation with other socio-economic variables.

The peripherality concept was expressed in terms of accessibility to centres of economic activity and therefore depends on both the geographical distribution of these centres and the distance between each region and the others. An attempt was thus made to show that differences in accessibility between regions were a basic factor in the theory of the location of wealth. In the subsequent sections we shall refer to the main accessibility indicators used by Keeble in his various publications.

These analyses made it possible to make a comparative assessment of the disadvantages of the most peripheral regions compared with the central regions in the EC located near what is called the "golden triangle" and to study the successive effects of the various enlargements of the Community as seen in the increase in regional imbalances and in the number of peripheral regions. It has been observed, however, that accessibility is tending to improve in the regions of southern Europe in general and to decline in northern Germany and in the Netherlands which, to some extent, is shifting the European centre of gravity to the south and gives an initial idea of what could be seen in the future as the Mediterranean sun belt.

Although these analyses have been used to establish the initial basis for regional policy and the allocation of structural funds on the basis of the peripherality and under-development of the regions, the concept of economic and social cohesion -- in the new spatial context which is being determined by technological changes and which will be finally formed by the internal market -- adds, however, a new dimension, as shown by the "Europe 2000" report (2) mentioned above and the Council Resolution on transeuropean networks of 2 January 1990 (4).

The new factors on which economic and social cohesion should be based are the development and interconnection of transeuropean networks, with special emphasis on peripheral zones; the overall approach to development and the use of Community territory; and the improvement of connections between peripheral zones -- a question that so far has been ignored. As we shall show in the next section, the new spatial pattern that is starting to take shape and the new distribution of flows now emerging are reducing the importance of the concept and measure of the peripherality of regions and emphasizing better and more extensive connections between them and the various transnational networks. Accordingly, the concept of accessibility as a peripherality indicator is slowly giving way to that of accessibility as an indicator of linkage with communications networks.

1.3. Accessibility in support of the internal market and the new framework as from the year 2000

Although, as we have stated in the preceding sections, the changes that occurred in the 1970s have resulted in a new approach to planning and in the definition and development of regional policies at both national and Community level, the changes that are now taking place, following the policy commitment by EEC Member States in 1985 to set up an internal market in 1993 and the strengthening of competition among European firms, are giving rise to a new type of spatial and communications structure in which, as shown by Turró and Ulied (5), what counts is not so much being located in a particular place but being connected with basic transport and telecommunications networks and systems.

In the new Community system of an area without frontiers or barriers in which persons, goods, capital and services move freely, the transport sector and the regional system will undergo a series of changes due to a number of circumstances, including:

-- The liberalisation of international transport as an immediate requirement for the establishment of the internal market;

-- The liberalisation of cabotage;

-- The elimination of distortions in competition or harmonization of the terms of competition among the different transport modes at both national and Community level;

-- The liberalisation and, to a large extent, the privatisation of national transport in connection with the current deregulation process and greater participation by the private sector in the funding and operation of public infrastructure and services;

-- The development of the Community into a new European economic area;

-- The internationalisation of activities, the changes in the location of production centres and the expansion of national and international markets;

-- The growth in trade;

-- The adoption and wider use of logistics within the productive sector, as a comprehensive system of managing flows of goods and information, as well as the application of JIT and similar techniques in response to new requirements on the demand side;

-- The dispersion of traffic departure and arrival points and the wider dissemination of goods flows that require greater continuity in the provision of services;

-- The development of commercial networks and integrated freight terminals which will facilitate logistical operations;

-- The extensive development of information and communication technologies and their practical application to transport.

All these factors will be, and already are, resulting in a substantial increase in transport flows -- to a greater extent at intra-Community than at national level -- in a new conception of the carriers' activity and transport which is seen as a link in the logistical chain, and in a new location of economic activities, which means that traditional transport undertakings will have to be reorganised and infrastructure geared to new quantitative and qualitative needs on the demand side.

The rapid development of telematics works and the improvements in both transport infrastructure and equipment are bringing production and consumption centres closer and facilitating the mobility of economic activities in which the new location factors, according to the "Europe 2000" report (2), are: rapid and efficient communications systems; the availability of skilled labour; access to local educational and research centres; the presence of high-quality business services; the quality of the physical, social and cultural environment, etc.

As Borja (6) says, all this makes for a new kind of area which consists rather of networks than hierarchical structures, and in which good accessibility, i.e. as the possibility of connecting up with these networks, plays a very important part in the development of a region, independently of its peripheral location.

Accordingly, the main objective of the European Community's regional policy up to the year 2000 should be to ensure that peripheral regions have accessibility levels that will at least enable them to be connected easily not only with the central zones and centres of activity, but also with the other peripheral regions, and also make it worthwhile to set up new activities and establishments that would contribute to economic development and thus to reducing regional imbalances.

This procedure therefore means that accessibility indicators have to be worked out for regions to show their linkage with communications networks and the levels of existing services, so as to be able to analyse objectively the contribution by transport systems to the regions' development potential.

However, these accessibility indicators should not simply quantify these effects, but serve as an important instrument in the new policy for economic and social cohesion, since it must be possible to use them as a basis for national and Community economic aid policy.

When assessing the benefit to the Community of projects eligible for Community funding, both the Community and individual States should therefore include in their objectives and criteria the contribution of these projects to improving the accessibility of the most disadvantaged or most peripheral regions. The TASC ((Transport Assessment System for the Community) system itself should include multicriteria analysis in its evaluations so as to emphasize accessibility.

The latest work to be carried out by CITRAME[1] and by CEDRE[1] should be mentioned, as it makes an important contribution to this subject.

CITRAME has produced a study (7) which defines quantitative indicators for regional accessibility and their application to land-locked areas in Mediterranean Europe, the aim being to contribute to the definition of objective criteria for the allocation of development aid (see Annex).

CITRAME selected as a regional accessibility indicator linkage with the main communications networks as measured by minimum access time -- which is adjusted upwards on the basis of the other connection possibilities for each system, the overall level of available services and capacity -- and not, as in the previously quoted studies by Keeble, the concept of peripherality in relation to the European urban and economic system.

The results made it possible to identify the zones where connections were the most difficult and to propose alternative routes for new transport infrastructure which, while also improving inter-regional communications and providing the additional capacity required for the coast, would help to open up the most isolated or least well-equipped zones.

The second study -- carried out as part of the forward planning study for the Atlantic Region, which was in some ways similar to the preceding one and refers to the Atlantic Axis -- was sponsored by the Directorate-General for Regional Policy (DG XVI) of the EEC and co-ordinated by CEDRE, which used the methodology developed by the Polytechnic University of Catalonia[2].

The accessibility indicator used is similar to the preceding indicator, even if there are some differences as regards the measurement of linkage with the other networks and the weighting of the various factors involved.

As in the preceding case, the results obtained make it possible to analyse the soundness of strategic regional projects and include accessibility as an objective in multicriteria analysis.

2. MEASURING ACCESSIBILITY IN REGIONAL PLANNING

The preceding sections clearly show that knowledge of a region's accessibility is essential for planning authorities, geographers, town planners, etc., since they must have data on the proximity and convenience of communications between two points. An estimate of this parameter will make it possible to identify the zones where mobility is inadequate (and which, therefore, are in most need of infrastructure and transport services), compare alternative plans, assess the consequences of each alternative and show the results in a way that is easy to understand. This parameter is also sometimes decisive in the location of certain activities. It is for this reason, as we have already said, that various accessibility concepts and yardsticks have been developed to analyse transport networks and their structural effects on the region concerned.

2.1. Concept and measurement of accessibility

It can therefore be said that all accessibility indicators seek to measure the distance between human activities or communities that are connected with one another by means of a transport system [Monzón, (8)]. This definition enables us to deduce the main components in any accessibility index: the measurement of the distance between any two points; the connection with the communications system which makes it possible to cover the distance between them; the "effort" (time, cost, etc.) required to cover the distance, and the connection with the particular type of activity in which the user wishes to take part.

Attention should also be drawn to the possible applications in economic geography where accessibility has been used to analyse the effects of transport and urban development plans, etc. In this case, correlations should be worked out between accessibility indicators and socio-economic or regional variables. If there is a good correlation, it will be possible to see the regional effects of improving the transport network or removing certain barriers.

Once this correlation has been worked out, accessibility can be used as an instrument for forecasting the trend in the number of business and industrial permits [Izquierdo, *et al.* (9)], the increase in population and salaries [Wendt and Kau (10)], the geographical distribution of employment [Black and Conroy (11)], population density [McDougall (12)], and economic development following the removal of barriers in the EC [Clark, *et al.* (13)].

It is not easy to describe the different yardsticks of accessibility that have been used so far since the range of cases has resulted in greatly differing formulations that seem to have little in common. Pirie (14) said it was possible that accessibility meant the same thing to everybody and that, quite simply, it could be measured in different ways, or had to be measured differently depending on the particularities or the limitations of the problem.

Looking back on the series of studies which have used accessibility indicators, we can say that this term has had the following meanings:

1. In the first studies, it simply meant the distance from one point to all the others in the reference zone. The accessibility of a point thus depended on its position in relation to the other points in the system. Accessibility therefore simply indicated proximity in the strict sense (distance) or the generalised sense (cost or time).

2. In later studies, accessibility was considered as the existing number of possibilities of taking part in certain activities. The concept had therefore widened, since it included not only the transport network, but also the need to analyse the profile of users and how attractive the various potential destinations were for them.

3. The most recent studies have identified accessibility with the net benefit accruing to a group of persons who find themselves in a given situation and are able to use a specific transport system.

The first two concepts involve a more empirical and intuitive notion of accessibility. The third is a macroeconomic type of concept complying with the theory of utility applied in regional and transport system analysis.

To sum up, it may be said that researchers have gradually developed the accessibility concept into one making it possible to explain the interrelationships between human activities, the environment and the transport system. Physical distance has thus been expanded to what might be called a "social distance" concept. This is the approach taken by Burns in his definition of accessibility (15) as a measure of people's freedom to take part in various activities (work, shopping, etc.).

2.2. The most common types of indicators

It is not easy to classify types of measurement of accessibility, since the indicators often include characteristics common to different types. However, for methodological purposes, we shall define three groups of measurement which can be divided into several types of indicators.

MEASUREMENT GROUPS	TYPE OF INDICATOR
A. Topological	-- Existence/non-existence -- Density -- Route factor
B. Aggregated	-- Gravity -- Utility
C. Disaggregated	-- Accumulated opportunities -- Life-path

2.2.1. Topological measurements

The topological measurements are the simplest and the point they have in common is that they take into account only the transport or communications network in the reference zone.

a) Existence/non-existence

The simplest type of indicator in this group is the "existence/non-existence" type. In an analysis of this kind, the reference area is divided into different sub-zones corresponding to territorial units -- municipalities, regions, types of vegetation, etc. -- or the zone is divided, for example into squares, by placing a polygonal grid on the map of the territory.

In the most recent version of the indicator, a value (1 or 0) will be allocated to each square depending on whether a means of communication exists or not. It is also possible to classify types of communications systems and use a code to denote the importance of each of them.

This indicator can be improved by weighting not only the importance of a communications system but the number of times each type of system appears in the sub-zone, or its length within the sub-zone. The result is a "composite existence/non-existence index", which brings out either aspect by means of the weightings [Nutley (16)].

COMPOSITE INDEX WEIGHTING FOR ACCESSIBILITY OF PUBLIC TRANSPORT

- Non-daily bus service	1
- Daily bus service	2
- Services for travel to work or school	2
- Afternoon and evening services (leisure)	2
- Weekend services (leisure, shopping)	2
- Access and two-hour visit to town > 5 000 inhabitants	1
- Access and four-hour visit to town > 5 000 inhabitants	2
- Proportion of inhabitants with private car (depending on %)	0-2

b) Density

Under "grid density" indicators we can include those which give the number of roads, tracks and means of communication of any kind and the surface area of the zone served. The denser the communications grid, the shorter is the distance between any two points in the zone. As in the preceding case, the zone can be divided into sub-zones and each density level can be indicated by different shading or colours, a process whereby "zonal homogeneity" and "inter-communication" between zones can be shown.

The most usual formula for the density index is the following:

$$D = \frac{\text{km of network}}{\text{Area of reference zone}} \; (\text{km/km}^2)$$

As a measurement of transport infrastructure density in a zone, this accessibility index has many variants, the most common of which are described below.

The first group comprises indicators which relate the two basic variables of network size and area of the reference zone in different ways. Rada (17) uses the following index to classify the roads in the zone according to their characteristics:

$$D = \frac{1.5\,a + b + 0.4\,c}{S}$$

where:

a = km of road over 6 m wide and with surface in good condition;
b = km of road 4 to 6 m wide and in good condition;
c = km of compact earth or macadam forest track over 4 m wide;
S = area of the reference zone in km^2.

Another possibility is to compare the size of the communications network with a territorial variable other than area, i.e. the number of localities in the zone, population density, number of inhabitants, number of industries, etc. We can also measure the size of the zone with other parameters such as the diameter, and the size of the network with the number of arcs in the graph. By using various combinations of these possibilities, a whole series of density indicators, which have been studied by Kansky (18), can be produced. Some of these indicators are as follows:

$$\beta = \frac{e}{v}$$

$$\tau = \frac{e}{3\,(v-2)}$$

$$\alpha = \frac{e - v}{2v - 5}$$

where:

e = is the number of arcs or different shadings in the network;
v = is the number of centres (localities, industries, etc.).

These indices can be used to identify the shortcomings in the communications network and define strategies to provide homogeneous conditions in all zones.

c) Route factor

The route factor is an indicator which tries to measure the quality of the route, i.e. to establish how close it is to a straight line and determine whether the route permits satisfactory travel times and conditions. It is written as follows:

$$r_{ij} = \frac{d_{ij}}{d_{gij}}$$

where:

r_{ij} = route factor between points j and i;
d_{ij} = minimum distance via the communications network from i to j;
d_{gij} = geographical or straight line distance from i to j.

To calculate the value for each point or sub-zone in the reference zone, we calculate the route factor between this point or sub-zone and all the others:

$$R_i = \sum_j \frac{d_{ij}}{d_{gij}}$$

where R_i is the route factor for centre i, which is the sum of the values of each of the routes connecting centre i with the others.

Other variants of the route factor exist and are used mainly in the study of road networks. The path-speed index (Ministry of Public Works and Urbanism,

MOPU, 1984) is one such variant which was used in the Spanish Government's General Road Plan (19). In this index, the route factor distances are replaced by travel time; the numerator takes into account actual travel time between the two points and the denominator includes the ideal time for travel in a straight line between the two points at average network speed. This index has also been used in the regional road plans (20) (see Annex).

Isoaccessibility curves are one traditional method of showing the results of accessibility studies. After the value of the indicator has been allocated to the points which represent each of the sub-zones, the curves connecting the points with the same value as the accessibility indicator are drawn by interpolation. The result is extremely instructive and offers a means of analysing accessibility in the same way as contour lines enable us to study the topography of the terrain.

Other kinds of isolines are used to show in diagram form some of the variables connected with accessibility -- distance, time and cost. Their purpose is to identify the possibilities of access to a centre in terms of distance, time or monetary cost. Accordingly, they reflect full accessibility, since they measure communication between one point and the other points in the same territory. Depending on their type, they are known as equal distance, isochrone or equal cost curves.

2.2.2. *Aggregated measurements*

They are so called because they provide joint information on a group of centres in the communications network and on their relationship with the other centres. These measurements are generally used to answer questions that are more complex than the mere location of the parts of the system within the territory. They usually include variables reflecting the behaviour of individuals, mobility standards, the main socio-economic variables, etc.

a) *Gravity indicators*

They are perhaps the best known indicators of this type and their name is derived from the similarity between their formulation and the laws of physics [Echenique, *et al.* (21)]. Their generic formula is as follows:

$$a_{ij} = \frac{O_i \, S_j}{T_{ij}^{\,x}}$$

where:

a_{ij} = zone i's relative accessibility to an activity in zone j;
O_i = origin zone i's potential for taking part in activity of j;
S_j = volume of activity in zone j;
T_{ij} = travel time, cost or distance from i to j;
x = factor describing the effect of the type of activity on the distance between i and j.

The variable representing the origin (O_i) is usually the section of the population in the zone who wish to travel to j, or the persons who may be interested in taking part in the activities at j. The variable which expresses the importance of the destination (S_j) will depend on the type of study to be carried out; it may concern the number of shops, the number of jobs, population size, hectares of forest, the number of industrial facilities, hotel capacity, etc.

b) Utility indicators

Utility models were devised to give gravity models a sounder conceptual basis. They are finally written in exactly the same way, but they are based on the measurement of the actual utility to users of potential trip destinations. Accordingly, this is a different approach from gravity models or, in other words, a different way of referring to gravity models, as the individual's decision process is examined more closely and his travel motivations are assessed.

According to Wilson (22) and Poulit (23), these indicators are written in the same way as an exponential type of gravity formula:

$$A_j = \sum_i \frac{S_j}{e^{c}_{ij}}$$

where S_j has the same meaning as the gravity indicators and c_{ij} is the cost of travel from centre i to j; e is the base of the Naperian logarithm.

The utility indicators are based on the economic theories of maximising net utility to the consumer, which is obtained by determining the entropy of the transport system [Wilson (24)].

Within this group we can include Keeble's previously mentioned peripherality measure which is written as follows:

$$P_i = \sum_{j \neq i} \frac{M_j}{D_{ij}} + \frac{M_i}{D_{ii}}$$

where:

M_i and M_j measure the volume of economic activity in the localities concerned; D_j is the distance between the two localities.

2.2.3. *Disaggregated measurements*

This group of indicators makes it possible to identify the possibilities of mobility at an individual origin point on the communications network and its possible destinations. They are used to analyse the number of destinations of a certain kind (opportunities) which can be reached from specific origin points.

a) *Accumulated opportunities*

The most common of the disaggregated measurements is the *accumulated opportunities* type. It is used to determine the number of destinations of a specific kind that can be reached within a given time by using a transport network. The basic characteristic of the individual points is their position.

According to Morris (1), these indicators are useful since they clearly show the attraction of destinations and the travel impedance, enable comparisons to be made between zones or transport modes and are both simple and instructive in diagram form.

They are generally written as follows:

$$A_i = \sum_j B_j F(C_{ij})$$

where:

B_j = the number of goods in zone j;

$F(C_{ij})$ equals 1 if $C_{ij} < C_k$
equals 0 if $C_{ij} > C_k$;

C_{ij} is the impedance measurement for the isochrone (or equal costs) with a value of k (10, 20, 30 ... minutes or monetary units).

b) Life-path type measurements

This type of accessibility measurement, developed by Hagërstrand and Thrift (25), shows the possibilities in terms of distance and time of reaching certain destinations. The accessibility measurement is given by the *prism* zone determined by daily mobility (life-path) graphs on the basis of travel possibilities and speed. It is a measurement that may prove useful in analysing specific cases of mobility from the geographical viewpoint.

2.3. Application to current planning

The above review suggests that accessibility indicators have been used in most cases on an *ad hoc* basis. The proliferation of different methods of measuring accessibility shows the lack of a generally accepted methodology. This lack of unity is obvious from the conceptual as well as the practical viewpoint.

The reason for this is perhaps that accessibility has been used to analyse quite practical problems, such as the position of shopping areas, transport centres, the path of public transport routes, or the construction of new road segments, etc. On the few occasions these indicators were used more actively in planning, it was in a sectoral context and they were very rudimentary and quite unsuitable for a precise analysis of the territorial system.

It is therefore necessary to develop sufficiently comprehensive indices that will take account of territorial variables as a whole and be flexible enough for use in the majority of cases. In addition, their application should start with strategic or inter-sectoral plans, where their full potential for territorial analysis and forecasting of future economic, social, regional development, mobility and other effects will be developed. Chapter 3 proposes some possible solutions for obtaining fuller and better results. These new models are consistent with the ideas discussed in the preceding chapter on the form that should be taken by accessibility indicators and the problems for which they should provide solutions.

As already pointed out in section 1.3, however, it must be stressed that accessibility indicators should not focus exclusively on regional analysis and the implications of possible measures as regards infrastructure, but should serve as a basis for the policy governing the allocation of economic assistance and thereby help to create the economic and social cohesion needed for the operation of the Community's internal market.

Accordingly, we consider it important to include accessibility among the criteria usually adopted in multicriteria analysis for project appraisal and selection and, for this purpose, to standardize the concepts and criteria for determining the indicators to be used in each case.

3. SHORTCOMINGS OF THE ACCESSIBLITY INDICATORS USED

In the preceding section we showed that substantial progress has been made in recent decades as regards the concept of accessibility indicators. However, most practical applications in transport planning have not taken full advantage of the indicators' potential for the purpose of regional analysis. The explanation is that, in some cases, the field of study was very limited -- to a town, a region, etc. -- while in others, not enough variables were taken into account to define adequately the complex socio-economic reality of the region concerned.

Some examples of accessibility studies conducted at European level are analysed in the following section.

3.1. Road and rail planning in Spain

For some years now, different types of indicator have been used in studies carried out in Spain concerning accessibility at both national and regional level. The relevant formulae are given in annex.

As in other countries, most of these studies focus on sectoral planning of roads and, while they have been of considerable help for decision-making, the indicators used have a number of limitations which have meant that they cannot really be used to make an accurate assessment of the territory.

First, they only take account of variables relating to topology and network capacity, such as the length of each section and the speed of its traffic. That is to say, from the standpoint of potential destinations, the same weight is given to zones which may have very good services -- and accordingly a high traffic potential -- as to less important destinations. The different reasons for travel should also be taken into account insofar as the same degree of need is not involved in every case. For example, home/work travel is much less flexible than travel for shopping or leisure.

Similar comments can be made on travel origins. Unless the population of each centre and the segments of this population who may be concerned by a certain type of travel -- such as the active population in the case of travel to work -- are taken into account, the results will not be reliable enough, since demand for mobility is directly connected with these data.

The restrictions imposed by the type of road and traffic conditions are not properly taken into account either, for there are factors which the driver allows for -- sometimes only intuitively -- and which define the "quality" of traffic. These are, for example, the degree of congestion on each section, the existence of black spots, carriageway characteristics -- number of lanes, shoulders, etc. -- the proportion of lorries, etc. These factors form what could be called each section's "opposition to traffic", which varies from case to case and may modify the minimum path sequence and even affect the decision to make a particular trip.

Everything that has been said so far refers to road planning accessibility studies. The only rail study of this kind was carried out for the Railway Transport Plan (PTF), which was approved in 1987 (26). It was a very rudimentary accessibility study and simply compared travel times on the Intercity network before and after the plan without taking account of the time spent on connections, waiting for trains and access to stations. It therefore simply analysed the reduction in travel time resulting from the new services and infrastructure improvements. In addition to the shortcomings of the road studies cited above, this study was also affected by others owing to the specific characteristics of rail operation. For example, it did not take into account the differing frequency of services on the various routes, trip time reliability, the number of intermediate stops, etc.

It can therefore be said that no sufficiently detailed accessibility studies have been conducted in Spain, for those carried out so far take account of infrastructure characteristics without referring to the territory concerned, the user classification, or the socio-economic characteristics of each of the network's main centres. This does not mean, however, that the studies have no scientific basis; the problem is that the complexity of an approach including all the above-mentioned variables is such that a detailed accessibility study is seldom warranted, especially in a very large territory, insofar as it is preferable -- at least initially -- to use only the more simple indicators so as to keep down costs and save time, even if the degree of accuracy of the results has to suffer.

3.2. Integration of European regions

Accessibility indicators have also been used to analyse the effects of the European integration process. Some studies have focused on the changes brought about in the economic situation and competitiveness of regions as new countries became signatories to the Treaty of Rome.

These studies include those conducted over twenty years ago by Clark, Wilson and Bradley, who pointed to the lack of competitiveness that would affect industries located in peripheral regions and used the following indicator to evaluate economic potential:

$$P_i = \frac{I}{M} + \sum_{j \neq i} \frac{I_j}{M + T_{ij} + F}$$

where:

Pi = potential of region i

I = income in the region

M = minimum costs

T_{ij} = cost of transport from i to j

F = price of transport.

The Department of Geography of the University of Cambridge continued the work along the same lines by assuming that economic potential also measured accessibility to economic life. Its staff worked out the following indicator [Keeble, *et al.* (3)]:

$$P_i = \frac{M_i}{D_{ii}} + \sum_{j \neq i} \frac{M_j}{D_{ij}}$$

where:

Mi and Mj measure the volume of economic activity (GDP);

Dij is the shortest distance from i to j.

$$D_{ii} = \frac{1}{3} \left(\frac{\text{area } i}{\pi}\right)^{1/2}$$

This same indicator was used to study the "peripherality" to which we referred in the first chapter.

Other studies have analysed the regional impact of specific European projects; for example, Vickerman (27) studied the impact on the economic development of the regions most directly affected by the Channel Tunnel.

Other researchers have focused on the study of certain European regions. M. Turró, of the Polytechnic University of Catalonia, has used accessibility indicators to analyse regional integration. The models constructed are a contribution to methodology which we shall explain subsequently. They endeavour to establish strategies for evaluating transport infrastructure investment so as to strengthen the overall cohesion of a zone with a view to its subsequent integration in Europe. Even if the model devised is an important theoretical contribution, its practical applications -- see Annex -- have proved unsatisfactory owing to the fact that the initial formulations used were oversimplified.

The research referred to in the paragraph above must also be improved. In the first place, sufficient allowance is not made for modal competition. In most cases, the road network is the only means of communication considered, while infrastructure capacity problems, which are very serious in certain corridors, are disregarded.

Finally, it should also be mentioned that the models used by the EC Commission, to assess the benefit to the Community of projects for which Member countries apply for funding, are inadequate to the task.

The TASC model, which is still at the experimental and review stage, does not provide in any way for accessibility. This model, which should in theory be used to allocate financial aid to projects benefiting the Community, is based on the conventional methods of measuring the consumer's "surplus" or analysing costs and benefits, without the use of multicriteria analysis.

It was only in certain studies -- conducted at the start of the TASC (1984, 1985) to see how the system worked -- that the economic assessment was supplemented by a simple multicriteria analysis that tried to incorporate the effects of projects in terms of accidents, environmental impact, regional development and energy consumption. This model never included the ways in which a project might affect the integration of a region into the Community nor criteria for estimating this effect by means of the establishment of appropriate accessibility indicators.

4. SOME MEANS OF IMPROVING THE ACCESSIBILITY MODELS USED

The shortcomings mentioned have led to work on more detailed methods of assessing accessibility, despite the fact that the problem thus becomes more complex.

Three years ago, Professor Monzón worked with Professor Izquierdo to develop a set of indicators for the assessment of accessibility for the Madrid Community Road Plan (28). An attempt was made to include in all of them the social and motivational inputs of travel. They therefore contained variables representing the influence of origin points and the attraction of destination points. An "impedance" function was also created to determine the obstacles to travel the user encountered on each section, which led to the definition of a new distance -- dij -- based on physical distance and weighted by a "friction factor" determined by a number of parameters: the width and state of the carriageway, traffic and the proportion of lorries, average speed, quality of service, level of danger, etc.

The accessibility indicators worked out for this case are written as follows:

Absolute accessibility: $$A^G_i = \sum_{j \neq i} \frac{H_i D_j}{e^{0.1d_{ij}}}$$

where Hi is a function of the origin point's population; D_j the destination and d_{ij} the generalised distance or impedance.

Depending on the reason for travel, D_j will be determined by the population of j (all travel), the number of jobs (home/work travel), the number of shops (shopping trips), etc. This indicator can be used to assess various alternatives within the same territory.

The second indicator is used to measure the differences in potential accessibility for users in different localities. It is a method of comparing the relative advantages of users in certain locations compared with others who have greater difficulty in reaching a number of destinations. The generalised distance is also used to take each section's "impedance" into account. It is written as follows:

Individual accessibility : $A^{I}_{ij} = H_i + \Sigma_{j \neq i} \frac{D_j}{e^{0.1dij}}$

where the variables have the same meaning as in the preceding case.

Another interesting contribution to methodology is the one -- already mentioned (5) -- made by CEDRE and CITRAME in a study to define a measure for regional accessibility in the Mediterranean. The accessibility index obtained consists of various terms. The first term reflects access to localities of certain size (IURB) which have extensive services and facilities. The second term (ICONEC) assesses each travel mode's connections with the transport networks. The general form of the index is as follows:

$$IACC = \alpha\ IURB + \beta\ ICONEC$$

where α and β are the respective weights for mobility compared with access to urban services, which is assessed by means of macroeconomic indicators.

The term IURB is defined as the weighted sum of access times to the province's capital (the province is taken as a zoning criterion) and to the centres of over 50 000 inhabitants within a certain radius. It is written as follows:

$$IURB = IP_{u1} * TC_{u1} + IP_{u2} * TC_{u2} + ... + IP_{cr} * TC_{cr}$$

where:

TC_{ui} = the access time to urban centre i;
TC_{cr} = the access time to the region's capital;
IP_{ui}, IPcr = the relative weight of each urban centre i and the region's capital.

The second term -- ICONEC -- refers to the connection with the four main transport networks: road, rail, port and airport. Different methods of calculation are used for goods and passengers. Times are weighted by means of quality of service indicators (frequency and regularity) and time losses on congested sections are penalised. Without going into details on the definition of each of these weighting factors, we shall give the general formulation for ICONEC:

$$ICONEC = \Sigma_i (IP_i * TC_i)$$

where:

IP_i : represents the importance of transport mode i;

TC_i : is the minimum access time from each zone to mode i.

This methodology has been applied to the Mediterranean (7), but only with the use of part of the index, i.e. the term ICONEC, which has meant the omission of reference to the importance of origin and destination points. This is a serious omission in the case of the road network, but even more so in that of the other transport modes, which are less extensive. It is not possible to assess the structural effects of ports, airports and even some rail infrastructure without including all territorial variables. This methodology has also been used, with some variants, to study the Atlantic façade (29). The formulations used for these two studies and the results are given in annex.

The Spanish Ministry of Public Works and Transport (MOPT) is now conducting preliminary work on a study on accessibility to transport networks for the four main transport modes in Spain. For each transport mode, this study again uses a combination of indices:

A: indicator for accessibility to the transport network;

B: indicator for topological accessibility to measure network quality: rough calculation of the straight line distance, communication quality, etc.;

C: indicator for accessibility to the metropolitan networks considered as economic activity centres.

Once the study is completed, it will be possible to use accessibility to assess the territorial effects of any proposal to modify one or more transport networks and thus prepare alternative investment proposals for all the networks forming the Spanish transport system.

At present, I am supervising a Madrid Polytechnic University PhD thesis that proposes a more detailed model to assess benefit to the Community. The project requires a change to the TASC model by adding a module for calculating the increase in accessibility that would be provided by the infrastructure assessed.

The aim is finally to define a new assessment instrument that will give higher priority to infrastructure projects routed across the EC regions which have a lower accessibility index, as is generally the case in peripheral regions.

It is for this purpose that an accessibility study is now being conducted in which the Pattern and Electre methods (I, II and IV) are applied to four criteria, including accessibility, in order to obtain a series of conclusions that will help to define the new funding instrument.

5. CONCLUSION

The aim of this paper is to highlight the fact that accessibility indicators have so far been used very little in infrastructure planning, and to stress the need for a methodology to obtain indicators that reflect the isolation of peripheral or landlocked regions so as to incorporate them into multicriteria analysis models and allocate Community aid in a more rational way. In this way, more could be done to ensure Europe's economic and social cohesion, link up peripheral centres with transnational transport networks and interconnect networks.

ANNEX

ACCESSIBILITY INDICATORS USED IN SPAIN'S TRANSPORT PLANS

To supplement the theoretical information given in the preceding sections, we shall now describe the main practical operations carried out for road and rail plans in Spain.

The use of accessibility indicators is relatively recent in Spain. One reason for this is the lack of planning procedures prior to investment decisions. The earlier plans were more in the form of investment programmes in which there was very little place for the processes of analysis and diagnosis discussed previously. The general lack of disaggregated data concerning a large number of variables was an additional factor; it was thus decided to conduct only very rudimentary accessibility studies, or purely and simply to drop them.

1. Initial studies by the Highways Directorate

The earliest studies in which accessibility was used as a planning instrument were carried out by the Highways Directorate's Research Section almost twenty years ago.

The first of them (30) used the following potential accessibility model:

$$A_i = \sum_{i+j} d_{ij}$$

where: n is the number of nodal points on the road network graph;
d_{ij} is the distance from i to j in average trip time.

This model was applied to a simplified graph consisting of the country's network made up of segments connecting towns with over twenty-five thousand inhabitants. It was used to assess the improvements that would result from a motorway network covering the entire country.

Another study was carried out in the following year (31) to analyse access to Galicia. In this case, the network was defined by taking localities with over ten thousand inhabitants as nodal points. This model was applied to the four Galician provinces plus Leon and the Asturias. The localities were selected on the basis of a series of socio-economic variables (population, municipal budget, number of telephones) depending on income. A potential accessibility model, similar to the one in the previous study, was used and the changes to accessibility levels from improved access in the north-west of the Peninsula were studied by estimating the changes that would occur in the socio-economic parameters for each zone.

These two studies remained at theoretical level, since the motorway plan was not carried out, nor was access to Galicia improved. However, they laid the basis for the methodology to be used in subsequent studies.

2. General Road Plan 1984-91

This was the first Road Plan -- and to date the only one -- concerning the present road network, which became the responsibility of central government following the transfer of powers to the Autonomous Communities after they had been set up.

The accessibility studies were part of the Plan Advancement phase (19) and were based on the concept of potential accessibility, which has already been described. An accessibility study involved the successive calculation of minimum distances and times between each pair of nodal points. A second phase had been planned to assess the influence of tolls on existing motorways, but it did not materialise. The 436 main towns of the regions concerned were considered as nodal points.

The indicators used were the following:

$$\text{Route index: } It_i = \sum_{i \neq j} \frac{\text{minimum trip time from i to j}}{\text{straight line length from i to j}}$$

$$\text{Route-speed index} \quad : Itv_i = \frac{\sum_{j=1}^{j=436} t_{ij}}{\sum_{j=1}^{j=436} t^{\circ}_{ij}}$$

where t_{ij} is the minimum trip time from i to j using the road network and t°_{ij} the notional time necessary to cover the distance between these two nodal points at a constant speed of 64.44 km/h, the network's average traffic speed.

These indicators were used to prepare isoaccessibility contour maps showing the level of accessibility for these 436 regional main towns. The analysis was carried out before the plan was completed. A forecast was then made by taking account of the changes in length and traffic speed that were to be introduced on each section.

3. Regional road plans

Once the procedure for the transfer of responsibilities was completed, each region -- known as an Autonomous Community -- drew up its regional road plan. Almost all these plans start with an analysis of supply and demand. In most of them, the analysis of supply includes an accessibility study.

They generally use the methodology developed by central government to which we referred above. Some regions, however, have introduced changes which we shall discuss in detail below (32) and (20).

A new indicator appearing in the plans of three of the regions -- Andalusia (20), Navarra and Madrid -- must also be added. It is known as the zonal accessibility indicator and measures each locality's accessibility to the main and intermediate centres in its region. The purpose of this indicator is to assess the ease with which smaller centres can communicate with those that are well enough equipped to meet their needs for basic services. The indicators are the same, but coverage is limited to each zone, and the potential destinations are the regional centres.

Another contribution by regional plans is the weighted route-speed index which is written as follows:

$$\text{Weighted route-speed index: } IPtv_i = \frac{1}{n} * \frac{\sum_{j=1}^{j=n} t_{ij}}{\sum_{j=1}^{j=n} t°_{ij}}$$

where t_{ij} is the minimum trip time from i to j using the road network and $t°_{ij}$ the notional time needed to cover the distance between these two nodal points at average traffic speed, and n the number of nodal points in each region or zone.

4. Accessibility of Madrid

A particular case warrants special attention. The Autonomous Community of Madrid is a region in which the capital's importance is such that it is a centre of attraction and a destination for most travel in the region. It may be said that all localities have their sights on the capital, which provides high-quality facilities and services. In addition, access to Madrid is based on the radial, high-capacity road network serving it. Radial accessibility has therefore been analysed in the Madrid Road Plan (33), the aim being to define access to the centre of the region along radial routes.

$$\text{Radial accessibility} = T_i$$

where i is each of the localities, and T_i the access time to Madrid at the average speed on each section.

A value is thus obtained for each population.

5. Accessibility of rail transport

In the studies for the Railway Transport Plan (PTF) (26), the operational changes to services and infrastructure improvements provided for higher speeds, especially on the Intercity network. An accessibility study was carried out to compare the situations before and after implementation of the Plan.

Each provincial capital's accessibility was calculated by adding the times taken to travel from each of them to all the others.

$$\text{Rail accessibility: } A_i = \sum_{j=1}^{46} T_{ij}$$

Travel time -- T_{ij} -- between each pair of provincial capitals was calculated by adding the net travel times before and after the plan; in other words, connection times and other causes of delay were not taken into account.

6. Study of accessibility in the Mediterranean Basin

We said previously that the methodology of Turró and Ulied (5) had been used in a simplified form to study the Mediterranean Basin. The simplification consisted of omitting the factor referring to urban areas. The purpose of this study was to define a measure for regional accessibility in the Mediterranean Basin. The maps give the results of the study which make it possible to identify the zones where connections with the major transport networks are most difficult.

The model is designed to evaluate the time taken for access to the various transport facilities: motorways, railways, airports and ports. The study covers Italy, a large part of Spain, southern France and western Yugoslavia. The islands were given special attention since an insularity index was defined to supplement the regional accessibility index.

The regional accessibility indicator combines within a single factor (corrected time) the distances (expressed in time) to the main transport networks and the levels of service provided by them. It is written as follows:

$$ICON = \sum_{i=1}^{5} \mu_i \left[T_{mi} + \frac{U_i - \sum_{j=1}^{n} S_{ij} * e^{(Tmi-Tij)}}{U_i}\right]$$

where:

i = the five transport modes studied;
j = the nodal points in the zone;
μ_i = the relative weight of mode i;
U_i = the minimum satisfactory level of service;
S_{ij} = service actually available;
T_{mi} = the minimum time for access to mode i's network;
T_{ij} = the access time for alternatives to minimum access time.

An insularity coefficient (IINS) was defined for the islands. It consists of two terms: minimum travel time from the island to the nearest ports and airports; and average waiting time, which is calculated as the average frequency of existing sea and air transport services to the nearest ports and airports.

7. Accessibility in the Atlantic façade

The Mediterranean Basin study led to another study on the Atlantic façade. The zones covered by this study are the south, west and north of the Iberian Peninsula, western France, Ireland and the United Kingdom.

The regional accessibility index, referred to as IAR in this case, is similar in form to that of the Mediterranean but with some changes to measure the utility of the possible destinations in terms of their connections with each transport network.

Regional accessibility: $IAR = \Sigma_i\ \alpha(i) * ICON(i)$

where:

$$ICON = (1+Ps)\ (Tm + Tu + Pg * Tg)$$

$\alpha(i)$ is the relative importance of mode i;
Ps is the penalty factor when there is no connection with a given network;
Tm is the time taken for a connection with the reference mode's network;
Tu is the utility of the connection with the network as seen in available services;
Tg is the time lost through network discontinuities;
Pg is the penalty by type of discontinuity.

The final conclusions of this study had not yet been published at the time of writing.

In the case with which we are concerned, the study compares current accessibility with the situation as it would be following certain transport investments that would give greater continuity as regards the Atlantic façade.

NOTES

1. CITRAME (Inter-Regional Committee for Transport in the Mediterranean, based in Barcelona) was set up in 1985 under the auspices of CEDRE (European Centre for Regional Development, based in Strasbourg) to enable the European Mediterranean regions to study their transport problems jointly and work out an inter-regional co-operative policy that would make a tangible contribution to Community and national decisions concerning transport.

2. At the time of writing, the study -- for which the outline is given in annex -- had not yet been published.

BIBLIOGRAPHY

1. Morris, J.M., *et al.*: Accessibility Indicators for Transport Planning. Transportation Research A, Vol. 13, Australia, 1979.

2. Commission of the European Communities. Europe 2000: Outlook for the Development of the Community's Territory. Communication from the Commission, COM (90) 544 Final, Brussels, 1970.

3. Keeble, D., *et al.*: Peripheral Regions in a Community of Twelve. DG Regional Policy, CEE, 1986.

4. Council of Europe: Resolution on transeuropean networks (90/C27/05), Brussels, 22 January 1990.

5. Turro, M. and Ulied, A.: Modelo de evaluación de la accesibilidad regional. Aplicación a la cuenca del mediterráneo. XVI Reunión de Estudios Regionales. AECR, San Sebastián, 1990.

6. Borja, J.: Ciudades y territorio. Congreso sobre problemas de las grandes ciudades en la década de los noventa. Madrid, 1990.

7. CITRAME. Definición de una medida de accesibilidad regional. Aplicación a la cuenca mediterránea. Terceras Jornadas sobre el Transporte en el Mediterráneo desde la perspectiva regional. Alghero, 1990.

8. Monzon, A.: Los indicadores de accesibilidad y la planificación del transporte: concepto y clasificación. TTC, Vol. 35. Madrid, 1988.

9. Izquierdo, R., *et al.*: Accesibilidad demográfica y renta en municipios de Cantabria. XII Semana de la Carretera, AEC. Santander, 1980.

10. Wendt, P.F. and Kau, J.B.: Predicting transportation impact in Northeast Georgia. Transportation Research Record, No. 617, 1976.

11. Black, J. and Conroy, M.: Accessibility measure and the social evaluation of urban structure. Environment and Planning A, Vol. 9, Australia, 1977.

12. McDougall, G.S.: The use of alternative measures of accessibility in estimating spatial relationships. Regional Science Perspectives, Vol. 8, Washington, 1978.

13. Clark, C. *et al.*: Industrial location and economic potential in Western Europe. Regional studies, Vol. 3, Pergamon Press, 1969.

14. Pirie, G.H.: Measuring Accessibility: A review and proposal. Environment and Planning A, Vol. 11, Australia, 1979.

15. Burns, L.D.: Transportation, Temporal and Spatial Components of Accessibility. Lexington Books, Massachusetts, 1979.

16. Nutley, S.D.: Accessibility, Mobility and Transport-related Welfare: The case of rural Wales. Geoforum, Vol. 11, UK, 1980.

17. Rada, B., *et al.*: Ordenación integral de la comarca de Albarracin (Teruel). ICONA, sin publicar, Madrid 1978.

18. Kansky, K.J.: Structure of Transportation Networks, 1963.

19. MOPU: Plan General de Carreteras 1984/91. Madrid, 1985.

20. Junta de Andalucia: Plan de Carreteras de Andalucía. Sevilla, 1987.

21. Echenique, M.: Modelos matemáticos de la estructura espacial urbana. Ed. SIAP, Chile, 1975.

22. Wilson, A.G.: A Statistical Theory of Spatial Distribution Models. Transportation Research, Vol. 1, 1967.

23. Poulit, J.: Urbanisme et transport: Les critères d'accessibilité et de développement urbain. SETRA, Ministère des Transports, Paris, 1974.

24. Wilson, A.G.: Entropy in Uurban and Regional Modelling. Pion Ltd., London, 1970.

25. Thrift, N.: An Introduction to Time Geography. Geo Abstract Ltd., Vol. 13, Noruega, 1977.

26. RENFE: Plan de Transporte Ferroviario (PTF), Madrid, 1987.

27. Vickerman, R.W.: Accessibility, Attraction and Potential: A review of some concepts and their use in determining mobility. Environment and Planning A, Vol. 6, 1977.

28. Monzon, A.: (B) La accesibilidad individual como elemento de evaluación de los planes de transporte en la Comunidad de Madrid. Informes de la Construcción, Vol. 40, CSIC, Madrid, 1988.

29. Ulied, A.: Accesibilidad regional e infraestructura de transporte: proyecto prospectivo del Arco Atlántico. CE, DG XVI, CEDRE-Universidad Politécnica de Cataluña, Barcelona, 1991.

30. MOP: Conceptos de accesibilidad en su aplicación a estudios de carreteras. Dirección General de Carreteras, Madrid, 1974.

31. MOP: Los modelos de potencial y la selección de inversiones en carreteras. Dirección General de Carreteras, Madrid, 1975.

32. Generalitat de Catalunya: Plan Regional de Carreteras, 1985.

33. Comunidad de Madrid: Avance del Plan de Carreteras, 1985.

Sub-topic 3

INFRASTRUCTURE CAPACITY AND NETWORK ACCESS

R. MARCHE
L. PAPINUTTI
INRETS
Arcueil
France

SUMMARY

Arcueil, January 1992

1. INTRODUCTION

1.1. Ease of access and capacity are two major determinants of demand formation and infrastructure management

Ease of access, and often capacity, are important factors in determining the demand for a transport network

The factors that determine the demand for a given transport network (TGV, air or urban public transport) (see Figure 1) are:

-- Demographic, economic and social factors that are exogenous to the transport system and determine "potential" demand;

-- The level of door-to-door service provided by the network in question and the ancillary networks that provide access to it at the start and end of a journey. It is therefore necessary to take account of both the level of service provided by the main network and that provided by the "terminal" networks that connect to it (see Figure 2);

-- The level of service on other networks that are competing with it for traffic.

Traditionally, the concept of network access has meant the ease with which users can enter a network at the start of their journey, in other words, the quality of service provided by the terminal networks at the start of a journey. Indicators of ease of access can be simple magnitudes such as the terminal journey time or, as will be proposed below (section 3.2.), composite indicators (of "generalised" time or costs), which seek to measure not just time but the overall level of service on terminal networks.

Obviously, it is also necessary to take into account the ease of access to connecting networks at the end of a journey, i.e. when the user leaves the network. The level of service on a terminal network is usually treated as being more or less the same in both directions, i.e. for any given point, to be the same at the start and end of a journey.

The drawback of this narrow definition of network access is that it does not give a complete picture of the situation. As mentioned earlier, what is important for any given journey, i.e. for any given point of departure and arrival, is the level of door-to-door service on all the networks that will be used in the course of the journey. Network access can therefore be defined in the broad sense as the level of service between the point of departure and the point of arrival. Furthermore, the narrow definition can give a false picture of the situation: it is necessary to take into account not only the ease with which a user can get onto a network, but also the extent to which it brings him close to his destination.

Various definitions of network access are thus possible:

-- A narrow one, corresponding to the level of service on terminal networks;

-- An intermediate one, to which can be added the ease of entry and exit;

-- A broad one, corresponding to the level of service on the entire transport system between point of departure and destination.

But, irrespective of the definition used, ease of access is linked to the level of service; it is thus an important factor in determining the demand on a given network.

The capacity of a network consists of both the capacity of the infrastructure proper and that of the vehicles using it. It will be discussed only briefly here (its various facets will be examined in more detail later). For the moment, suffice it to say that it is often an important factor in determining the quality of service on a network:

-- Insufficient capacity can result in congestion (and thus in slower-moving traffic) or reduced passenger comfort;

-- The availability or frequency of service of public transport is an important factor in the quality of service. It can be determined by both the capacity of the infrastructure and the capacity of vehicles.

The main objectives of transport network management are to improve access and to increase capacity.

As a general rule, the aim of network management, which will be described in more detail below, is to enhance the level of service, in other words, to improve access and, if necessary, to increase capacity.

Some increase in capacity can be obtained without any infrastructure investment, merely by increasing the capacity of vehicles and by improving traffic management. Often, however, it is also necessary to build new infrastructure to meet the growth of demand.

As regards ways of improving access, a network authority can usually do little to improve the level of service on terminal networks. That said, however:

-- It can participate in the construction of more efficient terminal transport facilities; for example, the French domestic airline, Air Inter, contributed to the construction of Orlyval, a light transit system connecting Orly Airport to the suburban express rail network that serves Paris;

-- When a network is being extended, it is important optimally to site the new stations that will connect the terminal networks to it, and also to ensure good connections with other transport modes.

To illustrate the latter point, we shall take the example of two French public-interest projects; it has been questioned, however, whether the various partners will benefit from them:

-- At national level, the development of Roissy Charles-de-Gaulle Airport makes it possible to link up the air transport, TGV and motorway networks, to improve connections with the terminal suburban express rail system and bus networks, and to enhance the service within the airport itself;

-- At regional level, regional transport is being reorganised around the stations of the TGV network.

On the broad definition of network access, it is obvious that a network authority can intervene more directly to improve:

-- The flow of traffic through connecting stations;

-- The level of service to the extent that it is determined by the traffic on a network; the level of service, it will be recalled, can be determined by network capacity.

1.2. Coverage of the report

It covers all types of transport network

It was decided to examine all types of transport network:

-- Networks at different geographical levels, i.e. interregional, regional and local;

-- Passenger and freight transport networks; however, freight transport will be examined only briefly.

It was decided to do this because:

-- From the methodological standpoint, it was considered useful to see whether the various concepts and methods of appraisal could be applied to different types of networks;

-- At a practical level, door-to-door transport generally involves several networks at different geographical levels;

-- Passenger and freight vehicles often use the same infrastructure, which can mean that sometimes they are competing with one another for the use of that infrastructure; conversely, however, insofar as passenger demand and freight demand occur at different times, they are complementary and can ensure that optimal use is made of capacity.

Only traffic in the physical sense will be considered

We shall focus essentially on the physical movement of vehicles. In other words, we shall examine infrastructure and the "transport services network" (traffic). Other aspects of networks, such as "legal access" to them, user information networks and internal information networks for the purposes of network management, will be considered only to the extent that they impinge upon the efficiency of the network in terms of access and capacity.

A simple presentation

We have adopted the simplest possible presentation:

-- First, we examine the role of access and capacity in determining the level of service for a given service; a few conclusions are then drawn with respect to demand formation and the economic appraisal of infrastructure (Chapter 3);

-- Second, the various aspects of infrastructure management are examined in turn: in Chapter 4 we consider the use of existing infrastructure and in Chapter 5 the construction of new infrastructure.

However, it was considered useful to begin (Chapter 2) with a review of the main practical issues that arise today and that will probably arise again in the longer term, often on a broader scale.

We have drawn upon a large body of literature, notably the findings of recent and current research by our colleagues at the INRETS, and would like to take the opportunity to thank them.

We shall try to be objective. The ideas and opinions put forward are our sole responsibility: if some of them are open to question, we hope that this will serve to generate a debate at the Symposium.

1.3. Terminology

Definitions of the main terms used

In order to circumscribe clearly the scope of this report, the concept of access is discussed in the introduction. Narrow and broad definitions of the concept are given.

Level of service and quality of service are also distinguished. By definition (see Figure 2):

-- Level of service embraces all the aspects or attributes of a transport service as perceived by the user;

-- Within the level of service, the price (or cost for "own-account" vehicles, or private and company vehicles) will be distinguished from the other factors that constitute the quality of service.

The terms "demand" and "users" will be used interchangeably to denote actual, i.e. effective or satisfied, demand.

The terms "transport network" and "transport system" can be interpreted in various ways [see, for example, (1)]. For simplicity's sake:

-- The word "network" is used in a narrow sense, i.e. to designate both a particular type of infrastructure, the type of vehicles that use it (i.e. the traditional concept of transport mode) and the geographical area that it serves;

-- "System" will thus be used to denote a set of networks.

As said earlier, the analysis will be confined to the actual physical movement of vehicles: ancillary information networks (that provide information to users, or information to the network itself) will be discussed only to the extent that they affect the level of service on a network.

Lastly, we shall try to describe the various facets of the term "network effects", distinguishing the demand-related aspects from the infrastructure-management aspects.

2. REVIEW OF THE MAIN PRACTICAL ISSUES IN THE DEVELOPED COUNTRIES

2.1. The inevitable growth of demand

It is necessary to distinguish the various categories of transport demand, particularly that for passenger transport

Broadly speaking, the following distinctions need to be made:

a) Usually, infrastructure is used by different types of vehicles;

b) There can be large differences between the component demands for the same infrastructure as regards their formation (different growth potential, different level of service requirements) and the optimal management of the infrastructure (in particular with regard to the extent to which the public interest has to be taken into account).

The use of the same infrastructure by passenger and freight vehicles is referred to under a). Under b), in the case of passenger traffic it is necessary to distinguish:

-- "Business" travel, i.e. paid for by the company; as in the case of freight transport, the efficiency (in the usual sense of the term) of this type of transport contributes to the overall efficiency of the productive system;

-- "Personal" (or private) travel, the price (or cost) of which is borne by households.

Most travel between the home and place of work, school or university is on local and regional networks:

-- The cost of it is usually borne in part by households, so it is not included in business travel;

-- But it contributes to the productive system; in other words, a decline in the quality of service amounts to a outright waste of human resources.

As the growth of demand has many adverse effects (it causes congestion, it calls for costly investment), would it be realistic to predict weak growth of demand in the future?

"Transport growth in question" is the subject of Sub-topic 1. We shall therefore consider future trends of demand only with a view to clarifying the problems pertaining to infrastructure capacity and network access.

The volume, structure and past trends of freight and passenger transport, and thus the main problems of the various transport networks, are fairly well known.

Past trends are an important guide to future trends, although it is not always easy, over a short period, to separate cyclical changes from long-term structural changes.

Explanatory models are available that take into account the various factors that determine demand (demographic, economic and social factors; level of service of the transport system). They make it possible to draw up fairly reliable medium- and long-term forecasts. They will be described in more detail in section 3.4.

These models take account of:

-- The trend of household car ownership and use (2)(3);

-- The multimodal aspect of interregional demand (4);

-- Daily travel, and thus the demand for urban transport networks: public transport (5); car use, including the demand for toll road projects (6);

-- Freight transport.

The so-called developed or "advanced" countries wish to see their economies, household income and citizens' aspirations to freedom and mobility continue to grow.

It would therefore be unrealistic not to assume strong long-term growth of:

-- Freight transport, especially of road haulage;

-- Business travel, with increased national and international travel between companies;

-- Passenger travel, whether family, leisure or holiday;

-- Education and training-related travel.

It is more difficult to foresee the trend of daily travel between home and the work place, which accounts for a large part of morning and evening peak-hour traffic, whether by public transport or car. This is because it is necessary to take account of:

-- Changes in the labour force, distinguishing part-time work from full-time work. In the long term, the problem will be not only one of jobs but also of individual behaviour (pattern of female employment, the retirement age);

-- The fact that, even within a single generation, there may be a significant shift towards "teleworking";

-- The likelihood that in the long term there will be a significant reduction in the average full-time working week.

A reduction in the working week could help to alleviate peak-hour traffic congestion. It could take two forms:

-- A reduction in the working week from five to four days for industrial and service sector jobs. This would reduce the amount of travel per working day for the relevant part of the labour force by 20 per cent. A significant number of firms could also spread their activity over six rather than five days;

-- A shorter working day coupled with flexible working hours. This could help to spread peak-hour traffic over a longer period.

2.2. Different types of demand occur simultaneously on interdependent networks, although they compete with one another only at certain times and in certain places

Simultaneously-occurring demand on interdependent networks

Networks are interdependent because users usually use several networks in the course of a journey. For example, interregional travellers on the air or TGV network will also use regional or local terminal networks in the course of their journey.

The main cases in which different types of demand can occur simultaneously on the same network are:

-- Passenger and freight traffic on the main road or rail infrastructure;

-- Regional and interregional traffic using the same motorway network. It is well known that, on many sections of motorway, regional traffic accounts for the largest share of traffic;

-- Regional and interregional traffic on the same rail infrastructure (excluding new TGV lines), using different rail networks or the same trains;

-- Local networks that serve as terminal networks for regional and interregional networks.

Fortunately, the different categories of demand come into conflict with one another only at certain times and in certain places

At the present time, the various types of demand come into conflict with one another only during the morning and evening peak hours on working days, either in built-up areas (the road network and public transport networks) or in their vicinity, in which case peak hour local traffic is added to regional and interregional traffic.

Mention should also be made of a few other cases in which congestion arises or capacity is stretched:

-- At the start and end of holiday periods, a large part of the motorway network can be paralysed for a few days by interregional demand;

-- Although there is no freight traffic during weekends, road traffic is often held up near major conurbations by local and regional traffic consisting of car-drivers going away or coming back from the weekend;

-- The capacity of rail and air networks may also be stretched at the start and end of holiday periods, or on Friday evenings (when week-end departures are added to working day return journeys);

-- On a few sections of road, demand is such that peak periods are very long, or the roads are almost completely congested at all times of the day (this is the case on the Paris ringroad and on a few sections of motorway, usually where they enter and leave major conurbations).

On the other hand, the different categories of demand are often complementary over time, since some categories avoid peak hours or periods during which traffic is heavy. This is often the case for freight transport since:

-- Lorry drivers try to avoid morning and evening peak hours in built-up areas and do not drive during weekends and public holidays;

-- A substantial proportion of interregional road freight is moved by night;

-- On busy lines the railways run freight trains during the night.

2.3. The main problems facing transport networks

Problems relating to the current quality of service

As we saw earlier, the main problems regarding the quality of service -- poor access and inadequate capacity -- are most marked in conurbations and their vicinity at peak hours. The result is:

-- Road congestion resulting from the conjunction of different types of demand. In the case of road freight transport, congestion is more of a problem for lorries when they arrive at their destination (for deliveries to intermediate and final customers) than when they set off, since the point of shipment often has better road links than the point of arrival;

-- Possibly, a reduction in comfort on dedicated urban public transport infrastructure (underground railways, express suburban rail systems, commuter trains).

It should also be borne in mind that thinly-populated residential areas (some parts of suburbs, rural areas) are poorly served by public transport networks (users have to walk or to use their own means of transport to get to the station; bus and coach services are infrequent; users have to change to get to their destination in the conurbation). As a result, people prefer to travel by car even if the traffic is bad.

Problems involved in expanding network capacity

These are dealt with in Chapter 5. For the moment, it may be noted that:

-- The aim of extending a network may be to expand capacity or to improve access for regions or areas that are currently not served by a transport network;

-- But in either case, the investment, particularly the infrastructure investment, is costly in relation to the revenue that will be generated; it is particularly costly in the case of extensions to capacity in conurbations and their vicinity, the revenue (fare or toll) generated by the infrastructure being insufficient to cover the cost if demand is light.

These problems affect road infrastructure and urban, local and regional public transport networks.

The problem of financing interregional public passenger transport networks is not an insoluble one, at least in France, since a network will be extended only if it is capable of breaking even. This is so when there is a large existing demand that is translated into effective demand as soon as the extension comes into service and when a large growth in future demand, and by the same token, revenue, is expected.

3. NETWORK ACCESS, INFRASTRUCTURE CAPACITY AND LEVEL OF SERVICE

Accurate indicators of the level of service have many uses

In this chapter we shall look more closely at the concepts of network access and level of service. We shall consider a given transport system at a given time, whose features are obviously determined by the features of the corresponding demand (see Figure 1).

Indicators of level of service will be defined. These have many uses:

-- First, they measure the performance of a transport system;

-- Second, they make it possible to identify the supply-related factors in demand and to explain their role in its formation. Incorporated in demand models, they make it possible to explain and estimate demand formation;

-- Third, with the aid of demand models, they allow the cost-effectiveness of changes in the level of service to be appraised;

-- Indicators of regional (or local) benefits will be proposed. These are particularly useful for assessing projects designed to improve the level of service.

It will be seen that these regional indicators can supplement the economic and social appraisal of the impacts of projects whose aim is to improve transport infrastructure. In particular, they make it possible to highlight the issues for the various partners and provide grounds for their decision whether to participate or not in the financing of such projects.

"Quality of service" and "level of service" have already been defined in the introduction (see section 1.3.). Figure 2 shows their component elements.

3.1. Capacity and quality of service

Network capacity -- i.e. capacity of infrastructure and that of vehicles -- is related to the capacity of the various sections of the network and to the geographical area covered by it

There is no need to dwell on this point. Suffice it to say that:

-- At any given time, or more precisely, during a particular period of a given day (e.g. the morning peak-hour period of a working day), the capacity-related components of the level of service obviously depend on the demand. It is for this reason that analysis and modelling need to use "homogeneous" periods for both supply and demand. The effects of infrastructure capacity vary according to the sections of the network;

-- On road networks (carrying car, lorry, bus and coach traffic), inadequate infrastructure capacity results in congestion; capacity and demand determine journey times. In calculating journey times, it is not enough to consider only average times, since users are sensitive to the size of the margin of uncertainty surrounding their journey time;

-- In the case of dedicated public transport infrastructure, inadequate capacity can also result in deterioration of the frequency of service. However, while it is true that inadequate capacity does contribute to congestion, its main effect is to overload vehicles and to reduce passenger comfort, which is obviously a very important factor in the quality of service. Conversely, obvious considerations of cost dictate that vehicles on dedicated public transport networks must, as a rule, have a minimum capacity and a minimum load factor. If demand is weak, the service will be infrequent; the quality of this component of the quality of service will therefore be poor.

Whether we are talking about a network of infrastructure or a network of vehicles, an extension to the geographical coverage of a network is primarily a matter of improving access as defined in the narrow sense, i.e. access to a network. But other factors also have to be taken into account:

-- As mentioned earlier, the link between the volume of demand and the frequency of service;

-- To the extent that it makes the network more dense, an extension gives users a wider choice of routes, and can thus help to improve the level of service on routes other than those served directly by the network.

Main features of the network effect

Following on from the foregoing remarks concerning extensions to the geographical coverage of networks, we shall now try to describe the main features of what is known as the "network effect", i.e. aspects of the level of service as perceived by users.

It is, of course, possible to define network effects "in absolute terms", i.e. in terms of the features that characterise a given network. But, in our view, it is more useful to analyse changes in networks, and especially extensions. We shall therefore confine our analysis to this aspect.

In the case of a network that offers "all or nothing" access, such as a telephone network, the concept of network effect is very simple:

-- A new subscriber is connected to all the existing subscribers; conversely, all existing subscribers benefit from the network being extended to new subscribers;

-- In other words, the more developed the network, the more advantageous it is for a new subscriber to join it.

Transport networks have the same effect, although it is less clear cut since in the developed countries the existing transport system already makes it possible to travel from any one point to any other. Instead of access, therefore, it is more appropriate to talk about "accessibility". The network effect can therefore be described in terms of improvements to the level of service.

A very simple definition of the network effect can be proposed: "*the network effect is the improvement in the level of service that results from an extension to a network and that benefits all the users of the network.*" We have seen that the beneficiaries of an extension to a network are:

-- Primarily the people who travel by the routes directly concerned, i.e. who travel from or to the area to which the infrastructure has been extended. This is a generalisation of the simple network effect, i.e. for a network with all-or-nothing access. It may be called the "accessibility effect";

-- But if a network is sufficiently dense, and if an extension makes it even more dense (as is the case when an area that is already connected directly to some nodes is linked directly to other nodes), a second effect comes into play. This can be called the "network density effect". To the extent that it makes possible several routes from points A to B, an increase in the overall capacity of a network will benefit users on routes that are not directly served by the extension.

3.2. Indicators of ease of access and level of service

The advantages of simple indicators of the main components of the level of service

Simple indicators measure network access in the narrow sense, i.e. the level of service on terminal networks, or the level of service on a network proper. They characterise the various components of the level of service, i.e.:

-- Price;

-- Journey time;

-- Frequency of service;

-- Number of connections;

-- The time it takes to get onto and off a given network;

-- More qualitative aspects such as comfort, the users' perception of the safety of the service, the ease with which connections can be made and, in addition to average journey times, punctuality of service and fluctuations in journey times.

We shall not discuss these indicators or the methods used to compile them at any greater length. They are used primarily for comparing network access in the narrow sense; their main drawback is that they give only a partial picture of the level of service.

This said, however, by virtue of their very simplicity they have two merits:

-- They provide an approximate measure of the level of service that can be understood by everybody;

-- They can be used for transport planning precisely because they give a simple picture of concrete magnitudes.

To cite only one example, they have been used with remarkable effect in the Netherlands (7).

More composite indicators combine measurements of monetary costs and journey times

A number of components of the level of service are "physical" magnitudes that have a simple but important property -- they can be added up. They thus make it possible to measure the level of service on the different networks used in the course of a journey, and to aggregate the consecutive levels of service. These components are:

-- Expenditures, i.e. the price of transport (or costs in the case of own-account transport), and ancillary expenditure such as parking charges;

-- Time, which by definition determines the quality of service. This can be broken down into several sub-components: journey time, the time it takes to get onto and off a network, time spent waiting for a connection, and various other times such as the "margin of safety", i.e. the amount of leeway that a traveller allows him or herself to ensure that he or she arrives on time.

It may be noted that:

-- It is usually possible to calculate average values for these composite indicators; however, the problem of the weightings to be assigned to the various time components of the quality of service arises. It is well known that the time spent in terminal transport or waiting for connections is often perceived by the user as being a greater annoyance than the time spent in vehicles on the main network, underlying once again the importance of network access;

-- Average values obviously cannot give a precise measure of the level of service, since values often vary widely across users. Thus, there may be wide variations in both physical magnitudes (for example, the price of transport will vary according to the particular tariff structure adopted, times will be subject to uncertainty) and in the degree of annoyance experienced by users;

-- Other components of the quality of service, such as the passenger's perception of comfort (or discomfort) in the broad sense of the term, or of safety (or lack of safety), cannot be translated directly into monetary costs or time.

A global indicator of the level of service -- "generalised" cost

Transport economists have traditionally aggregated the components of level of service (expenditure, time and other factors) to get a "generalised" cost. Initially, they used to employ average generalised costs, and then, from the end of the 1950s, they started to use a statistical distribution of "individual" generalised costs to take explicit account of the dispersion of values referred to earlier.

Generalised cost c is usually defined as:

$$c = d + ht + a$$

where: d = expenditure
t = components expressed in time
h = unit cost of time (hourly cost if t is expressed in hours)
a = other aspects.

It is necessary to use individual generalised costs (i.e. a statistical distribution of the values of c) based on the statistical distributions for the random variables d, t, h and a. It is necessary to take account of the correlations between these variables, especially between h and a, which are correlated with the level of income.

Obviously, the form of the expression -- the addition of the three variables d, ht and a, and particularly the product ht -- is open to question.

Better forms could be constructed if adequate data were available. As regards the product ht:

-- As mentioned earlier, the various components of t can be given different weightings; t thus denotes a total time "equivalent" to journey time;

-- In a more general formulation, t could be replaced by a function f(t).

For a given transport network and a given journey from a to b, the level of service is thus defined by the statistical distribution of generalised costs. The average value of the distribution provides a fairly simple overall indicator -- the average generalised cost. However, it should be pointed out that the generalised costs for a given network are not determined solely by the infrastructure but also by the demand on the network and on competing networks, mainly because the values of h vary from one network to another.

Figure 3 shows a very simple example of a regularly-distributed network. It can be seen that the average ease of access changes as one moves away from the centre to the outlying poles.

The "generalised cost" makes it possible to design simple demand models

If we know the total demand on a given route from a to b (including the statistical distributions of the individual values, particularly of h):

-- The split of demand between modes, between routes and even between the times of transport services, mirrors the breakdown of minimum generalised costs;

-- It is possible to take account of the "new" (or "induced") demand in the modal split since it is shown by a demand curve that varies with the generalised cost.

Obviously, the complexity of such models will vary according to the statistical distributions of individual generalised costs that are selected, and because the individual generalised costs of different modes are correlated with one another. Furthermore, in setting the parameters of a model to reflect an existing situation, it is necessary to take account of induced demand.

Lastly, mention should be made of two familiar problems that arise when major modifications to transport infrastructure are envisaged:

-- How will the changes to the infrastructure on certain routes affect total demand (i.e. the total demand generated) and its split between destinations, i.e, the spatial distribution of demand?

-- How can due account be taken of the short and long-term effects of the modifications? It is assumed that the long-term effects resulting (at least partially, although to what extent it is not known) from the modifications, will be structural, i.e, that they will change the pattern of residence, the location of activities and the pattern of trade between locations.

Neither of these problems has been resolved satisfactorily because sufficiently detailed and comparable historical data covering a very long period are not available. In any case, an even more fundamental difficulty arises when one tries to separate the effects of the two categories of factors that determine demand -- demographic, economic and social factors, and infrastructure-related factors.

The economic appraisal of projects on the basis of generalised costs

In appraising a project, i.e. a modification to network infrastructure that will alter generalised costs, the generalised cost-demand curve referred to earlier (which, it will be recalled, takes account of the "diverted" demand and the "induced" demand that will result from the project) allows two major parameters to be estimated:

-- The network operator's revenue, which is equal to the volume of demand multiplied by the price of transport adjusted appropriately (e.g. by adding taxes);

-- The user or consumer surplus, which Jules Dupuit, engineer and economist, defined and applied to transport in the middle of the last century.

The user surplus is defined as the excess of the use value (the generalised cost that the traveller is willing to pay) over the generalised cost.

The demand curve is, by definition, the cumulative curve of use values.

It is thus simple, in principle, to estimate the user surplus from the demand curve.

Project appraisal also takes into account other factors that are components of the overall economic surplus (8):

-- For a given network -- the cost (investment and operating costs); the producer's surplus is the excess of revenue over costs;

-- For competing or complementary networks -- the producer's surplus and the user surplus;

-- The government's surplus in the form of the tax revenue generated by the project;

-- The "environmental" surplus, corresponding to the external cost of the disamenities resulting from the project.

Generally speaking, economic appraisal in the broad sense (also referred to as socioeconomic appraisal) usually gives a higher rate of return than the financial rate of return because of the high value that it assigns to the user surplus.

In other words, by taking into account the user surplus, it is possible to assess the overall benefit that will accrue to the community from a project; this benefit will exceed the financial return.

The benefit to the community can also take the form of "capital gains" on land or property. As the user surplus and capital gains are two sides of the same coin, they should not be double counted. However, Jacques Lesourne (9) has shown that it may be warranted to add some of the capital gains to the economic surplus.

3.3. Compiling indicators of regional benefits

It is proposed to calculate the user surplus on a regional basis

It seems useful to try to break down the benefits to the community that would result from a project, as measured by the user surplus, on a regional basis. For example:

-- In the case of an extension to the TGV network, the areas in question would be regions or *départements*. By adding up the regional benefits in individual countries, we would arrive at the national benefits that would result from a European project;

-- For a transport project in a conurbation, the relevant areas would be local authorities.

In the case of a journey from a region of residence A to another region B, it seems reasonable to consider that the user surplus benefits both region A (i.e. that the residents benefit directly) and region B, the beneficiaries here being households (relations or friends who are being visited) or businesses (including other types of personal trips and business trips).

Should the same user surplus be assigned to the two regions -- i.e. should it be divided equally between them? This question would need to be examined more closely.

However, it may be noted that if the same value is assigned to both regions, there is no need to reconstitute journeys in order to distinguish region A, i.e. the region of residence, from region B, i.e. the destination. All one has to do is to calculate the user value for each section of the journey; there is no need to distinguish the beginning and end of section.

We have concentrated on the user surplus. But obviously, it would also be necessary to calculate user costs and expenditures on a regional basis in order to ascertain more clearly the beneficiaries of a network or the beneficiaries of any extensions to it.

This kind of regionally-compiled data also makes it possible to describe another aspect of the network effect -- the regional structure of beneficiaries.

Figures 4 to 6 illustrate a very simple linear network which is progressively extended. They show:

-- the network effects as measured by the traffic on the various sections of the network (Figures 4 and 5);

-- the regional benefits that accrue to the various poles (Figure 6); it can be seen that the poles benefit from the network and from the extensions to it.

3.4. Demand models

Two models recently developed in France -- MATISSE and DAVIS-TRIBUT-Equilibre

These models were developed for the purpose of estimating satisfactorily the demand for two major types of infrastructure -- the TGV network and toll urban expressways.

The MATISSE model was developed by Olivier Morellet and his team (4). It was designed specially for estimating the multimodal structure of interregional demand (TGV, air, motorway and interregional coach networks). Applications to French and European projects are being developed.

The main features of the model are the following:

-- It is based on an estimate of individual generalised costs. The components of these costs that are determined by the characteristics of users and their journeys, and their correlated statistical distributions, are incorporated explicitly in the model;

-- It takes induced demand into account;

-- It makes it possible not only to estimate the daily demand for the main modes of transport (rail, air, car and coach) but also takes into account the class of rail travel, whether or not toll motorways are used, and simulates the time distribution of traffic during the day and night;

-- Currently, the software cannot estimate the user surplus. However, it could be upgraded to do so later.

The DAVIS-Equilibre model, and subsequently the TRIBUT-Equilibre model, were developed by François Barbier Saint-Hilaire (6). These models were used to estimate the demand for major toll urban expressway projects such as that on the northern section of the Lyons ring road, the completion of the western section of the Ile-de-France ring road (A86) and other projects in the Ile-de-France region.

Its main features are:

-- It is a static "capacity-constraint" model. The time distribution of traffic is assumed to be homogeneous. More precisely, it is assumed that the flow of vehicles remains virtually constant on each section of the network;

-- It is based on individual generalised costs as expressed by the following equation: $c = p + ht$, where p equals toll, h equals unit value of time, t is an "equivalent" time that sums all the other components (cost of traffic; journey time, for which the idea of "guaranteed" time is introduced; comfort and safety bonus). In practice, the model uses the generalised times $T = t + p/H$;

-- Currently, it does not take account of induced demand. In most cases, however, this will be fairly modest since it will be curbed sharply by the toll; it can thus be evaluated approximately later;

-- The output generated by the model makes it possible to draw demand/toll curves from which the induced demand and user surplus can be estimated;

-- Experience has shown that these demand curves can be approximated by means of simple exponential functions. With the aid of these functions it is easy (10) to estimate the elasticity of demand with respect to the toll, the optimum toll (i.e. that generates maximum revenue), the user surplus, and the sensitivity of the results of the simulation to the various parameters, particularly to the average value of the distribution of the unit values of time h.

Future areas for model development

In the medium term, the aim should be to develop models sufficiently robust to handle the problems and issues that arise. Two general comments may be made in this connection.

First, regarding the type of model needed, it will probably be necessary to develop "dynamic" models of urban traffic that take account of spatial and temporal changes in demand, traffic flows and the effects of traffic conditions on the level of demand and routes, and also the links and nodes of the network (11). It would be necessary:

-- not only to abandon the assumption of homogeneity on which static models are based;

-- but also to design the models for other purposes such as traffic control.

Naturally, these models should be developed from existing models. It would also be desirable to increase international co-operation in this area.

Second, it would be necessary to improve the estimates of the parameters of existing models, using either existing or new types of statistical surveys. In particular:

-- Regarding interregional passenger transport, the MATISSE model could be expanded by incorporating data from new databases, especially with a view to estimating European-wide "departure-destination matrices". Possible sources of data for interregional travel in France would be: the update in 1993-94 of the "Transports" survey by the INSEE, border surveys by the *Direction du Tourisme*, and the surveys to be carried out as part of the "before-and-after monitoring" for the Channel Tunnel and the TGV Nord;

-- Regarding toll expressways, it would be very useful to carry out a thorough "before-and-after monitoring" of projects that are soon to come into service (the Prado-Carénage Tunnel in Marseilles, the northern section of the Lyons ringroad), with a view to estimating better those parameters that are still subject to a very large margin of uncertainty, notably the unit values of time.

4. MANAGING THE CAPACITY OF EXISTING INFRASTRUCTURE

In this chapter, we shall look briefly (since they are dealt with under other sub-topics) at the ways in which the capacity of existing infrastructure can be increased, notably by introducing new technologies (section 4.1.) and, if capacity is inadequate, the ways in which demand can be better matched to supply (sections 4.2. and 4.3.).

4.1. New technologies

To what extent is it possible to increase capacity, particularly that of indicated public transport infrastructure?

There are obviously two possible ways of increasing capacity: one can increase the capacity of vehicles or the frequency of services.

An increase in the capacity of vehicles (aircraft, trains) is all the more advantageous in that it often makes it possible to achieve economies of scale on operating costs. However, there is a limit to the extent to which capacity can be increased in this way; for example, the length of platforms in underground stations sets a limit to increases in the capacity of underground trains.

Train traffic control systems make it possible to reduce the intervals between trains while seeking to improve safety and punctuality. Train speeds and the length of interval between trains are linked to one another, which means that, in seeking to optimise the quality of service, an operator may have to make a trade-off between journey times and the frequency of trains.

4.2. Regulating demand

The two chief features of the level of service on a network -- cost and quality of service (time and comfort) -- impinge upon demand either by changing its level (i.e. by inducing demand) or by changing the times at which people travel.

Advantages and drawbacks of charging for the use of infrastructure

Economic theory enables the issues to be set out clearly provided that the aims are clearly defined (8), i.e.:

- If the aim is to maximise public welfare as measured by the criterion of economic surplus, the charge for using infrastructure should be set at a level equal to the marginal cost of production and, more broadly, to the social marginal cost;
- If the aim is to balance revenue and expenditure, Ramsay-Boiteux-type pricing should be used.

In practice, the systems adopted may vary quite widely, depending on the circumstances. We shall look at a few aspects of infrastructure pricing that seem important to us.

Regarding the use of road infrastructure, it is useful to compare expenditure by users (travel costs, tolls, fuel taxes, etc.) with the social marginal cost (costs of road congestion and accidents, external costs) and to examine whether users' expenditures also cover the cost of network extensions. It is known (12) that:

-- Situations vary markedly from one country to another;

-- At national level, cars and light vehicles cover social marginal costs, and even development costs, by a wide margin. Lorries, however, do not;

-- Situations also vary from one area to another; it may be considered a desirable aim of regional development that one area should cross-subsidise another to a certain extent.

Interregional passenger (air and rail) transport seeks to balance revenues and expenditures and permits a large element of cross-subsidisation between areas.

A more detailed analysis should be made of the spatial structure of user costs, expenditures and surplus so as to:

-- Show the regional breakdown of user costs, expenditures and surplus (see section 3.3.);

-- Verify whether the spatial cross-subsidisation by the various transport modes is desirable from the point of view of promoting vigorous intermodal competition.

It seems to us that it is perfectly warranted to vary the price for the use of infrastructure according to the time that it is used, so as to spread peak demand over a longer period:

-- Such a system has been in use for many years for interregional air and train transport, and is warranted by the structure of costs -- i.e. the volume of investment (particularly for vehicles) is determined by the peak period volume of traffic, and operating costs;

-- In France, charges will soon be introduced on an experimental basis on very congested sections of motorways, particularly at the end of weekends. It will be interesting to see whether the structure of charges corresponds closely to social marginal costs.

Urban and local public transport services are usually highly subsidised by local authorities and by contributions from enterprises. Such subsidies:

-- have a social aim -- to ensure that the budgets of low-income households are not overburdened;

-- but reflect the local interests referred to earlier (see section 3.3.).

Urban road infrastructure both carries traffic and is used for parking. Parking charges can thus be used to increase the capacity of the road network. For example, Paris recently introduced a system of "red roads", i.e. with parking charges. The main factors to be taken into consideration are:

-- The cost of parking on the highway is very high; it is often necessary to add to the land value of the roads themselves the indirect cost arising from the fact that drivers who are looking for somewhere to park or to re-enter the flow of traffic disrupt traffic;

-- It is usually possible to expand parking capacity by building underground car parks. Admittedly, the costs are high but still about the same as the total costs of surface parking facilities.

If prices are to reflect costs properly, high parking charges are therefore needed:

-- By and large, car drivers are willing to pay high charges for short-stay parking. High parking charges could also reduce the demand for car travel to a certain extent;

-- Local authorities can introduce special low charges for residents.

Lastly, personalised charges could be introduced, with:

-- Reductions for regular users, as part of the infrastructure operator's commercial policy;

-- Reductions on social grounds for certain categories of the population.

To sum up:

-- Provided that it is founded on clear economic principles, infrastructure pricing has many advantages;

-- However, it may be warranted to limit its application in order to achieve clearly-defined objectives -- for example, general considerations of regional development, local interests, social goals.

A situation in which road traffic regulates itself by creating traffic jams is wasteful of resources

A crude indicator of the efficiency of the road infrastructure in a given area is the time wasted in traffic jams. However, we consider that it is more appropriate to appraise efficiency in terms of economic surplus. Francis Papon designed a general model (PRESSE) for appraising the impact of modifications to road infrastructure in built-up areas (investment, pricing), which takes account of the effect on the demand for public transport (13). This model was recently applied in the Ile-de-France area (14).

The results of the appraisal of the impact of an urban road toll were particularly eloquent. Assuming that the toll is proportional to the number of passenger-kilometres, in 1988 the maximum overall economic surplus would have been obtained with a toll of about FF2 per passenger-kilometre; compared with the existing situation without any toll, the surplus would be between FF5 and FF10 billion a year, say about FF7 billion given the uncertainty surrounding the values of some parameters, particularly the unit costs of time.

Merits and drawbacks of regulating access to networks

Here, we are talking essentially about restrictions on access to road networks.

Restrictions do exist for lorries. They are not allowed to use motorways during the weekends and public holidays, and deliveries in towns are restricted to certain times. Obviously, it can be argued that such restrictions reflect the fact that road freight transport does not bear all the costs of infrastructure use. And as mentioned earlier (see section 2.3.), lorry drivers try to plan their journeys so as to avoid the times when the roads will be busy. It is our view that more detailed analysis would be needed to estimate more precisely the direct and external costs of road transport. If the pricing of road freight transport reflected better the costs that such transport generates, it would not only promote intermodal competition but would also be in the long-term interests of the haulage profession.

Certain roads that feed into urban expressways are closed when traffic is heavy. But this is a very primitive way of controlling traffic. Admittedly, it improves greatly the flow of traffic and journey times on expressways, but to the detriment of the drivers who are denied access to them, and to users of local roads.

Lastly, as regards the use of parking restrictions to improve the flow of traffic, it is necessary to strike a balance between supply and demand, and to set parking charges at a level that reflects costs.

4.3. User information

The provision of clear information about traffic conditions can help users to choose their route and the best time to travel

It is necessary to improve the content and dissemination of information to users of the various transport modes, particularly of road transport, both before they set off and in the course of their journey. This could be done by introducing new technologies.

5. TO WHAT EXTENT CAN INFRASTRUCTURE INVESTMENT IMPROVE NETWORK ACCESS AND CAPACITY?

In this section we shall focus on the ways in which infrastructure investment can improve network access and capacity.

First, as regards capacity, ways of improving the management of existing capacity and decisions whether to make new investments need to be considered simultaneously within a coherent framework of appraisal, due account being taken of their spatial and temporal impacts, as mentioned earlier. The tools of economic analysis needed to make such appraisals do exist; notwithstanding the uncertainty surrounding certain parameters, it is possible to make at least an approximate appraisal.

Future transport modes, such as very high-speed trains or high-speed guided vehicles that would operate on motorways, will not be considered here. However, the tools that are used for appraising existing modes would also be valid for them.

5.1. Ease of access and capacity -- two conflicting or complementary objectives?

At first sight, the aim of expanding a network is either to improve access or to improve capacity; however, this statement needs some qualification

For networks like the TGV that were built relatively recently, access will improve as the network is gradually extended. This kind of extension involves expanding both the infrastructure (i.e. the new lines) and the services (i.e. the trains, which are run in part on existing, though possibly upgraded, infrastructure, often on the assumption that new lines will be built in the future).

In the case of networks that are already extensive, such as motorways, the aim of an extension may be to improve access for regions that have poor transport links (i.e. to promote regional development) or to increase capacity on links that cannot take any more traffic:

-- In taking an investment decision, it is thus possible to choose between these two objectives;

-- In fact, however, they do not necessarily have to conflict with one another but can also be complementary, by virtue of the fact that an extension will increase the density of the network; for example, in response to the need to increase capacity on north-south routes in France, rather than increasing the capacity of existing motorways, it was decided to build new north-south links that would simultaneously serve the Massif Central and the Alps.

Special mention should be made of "missing links" such as the alpine tunnels for the TGV network:

-- These would overcome a natural barrier and improve connections between two vast regions;

-- They would generate a large demand that would in turn generate revenue on many other sections of the European network (this could be called the "missing link effect"), which would make it possible to finance very costly infrastructure.

The toll urban expressway projects now being implemented, which were referred to earlier, may also be regarded as completing missing links, as were also the numerous toll viaducts and tunnels built in the past that made it possible to overcome natural barriers (estuaries, mountains). Examples of current projects are:

-- An expressway completing the northern part of the Lyons ring road; a similar road will probably be built later on the western section;

-- An expressway completing the Ile-de-France ring road to the west;

-- A project to increase capacity on the Paris ring road, which is highly inadequate on the southern and eastern sections, by building an underground bypass.

5.2. The need for a global view of the transport system and land use

We would like to make three remarks in this connection.

Projects should be appraised from a multimodal perspective

In appraising the economic aspects of a project, it is necessary to take account of its impacts on other modes and on projects that might be envisaged for other modes, due weight being given to the spatial and temporal considerations referred to earlier.

Demand models confirm that car and public transport users often constitute fairly distinct segments of demand, i.e. transport modes are more often complementary than in competition with one another. In other words, major road infrastructure projects do not necessarily rule out ambitious public transport projects.

Transport projects need to be appraised in the light of clearly defined land use objectives

Everybody agrees on this. In practice, however, things are less simple, especially in the case of transport projects in built-up areas:

-- Local authorities usually seek to attract as many economic activities as they can with the praiseworthy aim of creating jobs and of raising the income of residents; also, they often seek to attract population;

-- In the past, the rate at which land was set aside for transport infrastructure (for cars and collective surface public transport) in built-up areas was not sufficient to keep pace with the growth of the population and travel, the long-term expansion of which was underestimated; for this reason, it is now often extremely costly to extend surface infrastructure;

-- Paradoxically, surface land use can be improved by underground infrastructure projects. These make it possible to "claw back" part of the road network for other uses with a higher economic and social utility -- bus lanes, pedestrian precincts -- and to reduce traffic on secondary roads, with a corresponding improvement in the quality of life.

It is necessary to take a long-term view

First, it should be said that the future growth of demand and revenue on a network (TGV, toll roads) will often determine to a large extent whether the network will be financially and economically profitable.

Particularly in the case of transport infrastructure in built-up areas, short-term projects involving extensions to networks should be conceived within the framework of long-term transport needs based on an overall plan of land use and demographic and socioeconomic projections.

5.3. Effective and partially effective demand

Would it be feasible to ration telecommunications or electricity consumption in developed countries?

Of course not. But in that case, why should we hesitate to carry out transport projects that meet the needs of society (by contributing to the efficiency of the productive system and satisfying the desire for mobility and well-being), and for which there is an effective demand?

A good example of an infrastructure project for which the demand was only partially effective when it was decided is the expressway completing the northern section of the Lyons ringroad

This toll urban expressway, which is scheduled to come into service in 1994, is a good example of a project that was decided when the demand for it was only partially effective:

-- It consists chiefly of tunnels and a viaduct, and is dimensioned (clearance and number of lanes) to cope with all types of road vehicle, hence the high construction cost;

-- Even on the assumption that the toll, and thus revenue, will rise steeply in the future, the *Communauté Urbaine de Lyons* will still have to contribute to ensure that the project breaks even.

The fact that the local authority is willing to contribute to the cost of the project shows clearly that it has taken into account the benefits that will accrue to the community.

Underground toll expressway projects in the Ile-de-France region; the demand for the first projects will probably be effective

The two major projects referred to earlier -- the underground bypass for the Paris ringroad and the expressway completing the Ile-de-France ring road to the west -- are urgently needed. Both of them will probably come into service some time between 1995 and 2000.

They have been designed for cars and small utility vehicles; the design is based on the LASER concept proposed in 1987 by GTM-Entrepose, namely:

-- A tunnel ten metres in diameter, containing two roads on top of one another, one for each direction of traffic;

-- Once the tunnel has been in service for a few years, the main section could operate with three lanes. For the first few years, traffic could be limited to two lanes, the third being kept for use as an emergency shoulder in case of incidents or accidents. In the medium term, the decision whether to open a third lane or not would be taken on the basis of the number of incidents that had occurred;

-- A tunnel of the same diameter, which would be used by light vehicles and lorries and would have only two lanes.

-- The LASER concept thus makes it possible to achieve at least twice the capacity of a conventional structure for the same cost, the diameter of the tunnel being the main factor that determines the cost.

Despite the uncertainty referred to earlier concerning the hourly values of time, studies have shown that there would be an effective demand for these expressways even with fairly high tolls (about FF 2 to 3 per km) that would rise steeply later.

Other projects are under consideration, notably an underground urban expressway (MUSE) which is being built by the *Département des Hauts-de-Seine*.

With the aid of the PRESSE model referred to earlier, Francis Papon has shown (14) that an ambitious road infrastructure programme could be financed with a toll of about FF 2.5 per km, and that it would generate a substantial economic surplus that could exceed FF 10 billion a year.

5.4. Ways of financing investment

The road and rail projects that will be built in the next few decades will contain a lot of tunnels. The economic appraisal of such projects, in the present state of the art, is clearly subject to a large margin of uncertainty concerning:

-- The construction costs, notwithstanding the experience that has already been gained with large tunnels;

-- Estimates of demand and revenue in particular.

Three key determinants of the financial profitability of a project will be discussed below.

Reasonable interest rates, long pay-back periods and a steep increase in tolls over time

We shall show how these three factors affect the present worth of future revenue. The first year in which the project comes into service will be taken as the date from which revenue is discounted to present value. Interest rates and revenue are expressed in real, i.e. constant, terms.

First, we shall consider constant annual revenue equal to R:

-- With an interest rate as high as 10 per cent, over 20 years the length of the pay-back period n does not make much difference: the present worth of income rises from 9.4 R for n = 20 years to only 10.4 R for n = 30 years;

-- With a more realistic rate of 7 per cent corresponding to market rates (in our view, the "margins" for the project should not be decided on the basis of the interest rate), the length of the pay-back period has a more marked effect on revenue: R rises from 11.3 for n = 20 years to 13.3 for n = 30 years.

The optimum toll, i.e. which generates maximum revenue, rises steeply over time for two reasons (10):

-- It is reasonable to assume that the hourly values of time will rise with revenue, since the demand models show that an optimum toll is nearly proportional to the average hourly value of time;

-- The demand models also show that there is a high degree of elasticity of the optimum toll and revenue with respect to total demand; even a moderate growth of total demand, say 1 per cent a year, would result in a significant increase in optimum revenue, of about 2 to 3 per cent, in addition to the revenue effect.

It will therefore be assumed that revenue will grow in a linear fashion (linear growth being more realistic in the long term than exponential growth); we shall take the example of a 5 per cent rate of growth at the start of the pay-back period, between the first and second years, which corresponds to growth of 95 per cent from the first to the twentieth year, and 145 per cent from the first to the thirtieth year.

This rate of growth increases substantially the present worth of future revenue; with an interest rate of 7 per cent:

-- for n = 20 years, we would get R = 15.5;

-- for n = 30 years, we would get R = 19.8, i.e. more than twice the corresponding revenue for a pay-back period of 20 years with an interest rate of 10 per cent.

In Japan the toll roads in Tokyo and Osaka, and the Tokyo Bay project, were financed in a similar way, i.e.:

-- The interest rates are very low; the interest rate subsidies that were granted showed that the local authorities took account of the fact that the community would benefit from the projects;

-- The pay-back periods are very long, as much as 40 years;

-- The tolls will increase over time.

5.5. Political and social problems that have to be resolved

We shall take the example of urban expressways once again.

An important social aspect -- the redistributive effects of road pricing

Because the hourly values of time are correlated with level of income, infrastructure pricing has redistributive effects. A flat-rate toll on urban roads of the kind examined in section 4.2. would have very large redistributive effects.

But if tolls were charged only on new roads and users could choose between new expressways and ordinary roads, the effects would be more limited, since:

-- As most users of toll expressways would be business travellers, the main effect of the tolls would be to contribute to the efficiency of the productive system;

-- Users of both expressways and ordinary roads would benefit; most car drivers seem to have realised that there would be a PARETO-type gain, and are thus not hostile to pricing;

-- As was pointed out in section 5.2., the traffic siphoned off by the new roads would make it possible to "claw back" part of the ordinary road network for uses that are of more benefit to the community than toll-free car traffic.

The "political" problems are mainly local

The costs and benefits of a project, particularly savings on journey times, comfort, safety, noise and pollution, can be clearly identified. Even if they are quantified only approximately, this is enough for the purposes of decision-making and for allocating the financial risks and possible benefits reasonably and clearly between the various partners. Also, the experience gained on the first projects, notably with regard to demand and revenue, will allow subsequent projects to be defined more clearly.

On the long-term assumption that a network of efficient urban toll expressways (similar to an interregional motorway network) will gradually cover the suburbs of large towns, in those areas where it is still possible to do so land should be put aside accordingly. There are two obvious reasons for doing this: it would reduce, where possible, infrastructure costs and users of toll roads would not have to spend too long in tunnels.

It is at local level -- in the vicinity of cloverleaf junctions -- that the difficulties are likely to arise. Local communities would be apprehensive about the extra through traffic that would result from the construction of an expressway. Indicators of regional and local benefits of the type described earlier (see section 3.3.) could be constructed to help to clarify the issues. But within the perspective of the long-term expansion of the network, the problem of through traffic is likely to become less important.

6. CONCLUSIONS AND RECOMMENDATIONS

6.1. New problems call for innovative solutions within a long-term perspective

It is the scale, not the nature, of the problems that is new

The growth of travel and freight transport was underestimated in the past. Such growth is not an evil but a reflection of economic and social development.

Innovative solutions will call for new technologies, road pricing and new methods of financing

New technologies do not mean only new modes of transport. They also include innovations to improve safety and external costs, traffic control and user information systems and new infrastructure construction techniques.

In major conurbations it will be possible to meet demand only by implementing ambitious public transport and road infrastructure projects. Road pricing is fully justified, both economically and socially, especially if in the long term it is planned to have two networks -- one consisting of toll expressways, the other toll-free.

With regard to financing, we have underlined the importance of three factors: the need for realistic interest rates; the need for a long pay-back period on account of the long service life of the infrastructure; the need to raise tolls in line with income levels and the growth of demand.

6.2. New project appraisal methods and models

Satisfactory demand models exist but they need to be improved

Demand models are the basis of project appraisal. Earlier we mentioned the need for dynamic models to simulate traffic on congested roads.

Project appraisal can be improved primarily by improving the numerical values of certain parameters

Obviously, the main parameters concerned are the hourly values of time and external costs.

Indicators of regional and local benefits require more study

6.3. Information and consultation: the need for selection criteria that are defined clearly and accepted by the various partners

Project appraisal must first set out the costs and advantages

Information can be complete and meaningful only if:

-- All the costs and benefits (direct, indirect and external) are listed;

-- They are quantified, insofar as that is possible, and the basis on which they were calculated and the margin of uncertainty to which they are subject are stated clearly.

Naturally, the aim of project appraisal is to calculate the financial rate of return and the economic rate of return in the broad sense of the term

Of course, the financial appraisal of a project can be subject to wide margins of uncertainty given the uncertainty attaching to future demand. It is therefore desirable to evaluate these margins of uncertainty with a view to defining more clearly the "rules of the game" that will bind the various partners, especially as regards the allocation of risks and benefits, including the actual allocation in the future.

It is usually even more difficult to estimate indirect or external costs. But approximate values, or even proxies, should be sufficient to evaluate the "collective rate of return", to highlight the issues involved and to lay the basis for the possible participation of central and local governments.

FIGURES

Figure 1. **Factors that determine transport demand**

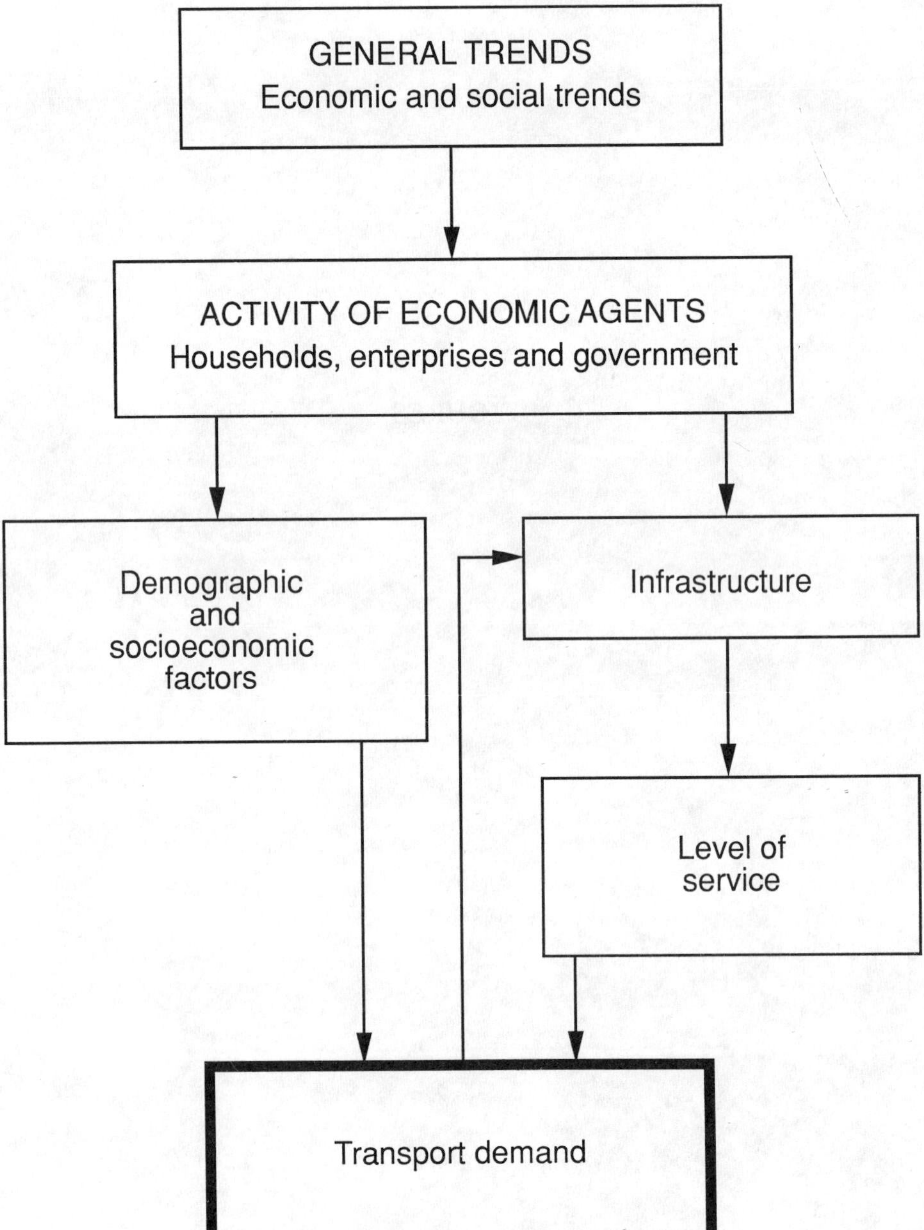

Figure 2. Level of service

(For a given network and its terminal networks)

1. TRANSPORT EXPENDITURE

2. QUALITY OF SERVICE

2.1. -- Time component

- Journey time, time spent in stations and waiting for connections;
- Waiting time imposed by the frequency of service;
- Margin of safety the user allows for a journey.

2.2. -- Comfort and safety component

- Number of changes and quality of changes;
- On-board comfort and safety.

Figure 3. **Indicators of ease of access in the broad sense in a hexagonal network with 19 poles**

Assumptions:

— Equidistant adjoining poles
(unit of measurement is distance = average generalised cost)

— The indicator of ease of access for a pole corresponds to the average distance between that pole and the other 18 poles.

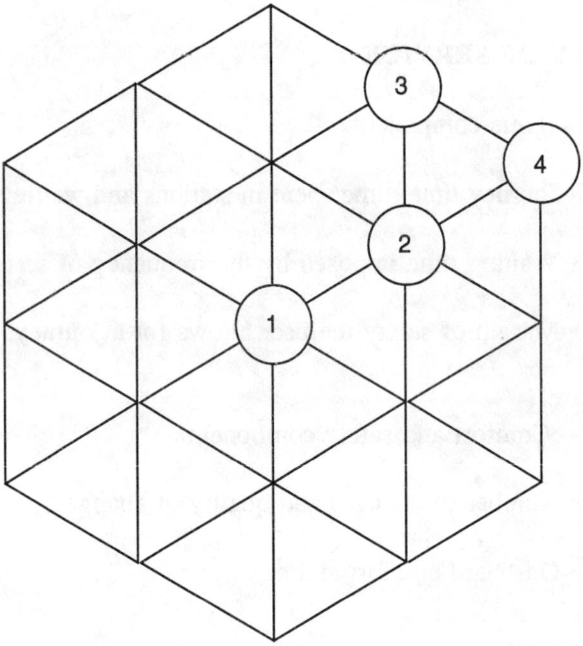

Type of pole	Number	Indicators of ease of access					
		Between poles			Avec somme des deux distances terminales = 1		
1	1	1,67	100,00	73,66	2,67	100,00	81,73
2	6	1,94	116,62	85,90	2,94	110,39	90,22
3	6	2,28	136,65	100,65	3,28	122,91	100,45
4	6	2,67	159,99	117,84	3,67	137,50	112,37
Total	19	2,263	135,8	100	3,263	122,4	100

Figure 4. **Network effects: extension to a linear network**

A. Traffic per link

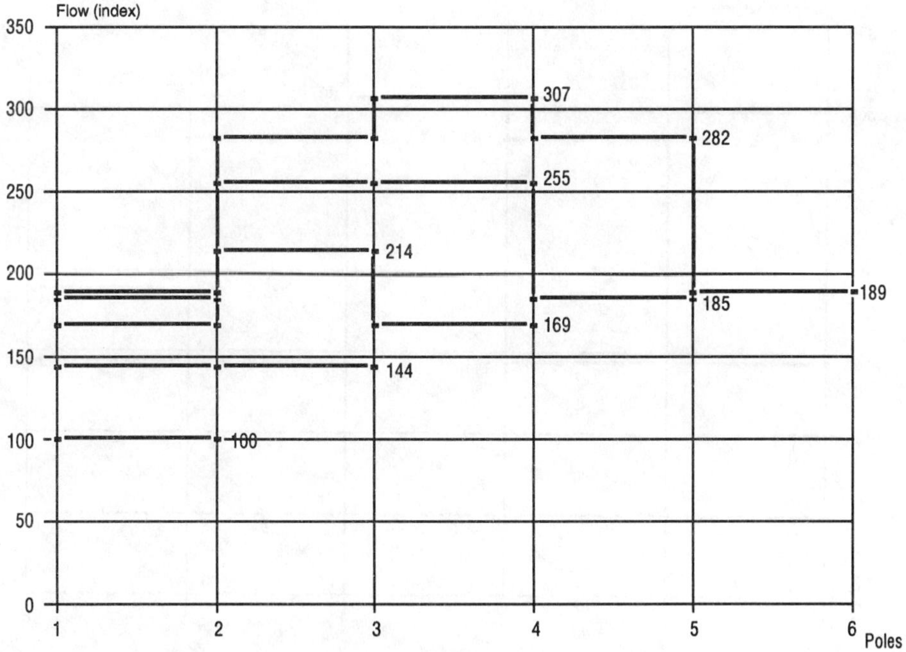

Basic assumptions (H) :

— Poles are of the same size
— Units are links of the same length (average generalised cost)
— Terminal transport is included: $d = d_0 + d_1 + d_2$ (example is with $d_1 + d_2 = 1$)
— Elasticity of demand (number of passengers) with respect to distance =-2 i.e. $D = k/d^2$.

Figure 5. **Network effects: extension to a linear network**

B. Traffic per link: missing link effect

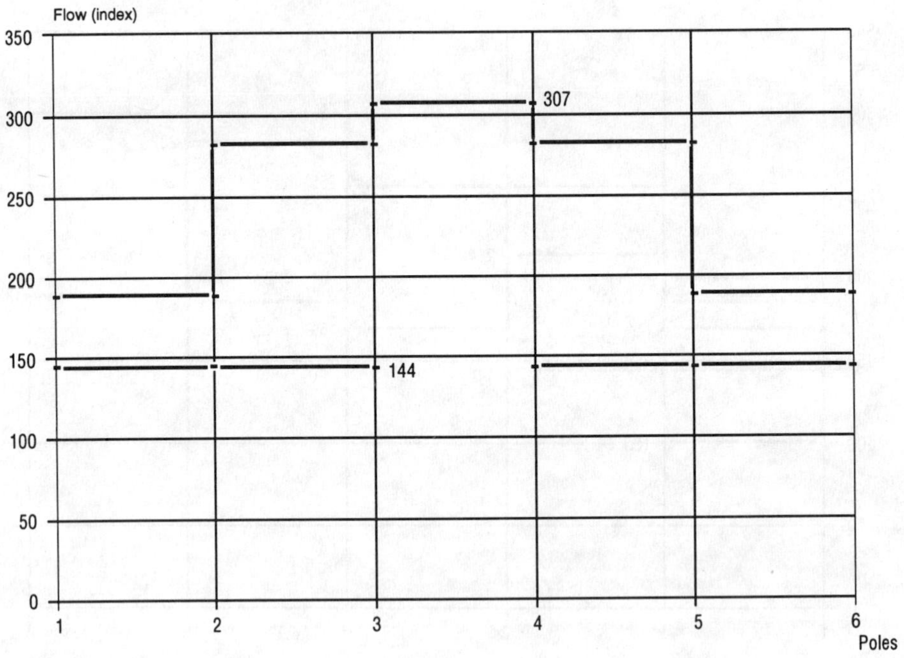

Basic assumptions (H) Cf. Figure 4.

Figure 6. **Network effects: extension to a linear network**

C. Indicators of regional benefits
Passenger-kms by point of departure (or destination)

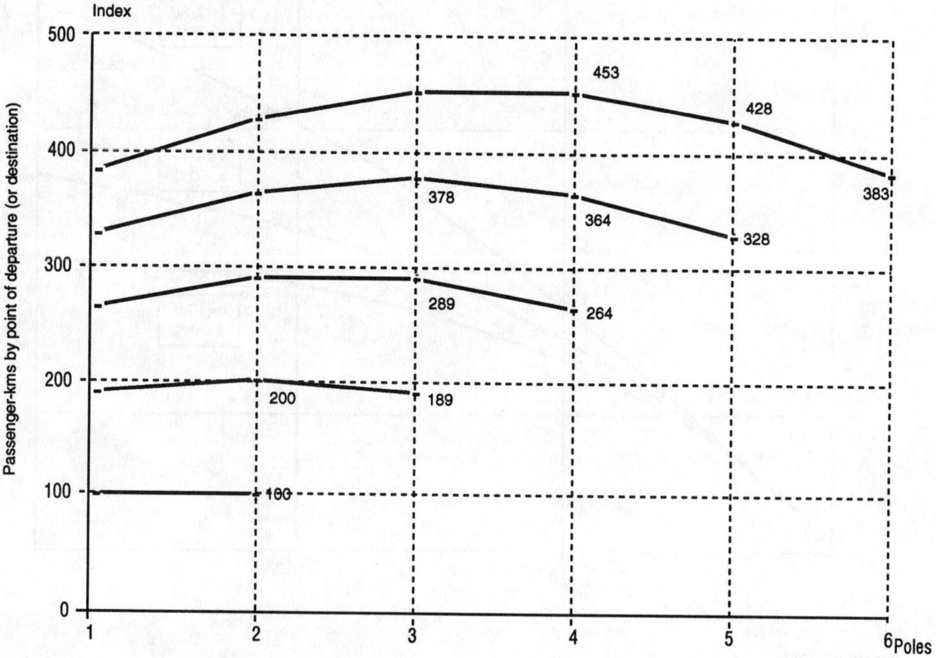

Basic assumptions (H): see Figure 4
Additional assumptions: Economic surplus is proportional to passenger-kms on the network.

Figure 7. **Present worth of revenue that rises linearly**

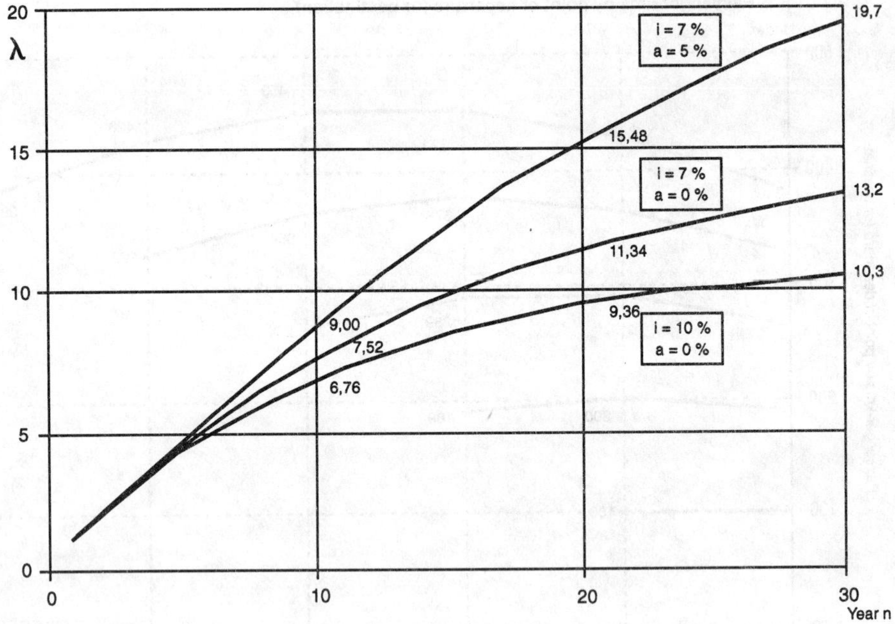

Assumptions:

— Actual income for year k: $R_1[1+(k-1)a]$

— Real interest rate = i ; r=1/(1+i)

— Present worth of revenue in year i : $Ai=\sum r^{k-1} R_k$

Result: ($\lambda=A_1/R_1=f(i,n)+a\ g(i,n)$)

$$\lambda= \frac{1-r^n}{1-r} + a \frac{r}{(1-r)^2} [1+ (n-1)r^n - n\ r^{n-1}]$$

Figure 8. **Margins of uncertainty for the revenue from new infrastructure**
The example of toll urban expressways

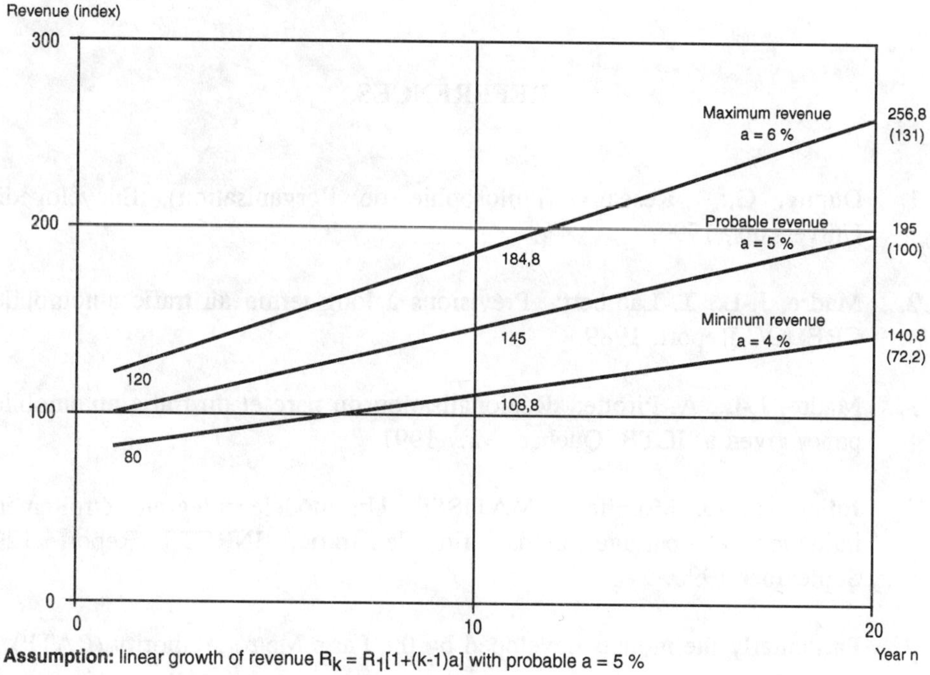

Assumption: linear growth of revenue $R_K = R_1[1+(k-1)a]$ with probable a = 5 %

REFERENCES

1. Dupuy, G.: Réseaux (Philosophie de l'organisation), Encyclopedia Universalis, 1990.

2. Madre, J.-L., T. Lambert: Prévisions à long terme du trafic automobile, CREDOC Report, 1989.

3. Madre, J.-L., A. Pirotte: Régionalisation du parc et du trafic automobile, paper given at ICTB, Quebec, May 1991.

4. Julien H., O. Morellet: MATISSE, Un modèle intégrant étroitement induction et partage modal fin de trafic, INRETS Report 129, September 1990.

5. Particularly the models developed by the Paris Metro Authority (RATP).

6. Barbier Saint-Hilaire, F.: Système DAVIS-Equilibre, INRETS Note, 1988.

7. The Netherlands: Second structure plan.

8. Quinet, E.: Analyse économique des transports, PUF, March 1990.

9. Lesourne, J., *et al.*: Etude des effets économiques indirects des investissements routiers et autoroutiers, SEMA, August 1976.

10. Marche, R., *et al.*: Boulevard périphérique Nord de Lyon, Appraisal Report (restricted), INRETS, March 1991. Methodological document in the course of preparation.

11. Leurent, F.: Notes sur l'utilisation des modèles statiques d'affectation du trafic routier urbain, ENPC and Université Paris XII, Mémoire de DEA, October 1991.

12. ESTI-ERT Seminar: La politique européenne en matière d'infrastructure de transport, Paris, 17th-18th January 1991.

13. Papon, F.: Les "routes de première classe", une tarification différenciée de la circulation en agglomération pour en améliorer l'efficacité économique de manière socialement équitable, INRETS, Doctoral thesis, September 1991.

14. Papon, F.: Les "routes de première classe", un péage urbain choisi par l'usager, Paper given at the "Journées Jacques CARTIER", Lyons, December 1991.

Sub-topic 3

INFRASTRUCTURE CAPACITY AND NETWORK ACCESS

P. NIJKAMP
Free University
Amsterdam

H. PRIEMUS
Delft University of Technology
Delft
The Netherlands

SUMMARY

Amsterdam/Delft, September 1991

1. PREAMBLE

It is increasingly recognised that our western economies are moving gradually toward an international network economy. This phenomenon has a demand aspect, related to international trade patterns, international service deliveries, international exchange of information, international tourism, etc., but also a decisive supply aspect, related to large-scale international physical infrastructure, the emergence of the new information technology and the rise of sophisticated telecommunication systems. Political developments such as the move toward Europe 1992, have acted as a catalyst for this irreversible and far-reaching process.

Seen from the above perspective, international network infrastructure will play a key role in the internationalisation processes of our economies. Such network infrastructures would have to serve the needs of a mobile society in which mobility/interaction of goods, persons and information are the clear exponents of a modern network economy (see ECMT, 1986; Nijkamp, *et al.*, 1990).

In the past decades, new infrastructure expansions and investments have, indeed, by and large followed the demand requirements: transport policy was chiefly demand driven and investments in transport infrastructure mainly followed the demand trends. Only the "jumps" in the system (e.g. airplanes, high-speed trains, etc.) were also caused by technology push motives.

However, the question we are facing nowadays is more complicated: if we take for granted the politically advocated and largely accepted objective of ecologically sustainable economic development, are then the needs of an extremely mobile network society for a drastic expansion of infrastructure compatible with the constraints imposed by environmental concerns, safety considerations and socio-economic equity objectives?

The answer to this question has far-reaching consequences. The conflicting nature of a demand-driven transport system evokes immediately the question as to the role of supply in terms of managing and expanding infrastructure. Here the fundamental question is: are ecological, safety and equity considerations prohibitive regarding network expansion? If so, then the question of capacity use of the existing material infrastructure in Europe has to be given due attention. If not, the question remains nevertheless whether a better use of existing capacity may not be an economically more viable option than an uncritical investment effort in conventional physical infrastructure.

Furthermore, the problem of capacity constraints should not only be considered from the viewpoint of separate bottlenecks in a given infrastructure component, but also -- and even more important -- from the viewpoint of the functioning of a network as a whole. Thus also, the relationship between infrastructure development and its use on the one hand, and the modal split on the other hand, is at stake here. This question also leads to complex trade-offs between investments and disinvestments at the same time in the transport sector. Transport policy should, in this context, serve to enhance efficiency and sustainability from the viewpoint of network operations [see also European Roundtable Secretariat (ERT), 1991]. Thus an important related question is: what kind of network policy can be feasibly developed so as to serve simultaneously the needs of a mobile society, the ecological paradigm and the socio-economic needs of the new mobility-deprived?

The previous questions make it evident that the notion of capacity and the idea of network management are critical parameters for a policy analysis of new infrastructures in Europe. In this report we will, in particular, call attention to the need for effective, efficient and creative capacity management of existing material infrastructure (including the need for a high-tech upgrading of, and a more market-oriented view on, such networks).

The paper is organised as follows. In Chapter 2 some empirical evidence regarding the discrepancy between supply and demand and the conflicts vis-à-vis environment and safety will be given. Chapter 3 will provide some background notions and conceptual reflections on network capacity which are necessary to provide the proper scene for the remaining part of this paper. Next, Chapter 4 will make the substantive point that management and upgrading of existing infrastructure networks is the heart of modern transport policy, as compatibility between transport, the environment and physical planning is of primordial importance. This will be followed (in Chapter 5) by a reflection on the interest and potential of current transport policy to achieve a better performance of transport systems at both the metropolitan and the European level. Finally, the European dimension will also be given due attention where, again, the point will be made that co-ordination and sophistication are critical success factors for an appropriate European transport policy.

2. SOME OBSERVATIONS ON SOCIAL COSTS OF TRANSPORT

Transport seems to have a double face nowadays. On the one hand, it is increasingly recognised that transport plays a vital role in building up an integrated European network economy and, on the other hand, there is a growing awareness of the high -- sometimes unacceptable -- social costs of transport (notably in the area of land use and the environment). Transport has become a focal point of research and policy interest because of the conflicting roles it plays in our modern society.

The previous observations indicate the transport field is fraught with conflicts. Transport policymakers in most European countries find themselves in extremely complicated choice situations. A large number of interest groups, ranging from multinational companies to local environmentalists, urges them to take action, however, often in quite different directions. Current discussions on the creation of mainports or the construction of high-speed rail links are illustrative in this respect. On the one hand, it has become obvious that the environment poses its limits on the volume, the character and the pace of the extension of the transport infrastructure. On the other hand, most business firms in (western) Europe are concerned about their competitiveness in a global context due to inadequate network infrastructure in Europe.

Transport thus forms the heart of our European network economy and the transport scene has shown significant changes. Mobility has drastically increased and, as a consequence, congestion has also increased in almost all transport modes, especially on motor roads and in the air. At the same time, the environmental burden of the transport sector far exceeds the carrying capacity of our environment and threatens ecological sustainability as advocated, amongst others, in the Brundtland Report.

The field of transport and communication is in full motion, not only at the local or regional level, but even more so at the (inter)national level. International commodity transport -- in terms of both volume and value -- is increasing, international passenger transport is rapidly rising and international telecommunication is increasingly gaining importance. From an international (i.e. cross-European) perspective the following developments at the European level may, *inter alia*, be observed:

-- Despite many institutional frictions, there is an increasing tendency towards an integrated and open European market, which by 1992 will have become the largest trade block of the world (with

320 million consumers). A further association with EFTA countries and east-European countries will increase its scope.

-- On a European scale, many initiatives are being taken to improve and expand the current infrastructure (e.g. the Channel Tunnel, the extension of the French TGV, the construction of the Trans-European Motorway, the design of an advanced European telecommunications system, etc.), so that all European countries will be linked to each other via a common and accessible network (see ECMT, 1989; Community of European Railways, 1989).

-- Internationally, the heartland of Europe seems to shift towards the south (see, e.g., Boeckhout and Romkema, 1989) and more recently also the east -- which has enormous economic and social implications for transport and mobility. Furthermore, many different kinds of border problems still have to be solved in Europe's unification policy.

-- Many countries have officially adopted a "basic right" principle towards peripheral or less accessible areas, which means that a certain level of accessibility is ensured on the basis of this equity paradigm. However, in the case of severe budget stress such principles tend to be easily neglected, particularly when accompanied by privatisation of (parts of) the infrastructure networks, public transport services, telecommunications, etc. This may lead to severe imbalances at the European level, especially for non-central areas.

-- Concentration tendencies in physical planning of facilities (schools, medical health care centres, high tech centres, etc.) have decreased the local level of services, thus causing a forced mobility in order to have access to these services. Here, the relationship between an equity oriented physical planning and an efficiency oriented transportation and infrastructure planning is at stake. In addition, new forms of spatial organisation seem to arise at a European scale, *viz.* a tendency towards the development of large metropolitan areas. Europe seems to become the home of metropolitan regions rather than of individual states.

-- The European trend toward more deregulation and decentralisation may seduce policymakers to wonder whether there is a case for planning at all; more particularly, the seemingly higher efficiency gains of a market oriented planning system need to be traded off against the social welfare gains of public interventions. This is especially important since a demand-driven transport system is increasingly advocated, even though the final results of such a market orientation are not always desirable (as is witnessed by the monopoly tendencies in the American airline sector).

-- International spatial interactions in the form of physical movements of persons or commodities are increasingly influenced by modern developments in the field of communication and information technologies (e.g. JIT systems, MRP systems, etc.).

-- The area of commodity transport is going through a rapid transition phase, especially due to the emergence of modern logistic systems. The transport sector is not only a "shipper" of physical transport, but increasingly an "organiser" of such transport. For both national and European freight transport this development has far-reaching consequences, not only in efficiency terms but also in terms of social consequences.

The previous observations demonstrate that transport has manifested itself as an extremely dynamic sector, at both the supply and the demand side. It is also clear that this sector is facing major bottlenecks caused by its pervasive nature. Everybody in society is -- directly or indirectly -- an interested party, as far as transport and mobility are concerned.

The factual development of both commodity transport and passenger transport (measured in terms of ton-kilometres and person-kilometres, respectively) has shown a continuous rise in the past twenty years. In both cases road transport has exhibited the strongest growth, as can be seen from Figures 1-3 concerning ECMT countries.

For commodity transport, we observe a slight decline for rail transport and inland waterways, but this is largely compensated by the high growth rates of road transport (and pipeline transport).

In passenger transport, private transport modes (i.e. the car) have become the dominant vehicle, while public transport has shown a much less high growth rate (although this situation seems to have improved recently in most countries).

It may now be interesting to confront the rapid rise at the demand side with the investments made at the supply side (see Figure 4). It turns out that in most European countries there has been a steady decrease in transport infrastructure investments in the past fifteen years (except in railways which has shown a relatively stable investment pattern). Thus supply has certainly not kept pace with the rise in demand. The combination of these two factors has led to various externalities (i.e. social costs):

-- Congestion costs;
-- Environmental costs;
-- Safety costs.

Various attempts have been made to assess the order of magnitude of these costs (*cf.* also Himanen, *et al.*, 1991; McKinsey, 1986; Vleugel and Van Gent, 1991). Congestion costs appear to be significant in all countries, but their order of magnitude varies drastically, depending on how a reference situation (without congestion) is defined and how time is valued by different road users. In a recent OECD report (1989), various estimates of environmental and safety costs of land transport can be found:

-- **Noise annoyance,** both damage costs (e.g. productivity losses, health care costs, decline in property values and loss of psychological well-being) and abatement costs (e.g. adjusted vehicle technology, anti-noise screens, double glazing, etc.). Studies in various countries show a relatively high level of social costs of traffic noise.

Social costs of traffic noise

Country	**Percentage of GDP**
France	0.08
Netherlands	0.10
Norway	0.06
USA	0.06 - 0.12

Source: OECD (1989).

-- **Air pollution,** both damage costs (e.g. damage to health, buildings or forests) and environmental protection costs (e.g. air pollution control, new vehicle technology, catalytic converters, etc). Numerical estimates of air pollution costs caused by transport show some variation, but all point in the same direction: social costs of transport are high.

Social costs of air pollution by traffic

Country	Percentage of GDP
France	0.21
Germany	0.4
Netherlands	0.2
USA	0.35

Source: OECD (1989).

-- **(Lack of) safety**, mainly resulting in accidents, leading to damage costs and recovery costs (including damage to vehicles, medical treatment, productivity losses, policy and emergency service expenditures, etc.). Various cost estimates have been made which show high financial burdens.

Social costs of road transport accidents

Country	Percentage of GDP
Belgium	2.5
France	2.6
Germany	2.54
Luxembourg	1.85
Netherlands	1.67
UK	1.5
USA	2.4

Source: OECD (1989).

The estimated figures lead to the conclusion that, on average, the social costs of road transport in developed countries fall in the range of 2.5 to 3.0 per cent of GDP. Recent estimates (see Himanen, *et al.*, 1989) suggest even much higher figures.

This relatively high figure has serious implications for transport and infrastructure policy. In order to make transport part of an ecologically sustainable economy, intensified efforts have to be developed to make the need for transport compatible with the need for a better environment in the European economies. This implies that market imperfections have to be removed by internalising the external (environmental) costs, e.g. by means of user charge principles which are increasingly accepted in European countries. A decline in the social costs of transport requires also a more efficient operation of current networks and a better, i.e. more coherent, design of new infrastructures.

The conclusion from the previous observations is rather straightforward: transport is increasingly facing severe constraints, in terms of both infrastructure capacity and environmental sustainability (reflected in external costs). Furthermore, it should be added that the social distribution of mobility is rather unequal; especially the trend towards large-scale mainport developments (e.g. the hub and spokes system) means a relative mobility deprivation for less central areas. Despite these observations, in the light of the relatively strategic position of the transport sector in a European network economy, it is difficult to claim that this sector should be phased out. But serious concern is warranted: the question of the right to mobility at all cost is at stake here.

In conclusion, the previous observations suggest, in any case, three important fields of research:

(a) The development and use of (new) infrastructures;

(b) The application of various types of user charge principles;

(c) The selective sustainability by means of modal split changes. These elements, which are also of a political nature, will be further discussed in Chapter 3.

3. MOBILITY AND SUSTAINABILITY: A VIEW ON CAPACITY AND NETWORKS

Mobility and transport are not an aim *per se*, but serve the goal of economic growth and welfare increase. However, there is not a linear correlation between mobility and transport on the one hand and economic development on the other. As shown in the previous chapter, as a result of external costs various negative feedback effects may occur. Thus there is essentially a conflict between three major policy orientations:

-- Economic development (ED);
-- Environmental sustainability (ES);
-- Network access (NA).

Depending on the size of transport flows, the specific modal split in a network, the vehicle technology used and the type of regulations, this conflict is more or less present in actual situations.

It is evident that the above conflicts are becoming more serious, as more traditional infrastructure investments -- in combination with more traditional mobility processes -- are allowed and realised. In this sense, a straightforward linear expansion of traditional transport systems is incompatible with sustainability and socio-economic/spatial equity considerations (see also Himanen, *et al.*, 1991). Whether or not this is politically unacceptable is a different question which, apparently, is given different answers in European countries.

In order to come to grips with the above-mentioned conflictual issues, it seems plausible to investigate the critical success factors for the planning and implementation of transport systems. In this context, reference can be made to the so-called pentagon model which has been used elsewhere to analyse and evaluate new European transport plans (see, *inter alia*, Maggi and Nijkamp, 1991 and Vleugel and Nijkamp, 1991). The edges of the pentagon (see Figure 5) represent five critical success factors for designing and operating transport systems.

These five factors have the following meaning:

-- Hardware (e.g. efficient technological standardization);

-- Software (e.g. use of compatible information systems);

-- Orgware (e.g. existence of effective management structures);

-- Finware (e.g. presence of private or public financial institutions):

-- Ecoware (e.g. environment-friendly systems).

This prism model may be particularly useful in evaluating new transport policies. Today, several projects concerning transport infrastructure or transport systems are being executed. An example in the field of large scale and transnational transport infrastructure is the Channel Tunnel (Chunnel), linking the transport infrastructure of the mainland of western Europe with that of England. The quality of the latter link, when finished, can be evaluated in the light of the five critical success factors mentioned above. With respect to the hardware, the value of the Channel Tunnel would be greatly reduced when through trains from the Continent to, e.g., London would be impossible. Partly, this reduced value might become reality when the French TGV is not allowed to attain its high speed on the English tracks due to the lack of sufficient infrastructure on the English side of the Chunnel. As the Channel Tunnel will be used by through trains and by shuttle services, orgware is a very important factor too. The timetables must be organised in accordance with the timetables of the French and English railways, while the shuttle services must be performed with a frequency that is sufficiently high to ensure its efficiency, which depends largely on the advantage of a strongly reduced travel time. Similar observations can be made regarding the finware (where the private financing of this project has caused major concerns), the ecoware (in terms of protection of vulnerable areas crossed by new tracks) and software (in terms of sophisticated information systems).

The previous notions may also be helpful in investigating policy alternatives regarding infrastructure capacity. Capacity is not only a technologically determined given stock (measured in terms of hardware), but may also be determined by route guidance systems (software) or smart traffic regulations (orgware), especially from the viewpoint of a network system's operation.

In the light of all these remarks, however, it makes sense to pay more thorough attention to the notion of **capacity of infrastructure**, not only on line segments but also -- and particularly -- in multi-modal networks. Infrastructure expansion is usually advocated on the basis of lack of capacity of existing infrastructure. And normally the claim is made that new infrastructure investment would lead to a rise in capacity (even though we know that -- according to Say's law "supply generates its own demand" -- after some time any new infrastructure will again manifest congestion phenomena). Therefore, the question is opportune: essentially, what is capacity? And is it conceivable that capacity management, technologically upgraded capacity and intermodal flexibility contribute more significantly to the solution of capacity problems than straightforward expansion? And last but not least: are we able to assess -- and charge to the user -- the right price of capacity use?

A closer analysis of the concept of capacity brings to light that capacity is essentially a multi-faceted phenomenon which cannot easily be characterised by means of a single indicator, but needs to be investigated from multiple dimensions. Therefore, the above-mentioned pentagon may also be helpful in identifying a proper definition of capacity (see also Kreutzberger and Vleugel, 1991).

In the context of searching for a new concept of capacity, the following reflection seems plausible. Capacity of infrastructure refers to the maximum volume of persons, goods, vehicles or messages that can use a given (part of) infrastructure in a given time period. The main question, however, is: what is maximum? This is not easy to answer as, for instance, a road segment may already have reached its environmentally sustainable maximum before it has reached its technical maximum. Consequently, the notion of capacity as a maximum use can only be delineated if the criteria determining a maximum are specified. Following the pentagon approach, the following indicators are possible:

- -- Technomax: The maximum volume that is possible, given the technical constraints on infrastructure;
- -- Enviromax: The maximum volume that is allowable, given the sustainability constraints;
- -- Orgmax: The maximum volume that is possible, given the regulatory system for the infrastructure at hand;
- -- Economax: The maximum volume that may be expected, given the economic efficiency and financial criteria;
- -- Infomax: The maximum volume that can be digested by the infrastructure, given the available information (road conditions, congestion, etc.).

These notions clarify the point that capacity has to be viewed as a multidimensional constraint, not only in a traditional technical sense, but much more in a broad sense in which policy intervention and human behaviour play a critical role. This leads to the important conclusion that capacity problems are not necessarily and predominantly solved by physical (hardware) expansion, but by a smart combination of different constituents that, altogether, make up a series of constraints on the use of infrastructure.

The previous considerations have been studied and tested for various transport fields in the Netherlands (e.g. railways, commodity transport, inland waterways, airlines). These concepts appeared to be extremely helpful in identifying the preponderant bottlenecks in existing infrastructures without leading immediately to a plea for physical expansion. In many cases, the limitations caused by technical or environmental barriers might even be overcome by a better organisation of the transport system in a broad sense (e.g. better route guidance systems). Thus the focus on the multidimensionality of the capacity concept prevents us from thinking, exclusively or mainly, in terms of physical technical capacity. Even if expansion of infrastructure would be necessary, the question would arise: which type of infrastructure should be expanded and which type reduced, looking also into economic efficiency or performance indicators of infrastructure?

It is clear from the above strategic considerations that Europe should increase its efforts and selective investments in improving the quality and performance of transport and communication infrastructure in order to increase its competitive power. Despite the urgency in some areas, the extra efforts should be allocated with care for both economic and environmental reasons. This raises an extra difficulty, as sufficient care is usually incompatible with swift action. Short-term solutions -- as advocated by some, mostly business-oriented, interest groups -- will heavily rely on a further massive extension of the European motorway system. This option may make some sense for southern and eastern Europe, but for western Europe this option does not seem viable in the long run. Time and again, Say's Law has proven its validity concerning the motorway system. Therefore, any extension beyond the level of relieving some unfortunate bottlenecks will only create a next era of congestion on a higher level. Such scenarios will likely become reality, even if additional measures such as road pricing were introduced. Furthermore, it will be detrimental to the spatial organisation of most urban areas as well to the ecology in western Europe.

There is another element which deserves full-scale attention in this context. Capacity should not only be considered in relation to a separate infrastructure segment, but as a feature of a multi-layer and multi-modal network. Thus the interface between different spatial interaction modes becomes increasingly important, so that the attention has to be focused on nodes (or centres) and connections (edges) in both physical and non-physical networks. Also the hierarchical structure of infrastructure connections (e.g. motorways, provincial roads, local roads, etc.) deserves attention here. Multi-modality of a network is an important way of coping with capacity problems (e.g. peak hour congestion) in some modes, as this allows for inter-modal substitution and complementarity, through which both the economic efficiency and the environmental sustainability, as well as socio-economic equity, may be increased (see van den Hanenberg, 1990). Here also, the potential of telecommunication (including telematics) has to be mentioned (see Giaoutzi and Nijkamp, 1989). The identification of the optimal mix of necessary infrastructure modes in view of reaching given objectives (the so-called packaging problem) is a major issue in this context.

The network configuration (including its links to all other modes) is decisive for network access, the efficiency of the network, and its load structure. The main problem is that, in the past, network planning has mainly taken place on the basis of segmented infrastructure planning rather than system-wide optimisation.

Such piecemeal approaches have mainly led to second-best solutions, in which none of the prevailing interests were fully accounted for.

From the viewpoint of system-wide network optimisation, it makes sense to pay particular attention to specific bottlenecks, such as transit points, variety in interaction/communication speed, intermodal connections, information systems regarding network operation, peak load and peak use, flexible working hours, new logistic systems, the position of mainports, standardization in transport systems technology, hierarchical functional divisions in networks, etc. Combined transport may often be regarded as an efficient way of overcoming current limits, by improving intermodal transit potential, rather than physically expanding the whole infrastructure. This also allows a much better use of existing capacity, so that through chain connections the above-mentioned socio-economic equity problem of limited network access can be relaxed.

Finally, the transport aspects of non-transport policies (e.g. urban policy, industrialisation policy, recreation policy, retail policy, etc.) also have to be mentioned. Since transport is a derived demand, significant consequences of non-transport policies for the mobility of people and goods may sometimes be expected which are hard to control (see also Louw, *et al.*, 1991). Consequently, the notion of instrument systems (i.e. packages of direct and indirect control measures) is relevant here.

4. MANAGEMENT AND UPGRADING OF EXISTING NETWORKS

The previous chapter has emphasized the need for an alternative view on network capacity (and hence network expansion). Rather than seeing capacity problems as a technical hardware problem (which might only be solved by means of material extension of existing infrastructure types), it has been argued that capacity has to be viewed from the multidimensional potential of a multi-modal network, with a focus on organisation/management, financing, ecological sustainability and information systems access.

The present chapter will take up this point a little further and will also call attention to ways of improving the economic efficiency of networks without doing harm to the other aspects summarised in our pentagon. It is important to do so, as the transport sector is exhibiting a strange paradox. It is, on the one hand, a cost factor (incorporating both private and social costs), so that its use would have to be minimised. On the other hand, transport is an important economic sector which in most countries provides a significant contribution to national income (up to 5-7 per cent in many countries), so that it would be tempting to maximise its use. However, recent statistical evidence also demonstrates that the profitability of the transport sector is relatively low (see Roschar *et al.*, 1991), so that the transport sector tends to become a (sub-)marginal sector, which is only a necessary evil in view of its strategic role in a competitive European situation.

The only way to improve this situation is not a straightforward expansion of conventional physical infrastructure, but to develop new transport systems which would increase the economic position of the transport sector without violating the constraints incorporated in our pentagon model. The main strategies to be pursued here are:

- Avoidance of any unnecessary physical transport, by improving the transport systems efficiency through more appropriate information systems, telematics, new logistic and management concepts for fleet guidance and management, etc.

- Operation of necessary physical transport systems against lowest social costs, by using the best available technology (route guidance systems, better vehicle technology, etc.), or by developing and using more environment-friendly means of transport.

Unfortunately, most existing infrastructures are so strongly embedded in our production and mobility patterns that the shift toward new systems (e.g. Maglev, underground vacuum tunnels, etc.) is extremely difficult due to almost prohibitive transition costs. Furthermore, new transport systems need to be linked to existing ones, in order to ensure a minimum critical mass of operation (the "connectivity" problem).

With respect to the integration of new transport infrastructures and transport systems into the existing infrastructures and systems, two different aspects of integration can be distinguished. In the first place, there is the aspect of the compatibility of the new system with the existing ones (e.g. in terms of technological standardization). This is an important aspect, considering the importance of the network effect. Secondly, one should recognise the competitive aspect of integration: since several transport systems exist already with a given market share, new systems will, in general, be more or less competitive.

Given the need for compatibility with existing transport infrastructures, the hardware, software and orgware factors of new infrastructures are of great importance. An example of a new transport infrastructure that, in itself, was not compatible with the existing infrastructure on the hardware level is the Japanese Shinkansen. To ensure that the new system did not become, in fact, a stand-alone system, software and orgware factors had to be fully synchronised. This means that the departure times of the trains have to be based on the arrival times of connecting trains. When a slight delay in the arrival of a train occurs, this information must be used to delay the departure of connecting trains accordingly. The TGV and the ICE are both compatible with the existing railway infrastructure. The new trains even partly use the existing infrastructure. This can only be made possible when the timetables of the TGV and the ICE are completely integrated in the timetables of the existing railway systems. If, in the future, a European railway network has to be developed, the national projects must be co-ordinated at a European level, to ensure the compatibility of at least the hardware, software and orgware of these projects. The compatibility problem is even more evident for the Maglev system. Thanks to its high speed and its excellent comfort, it is potentially an important competitor for the high-speed trains. However, the lack of integration of the system largely reduces the advantages compared to rail, so that the benefits of the system become debatable, and hence the difficulties to establish a real commercial line.

Although the objective of a new transport system will not be to compete with existing systems, it is hardly possible to avoid competitive behaviour completely. Usually the objective will implicitly encompass some aspects of competitiveness. For instance, when a new transport system is introduced with the objective to diminish the use of the private car, this new system has to be competitive with the car, and hence its production will be a (indirect) competitor with the automobile and gasoline industries. Two interesting examples can be found in the introduction of the Shinkansen and the TGV line between Paris and Lyons. In both cases the use of air transport diminished considerably in favour of the new railway systems. Analogously, the Channel Tunnel also will be competitive with the ferry services.

Thus, the construction of new advanced infrastructure networks is fraught with many difficulties, which may only be overcome if all conditions implied by the pentagon are satisfied. A straightforward expansion of existing infrastructure (more of the same) does not seem to be a logical or plausible strategy in many countries. Upgrading of existing infrastructure using modern information and telecommunication technology -- in combination with a selective transport volume policy -- seems to be the best viable policy. Thus, it has to be recognised that infrastructure is a prerequisite for a further economic development and integration of the European network economy. An effective (and official) recognition of the basic role of infrastructure for economic growth would allow new strategic explorations, *inter alia*, concerning the necessary upgrading of the current service level of transport systems or the design of new infrastructure systems. Quality is apparently nowadays of more strategic relevance than quantity, and therefore infrastructure and transport systems planning ought to take pre-specified performance and service quality levels as a strategic point of departure.

A choice for operational performance levels would need a coherent multisectoral European -- rather than a sectoral nationalistic -- view. Only in this context can sound financing and an environmental approach to infrastructure be reached. Such a European view is also necessary to cope with the phenomenon of missing networks in a pluriform European society (see ERT, 1991).

In the same vein, the problem of technological standardization may be seen. Standardization does not only pertain to hardware (like voltage systems in railways) but also to software (e.g. information systems for international customs procedures) and orgware (e.g. common carriage on European rails).

Finally, of strategic importance for commodity transport is a further development of multi-modal transport solutions (such as piggy-back systems and containerisation). But, especially in this field, a fine tuning in terms of hardware, software and orgware is necessary.

The conclusion from the above observations is that there is a need for strategic and anticipatory research, by taking long-run sustainability criteria as a point of departure and linking design and operation of networks to these criteria. This would also bring to light the (potential) success and failure of transport policy in different regions and nations in Europe.

5. THE INTEREST AND POTENTIAL OF EUROPEAN TRANSPORT POLICY

Transport policy in European countries, regions and cities cannot boast a high success rate, as transport policy is also trapped between a variety of mutually conflicting social goals.

The rapid dynamics of the transport sector in the context of the emerging European network economy has also clearly brought about, in the political arena, the awareness of the limits to growth: the European transport map is featuring various problematic developments and both local/regional and national/ international scales. Despite the increasing popularity of Just-in-Time (JIT) systems and related concepts, the actual practice of both commodity and passenger transport is disappointing and often frustrating. Severe traffic congestion phenomena at the urban or metropolitan level (e.g. Athens, Rome, Paris), unacceptable delays in medium- and long-distance transport during peak hours, unsatisfactory service levels of European railway systems (and public transport in general), unreliable airline connections due to limited airport capacity and slow technical and institutional renewal of air traffic control in Europe; all these phenomena illustrate the difficult position of the European transport sector. And there is no clear perspective for a drastic improvement of this situation.

On the contrary, it is increasingly claimed that a free European market (beyond the year 1992) and a further deregulation of the European transport may lead to unacceptable accessibility conditions in major regions in Europe. The development of the American airline sector into a monopolistic or oligopolistic market structure is illustrative in this respect.

Another important complicating factor will be environmental policy. In contrast to the deregulation with respect to the pure transport market phenomena, environmental policy is critically dependent on a great deal of regulations. In particular, more technical restrictions are likely to be imposed, e.g. limited emission levels of motorcars or even a prohibition of the use of certain transport modes.

Altogether, governments are facing a complexity of questions which may briefly be indicated as follows (see also Louw, *et al.*, 1991):

-- The role of the government in a deregulated market with respect to access, competition, financing/subsidising, safety and risks is an important issue. The effects of deregulation deserve a thorough analysis in order to remove monopolistic tendencies and to ensure a competitive market. This is particularly relevant for railway companies. They have the potential to operate in a more commercial way in combination with a high quality offer in terms of speed, reliability and comfort.

-- As far as commodity transport is concerned, deregulation of freight transport (e.g. scope and impacts on modes) also deserves full-scale attention in the near future.

-- In view of the international importance of transport infrastructure and freight transport, the possibilities of developing coastal transport and ro-ro (roll-on/roll-off) transport in Europe, as a partial solution to infrastructure shortcomings, have to be explored more intensively.

-- The consequences of the massive (auto)mobility growth are evident: on a European scale we have to face the problem of endless traffic jams and inaccessibility in and around urban areas. A main side effect is the serious environmental impact. Two different kinds of policy measures deserve analytical attention here:

i) Variabilisation of costs of car use as a compensation for environmental costs. In many countries the idea has emerged that the user should be charged for all (direct and external) costs. But since actors with different economic interests and aims use the same infrastructure, the question is: which user has to be charged for which use of scarce infrastructure? This question is at the heart of current debates on transport policy, as it reflects potential conflicts between business traffic, private traffic and public transport (including substitution possibilities between different modes). This issue has also been a focal point of recent policy interest in the Netherlands, especially because of the strong dominance of the commodity transport sector in the Netherlands, which is one of the strongest in Europe. Although in this field several experiments have been done with navigation systems and dashboard-mounted video display screens (especially in Japan), a practical European cross-frontier programme of electronic traffic aids on congested trunk roads is still missing (the new DRIVE programme may offer new perspectives here).

ii) Improvement of public transport. It is plausible -- in the light of actual choices made regarding modal split -- to assume that for short- and medium-distance transport (notably railways and private cars) most likely the environmental decay will not count as an argument in the choice between these two different modes, unless public transport will substantially improve its quality (in terms of fares, punctuality, comfort, etc.). Some important necessary conditions are: liberalisation of the European transport market, a reduction of the monopoly positions of (notably) railway companies, which implies a separation between infrastructure holding companies from transport operations; and (*ex ante*) evaluations of new transport projects in the light of their environmental effects.

-- Design of management information and planning systems, and satellite control of trains and vehicles under the condition of integration of national and international databases, is urgent.

-- In view of the "magical year" 1992, the analysis of possibilities for reducing border formalities and customs delays in both passenger and freight transport is also an important item on the list of planning research priorities. Harmonization of combined transport technologies in personal transport and in freight distribution seems in this respect to be the main precondition which has to be studied in order to find practical solutions. Of course, telematics plays a crucial role (as also the COST programme illustrates).

The foregoing observations have shown that there is a wide variety of transport policy options in coping with capacity and network access issues without immediately expanding conventional material infrastructure. The types of policy can be systematically distinguished as metropolitan-urban policies focusing on transport systems in main nodes (e.g. mainports) of a network, and cross-border policies focusing on European transport corridors.

As far as metropolitan-urban policies are concerned, three categories can be distinguished, *viz.* demand-oriented, supply-oriented and indirect transport policies.

1. Demand-oriented transport measures are mainly concerned with short- and medium-term ways of influencing (urban) transport behaviour in order to ensure a more efficient transport system or to reduce environmental or other external costs. Examples are:

   - Optimising urban transport network flows (e.g. co-ordinated traffic lights, electronic route guidance systems, etc.);

   - Road pricing, or user charge measures (e.g. the Singapore model, or the recent experiences in Oslo or Stockholm);

   - Auto restraint measures (e.g. closing of inner city areas, such as in Milan);

   - Car- or van-pooling and/or special lanes on motorways for car-poolers;

   - Information and communication campaigns;

   - Integration of fares systems in an urban area in order to enhance inter-system connections and thereby improving the accessibility and usefulness of public transport (e.g. the national "strip-card" for public transport in the Netherlands).

In various cases a combination of such management options is chosen. All these examples do not require a "hardware" solution, but originate from orgware, ecoware, finware or software types of policies.

2. Urban supply-oriented transport strategies refer to medium- and long-term measures which have a structural impact on the mobility pattern in urban areas from the provision of infrastructure. Examples are:

   - Improvement of public transport (e.g. in combination with deregulation, for example, Manchester);

   - More efficient management and organisation of transport systems technology;

   - Design of sophisticated new infrastructures (e.g. light rail, subterranean solutions);

   - Incentives for using telematics in transport systems;

   - Parking policy (in terms of volume, location and opening hours).

Also in this context the focus is more on management and organisation than on technomax expansion.

3. Indirect policies refer to measures which, outside the direct realm of the transport system, have a preponderant impact on the functioning of transport systems. Examples of such indirect policies are:

   - Alternative work schedules to avoid transport peak problems (analogous to electricity load management) (see also Tacken and De Boer, 1990);

   - Further introduction of telecommunications to favour telework, teleshopping, etc.;

   - Urban design, urban land use and urban street design (e.g. building permits for offices near terminals of public transport in the Netherlands).

We may conclude here with the observation that the strategic evaluation of the efficiency and the reduction in social costs of transportation as a result of new urban transport policy measures, is an underdeveloped field which, nevertheless, is of great importance for urban planners. Some illustrative examples of potential success measures may be given here for the city of Zurich (see Sommer, 1990):

	1995	2000	
Promotion of public transport/ parking	- 300	- 350	tNOx/year
Fiscal measures	- 150	- 150	"
Speed limits	- 500	- 400	"
Heavy vehicles	- 200	- 300	"
TOTAL:	-1 150	-1 200	tNOx/year

As stated above, next to metropolitan-urban policies there is a need for an effective **cross-border** policy initiative in order to pave the road to a unified European market. Without adequate infrastructure investments, the European economy will not be able to reap fully the fruits of the market integration. The need to develop a network strategy plan for Europe was recently advocated in a study (1990) by the Group Transport 2000 Plus, an advisory policy group of the Transport Commissioner of the European Commission. This group was given the task of compiling medium- and long-term definitions of the European Community's internal and external transport problems, as part of a wider outlook taking into account the upcoming Single Market, environmental protection, technological education and extension of present networks to central and eastern Europe.

In the necessary development of European transport systems, four issues deserve special attention:

-- Integration of ecology into transportation planning;

-- Energy efficiency of vehicles;

-- Spatial implications of transport infrastructure;

-- Social dimensions of spatial mobility;

The study makes a plea for fair competition in the transport sector by charging all infrastructure and external costs to the user, by making the cost structure more transparent, by avoiding manifest and indirect subsidies, by favouring market harmonization and by stimulating logistics and telematics.

The negative externalities have to be coped with by abatement at the source with the best available technology regarding emission reduction, noise abatement energy savings and safety.

Intermodal transport for commodities has a good potential and has to be strongly favoured. Temporary subsidy -- based on the "infant industry" argument -- may be allowed to ensure viability in a competitive multi-modal transport market.

The quality of decisions in the transport sector has to be improved by favouring more active and efficient institutional procedures at all levels of decision-making; in a European setting the subsidiary principle is a valid policy paradigm.

Also the financing aspects of European transport systems deserve due attention. Variabilisation of transport costs and road pricing are regarded as appropriate instruments. Furthermore, it is suggested to create a European Infrastructure Fund in order to finance missing links or missing networks in Europe's infrastructure.

It is interesting to observe that most bottlenecks facing the European network system can apparently be described by means of the considerations/indicators incorporated by the pentagon concept. European transport problems are not, in the first place, a matter of lack of technical capacity, but are related to management and organisation.

The latter message is also reflected in a Community document on trans-European networks (see EC, 1990).

This Community document contains a European programme of action in the transport sector. The argument is put forward that the emergence of trans-European networks is a necessity and deserves high priority, especially because current infrastructures in Europe are suffering from many insufficiencies. Furthermore, new transport systems developments have to be compatible with ecological constraints.

At present, many barriers to the emergence of trans-European networks can be observed, notably:

-- Difficulties of transfrontier interoperability;

-- Inadequate legislative environment;

-- Constraints linked to competition;

-- Lack of an overall view at the European level regarding the expected increase in demand and the resulting necessary infrastructures;

-- Shortage of statistical data collected on common bases.

This Community report then continues by concisely reviewing some problem situations in air transport, road transport, railway transport, inland waterways, sea shipping, coastal transport, telecommunications and telematics. The report recommends to draw up comprehensive schemes for developing trans-European networks, to rapidly introduce rules needed for the realisation of such networks, to reinforce standardization programmes (both technologically and institutionally) and to grant a declaration of European interest in such new infrastructure concepts.

The previous observations on the need for an intensive interest in the non-hardware aspects of European infrastructure networks also imply that the current trend of declining infrastructure budgets is detrimental to a sound and sustainable development of the European economy. The creation of a sophisticated infrastructure requires a maximum attention to the orgware, software, ecoware and finware aspects for transport in Europe.

6. THE NEED FOR EUROPEAN CO-OPERATION

A successful international spatial and transport policy also requires an effective infrastructure policy. The role of infrastructure as a catalyst for economic development has long been recognised by the European Communities: witness the huge subsidies for infrastructure projects in European countries. Clearly, it is not an easy task to establish priorities regarding infrastructure projects, but the limited financial resources force governments to find a compromise between efficiency and equity, a dilemma which is often reinforced by the predominance of national interests in European infrastructure planning.

The interest in a real European transport policy does not only rest with governments, but also with the industry in Europe (see ERT, 1988). In this context it is worth calling attention to a recent study on missing networks in Europe, commissioned by the ERT (1991). This study has been carried out by NECTAR (Network on European Communications and Transport Activity Research), a research group which acts in liaison with the European Science Foundation (ESF) in Strasbourg. Based on the above-mentioned pentagon of critical success factors, NECTAR (1991) has analysed various European-oriented transport systems (including multimodal options).

The field of international transport and communications is characterised by ad hoc and partial policy strategies and measures. Government actions tend sometimes to be taken more in response to crisis situations, rather than as part of a co-ordinated and pro-active policy programme which is strategic, holistic and anticipatory in nature (see Vleugel and Nijkamp, 1991).

A major reason for the emergence of missing networks is thus the inevitable tendency for national governments to protect their own manufacturing industries and to maintain their own transport enterprises. Only when a mutual benefit can be derived by all parties, will different countries come together to tackle problems at the international front. The importance of international policy forums such as the EC, the United Nations Economic Commission for Europe, the ECMT, Benelux, the OECD (Organisation for Economic Co-operation and Development), etc., is worth mentioning in this respect. Even here, however, agreements are often difficult to reach. While part of the problem often lies in a disagreement on the nature of common actions [e.g. resolving "the customs problem" or agreements on joint standards for electronic data interchange ("harmonization") etc.], it also stems from fundamental differences in national attitudes to transport policy. The problems of finding satisfactory forms of transport policy co-ordination at the international level are often even more severe for those countries which have significant regional variations or where the administrative system is of a federal nature (e.g. Austria, Switzerland).

In the sequel to this study, a summary of six case studies based on the above-mentioned NECTAR (1991) study on various transport fields will be given, each giving a sketch of bottlenecks in a given network followed by an outline of a new strategy which is not necessarily oriented towards technomax solutions. These policy fields are:

-- Freight transport on roads and rails;
-- Airline systems;
-- High-speed rail networks;
-- European common carriage;
-- Coastal transport and inland waterways;
-- Telecommunication networks.

In sections 6.1. to 6.6. these fields will be briefly described.

6.1. Freight transport and roads and rail

6.1.1. A sketch of bottlenecks

The current bias towards passenger transport (e.g. the planning of high-speed trains, Maglev systems and electrocars) may prove to be fatal if it reduces awareness of the forthcoming problems in the domain of goods transport. A continuation of the vast growth of freight transportation (especially by road vehicles) must be expected. This increase will be amplified by the liberalisation of trade in Europe. Because of this, urgent attention must be given to this area in the light of the existing bottlenecks in freight transportation in Europe.

Bottlenecks in European freight transport can be identified at all layers of our pentagon of concerns. They relate to the capacity of road and rail networks and goods terminals. An important number of problems have been identified on the orgware level which relate to the inefficient use of the existing networks. The national orientation of the planning and operation of railways in Europe, the lack of separation between network and operation, the absence of a clear, Europe-wide tariff structure, the insufficient planning of the spatial structure of the freight transport network in terms of hubs and spokes for multi-modal solutions, are together responsible for the under-use of the existing transport infrastructure in Europe. Concerning software, the absence of logistic strategies as well as all instruments of combined transport to control the European wagon and truck fleet on road and rail are the most important shortcomings. In the finware domain, problems arise with the funding of infrastructure projects which have a European impact while being planned by national companies. A European approach to the integrated treatment of funding, on the one hand and the equalisation of economic and environmental benefits and costs, is urgently needed.

6.1.2. *New networks*

A solution for many of the current problems is the realisation of a multilayer network which combines transport on road and rail. The first layer would consist of a combined transport network, where the nodes would be central European freight terminals near the big European agglomerations and the links would be used by block trains running according to a strict timetable between these terminals using standardized container technology.

A second layer will have to be installed, based on what might be called soft technologies in combined transport. The nodes of this network will be the existing freight stations in Europe. These stations can be used for combined transport due to the use of transhipment techniques which allow drivers to change their loads. The links will consist of piggy-back trains. This network links smaller centres all over Europe.

This two-layer system requires an advanced logistic system. A future integrated European Electronic Data Interchange (EDI) system for combined transport is urgently required, which deals with the movement of freight on road and rail at the same time. Logistic centres placed at the terminals should provide services on a commercial basis to any haulier who wants to operate combined transport.

Another solution concerns road haulage. Given important capacity limits on the European road network, measures must be found which allow for a more efficient use of existing roads. A solution might be a satellite-based network of mobile telecommunication for the European truck fleet (orbital truck fleet management). The installation of such a system would lead to a considerable reduction of the movement of empty trucks in Europe, increase the efficiency of road transport and thus increase the capacity of the existing network enormously. In the case of trucks, this network solution could be combined with the electronic customs facilities mentioned in the telecommunications case study.

A great deal can be realised through the reorganisation of the transport and logistic divisions of large European companies. The case of the mergers of various large-scale retail companies in Switzerland shows that there is an enormous transport cost savings potential in merging the goods distribution of several companies. A new network might be created if the transnational companies combined their logistic efforts and founded a European clearing house to make the most efficient use of their fleets.

6.2. Airline systems

6.2.1. A sketch of bottlenecks

The European airline system consists of a series of overlapping networks. These are the product of bilateral intergovernmental agreements on route authorities, (ambiguous) fare structures, etc., infrastructure (hardware) networks with airports and airport access facilities normally under the national authority, the software of air control and communication systems. This complicated network is likely to change after the European integration, with various mergers, strategic coalitions, etc., which may improve the efficiency of the European airline sector. Financing in general is typically a question of national public investment or public subsidies to the national airlines. Finally, air traffic results in important social costs from noise and air pollution.

There are various forms of air transport networks, but none of them are complete. The key organisational network required to co-ordinate the overall system is entirely absent and aviation is overseen by a variety of agencies. Where networks exist, they are characterised both by the total absence of some facets (such as a common technology for air traffic control) and the lack of networks of sufficiently high quality provision (such as the adequacy of access to airports on the ground).

The European air traffic control is a patchwork of twenty-two systems operated out of forty-four en-route control centres. Some limited co-ordination exists in the framework of EUROCONTROL. The control system itself involves verbal contacts between ground control and pilots. This presents no problem in the US but leads to serious difficulties in air traffic control in Europe because of the multiplicity of languages used. Automated systems are available but the necessary network of computerised infrastructure is missing. Another bottleneck is the shortage of experienced air traffic controllers.

6.2.2. New networks

The solution which would be compatible with a new network look at European air traffic control is the reduction of the number of air control centres. These will have to be equipped with a powerful standardized main-frame computer (as in the US) and the installation of a Central Flow Management Unit (CFMU). The main focus in the case of air traffic is thus on air traffic control and organisational and logistic solutions which will bring about a new European network.

Another weak element in air transport is the extremely unfavourable time-loss because of pre- and post-transport (by buses, taxis or trains). Rapid railway links from airport to major cities and the eventual interlinking with the new rapid train network might bring improvements.

6.3. High-speed rail networks

6.3.1. A sketch of bottlenecks

High-speed travel on rail is an excellent solution for many of the passenger transport problems in Europe because the distances between the major cities range from two hundred to one thousand kilometres, distances for which the rapid train is very competitive. Conscious of this challenge, the Community of European Railway Companies of the twelve EC Members plus Austria and Switzerland presented, in 1989, a project for a European high-speed network (Community of European Railways, 1989). This project redraws the European railway network map.

Such a project, in principle, introduces a network which has so far been missing. However, taking a multi-layer, multi-national perspective, some problems become immediately obvious. At the hardware level most technical problems have been solved, but the existing solutions are national ones. The only regularly running rapid train network -- the French TGV -- is running on tracks built exclusively for rapid passenger transport, while the German ICE is planned for both passenger and freight transport. Hence the effort of putting the national plans for improvement of rail transport in Europe onto a map does not in itself guarantee the achievement of a European network solution. To reach such a solution, important problems have to be solved on the orgware level and the ecoware level. It is doubtful whether a European rapid train system will ever come into being if its planning is left in the hands of the national railway companies and their related segmented ministries.

6.3.2. New networks

A co-ordinating body, to operate the services and/or distribute operations between companies according to competitive principles, should be foreseen at a very early stage. The planning of the infrastructure, which is not independent of the chosen system, must also be undertaken by a centralised body, unless the national railway companies can agree on a common standard.

In the short term, the realisation of the northern TGV could serve as a test bed for the multilateral co-ordination of rapid train planning involving several states. In the medium term, an integrated approach is required and the European Community has a clear responsibility if this network is to come into being. The basic problem in this field is to find a compromise between national and Community interests, mainly on the level of orgware and finware. A co-ordinating European infrastructure bank might be used to finance these high-speed projects.

Before the funding problems can be solved, a solution to the incompatibility of the different national systems must be found. Otherwise the new train will experience the same difficulties as the traditional trains with all the problems which arise at border crossings.

6.4. European common carriage

6.4.1. A sketch of bottlenecks

From an economic point of view, the idea of separating carriage and infrastructure in high-speed rail transport is based on the idea that networks have many of the characteristics of a natural monopoly. Consequently, if competition within a given mode is to be favoured, they should be separated from the use of the infrastructure, thereby realising a European concept of common carriage. Solving orgware and finware problems is essential for the realisation of such a strategy.

The development of the concept of common carriage must take account of many of the problems cited in the context of rail freight transport and the future rapid train system. In the process, many standardization questions have to be solved.

6.4.2. New networks

The concept of common carriage on European rail can only be realised for transport between high-ranking central places in Europe. Regional and national transport will be organised at the appropriate levels. At the European level, a European common carriage organisation will be necessary. This organisation will set standards and distribute slots on the rail system. Common carriage implies an integrative view to additions to the European train network, the closing of gaps, the retooling of certain tracks, especially with a view to the eastern European countries. Authority should be given to the European common carriage organisation with free entry to (private and public) parties meeting certain standards. Priority rules need to be set with respect to freight and passenger transport, feeder systems and regional traffic, and rules for concessions are needed which define bidding systems for routes and time schedules. However, overregulation should be avoided by limiting the power of this body.

6.5. Coastal transport and inland waterways

6.5.1. A sketch of bottlenecks

Changes in the international division of labour are concomitant with a new pattern of international trade flows, especially by sea and waterways.

Existing natural barriers, though, seem to impede the development of a European unitarian vision of the latter mode (inland waterways), while issues of strong competition between harbours within the European region have failed to develop the idea that they are part of a European network. In view of the above problems, the European Community has been recently engaged in an effort to develop the inland waterways network.

In the context of our analysis, we deal with three different types of networks: inland waterways, coastal transport, and mediterranean transport.

From the large number of bottlenecks in this field we may mention, *inter alia*, lack of standardization and network integration (e.g. lack of standardized vessels in transit areas); lack of harmonization of regulations (cabotage) -- also because national regulation is used to support national firms; lack of investment and planning of new networks or upgrading existing ones; lack of investments in fleet modernisation (also because of environmental reasons); lack of compatibility between barges, cargo specifications, train terminals and port facilities (necessary for multi-modal transport).

And if new infrastructure is eventually being built -- as is currently the case with the Rhine-Main-Danube Canal -- both planning and investment periods are very long.

6.5.2. New networks

To solve missing networks, policymakers should especially concentrate on (transnational) plans for main transport axes connecting at least Europe's major industrial areas with each other. Firms in each industrial area should be able to choose between road, rail and water as means of transport. Integration and harmonization of national policies and regulation (cabotage, labour, etc.) and standardization of hardware and software should also be favoured. Informatisation is also called for to ensure just-in-time transportation.

6.6. Telecommunications networks

6.6.1. A sketch of bottlenecks

The main problems in this field are thc following.

At the hardware level, there is an extreme kind of diversification between EC Members. This is particularly evident in the differences in developing infrastructure (ISDN) and differences in transmission capacity, etc., incompatibility and lack of interconnection.

At the orgware level, the main problems lie in the lack of standardization between national norms and standards for equipment, approvals etc. and -- most important -- in the way and pace in which European standardization is eventually achieved. Given the non-existence of a common European market in telecommunications, national priorities will then determine the kind of response to market needs. Another problem lies in the asymmetric way of price setting in telecommunication, determined by national considerations. For instance, high international telecom prices are often used to subsidise national users. Consequently, prices and costs are then more or less unrelated.

At the software level, a major problem lies in the absence of demand for sophisticated services using the telecom network. As long as this situation continues, suppliers of such services will not develop new applications.

Finware bottlenecks are also very important, since large investments are needed to develop a basic European telecommunications network.

Because of these problems, there is a real danger of a Europe *à deux vitesses*, with a clear division between those countries and/or regions having access to recent technology and those that have not. The socio-economic impacts of such developments are considerable, since existing differences in wealth and business opportunities will be accentuated.

6.6.2. *New networks*

The introduction of a European telecom base network, including standard facilities, services and uniform rules and tariffs, is necessary. Local networks should be at least hardware-compatible with this base network. Management and ownership should take the form of a public-private partnership in which governments, operators and users participate. Developing such a network will be very expensive, but will have positive economic impacts both for the users as well as for the industry; the use of EC (development) funding is needed.

A separation of responsibility between regulators (government; policy) and operators (implementation) is needed. Besides, avoidable barriers to entry should be minimised; the existence of monopolies should be avoided.

Since delivery technologies are changing too fast, a sustainable basis for regulation is missing. Improving competition should then be the keyword. Telecom prices should be cost-related. Furthermore, it would be necessary to use the outcome of current ENS-applications (e.g. the European NERVOUS-system) in transportation (EDI, ATMOS, FTM, Single Document, etc.), banking, environmental protection, health care and education, in order to develop European-wide applications.

Possible solutions include:

a) The use of new teleports as an operational planning tool for connecting telecommunications with physical goods transport or passenger movements (*cf.* the Amsterdam teleport success story);

b) The introduction of new networks;

   i) Substitution of postal services by more efficient and faster express mail: express mail services are booming, but the lack of a true network and, thereby, inefficient competition leads to very high prices;

   ii) The combined use of deregulation of national PTT services and the introduction of new standardized telecom services. The French Minitel might be used as a basis for such a European network (software, orgware). Experimentation with telecom zones in rural areas between two or three countries (orgware) is also an option in line with deregulation;

iii) Where substitution is impossible in goods transportation, options include the use of orbital fleet management in relation to electronic customs (replacement of physical border controls by standardized electronic vehicle identification at the big European freight terminals, ports and airports).

It is interesting to observe from the above case studies that the real heart of modern transport systems policy lies essentially in the co-ordination of multimodal systems, seen from the multi-dimensional viewpoint of five critical success factors. Expansion as a first logical choice is not plausible and does not solve the essential problems inherent in our modern network economies. Based on the previous case studies, three messages can be extracted for European policymakers.

The first message from the report concerns the predominance of national perspectives in transportation planning. Missing networks in Europe exist because transportation systems have been developed in a segmented way, each country and each transport mode seeking for its own solution without considering the synergetic effects of co-ordinated design and the use of advanced infrastructure. Because all economic development in space involves interacting networks, missing networks will, sooner or later, translate into missing economic development. Because of segmented national planning, there are European failures at the same time as national successes. New networks are created at the national level -- the national rapid train systems are an excellent example -- but the corresponding European network exists only as a fanciful map.

The second message of the report is the importance of a European perspective in the analysis and resolution of transport and communication problems in European countries. This is not only a question of formulating a co-ordinated standardization. Lack of standardization creates bottlenecks on all transport models with the exception of air transport. These problems range from a lack of technical standardization of cargo in combined transport on road and rail to problems with the width of canals and sluices on inland waterways. The greatest potential for standardization is in rail transport (differences in gauges, voltages, frequencies and supply type, signalling systems and norms for using foreign traction on domestic rails as well as in free profiles, etc.) and in telecommunications where the policies of the national PTT companies and developments in the NIT industries have led to the presence of an enormous variety of standards.

The third important message of this report is the need for multi-modal solutions. Although there are many success stories concerning uni-modal solutions at the national level, multimodal approaches are rarely found and, if present, are only of minor importance in terms of market shares. Nevertheless, it can be argued that the huge demand for additional transport capacity in Europe can only be met if multimodal solutions are also pursued. This holds for passenger transport (e.g. rapid trains for medium distances combined with air traffic for long distances) as well as for goods transport (e.g. rapid trains for medium distances combined with air traffic for long distances). The final message of this report, therefore, is that in looking for new network solutions, a multimodal view is essential.

The previous caveats suggest that infrastructure be declared as of a basic economic interest for Europe, so that a strategic priority plan from a European viewpoint has to be designed. Some necessary conditions for an efficient and effective European transport policy are a European institute for standardization, a European infrastructure bank, but also more strategic and co-ordinated transport research on a European level. Finally, technological progress should be stimulated in order to fully benefit from qualitatively advanced transport infrastructure.

7. CONCLUDING REMARKS

The previous observations have called attention to the development of European infrastructure in a highly dynamic, political, economic, social and technological context. Many uncertainties seem to prevail in the area of transport and infrastructure planning, such as the expected impacts of the completion of the internal market in Europe, the consequences for transport systems of deregulation and privatisation, the effects of stringent policies in favour of ecological sustainability, the potential of new infrastructure technologies, the flexibility (or rigidity) in human responses to transport policy measures, etc.

This also leaves us with an enormous research task regarding the design, use and access of European networks. Important research directions would have to be explored, such as:

-- Financing modes of new (transnational) infrastructure networks;

-- International co-ordination, harmonization and standardization of transport and communications systems;

-- Assessment and charging of social costs (and benefits) to various user categories and modes of transport;

-- The development of co-evolutionary planning principles between efficiency, equity and sustainability;

-- Cost-effectiveness analysis of network expansion *vis-à-vis* improved capacity use of existing networks;

-- Feasibility analysis of various types of user charge and road pricing measures;

-- The substitution possibilities between different transport modes in the light of their (realised or expected) performance, in terms of financial-economic, structural-economic and environmental consequences (e.g. intermodal transport);

-- The need for large-scale subsidisation of various types of transport (both public and private);

-- Experimental studies on separating property rights on infrastructure from operation and management of such networks;

-- The resilience of users of transport systems against changes and control measures impacting on human behaviour.

In terms of policy initiatives, the following strategy for the various planning levels (regional, national and European) regarding all transport and communication modes may be considered:

-- Declaration of infrastructure (development) as of basic economic interest for Europe; such a status should, for instance, include access to the various fiscal and financial instruments of the EC for R&D and pilot projects in this field;

-- Definition of a priority plan of base European networks (road, rail, air, waterways and telecom) in terms of network quality and performance (e.g. maximum travel time, reliability of transportation, etc.). Such a network would, of course, need sound links with lower level national and regional networks;

-- Strategic policy analysis of how to implement such a European network; for instance, coupling existing national networks is only a first step in this process, since nationalistic planning failures and thinking have strongly prevented the European network vision from emerging;

-- Creation of efficient decisionmaking procedures for European infrastructure (e.g. a co-ordination via a European institute for standardization), since current procedures are far from ideal. Growing constraints on infrastructure (e.g. financial, environmental, technical, etc.) have helped to create a climate in Europe which seriously affects its competitive position;

-- A clear strategy on prioritisation of European infrastructure projects, including a sound transnational financing (e.g. on the basis of a European infrastructure bank associated with a co-ordinating body for European transport policy).

Such initiatives are not in the first place addressed to the planning of infrastructure in the short term, but are focused on medium- and long-term projects, and form thereby a contrast with the well-known short-term, demand-oriented planning failures of the past. The emerging European network economy is faced with a large number of transportation bottlenecks, of which an important number may be ascribed to the absence or inefficient operation of vital physical and non-physical networks. From this study, the fundamental causes of missing networks have become more clear. One of the most important causes appears to be the nationalistic and/or unimodal way of organising and planning of infrastructure networks. A necessary condition for a competitive European network economy is a multi-modal European view on infrastructure, taking into consideration the five critical success factors discussed in this study. Europe's transport policy should thus be more strategic in nature.

FIGURES

Figure 1. **Development of European Commodity and Person Transport**
Index 1970=100

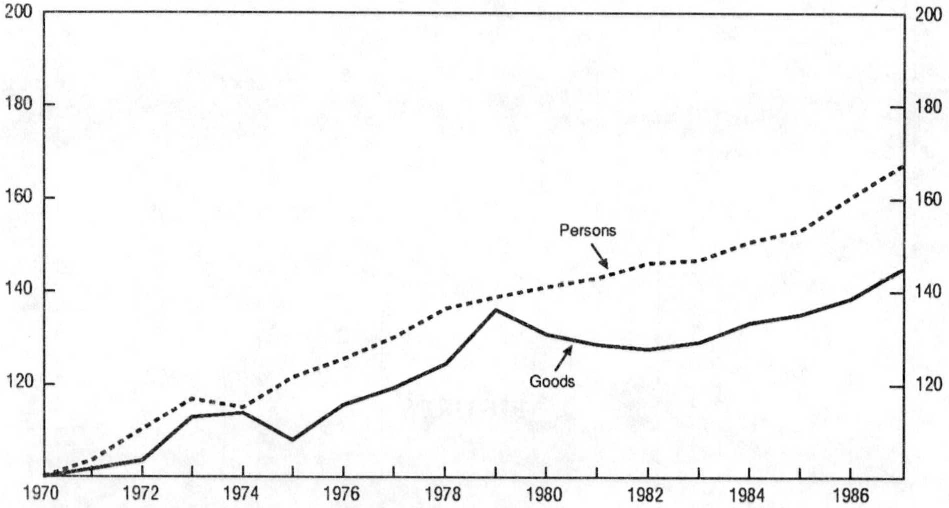

15 countries : A, B, DK, SF, F, D, I, L, NL, N, E, S, CH, TR, UK
Source : ECMT, 1990.

Figure 2. **Modal Split of European Commodity Transport**
Index 1970=100

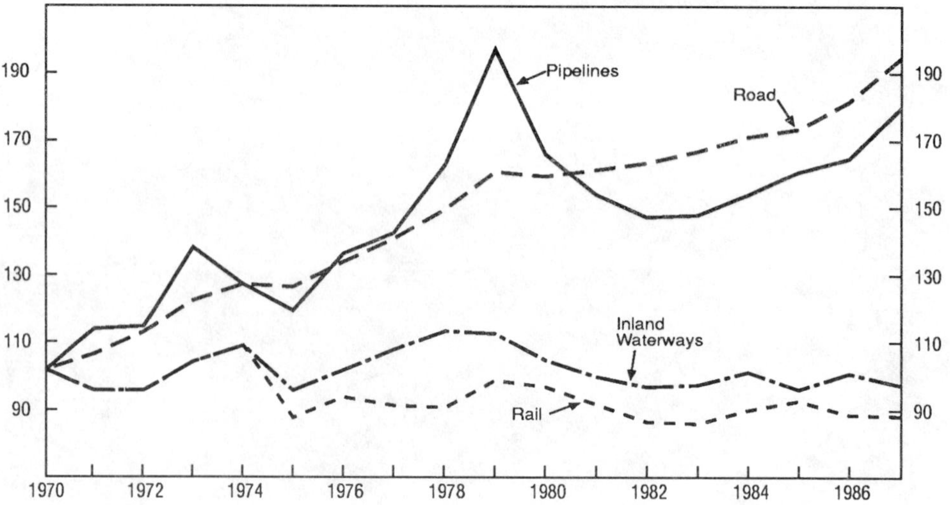

15 countries : A, B, DK, SF, F, D, I, L, NL, N, E, S, CH, TR, UK
Source : ECMT, 1990.

Figure 3. **Modal Split of European Passenger Transport**

Index 1970=100

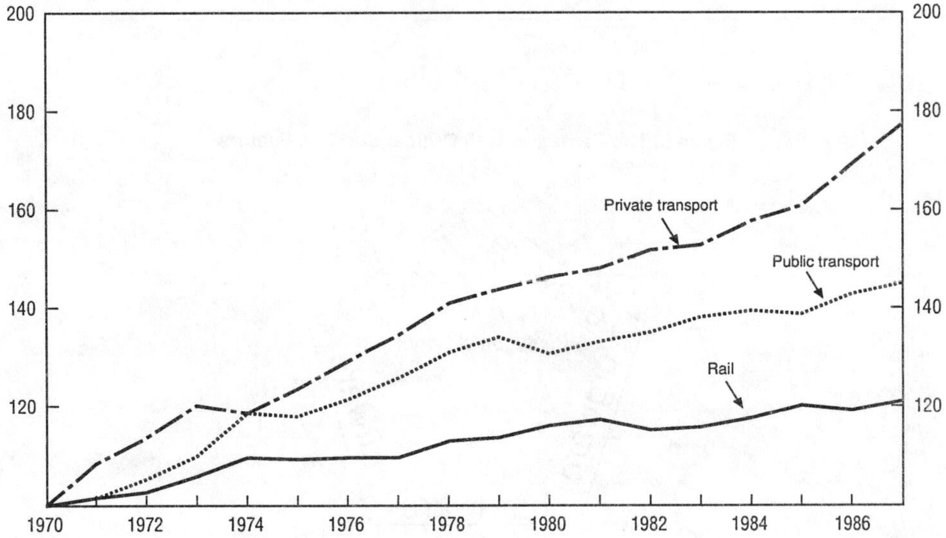

15 countries : A, B, DK, SF, F, D, I, L, NL, N, E, S, CH, TR, YU.

Source : ECMT, 1990.

Figure 4. **Development of European Transport Infrastructure Investments**

Index 1975=100

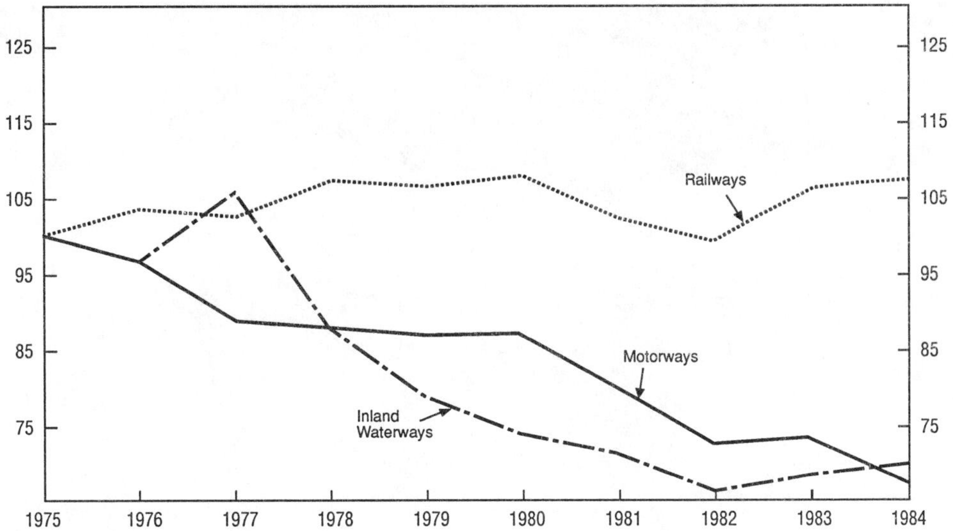

18 countries : A, B, DK, SF, F, D, G, IRL, I, L, NL, N, P, E, S, CH, UK, YU.

Source : ECMT, 1990.

Figure 5. **The Pentagon with Critical Success Factors**

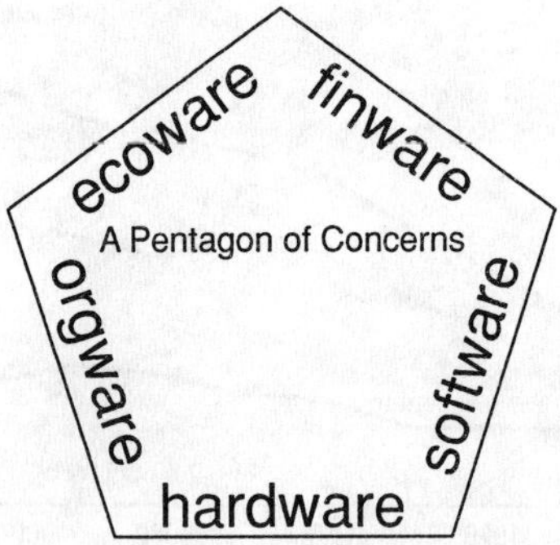

REFERENCES

Boeckhout, I.J. and S.A. Romkema (1989), Verschuiving van economische zwaartepunten in Noordwest-Europa: fictie of realiteit?, Rotterdam, NEI.

Community of European Railways (1989), Proposals for a European high-speed network.

Duenk, F.H.J. (1991), Het infrastructuurbeleid van de Europese Gemeenschap, Delft (DUP).

ECMT (1986), International Traffic and Infrastructural Needs, Paris (OECD).

ECMT (1989), Rail Network Co-operation in the Age of Information Technology and High Speed, Paris (OECD).

EC (European Community) (1990), Towards Trans-European Networks, DG VII, EC, Brussels.

EC, Group Transport 2000 Plus (1990), Transport in a Fast Changing Europe, DG VII, EC, Brussels.

ERT (European Roundtable of Industrialists) (1988), Need for renewing transport infrastructure; proposals for improving the decision-making process, European Roundtable Secretariat, Brussels.

ERT (1991), Missing Networks: A European Challenge, Brussels.

Hanenberg, A.G.M. van den (1990), Infrastructuur: Netwerk en Interactie, Delftse Universitaire Pers, Delft.

Himanen, V., P. Nijkamp and J. Padjen (1991), Ecological Sustainability and Transport Policy in Europe, Transportation Research.

Himanen, V., K. Makela, K. Alppivuori, P. Aaltonen, and J. Loukelainen (1989), The Monetary Valuation of Road Traffic's Environmental Hazards, Technical Research Centre of Finland, Research Report 943, Espoo.

Konings, R., E. Louw and J. Visser (1990), Missing links in Europees verband: technische standaardisatie, Delft (DUP).

Kreutzberger, E. (1991), Ruimtelijke dynamiek en metatrends; naar een onderzoeksagenda, Delft (DUP).

Kreutzberger, E. and J. Vleugel (1991), Topcapaciteit, Delftse Universitaire Pers, Delft.

Louw, E., P. Nijkamp and H. Priemus (1991), Sturingssystemen voor Infrastructuur en Mobiliteit, Delftse Universitaire Pers, Delft.

Maggi, R. and P. Nijkamp (1991), Missing Networks and Regional Development in Europe, Paper, International Colloquium on Regional Development, High Tatras.

Marchetti, C. (1987), On transportation in Europe: the last 50 years and the next 20, IIASA, invited paper on First Forum on Future European Transport, Munich.

McKinsey and Co. (1986), Afrekenen met files, Amsterdam.

NECTAR (1991), Missing Networks in Europe, ESF, Strasbourg.

Nijkamp, P., S. Reichman and M. Wegener (eds.) (1990), Euro-mobile, Avebury, Aldershot, United Kingdom.

OECD (1989), The Social Costs of Land Transport, Environment Directorate, Paris.

Pauchet, C. (ed.) (1988), L'Europe des transports, les enjeux de l'Europe, Paris (La Fédération).

Roschar, F., L. Jonkers and P. Nijkamp (eds.) (1991), Niet bij Transport Alleen, SDU, The Hague.

Sommer, H.J. (1990), The Zurich Cantonal Action Programme on Air Quality, Paper, Council of Europe Conference, Gothenburg, June 1990.

Tacken, M. and E. de Boer (1990), Spreiding van werktijden, spreiding van de verkeersspits, een analyse van condities en gedrag, Delft (OSPA-TUD).

Vleugel, J.M. and P. Nijkamp (1991), Policy Strategies for Missing Networks in Europe, Paper, European Transport Planning Colloquium, Brussels, 1991.

Vleugel, J.M. and H.A. van Gent (1991), Duurzame Ontwikkeling, Mobiliteit en Bereikbaarheid, Delftse Universitaire Pers, Delft.

Sub-topic 4

IMPACT OF NEW TECHNOLOGIES ON EFFICIENCY AND SAFETY

K.H. LENZ
BAST
Bergisch-Gladbach
Germany

SUMMARY

Bergisch Gladbach, June 1991

1. BASELINE SITUATION

According to United Nations' estimates (1) there were about 5.1 billion people living on our planet in 1988. The number of motor vehicles is estimated at 534 million, of which about 408 million private cars (2). If we just look at the global figures, it would thus appear that a car is shared by about twelve people.

However, cars are far from being equally distributed over the globe. While in the United States there are now 575 cars per 1 000 inhabitants, in Egypt there are 9 per 1 000, in Japan 240 and in Australia 438. It should be pointed out, though, that in the countries with a low level of car ownership this is not a true indicator of the level of motorised transport ownership because motorcycles and mopeds are important modes of transport in these countries. Even within Europe itself there are big differences. In the western European countries there are 345 million people with over 127 million cars, or 369 cars per 1 000 inhabitants. In the eastern European countries, with 318 million inhabitants, the car ownership rate is significantly lower, for example, 112 per 1 000 inhabitants in Poland and 51 in the European part of the Soviet Union.

Car ownership is generally not a serious problem in itself, apart from parking, notably in the inner city. The problem becomes critical only if the cars are used.

In 1960, all the motor vehicles of the former Federal Republic of Germany covered a total of 110 billion kilometres. By 1970, this figure had already increased to 234 billion vehicle-kilometres and it went on rising to reach 342 billion in 1980 and 461 billion in 1990. In thirty years the number of kilometres covered by our cars each year has more than quadrupled.

Today we cover 1.3 billion kilometres every day in our cars in the old *Länder* of the FRG, an incredibly high figure, and yet the car ownership level has not yet reached a peak. According to the latest Shell forecast for the Federal Republic of Germany (and it should be pointed out that most forecasts to date have been considerably exceeded by the actual figures) the car stock in the old

Länder will rise from the present figure of about 30 million to 35 million if the economic growth trend remains positive and will remain at about 30.5 million only if there is disharmony in economic life. In the new *Länder*, rate of growth will be much more marked: while less than 4 million cars were registered there in September 1989, the figure had already reached 4.8 million by September 1990, an increase of 23.5 per cent in one year. If we assume that the standard of living will be the same all over Germany by 2010, then the indications are that we shall have to be prepared for a total car stock of about 44 million.

The motor traffic has an enormous impact. In the Federal Republic of Germany alone, there were about 11 000 road deaths in 1990; the costs of congestion are estimated at DM 15 billion a year; very substantial quantities of energy are used in this form of mobility, polluting the environment and, notably in the towns, people are increasingly opposed to traffic noise and exhaust emissions.

The extension of the road networks cannot keep pace with the rapid growth of road traffic anywhere. For example, over a period of twenty years, the main road network in the Federal Republic of Germany increased from 162 344 to 173 590 km, i.e. by 7 per cent, and even though the motorway network increased from 4 110 km in 1970 to 8 618 km in 1988, i.e. by 110 per cent, the number of vehicle-kilometres increased over the same period by 246 per cent, or almost twice as fast.

There are many reasons why we cannot expect future increases in traffic to be matched by further increases in road space. The hopes of many for mastering the problems of private transport in the future can be summed up in the following slogan: less asphalt in the countryside, so more chips in the car.

2. THE BEGINNINGS OF TRAFFIC CONTROL

Serious road traffic problems first appeared in the big cities. In 1913 an installation with red and green incandescent lamps was introduced to regulate road traffic in Cleveland (USA) and hand-controlled, three-colour signals were introduced to regulate traffic in Detroit and New York in 1918 (3). The starting point for the technical development of traffic light signal control in Germany was in the Berlin metropolis. In Potsdamer Platz, which was considered difficult from the traffic control standpoint, green/yellow/red electric light signals were introduced only in 1924. It was reported that motor traffic became accustomed to the new type of signals more rapidly than expected and ran much more smoothly than before. However, it was difficult to make the pedestrians accustomed to using crossings rather than dashing straight across the square.

With these comments, the chronicle represents an evaluation of the function of the new installation. It is clear that the introduction of the new technology modified the behaviour of those involved in traffic movement -- partly with success, as concerns the drivers of vehicles, partly in an unsatisfactory fashion, as regards the pedestrians. As early as 1924 therefore it was found that in evaluating new technologies with regard to their effect, no useful conclusions can be drawn without studying the possible behaviour of traffic participants and their reactions to these technologies.

Still another important lesson was learned as early as 1924: the chronicle reports that at the same time as installing the light signal equipment, the former six-way intersection had been modified to leave a single oblique-angled intersection, in the middle of which stood the traffic island with the signals. Thus in order to be able to successfully use the new technology, constructional alterations were required. The need for harmonizing construction and operation thus came fully into evidence for the first time here.

If we now carry out in-depth studies before introducing new technologies in road transport, this is partly due to the experience that we have gained over past decades, mainly through practical tests in actual traffic conditions and with only very slow growth of the corresponding scientific instruments for theoretical and empirical studies. It is interesting in this connection, however, that at that time it was merely said that the traffic flowed much more freely with the new system. There was not one word about road safety, but this certainly does not mean there was no safety problem at that time. In 1925, Berlin had 4 million inhabitants and there were 35 000 motor vehicles on the roads. The statistics for that year report 143 road deaths -- excluding accident victims who died later. This is a very high figure when we consider that in (West) Berlin in 1985, with 1.9 million inhabitants and 740 000 registered motor vehicles there were 150 road deaths, i.e. about the same number as there were in 1925 when there was only one-twentieth of the motor vehicle stock.

Therefore, it cannot be because there was no problem that the chronicle has nothing to say about road safety. It is also unlikely that the new signals had no effects on safety; after all, they brought order to the former chaos and obvious, clear behaviour patterns which are of great relevance to safety and, as we know from many later studies, this must have increased safety. It is also unlikely that the chronicler had simply forgotten to mention this positive influence on safety.

It is much more likely that improving road safety was not then considered to be one of the tasks of the State; it was not yet part of the general provision expected from the State. Safety was then the concern of the individual, not so much of the system, though in the final analysis this also has a decisive influence on safety. This is a major difference between evaluation methods then and now.

3. TRAFFIC INFORMATION BROADCASTING

In an agreement between the ARD broadcasting station and the highest police authorities, traffic broadcasting was introduced in Germany in 1973-74, first under the name "traffic broadcasting" and later "traffic warning broadcasting" (4). There had already been precursors during the sixties as VHF radio began to spread.

Data were collected by the traffic police, a systematic organisational structure being built up:

-- The lowest level is formed by the police patrol cars, linked to their control stations by voice radio;

-- The middle level is formed by the *Land* reporting stations (LMSt). Each *Bundesland* has such a reporting station, manned day and night, and the regional transmitters provide information about the present transport situation, give traffic recommendations or indicate exceptional weather conditions;

-- The highest level is the Federal reporting station (BMSt) in Düsseldorf, whose task is to collect traffic information for the whole of Germany. It is informed by the *Land* stations about any congestion or problems affecting broad areas, important trunk routes or frontier-crossing traffic. The BMSt then directs the reports to the regional transmitters concerned, nation-wide transmitters and, where appropriate, neighbouring countries.

The Federal station and the *Land* stations, which already use computers to some extent to process the detailed congestion reports, give the reports confirmed by subordinate centres to the regional transmitters concerned and to nation-wide German radio. In addition, information is sent, where appropriate, to automobile clubs, frontier stations and the traffic authorities of the neighbouring countries affected. There is also a two-way exchange of information with the Weather Office in Offenbach, through which congestion caused by weather conditions can be included in the traffic broadcasts.

In Germany the traffic information is generally transmitted to motorists via VHF transmitters that serve a particular region (*Land*). The stations concerned normally broadcast general programmes (music, news) and briefly interrupt their programmes for traffic announcements. This interruption of the main programme is generally well accepted, so that no stations have been specially set up for traffic information purposes.

Traffic announcements can basically be heard on any VHF receiver and, to some extent or at times also, on medium-wave receivers. If the road user desires greater comfort, the VHF receiver has to be fitted with a decoder that automatically switches on on receipt of a frequency-dependent signal from the station of interest to the driver, to receive messages concerning the traffic situation.

The traffic broadcasting system outlined above works, but the flow of information, from the detection of the problem through its evaluation or confirmation and its passing on in the form of a report to a transmitter, is essentially manual. The transmission methods used are radio telephone, telephone and telex or special data networks.

The results of questionnaires show that this service is well known and much appreciated by motorists: 85 per cent of the respondents considered the reports to be useful, two-thirds highly effective. Over half said they always or frequently followed alternative route recommendations, but 31 per cent had gone astray because the signposting was obviously inadequate.

Despite the good organisation, the present information path is cumbersome. According to a presentation by the Federal Roads Office (Bolte, 1985), it could take over thirty minutes for a report of congestion caused by an accident to reach the *Land* reporting station. The time lag can be even longer when the problem is not caused by an accident and the police are not directly brought in.

Radio reports have the disadvantage that the driver has to filter out what is relevant for him from a great deal of other spoken information and that foreigners do not understand a message in what is, for them, a foreign language.

This disadvantage can be overcome if the reports are standardized and transmitted over existing medium-wave and/or VHF broadcasting networks in the form of additional coded digital signals.

Car radios with the appropriate additional circuitry can filter out the relevant information if instructed to do so by the driver and pass it on through synthesised speech (in the mother tongue of the driver concerned). Furthermore, the information can be retrieved and repeated at any time.

One transmission path could be the Radio Data System (RDS) introduced by the European Broadcasting Union (EBU) and in virtually Europe-wide operation since mid-1989, even though at present most of the broadcasting stations transmit only unchanging data for station recognition, etc. (static phase RDS).

The planned "Traffic Message Channel" (TMC) of the RDS is to be used to transmit traffic messages continually and inaudibly at the same time as and independently of the normal programme, so that there is no interruption in it, these messages being made audible by a special device in the vehicle.

Preliminary discussions and planning for the use of FM-RDS and AM-RDS Traffic Message Channels is already well under way in the European Conference of Ministers of Transport (ECMT), the European Broadcasting Union (EBU) and the Association of German Broadcasting Stations (*Arbeitsgemeinschaft der Rundfunkanstalten der Bundesrepublik Deutschland* -- ARD). In addition, in the context of the DRIVE research programme, concrete proposals for the coding of message texts, locality indicators and message management have been prepared. On the road and traffic management side, planning and the first steps towards traffic data collection on federal motorways have begun.

In Germany, the static part of the FM-RDS system was introduced on 1st April 1988. The dynamic parts have not yet been tackled.

In 1987-88, there were a number of field tests on the transmission of additional digital information through AM radio stations in Germany. The reliability and error structure of the data transmission was tested and evaluated with the aid of devices specially developed for this purpose under different operating conditions using a number of transmitters and in one special case, using two transmitters on the same frequency, the compatibility between additional signals and programmes was investigated. The findings indicate that a sufficiently reliable additional data transmission system is possible with a data transmission rate of up to 200 bits per second without any unacceptable deterioration of programme quality.

A field test is now being prepared in the Rhine area of Germany to investigate many aspects, such as technical questions, administration, operating problems, software, transmission methods, ease of use, acceptance, economics, etc.

4. ALI (GUIDANCE AND INFORMATION SYSTEM FOR MOTORISTS)

The ALI system was an initial traffic influencing system aimed at the individual driver (5). On the basis of a comprehensive traffic data collection system using roadside communications equipment, the individual driver is given directions for the choice of the best route to his destination at various decision points through a device fitted in the vehicle. At the same time, however, other data, for example concerning present road conditions and the traffic situation further ahead, can be transmitted.

The possibility of the ALI system for individual guidance to a destination and the transmission of special information can be used at variable levels in an overall package. The individual user can benefit from a reduction in the psychological and physical burden during the journey thanks to the provision of targeted information. For road users as a whole, there can be a reduction in the economic cost and improvements in road safety. Overall, better utilisation of transport infrastructures and reduction of road occupancy times can be achieved. For the authorities there are advantages to be expected in the implementation of tasks like planning, building and operating the road network.

From the technical standpoint it turns out that traffic influencing systems aimed at the individual, such as the ALI system, contain many components that can also be used by other systems. Systems aimed at the individual are therefore to be seen as complementary systems that can make a substantial contribution to improving the exchange of traffic information.

The main technical components of the system are: on-board communications equipment consisting of destination input and output devices and transmitting and receiving equipment; roadside communications equipment consisting of induction loops in road lanes before branching-off points and the associated sending and receiving equipment and microprocessors with data storage.

In order to analyse the efficiency of the ALI system, on the one hand the costs were compared with the expenditures that could be saved through the advantages of the system which could be expressed in monetary terms; on the other hand, in the context of a cost-effectiveness analysis, its suitability as an aid to decisionmaking and to reduce the psychological and physical burdens of driving was investigated.

The cost of fitting the Federal motorway network (6 000 km) with the ALI system would involve a one-off investment cost of DM 345 million. Converted to annual costs, this amounts to DM 16.5 million a year, to which must be added operating costs of about DM 10.7 million. The total annual costs of the ALI system for the motorway network would thus amount to DM 27.2 million or, given the length of the network, DM 4 500/km.

The costs for vehicle owners, assuming a fitting rate of 20 per cent for ALI equipment, would amount to DM 1 400 million or, converted to annual costs, about DM 140 million a year. For the individual vehicle owner the cost, assuming a price below DM 350 per ALI unit, would be two or three per cent of the vehicle price.

Since the costs for the individual vehicle owner are relatively low, the decision to buy depends less on the monetary advantage than on the convenience and performance of the guidance and information system as an aid on the road.

Two different approaches were therefore used to analyse the efficiency of the ALI system:

-- First, cost-effectiveness analysis was used to investigate the suitability of the ALI system as a decision and driving aid to reduce the psychological and physical burden on the driver. The results for the area investigated, the Rhine-Main motorway network, show that for all the different preference structures, comparing the ALI system with the two other systems analysed [traffic broadcasting (ARI) and alternate route indications], even with the low fitting rate of only 20 per cent of all vehicles, ALI can be just as effective as these other systems. With a higher fitting rate ALI would surpass the other systems with the same cost to the authorities.

-- Second, in order to evaluate the cost side of the ALI system, its costs were compared with expenditure in the fields where it brings advantages that can be expressed in money terms: accident reduction, vehicle operating costs and travel time costs. This not only showed the relationship between the costs of the ALI system and the advantages achieved, but it showed at the same time that even small savings in these fields could compensate for the costs of implementing the ALI system.

Since there are no known reduction factors for the effects of the ALI system on the benefit areas considered -- accident reduction, vehicle operating costs and journey time costs -- the expected benefits were designated as variables in the model.

The analysis shows that, even using a very conservative approach for the monetary effects of the ALI system, with a 20 per cent fitting rate, the annual savings are:

Accident costs	DM 27 million
Vehicle operating costs	DM 18 million
Journey time costs	DM 21 million

i.e. a total of DM 66 million in monetary benefits, or about 40 per cent of the total annual costs for the ALI system of DM 167.2 million. It appears justifiable to regard the remainder of the annual costs not covered as payment for the enhanced comfort for the individual driver brought about by the use of the ALI system.

On the other hand, an alternative comparison of the costs of the ALI system with the costs incurred in the areas of accidents, vehicle operation and journey time shows that a reduction in rear end collisions and accidents caused by ice and fog of 30 per cent, or a reduction in the operating costs of all vehicles of 2 per cent, or of ALI-equipped vehicles of 10 per cent, or travel time savings for all vehicles of 3 per cent, would exceed the total annual costs of the ALI system.

Even though there is much to indicate that ALI would be successful from the cost-benefit standpoint, it must now already be considered as belonging to history. Through avoiding certain disadvantages and exploiting technical progress, the basic idea of this system has been further developed to become ALI-Scout (see LISB below).

5. AICHELBERG QUEUE WARNING SYSTEM

The development of the Aichelberg queue warning system (StWA) was a response to the problem of designing and testing a fully automatic, effective road safety system for motorway stretches subject to congestion (6). The design was to be decided in co-operation with the authorities of the *Land* Baden-Württemberg responsible for the situation of the A8 Stuttgart-Munich federal motorway at the foothills of the Alps, in order to make the traffic flow safer on the stretch before the climb to the Alps, a stretch particularly subject to congestion and accidents. Queues build up here regularly due to the Aichelberg viaduct bottleneck at the beginning of the climb with a 7 per cent gradient and a curve radius of 400 metres. In addition to this restriction of the efficiency of the motorway due to the routing, problems are often caused by broken down vehicles as there is no hard shoulder.

The stretch to be covered by queue warning signals is about 8 kilometres long. It is so dimensioned that about 85 per cent of all queues can be covered, but not individual very long queues, for example at peak holiday periods, because the extension of the experimental installation would not be economically justifiable.

The queue warning area is divided into a total of fifteen blocks about 500 metres in length. Each block is fitted with variable message signs and vehicle detectors connected to a central traffic computer in the motorway control centre in Kirchheim/Teck (integrated system).

The variable message signs are fibre optic matrix signs constructed as a micro-raster, on which "100", "80", "60" and "STAU" (QUEUE) can be displayed. The speed indications are recommended maximum speeds, exceeding which is not punishable. The signs are fitted on gantries across the road and the displays are co-ordinated so that appropriate speed sequences can be established. To measure traffic density double-loop inductive detectors are used to determine the vehicle count, vehicle speeds and loop occupancy. The impulses from the detectors are transmitted unreduced by cable, using an audio frequency multiplex system, to the central computer where the information is processed and analysed. Using a pre-established control model, the computer sends switching commands as required to the individual variable message signs and receives the corresponding switching response signals together with any failure reports there may be from any of the components of the installation.

The aim of the queue warning is, above all, to improve road safety as a queue starts to form. The accident statistics thus provide data against which the effectiveness of the queue warning system can be assessed with respect to its aims. 1975 was used as the reference year for the situation without the queue warning system ("before"), which was introduced on 31st March 1976.

Assuming continuation of the existing accident rate trend on the motorway leading to the Aichelberg, the extrapolated accident figures can be used as the reference figures for the situation without the queue warning system. The extrapolated accident rates and vehicle kilometre figures make it possible to calculate the absolute accident figures "without queue warning system", Prognosis 1. These figures are given as the upper limit.

If it is assumed that the accident rate would not have grown any more even without the queue warning system, but would have remained constant at the 1975 figure, this represents the lower limit, Prognosis 2.

The actual accident figures are substantially below the values in both prognoses; the reduction in the number of accidents as compared with Prognosis 1 over the period 1976 to 1980 amounts to 243 accidents; as compared with Prognosis 2 it amounts to 173 accidents.

If we compare the actual trend in accident rates under the influence of the queue warning system with those of the prognoses without this system, the positive effect of the queue warning system is particularly clear: the accident rate fell to 57.5 per cent (Prognosis 1) and 65.6 per cent (Prognosis 2) of the extrapolated values, i.e. a reduction in the accident rate of 42.5 and 34.4 per cent respectively.

An analysis from the traffic engineering standpoint was carried out to provide information about how the signals in the queue warning system affect traffic movement:

-- It was demonstrated that the signals had a marked influence on traffic speeds;

-- The signals "100" and "80" led to a slight reduction in average speeds, but there was a marked fall in the proportion of vehicles travelling at high speed;

-- The reduction in the standard deviation of the speeds leads to the conclusion that there was a positive effect upon traffic flow;

-- The "80" signal tended to lead to better lane use and hence to a more even average loading.

A cost-benefit comparison provided information about the profitability of the measure. Only parameters that could be measured in monetary terms were taken into account here.

	Upper limit	Lower limit
Costs: Investment and maintenance costs	DM 5.6 million	
Benefits: Avoidance of accident and congestion costs	DM 13.3 mil	DM 6.9 mil
Difference: Benefit surplus	+DM 7.7 mil	+DM 1.3 mil
Benefit/Cost ratio	2.38:1	1.23:1

The result for the period 1976 to 1980 shows a clear benefit surplus (see table), even though the total cost of the system is here fully written off over the period of only five years and the actual "remaining value" of the installation is not taken into account.

6. KÖLN/AACHEN TRAFFIC INFLUENCING SYSTEM

At the end of 1988 a traffic influencing system came into operation on the motorway between Köln and Aachen. The stretch is about 52 kilometres long and has two lanes with a hard shoulder in each direction and runs through level and sometimes slightly rolling country. The average daily traffic load was around 55 000 vehicles per 24 hours. The installation comprises 27 signal gantries each with three matrix traffic signs so that signals can be given for each lane and for the entire carriageway through an additional matrix (e.g. speed limits, ban on overtaking, queue warning, etc.). It is intended to complete the installation by means of automatic traffic counting and control. A report by the operator (7) includes a study of the extent to which accidents have been reduced as a result of the installation.

The overall accident rate over this stretch had worsened by 10.1 per cent between 1987 and 1988. After the system came into operation the accident rate fell by 3.8 per cent between 1988 and 1989. It should be pointed out here that over the rest of the network in North Rhine-Westphalia there was an increase of 0.4 per cent over the same period. If we take injury accidents, the positive influence becomes even clearer: over the stretch covered by the installation, injury accidents fell by 9.8 per cent while in the *Land* as a whole they increased by 3.8 per cent.

The positive influence of the installation can also be seen in the accident costs: unlike 1988, when accident costs rose by 15.5 per cent over the previous year's figure, there was a fall of 23.2 per cent in 1989 as compared with 1988.

7. RHINE-MAIN ALTERNATIVE ROUTE SYSTEM

The Rhine-Main motorway network to the south-west of Frankfurt runs between Frankfurt and the towns of Wiesbaden and Darmstadt, connecting with the long-distance motorways from Cologne, Dortmund, Hanover, Munich, Stuttgart and Basel. This sub-network is characterised by the close mesh typical of conurbations which stems from the coming together of long-distance, feeder and link motorways. It is approximately forty kilometres in diameter. Corresponding to the rather polycentric structure of the Rhine-Main area, the sub-network fulfils the typical conditions of such a network, unlike the two stretches to the south that have the typical form of a "corridor" between Darmstadt and Walldorf in Baden (8).

For each journey (transit) between the seven external nodes of the Rhine-Main network, there is at least one alternative route available apart from the normal route that makes it possible to bypass one or more stretches of the normal route. However, the additional distance is sometimes considerable as compared with the shortest link that is taken as the normal route and used as the reference value.

In the Rhine-Main area the ordinary main road network (secondary network) is structured in the same way as the motorway network (primary network) and in no case are there frontage roads running alongside the motorways, as is fairly typical of city motorway networks in the United States, for example. The roads that do run more or less parallel have such a difference in capacity, corresponding to their normal function, that they cannot be considered as alternative routes for the motorways, but only as emergency deviations in case of need.

A temporary closing of a section of motorway or ramp control to relieve a bottleneck, forcing a deviation of traffic through the secondary network, therefore has to be excluded as a regular feature of traffic management.

Because of the geographical situation of the Rhine-Main area, the sub-network, and notably the transit motorways crossing it, carries a high proportion of through traffic which increases very considerably in holiday periods and becomes the major determinant of traffic flows. This long-distance traffic comes on top of the regional traffic and the commercial traffic almost typical of urban roads. Because of the different types of nodes, these traffics vary greatly not only with the location, but also with time. This means that when one stretch is overloaded there are almost always certain reserve capacities on parts of alternative routes.

Experience gained through the use of temporary diversion arrangements led in 1969 to the design of remote-controlled alternative route signs at the Rüsselsheim junction and Mönchhof junction nodes rather than stationary signs to relieve the bottleneck at Weilbacher Berg and Mönchhof junction. The aim was to be able at peak periods to divert traffic flowing from the east to the Mönchhof junction and from the south to the Rüsselsheim junction and heading for Cologne over the alternative route Mainspitz junction and the Wiesbaden-Mainz road. The necessary equipment was installed at relatively low cost and came into operation in 1970.

The direction indicators at both nodes were so constructed that the display area for the destination was formed by one side of a four-sided prism that could be revolved about the longitudinal axis. This made it possible to retain the fully retro-reflective traffic sign usual in Hessen and to display four different destinations independently of one another. The display was under program control, i.e. electronic and electrical switching was arranged to display five prism side combinations in each chain of direction indicators, controlled as a "program" from the Rüsselsheim motorway control centre.

Since distant destination information at a motorway node is not addressed to traffic terminating at following exits, only through traffic between the nodes at which the normal and alternative routes separate and rejoin can be used as the reference value to determine the degree of compliance, the proportion of this through traffic that follows the diversion signs being defined as the "compliance ratio". The amount of traffic actually to be diverted also depends on the proportion of through traffic in total traffic.

The compliance ratios for the variable route signs at the Rüsselsheim and Mönchhof junctions have been determined in several follow-up surveys, taking account of variant displays and the actual shift of traffic flows on the roads running from the nodes concerned.

The important findings and those showing the way ahead are:

-- Depending on the type of display, the compliance ratio lies between 0.5 and 0.8;

-- The compliance ratio for the diversion program is clearly greatest with the normal display (0.8), while unusual displays cause a significantly reduced compliance (Z 250 only 0.5);

-- The actual volume of traffic diverted is considerable: 30 per cent turning traffic before the deviation, 80 per cent during the deviation.

These measured results thus show that the use of changed route indications using traffic signs with strictly the same characteristics as normal signs can achieve significant traffic deviation. Over the short stretches considered here, the proportion of responsive through traffic is so high that a significant shift of traffic flow can be achieved.

For the particular problem involved, the operation of these first two variable route sign installations proved to be an effective measure for the rapid reduction of queues caused by overloading, with a detour time of about ten minutes in each case. However, since switching was dependent on observations by the police, own staff and a remote-controlled TV camera, it was possible only to relieve already overloaded roads and not to prevent queue formation, thanks to a knowledge of traffic build-ups.

Taking into consideration certain preconditions and on the basis of a modelling concept, the results of effectiveness analyses for the Rhine-Main alternative routing system (known as WWW -- *Wechselwegweisung*) can clearly be seen (9):

-- Cost-benefit analysis: *ex-post* analyses over a period of ten years. Because the system was operated at full capacity for only a short time compared with the total period, benefits did not cover costs. On the other hand, if development costs amounting to about 25 per cent of the costs of the WWW installation arising over the analysis period in the

Rhine-Main test area are assumed, costs are covered when the residual value is taken into account.

-- Cost-benefit analysis: *ex-post* analysis for operating year 1976-77. Taking into account the annualised investment cost and operating costs, there was a net benefit of about DM 2.9 million for the year.

-- Cost-effectiveness analysis: *ex-post* analysis for operating year 1976-77. There were very different results according to the group studied and the target. With the weighting from the standpoint of the motorist (speed has high value), the WWW was assessed positive by all groups. With the weighting from the standpoint of the operator and the economy (expenditure has high value) the installation was assessed positive only for the whole of the diverted samples and those achieving transport cost savings thanks to the on-line switching.

-- Utility analysis: *ex-post* analysis for operating year 1976-77. The high investment costs affect the result with weightings from the standpoint of operator and the economy as a whole. Positive evaluation of the system from the standpoint of the driver.

-- Cost-benefit analysis: *ex-ante* analysis over a period of twelve years. The results vary depending on the traffic flow model used. If a model is selected whose effects correspond roughly to those found in the sample survey in the analysis year, profitability is achieved after about ten years.

Even today, fifteen years after the first stage came into operation, the system is not yet obsolete and is to be used for routing traffic to the extended Rhine-Main airport.

8. LISB (BERLIN ROUTE GUIDANCE AND INFORMATION SYSTEM)

In (West) Berlin the LISB route guidance and information system has been under test for some years now. The difference between LISB and conventional traffic control is obvious: not the collective, but the individual vehicle is the target, actor and user of the traffic influencing system, and this in a kind of barter system. The driver announces his desired journey by entering the destination through a display to a central computer. He begins his journey and passes special beacons at intersections, through which he receives route recommendations, but the vehicle also transmits information about the time taken to cover the distance between beacons, waiting times at traffic lights, etc. From this information the computer draws conclusions about traffic density and the risk of queue formation, searches for the best route and displays it as a message on the screen inside the vehicle. Bottlenecks can thus be avoided.

The message on the small screen in the vehicle is certainly clear and simple, but it still diverts the eyes from the road. Fortunately, audible information has therefore also been introduced into the system. Many studies have been carried out to evaluate the road safety aspect and to investigate acceptance by the individual. The 1990 intermediate report for drivers not familiar with the area (10) indicates the following.

A field test was carried out in the form of a competition involving eighteen male and female drivers of different age groups, all unfamiliar with the area. This made it possible to create a time pressure comparable to the natural situation when using a guidance system. In order to be able to make comparisons between traditional street maps and the LISB system, fixed source-destination links were to be covered. This guaranteed roughly equal stretches for the different participants and comparable navigating difficulties.

Subjective and objective criteria were used to measure the different navigating aids. The recording of eye movements showed the duration and frequency of diversion of the eyes away from traffic events; a comparison of journey times using street maps and LISB showed the objective time savings for drivers unfamiliar with the area. The road safety impact was evaluated by a specially developed procedure using a traffic conflict technique. Demands on the driver were measured by means of subjective ratings and the physiological measurement of pulse rate. Acceptance and control were assessed on the basis of questionnaires and interviews.

In the case of journeys using LISB, participants looked at the display for 17 per cent of the total journey time. For an average journey of 22 minutes this meant 3.7 minutes. This high value during the journey was due, among other things, to the fact that when the vehicle is stopped no new information is received. In the case of journeys using maps, the reading of maps while the vehicle was moving was forbidden.

Remarkably enough, there was no difference between older and younger drivers as regards visual behaviour. Switching between "traverse navigation" in which only direction and distance to the destination was given and "real" guidance information through LISB did not change visual strategy either. The frequency of looking at the screen fell during the experiment, however, showing a familiarisation and practice effect, the end point of which is difficult to estimate.

The evaluation of driving behaviour and infringements of the rules generally showed better values for LISB. The use of the LISB system had a standardizing effect on speed, which was welcome from the road safety standpoint. Infringements of the rules and traffic conflicts were also seen less frequently than in the case of driving with the street map. There are two observations to set against this positive evaluation on the quantitative side, however. In journeys using LISB there was an above-average number of manoeuvres begun in uncontrolled fashion and, as a result, rather more traffic conflicts of a fairly serious nature. However, the total number of serious conflicts was too low for this finding to be regarded as certain.

The use of the LISB system significantly reduces journey times as compared with the use of a street map. The substantial variance observed with street map journeys over many stretches shows the influence of personal and situation variables. The help provided and route optimisation through LISB resulted in a smaller variance in journey times when this system was used.

The data also showed greater problems with map use in the case of older drivers and therefore substantially longer journey times. The benefits of a guidance system like LISB as regards journey time and hence risk exposure were particularly marked for the older driver group.

Analysis of the demands made on drivers initially showed inconsistencies between the subjective judgement and the physiological data. Subjectively, almost 90 per cent of the experimental group found street map use more demanding, while objectively (as measured by pulse rate) no difference could be observed at first. Traffic and personal methods could explain this result, but splitting the data into "in motion" and "stationary" showed the real reason for the discrepancy: studying the map while stopped was very demanding (highest pulse rate), while the same situation with LISB led to substantial relaxing (lowest pulse rate). While moving, the differences were evened out because of the stress caused by traffic. The falling pulse rate as the experiment progressed also indicated an effect caused by the experimental situation itself. Thanks to the design of the experiment, however, this effect worked on street map and LISB journeys in the same way and can therefore be ignored when comparing the two.

The question regarding the acceptance of the two types of orientation aid showed very different opinions regarding the street map, as against unanimous approval of the LISB system. Consistent with this, drivers found no loss of control through the electronic guidance system and felt more secure with LISB. It should be borne in mind, however, that the responses of the participants may have been to some extent distorted in favour of LISB by the tendency to give what were thought to be the desired answers.

Because of the relatively good guiding properties of LISB, drivers developed high expectations of the system and a kind of "blind trust" in it. However, as there are in fact a number of weaknesses in the system, drivers were for the most part quite helpless in such situations.

Drivers unfamiliar with a place are more at risk than locals. To what extent this risk can be reduced by a guidance system like LISB is not sufficiently clarified by the experiments carried out to date. The strategy for further research is therefore aimed in two main directions:

i) Analysis of whether financially acceptable technical changes or improvements in the man/machine interface can positively influence the road safety aspects of LISB;

ii) Evaluation of the safety gains of an ideal guidance system for drivers unfamiliar with the area.

9. PROMETHEUS

PROMETHEUS (Programme for a European Traffic System with the Highest Efficiency and Unprecedented Safety) is a research project funded by seventeen European car manufacturers, aimed at achieving a more efficient and safer future private transport system, with the main technology thrust in the fields of microelectronics and sensors and extending to their use in artificial intelligence systems. It is, without a doubt, the most spectacular transport project ever, a truly unique event in international industrial co-operative effort, supported by governments, an impressive approach to the combination of the engineering spirit and creativity. Some DM 1.3 billion are available for the first eight-year period, 35 per cent of this sum being from German sources.

PROMETHEUS is aimed at:

-- enhancing safety;
-- reducing undesired environmental impacts;
-- improving efficiency and economy.

The programme is so broad and all-embracing that even listing all the individual research topics would go beyond the scope of this paper. We therefore limit ourselves in what follows to a few selected road safety aspects. Here it should be pointed out that the individual components of PROMETHEUS are still being developed and are therefore not available for practical testing. The following method was therefore used to estimate possible safety gains (11).

The abstract descriptions of functions and effects of the electronic information and guidance systems discussed in the PROMETHEUS programme were used to evaluate the safety impact. The following functions were selected for this purpose: trip planning, route guidance, speed keeping, car following, lane keeping, overtaking, intersection control, accident detection, security and obstacle detection.

The first question is, what sorts of accidents can be influenced at all by the different PROMETHEUS modules. Here the categories used in the German accident statistics, with the division into category, type and cause, provide a sound basis. A whole series of hypotheses are to be considered when trying to answer the key question of how many accidents could possibly be prevented by a given PROMETHEUS module. The main ones are discussed below:

-- An assumption has to be made about the required and, within a reasonable time span, achievable level of vehicle and roadside technical infrastructures. Thus it is scarcely conceivable that every single intersection and every metre of road between the North Cape and Sicily would be cabled.

-- Assumptions have to be made about the technical efficiency of the module. For example, even an electronic camera for obstacle detection cannot yet distinguish between a person's shadow and the person himself.

-- There is also the question of whether the volume of data to be exchanged will increase more than proportionally with the increase in the number of PROMETHEUS users, and can still be successfully handled by the infrastructures outside the vehicle, on which there will be increasingly heavy demands.

-- An important, but still largely open, question is how drivers will get on with this technology, especially in view of the ageing of our motoring population. How will it influence their behaviour, to what extent will they accept it? The degree of intervention of the module is thus certainly of importance. Among the measures there are some that simply inform, others that warn and others again that more or less seriously impinge on the driver's sovereignty. The conceivable final stage is partial or even complete automation of road traffic.

-- Assumptions have to be made about whether the module appears suitable and feasible for all locations (urban streets, main roads, motorways).

-- Lastly, the authors (11) work on the basis that at first only cars and trucks can be fitted. Extension to other vehicles (e.g. motorised two-wheelers and eventually even cyclists) can be envisaged under certain conditions, but in this author's opinion only in the distant future. At present, equipping the pedestrian is considered to be out of the question.

With the exception of the last one, the above assumptions were considered anew for each module, for even if the aim is an initial rough estimation of the potential, the assumption of a universal infrastructure covering both roads and vehicles, working optimally at all times and in all places, with all acceptance and attitudinal problems having been solved, does not seem very useful. Nevertheless, the findings are fairly optimistic regarding the effectiveness of PROMETHEUS: even where the limits of applicability of a module are considered from a sceptical standpoint, the potential benefits still appear. This applies, for example, to intersection control in urban areas. Just how the many-faceted and confused information and communication links between road users and heavily-trafficked inner-city intersections -- taking account of the structural characteristics -- can be handled by PROMETHEUS in a completely conflict-free and harmonious fashion, lies beyond our powers of imagination at present.

It was not possible to deal with questions of the "error-proneness" of such systems and the associated "shifting of responsibility" to technology.

Because of the many complementary and substitutive relationships between the modules, the authors did not consider themselves to be in a position to combine the estimated possible effects of individual modules into a global effect.

The extent to which an accident could be influenced by a given module was estimated using three different databases, established by:

-- Special processing of the accident data collected for the official statistics;

-- Processing of the "investigations at the scene of the accident" carried out by the Hanover Medical University;

-- Processing of accidents in Rhineland Palatinate using the extended catalogue of accident categories.

These were classified according to locality: built-up area, outside built-up area and federal motorway. Thanks to the three databases, it was possible to make three approximations (estimates) to assess the effectiveness of the module.

It emerged from this process that the use of the modules for built-up areas had to be, as a rule, excluded or considered only partially effective. One reason for this was constructional characteristics, where active "seeing" round corners, under bridges or through tunnels is possible only to some extent if at all. What is more, the complexity of urban road traffic and the many interactions with parked vehicles or road users not equipped with PROMETHEUS, such as pedestrians, cyclists and motorcyclists, restrict use so much that no positive safety effect can be expected.

The individual modules vary considerably as regards their estimated average safety impact, as shown in the following table:

Module	Estimated effectiveness (percentage reduction in death and injury accidents)
Trip planning	(*)
Route guidance	0.4 - 1.4
Speed keeping	14.0 - 16.0
Car following	2.3 - 3.0
Lane keeping	0.8 - 2.6
Overtaking	1.7 - 2.9
Intersection control	4.3 - 4.5
Accident detection	0.1 - 0.2
Security	ca. 2.0
Obstacle detection	0.2 - 0.6

(*) No potential benefit could be estimated.

The range in the estimated effectiveness results from the different assumptions and framework conditions taken into account in the individual estimates, such as whether it was made on the basis of the type or category of accident. In evaluating the effectiveness of the individual modules it can be seen that, with but few exceptions such as speed keeping and intersection control, the estimated effects are very limited. We would again point out that the data on effectiveness are not to be seen as a precise result (even given the range), but merely as an estimate to determine the general order of magnitude. It is therefore not permissible, apart from the speed keeping and intersection control modules, which stand out somewhat from the others, to establish a ranking for the modules. It is not permissible, for example, on the basis of these results to conclude that the overtaking module would be more effective than the lane keeping module. An effectiveness estimate that allowed this type of attribution of priorities would require first of all detailed data on the extent of the impact of the module and then comprehensive information about the rest of the technical environment of the vehicle and road.

No attempt was made to sum the effects of the individual modules. The overlapping of module functions (e.g. between car following and speed keeping) would lead to double counting and thus argues against addition. A further reason is the impossibility of precise enough delimitation of the accident statistics parameters and the way they fit the description of the effects of the module. Even the different assumptions for the individual modules regarding whether an accident is PROMETHEUS-relevant or not can lead to error if the figures are added. Here a detailed discussion of the limiting factors would be necessary.

Which possible failures of the module could occur and how the possible accident consequences looked was not investigated. Like any technical installation, a module has a certain degree of reliability. The requirement of a high level of reliability in functions relevant to safety means some redundancy must be accepted.

Communication between vehicles is not error-proof either. Thus, with the use of electromagnetic waves to transmit information, outside signals or signal blocking through interference can cause errors.

All in all, the *status quo* nature of this study (11) must be stressed once again. This is clear from the dispersion of the aims and is due above all to the problem of trying to evaluate the actual accident situation using criteria that imply far-reaching technical innovations in vehicles and infrastructures (e.g. roads). It has not been clarified so far at what level the modules will operate: as information, as warnings or as active intervention in the operation of the vehicle. In particular as regards the last stage, it is still an open question to what extent automatic intervention -- affecting vehicle speed for example -- has any chance of being accepted in our society.

10. SUMMARY AND OUTLOOK

Germany's experience with new technologies to improve motor traffic efficiency and safety, described in the above report, make it clear that improvements in road traffic can be achieved with these technologies. Improvements can be achieved in both efficiency and safety, but the extent of the improvement must not be overestimated and depends not only on the system used, but also on local conditions, driver behaviour, the availability of alternatives, etc. These improvements are not provided at "null tariff" either, which means that in each case it is necessary to carefully weigh up, on the one hand, what costs are involved for the State or the user and, on the other, what benefits are obtained. In general it can be seen that the new technologies can certainly help with the traffic of the future and some systems have even proven themselves in field tests, but in the present state of the art no global solution to the future problems of private transport can yet be seen.

The use of present technologies is concentrated mainly on solving the problem of private transport; the networking of all transport modes into an overall system is not under consideration. Initial research approaches are to be seen in Germany, in Munich and Stuttgart, but as yet no results are available. It is likely that potential can be activated here, but the question again arises of the costs involved in introducing this kind of system. However, whether cost will continue to be the determining factor in the future, or whether other criteria such as environmental protection, energy consumption, urban planning, etc., will take on increasing importance, must remain an open question for the moment.

BIBLIOGRAPHY*

1. United Nations: Annual Bulletin, Geneva, 1989.

2. Verband der Automobilindustrie: Tatsachen und Zahlen aus der Kraftfahrzeugwirtschaft, Frankfurt, 1989.

3. Lapiere, Obermaier: Entwicklung der lichtsignalsteuerung in städtischen Straßennetzen, 88 Jahre Straßenverkehrstechnik in Deutschland, Kirschbaumverlag, Bonn, 1988.

4. Giesa, S., Everts, K., Schneider, H.-W.: ARIAM -- ein Verfahren zur Aktualisierung der Verkehrsfunk-Meldungen, Sonderdruck aus Straßenverkehrstechnik 30, Nr. 5 Kirschbaumverlag, Bonn-Bad Godesberg, 1986.

5. Bolte, Brägas, Keller, Kumm, Ottenroth, Pollmann, Tafel: ALI -- autofahrer Leit -- und Informationssystem Studie über ein individuell wirksames Verkehrsbeeinflussungssystem, Cologne, 1977.

6. Bolte, F.: Die Wirksamkeit der Stauwarnanlage Aichelberg, Straße und Autobahn 33, Nr. 7, Kirschbaumverlag, Bonn-Bad Godesberg, 1982.

7. Mechtersheimer, R., Sommer W.: Unfallauswertung der BAB A4 im Bereich der Verkehrsbeeinflussungsanlage zwischen AK Köln-West und AK Aachen, Der Regierungspräsident, Cologne, 1990, unveröffentlicht.

8. Wechselwegweisung in Hessen, Der Hessische Minister für Wirtschaft und Technik, Wiesbaden, 1976.

NB. While writing this report, many extracts have been borrowed from bibliographic references and have been quoted textually in order to report these results as faithfully as possible.

9. Hampe, Keller, Müller: Bewertung von Verkehrsleitsystemen, Heft 348, Bonn/Bad Godesberg, 1981.
Forschung Straßenbau und Straßenverkehrstechnik herausgegeben vom Bundesminister für Verkehr.

10. PROMETHEUS, Pro-General, LISB, Zwischenbericht 1990. Steierwald Schönharting und Partner GmbH, Stuttgart, October 1990.

11. Marburger, Klöckner, Stöcker: Abschätzung der möglichen unfallreduzierenden Wirkungen ausgewählter Prometheusfunktionen. Bundesanstalt für Straßenwesen, Bergisch Gladbach, December 1988.

Sub-topic 4

IMPACT OF NEW TECHNOLOGIES ON EFFICIENCY AND SAFETY

F. CROWLEY
Environmental Research Unit
Dublin
Ireland

SUMMARY

Dublin, July 1991

ROAD TRAFFIC ACCIDENTS IN IRELAND

Characteristics of the Problem and the Development of Couternmeasures

1. HISTORICAL TRENDS

The population of Ireland dropped from 2.96 million in the immediate post-war years to 2.82 million in 1961, before rising to an estimated 3.52 million in 1984. Corresponding to this increase in population, and the increased availability of motor vehicles, the number of registered vehicles rose from 75 000 in 1946 to a peak of 950 000 in 1981 (Fig. 1). The number of registered vehicles in 1989 was 1 020 000.

The number of registered vehicles per 100 population has increased from 2.4 in 1946 to 25.7 in 1984, having peaked at 27.6 in 1981. This level of motorisation is not far below that of other European countries.

The number of persons killed on Irish roads rose from 160 in 1946 to the peak of 640 in 1972, with a secondary peak of 628 in 1978 (Fig. 2). Since then, reported road deaths have declined steadily to 460 in 1989, a figure of the same order as for the late 1960s.

The Irish rate of persons killed per 10 000 population increased from 0.6 in 1946 to 2.1 in 1972 and declined to 1.2 in 1985 (Fig. 3).

Irish rates per registered vehicle are now (Fig. 4) *half* of what they were between 1970 and 1972, when fatal accidents reached their peak in recent years for this country (the rates were 10.03, 10.06 and 10.68 respectively) and a quarter of the figures for the 1940s.

2. INTERNATIONAL COMPARISONS

Ireland's record in terms of road deaths per 10 000 population is close to the EC average (Fig. 5) and higher than our nearest neighbour, the United Kingdom.

3. CATEGORY OF PERSONS KILLED AND INJURED

Currently, the number of persons killed each year stands at 460 (Fig. 6) and approximately nineteen times that number are reported injured.

The detailed analysis of these statistics presented in the annual publication of the Environmental Research Unit (ERU), *Road Accident Facts*, reveals the following general picture:

- Of those killed in road accidents each year, one in ten is a pedal cyclist, one in ten a motor cyclist, four in ten are pedestrians and the remainder are mainly car occupants (Fig. 7);

- The hour of day and day of week distributions of road accidents show little change from year to year. The frequency distributions show a peak in the hour before midnight (Fig. 8) and at weekends;

- As measured by the ratio of persons killed to persons injured, the severity of Irish road accidents appears to be greater than in other European countries. Whilst this may be partly a reflection of the under-reporting of injury accidents, it is probably also a function of the high proportion of travel on rural roads in Ireland, and of the higher speeds on rural, as distinct from urban, roads.

Accident data are reported by *An Garda Siochana* (the National Police Force) to the Road Safety Records Bureau, ERU. Whilst all fatal accidents are reported, it has been estimated (Fuller and Hearne, 1977) that less than half the accidents involving injuries are reported. This is somewhat similar to the situation in other European countries (Roosmark, 1970).

Some important categories of Irish road accidents are listed below.

3.1. Pedestrian Accidents

Four in ten of those killed on roads are pedestrians, as is one in five of those injured. Pedestrian accidents, as measured by the ratio of fatalities to injuries, are at least twice as severe as other accidents (Fig. 7). When injury accidents are considered, three in every four pedestrian accidents occur inside built-up areas. When fatal accidents are considered, one in two pedestrian accidents occurs inside built-up areas.

3.2. Child Accidents

In many countries, road accidents have in recent years become the largest single cause of child deaths. Road accidents involving children in Ireland are mainly pedestrian accidents which usually happen between noon and six in the evening, when children are either on their way home from school, or playing afterwards (Golden, 1979). Children between the ages of five and nine years have higher accident rates than younger or older children, and for all age groups accidents involving boys outnumber those involving girls. In four out of five accidents involving children crossing roads, the children are unaccompanied by adults (Brangan, 1976).

3.3. Young Driver Accidents

Less than one in fifty deaths is due to a road accident. However, in the age group 15 to 24 years, the number of deaths due to road accidents is dramatically higher, amounting to as many as two out of every five deaths (Fig. 9). This proportion is higher than the proportion due to all medical causes combined. Almost half the male deaths in this age group are due to road accidents. Moreover, the numbers of persons killed and injured in road accidents per 100 000 population are higher for this age group than for any other and are over twice the average for all age groups.

3.4. Motor and Pedal Cycle Accidents

Motor cyclists in Ireland comprise a very high-risk group with an accident rate per kilometre travelled about ten times that of car drivers. Although the number of motor cycles has declined over the last decade, the number of motor cyclists killed has remained constant (Fig. 10). Pedal cyclists are also a high-risk group. The likelihood of the pedal cyclist being injured in a road accident is over twice that of a car driver, and on the high-speed roads it is seven or eight times that of a car driver.

When motor cyclist deaths per 10 000 cycles are computed, Ireland has far higher rates than other countries.

3.5. Accidents at Night

Almost half of Ireland's road accidents occur at night (Fig. 12). This is appreciably higher than in most other European countries. In Great Britain, Belgium, Denmark and the Netherlands, about one-third of road accidents occur at night, whilst in France, Finland and Italy night accidents represent only one-quarter, or less, of the total number. The relative risk per km travelled on the national routes in Ireland at different times of the day is illustrated in Fig. 13, which clearly demonstrates that the probability of an accident is almost four times higher at night (10 p.m. -- 6 a.m.) on these roads in Ireland than in daylight (6 a.m. -- 6 p.m.).

3.6. Accidents on National Routes and in Urban Areas

One-third of fatal accidents, together with half of the injury accidents, occur in built-up areas which account for only four per cent of the Irish road network. A further one-third of fatal and one-fifth of injury accidents occur on rural national routes, which again represent only six per cent of the road network. Thus, some two-thirds of fatal accidents and the bulk of injury accidents are concentrated on one-tenth of the road network (Fig. 14). Countermeasures directed at road factors should initially be concentrated on these parts of the network.

3.7. Wet Road Accidents

One-third of Irish road accidents occur on wet roads and, of these, one in three involves a skidding vehicle. Because the road is wet for a high percentage of time in Ireland, and because of the relationship between skid resistance and the occurrence of skidding accidents (Crowley, 1970), it is important to provide and maintain high friction levels on wet road surfaces.

4. THE ANALYSIS AND PREVENTION OF ROAD TRAFFIC ACCIDENTS IN IRELAND OVER THE PAST TWENTY YEARS

4.1. Introduction

The main contribution of research to road accident prevention activity has been to develop a methodology to deal systematically with aspects of the road accident problem and to assess the effectiveness of currently implemented countermeasures.

Historically, the Poisson distribution was the first used to express, in terms of theoretical probabilities, the distribution of accidents among individuals exposed to equal risks of incurring an accident (Bortkiewicz, 1898). The most important development in this formulation was reported by Greenwood and Woods (1919) and Greenwood and Yule (1920). They assumed that for each individual considered separately, the Poisson distribution described adequately the distribution of accidents, but that the mean accident rate varied considerably between individuals. The resulting distribution for overall accident occurrence was the Negative Binomial Distribution. The importance of this development was that it became possible to establish priorities for road accident prevention work. Once the individual persons, road sections or vehicles with relatively high accident rates were identified, attention could then be paid to specifying the reasons for the high rates, with a view to reducing them, and consequently the overall accident rate. Subsequently, considerable work has gone into criticising, refining and developing this approach (e.g. OECD, 1970). Two essential points have been retained:

a) Under conditions of equal risk in an unchanging environment, the frequency distribution of accidents will be approximately Poisson, characterised by the mean accident rate in unit time (OECD, 1976).

b) The mean accident rate increases and decreases with increased or decreased risk, which is a function of (i) exposure to traffic hazards and (ii) differing individual accident liabilities (e.g. Wass, 1977).

The above formulations proved sufficiently general to be applied to large parts of the road accident problem and to establish priorities for accident prevention activity.

There remain substantial areas where no adequate theory exists. Further, the establishment of priorities does not in itself indicate why accident rates are high.

Consideration must be given to the causes of road traffic accidents, in order to identify those causes which, if prevented from recurring, would reduce accident occurrence.

4.2. Causes of Traffic Accidents, and Accident Prevention

The specification of causes of road accidents can be more complex than in many other fields. An accident cause is usually defined as a condition necessary, but not sufficient, for the accident to happen. It is only in conjunction with all the other circumstances of the accident that its satisfaction is sufficient to cause the accident. Not surprisingly, therefore, many such causes can be assigned to an accident, the non-occurrence of any one of which would have prevented the accident. To emphasize the lack of sufficiency, such causes are also called contributory "factors" to the accident.

It is rarely possible, or even useful, to identify all such factors. However, it is sometimes possible to identify a particular factor or combination of factors which increase accident risk and the recurrence of which it is possible to prevent by known, or perhaps new, countermeasures. Such factors are usually identified by a retrospective examination of accidents at particular sites or over larger areas.

In road safety work it is usual to distinguish between three types of accident factor, corresponding to the three elements present in every accident: the road, the road user(s) and the vehicle. From detailed, on-the-spot accident investigations, it has been suggested that in nine out of ten accidents, at least one road user factor is present; in at least one in four, a road factor is present; and in one in eight, a vehicle factor (OECD, 1975). A similar distribution of factors in Irish accidents is suggested by the results of a detailed study of accident report forms (Hearne, 1979).

5. ROAD FACTORS IN TRAFFIC ACCIDENTS

Considerable work has been done in applying the above models to identify high-risk sections of the Irish road network. However, this application is possible on a systematic basis only where sections of road are compared under conditions of homogeneity of exposure to risk.

This is possible on those parts of the rural network where the Annual Average Daily Traffic (AADT) figures are available as a measure of exposure to risk. Other methods are used in urban areas.

Work carried out on both rural and urban roads has identified the extent of the wet-road skidding problem, and its relation to low skid-resistance and increased accident risk.

5.1. Identification of High Accident Sections on Rural National Routes

The rural national routes comprise six per cent of the rural network. On them, half the rural fatal and injury accidents occur. The routes were classified into some 1 800 sections of varying length, where throughout each section the geometric characteristics and the traffic flow are uniform. The geometric characteristics include carriageway width, nature and width of verges, operating speed, design speed, the design hour volume and capacity and the percentage of the section with passing sight distance in excess of 800 ft. and of 1 500 ft. The number of junctions, of major developments such as factories, of houses and of field gates opening onto the section was also noted. These were combined using arbitrary weightings to give a "development index-number" for each section length.

The number of sections with 0, 1, 2, ... accidents in the time periods 1971-73, and 1974-76 was found to follow the Negative Binomial Distribution, consistent with the view that some sections have greater inherent accident risk than others (Figs. 15, 16, 17).

On these sections annual average daily traffic figures were available, and so it was possible to take account of the change in risk on each section arising from different traffic flows. However, after traffic flow was taken into account, many sections were identified as having significantly more accidents than anticipated. It was concluded that these sections had much higher than average accident risk, and should be priority areas for accident prevention work. Detailed reports on the rural national routes, indicating the relative safety for each section, have been published. In the latest period, 1984-87, sixty-two sections (137 miles in total length) on which one in nine of the accidents occurred were identified as having high accident occurrence.

An example of the format in which the results from the reports are shown is given in Fig. 18, where the + sign indicates a high accident section, also called a "black spot".

These techniques identify high accident sections and indicate priorities for investigation and improvement. They do not explain why these sections are unsafe, nor do they suggest remedies. The next stage is the detailed examination of accident reports and of the physical characteristics of these high-accident sections ("black spots" or "lengths"). A detailed examination of all 77 high-accident sections on the national routes was undertaken in 1985. The principal findings were:

-- Accident risk on the high-accident sections = 3 x average risk;

-- The 77 sections break down into:

  • 7 improved village sections,
  • 17 sections adjoining built-up areas (12 improved, 5 unimproved),
  • 54 rural sections (30 improved, 24 unimproved);

-- Accident-related road factors were detected in 67 out of 77 sections;

-- In all, 118 road factors were detected (2 per section).

A summary of the road factors identified showed that:

-- 61 per cent of road factors relate to how visually absorbed information is presented to drivers. Failure to cope;

-- 13 per cent of road factors relate to poor skid resistance;

-- 12 per cent relate to approach speeds being too fast and excessive width;

-- 6 per cent relate to too little width on narrow roads without shoulders;

-- 6 per cent relate to defects in setting out and construction.

5.2. Effect of Geometric Characteristics on Accident Risk

In the published reports, traffic flow figures have been used as the only measure of exposure. However, as already stated, information was available from the detailed inventory of the national routes on the various geometric characteristics and it may be asked what effect these characteristics might have in increasing accident risk on the sections.

A detailed examination was made of the relation between the geometric characteristics and average accident rates. A regression model was used with the geometric elements as independent variables. Maximum likelihood estimators were used to estimate the appropriate constants, with a Poisson error term (Weber, 1971). The only variables which affected accident rates to an important degree, besides AADT which was the dominant variable, were the presence or absence of hard shoulders and the development index on the section (Hearne, 1976). Rates were higher on sections without hard shoulders. An illustration of the increased accident rates due to an increase in developments along the road is shown in Fig. 19, given a traffic flow of 1 500 vehicles per day, and no hard shoulders.

5.3. Other Rural Roads

On Irish rural roads other than rural national routes, accidents are quite scattered. Information on road geometrics and on traffic flow is sparse. The simple and useful model for the identification of the critical parts of the road network described above becomes inoperable since no measure of exposure is available. It has been observed, however, that accidents cluster at a number of places even on those roads where traffic is light. A sophisticated computer mapping technique has been developed, on the lines of the National Grid co-ordinate system, to plot the location of all accidents to within 100 metres, using computer-drawn transparent overlays on the ½" Ordnance Survey maps (Holland, 1973). Provided that accident data are available for a time span sufficiently long to reveal clustering, all such locations can be identified easily by inspection of the overlays (Fuller and Holland, 1974).

5.4. Urban Areas

Whilst accidents occur much more frequently in built-up areas than in rural areas, lack of adequate exposure measures prevents the use of the "black spot" identification techniques applicable to the rural national routes. However, the density of population, of traffic and of accidents, makes it possible for the responsible road authority to consider the accident data provided by *An Garda Siochana* in detail and as relevant to local needs. Detailed studies can be carried out at local level to identify accident patterns on the busier urban roads (Holland and Wall, 1970). In residential areas having less traffic, the consideration of accident risks and road safety has led to the conclusion that, in large measure, road accident prevention is a matter of estate design (Dalby, 1979).

There is close co-operation between engineers, *Gardai* and road safety research workers in accident prevention activities in the Dublin County Borough, where a road safety unit has been set up in the traffic department. Lists of roads with high absolute numbers of accidents, as well as high proportions of accidents of particular types, are provided to the unit on a yearly basis (Curran and Newell, 1973: Golden, Curran and Brown, 1974). The road safety unit examines in detail the accident report forms for these areas with a view to identifying causative factors for accidents.

Action is then taken in an attempt to prevent the recurrence of these accidents (McEntee, 1975). As a further aid, computer mapping techniques to plot the different types of accident in Dublin have also been developed.

In respect of towns in Ireland, four model studies were undertaken (Crowley, 1983, 1984, 1986, 1986) at *An Foras Forbartha.* These studies covered four typical towns which lie on the National Roads in Ireland. The main findings were:

	Population	Injury Accident Rate per Pop.
Dundalk	25 000	44
Fermoy	3 200	70
Mitchelstown	3 000	29
Athy	4 750	19

Findings:

- 75% of accidents on through route;
- 50% involve pedestrians;
- 15% involve pedal cyclists.

In respect of towns on national roads, the proportion of accidents generated by through traffic has been quantified (Hearne, 1980).

5.5. The Skid Resistance of Wet Road Surfaces

The skid resistance of wet road surfaces is, in general, much lower than that of dry surfaces (Kummer and Meyer, 1967). As a consequence, stopping distances are longer and the incidence of skidding is much more frequent on wet road surfaces. A detailed survey of the skid resistance of road surfaces in relation to the occurrence of skidding accidents established the extent of the problem in Ireland (Crowley, 1970). It was found that the risk of skidding on wet surfaces was greater by half on rural as compared to urban roads, and that the risk on the National Primary Roads was approximately twice as great as the risk on urban roads. Overall, one-third of accidents occur on wet roads in Ireland and at least one in three of these involves skidding. A sample survey of skid resistance readings, measured by using a portable tester, showed significantly lower values for road lengths where wet skidding accidents clustered than for a normal road length.

A method has been developed for designating sections of national routes as wet road skidding accident "black spots" (Crowley and Fuller, 1978). The method is applied to a three-year block of accident data and results in the designation of approximately ten per cent of the length of the national routes as sections with high occurrence of wet skidding accidents.

Work by Plant (1972) established the polished stone values of road-making aggregates then available in Ireland. The polished stone value is a useful predictor of the performance, in terms of skid resistance, of a road surfacing aggregate.

In 1972, the Road Safety Section of *An Foras Forbartha* acquired SCRIM, the Sideways Force Coefficient Routine Investigation Machine. This machine is suitable for use in measuring the skidding resistance of road surfaces over an extensive road network. The essential components of SCRIM, which are mounted on a lorry chassis, are the test wheel unit, a water tank for wetting the road in front of the test wheel and the recording unit. A computer program was developed in *An Foras Forbartha* to process the output from the records (Curran, 1972). The computer printout presents the results in graphical and numerical format (Fig. 20).

From Fig. 20 it can be seen that SCRIM provides a continuous record of skidding resistance. It is, therefore, suited both to detailed measurement at specific location and the monitoring of skid resistance of the national and other road systems. The main types of testing undertaken by *An Foras Forbartha* are as follows:

i) Systematic testing of the national and other road systems. Results are processed and made available to local authorities and the Department of the Environment in both detailed and summary form (Golden and

Marry, 1978). In addition, aids to interpretation of results are also made available (Curran, 1975).

ii) Research testing: detailed and repeated tests are carried out on experimental surfaces with a view to assessing the safety performance of roadstones and binders.

iii) Request testing: Sideways Force Coefficient measurements, which are related to wet road friction values, are taken for local authorities in connection with their annual surface dressing programmes.

A large research effort has been devoted to relating the output from the SCRIM programme to the geometric and traffic characteristics of road sections and to the risk of accidents, with particular reference to wet skidding accidents. This has, to date, resulted in the publication of guidelines for engineers in respect of minimum skid resistance requirements for national primary roads (Crowley, 1976) and suburban arterial roads (Crowley, 1978). In addition, a note on differential friction has been prepared (Curran, 1987).

6. HUMAN FACTORS IN TRAFFIC ACCIDENTS

Human factors play a central role in accidents. As outlined above, the methods developed by Greenwood can be applied to the identification of road sections with high accident risk. The application of the method to the problem of identifying persons with a high risk of being involved in a traffic accident has met with less success, with the exception of those studies confined to professional drivers, such as bus and tram drivers (Hakkinen, 1958; Cresswell and Froggatt, 1963; Shaw and Sichel, 1971). Indeed, little work has been done in establishing general levels of risk-taking in driving, as compared with other human activities (Starr, 1969). Thus, it is now generally accepted that a substantial reduction in road accidents would not be achieved by identifying and removing accident-prone drivers (Cameron, 1975; Klein, 1973). Attention is directed instead to both the elimination of behaviour conducive to increasing accident risk and to the promotion of behaviour conducive to decreasing the risk or severity of accidents. In addition, therefore, to general rules governing road behaviour, legislative measures concentrate on prohibiting known high-risk behaviour, such as driving at high speed or with a high blood alcohol content, and promoting severity reduction measures, such as the wearing of safety belts. The principal Irish legislative measures enacted in recent years are considered below.

6.1. Speed

As illustrated in Fig. 21, a twofold reduction in the speed of a vehicle from 60 to 30 miles per hour results in more than a threefold reduction in stopping distance on a road with a good dry surface or as much as a fourfold reduction on a wet, smooth surface (Golden, 1975). Moreover, as would be expected, the severity of road accidents, especially those involving pedestrians, is influenced by the impact speed (Fig. 22).

Based, therefore, on the conclusion that lower speeds imply few and less severe accidents, legislation governing speed limits in built-up areas (30 and 40 mph) was introduced in Ireland in 1963. On the basis of a study carried out in 1969 (*An Foras Forbartha*, 1969b), a general speed limit of 60 mph was introduced for rural roads (regulations introduced under Road Traffic Act, 1961 and Road Traffic Act, 1968). Whilst a detailed assessment of the effects of the 30 and 40 mph limits on accidents in built-up areas has not been undertaken, some reduction in accident rates in built-up areas is suggested from the general accident statistics. Regarding the more recent general 60 mph limit, a study undertaken for the period prior to and following its introduction (Hall, Hearne and O'Flynn, 1970), showed that the limit did not result in a reduction in car speeds (Fig. 19) and that there was no observable effect on accident occurrence.

6.2. Safety Belts

In many countries the compulsory wearing of safety belts, supported by propaganda and an appropriate level of enforcement, has achieved a significant reduction in accident severity (Karin, Bernard Anderson, 1978). The first survey of safety belt usage in Ireland, undertaken in 1968 (Flynn, 1969), showed that whilst 12 per cent of cars were fitted with safety belts, the actual wearing rate was of the order of 5 per cent overall. Regulations making it compulsory to wear safety belts while driving were introduced in February 1979 (regulations introduced under the Road Traffic Act, 1968). At that time it was estimated that perhaps one in five car drivers wore safety belts. Examination of accident forms suggested that the figure had risen to one in two shortly after the introduction of the legislation. Whilst not under-rating the importance of this improvement, nonetheless, the available statistics reveal no notable effect on accidents. In particular, the proportion of car drivers killed in single vehicle accidents (no other vehicle being involved), which are the fatalities most likely to be reduced by the universal wearing of safety belts, has not significantly decreased. This suggested that much higher wearing rates than one in two would be necessary in Irish conditions before any worthwhile decrease in accident severity is manifest.

6.3. Alcohol

The association between drinking and increased accident risk is widely accepted (OECD, 1978). As illustrated in Fig. 24, the likelihood of being involved in an accident increases with blood alcohol content, regardless of age group. A blood alcohol level equivalent to the current Irish limit increases the accident risk of young drivers, especially the high-risk age group of 18 to 24, about sixfold compared to less than a twofold increase for those in the age group 35 to 54. The association between alcohol consumption and night accidents in Ireland is supported by two studies. One (Edwards, *et al.*, 1973), concerning traffic accident casualties involving 196 drivers and 147 pedestrians, revealed that one in five of driver casualties, and one in four of pedestrian casualties, had Blood Alcohol Content (BAC) in excess of 125 mg/100 ml of blood, the legal limit for drivers at the time. However, these ratios rose to one in three and one in two respectively, for accidents which occurred between 10 p.m. and 1 a.m. The second study (Hickey, Bofin, O'Donnell and Hearne, 1975) concerning accident fatalities involving 176 drivers and 97 pedestrians, showed that two in five of driver fatalities and one in two of pedestrian fatalities had BACs in excess of the then legal limit for drivers of 125 mg/100 ml of blood and, again, the proportions were higher for night accidents.

Within the last decade, many OECD countries have introduced legislation making it an offence to drive with a blood alcohol level in excess of certain limits. In Ireland a blood alcohol limit of 125 mg/100 ml was introduced in 1969, as compared with 50 mg/100 ml in Norway, Sweden and Denmark and 100 mg/100 ml in the USA. During the succeeding nine years, legal difficulties and a low level of compliance and enforcement attenuated the effect of the law. There was no measurable effect on accidents during this period. The level was subsequently lowered to 100 mg/100 ml in July 1978, and the reintroduction was accompanied by considerable publicity. For the remaining five months of 1978 fatal accidents dropped 5 per cent compared to the predicted level. Even more significantly, for the high-risk period from 9.00 p.m. to 3.00 a.m., fatal accidents were reduced by 8 per cent, and injury accidents by some 13 per cent (*An Foras Forbartha*, 1979).

Another facet of drinking and road safety of particular concern in Ireland is the high proportion of pedestrian fatalities, especially after dark, in which the victims have elevated blood alcohol levels (Hickey, Bofin, O'Donnell and Hearne, 1975). In more than one out of every two pedestrian fatalities involved in night accidents, the victim had a blood alcohol level in excess of the then legal limit, compared to one in ten for day accidents (Fig. 25). Indeed, almost one in ten pedestrians killed during darkness seems to have been actually lying on the road prior to the collision (Hearne, 1979). In general, pedestrians with elevated blood alcohol levels, coupled with the low visibility to drivers of pedestrians at night, constitute one of the major road safety problems in Ireland. The problem is particularly acute under wet weather conditions and on rural roads on which some 80 per cent of driving is concentrated.

Research indicates (OECD, 1978) that drugs are also a contributory factor to increased risk of involvement in road accidents. This extends not only to illegal drugs, such as heroin, LSD and marijuana, but to tranquillisers, such as Vallium, Librium and the barbiturates. However, no detailed information is available for Irish conditions.

6.4. Young Drivers

Research indicates that the time taken to gain adequate driving experience is some seven to eight years (OECD, 1975). In terms of both single vehicle accidents and other collisions, those in the under twenty-five age group, who represent over half of Ireland's population, are a high accident risk group. As illustrated in Fig. 26, the relative risk of a single vehicle accident is high at age 18, declines sharply between eighteen and thirty years of age, and subsequently declines more slowly. In terms of all collisions, however, the lowest accident risk is that of the middle age group (Carr, 1969).

In addition to undertaking a greater proportion of their driving at night and weekends, the relatively high accident risk for young drivers reflects the greater concentration in this age group of motor-cycle riders -- motor-cycles are intrinsically more risk-prone than cars (Fig. 27) -- as well as their greater susceptibility to alcohol.

Evidence from the UK indicates that more stringent driving tests can help to reduce accident rates (Hoinville, Berthaud and Mackie, 1972). Further to this, an OECD Report, entitled Young Drivers, recommends that driving tests should include comprehensive training under such conditions as high-density traffic, night, rain, fog and high speeds, etc. In Ireland, a mandatory driving test of thirty minutes' duration and covering vehicle manoeuvring in traffic, as well as knowledge of the rules of the road, was introduced in 1964. The effects of the test on the general accident rate and in particular the driving ability of the young driver are, however, difficult to ascertain.

6.5. Recent Developments

In September 1990, the Minister for the Environment announced that a new initiative was to be undertaken to reduce accidents. This initiative would concentrate on the three areas of seat-belt wearing, speeding and drink-driving. The ERU was asked to assess driver attitudes in these areas. A sample survey was undertaken (Crowley, 1991), which has just been published. The principal findings are:

-- 54 per cent of drivers take an alcoholic drink at least once a week;

-- 74 per cent of drivers who drink, drink at the week-end -- Friday to Sunday inclusive;

-- 72 per cent of drivers who drink are mainly beer drinkers;

-- Of drivers who drink, 47 per cent said they would never drive when they had up to two alcoholic drinks, 80 per cent when they had between three and five drinks and 95 per cent said they would never drive when they had more than six drinks;

-- Of all drivers surveyed, 69 per cent said that they always wore their seat belt;

-- Overall there was low awareness of the proportion of accidents caused by drivers who had been drinking alcohol, indeed opinion was spread across the spectrum for "less than a quarter" to "over three-quarters". One-fifth of the respondents were unable to estimate the proportion of accidents where drivers had consumed alcohol and, as is often the case, those least likely to know or to offer an answer were DE (Department of the Environment) respondents (25 per cent), those aged 45 years or over (23 per cent) and females (23 per cent).

In the months leading up to Christmas 1990, an intensive publicity campaign conducted by the National Safety Council on the consequences of drink-driving was supported by an increased enforcement effort by *An Garda Siochana*. Early indications are that this campaign has been successful in reducing the number and severity of accidents over the period.

National surveys of seat-belt wearing and speed behaviour are being conducted in the current year (1991). These will be reported in due course.

7. VEHICLE FACTORS IN TRAFFIC ACCIDENTS

Information on the contribution of vehicle factors to road accidents is much less complete than that on road or human factors. Within OECD countries, it has been estimated that a car factor is contributory to one in eight road accidents (OECD, 1975). Examination of Irish accident report forms suggests that, as a lower limit, in one in twelve accidents on Irish roads a contributory vehicle factor was present (Hearne, 1979). A sample survey, undertaken between 1972 and 1975 by *An Foras Forbartha*, concluded that one in ten cars had a major defect, that is, a defect which could precipitate an accident. It was also found that cars over six years old were in considerably worse condition than newer cars, and were involved in more fatal accidents per mile travelled. It was tentatively concluded that a reduction of 5-10 per cent in road accidents could be obtained in Ireland if a national effort were made to eliminate safety defects in cars (*An Foras Forbartha*, 1975b).

Whilst heavy goods vehicles have, on average, a 20 per cent lower accident rate per mile travelled than cars (*An Foras Forbartha*, 1978), a preliminary survey suggests that they may be in somewhat inferior mechanical condition (Byrne, 1979). Whilst this observation is obviously a cause for concern, especially in view of the high severity of accidents involving goods vehicles, the problem may be alleviated by the proposal to introduce a compulsory inspection scheme for goods vehicles.

A further aspect of goods vehicle safety arises with the problem of overloading. A pilot study has indicated considerable overloading of heavy goods vehicles (Marry and O'Sullivan, 1976). Overloading of goods vehicles is not readily apparent, since only four of the goods vehicles involved in fatal accidents in 1977 and three in 1978, were stated by the investigating *Garda* to be overloaded.

8. APPLICATION AND EVALUATION OF COUNTERMEASURES

As outlined in previous sections of this review, the characteristics of the Irish road accident problem are now sufficiently understood to permit the identification of those aspects amenable to correction through the application of established countermeasures. It is generally accepted that the road and vehicle elements can be modified independently of the human element, and that the modification of these elements is both more effective and gives a better return for investment.

The contribution of the road element to accident occurrence in Ireland has been broadly quantified. The locations on the national routes, which should be given priority in any systematic programme for modifying the road element, have been identified. In rural areas the greatest potential for accident reduction lies in the application of specific, low-cost engineering countermeasures to these identified locations, many of which are scheduled for major reconstruction in the long term. In urban areas the greatest potential for accident reduction lies in the detailed study of pedestrian safety requirements in existing networks and the design of new residential areas so as to segregate, as far as possible, the pedestrian from motor traffic.

In respect of road-related countermeasures, the following are the most recent estimates of first year rates of return for the national routes:

Countermeasure Type	1st Year Rate of Return (Acc. Savings as % of Capital Cost)
Low Cost Rural Site Specific	1 108 %
Low Cost Urban Site Specific	665 %
Provide High SFC at "Difficult" Locations	207 %
Alter Approaches to Towns	220 %
Upgrade Darkness Definition	44 %

The contribution of the vehicle element to accident occurrence in Ireland has also been broadly quantified. The main problem in this area is to specify an economic procedure for detecting and rectifying safety related defects in the vehicle population.

The potential for reducing the contribution of the human element to road accidents is also high. It is a long-term strategy, however, because of the underlying difficulty of ensuring general compliance with safe behaviour, whether through propaganda, legislation or a combination of both. The primary objective of road safety education and propaganda should be to promote greater and sustained public awareness of the gravity and magnitude of the road accident problem so as to create a climate of greater compliance with specific behavioural countermeasures. Within this framework, road safety programmes should be directed specifically towards those aspects of road user behaviour which have a good possibility of general compliance and a high potential for reducing accidents. The use of legislation to change human behaviour relies, firstly, on the legislation having a substantial public acceptance and, secondly, on the appropriate degree of enforcement. The actual attainment of these pre-conditions can, in practice, be much more difficult than is generally realised. Best results have been achieved abroad where the propaganda, legislative and enforcement elements associated with a particular countermeasure were designed in advance and synchronised in application. Above all, a flexible approach to the timing and application of human element countermeasures is required.

All road accident countermeasures, whether aimed at the road, vehicle or human elements, are expensive, yet with some exceptions, there are inadequate data as to their cost effectiveness or even effectiveness. Continuous research is required to monitor the effectiveness of existing countermeasures and to evaluate future options, if necessary using pilot schemes prior to their general introduction.

FIGURES

Figure 1. **Total Number of Registered Vehicles by Year**

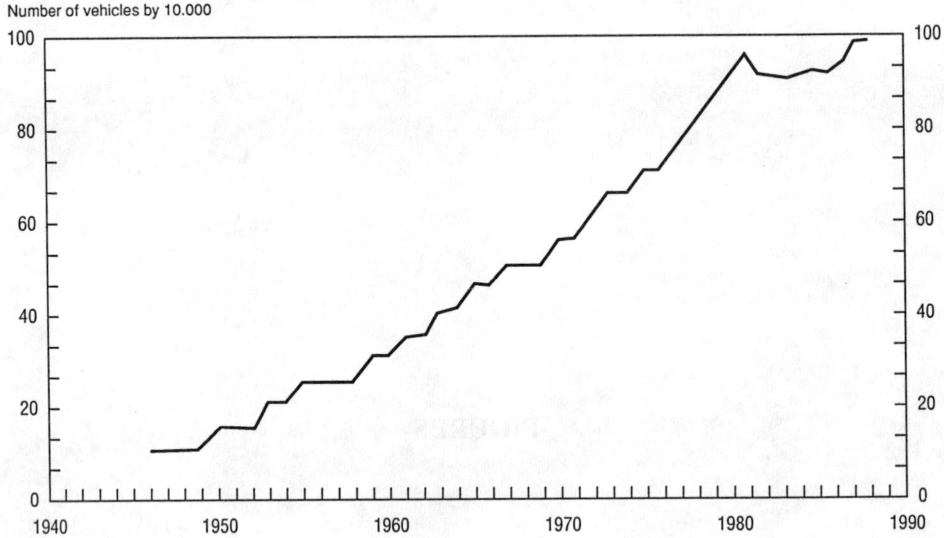

Figure 2. **Total Number Killed by Year**

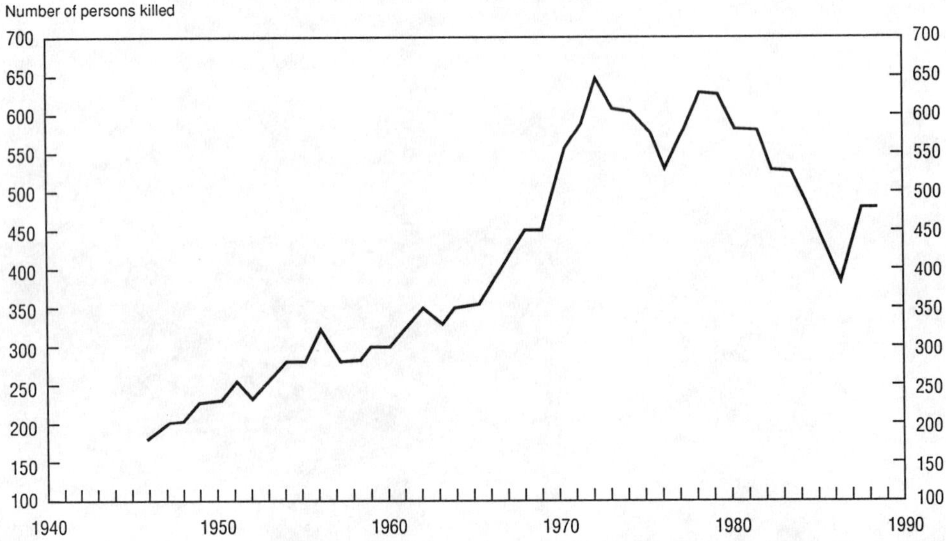

Figure 3. **Number Killed per Ten Thousand Population**

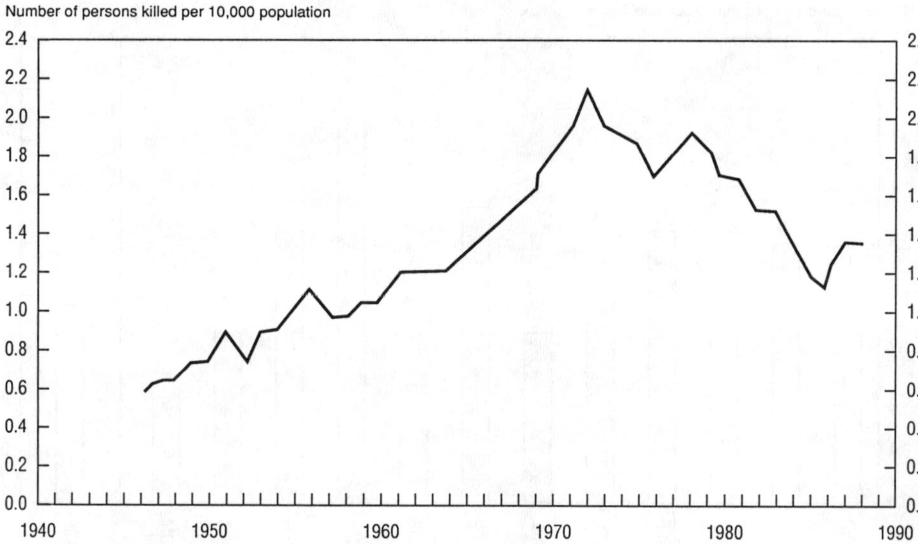

Figure 4. **Number Killed per Ten Thousand Registered Vehicles**

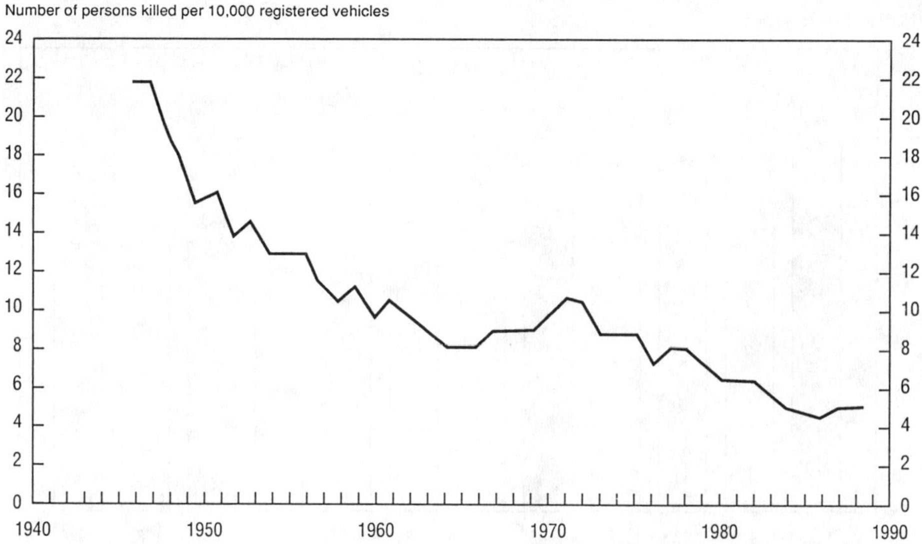

Figure 5. **Road Deaths in Ireland Compared with other E.C. Countries in 1988**

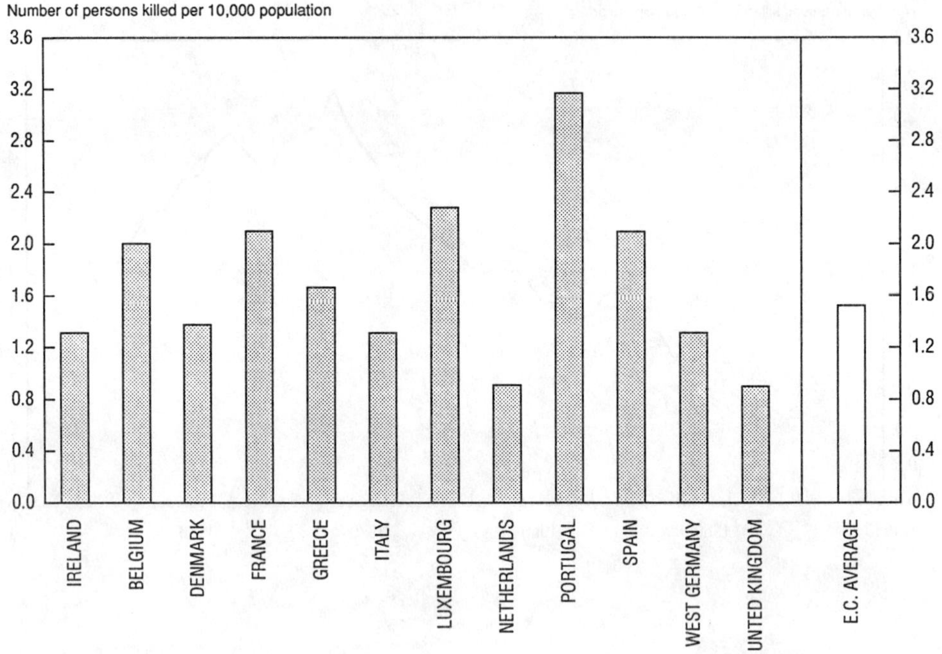

Note: Figures for Greece refer to 1987

Figure 6. **Number of Persons Killed 1978 to 1989**

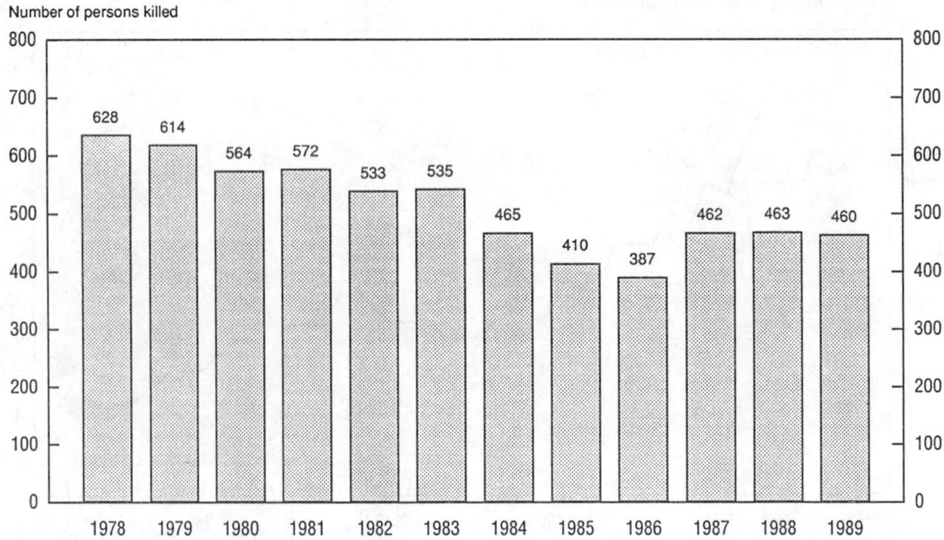

Figure 7. **Casualities Classified by Road User Type**

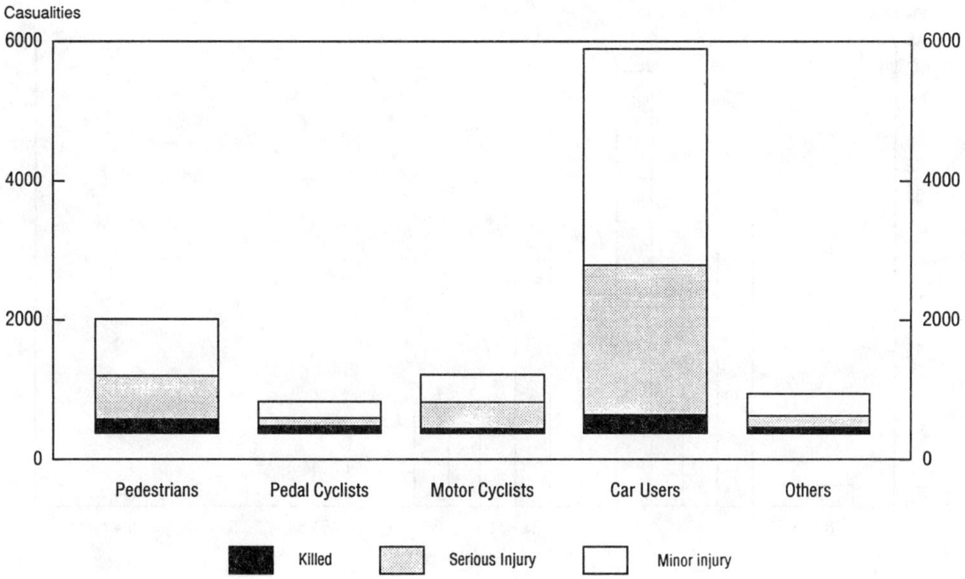

Source : An Foras Forbartha.

Figure 8. **Accidents by Hour of Day**

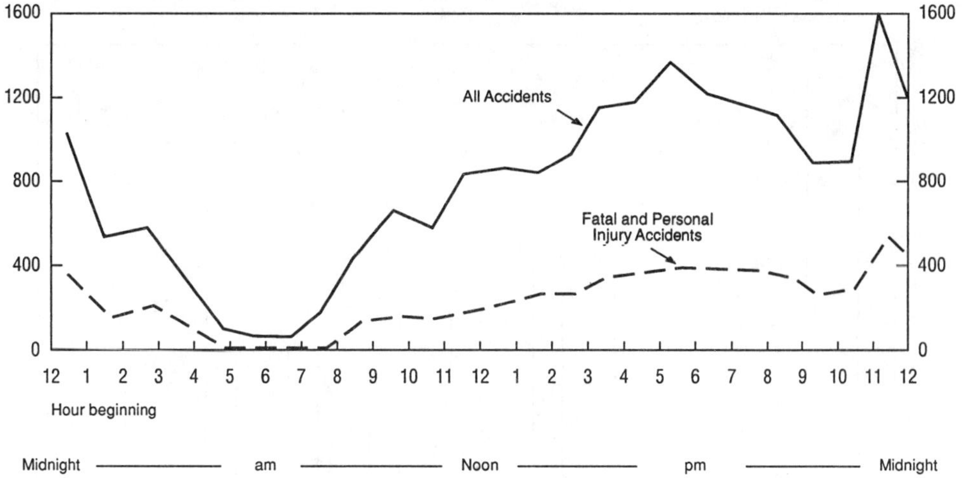

Source: An Foras Forbartha

Figure 9. **Number of Persons Killed in Road Accidents as a Percentage of all Persons Who Died by Age Group**

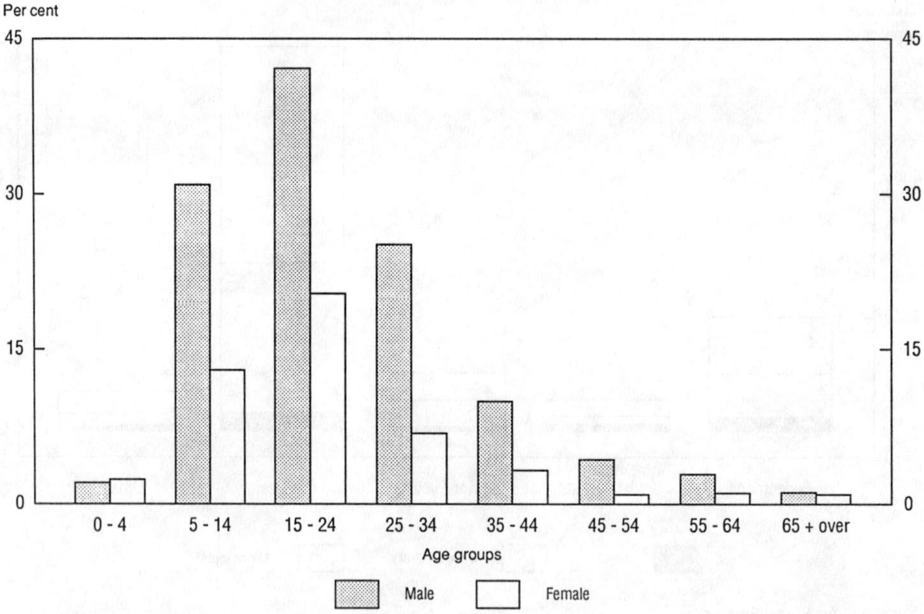

Source: An Foras Forbartha.

Figure 10. **Motor-cycle User Deaths: Some International Comparisons** (Moped users excluded)

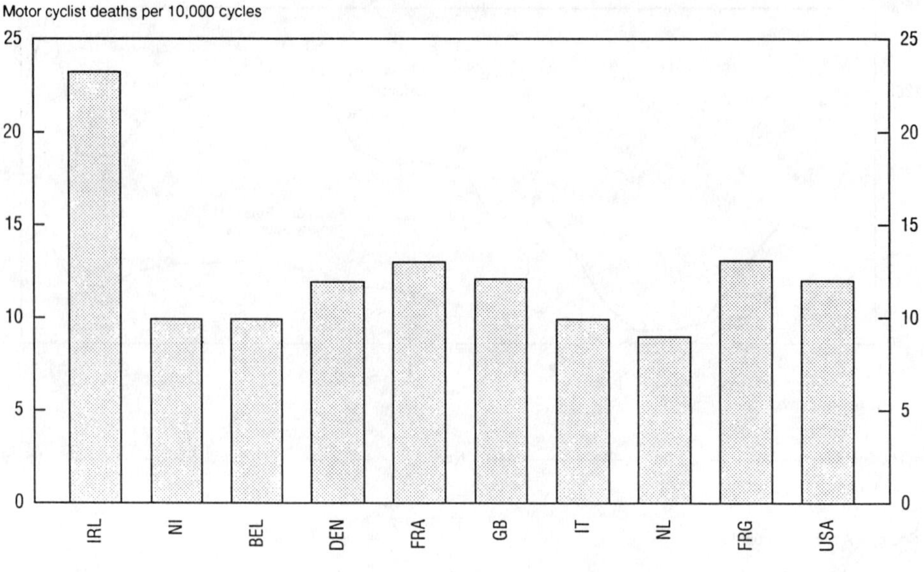

Figure 11. **Persons Killed by Road User Type**
1980-1989

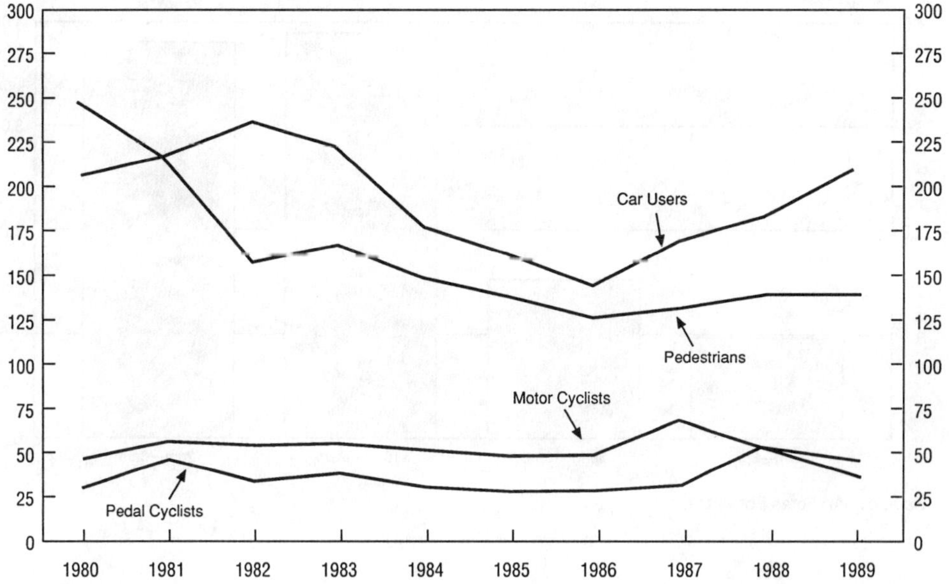

Figure 12. **Percentage of Fatal & Injury Accidents at Night in some European Countries** 1977

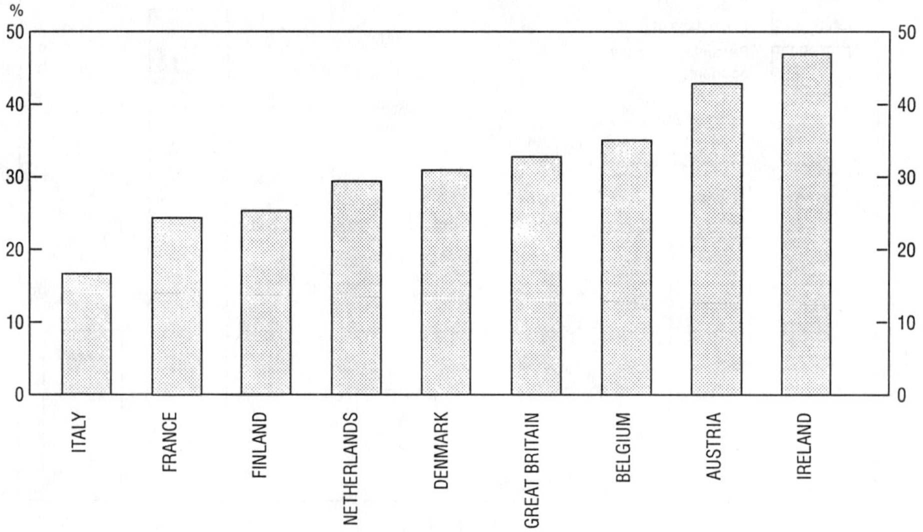

Source: An Foras Forbartha.

Figure 13. **Accident Risk per Mile Travelled at Different Hours of the Day, where the risk between 6am and 6pm is taken to be unity**

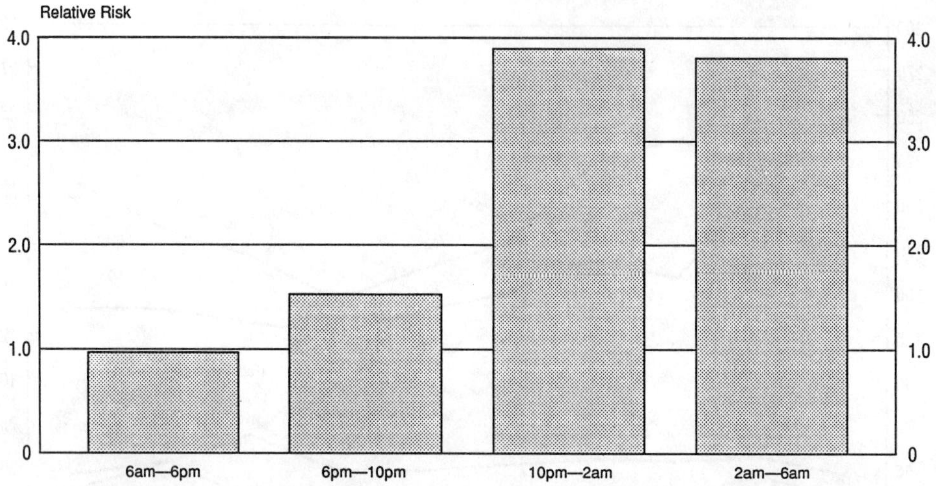

Source: An Foras Forbartha.

Figure 14. **Percentage of Accidents by Network**

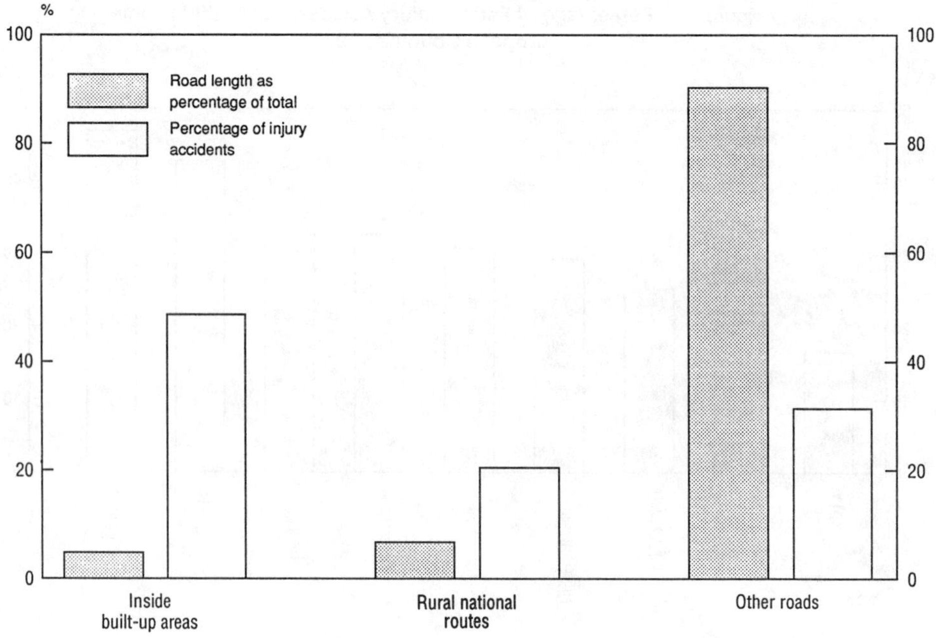

Source: An Foras Forbartha.

Figure 15. **Empirical Distribution of Sections**

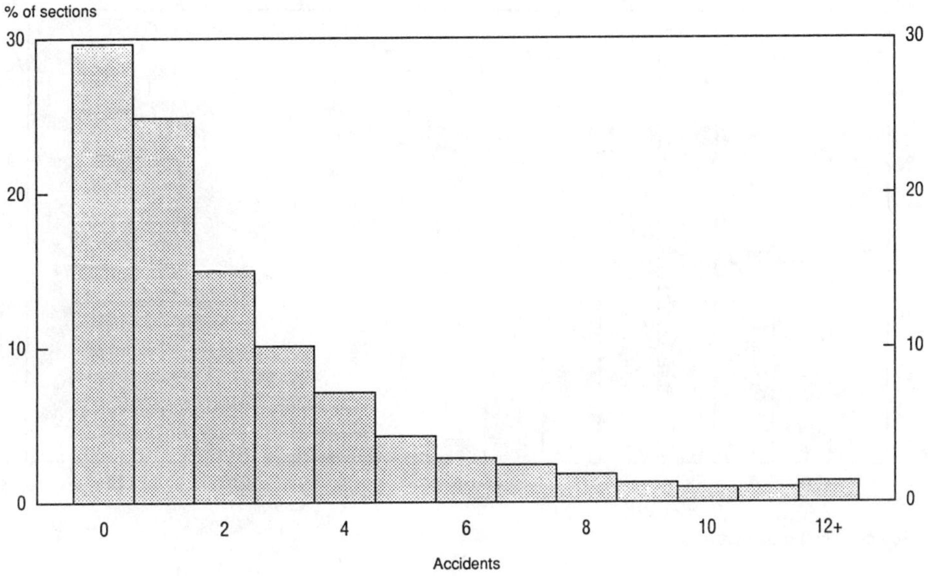

Figure 16. **Negative Binomial (unequal risk) Distribution of Sections**

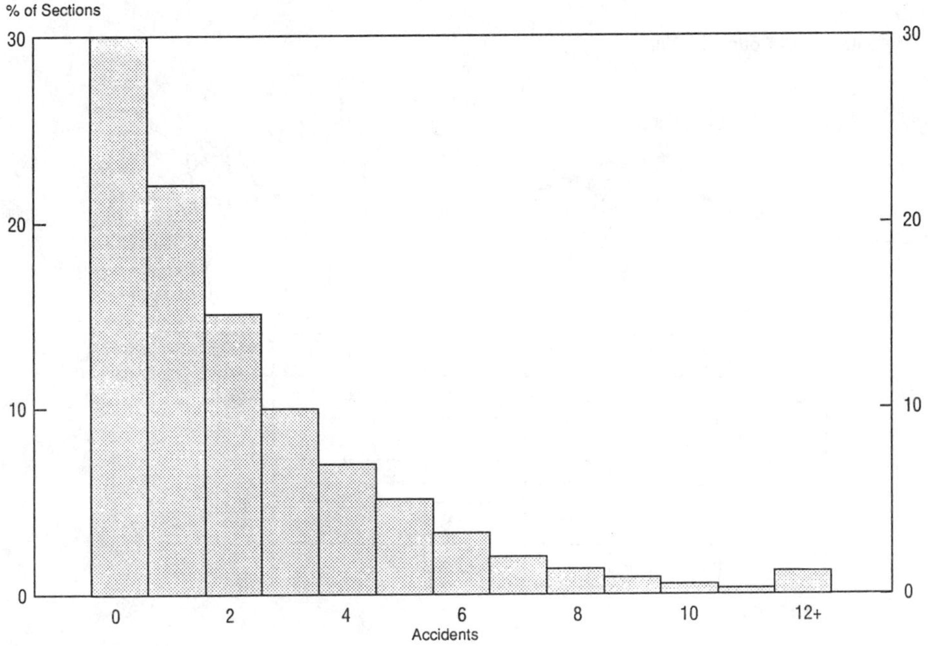

Source : An Foras Forbartha.

Figure 17. **Poisson (equal risk) Distribution of Sections.**

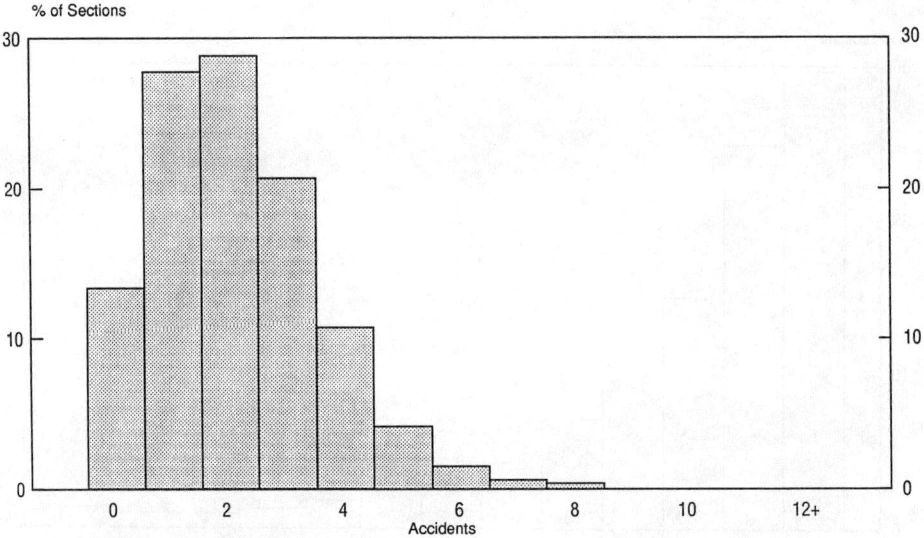

Source : An Foras Forbartha.

Figure 18. **Example of High Accident Location Map**

Route No. N1 County Dublin

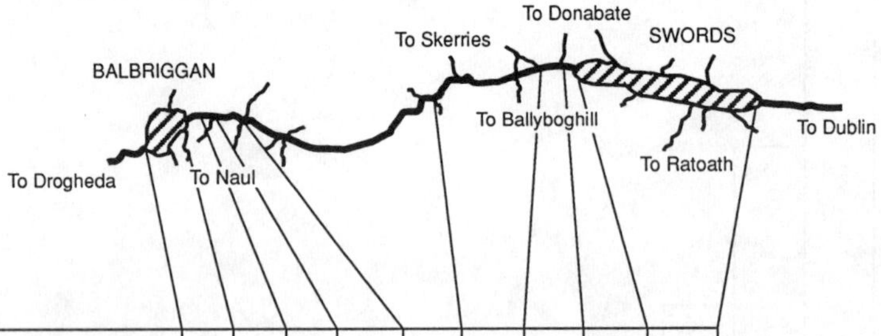

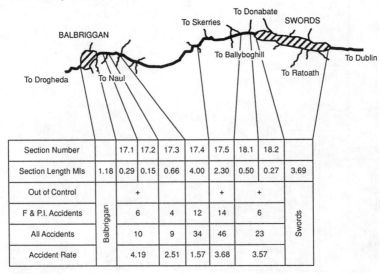

Section Number		17.1	17.2	17.3	17.4	17.5	18.1	18.2	
Section Length Mls	1.18	0.29	0.15	0.66	4.00	2.30	0.50	0.27	3.69
Out of Control	Balbriggan	+				+	+		Swords
F & P.I. Accidents		6		4	12	14	6		
All Accidents		10		9	34	46	23		
Accident Rate		4.19		2.51	1.57	3.68	3.57		

+ High Accident Location

Source: Fuller, T. (1975)

Figure 19. **Accident Rates and Roadside Development**

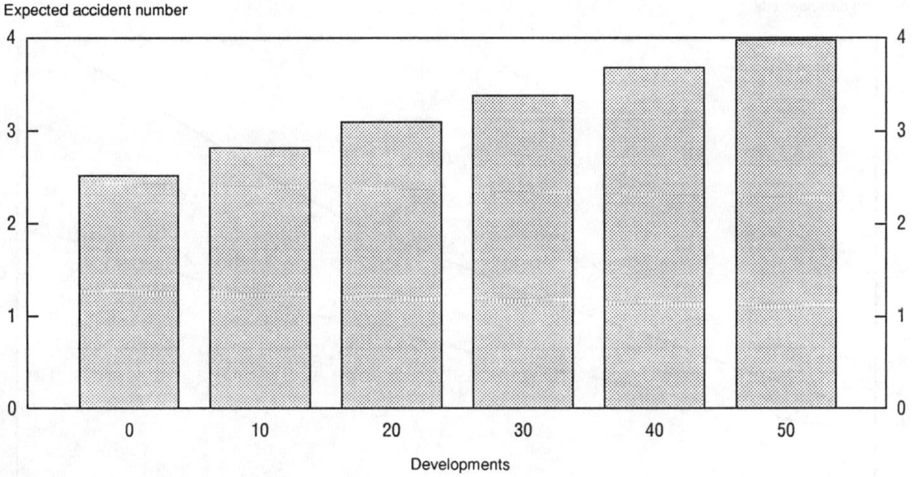

Lenght of section 3.5 km
AADT 1500
No hard shoulders
Carriageway width 22'
Source: Hearne, R. (1976)

Figure 20. **SCRIM Output**

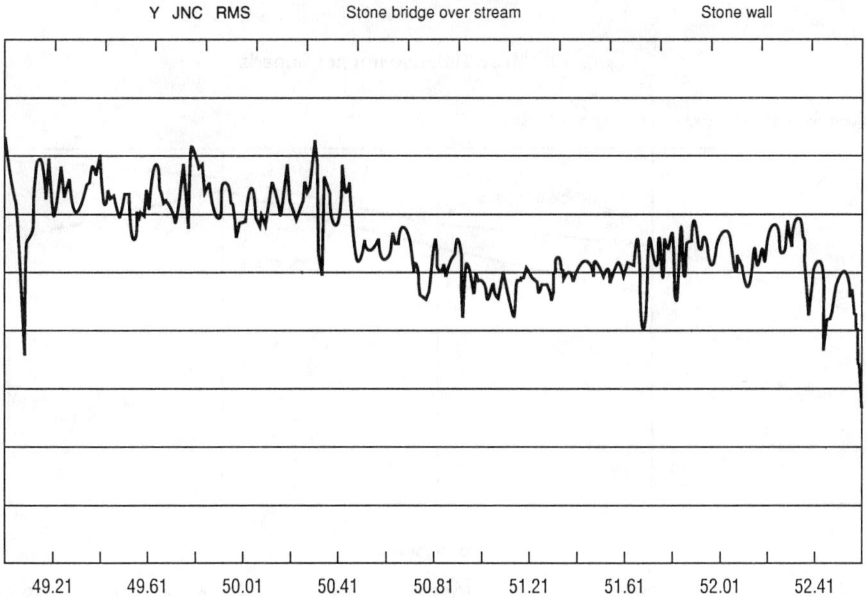

Figure 21. **Total Stopping Distance (in yds.) at Different Speeds**

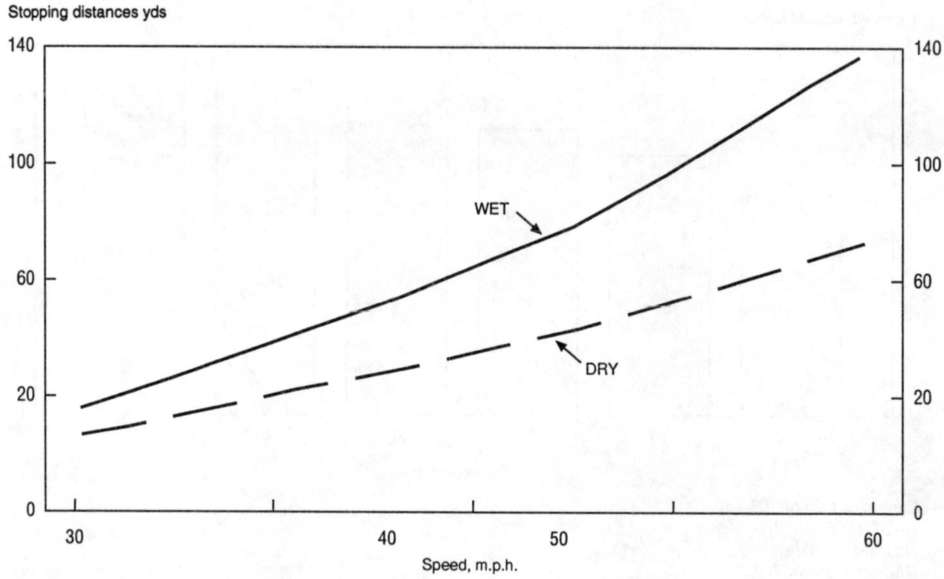

Source: Golden, M. J. (1975)

Figure 22. **Mean Relative Impact Speeds**

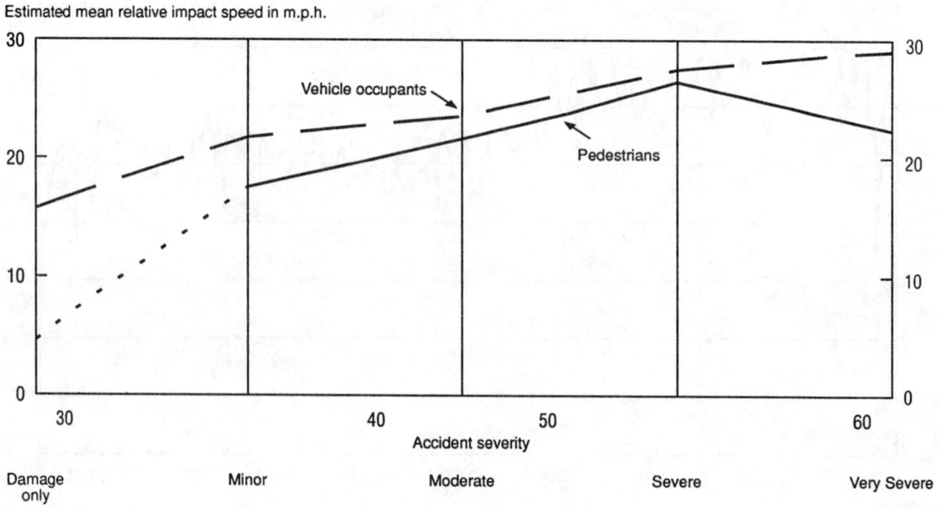

Source: Golden, M. J. (1975)

Figure 23. **Car Speeds Before and After Introduction of General Speed Limit (41)**

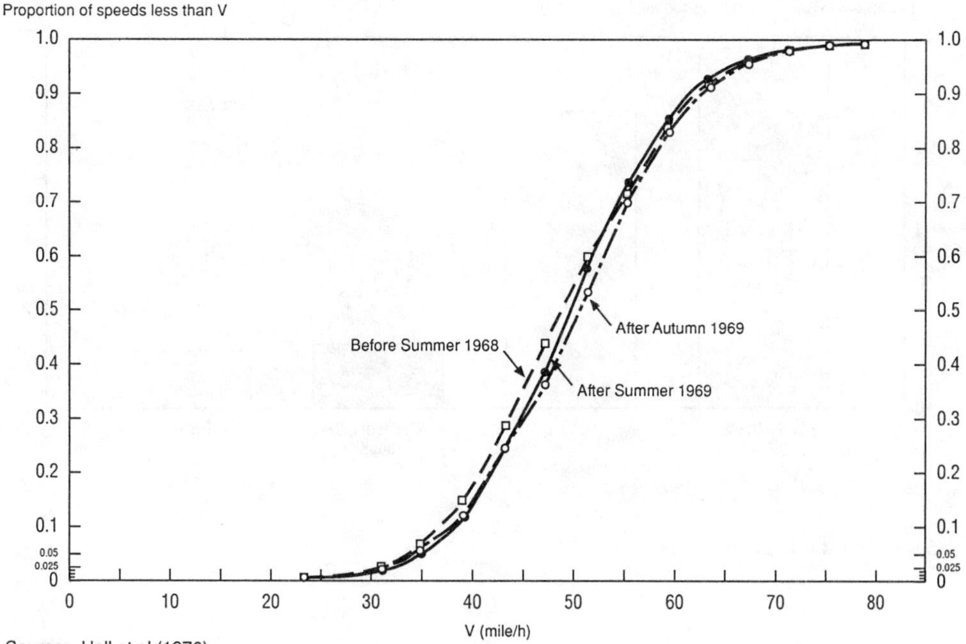

Source: Hall et al (1970)

Figure 24. **Relative Risk of Being involved in an Accident by BAC**

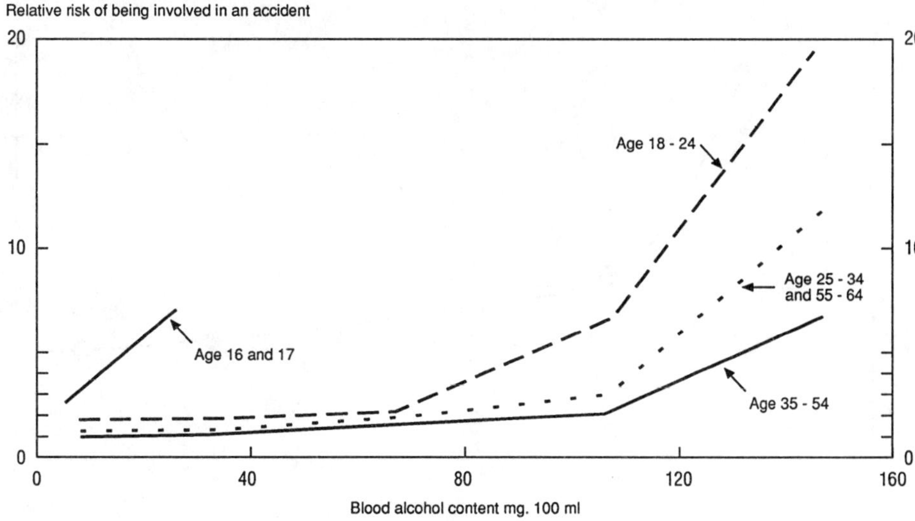

The increased risk applies to every age group.
Source: OECD (1978).

Figure 25. **Percentage of Facilities with BAC over 125mg/100ml**

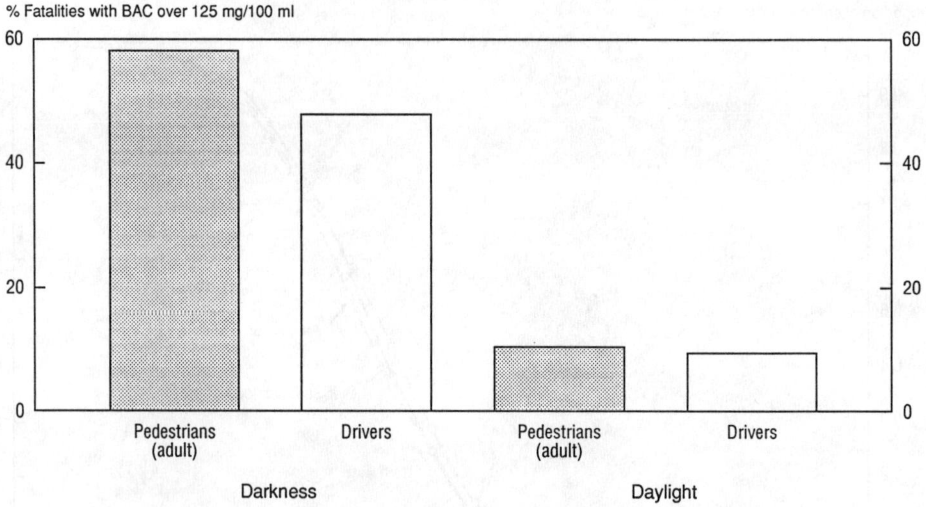

Source: J.I.M.A. (Dec. 1975)

Figure 26. **Risk of Single Vehicle Collision Relative to Other Collision, by Age**

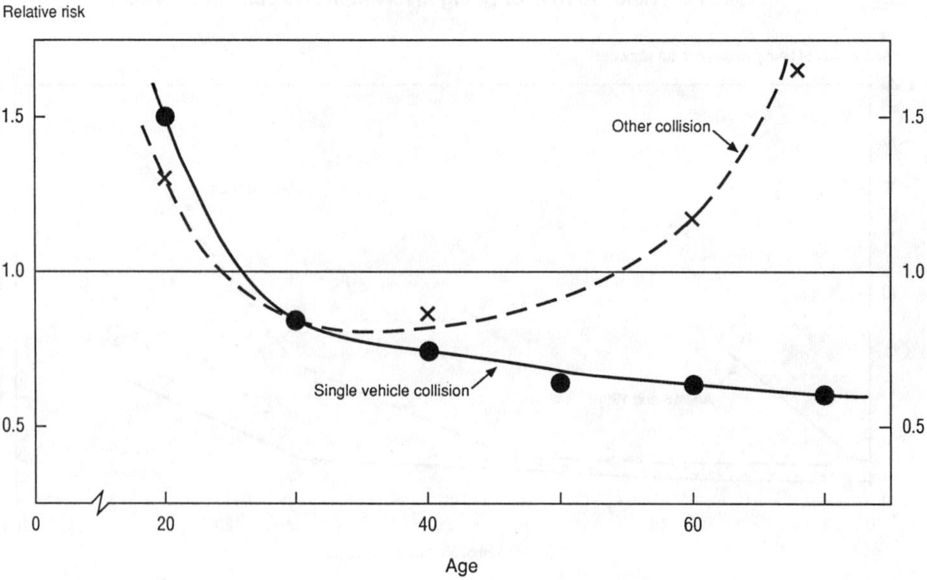

Source: Carr, B. (1970)

Figure 27. **Injury Accident involvement Rate per Mile Travelled in Different Vehicle Types, where the involvement rate for cars is taken to be unity**

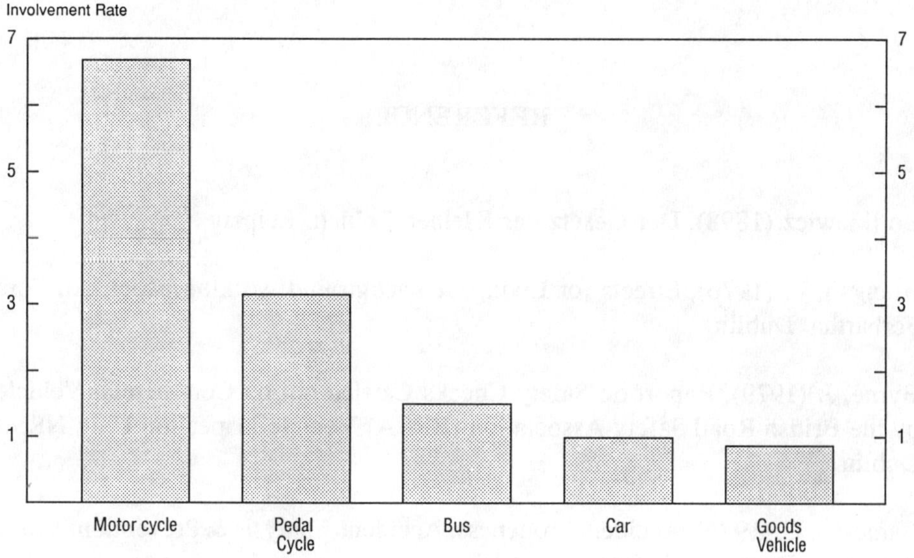

Source: An Foras Forbartha.

REFERENCES

Bortkiewicz (1898), Der Gesetz der Kleinen Zahlen, Leipzig.

Brangan, E. (1976), Streets for Living, A background working paper, An Foras Forbartha, Dublin.

Byrne, J. (1979), Report on Safety Checks Carried out on Commercial Vehicles by the British Road Safety Association (BRSA) Vehicle Inspection Unit, NRSA, Dublin.

Cameron, C. (1975), Accident Proneness, Accident Analysis & Prevention, Vol. 7, Pergamon Press, 1975, Oxford.

Carr, B.R. (1969), A Statistical Analysis of Rural Ontario Traffic Accidents Using Induced Exposure Data, Paper delivered at Transport and Road Research Laboratory (TRRL), Crowthorne, Berks., April 1969.

Cresswell, W. and Froggat, P. (1963), The Causation of Bus Driver Accidents, Oxford University Press, London.

Crowley, F. (1970), Skidding Accidents in Relation to the Characteristics of Road Surfaces in Ireland, RS.68, An Foras Forbartha, Dublin.

Crowley, F. (1976), Road Surface Characteristics in Relation to Skidding Resistance, RS.195, An Foras Forbartha, Dublin.

Crowley, F. (1979), Road Factors in Relation to an Unimproved Section of Road, RS.243, An Foras Forbartha, Dublin.

Crowley, F. and Fuller, T. (1978), Wet Road Skidding Accident Black Spots on the National Road Network, Based on Accident Data from the Period 1974 to 1976 Inclusive, RS.227, An Foras Forbartha, Dublin.

Crowley, F., Fuller, T. and Goss, J. (1973), A Study in Detail of Traffic Accidents on Selected Sections of the National Routes, RS.144, An Foras Forbartha, Dublin.

Crowley, F. (1978), Skid Resistance of Suburban Arterial Roads, RS.217, An Foras Forbartha, Dublin.

Crowley, F. (1983), Dundalk Traffic Accident Study, RS.298, An Foras Forbartha, Dublin.

Crowley, F. (1984), Athy Traffic Accident Study, RS.320, An Foras Forbartha, Dublin.

Crowley, F. (1986), Fermoy Traffic Accident Study, RS.348, An Foras Forbartha, Dublin.

Crowley, F. (1986), Mitchelstown Traffic Accident Study, RS.349, An Foras Forbartha, Dublin.

Crowley, F. (1987), Report on High Accident Locations on National Routes, RS.374, An Foras Forbartha, Dublin.

Crowley, F. (1988), Traffic Accidents -- Low Cost Remedial Engineering Methods, RS.377, An Foras Forbartha, Dublin.

Crowley, F. (1989), Speed Reducing Devices, RS.387, Environmental Research Unit, Dublin.

Crowley, F. (1991), A Survey of Driver Attitudes in Respect of Seat Belt Wearing, Speeding and Drink Driving, RS.400, Environmental Research Unit, Dublin.

Curran, A.J. (1972), A Computer Programme to Analyse SCRIM Data, RS.116, An Foras Forbartha, Dublin.

Curran, A.J. (1975), The Interpretation of SCRIM Results, RS.181, An Foras Forbartha, Dublin.

Curran, A.J. and Keogh, W. (1975), Measurements of Lighting Levels in Dublin City Streets, An Foras Forbartha, Dublin.

Curran, A.J. and Newell, M. (1973), City Accident Black Spots (1973), RS.125, An Foras Forbartha, Dublin.

Curran, A. (1984), National Speed Survey, RS.318, An Foras Forbartha, Dublin.

Curran, A. (1987), Differential Friction, RS.362, An Foras Forbartha, Dublin.

Dalby, E. (1979), The Use of Area-Wide Measures in Urban Road Safety, Transport and Road Research Laboratory (TRRL), Crowthorne.

Edwards, Carmody, Hoey, Lucas, O'Callaghan (1973), Road Traffic Accidents -- A Six Months' Review, JIMA, Vol. 66.

An Foras Forbartha (1969 to 1991), Road Accident Facts 1968-1990, Annual Publication, Dublin.

An Foras Forbartha (1969b), General Speed Limits, RS.39, Dublin.

An Foras Forbartha (1975b), Motor Car Defects in Ireland, RS.180, An Foras Forbartha, Dublin.

Fuller, T. (1975), High Accident Locations IV, The National Routes, 1971-1973, RS.160, An Foras Forbartha, Dublin.

Fuller, T. (1979), High Accident Locations V, The National Routes, 1974-1976, RS.234, An Foras Forbartha, Dublin.

Fuller, T. and Hearne, R. (1977), The Reporting Level of Traffic Accidents, RS.208, An Foras Forbartha, Dublin.

Fuller, T. and Holland, T. (1974), Map Overlays of Accident Locations, RS.152, An Foras Forbartha, Dublin.

Golden, J.M. (1975), Estimation of Stopping Distances, RS.183, An Foras Forbartha, Dublin.

Golden, J.M. (1980), Pedestrian Accidents, RS.225, An Foras Forbartha, Dublin.

Golden, J.M., Curran, A.J. and Brown, G. (1974), Dublin and Dun Laoghaire Accident Lists, RS.156, An Foras Forbartha, Dublin.

Golden, J.M., Hearne, R. and Staunton, M. (1978), A Preliminary Assessment of the Operation of Pelican Crossings in the Dublin Area, R.76, An Foras Forbartha, Dublin.

Golden, J.M. and Marry, A. (1978), Skid Resistance on the National Primary Routes, RS.229, An Foras Forbartha, Dublin.

Golden, J.M. (1990), High Accident Locations VIII, RS.393, Environmental Research Unit, Dublin.

Greenwood, M. and Woods, H.M. (1919), A Report on the Incidence of Industrial Accidents upon Individuals with Special Reference to Multiple Accidents. Ref. Industr. Fat. Res. Bd., London, No. 4.

Greenwood, M. and Hule, G.V. (1920), An Inquiry into the Nature of Frequency Distributions Representative of Multiple Happenings, etc. JRSS 83, 255-279.

Hakkinen, S. (1958), Traffic Accidents and Driver Characteristics, Finland's Institute for Technology, Scientific Research 13.

Hall, P., Hearne, R. and O'Flynn, J. (1970), The 60 mph General Speed Limit in Ireland, RS.62, An Foras Forbartha, Dublin.

Hall, P., Hearne, R. and Holland, T. (1971), High Accident Locations, Vol. 1, RS.71, An Foras Forbartha, Dublin.

Hearne, R. (1976), Selected Geometric Elements and Accident Densities, RS.167, An Foras Forbartha, Dublin.

Hearne, R. (1979), Contributory Factors in Road Accidents Identified from a Sample of Garda Siochana Accident Report Forms, RS.212, An Foras Forbartha, Dublin.

Hearne, R. (1980), Accidents Due to Through Traffic in Irish Towns, RS.244, An Foras Forbartha, Dublin.

Hearne, R. (1980), Small Scale Surveys of Safety Belt Wearing Rates 1978 & 1979, RS.254, An Foras Forbartha, Dublin.

Hearne, R. (1980), A Preliminary Assessment of the Effectiveness of the Safety Belt Legislation, RS.255, An Foras Forbartha, Dublin.

Hearne, R. (1982), High Accident Locations, Vol. VI, RS.298, An Foras Forbartha, Dublin.

Hearne, R. (1983), High Accident Locations, Vol. VII, RS.310, An Foras Forbartha, Dublin.

Hearne, R. and Marry, A. (1984), Car & Truck Speeds on National Roads, RS.330, An Foras Forbartha, Dublin.

Hearne, R. (1986), Note on Fatal Accident Trends in Ireland 1946-1984, RS.351, An Foras Forbartha, Dublin.

Hickey, M., Bofin, P.J., O'Donnell, B. and Hearne, R. (1975), Blood Alcohol Levels in Road Traffic Fatalities, JIMA, Vol. 68, 579-582, Dublin. (These figures were updated in a lecture given by Hickey to the WMA in 1977.)

Hoinville, G., Berthaud, R. and Mackie, A.M. (1972), A Study of Accident Rates Amongst Motorists Who Passed or Failed on Advanced Driver Test, LR.499, TRRL, Crowthorne.

Holland, T. (1973), Map Overlays of Accident Locations (1970-1972), RS.151, An Foras Forbartha, Dublin.

Holland, T. and Wall, W. (1970), HAL in an Urban Area, RS.66, An Foras Forbartha, Dublin.

Karin, Bernard Anderson (1978), Use and Effects of Seat Belts in 21 Countries, Institute of Transport Economics, Oslo.

Klein, D. (1973), Accident Proneness Revisited, Contemporary Psychology, 18.

Kummer, H.W. and Myer, W.E. (1967), Tentative Skid Resistance Requirements for Main Rural Highways, National Co-operative Highway Research Program Report 37.

McEntee, M.J. (1975), Identification and Easement of High Risk Locations in Dublin City, Dublin Corporation.

Marry, A. and O'Sullivan, D. (1976), HGVs -- Pilot Survey of Gross Weights and Axle Loadings, RS.200, An Foras Forbartha, Dublin.

McCarthy, M. (1984), The Nature & Extent of the Child Accident Problem, RS.319, An Foras Forbartha, Dublin.

NRSA (1979), The Voluntary Car Inspection Programme in 1978, NRSA, Dublin.

OECD (1970), Statistical Methods in the Analysis of Road Accidents, Paris.

OECD (1975), Young Driver Accidents, Paris.

OECD (1976), Hazardous Road Locations, Paris.

OECD (1978), The Role of Alcohol and Drugs in Road Accidents, Paris.

O'Flynn, J. (1969), Safety Belts, RS.56, An Foras Forbartha, Dublin.

Plant, J.E. (1972), Polished Stone Values and Engineering Properties of Road-Making Aggregates in Ireland -- 1972, RC.104, An Foras Forbartha, Dublin.

Rayner (1975), The Work and Development of the Greater London Council Road Safety Section, PTRC Seminar, June 1975.

Roosmark (1970), Interview Investigations of Traffic Accidents, OECD, Paris.

Shaw, L. and Sichel, H. (1971), Accident Proneness, Pergamon Press, Oxford.

Starr (1969), Social Benefit Versus Technological Risk, Science, September 1969.

Swali (1973), Selection, Analysis and Treatment of Accident Black Spots in Urban Areas, Presented for the Greater London Council at PTRC Seminar in 1973.

Wass, C. (1977), Traffic Accident Exposure and Liability, ROC, Rungsted, Denmark.

Weber, D. (1971), Application of Multiple Regression Analysis to a Poisson Process, JASA, 66.

International Road Federation (1978), World Road Statistics 1973-1977, Washington DC.

Sub-topic 4

IMPACT OF NEW TECHNOLOGIES ON EFFICIENCY AND SAFETY

J.P. BAUMGARTNER
Lausanne
Switzerland

SUMMARY

Lausanne, February 1991

RÉSUMÉ

Fundamental or revolutionary technological innovations are rare, but there are a great many technical innovations of a more limited nature which build up in the sector over time and help to reduce the price and raise the standard of transport.

Technical innovation is not an end in itself but is a service to the customer and user of transport.

The efficiency of technological innovation is expressed and assessed essentially in terms of modal split.

The only techniques which establish a lasting place on a transport market worthy of that name are those which show an economic return.

1. INTRODUCTION

People were travelling at the same speed in the early eighteenth century as they were in the second century on Roman roads, i.e. about twenty to thirty kilometres per day. What small volume of goods was carried on the backs of mules or in horse-drawn carts travelled at speeds of ten to twenty kilometres per day.

Improvements came after some sixteen centuries of little or no progress: for example, it took a stage coach ten days to travel from Paris to Lyons at the beginning of the eighteenth century, four days under the First Empire and seventy-five hours under Louis-Philippe.

In the middle of the nineteenth century, the railways (i.e. steel-wheel on steel-rail and the steam locomotive) represented the greatest progress in relative terms ever recorded in transport. At a single stroke the railways:

-- Increased tenfold the commercial speed of passenger and goods transport;

-- Reduced tenfold the price or cost of passenger and goods transport;

-- Increased transport capacity one hundredfold and, quite rapidly, by a thousandfold;

-- Increased a thousandfold the geographical areas of industrial and commercial markets.

The early twentieth century saw the development of road motor vehicles (more precisely, the marriage of the petrol-driven motor with the pneumatic tyre). After the Second World War, road transport became the mode of land transport looked to as a point of reference. The progress it offered in terms of price and capacity was only marginal. Its benefits lie elsewhere. For the first time in the history of transport, the possibility of individual travel was offered to almost everybody. In contrast with the railways, moreover, road transport enabled and promoted almost unlimited geographical decentralisation of housing and of most industrial, commercial and recreational activities.

Commercial airlines developed after the end of the First World War and expanded rapidly after the Second World War. Air transport increased the commercial speed of travel tenfold but, with certain exceptions, did not change the order of magnitude of the average price for transport.

The railways, road transport by car and lorry and air transport are the three examples of genuine mutations (in the biological sense of the term) in the transport sector.

Spectacular though they have been, these mutations must not conceal from us another vector of the technique of transport, modest in the short term, but singularly efficient in the long run.

In each mode of transport there is an ongoing improvement in the standard of service offered and in the productivity of labour. The annual rates of increase in these indicators are low, but a large number of small technical improvements, carried out incessantly, each reinforcing the other over time, finally result in remarkable progress.

Between 1960 and 1990 in Switzerland, for example, it may be noted that in real terms (calculated in Swiss francs of 1990, i.e. the level of prices in 1990) as a rough estimate (see Table 1):

-- The purchase price of a car was reduced by half;

-- A car's running or marginal costs (fuel, oils, tyres, maintenance, repairs and part of the depreciation) were reduced by about three quarters;

-- The total cost of running a car in terms of kilometres travelled was reduced by two-thirds; in other words, over a thirty-year period, the real cost (in constant prices) of private transport diminished by some 3.6 per cent per year or, in terms of efficiency -- i.e. the inverse ratio of total charges to kilometrage -- showed an increase of 3.7 per cent per year.

This progress has not been achieved by any sudden introduction of new and revolutionary techniques. Today's car is fundamentally no different from that of thirty years ago. However, competition among manufacturers has promoted research and development and the application of numerous small technical improvements.

The trend in real costs is less spectacular in the freight sector but is no less clear cut. Table 2 shows that in Italy between 1960 and 1989 in real terms (calculated in lira of 1989, i.e. in 1989 prices) and as a rough estimate:

-- There was no change in the purchase price of a heavy goods vehicle (lorry and trailer or articulated vehicle) as expressed in relation to the capacity in tonnage;

-- The total remuneration of a driver (wages, social contributions, etc.) doubled;

-- In relation to capacity, total annual charges excluding kilometrage running costs (interest, depreciation, wages and social contributions of two drivers, taxes and duties, insurance, garage) increased by about 25 per cent;

-- On the basis of output in tonne-kilometres, costs per kilometre or marginal costs (diesel, oils, tyres, maintenance and repairs) were reduced by two-thirds;

-- In relation to output in tonne-kilometres, total costs were reduced by about 40 per cent.

Accordingly, between 1960 and 1989 the cost of medium and long-haul road haulage in Italy was reduced -- all other factors being equal -- by an average of 1.75 per cent per year in real terms. Or, alternatively, the efficiency of road haulage, i.e. the inverse ratio of cost to kilometrage, showed an average increase of 1.8 per cent per year.

Technical innovation is one of the two decisive factors contributing to progress in the transport sector.

The other decisive factor is competition between modes and among carriers within each mode. However, such competition must be subject to the constraint of a balanced budget for each mode (for both infrastructure and vehicles), each carrier and each customer or user. Unfortunately, however, competition in the transport sector has always been far from perfect, although it is also fortunate that it does not have to be perfect to be effective to some degree. Technical progress is curbed or eliminated without competition, which alone ensures gradual improvements in quality and a reduction in prices.

The perfect market of economic theory does not exist, but the efficiency of the transport market can always be improved, essentially by encouraging technological innovation along the following lines, for example:

-- Providing more and better technical and commercial information for transport users (passengers, freight shippers and consignees) and carriers;

-- Explaining and clarifying the operation of the price mechanism on the transport market;

-- Combating cartels or *ententes* among carriers or partial monopolies of particular carriers and public services;

-- Avoiding or eliminating bans and quota and allowance measures, etc.;

-- Ensuring the freedom of choice of transport users (passengers, freight shippers and consignees) among modes and carriers and also between transport for hire or reward, on the one hand, and personal transport and own-account transport, on the other;

-- Restricting or avoiding transfers (specific taxes and duties, or specific subsidies), irrespective of what they are called for accounting purposes and what reasons or pretexts are given for them;

-- Avoiding a policy-based system of pricing.

2. ASSESSING EFFICIENCY AND SAFETY IN THE TRANSPORT SECTOR

The economy consists of all the activities that serve to put goods at the disposal of those who want them.

The efficiency and safety of a transport mode or technique is the expression and measure of its capacity to cater for demand for travel or the carriage of freight.

2.1. The carrier's view

The carrier, that is to say, an undertaking providing transport for hire or reward or a public transport service, may use a set of criteria, indicators or partial technical and physical ratios in order to assess and analyse the efficiency and safety of production, essentially for example, with reference to:

-- Labour productivity, calculated in terms of transport output sold to users by working hour or by worker during a year;

-- Energy consumption, as it relates to transport output sold to users;

-- Average speed of vehicles used;

-- Duration of use and kilometrage travelled each year by vehicles;

-- The percentage of empty runs in total vehicle runs;

-- The load factor of laden vehicles;

-- Vehicle availability factor, i.e. the percentage of roadworthy vehicles in the total fleet;

-- In the case of passenger transport, casualties (killed or injured) as a percentage of total passengers carried.

The criteria, indicators or technical ratios in question differ in character. They are not independent but cannot be aggregated. Taken individually, each criterion may be conducive to sub-optimal decision-making.

A carrier may therefore use a number of partial indicators or ratios expressed in monetary values such as, for example:

-- The ratio of the revenues obtained solely and directly from the sale of transport services in relation to the total personnel employed by the carrier;

-- The ratio of revenues obtained solely and directly from the sale of transport services in relation to the overall expenditure on personnel (wages, bonuses, social contributions, miscellaneous charges, indirect expenditure, etc.);

-- In the case of freight transport, the ratio of compensation paid to users as a result of pilfering, loss and damage during transport in relation to gross revenues from transport output.

However, only a profit and loss account can provide a full view of the efficiency of a carrier's activity. Such an account would, moreover, have to be drawn up correctly, that is to say, the legal or regulatory account must be adapted to the particular requirements by, for example:

-- Taking account of the interest charges of all capital invested in equipment (infrastructure and vehicles) which is used to produce services; the interest rates must be those normally obtaining on the capital market;

-- Eliminating subsidies for investment;

-- Including only revenues obtained solely and directly from the sale of transport services to users (passengers and freight shippers or consignees);

-- Ensuring that subsidies, compensation, etc. -- regardless of what they are called or why they are paid -- and grants to offset deficits are not accounted for with revenues or entered under the heading of "income".

The efficient carrier is the one who ensures that this adjusted profit and loss account is in balance. There is one exception. A public transport service is by definition not subject to the constraint of a balanced budget. There are no criteria available for measuring the overall efficiency of a public transport service in quantifiable and verifiable terms. Judgement can be passed on the efficiency of such a service only from a policy standpoint.

An adjusted profit and loss account makes it possible to assess the efficiency of the management of a transport undertaking in a previous financial year.

The carrier himself has to resolve a more specific problem, namely that of preparing a decision. The solution envisaged is justified from the moment at which the discounted future returns, obtained solely and directly from the sale of transport services, seem likely to exceed the discounted total future expenditure. In other words, the decision-making criterion of the carrier is that of profitability.

In the case of a public transport service, whose aims and functions are by definition not of an economic nature, only policy criteria count.

2.2. The user's view

The user expresses a demand. In the economic sense of the term, the demand associates quantity, quality and price.

2.2.1. Assessing efficiency in passenger transport

Passengers weigh up the quality of their journeys on the basis of criteria such as the following, in particular:

-- The price or cost, calculated from the start of the journey to the destination;

-- The overall time taken, that is to say, from door to door (or in other terms, the average speed of the journey from door to door);

-- The reliability of the journey (for instance, being on time);

-- The frequency of the services or, alternatively, the interval between two successive services; in more general terms, the availability of transport;

-- The number of interchanges (connections, change of mode or vehicle);

-- The probability of strikes by the carriers' personnel;

-- The ease with which a particular volume of baggage may be carried;

-- Comfort, atmosphere, prestige;

-- Whether or not there is the opportunity to select the travel companions and avoid contact with people considered disagreeable;

-- The security offered by the mode or by the carrier, etc.

The indicators or criteria in question are not uniform. It is solely up to each individual user to make his own personal assessment of all the elements in each particular case. No-one can do it for him. On the transport market in the broadest sense of the term, i.e. including private transport, each user chooses in the light of his personal requirements in each case.

2.2.2. *Assessing efficiency in freight transport*

Freight shippers and consignees essentially take account of factors such as the following when taking decisions:

-- Price or cost of transport (including all ancillary items: terminal charges, transfers of load, intermediate storage, packaging, etc.);

-- Total transport time or, in other terms, the commercial speed of the transport operation from point of departure to destination;

-- Reliability of transport, i.e. keeping to agreed, planned or programmed delivery times;

-- Goods lost, pilfered and damaged;

-- Stability to fit in to the production process, in the economic sense of the term, as and when required (concepts of just-in-time, zero stock, etc.);

-- Probable frequency and length of strikes of personnel of the various modes, etc.

The indicators and criteria concerned are not cumulative, but the decision-making methods are improving and in each particular case informed decisions can be taken essentially by means of such methods as computer-aided multi-criteria analysis (necessarily, of course, in a market economy with decentralised decision-making in which the freedom of choice of the user is not restricted by the legal, regulatory or fiscal framework).

2.3. Modal split

In a market economy -- as pointed out where decisions are decentralised and it is assumed that the user or customer has freedom of choice -- the relative efficiency of the different modes of transport is expressed by the choice of the users and can accordingly be assessed in these terms.

Modal split may take two forms:

-- the overall average for a given country;

-- the specific modal split for a particular case.

2.3.1. *National modal split*

As a general rule, one calculates the transport output by the number of passenger-kilometres or tonne-kilometres recorded in a country. The national modal split clearly and simply quantifies the relative efficiency of the different modes at any given time and in a chronological series. It also measures the extent to which the demand of transport users has been met.

For example, Tables 3 and 4 clearly show the present preferences of transport users.

2.3.2. *Specific modal split*

In order to enable carriers to take informed decisions and to assess the effects of such decisions, it is necessary to determine or estimate the modal split for each particular case, notably for example, for each route specified in terms of point of origin and destination, for each particular time and for each reason a passenger travels and for each category of freight to be carried. This is the specific purpose, for example, of econometric forecasting models, some of which give satisfactory results in the light of the assumptions and scenarios selected.

3. SOME EXAMPLES OF THE IMPACT OF NEW TECHNOLOGIES ON EFFICIENCY AND SAFETY

We shall specifically exclude consideration of the many technological innovations in the sphere of electronics, information technology and telematics -- which have so many applications in the world today since their effects go far beyond the transport sector as such -- and confine ourselves for present purposes to a few technological innovations specific to transport.

If a technological innovation is to be effective, it will not suffice for it to be interesting, ingenious and elegant from the scientific and technical standpoint since it must also cater for a demand in the economic sense of this term. An effective technological innovation is one which arrives on the transport market at a price which establishes the equilibrium between supply of and demand for transport services, the transport users on the one hand and carriers on the other being subject to the constraint of maintaining a balanced budget. As it is assumed that users are free to choose, a technological innovation will replace an existing technique when it enables the price of a given service to be reduced or provides a better quality service for the same price.

3.1. The "rolling road" through the Alps

The governments of a number of countries are trying to ensure that the "rolling road" (*rollende Landstrasse* or *rollende Autobahn* as it has been named by its promoters) is used for the carriage by rail through the Alps of lorries, coupled combinations (lorries and trailers) and articulated vehicles (tractors and semi-trailers) together with their drivers. More particularly, the rolling road calls for the use of special wagons equipped with 8, 10 or 12 axles with 16, 20 or 24 small wheels. During the rail transport, the road motor vehicle (i.e. the expensive vehicle) and its driver are inactive. The tares of both the wagon and road vehicle have to be added together in the rolling road technique, which increases the unit consumption of energy.

The rolling road technique would be adopted if the cost of carrying the road vehicle by rail was less than the cost of the road journey being replaced. However, the rolling road through the Alps is more expensive than the road transport it is to replace (Table 5), but it has developed to some extent by means of subsidies, i.e. thanks to transfers of income organised by governments at the expense of all taxpayers and thanks to a set of legal and regulatory steps (traffic bans, limits on permissible total weight, etc.). The rolling road is an example of an inefficient technique which is therefore both useless and harmful.

3.2. The electric car

Petrol is a limited and non-renewable natural resource. In the long term the real price of petrol is bound to rise substantially, so it is worth thinking about an engine that can replace the petrol engine. The first idea that comes to mind is that of the electric motor using batteries which would themselves be recharged from a national grid.

As one example among others, an electric car of the Larel type may be compared with the Fiat Panda car. The Larel (manufactured and sold on a small scale) is a Panda equipped with an electric motor instead of a petrol engine. Since the batteries are heavy and take up a lot of room, the Larel has only two seats (instead of the four or five places in the Panda) and can carry only 30 kg of baggage. The Larel can travel 53 km at an average speed of 45 km/h without recharging. Recharging the batteries then takes seven hours. The total weight of the batteries is 250 kg; they have a life of 15 000 km and cost SF 3 400 (ECU 2 000).

The Larel's purchase price is SF 36 500 (ECU 21 500). Power consumption amounts to 17 kWh per 100 km, i.e. a cost of SF 3 (ECU 1.8) per 100 kms. Maintenance costs are about the same as those for a Panda. Total cost for the Larel (electric power, oils, tyres, maintenance and repairs, yearly interest and amortization, insurance, taxes and duties, etc.) amount to SF 1.72 (ECU 1) per kilometre for an annual total of 5 000 km. For 10 000 km per year they are SF 1.06 (ECU 0.63) per km as compared with SF 0.47 (ECU 0.28) per km for the Panda.

At the present stage of development and on the assumption that the price of petrol escalates steeply, it is conceivable that the electric car might be useful in urban traffic. Given the present state of the art, however, it cannot be used in inter-city traffic.

A fundamental aspect of the problem arising in connection with the electric car calls for further consideration, namely the replacement of petrol by electricity. If the electric car is to replace the petrol-driven car, i.e. if one day we are to have as many electric cars as petrol cars today, there would be increased demand for electric power. If the additional electricity is generated with natural gas, coal, lignite or diesel oil, this would produce very little less CO_2 than the petrol-driven cars that were replaced. The other alternative would be to generate electricity needed in nuclear power stations, a solution that cannot be said to meet with unanimous approval. What remains are, for example, particular sources such as geothermic, wind and solar energy. As matters now stand, science still has to resolve the related problems, but we must not give up. What is at stake is enormous.

3.3. The high-speed train travelling on specialised dedicated infrastructure

If the railways wish to increase their share of domestic and international inter-city transport, they will have to begin by offering their passengers a station-to-station commercial speed that is competitive, i.e. at least 200 km/h. To do so, a maximum running speed of at least 250 km/h -- and preferably 300 km/h -- is called for in commercial service.

To remain competitive in the medium term the railways must offer a station-to-station commercial speed of 250 km/h or more on inter-city links, so a nominal speed of at least 300 km/h will have to be selected.

Fast inter-city trains can travel at speeds of 300 km/h or more in commercial service only on new, purpose-built track.

There are two categories of new railway line: new lines for mixed traffic and new, specialised lines for passenger traffic.

New lines for mixed traffic (both passenger and freight traffic) can never be anything more than a development of the conventional railway. More particularly, a new line combining high-speed and mixed traffic is not and cannot be a satisfactory response from either the technical or economic viewpoints to the following two problems:

-- On curves, is the cant of the track to be adapted to both a speed of 300 km/h (motor sets) and a speed of 100 to 120 km/h (freight trains)?

-- Can sufficient intervals of time be left open for inspection, maintenance and renewal of the track and overhead line?

Accordingly, new lines for mixed traffic will not be examined in this context, since only those specialised for passenger traffic offer a new technology, namely the B1 lines of the AGC (European Agreement on Main International Railway Lines, signed in Geneva in 1985 under the aegis of the Economic Commission for Europe; Annex II, Table 1). The nominal minimum speed for these lines is 300 km/h.

The new specialised lines for passenger traffic (category B1 of the AGC) have the following characteristics:

-- Separation of services: passenger traffic between large urban centres is exclusively on new high-speed lines, while freight trains travel solely on existing conventional lines that run more or less parallel with the new high-speed lines;

-- Specialisation of lines: the new high-speed lines are reserved solely for high-speed passenger trains between major urban centres; the existing lines of the conventional network, running more or less parallel with them, are used by all freight trains;

-- The inspection, maintenance and renewal of fixed installations on the new high-speed lines is carried out on a rational, efficient and economic basis during the intervals of time left open each day.

In passing, it may also be pointed out that a specialised new line reserved for passenger trains might also be used by motor sets carrying mail, parcels, pallets and appropriate containers, etc., provided that they keep to the same timetable (the same running times) as the passenger motor sets. In other words, motor sets for freight forwarding, which calls for and can pay for high speed, should offer the same maximum speed in commercial service and the same mechanical and electrical facilities as high-speed motor sets for passengers (the same facilities in terms of traction and braking power, the same braking, running and suspension gears, the same maximum axle load, etc.). High-speed motor sets for mail and parcels are already in service in France.

For both the new, specialised high-speed line and the existing more or less parallel line taken together, it is found on each of the two lines that specialisation narrows or eliminates the differences in speeds of the fastest and slowest trains. Specialisation is therefore a means of achieving maximum capacity for both inter-city passenger traffic and freight traffic. Specialisation enables freight trains to travel at the highest possible station-to-station commercial speed and provides for the greatest precision in movements of both passenger traffic on the new line and of freight traffic.

In the last analysis, moreover, it is conceivable that the need to increase the commercial speed and reliability of freight trains may in itself indicate in some cases the separation of traffic, the construction of high-speed lines solely for inter-city passenger trains, and the specialisation of existing conventional lines for freight.

The Japanese and French railways have decided on the separation of services and the associated specialisation of lines. Their experience has proved to be positive in every respect.

From the competitive standpoint, the limitations of high-speed passenger trains on new specialised lines are quite evident. It is pointless to try to compete with the private car for high-speed journeys of less than one hour, or to compete with the airlines on journeys where the high-speed train takes more than three or four hours. In any event, a succession of stops at intervals of less than an hour is not, by definition, suitable for a high-speed train.

A new high-speed line calls for large-scale investment. From an economic standpoint, only investment showing a satisfactory return is warranted. If such a line is to offer or promise an industrial and financial internal rate of return that is adequate, it must cater for demand from a large number of paying passengers, demand which exists solely on a limited number of inter-city links, that is to say between those large cities which, for example, each have one or more continental or intercontinental airports.

Priority should be assigned to the construction of large-volume, high-speed lines between the major European urban areas, between which the journey time will not exceed three hours.

The high-speed train travelling on a specialised, new high-speed line -- and so reserved for passenger traffic -- has shown that it can offer a very high level of safety. Absolute safety does not exist but, since 1964 (commissioning date of the first Shinkansen line) and since 1981 (commissioning date of the TGV Paris/Sud-Est) up to the time of writing this paper, neither the Japanese railways (which have carried more than 3 billion passengers on the Shinkansen) nor the French have had any casualties for which the railway was responsible on the high-speed lines.

The high-speed passenger train that runs on a new high-speed line reserved for passenger traffic can today be regarded as both an advanced technology and as a technique tried and tested in commercial service.

3.4. Transport by means of magnetic levitation and driven by linear motors (Maglev)

This form of transport is best known under the popular and prestigious name of Maglev, a technique researched, developed and offered essentially by the Japanese and German industries which has the following characteristics:

- The infrastructure consists of a track in each direction in a T, inverted T or U shape, in most cases as a viaduct;
- Magnetic levitation of vehicles;
- Vehicles driven by linear motors;
- Maximum running speed of some 400 to 500 km/h is planned in commercial service;
- Minimum radius of curves on a level and an undulating track and maximum gradients are the same as those for a railway line designed for the same nominal speed.

A Maglev train might be compared with an aircraft bereft of its wings and turbo reactors and moving on a continuous infrastructure at ground level, i.e. at the altitude at which the atmosphere is most dense and aerodynamic resistance is greatest.

The track is appreciably wider and higher than that of the conventional railway.

As in the case of the high-speed train, the market slot in which Maglev might be competitive is limited over shorter distances by the higher average door-to-door speed of the car and, over medium to long distances, by the higher average door-to-door speed of air travel.

There is little or no difference between the maximum commercial speed of high-speed rail and the Maglev technique.

Infrastructure investments per km for a Maglev double-track line, in open country with all factors being equal, are on the same scale as those for a railway line designed for the same nominal speed. However, a tunnel which has to take a Maglev-type track must provide exceptional clearance owing to the greater dimensions. Accordingly, in regions with difficult topography, in those with high population density and especially in suburban and urban areas, the investment called for by the Maglev technique would in some cases seem to attain prohibitive levels.

In any event, from both the economic and financial standpoints, use of the Maglev technique can only be warranted to cater for demand requiring an extraordinarily high throughput (as measured in passenger-kilometres per kilometre of route and per year).

3.5. The "Swissmetro"

Like the Maglev technique, Swissmetro uses magnetic levitation and is driven by linear motors, although it differs from Maglev in two fundamental ways:

-- Swiss metro vehicles travel in two parallel underground tubes (one in each direction);

-- A relative vacuum is maintained in the tubes by means of moderately-powered electric pumps. The vehicles move in a partial vacuum similar to that in which aircraft travel at an altitude of about 15 000 metres.

The partial vacuum in the tubes (about ten Torr), or the resulting absence of aerodynamic drag, means that the clearance left for the vehicle in the tube can be reduced, so the inside diameter of the tube can be kept to about 3.7 metres. The total width of the two tubes used for Swissmetro is therefore three times narrower than a double-track rail tunnel or one of the two dual carriageways of a motorway (or, more particularly, the two tracks required by the Maglev technique).

Since the vehicle moves in a vacuum it is possible to save all the energy that other modes of land transport use simply to overcome air resistance. At ground level and at high speeds, when a vehicle is travelling on the flat at a constant speed it is aerodynamic drag that consumes the most energy (for example, up to 90 per cent at a speed of 500 km/h).

In these circumstances, Swissmetro might very well have a maximum running speed in commercial service very much higher than 500 km/h if and when necessary. For example, Swissmetro promoters are suggesting a standard running time of twelve minutes for distances of 50 to 100 km between two successive stops. Swissmetro stations may be located in the centre of urban areas or on their outskirts, with no change in the investment involved as the stations are under ground in each case.

The Swissmetro technique creates no disamenities: no noise, air pollution or visual intrusion. It calls for very little in the way of land purchases and keeps down the amount to be paid for expropriations.

Swissmetro is not competitive with the car over short distances nor with air travel over long distances. It would seem most appropriate for catering to demand for inter-city travel in very densely populated areas in which the major cities are not very far away from each other.

3.6. General comment

On the basis of the foregoing examples, it is reasonable to say that the characteristics of the new technologies are dissimilar. No common denominator can be found. The efficiency and safety of each has to be examined separately, case by case, each in the light of its own merits.

In any event, there is no new technology which at present poses a threat to the technical and economic advantages of the car over short distances or of air travel over long distances.

4. CONCLUSIONS

Only the combination of three factors can increase the efficiency and safety of transport:

1. The art and science of the engineer, that is to say, research, development and the application of technological innovations;

2. The free choice of the user;

3. Competition among modes of transport and, within each mode, among the largest possible number of carriers.

On any transport market worthy of that name, the only techniques that can find their place and survive are those which show an economic return.

TABLES

Table 1. Comparison of car prices, costs and charges for the user in Switzerland in 1960 and 1990 at 1990 prices (SF of 1990)

Type of car : cylinder capacity (cc)	1 000		1 500	
Year	1960	1990	1960	1990
Purchase price in SF	25 000	10 000	32 000	16 000
Cost of petrol in SF/litre	1.60	0.96	1.60	0.96
Petrol consumption in litres/ 100 km	9	6.5	10	7.5
Annual charges in SF excluding running costs per km (proportion of depreciation, interest, taxes and duties, insurance, garage, parking fees)	4 500	3 400	5 750	5 000
Running costs in SF per km (proportion of depreciation, fuel, oils, tyres, maintenance and repairs)	0.68	0.13	0.72	0.16
Total annual costs per kilometre travelled for 15 000 km/year in SF per km	0.97	0.35	1.66	0.50

Table 2. **Comparison of HGV prices, costs and charges in Italy in 1960 and 1989 in terms of 1989 prices (lira of 1989)**

Year	1960	1989
Type of vehicle	Coupled combination (lorry and trailer)	Articulated vehicle (tractor and semi-trailer)
Gross tonnage	32	37
Total capacity in tonnes	21	25
Purchase price	162 x 10^6 ITL	155 x 10^6 ITL
Drivers' wages ITL/year	19.6 x 10^6 ITL/year	37.4 x 10^6 ITL/year
Diesel consumption	43.5 l/100 km	38 l/100 km
Diesel price	1 660 ITL/L	730 ITL/l
Annual kilometrage	70 000 km	100 000 km
Depreciation period	9 years	7 years
Annual costs excluding kilometrage costs	80.3 x 10^6 ITL/year	125.1 x 10^6 ITL/year
Kilometrage or marginal costs	1 316 ITL/km	507 ITL/km
Total annual costs per km	2 463 ITL/km	1 758 ITL/km
Total annual costs per tonne/km of output	117 ITL/TKO	70 ITL/TKO

Table 3. Modal split of passenger traffic in ECMT countries (passenger-kilometres)

Year	Rail	Road		Total
		Public transport (buses and coaches)	Private transport (cars)	
	%	%	%	%
1965	13.1	15.8	71.1	100
1970	10.1	13.0	76.9	100
1980	8.3	11.9	79.8	100
1988	7.0	10.0	83.0	100

Table 4. Modal split of freight traffic in ECMT countries (tonne-kilometres)

Year	Rail %	Road %	Inland waterways %	Total %
1970	31.2	55.0	13.8	100
1975	25.2	62.7	12.1	100
1980	23.0	65.9	11.1	100
1987	18.9	71.8	9.3	100
1988	18.4	72.5	9.1	100

Table 5. **Costs of the "rolling road" through the Alps**

Comparative costs in ECU (1990) for a road combination or articulated vehicle carried through the Alps	**Distance between loading and unloading terminals**	
	500 km	1 000 km
Road combination or articulated vehicle with a permissible total weight of 40 tonnes travelling on motorways and roads: diesel, oils, tyres, maintenance and repairs	218	435
Road combination or articulated vehicle with a permissible total weight of 40 tonnes carried by rail ("rolling road"): interest and amortization of capital invested in rolling stock (locomotives, wagons and coaches), rolling stock maintenance and repairs, locomotive driving crews, traction energy	334	635
Additional cost for the use of the "rolling road" through the Alps	+ 116 (+ 53 %)	+ 200 (+ 46 %)
The following are to be added to the above costs for the "rolling road": -- investment and operating expenditure for terminals; -- time losses: waiting before loading, loading, waiting before departure of train, waiting between arrival of train and unloading.		

BIBLIOGRAPHY

Revue Automobile, Numéro catalogue, Hallwag, Berne; Edition 1960, Trois budgets d'utilisation, p. 134; Edition 1990, Calcul des frais d'exploitation, p. 100.

Armani, F., Gli autotrasporti italiani nell'anno 1959, Costo del trasporto con alcuni tipi di autocarri, autoarticolati ed autotreni a gasolio al 1 gennaio 1960, Ingegneria ferroviaria, Rome, No. 4, April 1960, p. 314.

Armani, F., Gli autotrasporti italiani nell'anno 1959, Costo del trasporto con alcuni tipi di autotreni ed autoarticolati al 1 gennaio 1989, Ingegneria ferroviaria, Rome, No. 5, May 1989, p. 256.

Short, J., Aspects of Intermodal Competition, ECMT, Paris, October 1989.

La voiture électrique Larel, Touring, Geneva, No. 15, 19 July 1990, p. 7.

Eisenmann, J., Auswirkung eines Mischverkehrs auf den Eisenbahnoberbau, ETR, Darmstadt, H. 1/2, January-February 1987.

Hartkopf, R., Probleme des Mischverkehrs auf Neubaustrecken, Die Bundesbahn, Darmstadt, H. 11, November 1989, p. 981.

European Agreement on Main International Railway Lines (AGC). United Nations Economic Commission for Europe, Inland Transport Committee, Geneva, 31st May 1985. More particularly, Annex II: Technical characteristics of main international railway lines, Table 1, column B1 (for passenger traffic only).

Duchemin, J., Very High Speed Trains: A New Philosophy, Directorate-General for the Internal Market and Industrial Affairs, Commission of the European Communities, Brussels, July 1990.

Swissmetro, Départements de génie civil, d'électricité et de physique, Ecole polytechnique fédérale de Lausanne, Fascicule A4, September 1990.

Sub-topic 5

ENVIRONMENT, GLOBAL AND LOCAL EFFECTS

R. KÜRER
Umweltbundesamt
Berlin
Germany

SUMMARY

Berlin, September 1991

1. TRANSPORT AND THE ENVIRONMENT

Environmental protection and an adequate transport supply are equally important requirements for living in our type of society. A fundamental feature of a policy aimed at the general good is that transport need should be satisfied with the least possible environmental pollution. Environmental considerations take first place, however, where the health of the population is endangered or if there is reason to fear substantial or permanent damage to the natural conditions for life.

With new technology and ever more stringent legislation it has certainly been possible to build and operate ever more environmentally friendly vehicles and transport facilities but, because of traffic growth, the reduction in pollution has been at least partially wiped out, so that the pollution caused by transport has not been reduced to the desired extent and in some cases has even increased.

Transport is still causing danger to health and the environment. The risks can be durably reduced to an adequate extent only if, in addition to the technical measures, steps are taken to influence the volume of traffic and modal choice.

1.1. Main types of transport-induced environmental pollution

There are signs that transport is contributing to quite alarming global, regional and local environmental damage. Examples are:

-- Climatic change, greenhouse effect

- CO_2 emissions, mainly due to increased energy consumption, are leading to climatic changes and hence to an increase in the mean sea level and a shift of vegetation zones;

-- Damage to forests

- NO_x and HC emissions are leading to increased regional ozone concentrations, increased acid and nitrogen depositions and the build-up of noxious substances in soils and waters.

-- Health risks in conurbations due to local excessively high air and noise pollution:

- High NO_2, particulate and CO concentrations, carcinogenic pollutants and prolonged exposure to loud noise on heavily trafficked roads, together with high ozone concentrations on the periphery of conurbations, are giving rise to health risks;

-- Losses to the community as a whole

- High noise levels on main traffic axes lead to reduced property values, while high concentrations of pollutants lead to the deterioration of buildings and monuments through material damage.

Table 1 summarises the causes and effects of air pollutants generated by transport (1).

2. ENVIRONMENT-RELEVANT TRANSPORT TRENDS

Emissions, resource consumption and many other types of environmental pollution caused by transport are mainly due to the transport conditions listed below. Measures to reduce the problems must therefore be concentrated above all on these basic conditions:

a) Mobility and transport needs;

b) Supply and quality of vehicles and equipment;

c) Transport organisation, modal split and operation.

Environmental policy measures to reduce pollution have so far been concentrated on improving the technical quality of vehicles and transport infrastructures, but since the reductions in pollution achievable by these methods have proved insufficient, it is important to observe the environmentally relevant transport trends in order to be able to influence them, in full knowledge of the facts and in the most effective way.

2.1. Past trends

If we consider the transport data for Europe (2,3), it is clear (Figures 1-4) that growth has been above all in the field of road traffic (private cars and goods vehicles) which in some cases has increased by over 100 per cent in the past twenty years. Despite all past forecasts of a reduction in traffic growth (saturation), this has still not come about. Table 2 summarises the data shown in graphic form in Figures 1-4.

There is concern about the ever-increasing transport output of both trucks and cars. As will be shown below, this means that the greatest growth is unfortunately in precisely the transport modes that cause the greatest pollution. What is more, it is precisely the roads on which, because of high speeds, air and noise pollution is the greatest and most fuel is consumed (motorways) that traffic is increasing most rapidly (4).

The figures and Table 2 also give the data for Germany for purposes of comparison. The trend in Germany is for the most part similar to that of Europe as a whole, though with a rather less rapid rate of increase. It can be seen, however, that despite a significantly lower rate of increase in truck numbers and truck-kilometres in Germany, road freight transport output is growing at about the same rate as the average for Europe as a whole. This is mainly due to an over-proportional increase in the number of heavy goods vehicles (over 9 tonnes payload) and highly efficient articulated trucks and trailers. It would appear to be justifiable to base what follows mainly on surveys carried out in Germany. The vehicle stock in the rest of Europe must be even more detrimental to the environment.

2.2. Future trends

All past forecasts of traffic trends have been substantially exceeded by reality, notably in the case of road and air transport. What follows is therefore to be understood as a rough indication of trends and a basis for pollution reduction strategies necessary from the environmental standpoint. The discussion is partly limited to road traffic as this causes the greater part of transport-induced environmental pollution.

2.2.1. *Vehicle numbers*

In Germany the car ownership rate is now almost 500 cars per thousand inhabitants, as compared with the European average of about 320. These rates are substantially lower than in the United States (about 600 cars per thousand inhabitants), but even in the United States there is still no sign of saturation. If we assume an average car ownership rate of 400 per thousand inhabitants in Europe by the turn of the century, there will be some 175 million cars on European roads (up 33 per cent as compared with the roughly 130 million in 1987).

In the case of trucks, the imminent deregulation within the single European market and the increasing east-west traffic will no doubt result in significantly higher vehicle numbers. In Germany, just on 2 million trucks are expected by the turn of the century, as compared with the present 1.3 million. The particular conditions in Germany mean that this kind of increase cannot be extrapolated to the rest of Europe, however. In any discussion, the reasons for the deviations from trends in other parts of Europe, as shown in Table 2, must be borne in mind. Nevertheless, an OECD Europe truck stock of some 20 million vehicles by the turn of the century (up 38 per cent on the 1987 figure of 14.5 million) is quite on the cards.

2.2.2. *Vehicle use (kilometres covered)*

The most important factor with regard to transport-induced environmental pollution is vehicle-kilometres. In its prognoses for the transport-induced environmental pollution up to 2005, the German Environment Office assumes an average increase of 1.6 per cent a year in car use and 2.5 per cent a year in truck use, with a falling trend. If we thus assume some flattening of the trend as compared with the 1987 situation, it would appear that in Europe total vehicle-kilometres by the turn of the century will be up 20 per cent (on the 1987 figures) for cars and up 30 per cent for trucks.

There would then be 1 900 billion car-kilometres a year in the European OECD countries (430 billion in Germany) and 410 billion truck-kilometres (47 billion). Here we are working on the basis solely of the saturation tendency in traffic and not considering the effects of any deliberate reduction in road traffic or modal shift from road to rail.

2.2.3. Transport output (passenger-km and tonne-km)

In traffic forecast scenarios a distinction is made between data resulting from the extrapolation of past trends (trend scenario) from the figures that can be achieved through a targeted package of measures to reduce environmental pollution (reduction scenario). These measures are mainly those that promote the more environmentally-friendly rail and public road traffic and the general avoidance of unnecessary traffic.

Such scenarios were commissioned by the German Bundestag Commission of Enquiry into the protection of the earth's atmosphere (5). Table 3 shows the published prognoses of this enquiry [taken from (6)].

It can be seen that even in the trend scenario the road transport output is forecast to grow much more slowly than for the period to 1987 shown in Table 2. It can also clearly be seen that in the reduction scenario the reduced road transport output leads to a considerable increase in the transport output of the more environmentally-friendly, rail and inland waterway modes. Modal shifts of this kind, however, require considerable efforts to expand the rail transport capacities and there are even some experts who doubt that this is possible.

In the context of the present report it is not possible to say to what extent the reduction scenario measures could lead to a slower rate of increase in road traffic and a shift of transport output in the rest of Europe too. The problems caused by traffic are now very similar in all highly-industrialised countries, however, and it would therefore be desirable to reduce road traffic and switch to the less polluting modes in Europe as a whole. Table 3 shows a first approximation to the rates of change that could be achieved (trend and reduction scenarios), again with respect to the 1987 situation of Table 2.

Air traffic is also included in the German scenarios, even though the air share of total transport output is still very low in 2005. The important factor here is the particularly serious environmental pollution (CO_2 emissions and noise) and there is reason for concern in this respect even with the rates of increase in the reduction scenario.

3. ENVIRONMENTAL POLLUTION CAUSED BY TRANSPORT

The traffic trends described above have led to transport now being a major polluter. While in the case of industrial plants and power stations stringent environmental regulations have had considerable success in reducing pollution, the successes in reducing transport-induced pollution are still far too modest, mainly due to transport growth.

-- Air pollutants such as CO_2, NO_2, volatile organic compounds, etc., that damage vegetation and affect the climate are, to a large extent and in some cases even predominantly, caused by traffic. Emissions of heavy metals and persistent substances lead to the build up of noxious substances in soils and water. In and around the conurbations, transport emissions are the main cause of pollutant concentrations that may cause health problems. Carcinogenic substances (including diesel particulate and benzene) warrant particular attention here.

-- In the case of noise too, traffic is the main source. Residents of heavily-trafficked streets suffer particular disamenity and are also even subject to increased health risk. This causes people to move (flight from the city) and results in lower property values on major axes.

-- The areas of land required for transport infrastructures lead to substantial destruction of the countryside which means, among other things, reduction of the area under vegetation, the sealing of large surfaces, the division of land with a resulting loss of living space and further damage to the natural economy as well as the urban and rural landscape.

Most of this damage and risk is mainly due to road traffic. Only in the case of noise are the emissions from air and rail traffic already of significance today (1,8).

3.1. Air pollutants and CO_2

Air pollution is caused by many different human activities, but the greatest pollution results from the combustion of fossil fuels in stationary and mobile plants (transport). The transport share of total emissions in the Federal Republic of Germany in 1988 (road traffic share in brackets) was (1,7):

Carbon monoxide	(CO)	74%	(70%)
Hydrocarbons	(HC)	53%	(42%)
Nitrogen oxides	(NO_x)	65%	(57%)
Soot particles/dust		34%	(25%)
Sulphur dioxide	(SO_2)	4%	(3%)
Carbon monoxide	(CO_2)	20%	(17%)

It is clear from these data how high the transport share of total pollutant emissions is and that road traffic is responsible for by far the greater part of these emissions.

Mention must also be made of the pollutants emitted by transport, such as benzene, polynuclear aromatic hydrocarbons (PAH), lead, formaldehyde, toluene, ammonia, nitrous oxide, cyanide, hydrogen sulphide, ethylene and dioxin. These emissions do not all come from vehicle exhausts, but are caused through the carburation of fuels, oil loss or wear of materials, such as brake linings, tyres and road surfaces.

Substantial quantities of energy (CO_2 emissions) are also necessary in vehicle manufacture and disposal, causing pollution that cannot be attributed to vehicle use but is directly connected with it.

3.1.1. Transport-specific emissions

Tables 4 and 5 show the transport output related specific pollutant and CO_2 emissions for different vehicles and transport outputs (1). It can clearly be seen, that the specific emissions of road vehicles, (including buses) pollute the environment most. In addition, by far the greater part of total transport output is produced by road vehicles. It is thus obvious that, from the environmental standpoint, it is absolutely essential to try to reduce the highly-polluting road transport share of total transport output.

While the transport mode with particularly high specific CO_2 emissions (air transport) does not (yet) account for any substantial part of total transport output (see also Table 3), it nevertheless needs to be very carefully monitored and if necessary control measures should be introduced.

3.1.2. Emission forecasts

In the latest scenario calculations for traffic in the former FRG for the years 1998 and 2005, the air pollutant emissions expected by the German Environment Office are based essentially on the following assumptions (7):

-- Transport output:

- For cars, an annual average increase of 1.9 per cent until 1998, then of 1.2 per cent;

- In the case of trucks a distinction is made according to the type of road: motorway transport output is assumed to go up by 3 per cent a year until 1998 then by 2 per cent, while on other roads an increase of 0.5 per cent a year is assumed.

-- Emission factors:

- In the case of cars, two sharp reductions in exhaust gas emission limits are assumed as compared with the 1992 EC regulations (see Table 6).

- In the case of trucks, three further reductions are assumed as compared with the status quo value (see Table 7).

-- Scenarios:

- In the scenarios calculated by the Environment Office there are several variants in which deadlines are established (at intervals of four to five years) as from when the above mentioned reduction in emission factors become binding for new registrations. In addition, transition periods are given in which the early introduction of new technologies (i.e. before lower limits are made compulsory) is promoted by tax incentives.

- These are thus scenarios for the phased introduction of **technical** emission reduction measures. For the sake of clarity, Table 8 shows only the results (relative change with respect to 1988) for the most ambitious limit value reduction scenario (for the former FRG only).

In earlier Environmental Office prognoses (1) sulphur dioxide and carbon dioxide emissions were also forecast. This provided the data for the relative change with respect to 1988 also shown in Table 8. The assumptions in these earlier prognoses concerning vehicle-kilometres were the same as those set out above.

The changes in vehicle SO_2 emissions are mainly due to a reduction of the sulphur content of fuels. In the case of CO_2 emissions, it is assumed that the average fuel consumption of the car stock will be reduced by 16 per cent between 1987 and 2005. This is a moderate assumption and quite probable from the technical standpoint, for the reduction possibilities for the typical car are somewhat greater. These vehicle-specific savings can be only partially achieved in Germany at present, however, because of the emerging trend to bigger, more powerful vehicles and fast leisure driving. In addition, the average speeds on motorways and thus consumption per kilometre will increase, as will the amount of time spent in fuel-inefficient queues or stop-and-go traffic.

In the case of goods vehicles a reduction in per kilometre consumption with respect to 1989 is assumed to be 1.3 per cent by 1998 and 3.6 per cent by 2005. This equally moderate reduction already takes into account possible consumption changes due to more stringent NO_x limit values.

Vehicle emissions at present not subject to legal limits

In what follows, some selected representatives of the many other pollutants which are not so far subject to any legal limits ("unregulated") are discussed [see also (9) cited from (1)]. In each case an attempt is made to give the present emission situation, the future trend and the technical background. The quantitative data refer to traffic in the former FRG.

Benzene

Some 90 per cent of the total benzene emissions in the former Federal Republic are caused by traffic, and in particular gasoline engined cars. Total emissions in 1986 amounted to some 40 000 tonnes. Benzene emissions have since been reduced by about 85 per cent thanks to the introduction of catalyst technology. Another planned emission reduction measure is further reduction of the benzene content in gasoline: the present value is between 2 per cent and 3 per cent and it is planned to reduce this to 1 per cent.

Toluene

Toluene emissions from motor traffic are about twice as great as benzene emissions. Road vehicles are probably the biggest emission source, but the regulated three-way catalyst can reduce toluene emissions by some 90 per cent.

Polynuclear Aromatic Hydrocarbons (PAH)

At present motor traffic emits about 6 to 7 tonnes a year of PAH or about 20 per cent of total emissions. Three-way catalyst technology can reduce PAH emissions from internal combustion engines by 95 per cent to 97 per cent.

Formaldehyde

Some 80 per cent of total formaldehyde emissions is caused by motor traffic (some 12 000 tonnes a year). A regulated three-way catalyser can reduce this by over 90 per cent. Increased formaldehyde emissions could appear, however, through the use of methanol as motor fuel. At present gasoline must contain no more than 3 per cent methanol.

Cyanide, hydrogen sulphide

There are at present no reliable emission data for these compounds, but here again a three-way catalyser can cut emissions very substantially. Like benzene they appear more in the "rich" area of the gasoline/air mix (lambda lower than 1 in full load and cold-start enrichment).

Dioxins

Dioxins are formed, among other things, by the combustion of the additives in leaded fuels. This type of emission can be prevented through the use of lead-free gasoline, while the three-way catalyser can reduce any remaining dioxins by 90 per cent. Remaining emissions could therefore be reduced to only 1 per cent.

Discussion of the findings

In order to reduce the potential danger through CO_2 and air pollutants to a reasonable level, the German Ministerial Conference of Ministers of the Environment decided on the emission reduction targets for **transport** in the FRG as set out in Table 9 (10).

If these targets are compared with the emission reductions that can be achieved according to the Environment Office scenario calculations (see Table 8) this confirms the opinion that important goals apparently **cannot** be achieved through **technical** measures alone! This applies, for example, to nitrogen oxide (NO_x) emissions for which the 2005 target cannot be achieved, mainly due to the insufficient reduction of truck emissions, and in particular to CO_2. Here the problem is that the increase in vehicle-kilometres more than compensates for the technically achievable CO_2 reduction (lower fuel consumption). In the Environment Office forecasts it should be borne in mind that the assumed increases in vehicle-kilometres must be considered as rather moderate (*cf.* Section 2.2.2.) so that action is probably even more urgently required.

Table 10 shows what additional reductions need to be achieved by measures other than the (technical) measures outlined. These "non-technical" measures will have to cause a change in the transport conditions listed in Section 2. On the possible and required measures, see for example (8, 11 and 12).

For the unregulated air pollutants and diesel particulates no requirements have so far been calculated. Because of the increased cancer risk caused by these substances, what is required here is above all minimisation, i.e. "as little as possible"! As pointed out above, the progressive three-way catalyst technology has distinct advantages as regards the minimisation of unregulated air pollutants.

3.1.3. Air quality

In this chapter we discuss the air pollution caused mainly or to a large extent by road traffic. This includes essentially the generally monitored components: CO, NO_x and hydrocarbons, as well as lead and CO_2, soot particles and formaldehyde. Because of its effect on human health, benzene should be singled out among the hydrocarbons as this, like soot particulate, has a carcinogenic potential. The carcinogenicity of toluene is at present being examined.

Through its emission of air pollutants, transport contributes to global climatic change through increasing the greenhouse effect. This applies above all to CO_2, but also to chlorofluorocarbon (CFC) emissions, for example (13). Because of the high and globally rising consumption of energy from fossil fuels at the same time as the destruction of carbon dioxide converters (deforestation) there is a clearly increasing proportion of CO_2 in the atmosphere. Since 1958, the CO_2 concentration in the earth's atmosphere has increased by over 10 per cent. As the concentrations of other trace gases in the atmosphere is also increasing, the recently observed global temperature rise is attributed to the greenhouse effect caused by these pollutants. Experts believe that it is possible that if temperatures continue to rise as feared, the mean sea level could rise by between 25 cm and 165 cm over the next 50 to 100 years, with quite disastrous effects (14).

Of regional and trans-regional importance in conurbations and over larger areas are the products dangerous to animal and plant health formed in the atmosphere through reactions with the primary emissions, notably NO_x and hydrocarbons: examples are the photochemical oxidants, with ozone as the major component. Lower crop yields due to ozone pollution are estimated at 3-5 per cent in the Netherlands (7). Nitric acid as a compound formed from NO_x emissions is important as a component of acid deposition.

Of importance in causing **local** health risk are above all the high concentrations of NO_x and the carcinogenic diesel particulate and benzene in the air of streets lined with high buildings.

The monitoring network of the German *Länder* and Environment Office comprise over 400 air pollution measuring stations. This network of stations is the most comprehensive automatic continuous air pollution monitoring system in Europe. For historical reasons and concern with covering the whole country, monitoring stations were only seldom set up at points exposed to motor traffic. Figures are given for rural and urban areas, inside vehicles and inside buildings (1).

Rural Areas

The measurements of motor vehicle related **hydrocarbons** in rural areas are very incomplete. The findings lie in the lower concentration levels and are of little relevance to the impacts. Environment Office measurements reveal that the concentrations of the motor vehicle specific hydrocarbons **isopentane, pentane, hexane and toluene** are well below 2 ug/m^3. By analogy it can be assumed that the average values for benzene also lie below 2 ug/m^3.

Our present knowledge about the **nitrogen oxide** concentrations in rural areas may be summed up as follows:

-- Along motorways and trunk roads there are high concentrations of the compounds emitted by motor vehicles even in rural areas. However, these are found only within a strip about 200 metres wide (concentrations directly on the road are similar to those found in heavily-trafficked city streets).

-- At a greater distance from the roads, no direct influence of motor traffic on NO concentrations can be detected.

-- NO_2 concentrations are also relatively low, the annual average lying between 4 and 20 ug/m^3 (the WHO guidelines for the protection of sensitive plants being 30 ug/m^3). The 98 percentiles of NO_2 concentrations lie between 18 and 50 ug/m^3 and are thus significantly lower than the corresponding values in urban areas (EC limit value 200 ug/m^3).

-- The NO_2 concentrations monitored over the years in Environment Office rural background stations show a slight but statistically significant increase since monitoring began in 1968.

In rural areas the primary pollutants emitted from motor vehicle exhausts are not so important as the secondary products formed through photochemical processes, above all ozone but also nitric acid.

Our present knowledge about ozone concentrations in rural areas may be summed up as follows:

-- The annual average for flat country lies between 40 and 90 ug/m^3, while mountain stations show significantly higher concentrations, between 70 and 120 ug/m^3 (the WHO guideline for the growing period for the protection of terrestrial vegetation is 60 ug/m^3). The differences in concentrations caused by altitude disappear with the 98 percentile. Here the flatland stations sometimes have the highest concentrations.

-- There is as yet no clear annual trend detectable for ozone concentrations at the Environment Office background monitoring stations since the beginning of measurements in 1980.

-- As compared with concentrations at urban stations, there are much smaller variations over the course of the day in rural ozone concentrations. This means that the ozone dose in rural areas is generally higher than in the conurbations. This is important mainly because of possible damage to vegetation.

Another important pollutant largely due to motor vehicle exhaust gases is the deposit of nitrogen compounds. These are mainly the dry deposit of NO_2 and the wet and dry deposit of nitric acid/nitrates.

The rate of deposit for nitrates in open country is about 5 to 10 kg N per hectare per year. In forest areas because of the filtering effect of leaves and pine needles, the rate of deposit is somewhat higher: about 5 to 12 kg N per hectare per year in the case of deciduous forests (birch) and 8 to 20 kg N per hectare per year for fir forests (spruce). The rate of deposit is fairly even over a broad area and there are no great differences between urban and rural areas.

Urban Areas

The pollutant concentrations considered here are measured away from the direct street area, for example in residential districts. In addition, some data is given about the values measured directly at the edge of inner-city streets.

Table 11 shows the values observed by the corresponding German monitoring stations in recent years. It can be seen that in central residential areas and on inner-city streets, the NO_2 concentrations are several times those found in the open country. On heavily-trafficked city streets the EC limit value (200 ug/m^3 for the 98 percentile) is in some cases exceeded. On the other hand, the ozone concentrations in urban areas are lower than in rural areas. The trend over many years is for CO concentrations to remain the same and NO to rise in some cases.

In-vehicle Concentrations

High concentrations of pollutants emitted by the engine are found inside motor vehicles in both urban traffic and in motorway conditions. While on the motorways the main pollutants are nitrogen oxides and certain hydrocarbons (e.g. benzene), in urban traffic carbon monoxide concentrations are also of importance from the standpoint of health. Table 12 shares the values measured by the Environment Office in 1989 for motorways and major commuter routes.

Investigations of the trend from 1977 to 1989 showed no significant changes in concentrations.

Air pollution in buildings caused by motor vehicles

Research by the Bavarian Environmental Protection Office in 1988 [cited from (1)], revealed that average air pollution levels inside buildings were only slightly below the concentrations outside. It was still possible to show the influence on interior concentrations of opening windows for ventilation, however.

With high CO, NO and NO_2 concentrations in the outside air, concentrations inside buildings with closed windows were 55-74 per cent lower than outside and with mainly open windows only 10-20 per cent.

With low outside concentrations, with closed windows the interior concentrations are higher than those outside. When there is smog and during the peak emission periods in the rush hours, the findings of this research indicate that windows should be kept closed in order to keep the inside air as clean as possible. Windows should be opened for ventilation during the midday break and after the evening rush hour.

Effectiveness of transport emission reductions with respect to ozone concentrations

An urgent task of clean air measures is to reduce excessively high ozone levels. Ozone is a secondary pollutant formed by the photochemical conversion of the NO_x and volatile organic compounds (VOC) emitted mainly by transport. Because of the complex, non-linear chemical reactions in the formation of photo-oxidants, measures to reduce emissions do not have the same effect on reducing ozone concentrations. Emission reduction measures at local and regional level are not sufficient to effectively reduce the oxidant level in specific regions. In a German-Dutch programme known as PHOXA (Photochemical Oxidant and Acid Deposition Model Application within the Framework of Control Strategy Development), it was possible to assess emission reduction measures over the whole of Europe.

The PHOXA instruments have been used several times in periods of increased oxidant concentrations. Among other things the effects of (hypothetical) emission reductions on oxidant concentrations have been studied with the following results (38).

The findings of computer modelling showed that the effects of the reduction of nitrogen oxide (NO_x) and volatile organic compound (VOC) emissions on ozone concentrations both near the source and at greater distances from the emission area are not proportional. A VOC reduction always leads to a reduction in the peak ozone values while an NO_x reduction reduces ozone concentrations in regions with low NO_x emissions. In and around conurbations with high NO_x emissions, a local reduction of NO_x emission can lead to an increase in peak ozone values. However, in such regions the absolute ozone concentrations are normally relatively low. A combined reduction of both types of primary emission always has the effect of weakening the negative effects of an NO_x reduction alone.

It also turned out that with a reduction of emissions of about 50 per cent, VOC reduction was more effective in lowering the ozone concentrations near the ground than a corresponding NO_x reduction. The most effective measure at this level of reduction is always the simultaneous reduction of both primary emissions. In the case of greater reductions (75 per cent and over) NO_x reduction becomes increasingly more effective than VOC reduction.

All in all, the findings of the model investigation for large areas show drastic reduction measures are necessary if high peak ozone levels are to be significantly reduced (38).

In order for no increased ozone to appear even under unfavourable conditions, the research findings show that NO_x and VOC emission reductions of up to 80 per cent are required (7). The German Conference of Environment Ministers has set reduction targets (see Section 3.1.2., Discussion of the findings) of 60 per cent for NO_x and 70 per cent for HC by the year 2005 (10).

3.1.4. Concentration limits and guidelines

A table taken from a communication from the Hamburg Senate (37), on its Expert Report on Clean Air Measures in Hamburg, suffices to show the multitude of air pollution limits in force or proposed.

Pollutant (ug/m^3)		Lowest threshold	Country/ institution	Hamburg actual	Hamburg target value
SO_2	1W1	25	Finland/IUFRO**	27	25
		(140	TA Luft)		
	$1W2^{98}$	$75^{97.5}$	IUFRO**	109-250	100
		(400	TA Luft)		
NO_2	1W1	30	Switzerland/WHO	39	30
		(80	TA Luft)		
	1W2	146*	Switzerland	76-108	70
		(200	TA Luft)		
CO	1W1	10 000	TA Luft	692	
	1W2	30 000	TA Luft	2 000-3 800	
Dust in suspension					
	1W1	40	EC (Guideline)	51	40
		(150	TA Luft)		
	1W2	250	EC (Guideline)	165-146	
		(300	TA Luft)		
O3	1W1	30	Canada (target)	38	120
	1W2	120	MIK/FRG	135-146	

Notes:

* These values are converted to the 98 percentile level, given in 95 percentile. Conversion according to Münch/Müller (Dornier 1983).

** IUFRO = International Union of Forest Research Organisations (reference value that serves for maintaining the protection and social functions of the forest in extreme locations).

3.2. Noise

Noise, especially traffic noise, is becoming an increasingly serious problem in the industrialised countries, including Germany. The opening of frontiers in Europe, growing production of goods, ever increasing demand for goods and the desire to ever greater mobility results in ever increasing transport output. The extension of transport networks both opens up and brings problems to hitherto peaceful remote areas. Increasing numbers of people want to live in "peaceful" areas outside the town or find no suitable dwelling in the city and have to travel long distances to work every day.

Because it is perceived directly, noise is the form of pollution that people feel most affected by [see Table 13 taken from (15)]. As shown by a recently published French study (16) Germany is not the only country where this is so.

People do not only feel noise to be a nuisance and disamenity, but the great majority of the German population regard it as a potential danger to health [see Table 14 taken from (17)]. In a traffic study commissioned by Uniroyal (18) it was found that about one-fifth of the German population suspected that road traffic was affecting their health.

As early as 1978, the German Government's Expert Committee on Environmental Issues established that noise is the leading factor in the perception of environmental pollution (19). The significance of this is that to the extent that a person gets annoyed about noise, he will become aware of other forms of environmental pollution and will then judge them critically. Originally concerned about noise, he becomes concerned about pollution in general. Politicians must be made aware of this if they have in the past paid too little attention to noise in setting their environmental policy priorities.

In order to assess the extent to which people are affected and how those affected react, a distinction needs to be made between two levels:

-- The objective situation, which in the case of noise can be determined by objective methods (calculation or measurement);

-- The subjective perception, assimilation and judgement. In the case of noise this means personal feelings of disamenity or even fear of health impairment.

In what follows, we first describe the objective presence of noise. We then go on to discuss the extent of the impact of noise on the population and the reactions to it.

The discussion is based essentially on the results of German studies, but the basic findings no doubt apply to other European countries with similar traffic and social structures.

Key Values

Noise intensity is now expressed internationally in A-scale decibels, or dB(A). The decibel scale means that the relationship of the noise pressure concerned is logarithmically scaled to the hearing threshold and the A-value that the proportion of a sound at different frequencies takes into account the sensitivity of the ear to these frequencies.

Figure 5 shows the dB(A) values (noise intensity) for some common noises. Thus someone using a motor-mower is exposed to a noise of about 70 dB(A) and someone at the side of a city street is exposed to about 85 dB(A) when a truck passes, that is a noise intensity ten times higher [i.e. 10 dB(A) higher] than that of a car [75 dB(A)].

In order to describe noise that varies over time it is usual to give the average value for the period for the different sound intensities (energy-equivalent average level). The various noise components are included in this figure according to their intensity, frequency and duration. Noises with the same average level may have completely different time patterns. This can therefore sometimes result in completely different impacts. Thus, in the periods between the very loud noise of a passing train it is possible to hear natural background noise, whereas with road traffic noise of the same average level there is scarcely a quiet moment. Therefore different types of noise have to be distinguished not only according to the average level expressed in dB(A), but also verbally with regard to their particular characteristics, i.e. the type of noise (for example, road, rail or industrial noise).

3.2.1. Transport-specific emissions

In describing traffic noise a distinction is made between the noise emission of the individual vehicle and that of a transport infrastructure (for example, a road) with many different vehicles.

In simplified descriptions, the noise emission of a single vehicle is usually expressed as the passing noise level and that of a transport infrastructure by the energy equivalent average level. As mentioned above, this average value for a given period includes all noise events according to their amplitude, duration and frequency.

Vehicle passing noise

Even vehicles of the same category can make noises of very different intensities when they pass. As an example of this, Figure 6 shows the results of a statistical evaluation of measurements for a number of motor vehicles of different categories. A distinction is made between urban conditions (30 to 60 km/h) and the open road (60 to 100 km/h). The figure shows the average L_{AR} of the passing noise and the L_{95} values, exceeded by only 5 per cent of passing vehicles (all at 7.5 metres distance) (20).

If the data for different vehicle categories as shown in Figure 6 are compared, this confirms -- as is scarcely surprising -- that trucks are by far the noisiest road vehicles, followed by motorcycles. A single truck is on average as noisy as ten to twenty cars together [noise level difference of 10 to 13 dB(A)]. The difference in noise levels between trucks and cars is smaller on the open road than in towns.

This type of comparison of passing noise levels does not take into account the different transport output performance of the different transport modes and categories of vehicle, however. Tables 15 and 16 therefore show passing noise level at a distance converted to a uniform 25 metres for the specific vehicle noise emission with the usual average load (passing noise level per person or tonne carried) for different transport modes.

Every 3 dB of difference means that twice or half as much noise is emitted. If the passing noise is converted to other distances it changes by at least 6 dB with a doubling or halving of this distance; if other loadings are assumed, the load-specific passing noise changes by 3 dB for each doubling or halving of the number of persons or tonnes carried.

Here again, it can be seen that trains and buses have very clear advantages: using public passenger transport more people can be carried before the person-specific passing noise of the private car is reached, while in long-haul goods traffic, the railways can carry much more freight before reaching the load-specific passing noise of a truck.

From the standpoint of a desirable reduction of noise it is therefore essential to make efforts to reduce the number of kilometres covered by the highly polluting road vehicles (cars and trucks).

Average noise intensity

In order to compare the noise nuisance caused by the different transport modes, it is possible to calculate the average noise intensity for the same transport output. Tables 17 and 18 show the average noise level per hour for the carriage of 1 000 people or 1 000 tonnes by different modes. In comparing the findings it should be borne in mind that the number of vehicles passing for the same total transport output can be up to 100 times greater for private cars and trucks than for buses and trains. What is more, railway noise is, as a rule, considered to be more tolerable than road traffic noise so that, even with a somewhat higher average noise intensity, rail transport is better from the standpoint of noise nuisance.

To show the extent to which road noise emissions generally appear, Figure 7 shows cumulative frequencies for the average noise intensity at 25 metres from German motorways and trunk roads. It can be seen that noise intensities of 75 dB(A) for motorways and 68 dB(A) for trunk roads are exceeded along over 50 per cent of the length of these roads.

From the 25m average noise level it is possible to calculate approximate levels for other distances in free noise propagation conditions by assuming a 3 dB(A) change for a doubling of distance. Thus, for example, it is possible to establish that within a strip over 200 m wide along a motorway with a medium traffic volume the average noise intensity during the day exceeds 65 dB(A). With long-term exposure to noise of this level the people affected have a significantly increased risk of heart and circulatory diseases (see Section 3.2.3.).

3.2.2. Noise exposure data

Comparative data for traffic noise in different countries have been published by the OECD (21). Figure 8 is taken from this publication. In the author's opinion, however, the differences to be seen here are not only true differences in noise levels, but are also partly due to differences in survey and evaluation methodology. This is true at any rate for the comparison of OECD countries with similar traffic conditions, for example the European countries shown in Figure 8. In what follows we base the discussion on German studies.

Data concerning the noise exposure suffered by the population are important aids to policy decisions. The German Environment Office commissioned the Battelle-Institut in Frankfurt (22) to construct a model for noise exposure that could be used to determine representative present and expected future noise levels for the then (1981) Federal Republic of Germany. For this model, 57 municipalities or districts of different sizes over the entire country were originally selected for study. The actual noise exposure situation was determined in this way. Thanks to the choice of a representative sample, these data could then be extrapolated to the whole country.

To express the exposure of the population to traffic noise, the above mentioned average noise levels were used, split into daytime (0600 to 2200) and night-time (2200 to 0600) values.

The first values determined by the noise exposure model for different noise sources were already in the documents volume of the Second German Government Immissions Protection Report (23). This initial analysis revealed, as was to be expected, that during the day traffic is **the** dominant noise source. This also corresponds with the survey findings concerning noise nuisance from different sources [see Figure 9 derived from (24)]. It also turns out, however, that at night rail traffic causes almost as much noise as road. But as exposure to rail noise causes less nuisance, the following discussion is to be understood as referring above all to road traffic.

The base data were the traffic and noise emission data for 1979. To establish the data for the new base year of 1985 for all subsequent work, the 1979 values were extrapolated using our knowledge of the changes in vehicle noise emissions (25) and the traffic trend (26). The results showed a slight fall in emissions but a marked increase in vehicle numbers and total vehicle kilometres. Because of these two opposing trends, there was no significant change in traffic noise exposure between 1979 and 1985.

Figure 10a/b shows the road traffic noise exposure calculated for 1985 as a percentage of the total population (61.5 million) exposed to different noise levels [classes of 5 dB(A) intervals]. The figures are given in Table 19.

Since its construction in the early eighties, the model has been further developed by the German Environment Office and can now be used to evaluate the effectiveness of noise abatement measures at local and national level. Some examples follow [see also (27,28)].

If we want to study the possibilities for reducing road traffic noise, the first aspect to consider is what roads the most affected people live on. Figures 11a/b show noise exposure, again in 5 dB(A) classes, but this time according to road category. It can be seen that the least number are affected by motorways and that those exposed to noise levels representing a health risk [average daytime level greater than 65 dB(A)] are mostly on main traffic routes. These findings are scarcely surprising, but what is to be noted and is of importance regarding possible measures is that in the medium daytime noise range of 55 to 65 dB(A), precisely the range to which the biggest numbers are exposed, most of those affected are on side streets.

Among other examples of the use of the model was a study of whether and to what extent the introduction of a side street limit all over the country of 30 km/h ("Tempo 30") would improve the noise situation. The calculations showed that a measure of this type, which is important above all for road safety reasons, also has distinct advantages from the standpoint of noise reduction.

Figure 12a shows first the percentage of people affected by size of community, then Figure 12b shows how the picture would change with the above-mentioned introduction of Tempo 30. It can be seen that it would, above all, bring significant improvement for the larger communities (over 20 000 inhabitants). In the important exposure range of 60 to 65 dB(A) and from 65 to 70 dB(A), the number of people affected could be reduced by between 3 and almost 5 per cent (each percentage point meaning something over 600 000 people).

The German Environment Office has also investigated various scenarios for how technical measures to reduce vehicle noise are likely to affect the noise exposure situation in 1995 (27). The scenarios vary mainly in the rate at which vehicles meeting the more stringent EC limit values are introduced on the market. For the sake of simplicity, only the data for the scenario with the biggest reduction are presented here.

This scenario assumes a 30 per cent increase in transport output between 1979 and 1995. The assumed changes in noise emissions are given in Table 20. Vehicle life is taken to be about ten years. In addition, account was taken of the fact that on motorways tyre noise is the dominant one, so that here the reduced drive train noise will have less effect.

This "more stringent limit values" scenario shows (Table 21) how road traffic noise exposure will change with respect to 1985 (see Table 19).

Thus the large-scale introduction of quieter vehicles could reduce the proportion of people exposed to daytime noise levels of over 65 dB(A) from the 1985 figure of 12.5 per cent to 7 per cent in 1995 and to night-time levels of over 55 dB(A) from 14 per cent to a still substantial 8 per cent.

If this technical scenario were combined with the introduction of Tempo 30 on all urban side streets, it would be possible to reduce the proportion of people exposed to a daytime level of 65 dB(A) and a night-time level of over 55 dB(A) by about half.

The German Environment Office also used the model to determine how noise levels outside built-up areas had increased due to more roads. In individual cases, for example, where a by-pass is built round a village, a new road may reduce noise exposure for the inhabitants, but new roads generally mean:

-- Greater distribution of noise sources over the area, and hence

-- Noise in hitherto peaceful places.

Figure 13 shows that the area outside built-up areas exposed to a daytime noise level of over 60 dB(A) and a night-time level of over 50 dB(A) has increased by about 30 per cent since 1973. The recreational value of areas subjected to such noise is significantly reduced.

3.2.3. Noise impacts and number of persons affected

Noise has a considerable impact on people's lives: it impairs sleep and rest, causes headaches and listlessness, activates the vegetative nervous system, reduces physical and mental performance, interferes with conversation, upsets the human environment and forces people to change their everyday living and leisure behaviour.

Table 22 [derived from (29)] shows the relationship between different noise levels and the proportion of affected persons who suffer specific noise effects. If we now also take the data in Section 3.2.2. concerning the number of people affected by specific noise levels, we can determine the number of people in Germany who are subject to specific psychosomatic noise effects as a result of road traffic (see Table 23).

Regarding the effects of noise on sleep, the German Environment Office Interdisciplinary Working Party on the Effects of Noise has determined that disturbed sleep due to traffic noise can generally be avoided if the average noise level at the sleeper's ear does not exceed 30 dB(A) (30). In the case of 14 per cent of the population this value cannot be achieved with windows of normal noise-damping effect [difference of 25 dB(A)] closed. In 1985 therefore, almost 8.5 million German citizens could only sleep undisturbed by road traffic noise with closed, sound-proof windows.

The Interdisciplinary Working Party also found (31) that good speech comprehension inside rooms is possible only if the short period average disturbing noise level does not exceed 40 dB(A). This requirement cannot be met in daytime by 27 per cent of the population even with normal windows shut. Over 16 million citizens of the former Federal Republic of Germany can therefore hold a normal conversation undisturbed by traffic noise only behind closed, sound-proof windows.

Noise is also a health risk: the findings of epidemiological research greatly increase the suspicion that there is a connection between constant exposure to road traffic noise and high blood pressure, so that it increases the risk of heart and circulatory system diseases, one of the most frequently found health problems in Germany (some 6 million sufferers). According to German Environment Office findings (32), there is an increased risk of heart or circulatory system disease with exposure to outdoor, daytime average noise levels of over 65 dB(A). According to the results of the noise exposure model, road traffic alone would have caused about 12.5 per cent of the population, i.e. almost 8 million citizens, to be exposed to such noise in 1985.

People react in many different ways to the effects of noise. Some of the most important are indicated below (33):

-- Younger and rather better-off families leave the city centres wherever feasible and move out to places as peaceful as possible, surrounded by greenery;

-- Along heavily trafficked roads leading to the city centre there can be shifts in the social structure that are undesirable from the population policy standpoint;

-- Noise can reduce real estate values: land price reductions in the order of 1.5 per cent per dB(A) of average road traffic noise level in the 50 to 70 dB(A) range and rent reductions of up to 30 per cent as a result of road traffic noise have already been observed.

3.2.4. Limit values and guidelines

Table 24 presents data about the noise emission limit values being introduced in Germany. The first column shows guideline figures recommended by an expert committee of the German Standards Institute concerned with noise protection in urban development (34). These values form the basis for planning purposes, but are not limit values.

The limit values in the second column are those laid down by environmental protection Ordinance 16.BImSch (35). They are to be respected in new construction and in major changes in transport infrastructures (road and rail). Where they cannot be respected, noise protection measures must be taken for the buildings affected.

The third set of values was established for the last time in 1986 as Federal Ministry of Transport internal guidelines (36). These are the limits as from which noise reducing improvement measures for existing roads can be financed out of Federal funds, within the limits of the budget resources available. Some *Länder* and municipalities have similar rules.

3.3. Other environmental pollution

It should be explicitly said that this report is not concerned with the deaths, injuries and damage caused by transport (in the former FRG in 1987 there were almost 8 000 deaths, over 400 000 injuries and accident costs of DM 49 billion). The environmental pollution thus caused is admittedly not designated as such, but it really should be to a large extent!

In addition to the air and noise pollution problems described above in detail because of their particular importance, transport causes a number of other kinds of serious environmental pollution. The most important among these are: consumption of space, waste disposal problems and water and soil pollution. We shall briefly present some data on these, while other types of pollution are simply mentioned here as a reminder: vibration, release of pollutants in the case of goods vehicle accidents, splitting of areas of land and impairment of biotopes, landscapes and urban landscapes.

3.3.1. Consumption of space

The amount of space consumed is an important indicator of the impairment of nature and the countryside through transport vehicles and infrastructures.

Substantial pollutant emissions are generated by transport areas, contaminating soils and the crops produced in their vicinity.

The total area covered by sealed roads has increased by some 30 per cent over the past thirty years. The transport area (used for road, rail, air and water transport) covered 41 per cent of the built-up areas and 4.9 per cent of the total area of the FRG in 1985. In the densely populated regions (some 470 000 hectares or 4.9 per cent of the total area) the proportion of land used for transport purposes is significantly higher than in more rural regions (some 330 000 hectares or 3.9 per cent of the total area).

3.3.2. Resource consumption and waste problems

Substantial resources are consumed in the manufacture, use and disposal of vehicles and the construction and maintenance of transport infrastructures, and many types of waste problems arise. Here again, road transport is the biggest culprit.

Motor vehicle manufacture at present accounts for between about 10 and 20 per cent of total metals consumption and 7.5 per cent of plastics. It is thus clear that, in addition to the possibilities for saving raw materials in the manufacturing stage, recycling through the recovery of parts and spares and appropriate scrapping processes are of great importance. It is encouraging to see that, in response to pressure by the German Minister for the Environment, the automobile industry has recently been more prepared to build new cars in such a way that the manufacturer can take them back and use the materials again.

In 1987, 2.3 million motor vehicles were taken out of service in the FRG; in other words, they had to be disposed of. With an average vehicle weight of 1 000 kg, this means 2.3 million tonnes of waste a year. A particular problem is the disposal of difficult substances like fuels, greases, oils, cooling fluids, etc., which total some 63 000 tonnes a year.

3.3.3. Water and soil pollution

Transport, and in particular road traffic, has many impacts on the soil, run-off waters and groundwater. These extend from the breakdown of mineral and other raw materials, leaching out of road surface materials, to water and soil pollution caused by vehicle washing and road safety measures (salt application in winter).

In addition, substantial pollution is caused by road wear (6.5 million tonnes a year), tyre wear (24 000 tonnes) and brake wear (6 000 tonnes) in the FRG. No reliable figures are available for oil and fuel losses.

4. SUMMARY AND OUTLOOK

This report shows that in some areas transport has increased in quantitative terms by over 100 per cent over the past twenty years (2). It also shows that rapid growth will no doubt continue beyond the turn of the century. It will be very difficult to prevent the particularly polluting road traffic from going on growing at the fastest rate, as it has in the past.

In view of the trend of recent decades and the further increase of traffic to be expected due to political and economic circumstances, it is now more necessary than ever to highlight the resulting environmental pollution and the extraordinarily high consumption of resources.

Transport accounts for over 30 per cent of total energy consumption (3). Today, the well-known air pollutant emissions caused by transport (CO, HC and NO_x) account for well over 50 per cent of total noxious emissions. Transport in Germany accounts for 20 per cent of the total CO_2 emissions that contribute to the greenhouse effect. Road traffic noise pollution alone affects over two-thirds of the German population, and almost one-quarter substantially.

The German Conference of Ministers for the Environment considers it necessary to drastically reduce this environmental pollution. It is intended to achieve the following reductions by 2005 as compared with the 1987 figures:

NO_x	: -60 per cent
HC	: -70 per cent
CO_2	: -10 per cent

It should be clear from the report that in order to achieve these goals, even very demanding technical measures are not enough on their own. In addition it is necessary to introduce measures to:

-- Shift road transport output to more environmentally friendly modes;

-- Reduce vehicle-kilometres through more efficient transport operation and organisation;

-- Make the remaining road traffic less polluting;

-- After examining the causes of transport operations, to reduce the need for transport wherever it is not absolutely essential.

TABLES

Table 1

Origin and impact of transport related air pollution and noise

POLLUTANT	SOURCE	EFFECTS ON:			
		People	Vegetation and ecosystem	Climate	Materials and buildings
HYDROCARBONS (HC)	Incomplete combustion, carburetion	Direct, notably carcinogenic effects of individual components	Through build-up in soil, feed and food crops	High greenhouse potential (methane), ozone formation	
NITROGEN OXIDES (NO_x)	Oxidation of N_2 and N-compounds in fuel additives	Irritation, morphological changes in the respiratory system	Acidification of soil and water, over-fertilizing, increased risk of leaf and root damage	Very high greenhouse potential (NO_2), ozone formation	Weathering, corrosion
OZONE (0_3)	Photo-chemical oxidisation with NOx and HC	Irritation of mucus and respiratory system, premature aging of the lungs	Increased risk of leaf and root damage	Very high greenhouse potential	Decomposition of polymers
CARBON MONOXIDE (CO)	Incomplete combustion	Inadequate oxygen supply, in particular heart/circulation and central nervous system		Indirect through ozone formation	
PARTICULATES	Incomplete combustion, source-specific emissions, dust thrown up	Damage to respiratory system, toxic contents with broad range of effects	Reduced assimilation		Dirty buildings
SOOT	Incomplete combustion	Carcinogenic			Dirty buildings
CARBON DIOXIDE (CO_2)	Combustion			Quantitatively important greenhouse gas	
NOISE	Engine, drive and rolling noise	Substantial nuisance, higher health risk			Reduced value

Source: Umweltbundesamt, 1990 (1).

Table 2

Environment relevant European transport data

PASSENGER TRANSPORT	1970	1987	Percentage change (1987 re 1970)
CARS (million vehicles)			
OECD Europe	64	130	+ 104
Germany	14	28	+ 101
VEHICLE USE (Billion vehicle-kilometres)			
OECD Europe	856	1 574	+ 84
Germany	201	357	+ 77
TRANSPORT OUTPUT (Billion passenger-kilometres)			
ECMT rail	221	271	+ 23
ECMT public road transport	247	353	+ 43
ECMT private car	1 542	2 685	+ 74
Germany rail	37	43	+ 16
Germany public road transport	49	53	+ 9
Germany private car	351	531	+ 52
FREIGHT TRANSPORT	**1970**	**1987**	**Percentage change (1987 re 1970)**
TRUCKS (million vehicles)			
OECD Europe	8	14.5	+ 77
Germany	1	1.3	+ 30
VEHICLE USE (Billion vehicle-kilometres)			
OECD Europe	178	313	+ 76
Germany	27	36	+ 34
TRANSPORT OUTPUT (Billion tonne-kilometres)			
ECMT rail	274	251	- 8
ECMT road	439	825	+ 88
ECMT inland waterway	113	110	- 3
Germany rail	70	58	- 18
Germany road	78	141	+ 80
Germany inland waterway	49	50	+ 2
ROAD LENGTH (thousand kilometres)	**1970**	**1987**	**Percentage change (1987 re 1970)**
ALL ROADS (thousand kilometres)			
OECD Europe	2 876	3 131	+ 9
Germany	441	494	+ 12
MOTORWAYS (thousand kilometres)			
OECD Europe	14.5	35.3	+ 143
Germany	4.5	8.6	+ 93

Sources: OECD 1989 (3), ECMT 1990 (11).

Table 3

Forecast transport output in Germany

PASSENGER TRANSPORT	1987	2005		Percentage change (2005 re 1987)	
		T[1]	R[1]	T[1]	R[1]
TRANSPORT OUTPUT (Billion passenger-kilometres)					
Rail	39.9	44.9	74.2	+ 13	+ 86
Public road transport	69.7	64.5	95.4	- 7	+ 37
Air transport	14.7	24.2	20.2	+ 65	+ 37
Private car	533.4	605.8	499.2	+ 14	- 6
FREIGHT TRANSPORT	1987	2005		Percentage change (2005 re 1987)	
		T[1]	R[1]	T[1]	R[1]
TRANSPORT OUTPUT (Billion tonne-kilometres)					
Rail	57.8	68.5	102.9	+ 19	+ 78
Road	145.0	205.9	168.7	+ 42	+ 16
Inland waterway	49.7	60.1	65.9	+ 21	+ 39
Air transport	0.4	1.0	0.7	+ 250	+ 175

1. T = Trend scenario; R = Reduction scenario.

Source: DIW, 1990 (5).

Table 4

Transport related specific emissions in Germany (1986)
-- Passenger transport --
(g/pkm)

		CO	CO_2	HC	NO_x	SO_2	Particulate/ Dust
CAR:	Gasoline[1]	14.40	180	2.50	2.40	0.03	0.01
	Diesel	1.40	150	0.30	0.60	0.19	0.18
BUS:	Local	0.60	65	0.50	0.90	0.09	0.20
	Long-haul	0.05	20	0.05	0.40	0.03	0.02
RAIL:	Local	0.02	105	0.01	0.30	0.70	0.04
	Long-haul	0.01	45	0.01	0.15	0.30	0.02
AIR:		2.20	465	0.40	1.80	0.15	0.07

1. Without catalyser.

Source: UBA 1991 (1)).

Table 5

Transport related specific emissions in Germany (1986)
-- Freight Transport --
(g/tkm)

		CO	CO_2	HC	NO_x	SO_2	Particulate/ Dust
ROAD:	Local	1.86	255	1.25	4.1	0.32	0.30
	Long-haul	0.25	140	0.32	3.0	0.18	0.17
RAIL:	Merchandise	0.15	48	0.07	0.4	0.18	0.07
INLAND WATERWAY:		0.18	40	0.08	0.5	0.05	0.03

Source: UBA 1991 (1).

Table 6

Car emission factor reduction rates for the Umweltbundesamt pollution scenario calculation 1998/2005 (relative reduction with respect to the EC 1992 requirements)

	CO	HC	NO_x
2nd stage	5 to 20 %	0 to 50 %	10 %
3rd stage	20 to 40 %	40 to 90 % 60 % (carburetion)	20 to 40%

Table 7

Truck emission factor reduction rates for the Umweltbundesamt pollution scenario calculation 1998/2005 (relative reduction with respect to the 1990 status quo)

	CO	HC	NO_x	Particulate
1st stage	0 %	0 %	30 %	15 %
2nd stage	10 %	12 %	60 %	65 %
3rd stage	55 %	50 %	80 %	80 %

Table 8

Forecast of the relative change in air polluting emissions in Germany in 1998 and 2005 with respect to 1988

EMISSIONS	1988	1998/1988	2005/1988
CO **Total ('000 tonnes):**	8 701 100%	- 40%	- 56%
of which:			
Total transport	6 441 100%	- 51%	- 69%
Road transport[1]	6 092 100%	- 53%	- 70%
of which: Car	5 954 100%	- 54%	- 71%
Truck	138 100%	+ 18%	- 14%
HC **Total ('000 tonnes):**	2 436 100%	- 45%	- 63%
of which:			
Total transport	1 286 100%	- 51%	- 73%
Road transport[1]	1 025 100%	- 52%	- 76%
of which: Car	913 100%	- 61%	- 84%
Truck	112 100%	+ 21%	- 8%
NO_x **Total ('000 tonnes):**	2 848 100%	- 34%	- 48%
of which:			
Total transport	1 838 100%	- 30%	- 51%
Road transport[1]	1 623 100%	- 34%	- 57%
of which: Car	1 068 100%	- 52%	- 70%
Truck	555 100%	+ 1%	- 34%
Particulates			
Total ('000 tonnes):	224 100%	- 22%	- 45%
of which:			
Total transport	76 100%	- 24%	- 56%
Road transport[1]	62 100%	- 26%	- 63%
of which: Car	23 100%	- 50%	- 67%
Truck	39 100%	- 13%	- 62%
SO_2[2] **Total ('000 tonnes):**	1 286 100%	- 35%	- 47%
of which:			
Total transport	56 100%	- 57%	- 55%
CO_2[2] **Total ('000 tonnes):**	708 100%	+ 2%	+ 1%
of which:			
Total transport	143 100%	+ 13%	+ 16%
Road transport[1]	121 100%	+ 15%	+ 18%
of which: Car	93 100%	+ 12%	+ 13%
Truck	28 100%	+ 25%	+ 36%

1. Cars and trucks only.
2. From the Umweltbundesamt prognosis (1) 1990.
3. For the Symposium in May 1992, the latest forecasts for Germany (former FRG and GDR) and for CO_2 will be available.

Source: UBA (1) 1990 and (7) 1991.

Table 9

Reduction targets for transport related air pollutant and CO_2 emissions (Reference year 1987)

Year	NO_x	HC	CO_2
By 1998	- 30%	- 50%	- 5%
By 2005	- 60%	- 70%	- 10%

Source: Umweltministerkonferenz (10).

Table 10

Desirable additional reduction targets for transport related air pollutant and CO_2 emissions through traffic influencing measures (Reference year 1987)

Year	NO_x	HC	CO_2
By 1998	- 8%	- 2%	- 20%
By 2005	- 17%	- 1%	- 28%

Source: UBA 1991 (8).

Table 11

Air pollutant concentrations in urban residential areas and city centre streets (ug/m^3)

Pollutant	Residential areas		City centre streets	
	Annual average	98 percentile	Annual average	98 percentile
NO	40 to 60	200 to 300	80 to 200	350 to 800
NO_2	40 to 60	100 to 150	50 to 100	120 to 260
CO	1* to 2*)	3* to 5*)	3* to 5*)	5*) to 15*)
Soot (BS)	10 to 20	40 to 70	20 to 40	70 to 140
Benzol	5 to 20		15 to 35	46
Toluol	8 to 35		25 to 50	70
NMHC	60 to 200	200 to 700	90 to 1.2*)	400 to 3.7*)
Lead	0.2 to 0.4		0.3 to 0.8	
Formaldehyde	1 to 5		5 to 10	
Ozone	20 to 50	50 to 170	10 to 30	40 to 120

*) mg/m^3.

Source: UBA 1991 (1).

Table 12

Transport related pollutant concentrations within vehicles (mg/m^3)

Pollutant	Motorway	Commuter route
NO	0.5 to 1.4	0.4 to 1.2
NO_2	0.15 to 0.22	0.05 to 0.11
CO	3 to 12	9 to 15
Benzol	0.02 to 0.06	

Source: UBA 1991 (1).

Table 13

People directly affected by different types of pollution (Percentage of respondants)

Type of Pollution	Directly affected	Ranking
Noise	54	1
Road traffic	50	2
Air pollution	49	3
Water pollution	31	4
Waste disposal	26	5

Table 14

Assumption of a health risk with different types of pollution (Percentage of respondants)

Type of Pollution	Assumption of a health risk
Road traffic	91
Air pollution	89
Noise	80
Water pollution	78

Table 15

Passenger transport mode specific noise emissions in Germany (Passage at a distance of 25 m)

Mode	Type of traffic/location	Passing speed (km/h)	Average passengers per vehicle	Noise level dB(A)	Mode specific noise dB(A)/person
Car	Built-up	30 to 60	1.3	61*)	59
	Open road	60 to 100	1.5	67*)	65
Bus	Built-up	30 to 60	30	70*)	55
	Open road	60 to 100	35	72*)	56
Rail	Tram	50	100	77	57
	S-Bahn	100	350	85	60
	Intercity	150	200	89	66

*) L_{AR} from Figure 6.

Source: FIGE (20), UBA (40).

Table 16

Freight transport mode specific noise emissions in Germany (Passage at a distance of 25 m)

Mode	Type of traffic	Passing speed (km/h)	Average tonnes per vehicle	Noise level dB(A)	Mode specific noise dB(A)/tonne
Truck	Local	30 to 60	5	71*)	64
	Long-haul	60 to 100	9	74*)	64
Rail	Long-haul	100	500	90	63

*) L_{AR} from Figure 6.

Sources: FIGE (20); UBA (40).

Table 17

Passenger transport mode specific noise emissions in Germany [level calculated according to DIN 18005 1987 and Schall 03 (4) for 1 000 passengers per hour and usual occupancy rate]

	CAR			BUS		RAIL		
	Urban	Open Road		Urban	Other	Tram	Rail S-Bahn	IC
Pass./unit	1.3	1.5	1.5	30	35	100	350	200
Units/hour	770	667	667	33	29	10	3	5
Train length (m)						25	150	300
Speed (km/h)	50	80	120	50	80	50	100	150
Noise level at 25m (dB)	59	63	67	60	62	54	62	68

Table 18

Freight transport mode specific noise emissions in Germany [level calculated according to DIN 18005 1987 and Schall 03 (41) for 1000 tonnes per hour and usual capacity utilisation rate]

	TRUCK		TRAIN
	Local	Long-haul	Long-haul
Tonnes/unit	5	9	500
Units/hour	200	111	2
Train length (m)	-	-	500
Speed (km/h)	50	80	100
Noise level at 25 m (dB)	68	67	70

Table 19

Road traffic noise suffered by the German (former FRG) population (percentage of 61.5 million inhabitants)

Noise level in dB(A)	45-<50	50-<55	55-<60	60-<65	65-<70	70-<75	>=75
DAY	not calculated		18.3	14.2	7.4	4.0	1.1
NIGHT	18.1	13.8	8.0	4.0	1.7	0.2	0.1

Source: UBA 1989 (27).

Table 20

Assumptions for the reduction of noise emissions for road vehicles by 1995 in Germany (former FRG)

Type of vehicle	Urban traffic	Motorway
Car	for 60% 5 dB(A)	for 60% 2dB (A)
Car	for 40% 3 dB(A)	for 40% 1dB (A)
Truck	for 60% 7 dB(A)	for 60% 3dB (A)
Truck	for 40% 3 dB(A)	for 40% 1dB (A)

Source: UBA 1989 (27).

Table 21

Forecast of noise pollution as a result of the technical reduction scenario of Table 20

Noise level in dB(A)	45-<50	50-<55	55-<60	60-<65	65-<70	70-<75	>=75
DAY	not calculated		14.3	10.8	4.9	2.0	0.2
NIGHT	14.9	11.7	4.3	3.0	0.2	0.1	0.1

Source: UBA 1989 (27).

Table 22

Effects of different volumes of road traffic noise

Noise level in dB(A) (Day 0600 to 2200, outdoors)	55	60	65	70	75
Number of motor vehicles/hour (10% trucks, 50 km/h, 12.5 m distant, buildings well back from roadway)	43	140	430	1 400	4 300
Substantial disturbance of home activities (percentage of people affected)	29	41	53	65	77
Psycho-vegetative effects (percentage of people affected)	15	24	32	41	49
Perception of the situation as "unbearable" (percentage of people affected)	9	21	33	45	57

Source: UBA (29).

Table 23

Number of people affected by road traffic noise (million inhabitants)

Noise level in dB(A) (day 0600 to 2200, outdoors)	55*	60*	65*	70*	75*
Total number affected	11.6	9.2	4.6	2.7	0.8
Number substantially disturbed in home activities	3.3	3.6	2.4	1.6	0.5
Psycho-vegetative effects	1.7	2.1	1.5	1.0	0.3
Perception of the situation as "unbearable"	1.0	1.8	1.5	1.1	0.4

* Instead of the 5dB intervals the lower limits of the noise level intervals were used.

Source: UBA (29).

Table 24

Guidelines and limit values for road and rail traffic noise

	Guide values (DIN 18005)		Not to be exceeded in building/renovation (16.BImSchV)		Noise reduction measures required (BMV Guidelines)	
	Day	**Night**	**Day**	**Night**	**Day**	**Night**
Hospitals	50	40	57	47	70	60
Residential areas	55	45	59	49	70	60
Mixed areas	50	60	64	54	72	62
Industrial areas	65	55	69	59	75	65

Sources: DIN 18005, 1987; 16.BImSchV, 1990; BMV, 1986.

FIGURES

Figure 1. **Road vehicle stocks**

Relative change of vehicle numbers in relation to numbers 1970 OECD-Europe and FR Germany

Passenger cars (change in percent re 1970)

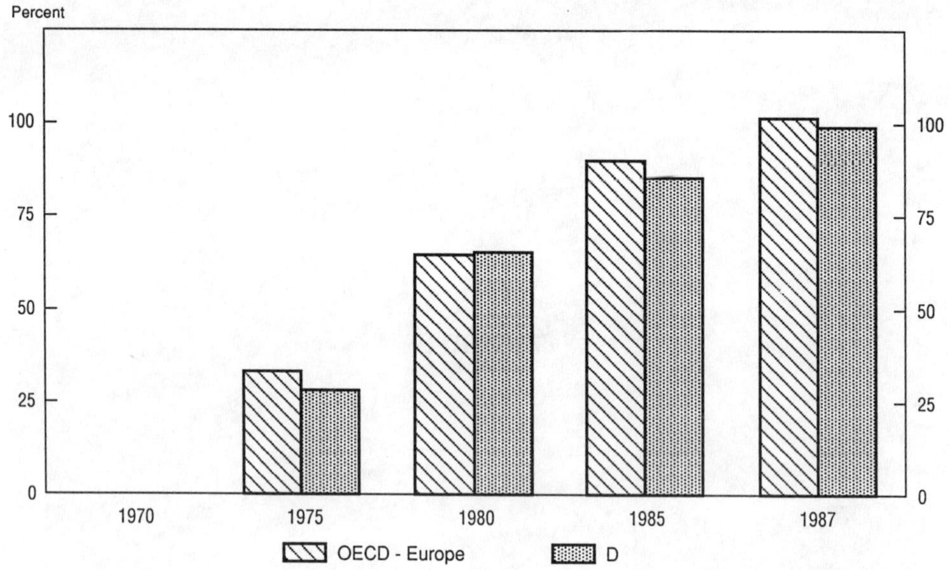

Goods vehicles (change in percent re 1970)

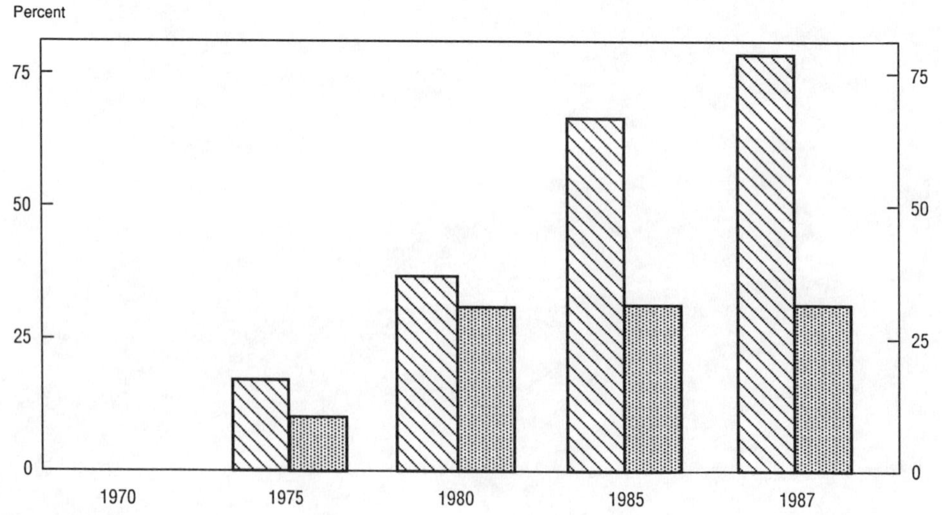

Source: OECD 1989 /3/, ECMT 1990 /11/.

Figure 2. **Road traffic volumes**

Relative change of vehicle-kilometres in relation to volumes 1970 OECD-Europe and FR Germany

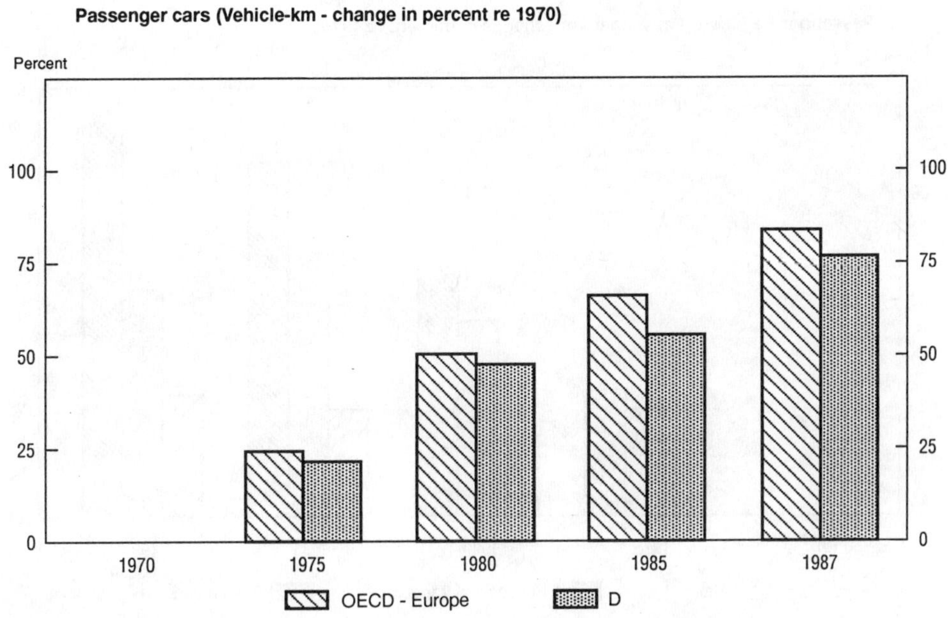

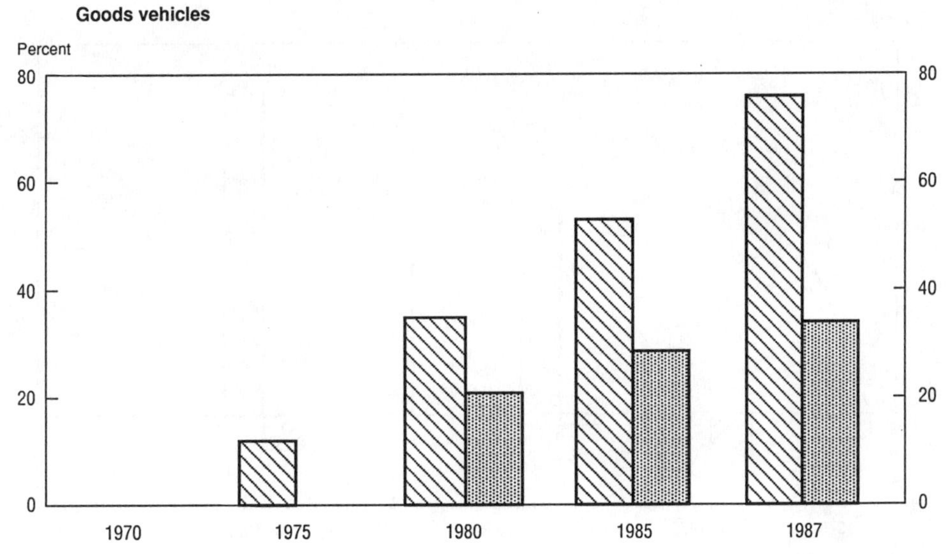

Source: OECD 1989 /3/, ECMT 1990 /11/.

Figure 3. **Transport**

Relative change of passenger-kilometres and tonne-kilometres in relation to transport 1970 OECD-Europe

Passenger transport (Passenger-km - change in percent re 1970)

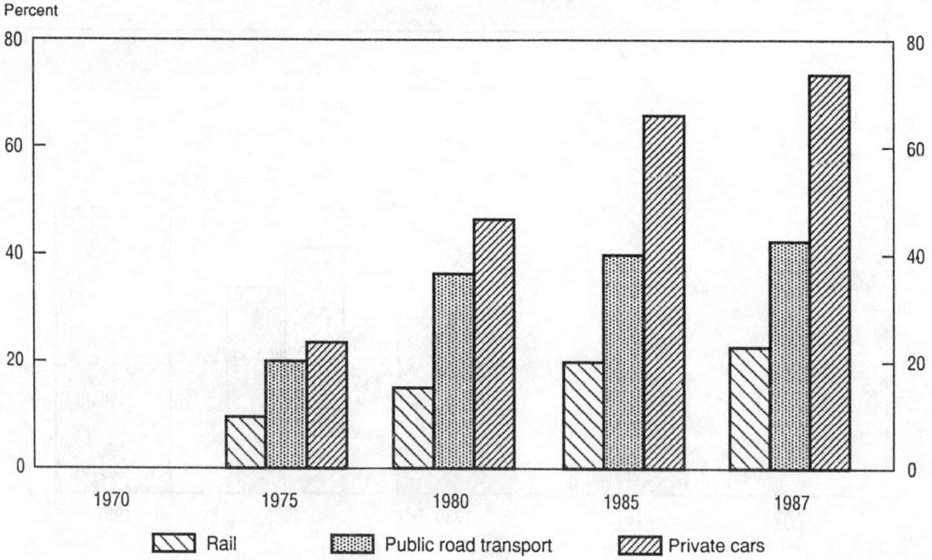

Freight transport (Tonne-km - change in percent re 1970)

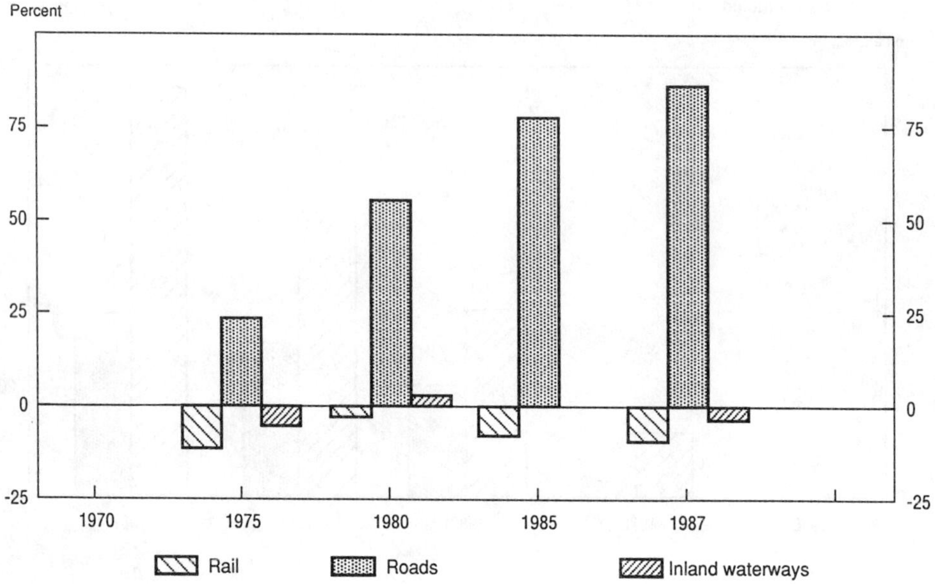

Source: OECD 1989 /3/, ECMT 1990 /11/.

Figure 4. **Road network length**

Relative change of road length in relation to length 1970 OECD-Europe and FR Germany

Road network length : all roads (km - change in percent re 1970)

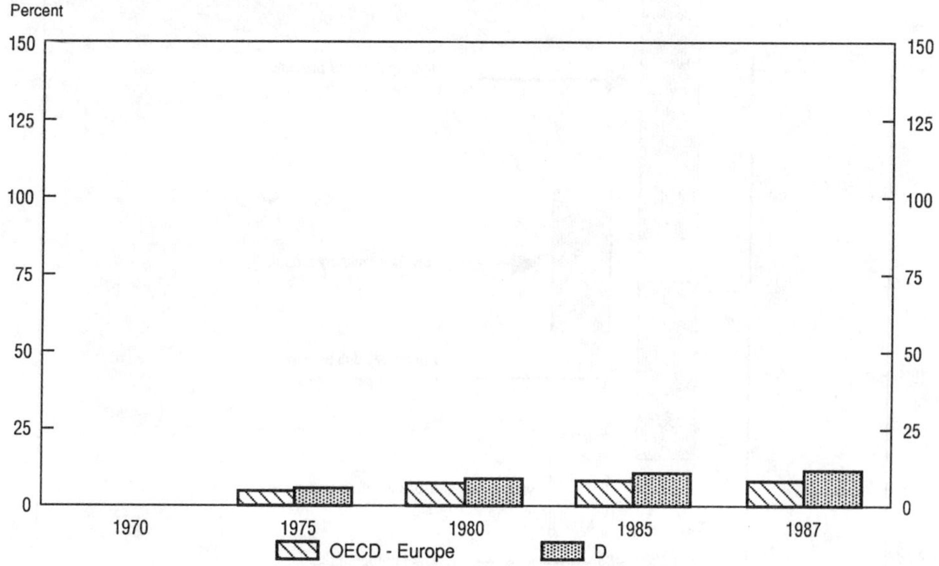

Road network length : motorways (km - change in percent re 1970)

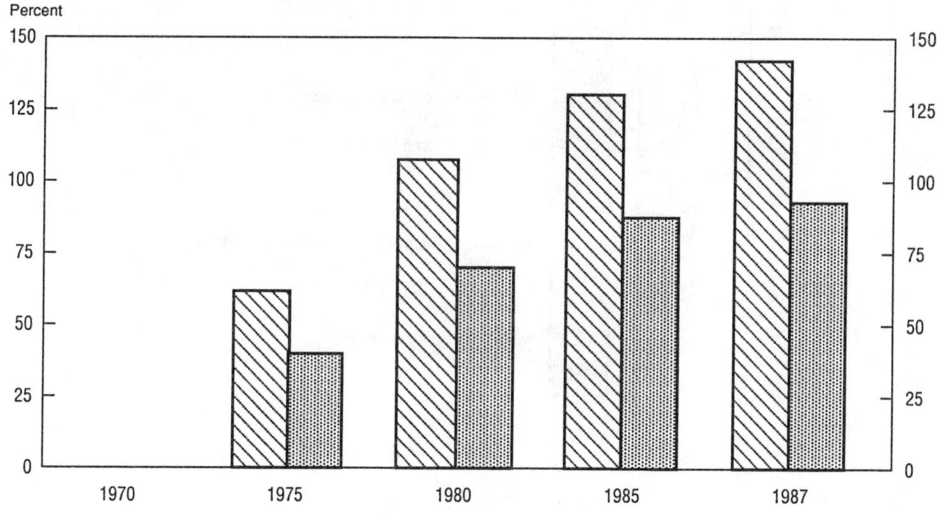

Source: OECD 1989 /3/, ECMT 1990 /11/.

Figure 5. **Noise pressure level of common environmental noises**

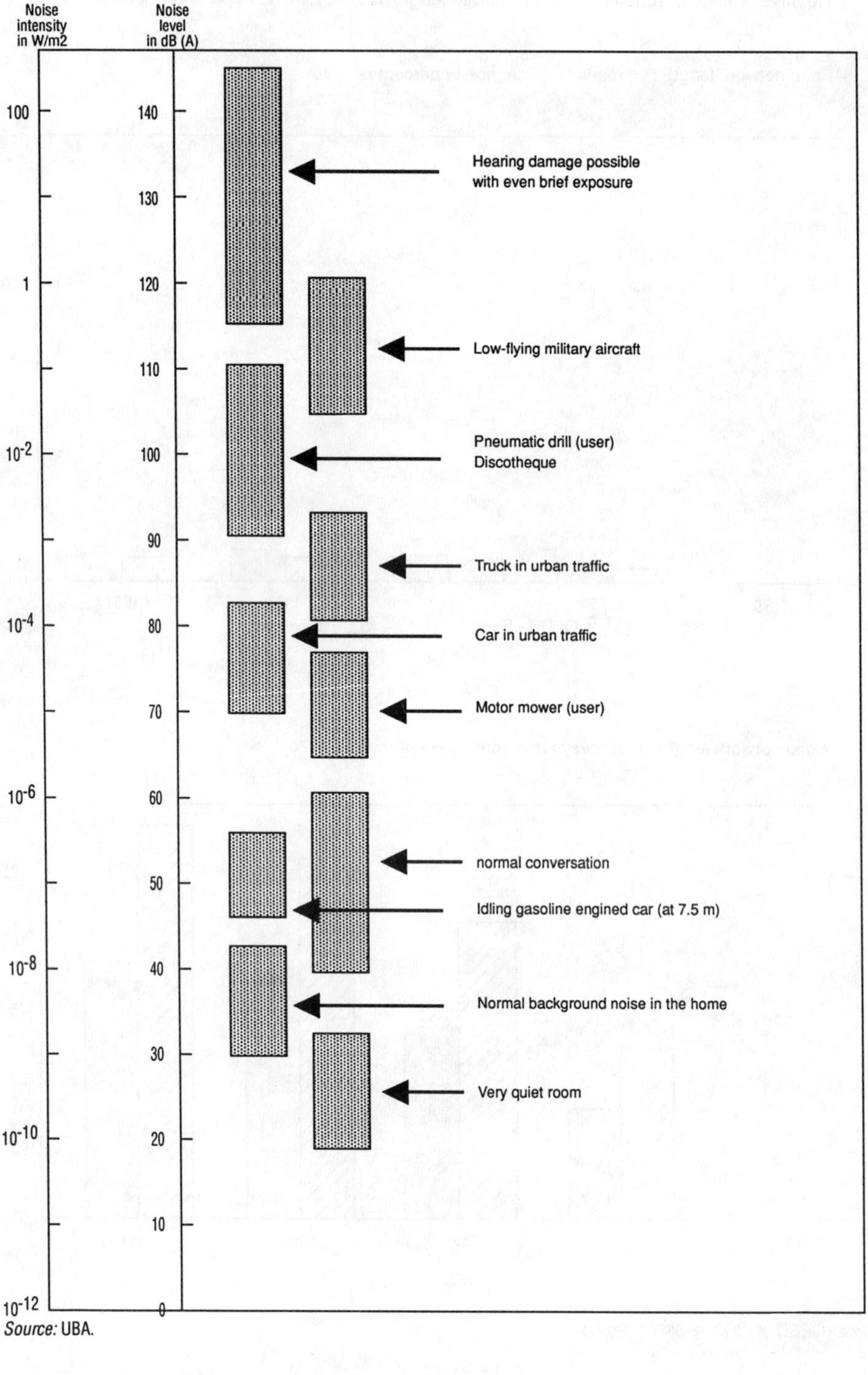

Source: UBA.

Figure 6. **Noise level of passing vehicles**

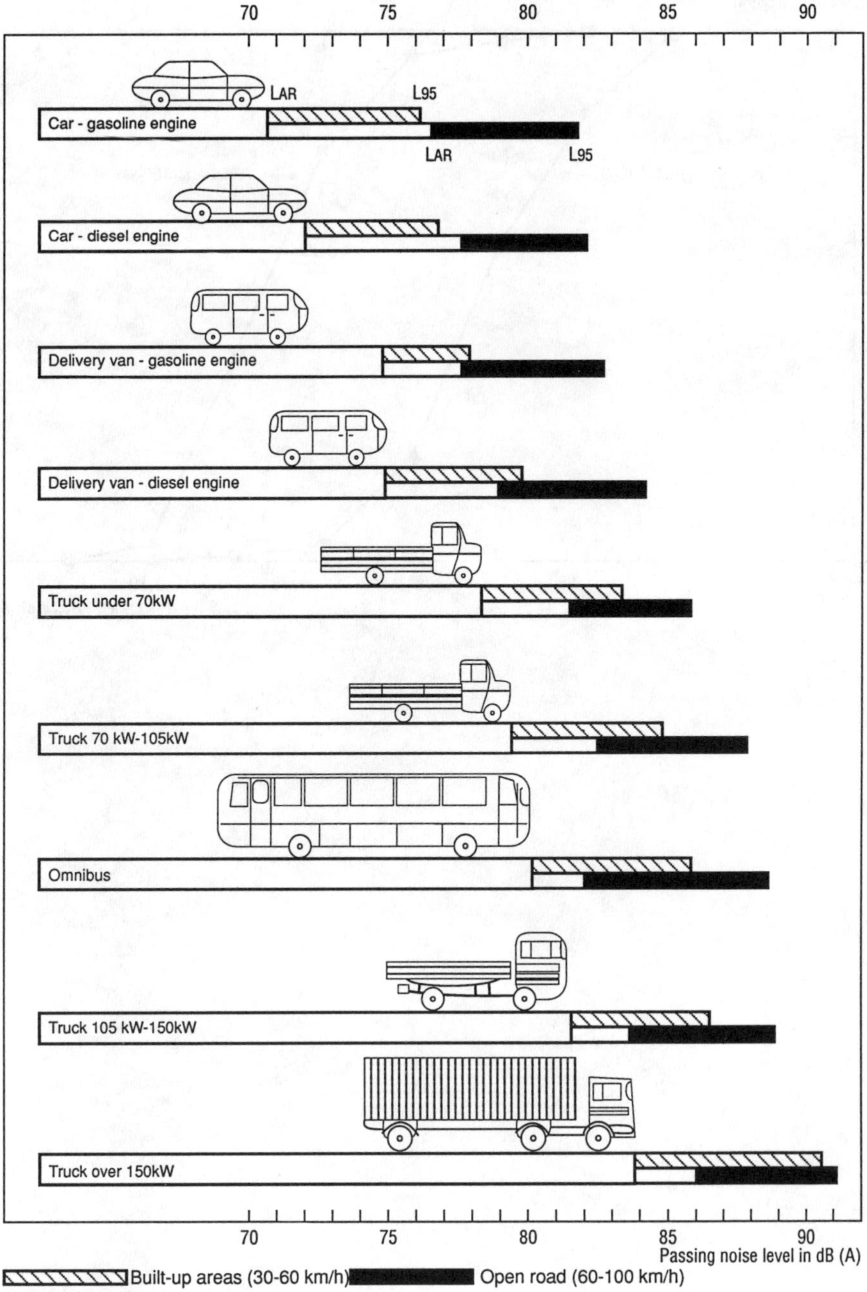

LA R = Arithmetic mean

L9 5 = Value exceeded by only 5% of vehicles

Source: FIGE (20).

Figure 7. **Day noise level on trunk roads and motorways in Germany**

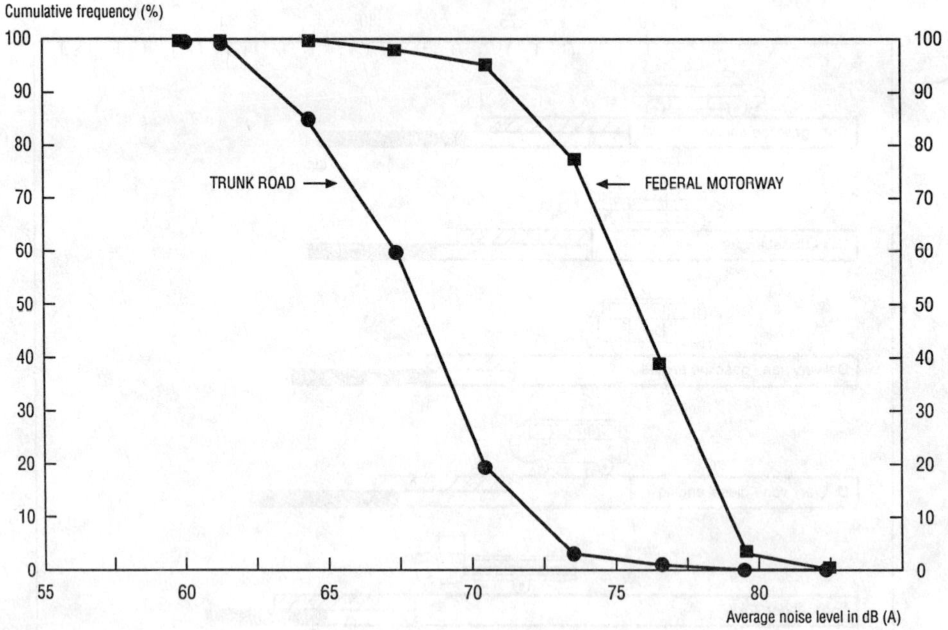

Source: UBA 1989 (39).

Figure 8. **Population exposed to road traffic noise**

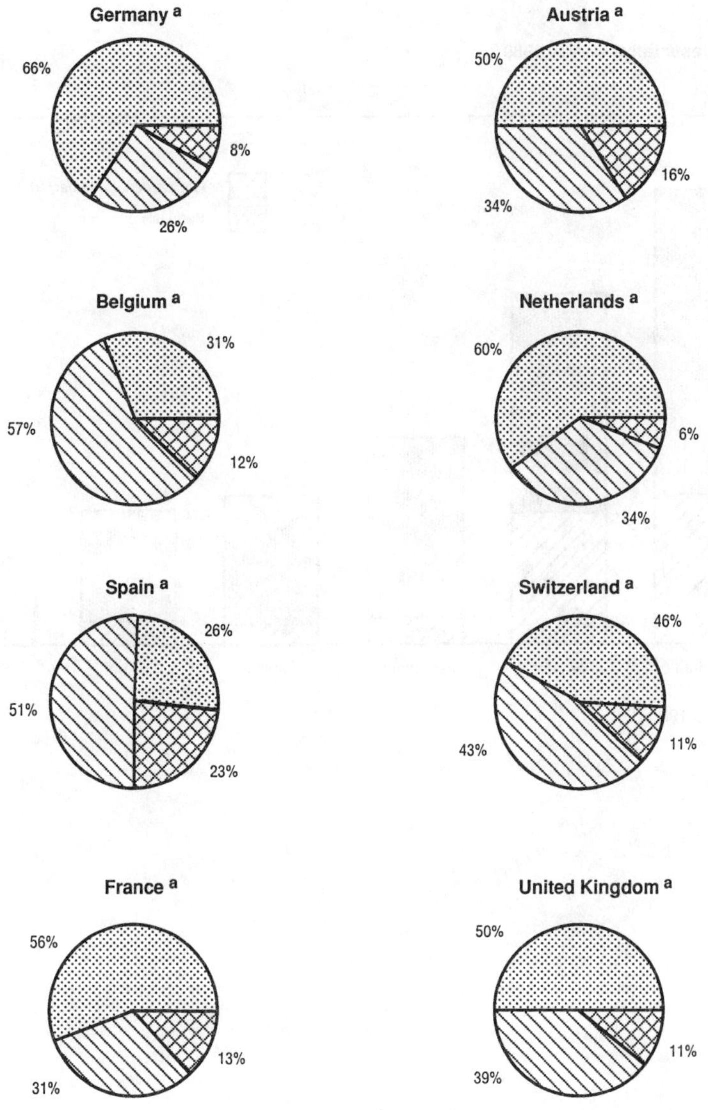

Légend: Leq<55 dB(A) Leq 55-65 dB(A) Leq>65 dB(A)
a = Leq day time
b = Leq 24 hours

Source: OECD 1985 /21/ .

Figure 9. **Percentage of people affected by noise in Germany**
Percentage of the total population of 61,5 million in 1989

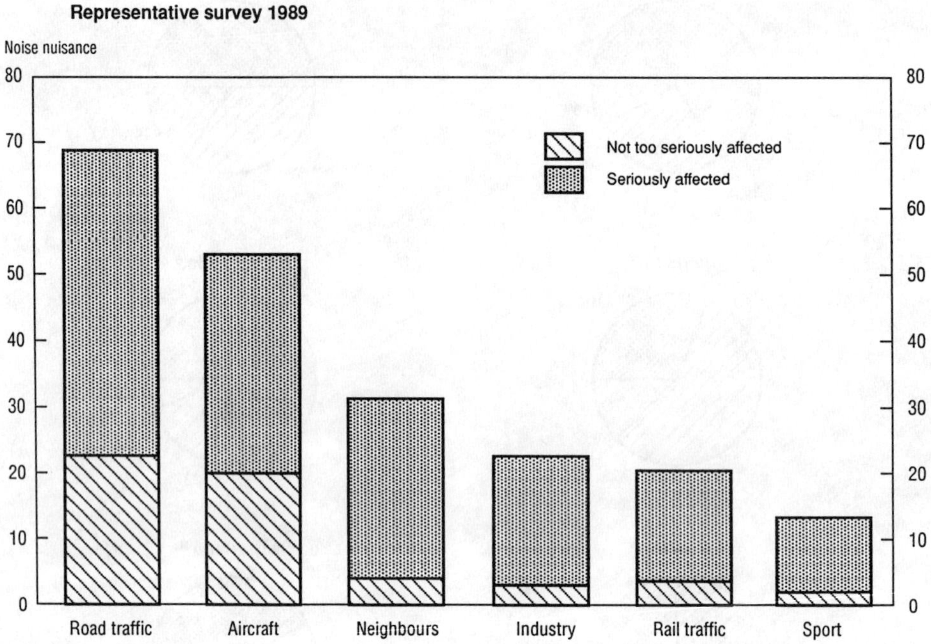

Source: IPOS 1990 (24).

Figure 10. **Percentage of people affected by road traffic noise in Germany - all roads**
Percentage of the total population of 61,5 million in 1985, former FRG

Noise nuisance due to road traffic

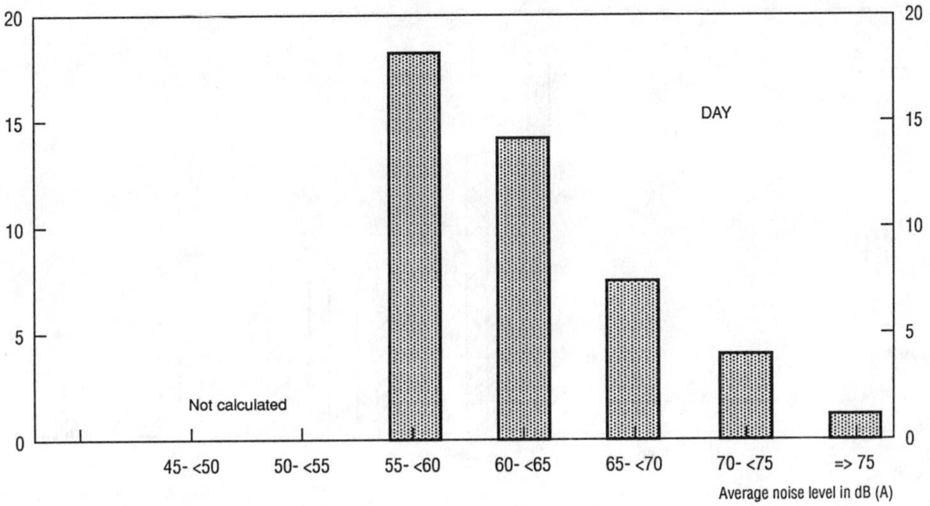

All roads

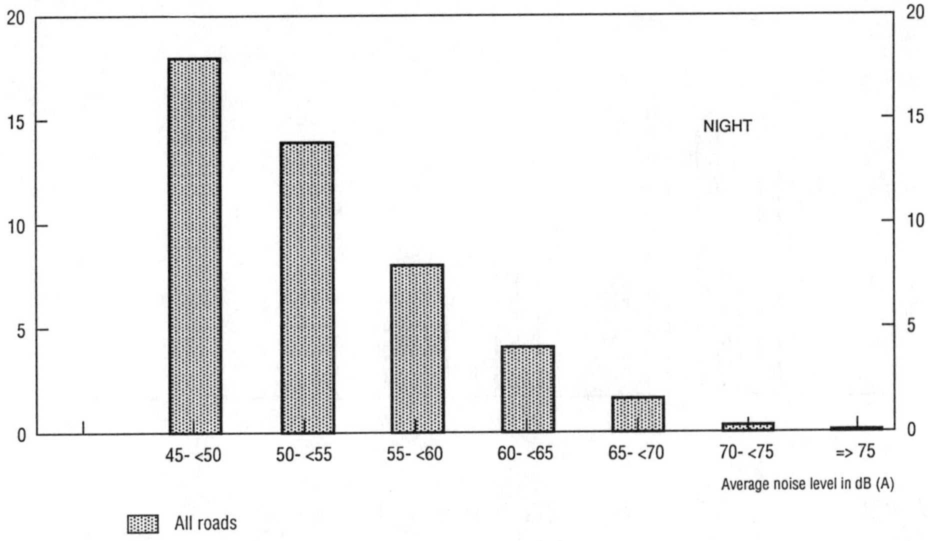

Source: UBA 1991 (28).

Figure 11. **Percentage of people affected by road traffic noise in Germany by type of road**
Percentage of the total population of 61,5 million in 1985, former FRG

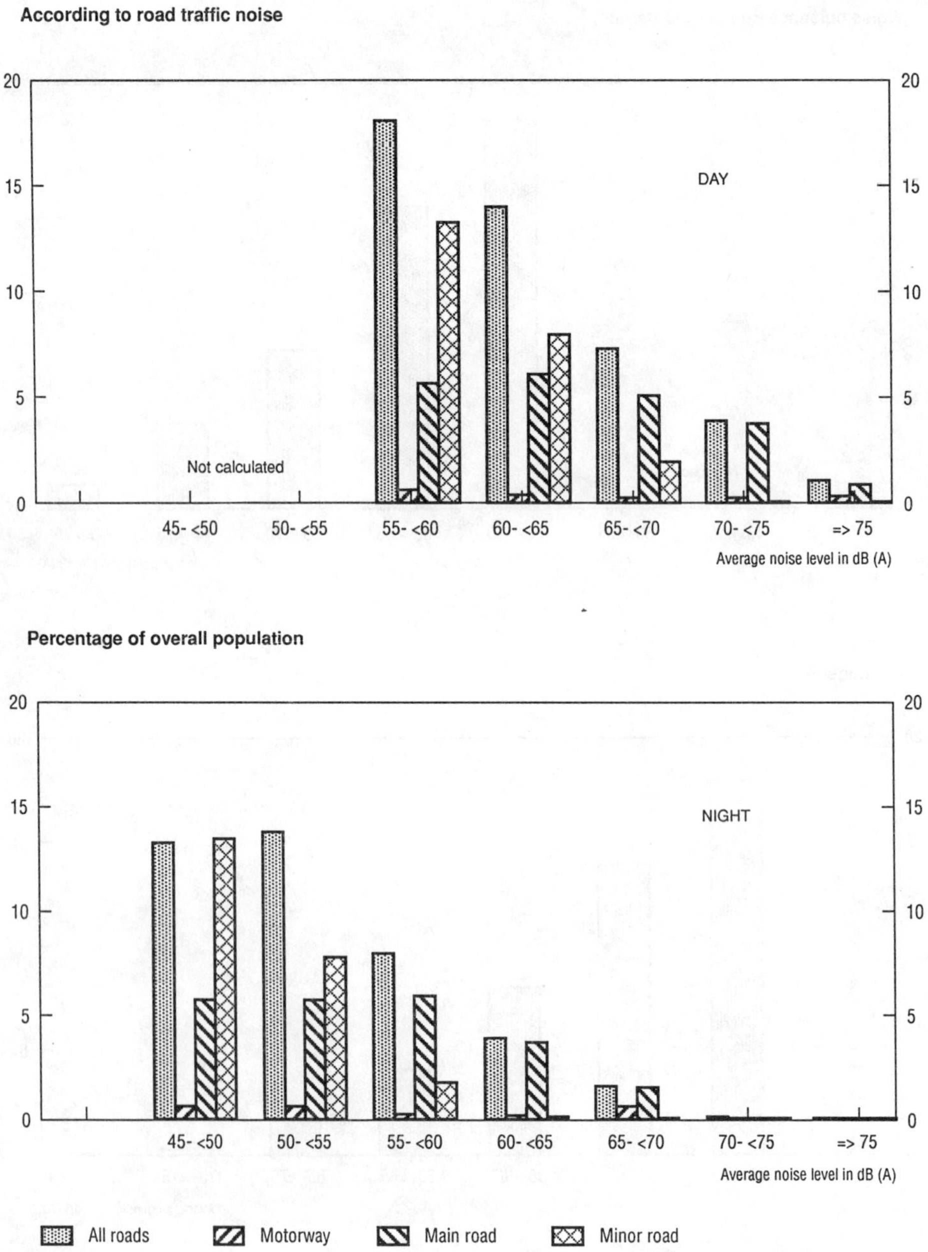

Source: UBA 1991 (28)

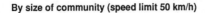

Figure 12. **Percentage of people affected by road traffic noise in Germany**

Percentage of the total population of 61,5 million in 1985, former FRG

By size of community (speed limit 50 km/h)

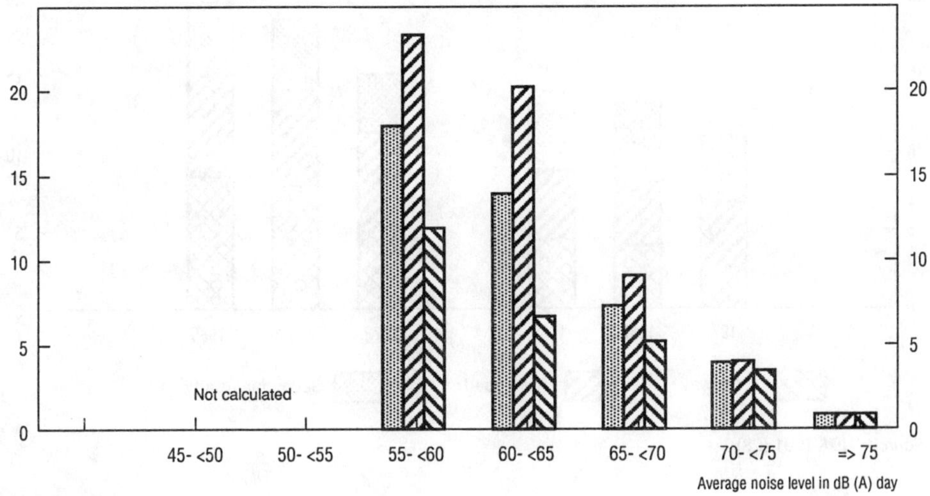

With a 30 km/h limit on all minor roads

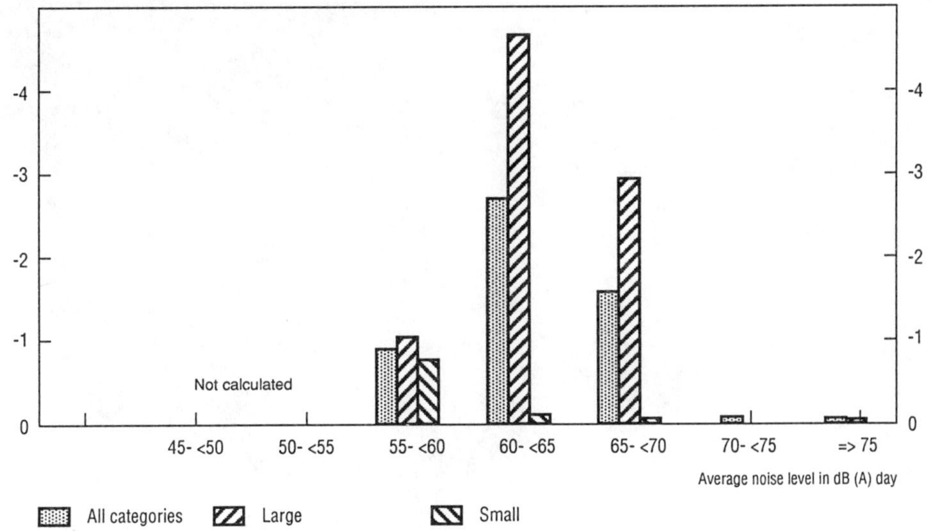

Source: UBA 1991 (28)

Figure 13. **Area outside built-up areas with high traffic noise in Germany**

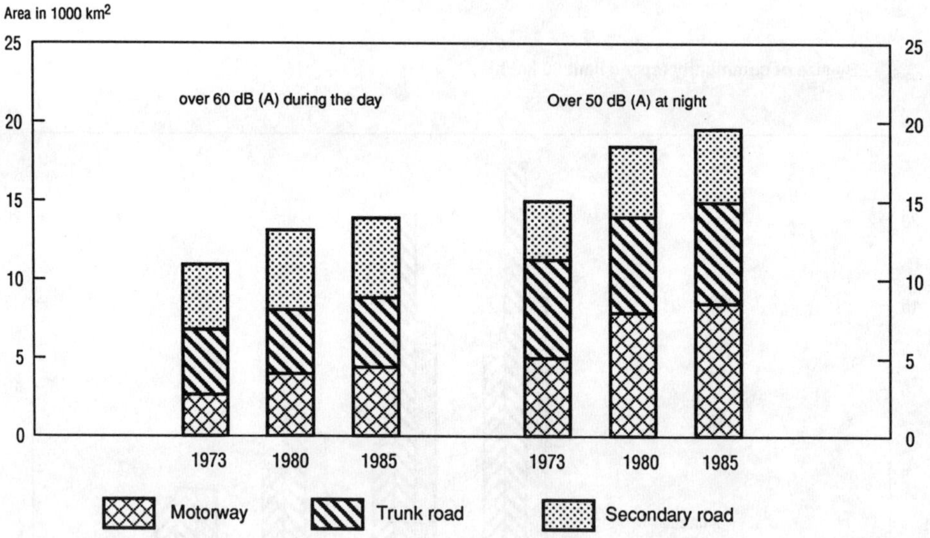

Source: UBA 1991 (28)

REFERENCES

1. Umweltbundesamt: "Verkehrsbedingte Luft- und Lärmbelastungen - Emissionen, Immissionen, Wirkungen", UBA-Texte 40/91, Berlin 1991.

2. Statistical Trends in Transport 1965-1987, European Conference of Ministers of Transport (ECMT), Paris 1990.

3. OECD Environmental Data, Compendium 1989. Organisation for Economic Co-operation and Development (OECD), Paris 1989.

4. Umweltbundesamt: Jahresbericht 1986, p. 58 and Jahresbericht 1987, p. 67, Berlin 1986-87.

5. "Konzeptionelle Fortentwicklung des Verkehrsbereichs" Bericht des Deutschen Institut für Wirtschaftsforschung (DIW) für die Enquete-Kommission "Vorsorge zum Schutz der Erdatmospäre" des Deutschen Bundestages, Berlin 1990.

6. "Reduzierung der CO_2-Emissionen in der Bundesrepublik Deutschland bis zum Jahr 2005", Bericht des Bundesministers für Umwelt, Naturschutz und Reaktorsicherheit, p. 47, Bonn 1990.

7. Ozon-Symposium München, veranstaltet vom Bundesministerium für Umwelt, Naturschutz und Reaktorsicherheit und dem Bayerischen Staatsministerium für Landesentwicklung und Umweltfragen, Munich 1991.

8. "Verkehrsbedingte Umweltbelastungen -- Analysen, Prognosen, Ziele, Minderungen", Umweltbundesamt (Hrsg.) Texte 26/91, Berlin 1991.

9. "Nichtlimitierte Automobilabgaskomponenten", Volkswagen AG (Hrsg.), Wolfsburg 1988 [zitiert aus (1)].

10. Beschluß der 35. Umweltministerkonferenz, Berlin, 1990.

11. Transport Policy and the Environment, ECMT Ministerial Session 1989, ECMT/OECD, Paris, 1990.

12. "Erstickt Europa im Verkehr ? -- Probleme, Perspektiven, Konzepte", Materialband zum Verkehrspolitischen Kongress der Landesregierung Baden-Württemberg, Stuttgart 1991.

13. MacKenzie, J.J. and M.P. Walsh: Driving Forces: Motor Vehicle Trends and Their Implications for Global Warming, Energy Strategies and Transport Planning. World Resources Institute, New York, Washington 1990.

14. "Daten zur Umwelt 1988/89", Umweltbundesamt, Erich Schmidt Verlag, Berlin 1989.

15. "Motivierung der Bevölkerung zu umweltbewußtem Verhalten", UBA-Forschungsbericht No. 101 07 051, p. 47; Socialdata, Munich 1984.

16. Maurin, M. and J. Lambert: Exposure of the French Population to Transport Noise. In: Noise Control Engineering Journal, No. 1 (1990), pp. 5-18.

17. Infratest "Gesundheitsforschung", 1986.

18. D. Ellinghaus: "Lärm auf den Straßen", Uniroyal Verkehrsuntersuchung, IFAPLAN, Cologne 1989.

19. "Umweltgutachten 1978" des Rates von Sachverständigen für Umweltfragen -- Unterrichtung durch die Bundesregierung Drucksache 8/1938 (Pkt.1370).

20. "Ermittlung von Fahr- und Betriebszuständen sowie Geräuschemissionen bei Stadtfahrten mit speziellen Kraftfahrzeugen" UBA-Forschungsbericht No. 80 -- 105 05 101; Forschungsinstitut für Geräusche und Erschütterungen (FIGE), Aachen 1980.

21. Strengthening Noise Abatement Policies, OECD Report, Paris, 1985.

22. "Belastung der Bevölkerung durch Lärm", UBA-Forschungsbericht 105 02 803/02, Battelle Institut, Frankfurt 1981.

23. "Lärmbekämpfung '81", Materialienband zum 2. Immissionsschutzbericht der Bundesregierung, Erich Schmidt Verlag, Berlin 1982.

24. "Einstellungen zu aktuellen Fragen der Umweltpolitik 1989", Bericht des Instituts für praxisorientierte Sozialforschung i.A. des BMU, Mannheim 1989.

25. "Ermittlung der Geräuschemissionsänderung -- Erfolgskontrolle von Grenzwertverschärfugen und Energiesparappellen" UBA-Forschungsbericht 105 05 128, FIGE, Aachen 1985.

26. Verkehr in Zahlen, Bundesminister für Verkehr, Bonn 1986.

27. Nolle A. and W. Pollehn: "Geräuschbelastung der Bevölkerung durch Straßenverkehr -- Bestandsaufnahme, Auswirkungen von Tempo 30 und Prognosen für das Jahr 1995", Zeitschrift für Lärmbekämpfung 36 (1989), pp. 95-104.

28. Kürer, R.: "Betroffenheit der Bevölkerung durch Verkehrslärm", in (7).

29. "Betroffenheit einer Stadt durch Lärm", UBA-Forschungsbericht Nr. 105 01 301, Physikalisch-Technische Bundesanstalt, Braunschweig, 1980.

30. Interdisziplinärer Arbeitskreis für Lärmwirkungsfragen beim Umweltbundesamt "Beeinträchtigung des Schlafs durch Lärm", Zeitschrift für Lärmbekämpfung 29 (1982), pp. 13-16.

31. Interdisziplinärer Arbeitskreis für Lärmwirkungsfragen beim Umweltbundesamt "Beeinträchtigung der Kommunikation durch Lärm", Zeitschrift für Lärmbekämpfung 32 (1985), pp. 95-99.

32. "Lärmbekämpfung '88 -- Tendenzen, Probleme, Lösungen", Umweltbundesamt (Hrsg.), Materialien zum 4. Immissionsschutzbericht der Deutschen Bundesregierung, Erich Schmidt Verlag, Berlin 1989.

33. Penn-Bressel, G.: "Belastung durch Straßenverkehrslärm und Standortverhalten der Bevölkerung in der BR Deutschland", Fortschritte der Akustik -- DAGA-Bericht 1987, p. 317.

34. DIN 18005 "Schallschutz im Städtebau", Teil 1 Beiblatt 1 (Ausgabe 1987).

35. 16. Verordnung zur Durchführung des zum BundesImmissionschutzgesetzes (Verkehrslärmschutzverordnung -- 16.BImSchV), 1990.

36. Richtlinien des BMV zum Lärmschutz an Bundesfernstraßen in der Baulast des Bundes vom 15.1.1986 (VkBl. 1986, p. 101).

37. "Luftreinhaltung in Hamburg -- Sachstandsbericht 1990", Mitteilung des Hamburger Senats an die Bürgerschaft, Drucksache Bürgerschaft Hamburg 13/6074 -- p. 19, Hamburg, 5.6.1990.

38. Umweltbundesamt: Jahresbericht 1990, pp. 182-183, Berlin 1991.

39. Kürer, R.: "Geräuschemissionen im Straßenverkehr und Minderungspotentiale", im Bericht zur Tagung "Umweltschutz und Verkehr" der Verkehrswissenschaftlichen Gesellschaft, Berlin 1989.

40. Giesler, H.-J. and A. Nolle: "Geräuschemission von Schienenfahrzeugen", Zeitschrift für Lärmbekämpfung 37 (1990), p. 157.

41. "Richtlinie zur Berechnung der Schallimmissonen von Schienenwegen -- Schall 03", Information Akustik 03 der Deutschen Bundesbahn, Frankfurt am Main, 1990.

Sub-topic 5

ENVIRONMENT, GLOBAL AND LOCAL EFFECTS

F. BEFAHY
Société Nationale des Chemins de Fer Belges
Brussels
Belgium

SUMMARY

Brussels, September 1991

1. INTRODUCTION

The current prospects suggest that personal mobility and the volume of goods to be carried will continue to increase substantially in the next few years, particularly over medium and long distances. Within the European Economic Community, this increase will be given further impetus by the opening of the single market in 1993. Substantial growth in trade between western and eastern Europe is also to be expected as a result of the recent political developments.

Transport stimulates economic and social life, but it also has a negative impact on our natural and human environment: it monopolises large surface areas, consumes a great deal of energy, is an important source of air pollution, generates noise and gives rise to many accidents, although in all these respects there are very marked differences between the transport modes.

Environmental protection is a growing concern which is today by no means confined to the industrialised regions. The problem is therefore to reconcile the greater mobility required for European integration and the pursuit of economic development with the safeguard of the natural and human environment, especially since the damage inflicted on it has already reached critical levels, particularly in some heavily populated and industrialised areas.

The railways are convinced that a policy based on rail traffic growth, particularly in densely populated regions, can help to meet expanding transport demand while also helping to safeguard our environment.

While the content of this report mainly concerns Belgium, its implications are by no means confined to that country.

2. TRENDS IN PASSENGER AND GOODS TRAFFIC IN BELGIUM

2.1. Past trends (1980-89)

In Belgium as in Europe as a whole, total passenger and goods traffic increased substantially over the past decade, especially during the second half of the period (see Table 1).

This overall increase was entirely attributable to the substantial growth in road and air traffic, whereas SNCB goods traffic remained at more or less the same level and passenger traffic even diminished.

In assessing these findings, account must also be taken of the major industrial restructuring operations that have taken place in recent decades, particularly since the mid-1970s, since these have led to a sharp decline in the inland transport of heavy bulk goods (mainly coal and ores) which account for a large proportion of rail traffic.

2.2. Future trends

The future increase in transport needs will mainly depend on trends in population and in economic and social policies.

All in all, demographic factors will have very little to do with the increase in demand for transport in Belgium and in neighbouring countries.

Economic growth, however, should continue and result in a marked increase in passenger and goods traffic, trends that will be consolidated by the establishment of the European single market in 1993 and the opening of frontiers between western and eastern Europe.

On the basis of the foregoing, it would seem realistic to forecast an overall increase of 40 to 50 per cent in transport demand in terms of passenger-km and t-km by the period 2010-2015.

The authorities will therefore have to work out a policy in response to both the expected increase in transport needs and the growing concern about protection of our environment.

The railways are convinced that they can do much to help carry through such a policy, provided they have the financial resources required to provide more and better services.

3. TAKING ACCOUNT OF ENVIRONMENTAL CONSTRAINTS IN MAJOR TRANSPORT INFRASTRUCTURE PROJECTS

3.1. Alternatives

In assessing the environmental impact of a given project, a number of alternatives have to be worked out beforehand so as:

a) To compare the foreseeable environmental effects of the various ways of carrying out the project;

b) To determine ways of reducing or avoiding negative environmental effects.

In a high-speed rail project, for example, the following alternatives should be singled out with reference to the order of priority of the decisions to be taken:

-- **The alternatives in terms of objectives** which relate to the end purpose of the project and society's major options. Should international flows, for example, be improved by facilitating personal mobility or by promoting the development of telecommunications systems?

-- **The alternatives in terms of means** which relate to the policy for achieving the established objective. Personal mobility can be improved by developing rail, air or road traffic;

-- **The alternatives in terms of methods** which relate to the various ways of carrying out the established policy. For example, should rail traffic be improved by modifying the existing infrastructure (realignment of parts of the track layout, laying of additional tracks, etc.) or by building new lines?

-- **The alternatives in terms of locations** which relate to the available options for the site of the proposed activity. In the case of a new line, the choice is between various possible routes;

-- **The alternatives in terms of technical** means which relate to the various ways of carrying out or planning the work at a selected location. For example, should a new line run across a particular site in the open or in a tunnel?

3.2. A comparative study and an environmental impact study on the TGV project in Belgium

In accordance with the Decision of the Commission of the European Communities of 22 December 1987, which was transmitted to the Kingdom of Belgium, the SNCB has carried out on the northern TGV project (Paris/London-Brussels-Cologne/Amsterdam):

-- A comparative study;

-- An environmental impact study for the part of the project concerning Belgium.

The comparative study weighs up the advantages and drawbacks of using different transport modes (train, aircraft, car and coach) for intercity travel in the Paris/London-Brussels-Cologne/Amsterdam corridor. The subjects covered by the study are as follows:

-- Surface area used;
-- Energy consumption;
-- Air pollution;
-- Noise;
-- Safety.

Accordingly, this study mainly concerns the alternative means referred to above.

The environmental impact study (EIS) deals mainly with the project's location and technical alternatives. Its main object is:

-- To provide the information needed to select the route which will be least detrimental to the natural and human environment;

-- To suggest general measures that could reduce or even offset negative environmental effects.

It should be stressed, moreover, that the Directive of the Council of the European Communities of 27 June 1985 and the decrees enacted in Belgium by the regional executives in accordance with this Directive require an EIS to be carried out for any public or private project that could have a notable environmental impact.

4. COMPARISON OF THE OVERALL IMPACT OF THE VARIOUS TRANSPORT MODES ON THE NATURAL AND HUMAN ENVIRONMENT

4.1. Preliminary comments

This chapter compares the overall impact of the various transport modes on the environment. The results for international passenger traffic are those obtained in the comparative study of the TGV project.

It should be stressed that some of the data given below differ, sometimes substantially, from those in other reports published abroad. These differences are due to the fact that this study concerns Belgium and that the basic assumptions are not always the same.

4.2. Surface area used

4.2.1. Transport infrastructure

The surface area used for transport infrastructure is not directly proportional to transport performance. It rises in stages and mainly depends on the volume of traffic to be carried in the busiest periods.

The average width of the land needed for a railway line in Belgium is about:

-- 25 metres for a conventional double line;

-- 35 metres for a new double line of the type planned by the SNCB for the TGV project.

These figures take into account not only the track bed itself, but also the area occupied by embankments, junctions, passing tracks and station buildings.

The hourly capacity of a railway line closely depends on the structure of traffic, and particularly on whether through trains and local trains use the same tracks. Taking the number of passengers carried by the SNCB during peak hours on the major lines running to Brussels, the following capacity figures are obtained:

-- About 4 900 to 8 100 passengers per hour and per track when it is used by through and local trains (seven to ten trains per hour and track);

-- Up to 12 500 passengers per hour and per track when it is used either by through trains only or local trains only (up to fifteen trains per hour and per track).

In Belgium, the average width of a 2 x 3-lane motorway site is about 75 m. This width allows not only for the bed itself but also the area occupied by the central reservation barrier, embankments, interchanges, rest areas, etc.

If minimum traffic safety and flow standards are to be observed, it is considered in Belgium that the maximum permissible flow is 1 500 traffic units per hour and lane, or 4 500 units per direction and per hour on a 2 x 3-lane motorway (one traffic unit equals one private car).

Taking an average occupancy of 1.7 passengers per car, the capacity of a 2 x 3-lane motorway is 7 650 travellers per hour in each direction.

It should be stressed that this average occupancy varies with the time and day: for example, it is about 1.4 to 1.5 on working day peak hours (from 7 to 9 a.m. and 5 to 7 p.m.).

4.2.2. Vehicle parking

The area used for passenger train stabling in storage sidings is about 250 m^2 per coach. Taking into account average seat occupancy and reserve coaches, an average value of 3.5 m^2 per passenger is obtained.

A parking area for private cars should include not only the area of the actual parking positions (2.5 x 5 m per vehicle), but also the area allocated to access (entry/exit) and to movements within the car park. We thus obtain a total necessary area of about 23 m^2 per car, which gives 13.5 m^2 per passenger with an average occupancy factor of 1.7 passengers per vehicle.

4.2.3. Comparison between the train and car

The following comparisons summarised in Table 2 on passenger transport can be made with the use of the above data:

-- A double railway line gives on average a capacity equivalent to or higher than a 2 x 3-lane motorway, but requires two to three times less space;

-- With regard to vehicle parking, the rail passenger requires about three to four times less space than a private car traveller.

4.2.4. Case of the TGV project in Belgium

The length of the lines used in Belgium by the TGV trains operating the London/Paris-Brussels-Cologne/Amsterdam route will be 310 km, including 165 km of new lines. A total area of 645 ha of land will be required for the construction of this network.

This area is about equivalent to that needed for 85 km of motorway (it should be noted that from 1965 to 1980, for example, 890 km of motorway became operational in Belgium, i.e. on average about 60 km a year).

This area can also be compared with:

-- The 1 650 ha occupied by Brussels National Airport (including its annexes) where total traffic in 1989 amounted to 7 320 000 passengers (inbound + outbound) and 322 000 freight tonnes (including mail);

-- The 762 ha which were returned by the SNCB to the Belgian Government Property Department in the period 1985-88 and became available for other purposes.

4.3. Energy consumption

Energy consumption has been expressed in megajoules (MJ) per traffic unit for a comparison between transport modes. It is also expressed as a primary energy equivalent, i.e. it takes into account the efficiency of power stations and oil refineries.

The equivalence factors used are as follows:

-- 1 kWh	= 10.5 MJ	(primary energy equivalent)
-- 1 litre petrol	= 34.8 MJ	"
-- 1 litre diesel	= 38.2 MJ	"
-- 1 kg diesel	= 44.9 MJ	"
-- 1 kg kerosene	= 42.0 MJ	"

Average energy consumption on the SNCB network for train traction and heating in 1989 was:

-- 1.40 MJ per passenger-km;
-- 0.59 MJ per t-km.

Average forecast consumption for the TGV is 0.83 MJ per passenger-km, a figure which is substantially lower than for the SNCB's total traffic at the present time. The difference is explained by the fact that higher consumption due to higher speed is more than offset by a considerably higher average seat occupancy (65 to 70 per cent for the TGV as against about 25 per cent overall on existing trains).

The road transport calculations concern private car travel and goods transport by lorries and semi-trailers with a payload exceeding ten tonnes (i.e. vehicles that can compete with rail and waterways).

Average private car fuel consumption for intercity travel is put at 8.9 litres/100 km for vehicles running on petrol (about seventy-five per cent of the fleet) and 6.8 litres/100 km for those running on diesel (about twenty-five per cent of the fleet).

The resulting average energy consumption is as follows:

-- 1.7 MJ per passenger-km with an average occupancy of 1.7 passengers per vehicle (total traffic, all travel motives combined);

-- 2.25 MJ per passenger-km with an average occupancy of 1.3 passengers per vehicle (home-work trips only).

In goods transport, it is assumed that average diesel consumption is 35 litres/100 km for lorries and 45 litres/100 km for semi-trailers with payloads exceeding ten tonnes in both cases. The average load factor (including empty runs) is about fifty per cent (*source*: INS).

This gives an average energy consumption of 1.48 MJ per t-km.

Since no data specific to Belgium are available for goods transport by waterway, we have used the value of 0.6 MJ per t-km which was calculated for the Federal Republic of Germany and appeared in the report prepared in 1987 by Prognos AG for Verkehrsforum Bahn.

The value used for air passenger travel is 2.34 MJ per passenger-km. It corresponds to the average consumption observed at the end of the 1980s on Sabena's European flights of less than 800 km, i.e. on distances also suitable for travel by car or train.

Table 3 compares the various transport modes' average energy consumption per traffic unit. On the basis of the same performance criterion, rail uses substantially less energy than the other modes, with the exception of waterways.

It should be noted, however, that technical progress will probably result in a significant reduction in unit energy consumption over the next few decades. But this trend will not be such as to modify the conclusions that can be drawn from Table 3.

4.4. Air pollution

4.4.1. Main pollutants

The main pollutants emitted by burning fossil fuels are as follows:

-- carbon monoxide (CO);
-- carbon dioxide (CO_2);
-- nitrogen oxides (NO_x);
-- hydrocarbons (C_xH_y);
-- sulphur dioxide (SO_2);
-- lead (Pb);
-- aerosols (fine particulates).

These individual pollutants as well as those produced by chemical reaction in the atmosphere have a direct or indirect, immediate or subsequent impact on:

-- Health, by irritating the respiratory system, producing mutagenic or carcinogenic effects, reducing immunity to infections, etc.;

-- The environment, with the acidification of soil and surface water, the withering of forests, the increase in the greenhouse effect, the corrosion of materials, etc.;

-- The comfort of daily life as a result of odours, poorer visibility, etc.

In industrialised countries, a high proportion of air pollution is attributable to the transport sector, which is responsible for 50 per cent or more of CO, NO_x and C_xH_y emissions.

CO_2, SO_2 and Pb emissions from vehicle combustion engines are virtually proportional to fuel consumption and the sulphur and lead content of fuel.

On the other hand, CO, C_xH_y, NO_x and aerosol emissions also depend on other factors: CO and C_xH_y emissions are caused by incomplete fuel combustion, while NO_x emissions depend on combustion temperature. With no change in energy consumption, these emissions can be reduced by technical improvements such as catalytic converters, anti-soot filters, etc. As strict standards were adopted in the early 1970s and subsequently tightened, it has been possible to reduce emissions per vehicle-km considerably. However, the improvements seen in many countries have been practically offset by the continual increase in traffic and have therefore not led to an overall reduction in emissions generated by transport. Moreover, it should be stressed that it is one thing to lay down emission standards but another to enforce them. Stricter and more intensive controls than at present should therefore be introduced.

4.4.2. Comparison between transport modes

The data in Table 4 are expressed in grams of pollutant emitted per traffic unit (passenger-km or t-km) and correspond to the unit energy consumption figures in Table 3. In the case of rail, they take into account the air pollution caused by power plants using fossil fuels (about 30 per cent of electricity in Belgium is generated by fossil fuel power plants and 70 per cent by nuclear and hydro plants).

The passenger transport data are based on the results of the comparative study for the TGV project. Moreover, they already take account of the European standards laid down at the end of the 1980s for new vehicles and therefore of the substantial reductions in CO, C_xH_y and NO_x emissions to which they should lead. The goods transport data are from the study carried out by Prognos for Verkehrsforum Bahn and have been adjusted to the unit energy consumption figures given in Table 3.

Table 4, in which the data should be seen as orders of magnitude despite their apparent precision, clearly shows that rail generates considerably less air pollution per traffic unit than the other modes and that this advantage will remain when the increasingly stricter emission standards imposed on them and particularly on road vehicles have been enforced. The advantage of rail is also attributable to its low unit energy consumption and its extensive use of electric traction.

4.5. Noise

Traffic is a major source of noise.

Correlations drawn between the average value of sound energy (an objective and measurable concept) and the annoyance effect (a subjective concept) have made it possible to define maximum values above which noise creates annoyance that is recognised by the medical profession (hearing troubles, loss of concentration, stress, etc.). In the case of regular and continuous noise (road traffic, for example), the maximum values generally permissible by day are loudness equivalent (Leq) levels of 60 dB(A) or 65 dB(A) depending on whether the environment is rural or urban.

As regards discontinuous noise, surveys on the comparison of different noise sources have shown that the Leq can often exceed that of continuous noise by several dB(A) before causing the same amount of annoyance. In the case of rail, this advantage may be as high as 15 dB(A).

For example, with the same number of passengers carried and at a distance of 25 m from the infrastructure, TGVs running at 300 km/h result in a Leq of 7 to 8 dB(A) higher than that caused by road vehicles driven at 100 km/h. However, taking into account the advantage for rail mentioned above, the TGV creates less disturbance than the car.

Where annoyance is concerned, however, a general comparison between transport modes is not very meaningful:

-- Annoyance is felt only near the noise source, so the location of the source in relation to residential, recreational and similar areas is all-important here;

-- The relationship between loudness equivalent and traffic intensity is logarithmic. Variations of several dozen per cent in the number of vehicles using a given infrastructure therefore have little influence on the Leq measured alongside the facility;

-- Every day each individual is subjected to many kinds of noise which occur either simultaneously or in sequence, and their real level and effects cannot be simply totalled but must be considered in overall terms.

As a result of the environmental impact study conducted in Belgium for the TGV project, the SNCB has increased the protective measures against noise it had already planned. The outcome is that the total number of persons disturbed by noise will rise slightly and that the number of inhabitants disturbed by noise from traffic may even decline along the new line's sections that run parallel with the existing infrastructure (mainly motorways).

4.6. Traffic safety

Personal safety also contributes to the quality of our natural and human environment. It must be acknowledged, however, that traffic gives rise to many accidents causing casualties. The facts again show that there are substantial differences between transport modes in this area.

4.6.1. Definitions

In **rail transport**, the number of casualties includes all SNCB passengers and personnel killed or injured as a result of accidents occurring on the railways, so the total consists not only of train collision or derailment casualties, but also persons who have been run over by a train or been injured when getting on and off trains, etc.

The statistics have been compiled for a period of ten years (1980-89) so the results are sufficiently representative.

In **road transport**, since only those travelling by private car and goods transport are included in this report, the number of casualties comprises:

-- The drivers and passengers of private cars and commercial vehicles;

-- Pedestrians, as well as cyclists and motorcycle drivers and passengers involved in an accident with the two categories of vehicles mentioned above.

4.6.2. Comparison between transport modes

The data in Table 5 show that rail is much safer than road transport.

As regards rail, if account is taken solely of train collision or derailment casualties, the results are even better since the passenger fatality rate is 0.08 per billion passenger-km.

Data compiled in recent years at international level also show that air transport (excluding acts of terrorism) and waterways transport have a safety level comparable to that of rail.

4.7. Conclusion

The comparisons above show that rail is much more environment-friendly than other modes, especially road transport. Only the waterway has comparable characteristics, but it is used exclusively for goods transport.

Considering the foreseeable growth in personal mobility and in the volume of goods to be carried, a policy to increase rail's services and market shares wherever this is possible or caters for economic needs can only improve the protection of our natural and human environment, especially since many rail routes still have considerable spare capacity.

5. BELGIUM'S RAILWAY DEVELOPMENT PLAN

5.1. Preliminary comments

The fact that rail is now usually considered to be an environment-friendly transport mode is not in itself enough to encourage the travelling public and firms to use this mode more frequently. The explanation is obvious: individual behaviour is very seldom based on what is in the general interest, but rather on the quality, convenience, reliability and price of available services.

In passenger transport, the rise in living standards will mean that people assign even greater importance to journey time and quality of service.

In terms of rail traffic, this trend will result in:

-- An increasing demand for high speed, mainly over long distances, and more frequent services, mainly over short distances;

-- Greater insistence on the reliability of journey times (and so on published times) on information and courtesy at stations and on comfort during the journey.

Goods transport will continue to see considerable structural change as a result of industrial transformations at both the European and world levels. The forecast increase in demand will relate to the carriage of semi-finished and manufactured products and not heavy bulk traffic.

The concentration and specialisation of production centres and the fact that lower volumes of stocks are being held, thus calling for just-in-time services, are resulting in particular in the need for greater reliability in the logistics chain to ensure the continuity of the production/distribution process.

The improvement in (door-to-door) commercial speed, the reliability of forwarding times, the flexibility of the transport chain and the possibility of real-time data exchange between carriers and shippers will be increasingly important factors in modal choice.

5.2. The SNCB's ten-year investment plan, 1991-2000

5.2.1. Context

In 1989, at the request of the Minister of Communications, the SNCB drew up its STAR 21 programme (acronym for *Spoor Toekomst/Avenir du Rail*, i.e. the future of rail), thus setting out the major quantitative and qualitative requirements on the supply side over the next twenty to thirty years whereby the Belgian Railways might cater for the forecast increase in demand and expand rail's market shares.

The ten-year investment plan worked out by the SNCB -- approved by the Belgian Government in July 1991 following consultation with the regional executives -- is the first phase in the implementation of the STAR 21 programme.

5.2.2. *Overview of investment planned for the period 1991-2000*

The total investment planned for the ten reference years amounts to ECU 6 186.6 million (1991 values), comprising ECU 4 276.4 million for infrastructure and ECU 1 821 million for rolling stock (*cf.* Table 6).

The TGV project, which is scheduled for completion in Belgium over the period 1991-98, accounts for about 38 per cent of the above total investment and therefore also explains why it is particularly high.

This ten-year plan is evidence of the SNCB's aim to develop both passenger and goods traffic by rail and it has the support of all levels of government in Belgium. Moreover, since the central government is convinced that rail has an important role to play in environmental conservation policy and that the SNCB's projects are sound, it has also decided to make a substantial increase in its contribution to investment in rail in the 1990s. It will finance about 55 per cent of this investment, i.e. an average annual total of some ECU 340 million (1991 values), or about 50 per cent more than in the second half of the 1980s.

High as the forecast investment seems in absolute terms, it is not, however, excessive. By comparison, public investment (by central government, the provinces and communes) in the road and motorway network even exceeded ECU 2 000 million a year (in 1991 values) at the start of the 1970s. The total volume of investment in rail infrastructure for the period of the ten-year plan is not therefore even equivalent to the funds provided for the Belgian road and motorway network over a 24-month period some twenty years ago.

5.2.3. *The TGV project*

Participation in the construction of the northern TGV link (Paris/London-Brussels-Cologne/Amsterdam), which forms part of the high-speed rail network planned at European level, is one of the priority objectives of the SNCB and will enable it to increase its market share on international routes considerably.

TGV infrastructure works

The infrastructure works and the dates planned for entry into service are as follows:

Works	Dates planned for entry into service
1. Between the French border and Brussels Midi (88 km):	
-- Construction of a new dedicated 300 km/h line up to Lembeek (72 km);	1996
-- Laying of two new tracks (200 km/h) along the existing Lembeek-Brussels Midi line (16 km).	1998
2. Construction of a TGV terminal and a train maintenance shop at Brussels Midi.	1993
3. Between Brussels Nord and the German border (142 km):	
-- Conversion to four tracks with increased speed (200 km/h) on the Brussels-Louvain section (30 km);	1998
-- Construction of new line sections between Louvain and Bierset (64 km) and between Chênée and Welkenraedt (28 km).	1998
4. Between Brussels Nord and the Netherlands frontier (75 km):	
-- Modernisation with increased speed (160 km/h) on the present line;	1998
-- Construction at Antwerp of a new station and a tunnel under the town.	1998

Rolling stock deliveries are planned as from 1993 for the cross-Channel TGVs and from 1995 for the continental TGVs (Paris-Brussels-Cologne/Amsterdam).

The TGV project defined above could be further improved without detracting from the utility of the works already approved. If justified by traffic volume and growth, other works to reduce trip time could be carried out after the year 2000:

for example, a new tunnel crossing Brussels and additional sections of new line north and east of Brussels could be built.

Journey times and number of travellers

The completion of the northern TGV project as planned by the year 1998 will give a very appreciable reduction in journey times, as shown below in the case of a few major station-station runs:

	Present situation (average times)	TGV operation (project completed by 1998)	Reduction in journey time
Paris-Brussels Midi	2 h 40	1 h 22	1 h 18
Paris-Cologne	5 h 38	3 h 12	2 h 26
Paris-Amsterdam	5 h 49	3 h 29	2 h 20
Brussels Midi-Cologne	2 h 46	1 h 45	1 h 01
Brussels Midi-Amsterdam	2 h 57	1 h 59	58 mn
London-Brussels Midi (without new line in the UK)	6 h 55	2 h 35	4 h 20

The reduction in station-station journey times and the time gains obtained by increasing service frequencies (in theory at least one train an hour per direction is planned for TGV operation) will result in a very sharp increase in rail travel. The SNCB's traffic forecasts used in its TGV profitability studies are as follows for the year 2000.

	Without TGV	With TGV	Difference
	(x '000 passengers in the year 2000 both ways)		
SNCF-SNCB	2 750	5 130	+ 87 %
SNCF-DB	630	1 350	+ 114 %
SNCF-NS	850	1 450	+ 71 %
SNCB-DB	750	1 220	+ 63 %
SNCB-NS	850	1 500	+ 76 %
BR-SNCB	600	2 800	+ 367 %
BR-DB	400	1 100	+ 175 %
BR-NS	600	1 350	+ 125 %
TOTAL	7 430	15 900	+ 114 %

Moreover, after the year 2000, the traffic growth differential between TGV and non-TGV operation is put at 2 per cent.

5.2.4. Improvement of domestic passenger transport

Considering the foreseeable trend in transport demand and the increasing problems of road congestion around and in the major urban centres and Brussels in particular, the SNCB estimates that between now and 2010-2015, its domestic passenger traffic will rise by 50 per cent or even more compared with the level in the late 1980s. This increase will, however, require higher commercial speeds and service frequencies. For this reason substantial investment has been provided for in the ten-year plan, for both infrastructure and rolling stock.

Maximum permissible speed will be raised on a number of lines. The main routes concerned are:

-- Brussels-Ghent, from 140 to 200 km/h;

-- Brussels-Antwerp, from 140 to 160 km/h, as part of the TGV project;

-- Brussels-Louvain, from 140 to 200 km/h, and Louvain-Liège from 140 to 300 km/h (new line), as part of the TGV project;

-- Brussels-Namur-Ciney, from 130 to 160 km/h;

-- Brussels-Charleroi, from 120 to 140 km/h.

The capacity of most lines converging on Brussels will be increased by building one or two more tracks. These works, which will also partly come under the TGV project, will make it possible to step up intercity service during peak hours and increase capacity on the suburban lines.

The construction of a few **junction curves** will give considerable time gains on certain routes. Infrastructure works are also planned for the closer integration of the Brussels Europe Area (where the headquarters of the European Communities is located) with the SNCB network.

In order to improve passenger facilities, the ten-year plan also provides for an extensive renovation programme for **station buildings** and their immediate environment (including car parks and connections with other public transport modes).

Rolling stock is to be purchased not only to replace older equipment but also to increase comfort and speed, which are essential if more passengers are to be won over, especially to long-distance travel.

5.2.5. Improvement of goods transport

The SNCB has provided in its ten-year plan for substantial investment to promote goods traffic.

It will continue to modernise **terminal facilities** in the major traffic-generating areas: the Antwerp, Zeebrugge and Ghent ports and the Liège, Charleroi and La Louvière-Mons industrial centres.

A basic network avoiding as far as possible the main passenger lines has been defined in order to ensure a rapid flow of traffic on major routes. This network links up the ports, industrial centres and the main frontier points which have been selected after consulting neighbouring railway authorities. Its lines will be progressively equipped to take trains running at 120 km/h with a maximum axle load of 22.5 tonnes. The works scheduled for this purpose in the ten-year plan mainly concern the following routes:

Zeebrugge		-- Charleroi -- (France)
	-- Louvain -- Fleurus	
Antwerp		-- Athus -- (G.D. Luxembourg and beyond

Wagon stock will be progressively modernised and modified for a speed of 120 km/h with an axle load of 22.5 tonnes. This operation will result in more rapid service and meet requirements for traffic growth while limiting the increase in stock.

The future of rail also lies in a **multimodal approach** to goods transport. Accordingly, further action will be taken to promote combined traffic (rail/road and large-container traffic) which has already seen marked growth in the last few decades and in 1989 accounted for about 11 per cent of Belgian Rail's total freight (expressed in tonne-km). The SNCB considers that a twofold increase in its combined traffic by the year 2010 is a realistic objective. It will therefore continue to fit out terminals and gradually adjust its main lines to the C gauge.

5.3. Assessing the environmental impact of major infrastructure projects

5.3.1. Preliminary comments

In accordance with the Directive of the Council of the European Communities of 27 June 1985 and the decrees implementing this Directive issued by the regional executives responsible in Belgium for land-use policy, from now on the SNCB has to carry out an environmental impact study (EIS) for new major infrastructure projects.

The TGV project is the first major infrastructure project to be the subject of such a study in Belgium.

5.3.2. Environmental impact study of the TGV project in Belgium

The EIS on the TGV project concerned:

-- The alternative locations for the project (mainly choice of paths);

-- The technical alternatives for the project (how it should be carried out at a given site).

An initial series of alternatives had already been proposed by the SNCB in a preliminary study phase. Others were defined during the study itself.

The project was sub-divided into six geographical sectors on the basis of their individual line and environmental characteristics and competent regional authority.

An engineering consultant was appointed for each sector to assess the environmental impact.

In order to guarantee the scientific quality of the studies and their homogeneity, the SNCB also appointed a panel of experts (*Groupe Interuniversitaire de Recherches en Ecologie Appliquée* and *Groep voor Toegepaste Ecologie*) to:

-- Work out the EIS methodology;

-- Supervise and monitor the consultants' work;

-- Draft a report summarising the findings.

After an initial phase in which the paths to be examined were defined, each of them was described in terms of :

a) The reference situation, i.e. the probable situation assuming the project was not carried out. It was deduced from a projection of the present situation, due account being taken of the other projects under consideration and present or foreseeable trends;

b) The rudimentary situation, i.e. the situation that would arise if the TGV project were carried out with no other steps taken to correct environmental impacts;

c) The improved situation, i.e. the situation arising if the TGV project were carried out with realistic corrective measures being taken.

In each case, the environmental systems examined were as follows:

-- The abiotic environment: sub-soil, soil, terrain, water, atmosphere, noise and vibrations;

-- The biotic environment: flora and fauna, the relevant communities and relationships between them;

-- Agriculture, livestock farming, fish farming and forestry;

-- Urbanised entities: built-up areas;

-- Traffic and transport;

-- Scenery and cultural assets (archaeological, historical and architectural);

-- Recreation (leisure activities).

In addition to being described in practical terms, the effects were expressed as impact scores for each system and for the rudimentary and improved situations.

On the basis of the EIS conclusions, the SNCB adjusted its project, stepped up local environmental protection measures and submitted the proposed route paths to the regional executives which have exclusive jurisdiction over land use planning in Belgium.

The regional executives held a public inquiry into these paths and some alternative paths on the basis of legislation on regional land-use planning. Following this inquiry, they adopted the paths proposed by the SNCB, subject to a few adjustments.

5.3.3. TGV Fund for the communes

The implementation of the TGV project and particularly the construction of new dedicated lines will generate disamenities in the communes on the TGV route but without providing any direct benefit for them.

In order to promote the TGV project in Belgium, it was decided to set up a TGV Fund financed by the SNCB for works that would reduce the local disamenities caused by the construction and operation of TGV lines.

The cost of these works, which include the implementation of the environmental protection measures recommended in the impact studies, is put at ECU 276 million (1991 values). The breakdown of works is given below:

Type of works	**Costs** ECU millions, 1991 values
(1) Renewal of existing road systems to give equivalent service	111.1
(2) Environmental protection (noise screens, tunnels, structures, etc.)	129.9
(3) New facilities for access to agricultural land	3.4
(4) Urban and rural projects for the integration of the TGV path in the immediate environment (modification of the terrain, planting of vegetation, modification of the path of certain road systems, etc.)	23.6
(5) Reconstruction of communal mains and lighting systems	8.0
TOTAL	**276.1**
of which: -- along new lines	**190.2**
-- along existing modified lines	**85.9**

The above-mentioned works to be carried out along new lines account for about 15 per cent of their total construction costs, which leaves no doubt as to the SNCB's and Belgian authorities' objective of including railway projects within a comprehensive environmental protection and land use policy.

6. GENERAL CONCLUSIONS

The current prospects suggest that transport needs will continue to increase in the next few years, since it is universally accepted that a close correlation exists between economic activity and transport demand. Economic growth generates an increase in travel needs and, conversely, improved mobility for people and goods stimulates the economy. At the same time, depending on how well it is geared to requirements, transport supply stimulates or slows down demand and, therefore, economic activity.

Environmental protection is a growing concern and will take an increasingly important place in transport policy. In this connection, it must be stressed that rail is more respectful of our natural and human environment than other modes: on the basis of the same performance criteria, it generally uses a smaller surface area, consumes less energy and causes less air pollution and fewer accidents.

Railway undertakings realise that they are by no means able to meet the forecast increase in demand by themselves. They also believe that the development of multimodal transport is increasingly necessary and that their role can be expanded considerably in the following fields:

-- Passenger transport over long distances (mainly from 100 to 800 km) by using high speeds;

-- Suburban services for major urban centres;

-- Goods transport between major economic centres, particularly by developing combined traffic.

Rail traffic growth and the increase in rail's market shares will require a quantitative and qualitative improvement in supply. Railway undertakings and the SNCB in particular have therefore drawn up major investment programmes.

Achieving these objectives will also require active participation by the authorities.

With regard to **land use planning**, the authorities will have to improve living conditions in town centres and encourage the development of residential areas and commercial, administrative and industrial centres in places that can be easily reached by rail.

In the **environmental field**, the same standards must be applied to each transport mode. Extensive action will be taken, particularly in Belgium, to integrate new rail infrastructure in its environment and reduce the disamenities caused by the construction and operation of this infrastructure. At the same time, however, such action must not lead to constraints, or to an excessive increase in the construction costs to be met by the railways and therefore to a brake on their traffic growth, which would finally run counter to the desired effect. A priority for rail is its demand for the internalisation of external costs for all transport modes, or at least the explicit inclusion of these costs in policy options.

Government policy will also have to be increasingly based on a **multimodal approach** to transport. In this context, the problem of funding the construction and modernisation of infrastructure warrants particular consideration. Since such investment usually does not pay off immediately but is essential for long-term economic development, substantial financial support from the authorities is also necessary and justified.

TABLES

Table 1. **Trends from 1980 to 1989 in passenger and goods traffic in Belgium**

	Units	1980	1985	1989	1989-1980 %
Passenger traffic					
Trains (SNCB)	mio VKM	6 963	6 572	6 400	-8.1
Private cars (of which on motorways)	mio VKM	65 376 (16 060)	67 361 (18 130)	78 173 (24 315)	+19.6 (+51.4)
Coaches, buses, trams, metros	mio VKM	9 075	8 965	9 450	+4.1
Total inland traffic	mio VKM	81 414	82 898	94 023	+15.5
Air passengers at Belgian airports (inbound + outbound)	1 000 passengers	5 365	6 148	7 726	+44.0
Goods traffic					
Rail (SNCB)	mio TK	8 036	8 277	8 066	+0.4
Road	mio TK	18 311	22 106	30 394	+66.0
Waterways	mio TK	5 853	5 063	5 322	-9.1
Pipelines	mio TK	1 802	810	1 011	-43.9
TOTAL	mio TK	34 002	36 256	44 793	+31.7

Sources: ECMT and *Institut National de Statistique de Belgique*.

Table 2. Use of surface area in passenger transport

	Train	Car
(1) Infrastructure	double line	2 x 3 lane motorway
- average site width	25 to 35 m	75 m
- hourly capacity each way	4 900 to 8 100 passengers on a line with mixed traffic and 12 500 passengers on a line with one type of traffic	7 650 passengers
(2) Vehicle parking		
- area per passenger	3.5 m^2	13.5 m^2

Table 3. Comparison of unit energy consumption by the various transport modes

Passenger-transport	MJ per V-KM
(1) Conventional rail (SNCB traffic in 1989)	1.40
(2) TGV on the SNCB network (forecast for the year 2000)	0.83
(3) Private car (intercity traffic)	
- with average occupancy of 1.7 passengers	1.70
- with average occupancy of 1.3 passengers	2.25
(4) Aircraft (flights of less than 800 km)	2.34
Goods transport	**MJ per T-Km**
(5) Rail (SNCB traffic in 1989)	0.59
(6) Waterway	0.60
(7) Lorries and semi-trailers with a payload exceeding 10 tonnes	1.48

Table 4. Air pollutant emissions by the various transport modes expressed in grams per traffic unit

	CO	CO_2	NO_x	C_xH_y	SO_2	Aer
	(grams per passenger-km)					
Passenger transport						
Conventional rail (SNCB)	0.008	48.7	0.120	0.003	0.209	0.074
TGV on SNCB network (forecasts)	0.005	28.9	0.071	0.002	0.124	0.044
Private car in intercity traffic:						
- with average occupancy of 1.7 passengers;	1.038	126.4	1.367	0.168	0.084	0.046
- with average occupancy of 1.3 passengers;	1.357	165.2	1.786	0.219	0.110	0.060
Aircraft (short- and medium-haul flights)	1.266	210.0	0.588	0.198	0.078	0.028
	(grams per t-km)					
Goods transport						
Rail	0.06	n.a.	0.40	0.02	n.a.	0.08
Waterway	0.20	n.a.	0.58	0.08	n.a.	0.04
Trucks and semi-trailers with a payload exceeding 10 tonnes	2.10	n.a.	1.85	0.92	n.a.	0.04

Sources: *Mens en Ruimte* (passenger transport); Prognos AG (goods transport).

Table 5. Comparison of the number of casualties in Belgium by billion traffic units

	Passenger transport (casualties per billion v-km)		Goods transport (casualties per billion t-km)	
	Fatalities[a]	Injured	Fatalities[a]	Injured
Rail (annual average 1980 to 1989)[b]	0.61	36.80	0.28	3.93
Entire road network (1989)	19.87	907.12	4.80	133.22
Motorways only (1989)	7.20	164.20	0.66	14.80

(a) Person killed in an accident or dying within 30 days following its occurrence.

(b) The data for rail include persons who were slightly hurt but did not require hospital treatment.

Table 6. The SNCB's ten-year investment plan, 1991-2000

	BF Mio (1991 values)	ECU Mio (1991 values)
I. Infrastructure		
1. Replacement and modernisation of the existing network	46 577	1 098.5
2. TGV project		
- construction of new lines	53 997	1 273.5
- increase in speed and capacity on the existing lines which will be used by the TGV and domestic network trains	27 126	639.8
- Brussels Midi TGV terminal and high-speed train maintenance facility	3 329	78.5
3. Increase in speed and capacity on main domestic passenger lines	16 094	379.6
4. Improved passenger service at stations	6 722	158.5
5. Increase in speed and capacity on main goods traffic lines	13 449	317.2
6. Equipment and modernisation of goods traffic terminal facilities	9 174	216.4
7. Workshops and miscellaneous	4 850	114.3
8. Total infrastructure investment	181 318	4 276.4
II. Rolling stock		
1. High-speed train sets	15 121	356.6
2. Locomotives	12 307	290.3
3. Passenger stock (coaches and rail motor vehicles)	33 281	784.9
4. Wagons	12 082	285.0
5. Workshops and miscellaneous	4 418	104.2
6. Total rolling stock	77 209	1 821.0
III. Computers, general administration and miscellaneous	3 786	89.3
IV. Total investment	262 313	6 186.6

ANNEXES

Annex 1

Main statistical data on the SNCB

			1980	1989
1.	**Work force**			
	(Average total)		65 652	46 703
2.	**Length of lines in service** (as at 31 December)			
2.1	-- Single-track	km	1 408	895
	-- Double-track or more	km	2 563	2 618
	-- **TOTAL**	**km**	**3 971**	**3 513**
2.2	-- Non-electrified	km	2 558	1 247
	-- Electrified (3kV, direct current)	km	1 413	2 266
	-- **TOTAL**	**km**	**3 971**	**3 513**
2.3	-- Open to passenger and goods traffic	km	2 959	2 797
	-- Open to goods traffic only	km	1 012	716
	-- **TOTAL**	**km**	**3 971**	**3 513**
2.4	-- Operational at 140 km/h or over	km	455	676
	-- Operational at 120 km to 130 km/h	km	1 063	1 343
	-- Operational at 90 km to 120 km/h	km	1 220	744
	-- Operational at less than 90 km/h	km	1 233	750
	-- **TOTAL**	**km**	**3 971**	**3 513**

3. Rolling stock
(as at 31 December)

3.1 Locomotives			
-- Single-system		222	330
-- Multi-system		27	51
-- Line diesel		481	287
-- Shunting diesel		448	377
-- TOTAL		**1 178**	**1 045**
3.2 Passenger stock			
3.2.1 Number of vehicles			
-- Electric motor units		1 146	1 428
-- Diesel motor units		94	25
-- Hauled units		2 401	1 850
-- TOTAL		**3 641**	**3 303**
3.2.2 Number of seats	10^3	317	295
3.3 Commercial service wagons			
-- Number		42 876	28 973
-- Tonnage	10^3	1 525	1 227

4. Operating performance and energy consumption

4.1 Passenger trains-km			
-- Electric traction	10^6	47.7	66.5
-- Diesel traction	10^6	26.3	8.0
-- TOTAL	10^6	74.0	74.5

4.2 Goods train-km			
-- Electric traction	10^6	8.7	12.8
-- Diesel traction	10^6	14.3	8.1
-- TOTAL	**10^6**	**23.0**	**20.9**
4.3 Energy consumption for train traction			
-- Electricity	10^6 kwh	744	1 017
-- Diesel	10^6 kg	146	69
5. Transport performance			
5.1 Passenger-km			
-- Domestic traffic	10^6	5 899	5 515
-- International traffic	10^6	1 064	885
-- TOTAL	**10^6**	**6 963**	**6 400**
5.2 Tonnes-km			
-- Heavy bulk traffic (solid fuels, ores, petroleum products, quarry products)	10^6	4 544	3 938
-- Other products	10^6	3 492	4 128
-- TOTAL	**10^6**	**8 036**	**8 066**

Map of the SNCB network

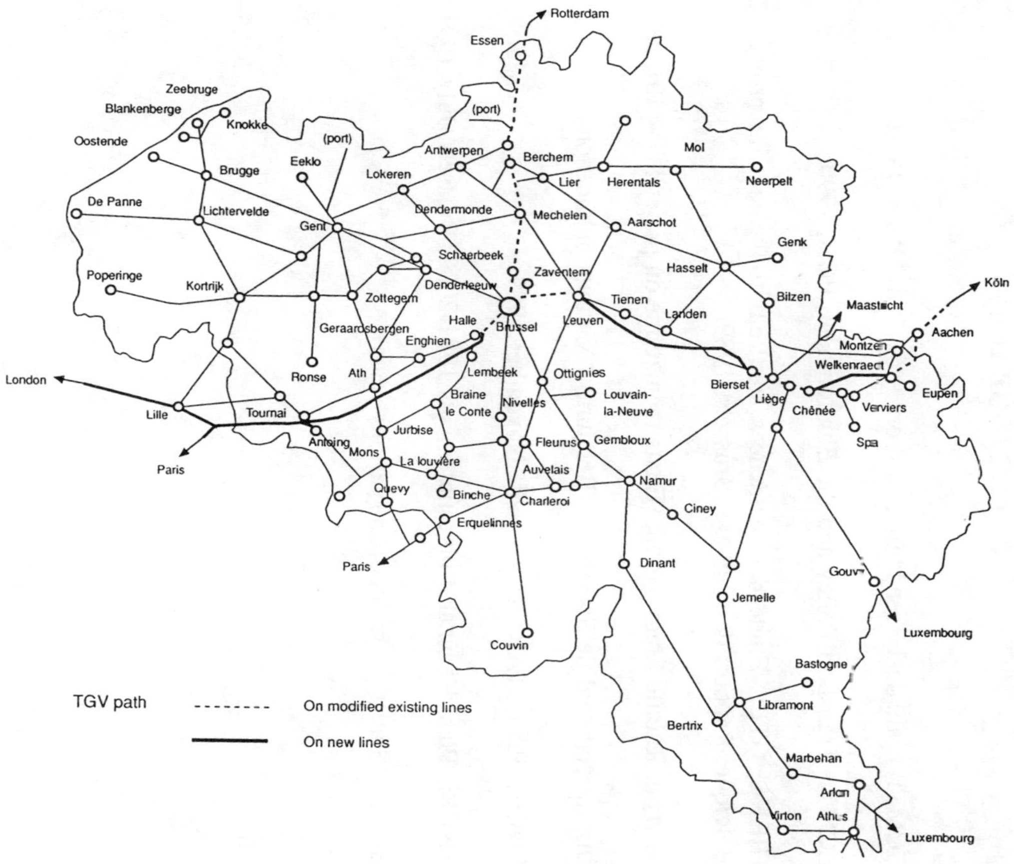

BIBLIOGRAPHY

ECMT: Statistical Trends in Transport 1965-1987, Paris, 1990.

ECMT: Transport Policy and the Environment, Paris, 1990.

GIREA, GTE: Etude des incidences sur l'environnement du projet TGV en Belgique. Rapport de synthèse, Brussels, 1989.

Mens in Ruimte Study group: Etude thématique du projet TGV, Brussels, 1989.

Institut National de Statistique (Belgium): Various publications.

SNCB: Plan STAR 21, Brussels, November 1989.

SNCB: Plan décennal d'investissements 1991-2000, Brussels, July 1991.

SNCB: Statistical handbooks (various years).

Sub-topic 5

ENVIRONMENT, GLOBAL AND LOCAL EFFECTS

J. SHORT
European Conference of Ministers of Transport
Paris
France

The views in this paper are the author's and do not necessarily represent those of the ECMT or its Member governments.

SUMMARY

Paris, January 1992

1. INTRODUCTION

That the environment is treated last in this Symposium may be accidental but is unfortunate since this has been the traditional response of transport policymakers. Environmental considerations may modify projects or policies but they are not central. Like catalysers they are added on afterwards. It is also unfortunate since it is essentially the environmental issue that prompted the title of the Symposium. Transport growth is a key problem since several environmental effects are directly related to traffic volumes. Indeed, even where significant environmental improvements are made, growth risks to swamp the achievements.

There is undoubtedly a growing hostility to traffic and its effects, whether it is expressed by blocking motorways, or traffic bans, or opposition to investment. This hostility is not everywhere the same and, as a recent car advertisement says, *"our love affair with the car is not yet finished."*

While the environment has become one of the major political topics in the last few years, the issues are not just narrowly environmental but also have significant industrial, social and economic aspects. The supply side interest groups are politically powerful, well organised and economically important. Consumers are often two-faced, favouring environmental protection in general but hesitating when they have to pay directly themselves.

This paper attempts to give an overview of how the growing importance of the environment is affecting transport policymaking. It begins by discussing the now widely known concept of "sustainable development". Then it looks at the measures countries are taking to reduce environmental harm from transport and the final section discusses the political challenges for the future.

2. SUSTAINABLE DEVELOPMENT AND TRANSPORT

The Brundtland Report (1) introduced the term Sustainable Development to a wide audience. Though there is no agreed definition, the most widely used is:

> *"Development that meets the needs of today without compromising the ability of future generations to meet their own needs."*

Somewhat more specific is:

> *"a process of change in which the exploitation of resources, the direction of investment, the orientation of technological development and institutional change are all in harmony and enhance both current and future potential to meet human needs and aspirations."* (p. 34, *op. cit.*)

These are very worthy but are of limited immediate use as guides to action. Despite this it is clear that development is a broader concept than economic growth and includes all factors that lead to increases in societal well-being.

Two main approaches can be identified in attempting to make these definitions more concrete. Simplistically, these could be called the "economic" approach and the "ecological" approach.

The "economic" approach puts the accent on maintaining the productivity of the total capital base (both man-made and natural assets) while the "ecological" approach focuses on maintaining the stock of natural assets.

Uncertainty about whether or not processes of environmental change are reversible, uncertainty about the risks and uncertainty about the possibilities to substitute man-made for natural products, are combining to shift the balance of political thinking more towards an "ecological" approach, though in practice most countries' actions are still very much based on an "economic", even "financial" concept of assets.

It is argued that the sustainability concept can be made more operational by paying particular attention to natural capital and by treating international aspects, in addition to attempting to increase the well-being of present generations. Thus, recent analysis concentrates on the need to transmit to future generations a stock of capital capable of maintaining prevailing rates of welfare growth. However, the extent to which reductions in the overall capital stock should be permitted and the degree of permissible substitution between environmental and man-made assets are unresolved.

While all of this is still not particularly concrete, the term "sustainable development" is here to stay. For the transport sector it is therefore worth asking what the concept might indicate. I do this in the next section and begin by looking at the link between transport and the economy.

2.1. Transport and the economy

Surface transport in Europe has grown steadily over the last twenty years and has been closely related to economic growth over the period. Table 1 presents data on trends in European economies and in surface transport since 1970. There are a number of caveats to these transport data; there are differences in coverage, the definitions and estimation methods vary; only surface transport is included and coverage is not complete, e.g. empty runs by trucks are not included. Finally, the GDP figures are for OECD Europe while the transport data exclude Greece, Portugal and Ireland for freight and Ireland and Luxembourg for passenger transport.

The data clearly show the close statistical relationship between transport and economic growth. Over the period, freight transport has grown slightly less and passenger transport somewhat more than GDP. In years where economic growth is greatest, i.e. 1973, 1988 and 1979, transport (especially freight) also grew most rapidly. Slower economic growth, for example in 1975 and 1981-82, resulted in freight transport reductions.

In summary, each 1 per cent growth in GDP has seen a concomitant growth of 0.93 per cent in freight transport and 1.24 per cent in passenger transport. Though not shown in the table, the corresponding elasticity figures for road freight and private car traffic are far greater. Each 1 per cent increase in GDP has been accompanied by an increase of 1.74 per cent in road freight transport and by 1.40 per cent in private car traffic.

Perhaps surprisingly, the late 1980s show higher elasticities than earlier periods especially for freight, as Table 2 demonstrates. The figures shown provide no clues to why this was so, but its explanation lies in a combination of factors like the anticipation of the creation of the single market, price declines with competition, changing logistical practices and more dispersed industrial and home locations. For road freight, for example, it is seen that about three-quarters of the increase in t/kms is due to longer hauls (6).

These overall figures for ECMT hide major variations between countries. Table 3 shows, for ECMT countries with data, economic and transport growth rates from 1970 to 1990. It can be seen that, in general, those countries with rapid economic growth also had rapid transport growth.

When looked at on a per capita basis for 1990 (Table 4), it can be seen that there is also a high correlation between the wealthiest and the most mobile countries. The five wealthiest ECMT countries, measured as per capita GDP at current purchasing power parities, are Switzerland, Germany, France, Sweden and Denmark, while the five with the highest mobility are Switzerland, Denmark, France, Sweden and Finland.

These relationships between transport and economic growth are important environmentally and politically. Environmentally, because transport growth is usually bad for the environment. Since road transport grows more rapidly and since it is the most harmful environmentally, the environmental consequences of rapid economic growth are of particular concern. Politically, by confirming that economic and transport growth are closely linked, they make it difficult to suggest that transport growth should be restrained.

However, the transport and GDP trends seen here are significantly different from those linking the economy to the energy sector generally. The "energy intensity" of OECD economies -- defined as the amount of energy needed to generate one GDP unit -- has declined sharply since 1974. Thus energy use and economic growth have become "decoupled". From the data shown, transport and the economy have become even more "coupled" and our economies have become even more "transport intense".

Published forecasts for the next twenty years from many countries indicate rapid transport growth, even in those countries where car ownership and use rates are already high. These forecasts tend to be based on the relationships described above, confirming the planners' views of the inevitability of transport growth when there is economic growth.

In this context the GDP concept is also limited since environmentally damaging activities can increase it. Nevertheless, it is a crucial transport and societal issue to find ways of increasing welfare without concomitant increases in environmentally harmful transport.

2.2. Transport and the environment

The environmental effects of traffic have been described (qualitatively at least) many times, e.g. (3), (4), (5).

Despite this information there remain serious gaps in knowledge about the health and other effects of present pollution levels; thus, estimation of the marginal benefits from air quality improvements (e.g. through improved engine design) are extraordinarily difficult, while the calculation of marginal costs is easier and concretely real.

It is also clear that the focus of discussion on environmental effects has been on the more quantifiable effects. There is evidence that the aspects of traffic that cause most annoyance are those that are less easy to quantify (6). If, as seems likely, these subjective annoyances are increasing, then even if traffic and emissions stabilize, new demands to reduce transport's adverse effects will arise.

Data at ECMT level on the environmental effects of transport are scarce. A document presented to Ministers of Transport in November 1991 concluded (7):

> *"as regards the quantifiable effects of transport on the environment, no reliable global figures are available. Because of rapid transport growth in the late 1980s and because, in many countries, catalysers have been fitted to only a small proportion of vehicles it is likely that total transport emissions of HC and NO_x increased. The timing of the turn-down in these emissions depends on factors like the rate of penetration of catalyser-equipped cars, the growth in traffic and the share of diesel cars and trucks in the fleet. With the widespread and rapid introduction of unleaded petrol, lead emissions continue to fall everywhere. CO emissions are also probably falling because of technology improvements. Noise has probably increased and there is little evidence that congestion has been reduced. Emissions of CO_2 certainly increased in the late 1980s."*

Contrast this with the United States:

> *"In the years after the passage of the Clean Air Act Amendments of 1970, considerable progress was made in reducing air pollution in the nation's urban areas. Average automobile emissions dropped from 85 grams per mile of carbon monoxide (CO) in 1970 to 25 grams per mile in 1988. Lead usage in gasoline dropped by 99 per cent between 1975 and 1988. From 1978 to 1988, transportation related emissions decreased 38 per cent for CO, 36 per cent for hydrocarbons, 15 per cent for nitrous oxides (NO_x).*

The reduction occurred despite a 24 per cent increase in vehicle miles of travel during the same period." (8)

Despite this progress:

"By 1988, 101 urban areas failed to meet national ambient air quality standards (NAAQS) for ozone, and 44 areas failed to meet the NAAQS for CO." (Op. cit.)

One can only speculate about the number of cities in Europe that would fail to meet these standards.

2.3. Transport and sustainability

Obviously, the environmental effects of the transport sector should be no more than man and nature can bear in the long term. Two factors are important in this regard: firstly, it must be remembered that many air pollution emissions are cumulative over time and secondly, a strategy of risk aversion should obviously be chosen since it makes little sense to test our systems to destruction.

One general principle might be that further environmental degradation is not acceptable. This would imply first, a stabilization of emissions and then, remembering the cumulative nature of much damage, gradual but steep reductions. Several countries have taken such a stance, either together in international agreements, for example, for NO_x, CFCs, VOCs, CO_2 or individually for other emissions like CO, CO_2.

However, such a principle is rather blunt. First, countries with small quantities of traffic or infrastructure may feel they can increase the damage they do to the environment, partly since they believe economic well-being will suffer if the transport sector is constrained but also since they say present emissions are at a low level. Moreover, though it is true that extra traffic will lead to additional environmental damage, the additional traffic may bring economic and other benefits. Firms locating in outlying areas may generate extra transport but will bring jobs and other benefits to the region. For this reason, traffic generation is still an implicit objective for many regions.

Nevertheless, attainment of existing international goals on emission reductions (CO_2, NO_x, VOCs, CFCs) would presumably represent one component of what sustainability should be. It is interesting that very few of the countries that are party to these agreements have sector-specific targets for particular emissions. It is not clear, therefore, whether transport is expected to reduce its emissions by the same proportions or whether more complicated arrangements will be made, e.g. involving equalisation of marginal costs of emission reductions.

For CO_2, an agreement along the lines of stabilizing total emissions by the year 2000 and reducing them 25 per cent by 2005 is being discussed. There is very little chance of the transport sector achieving these kinds of target, as Table 5 shows clearly.

Transport emissions have increased both absolutely (by 30 per cent) and relatively (from 23 per cent to 28 per cent of total CO_2 emissions). On this basis present transport trends are unsustainable.

For many cities, air quality standards are routinely exceeded, congestion is extreme and accidents common. Increasing car ownership is exacerbating these problems. Many cities now have worsening traffic and environmental problems, trends that are unsustainable.

In several areas, but especially the Alps, the amount of road freight transport has become unacceptable to the local population. Growth is consequently unsustainable.

The number of travel-to-work trips, alone in a private car, continues to increase in many places. These are inefficient in their use of scarce space, are environmentally harmful and pay neither the congestion nor other costs they cause. Growth in such trips is unsustainable.

A feature of both passenger and freight transport is that average trip distances are increasing. To what extent is this trend towards more dispersed location patterns for homes and businesses sustainable?

These examples show that large segments of the transport sector are growing in an unsustainable way.

Of course, the environment is not a new subject and countries have been taking steps to limit the harm transport causes. I now turn to look at some actions that have been and are being taken.

3. ACTIONS UNDERTAKEN

This section enumerates some recent measures taken in different ECMT Member countries. The countries cited are illustrative and it is quite probable that others also undertook action in the indicated domains. The information derives from a questionnaire sent to ECMT Members during 1991.

3.1. Air pollution from cars

EC countries are incorporating recent EC Directives (88/76, 88/436, 89/458) into national law. A new consolidated Directive 91/441 will result in equivalent standards for all classes of car. Other ECMT countries in the "Stockholm Group" (Norway, Sweden, Austria, Switzerland and Finland) have at present tighter emission standards, but a gradual harmonization is taking place towards similar standards. Catalytic converters will be required on all new cars in most ECMT countries from 1993.

As a result there will be significant reductions in car air pollution throughout the ECMT. Some countries are already seeing the downturn in total emissions despite traffic growth. Nevertheless, pressure to reduce emissions further will continue. A part of this pressure will come from the United States where the 1990 amendments to the Clean Air Act established yet tighter standards for HC, CO and NO_x emissions from cars and trucks. Under the Act, a clean fuel pilot programme in California requires the phasing in of tighter emission limits for 150 000 vehicles in 1996 and 300 000 in 1999 (9). The concepts of LEVs and even ZEVs (low emission vehicles and zero emission vehicles) have also been introduced in California.

One consequence for Europe of these developments is that it seems unlikely that the demands of manufacturers for a period of stable emission norms will be met.

3.2. Air pollution from trucks

New EC norms (91/542) come into force on 1 July 1992 for type approval and on 1 October 1993 for conformity of production. They will be substantially strengthened in 1995 and 1996. EC and "Stockholm Group" norms will be almost identical from the mid-1990s. This programme will result in the introduction of cleaner heavy goods vehicles virtually throughout the ECMT, in the latter part of the 1990s.

Nevertheless, for trucks progress has been slow. NO_x, CO_2 and noise emissions from trucks will remain a significant preoccupation since they will become relatively more important. Noise may be reduced but probably not below 78 dB(A) and heavy goods vehicle noise will remain a serious problem.

3.3. Maintenance and testing in-use vehicles

Several countries have mandatory vehicle inspections at regular intervals and/or at time of resale. These inspections focus mainly on safety aspects of the vehicle. Norway, Switzerland, Sweden, Germany and Yugoslavia have at present regular inspections of pollution levels. Belgium and France monitor CO at vehicle tests. The most ambitious programmes are in Sweden and Switzerland. Finland (1993), United Kingdom (November 1991), Portugal (1995 and 1998) and Spain and Hungary are introducing programmes of regular inspection, to include tests of some emissions. The Netherlands has a programme of random testing to check in-use compliance.

This is an area of great importance, especially as a small share of vehicles are usually responsible for a very large share of pollution. Introducing spot-checks on in-use vehicles would seem to be an essential additional element to such programmes, yet very few countries foresee this.

3.4. Diesel fuel quality

For most EC countries the maximum sulphur content of diesel fuel is 0.3 per cent by weight (87/219/EEC). Germany, Denmark, the Netherlands and most of the "Stockholm Group" apply 0.2 per cent. Belgium also intends to go to 0.2 per cent. Denmark uses economic incentives so that buses use light diesel (sulphur content less than .05 per cent by weight) and Germany states that the aim is to get to .05 per cent. A new EC Directive is under discussion and envisages .05 per cent in 1996. Sweden has introduced environmental categories for diesel fuel and the cleaner diesels have lower taxes. Turkey allows 0.7 per cent.

For central and eastern European countries, better fuel quality is central to environmental improvement. Without better grade fuels higher levels of vehicle technology cannot be used.

3.5. Investment policy

While it is increasingly being argued that all transport investment is bad for the environment, most countries and especially outlying regions still insist on the direct relationship between economic growth and transport investment, especially in roads. In such areas environmental considerations are not the limiting factor to additional investment.

Most governments claim that their investment policy is environmental as it focuses on the cleaner modes, or concentrates on reducing (or relocating) nuisances. The construction of by-passes or routes avoiding population centres (Portugal, Spain, Ireland) is the most frequently cited measure. Improved route landscaping and protection is also common.

Several countries concentrate on rail and combined transport investment (Switzerland, the Netherlands, France, Belgium, Germany, Sweden, Portugal). In some cases these investments will be very substantial, e.g. Switzerland where new tunnels at Loetschberg and St. Gothard will be built. A new United Kingdom programme to transfer traffic to the railways was published in May 1991. The Netherlands has changed its investment plans so that public transport investment will be increased and road investment decreased.

Investment in roads in ECMT countries, which declined about 30 per cent between 1974 and 1984, increased in the second half of the 1980s. Several ECMT countries are investing heavily in rail infrastructure and in some countries at the expense of road investment. Especially in urban areas, a more critical view of road investment is taking hold and the traditional cost-benefit methods are being increasingly questioned.

3.6. Investment appraisal procedures

The answers show that environmental appraisal (EA) is becoming more integrated in the process of project planning, and takes place at an earlier stage. Germany, in a 1989 Act that goes further than the 1985 EC Directive 85/337, requires that environmental impact be examined in the context of regional/corridor and land use planning. Countries now say that the EA has an important role in decision-making about projects. Consultation with the public and with concerned organisations is now widespread. Consultation takes place at an earlier stage than formerly and public inquiries are also a feature of many countries' procedures.

3.7. Urban traffic management

Several countries use direct measures to encourage increased use of public transport, including subsidies and investment aids. Amongst the examples are increased use of bus lanes (Finland, Denmark, Hungary, Ireland), increased investment (Sweden, Spain, Portugal, Hungary, United Kingdom), improved service frequencies (Switzerland, Sweden), better integration of public transport services (Switzerland, Spain), technical measures such as better fleet monitoring and synchronised traffic light control (Ireland, Switzerland, Spain) and park-and-ride facilities (United Kingdom, Switzerland, Spain). Switzerland uses "ecological subscriptions" to encourage public transport use. Belgium introduced a range of measures including fares incentives and integration of services to make public transport more attractive.

As regards the measures designed to discourage or limit car use, several countries focus on parking policies, including higher charges (Denmark, United Kingdom), restrictions (Finland, Hungary, Spain, Sweden) and intensified enforcement (Ireland, United Kingdom). The Netherlands will discourage car use through physical planning instruments, with a stricter policy on housing and office location.

The popularity of pedestrian zones is leading to their expansion in many countries (Denmark, Finland, Hungary, Portugal, Switzerland). Some countries (Denmark, the Netherlands, Hungary) mentioned improvements in bicycle facilities -- special routes and parking facilities. Zones with very low speeds (30 km/h) were mentioned also by Belgium, and France referred to the introduction of 50 km/h speed limits in urban areas.

Switzerland mentioned the intention to reduce the number of parking spaces available in several cities. France (Paris), Spain and Portugal, on the other hand, intend to increase the number of spaces available so as to help improve traffic flows.

This latter point illustrates that the perception of the problem is still very dissimilar. There are still many city or national governments that believe that supply (in this case parking) can be expanded to meet demand, even where traffic levels are already exceedingly high.

3.8. Economic/fiscal incentives

Unleaded petrol

Almost all countries now provide an incentive to buy unleaded petrol. Table 6 shows the market share achieved by sales of unleaded petrol in several ECMT countries as well as information on the price incentive that is given.

Price incentives, together with marketing and information campaigns, have resulted in unleaded petrol use rising rapidly in many countries. Southern and now eastern Europe are slowest to develop a full network. The effectiveness of the price incentive for unleaded petrol has been a successful way of convincing sceptical governments of the possibilities which economic instruments offer.

Catalytic converters

Several countries have given incentives to buy catalyser equipped cars (Austria, Switzerland, Germany, Finland, Norway, Sweden, Japan, Netherlands). The data in Table 7 show the size of the market for catalyser equipped cars. These data help to confirm the effectiveness of fiscal incentives, since the market penetration is highest in countries where incentives were provided.

This table also emphasizes the lengthy time lag before the measure takes full effect. This adds to the need for pollution checks on in-use vehicles.

3.9. Summary

It can be seen that substantial progress has been made in tightening emission standards and in improving investment appraisal practices. Moreover many traffic management measures have been introduced at local level. While these measures have had and will have positive effects, they have probably not been enough to halt the increase in environmental harm due to transport in Europe.

The next section looks at some policy issues that need to be addressed to achieve a "sustainable" transport policy.

4. POLICY CHALLENGES

Developing a more environmentally friendly transport system depends on a number of factors. I propose to discuss three -- the need for better information, the need to achieve acceptability and the need for a broader policy approach.

4.1. Information

Few countries have good data on transport and the environment. It is probably true that those that try hardest to collect and disseminate information are also those with the most active policies to reduce harm. This does not prove that information is a spur to action but there are several examples where new information on the environment has caused a rethinking of policy.

Most countries found it impossible to provide concrete factual information on what has happened in the two years since the ECMT Council adopted the Resolution on Transport and the Environment. Published information, including that by ECMT in Transport Policy and the Environment (5), contains numerous gaps and anomalies. Air quality information from cities, routinely available in the US, is rare in Europe.

Cities, governments and international organisations need to intensify their efforts to collect and disseminate comparable, coherent data on environmental quality and on transport's responsibility for it.

4.2. Acceptability

New measures need the support of those affected. Many groups are not convinced that they will gain from measures to reduce environmental harm from transport and therefore their opposition can be expected. The principal such measure being discussed at present is pricing and it is appropriate to say a few words about it.

That pricing should be used more as a means of regulating the total volume of traffic or its distribution has achieved a quasi-unanimity among researchers, academics and policy commentators. That pricing can work and can be acceptable politically is optimistically and persuasively argued by Goodwin in a report for ECMT on traffic management and the environment (10). Part of his argument is that the money raised through road pricing can "buy" acceptability (e.g. more road building, more public transport and more environmental measures).

So far, however, politicians have not been convinced and those places which have been considering pricing have not advanced much beyond that stage. Where there has been pricing, the reaction has not exactly been enthusiastic. In Oslo, opponents bombed the newly introduced toll plazas.

Of course, politicians reflect popular views. A major survey conducted recently for the EC and the UITP (11) asked a large sample of the population about their attitudes to public transport and to various forms of car restraint. While it is not surprising that the vast majority of people favoured public transport, the views on car restraint were more interesting.

Over 70 per cent favoured restrictions on car use in city centres. On the other hand, 65 per cent opposed road pricing measures and 80 per cent believed that increasing fuel prices was ineffective in solving urban problems.

An annual survey in the Paris area confirms this and goes further in that it shows a mounting opposition to additional charging for using roads. The proportion of people opposed to road pricing in Paris has doubled in ten years despite worsening congestion (12). A major part of this opposition comes from suburban dwellers who are not well served by public transport.

The scepticism of motorists may not be unexpected but perhaps more surprising is that business interests have not seen the potential benefits in terms of better deliveries and better services. These interests greatly fear that car traffic restrictions will reduce trade, since they believe that discouraged car drivers will probably not switch to other modes.

Convincing the population that pricing measures can work efficiently requires courage, time and effort. Because of this it is likely that such action will not be taken lightly or often. The traditional solution -- queueing -- will continue to be used in most places. The experiments under way, for example in Norway (Oslo, Bergen, Trondheim) and being (endlessly) considered, e.g. Stockholm or the Randstadt, will be followed closely by the rest of Europe.

I would now like to look at the role of two important interest groups -- road hauliers and manufacturers.

Road Hauliers

Road haulage is economically vital but is of growing environmental concern. Typical of some recent criticism is the trenchant view on road haulage from Whitelegg:

"The support of road transport by whatever means in the EC is a direct subsidy to an environmentally damaging activity." (13)

Reducing environmental damage from road haulage is a major challenge and will require, among other things, co-operation from the profession. So far it is sceptical. For example, the Secretary General of the IRU has written:

"Despite the constant tightening up of international regulations ... many ... are considered inadequate by ecological movements which are proving increasingly emotional and irrational in their demands." (14)

And yet, at the same time there have not been any significant extra costs.

"The regular year-by-year tightening of international standards on noise and on exhaust fumes has not so far given rise to any significant increase in the price of vehicles, as the cost of the new requirements has been easily offset by successive technological advances." (do.)

For the IRU, the solution lies in *"technological improvements to vehicles, road network planning, traffic control, better road infrastructures and improved carrying capacity and vehicle management." (Do., op. cit.)*

But:

"Additional vehicle production costs must be offset by improved productivity and technological progress." (Op. cit.)

In summary, hauliers do not like but can accept higher vehicle prices, though they expect something in return. They are more strongly opposed to increased operating charges (tolls, carbon taxes, abolition of refunds). The difficult competitive position of the industry (low profits, freer access) and its considerable influence makes the introduction of environmental charges politically difficult.

Price increases of 150 per cent and more have been suggested by some economists [see, for example, Summary by Gwilliam in (10)] as being necessary to reflect real costs. While increases of this order are not politically possible, ministers have given support to the idea that it is necessary *"to introduce systems of supplementary charging for environmental damage caused"* [ECMT Resolution of November 1989, see (4)].

In general, the profession could show more concern for the environmental problems it causes. For example, respecting existing regulations, maintaining vehicles in good condition and better driver training can all make financial sense as well as limiting environmental damage.

Manufacturers

Vehicle manufacturers have a crucial role but they cannot act alone; the framework provided by government is also central. So far, few countries have given signals to consumers that are strong enough to persuade them to buy environmentally better cars.

The differences between what is technically possible and what is likely, given present market trends, are substantial. Perhaps as much as a 40 per cent improvement in fuel economy is theoretically possible for cars. However, present trends towards larger, more powerful vehicles means that only a few per cent reduction is likely in the next five or six years (15). The recent announcement by the ACEA (Association of European Car Manufacturers) that they will guarantee fuel economy savings between 1993 and 2005 of 10 per cent, is welcome though it is a long way short of what is possible. While it might appear that the market potential for clean, quiet, fuel-efficient cars is enormous, consumer preferences do not yet favour environmentally friendly vehicles. Performance and comfort characteristics, not cleanliness and efficiency ones, are more important to the consumer. Prototypes with exceptional fuel performance characteristics exist, but the incentives for industry to produce them commercially are not yet sufficiently strong.

Governments are becoming aware of this. Consequently, in addition to further tightening of emission standards the introduction of various incentives (taxes, labelling, operating advantages) can be expected. This will not make conditions easier for manufacturers but it seems unlikely that their demands for long lead times and stable harmonized standards will be met.

4.3. Transport policy approach

For most countries, the transport policy approach to the environment is piecemeal and ad hoc. A few countries, including Sweden, Austria and the Netherlands, have comprehensive plans and numerical targets to reduce transport's harmful effects. In Sweden and the Netherlands these plans have been jointly prepared by transport and environment ministries and are "environmental" in that they set out specific targets for transport to achieve desired air quality standards.

Countries retain or even introduce policies that harm the environment. The pricing and taxation system provides many examples where transport or fiscal objectives run counter to environmental aims. Fixed taxes on vehicle purchase and low marginal charges for operation are widespread and encourage the use of vehicles once purchased. Charges per period of time for using infrastructure again encourage maximum use to get value for the charge. Many countries give travel incentives, usually for public transport, but sometimes also for car travel. The tax treatment of company cars is a prime example in many countries of where users pay no, or minimal, marginal costs. Public transport subsidies, to many an essential element of an environmental transport policy, mean that few users pay their full costs.

There are sharp differences in the statements that different countries have made. Contrast *"In the long term, measures may also be possible to reduce the need or demand for transport ..."* from the UK (16) with *"The simple need to ensure accessibility in major urban areas forces us to restrain the increase in road traffic ..."* from the Netherlands (17).

The lack of consistency between transport actions and environmental objectives is not surprising given the pervasiveness of transport, the range of objectives assigned to it and, until recently, the low priority given to the environment. In transport policy formulation, environmental consequences have been of secondary importance, drawn on as arguments to support decisions which had environmental benefits, but forgotten when the decisions went the other way.

Transport does not exist for itself. It is an intermediate good and consequently transport objectives have always been linked to objectives for the activities or locations which transport serves. Thus, transport actions have objectives in regional policy, housing policy, industrial policy, tourism policy and trade policy, even taxation policy. Moreover, transport is often assigned equity objectives and the "right" to travel has become a fundamental kind of freedom almost like freedom of expression or liberty itself.

Transport is a fact of economic and political life. Transport quality is highly regarded and often taken for granted. Economically, there is no first best solution which leaves everyone better off. Politically, we cannot start from scratch. People are attached to the benefits that transport has brought and to reduce them or even price them properly are not yet considered politically desirable or possible in many countries.

Transport ministers have an increasingly unenviable role. They are pressured on the one side by industry interests (vehicle manufacturers, road builders, trade and commercial interests) to expand capacity, to improve links, in general to meet all demands and now, on the other, by a growing hostility to traffic and its effects. Politically, this is a new position for transport ministers, since their traditional role has been mainly to facilitate traffic.

The dilemma for ministers is a reflection of society's double standards. We all wish to travel more without being bothered by other people doing the same. We all want a better environment and more mobility.

Faced with this dilemma we can see gradual changes in the attitude of transport ministers. First, some are beginning to argue strongly for the introduction of best available technology. This seems entirely logical since if emission reductions can be achieved technically less needs to be done in the political minefield of demand management. Second, there is a renewed emphasis on public transport investment and services. Many ministers are convinced that this is a sufficient answer, despite the mounting evidence that improving public transport attracts extra passengers, but not necessarily from cars. Third, some are taking an active part in encouraging research on new fuels or engines or on new ways of managing traffic. Fourth, some are beginning to say that private transport is too cheap, though few have made progress in reforming the pricing system to take account of the environment. The effectiveness of fiscal incentives, as on unleaded petrol, has convinced some countries of the case for making greater use of economic instruments. Fifth, there is a growing realisation of the institutional challenge that the environmental issue poses. As mentioned, some countries have brought together the various ministries (transport, environment, finance, land use planning, energy) to draw up plans for the sector. For many countries, however, traditional departmental responsibilities have been guarded and a co-operative approach has yet to emerge. Sixth, in a few countries, transport ministers are beginning to realise the importance of land use planning for mobility. It is right that they should insist on being party to decisions which may generate mobility. Transport ministers cannot oppose mobility, but it is entirely logical that they should insist that mobility does not damage the environment. Moreover, they should be prepared to propose minimum mobility solutions to land use planning problems.

CONCLUSIONS

Transport's effects on the environment are numerous and complex and efforts to reduce or limit these require actions in many domains. Comparing the actions in these domains by countries needs to take account of wide differences in the extent and perception of the problems, the existing transport system and the resources available. Certainly, most European countries have begun to accept that transport is a major and growing cause of environmental harm. Some have reacted more vigorously in trying to improve the situation but most have a relatively narrow view on what the challenge is. The threat of global warming has added a new dimension to the need to reduce transport's environmental effects. An international agreement to limit CO_2 emissions may emerge during 1992 to consolidate the commitments made within the EC and in some other countries. At present few countries have sector specific targets or plans to achieve CO_2 reductions. One thing is certain: with the continuation of present trends in vehicle use and purchase patterns, stabilizing and reducing CO_2 emissions will not be possible. New actions and policy measures will be required. These must include a strong push to take advantage of technical possibilities to step up the fuel efficiency of vehicles, but other measures, including carbon taxes, road pricing, land use measures and encouragement for other modes, are all needed. So far there is very little evidence of countries having come to grips with this issue. There is no convincing strategy to deal with the substantial traffic growth forecast for the next twenty years. Even countries with relatively comprehensive policies are finding that practical politics is forcing a more cautious approach.

REFERENCES

1. UN (1987), Our Common Future, Report of the UN Committee on Environment and Development, chaired by Gro-Harlem Brundtland, Prime Minister of Norway.

2. OECD (1989), this draws on an article by Jean-Philippe Barde, OECD Observer, No. 158.

3. OECD (1988), Transport and the Environment, Paris.

4. ECMT (1990), Transport Policy and the Environment, ECMT Ministerial Session, November 1989.

5. Motor Vehicle Contribution to Global and Transported Air Pollution. Michael P. Walsh and Curtis A. Moore; Paper to third US-Dutch International Symposium, May 1988.

6. ECMT (1991), "The Importance and Adverse Effects of Freight Transport", C.G.B. Mitchell, Freight Transport and the Environment, ECMT 1991.

7. ECMT (forthcoming), 1991 Annual Report, Follow-up to Resolution 66 of November 1989.

8. US Department of Transportation, 1990.

9. US Environmental Protection Agency, Summary Materials on the Clean Air Act Amendments.

10. ECMT (1991), "Managing Traffic to Reduce Environmental Damage", P. Goodwin, Freight Transport and the Environment.

11. International Research Associates. Eurobarometer 35.1, European Attitudes Towards Urban Traffic Problems and Public Transport, July 1991.

12. CREDOC, Enquête sur les conditions de vie et aspirations des français.

13. UNESCO, John Whitelegg, Impact of Science on Society, No. 162.

14. UNESCO, Impact of Science on Society, No. 152, pp. 115-125. A.J. Westerink, in Road Transport: an essential factor in economic development.

15. IEA, OECD. Low Consumption, Low Emission Automobiles, Proceedings of an Expert Panel, Rome, February 1990.

16. This Common Inheritance, Britain's Environmental Strategy, September 1990.

17. Second Transport Structure Plan, Netherlands, 1989.

TABLES

Table 1. Transport and Economic Trends 1970-90 (1970=100)

Year	Passenger Traffic (pass-kms)	Annual Change (%)	Freight (tkms)	Annual Change (%)	GDP (1)	Annual Change (%)
1970	100		100		100	
1971	106.6	6.6	101.0	1.0	103.2	3.2
1972	112.1	5.1	105.4	4.4	107.7	4.3
1973	118.3	5.5	113.2	7.4	113.8	5.7
1974	117.0	-1.1	116.6	3.0	116.2	2.1
1975	121.7	4.0	108.9	-6.6	115.2	-0.8
1976	125.9	3.5	115.0	5.6	120.3	4.4
1977	130.5	3.7	118.4	3.0	123.6	2.7
1978	136.7	4.8	123.9	4.6	127.2	3.0
1979	138.4	1.2	133.2	7.6	131.8	3.6
1980	141.6	2.3	131.6	-1.3	133.8	1.6
1981	142.3	0.5	130.6	-0.7	134.2	0.3
1982	145.9	2.6	129.5	-0.9	135.5	0.9
1983	146.4	0.3	131.4	1.5	137.7	1.7
1984	150.3	2.7	134.8	2.6	141.2	2.5
1985	152.6	1.5	137.0	1.6	144.9	2.6
1986	159.2	4.3	141.4	3.2	148.8	2.7
1987	166.5	4.6	146.5	3.6	153.2	3.0
1988	174.5	4.8	157.2	7.3	159.0	3.8
1989	180.4	3.4	163.2	3.8	164.1	3.2
1990	185.2	2.7	163.6	0.3	168.6	2.8

1. At constant 1985 prices and exchange rates.

Sources: ECMT, OECD.

Table 2. Annualised Growth Rates (%) for Transport and GDP, Various Periods, ECMT Countries

Period	Passenger Traffic		Freight Traffic		GDP
	Total	Cars	Total	Road	
1970-90	3.1	3.4	2.5	4.0	2.6
1970-80	3.5	3.8	2.8	4.5	3.0
1980-90	2.7	3.0	2.2	3.5	2.3
1985-90	3.9	4.4	3.6	5.1	3.0

Sources: ECMT, OECD.

Table 3. Transport and Economic Growth Rates (%), 1970-90 ECMT Countries

Country	Passenger	Freight	GDP (1985 prices and Exchange Rates)
Germany	55.0	34.5	61.0
Austria	44.0	50.9	78.0
Belgium	39.9	60.1	66.9
Denmark	61.1	14.8	52.8
Spain	119.1	162.7	89.9
Finland	78.4	63.8	92.6
France	86.8	12.0	72.1
Italy	135.9	142.1	81.5
Norway	90.6	145.3	102.2
Netherlands	86.9	31.7	59.1
United Kingdom	70.4	41.9	55.9
Sweden	53.9	31.4	47.1
Switzerland	67.1	60.3	117.1
Turkey	201.7	391.4	173.1

Sources: ECMT, OECD.

Table 4. Per Capita Transport and Income, 1990 (ECMT Countries)

Country	Passenger Transport (000 kms)	Freight Transport (000 tkms)	GDP(1) (000$)
Germany	10.8	4.5	18.3
Austria	9.9	3.5	16.6
Belgium	9.3	4.5	16.4
Denmark	12.9	2.2	16.8
Spain	5.6	4.3	11.8
Finland	11.8	7.6	16.5
France	12.3	3.4	17.4
Italy	11.3	3.6	16.0
Norway	11.0	2.7	15.9
Netherlands	10.7	4.5	15.8
Portugal	7.8	n.a	8.4
United Kingdom	11.1	2.8	15.7
Sweden	11.8	5.4	16.9
Switzerland	15.1	2.9	21.0
Turkey	2.5	2.1	3.3

(1) Current prices and PPPs.
Sources: ECMT, OECD.

Table 5. CO_2 Emissions OECD; 1973-88 (millions of tonnes)

Sector	1973	1978	1983	1988
Transport	596	688	665	773
Industry	1 037	994	857	923
Other	973	1 034	973	1 046
Total	2 606	2 715	2 495	2 742

Source: International Energy Agency, OECD.

Table 6. **Market Shares and Price Incentives for Unleaded Petrol (Mid-1991)**

Country	Market share for unleaded petrol June 1991	Price difference	
		(ECU)/l	%
Belgium	30	.04	6
Denmark	64	.1	14
Finland	50	.06	7
France	24	.03	4
Germany	77	.05	6
Hungary	6	.02	3.5
Ireland	25	.03	3.5
Netherlands	60	.05	
Norway	43	.08	8.5
Poland	<1	[2]	[2]
Portugal [1]	1.7	.05	6.8
Spain	2	.02	3.4
Sweden	55	.05	5.7
Switzerland	57	.05	7
United Kingdom	40	.06	8
Yugoslavia	1	0	

Notes:

1. For 1990.
2. Unleaded is 4 per cent cheaper than imported leaded, but 6 per cent dearer than local leaded.

Table 7. **Market Shares and Incentives for Catalyst Cars**

Country	Market share for catalytic equipped cars (petrol driven)		Tax incentives for catalytic convertors
	in new sales (1991)	in fleet	
Belgium	30		Yes (1)
Denmark	100 (Petrol)	5	No (mandatory)
Finland	81	5	Yes (2)
Germany	>90	21*	Yes (3)
Hungary			Yes (4)
Netherlands	75		Yes
Norway	100	8	No (mandatory)
Sweden	100	29	Yes (5)
Switzerland	100	45	No (mandatory)
United Kingdom	14.6	0.8	No

* Excludes former DDR.

1. 15 000 BF for 1 400 to 2 000 cc;
   20 000 BF for 0 to 1 400 cc.

2. 1 350 ECU tax relief.

3. For new cars the programme is finished. 550 DM to fit older cat. equipped cars with closed loop cat.

4. Lower customs (13 per cent instead of 18 per cent) and VAT are charged.

5. For cars going beyond statutory limits.

CLOSING ADDRESS

J. FERREIRA DO AMARAL
Minister of Public Works, Transport and Communications
of Portugal

Portugal is currently holding the Presidency of the European Communities, so it has been a very great pleasure to have received in Lisbon over the past three days the participants in the 12th Symposium of the European Conference of Ministers of Transport which is now coming to a close.

The significance of this meeting and the great interest shown in it have been clearly illustrated by the high scientific and technical level of the papers submitted and by the large number of highly qualified people attending which has exceeded all expectations, quite probably as a result of the fact that we are going through a period of profound economic and political change on a world-wide -- but more particularly European -- scale. These changes are reflected in the gradual deregulation of our economies and in the opening of markets, but they are at one and the same time both the cause and consequence of a faster rate of increase in movements of people, goods, services and capital.

This complex process of radical transformation of the economic and social realities has taken a number of forms. There is, for instance, the process of ratification and subsequent entry into force of the Maastricht Treaty, an instrument to consolidate firmer union among the peoples of the Europe of Twelve -- which is broadening its scope for action with respect to the economy and finance -- while at the same time providing for decisive steps in the sphere of social, political and security issues.

Under way at the same time is the formal process leading to the completion of the European Economic Area which will involve the extension to the EFTA countries of a range of Community norms that will promote greater inter-penetration of our economies in an increasingly broad and open geographical and political area.

Furthermore, the developments to be seen in the countries of Eastern Europe will make it possible to conclude agreements of association and co-operation between these countries and the European Communities. The Czech and Slovak Federal Republic, Hungary and Poland are already full Members of ECMT, and ECMT has also accorded observer status to the Community of Independent States, Bulgaria, Estonia, Latvia, Lithuania and Romania.

This climate of international change likewise includes the discussion of radical changes in the GATT which will inevitably lead to the reshaping of market organisation and the growth of passenger and goods traffic, a context in which it of course becomes imperative to analyse the problems arising for our modern societies as a result of such growth.

Our Symposium could not therefore have come at a better time since it seeks responses to these matters of concern by analysing changes in demographic and social behaviour, the rational utilisation of available resources, the location of points of congestion in infrastructure, the promotion and improvement of new technologies to increase the security of passengers and goods, and the conservation of the environment and existing energy resources.

We believe that the process of extraordinary development and profound change through which we are living must not be impeded through lack of capacity in the transport sector. Transport services must be geared to the new requirements while at the same time respecting the free choice of users and seeking solutions consistent with the specific requirements of each region.

The European Conference of Ministers of Transport comprises 22 European countries as full Members, five non-European Associate Member countries and seven observer countries, so it is an appropriate forum for discussing these issues in greater depth and for responding positively to the major challenges facing governments, enterprises and the general public where the development of transport is concerned. The work done during the past few days is a good example of what ECMT can achieve.

CONCLUSIONS OF THE SYMPOSIUM

A. BAANDERS
Vice-Chairman
of the ECMT Economic Research Committee

Mr. Chairman, *Senhor Ministro*, Ladies and Gentlemen,

"Transport Growth in Question", that was the theme of this 12th ECMT Symposium. We have heard presentations and discussions about demographic developments, social behaviour, economic developments and specialisation in transport, network capacity and access, the contribution of new technologies to efficiency and safety, and the consequences of transport for the environment.

Every participant will go home with his or her own impressions. I have looked at my notes and have concluded that I am not able to formulate for you one overall conclusion. The sessions have been too rich and varied; it would not do justice to the many contributors. Rather, I wish to give you some personal impressions, the ones that I myself will return home with.

1. I would like to formulate the first impression as follows: *A muito formosa cidade de Lisboa é um lugar ideal para a organisação dum congreso como éste.* (The very beautiful city of Lisbon is an ideal place to organise a congress such as this one). I am afraid my Portuguese will not get me much further, so I must change back to English.

   I am referring to the organisation, the hospitality, the many interesting things to see and do. But I also mean that we could have a direct experience here of the problems of transport growth.

2. The second impression is that the demographic and social developments in ECMT countries point to a continuing increase in the number of cars.

   The question is not if this trend will persist. Most contributors think it will. Nor is there a question of whether we can allow this growth to continue freely. It has been said that transport has become the victim of its own success. The concerns about the environment, safety, urban sprawl (the spatial organisation of human activities), and congestion have all been clearly stated.

   The notion of "sustainable development" is being accepted more and more. Technologies to reduce the environmental damage caused by cars are needed. But I got the impression that the most important question, and also the most difficult one, is: *through what measures should we limit car use in our countries?*

3. The third impression is that economic growth remains an important policy objective in ECMT countries. Economic competition is highly valued within and between countries. The wealthiest ECMT countries aspire to more prosperity. The less wealthy ones want to make up for the difference. And outside the ECMT we find large parts of the world that lack our standards of living even more.

   Transport is an activity derived from other economic and social activities; it is not a goal in itself. Therefore economic growth means a growth in the need for transport. Even if we put "transport growth in question", we do not put economic growth in question.

   As a consequence, the increasing need for transport has to be satisfied in ways that are different from those used up to now.

4. This leads to my fourth impression. It is a real struggle to find those different ways to satisfy the increasing need for transport. We have heard about:

   -- the prospects for technological innovation;

   -- the need for better spatial planning (urban and non-urban);

   -- the possibilities for network optimisation;

   -- the effects of specialisation in transport;

   -- the possibilities for better use of the transport modes;

   -- the pros and cons of combining the different modes, and so on.

   These all represent challenges that have to be met. But it is doubtful if these will be sufficient. It struck me that some of the participants, who have careers of twenty or thirty years in this field, found themselves discussing themes that they had already studied at the beginning of their careers.

   In market economies, the most logical way to satisfy increasing needs is through the mechanisms of the market. During the discussions, I suddenly remembered that I had been trained as an economist. If there is not enough supply of a commodity for which there is an increasing need, the price will go up, the theory says, thus limiting demand. But many contributors have noted that the real cost of using the car is going down all the time. Not all the costs that transport causes are paid for by those who consume transport. A part -- the externalities -- is transferred to others. The conditions under which the economic actors make their choices are not optimal. They would make different choices if prices were different. The statement that transport is too cheap, that the price is too low, was made several times. And no-one in this Symposium questioned it.

5. This explains my fifth impression. Government intervention, national and international, is needed to help the price mechanism. It was stated that there is a distorted equilibrium. Fair competition and efficient markets are only attainable if prices are fair. And that means including elements like damage to the environment, lack of safety and congestion.

This means taking measures that are, politically speaking, very unpopular. It was suggested that they are even more unpopular with the decisionmakers than with the public. But many feel that they are becoming more and more difficult to avoid.

If measures like road pricing were taken, they would have a great impact on the way the demand for transport is satisfied. The competitive position of the modes would change. The amount of need for transport that is translated into demand would diminish. It would cause the production and consumption units in the economy to use transport differently. New technological solutions would get a chance to develop which they would perhaps otherwise not have (and many technological solutions that might develop have been mentioned during the sessions).

However, we should not forget the international dimension to this problem. Because of international competition, no single country can afford to take measures that give others a competitive advantage if they do not take the same measures. Co-ordinated international actions are needed and the international organisations have a vital role to play in this respect.

6. My sixth impression concerns the transport research that is needed. It was generally agreed that it is not justified to hold back the political actions implied in the foregoing until more research has been done. Immediate action was called for. But I do not feel this means that research should stop. On the contrary, much research is needed to find the best ways to implement

those actions. But more cohesion between the different programmes was felt to be necessary. Here too, the international organisations have an important role to play.

7. The last and <u>seventh impression</u> is about the subjects that have not been discussed at the Symposium. We have covered the field very widely and thoroughly in these three days. We looked, in accordance with the character of ECMT, mostly at ground transport, but reference was made to sea and air transport. Still, we have not covered everything. Each of you will have your own impression of what has been missed. I will end by giving you my personal view.

-- The versatility of the truck in freight transport is as large as that of the car in passenger transport, when compared to the other modes, especially for shorter distances. How do we cope with this competitive edge?

-- If the use of cars is restrained (especially in urban areas), what kind of public transport must be offered as an alternative? I think that many actual public transport systems are better at generating new mobility (or turning pedestrians and cyclists into passengers) than they are at coping with the demands of the car driver.

-- Is safety only a concern to users of individual forms of transport? In many big cities, public transport passenger safety is also becoming a worry, e.g. for women (the group with the highest growth rate in driving licence and car acquisition) and the elderly (the group with the highest growth rate in the populations of most ECMT countries).

-- I have already mentioned the bicycle. In some countries, like the Netherlands, many people in the cities use it to travel to work every day (including myself). Those ECMT countries which have lost the habit of cycling, other than for recreational purposes, would be well advised to reconsider it.

-- Most of you have used a taxi during this Symposium. But we forgot to consider its role once we were inside this building.

-- Finally, we have seen that in the future we will have many more elderly people driving cars than we have now. You and I, for example. When talking about all those new information technologies in cars, are we sure that the elderly drivers will be able to use them?

That concludes my impressions of this Symposium. I would like to end by thanking, on behalf of all the participants, the organisers: the Portugese Authorities, and the ECMT Secretariat.

Muito obrigado pela vossa atenção.

SUMMARY OF THE DISCUSSIONS

C. PAULINO
Centre for Urban and Regional Planning
Technical University of Lisbon
Lisbon
Portugal

SUMMARY

Lisbon, July 1992

FIRST SESSION

DEMOGRAPHIC STRUCTURE AND SOCIAL BEHAVIOUR

Chairman:	A. Baanders (NL)
Rapporteurs:	A. Bonnafous (F),
	A. Van den Broecke (NL),
	D. Banister (GB)
Panel Members:	W. Brög (D),
	A. Marzotto Caotorta (I)

Mr. Van den Broecke began by agreeing with the other rapporteurs for this session about the main demographic changes taking place in most western European countries: populations are ageing and becoming more urbanised and prosperous.

He then described a new way of modelling long-term trends in car ownership (which can also be used for modelling long-term trends in mobility). This "cohort" model takes account of demographic trends, as well as external effects such as economic and socio-economic changes, thus providing a clearer picture of car-ownership dynamics and trends in the population over a long period. The cohort model examines the trends in two new ways:

-- The population is divided into cohorts of five birth years -- each cohort is then followed over time, instead of just comparing populations;

-- Decision units (singles and couples) are taken as units for car ownership instead of households as has usually been the case.

The concept of cohorts is similar to what Mr. Bonnafous and Mr. Banister call in their papers "generations", but cohorts pass the stages in their life cycles in different historical time periods, with different economic, social and educational levels. It also means that when age groups at varied points in time are compared, different generations and cohorts are compared under different circumstances.

Mr. Van den Broecke then presented some charts from a study for the Dutch Ministry of Transport where his model is used for estimating the potential growth of car fleets in the Netherlands in the next twenty-five years with different scenarios for economic growth, and on the understanding that there will be more older and middle-aged people in the future. This resulted in "unrestricted growth", to 2.4 million more cars in the year 2015 than in 1990.

Mr. Banister, the second rapporteur, pointed out in his analysis of mobility growth that it has increased in the last twenty or thirty years by nearly thirty per cent in terms of car ownership and traffic levels in OECD countries. He then summarised changes in travel patterns:

-- A steady growth in journeys made, increasing by 18 to 20 per cent in most western European countries;

-- Some trip rates have declined marginally (work and education trip rates);

-- An increase in other types of activities (social, entertainment, recreational trips);

-- Similarities between the aggregate journey patterns of men and women (16 to 59 years) and the elderly in car-owning households for non-work-related activities;

-- An overall significant increase in travel distances (up 42 per cent);

-- A strong correlation between mobility patterns and car ownership;

-- Distances travelled by those in non-car-owning households have remained stable.

These are the effects of what is known in the United States as "the motorisation revolution". The argument is that all age groups, particularly the elderly, have experienced the "motorisation effect" and this has affected both habits and expectations. The 1990s are the first decade in which the elderly have experienced full motorisation and this is compounded by the fact that individuals are now trying to maintain the ability to drive for as long as possible.

The conclusions reached are as follows:

-- There will be significant increases in car drivers and in the number of cars in the next thirty years, the trend being somewhat similar to the current pattern in the USA (about 550 cars per 1 000 population);

-- Much of this growth will take place in households already owning one car;

-- For men aged 20 to 70, the proportion of licence holders will probably remain stable, at about 85-90 per cent. The highest growth will be in the youngest and in the elderly age groups.

-- For women, growth is likely to be significant across all age groups, to somewhere between 70-80 per cent. The greater access of women to cars as drivers is likely to be a major source of new travel;

-- Young people will have greater expectations and will also aspire to car ownership, with a significant increase in demand for travel;

-- Perhaps the most important area of growth in demand for travel will be among the elderly, in view of the trend towards keeping their cars as long as possible, the significant growth that will occur in the number of elderly people and the major changes in this group with highly mobile, affluent elderly car drivers.

By means of dynamic analysis, some idea can be obtained of the range of increase that is likely to take place in travel among the elderly over the next fifteen years:

-- The number of journeys undertaken will increase by 23 to 24 per cent;

-- Distance will increase by 30 to 50 per cent;

-- There will be a switch in terms of modal choice from public transport to car use.

Many factors will prompt growth in car ownership:

-- The demographic factors already mentioned;

-- Young adults who still live with their parents but have their own car;

-- Increasing female participation in the labour force, leading to greater affluence, greater independence and car ownership.

-- A decline in household size (by about 20 per cent in Europe over the last thirty years, partly owing to lower fertility rates and a breakdown of the family unit) leading to increases in car ownership;

-- Suburbanisation, greater complexity of work journeys, the patterns of daily movement will be much more varied, making it difficult to provide public transport facilities;

-- Increased leisure time, estimated to be one of the largest areas of growth over the next 10-15 years;

-- Higher levels of affluence brought about by increases in real income levels and rising levels of inherited wealth will also result in growth in car ownership.

-- Migration, the great unknown, resulting from the Single European Market, the breaking down of barriers between East and West and the moving of populations.

This leads to the question: how can public transport in fact react to these fundamental demographic and other changes that are taking place in society? The traditional markets for public transport have diminished and new markets must be sought:

-- Greater priority should be given to public transport in urban areas;

-- The quality of public transport must be improved, with much higher quality services and integration of rail and bus services;

-- The design of public transport must be improved, particularly for the elderly age group; the vehicles must be made as user-friendly as the car;

-- The potential for public transport as a leisure mode should be exploited, and it should be used for cultural events or organised tours.

Mr. Bonnafous presented some graphs to illustrate certain trends:

-- Households with one car or more use public transport less than those without a car;

-- People from different income categories have different levels of car ownership;

-- The phenomenon of urban growth is tending to slow down or even be reversed, while rural communes are growing;

-- The phenomenon of growth into larger urban areas does not result in economies of scale in public transport; using a Quin-Quin model, it is possible to show that if a town increases in size by ten per cent, the number of trips offered by public transport needs to increase by much more than ten per cent (a logarithmic relation);

-- In areas with urban spread, the response of public transport will not be sufficient to cope with the situation adequately, so it will be necessary to invest in other types of solutions.

Mr. Marzotto Caotorta was the first panel member to take the floor. He pointed out that there are four very precise reasons for attaching greater importance to public transport:

i) Space: our towns are short of road space for parking cars, so it is necessary to reduce the number of cars occupying the space because public space should be used for mobility, not parking;

ii) Pollution: air or noise pollution is one of the main problems in our towns;

iii) Fuel consumption: in the last thirteen years fuel expenditure in Italy has risen from 8.5 billion liras in 1977 to 32 billion liras in 1990, and 40 per cent of this fuel is consumed in towns;

iv) Safety: 70 per cent of accidents occur in towns.

He concluded by stressing that mobility is a right, recognised in our constitutions, just as is education or health.

Mr. Brög had four comments, the first concerning the concept of mobility. Mobility is not a purpose in itself but a means of conducting activities outside of the home. This definition of mobility covers all vehicles, even non-motorised ones. If people have to travel greater distances to carry out their activities than in the past, perhaps mobility measured in travel distance is not truly positive. In the same way, changes in the traffic situation in the last twenty years (pedestrian numbers have declined and motorists are increasing) have led to a reduction in pedestrian areas.

Secondly, he pointed out that our behaviour is based on social standards and values. One of these standards is to consider the car as a symbol of human freedom. This car-oriented view is now a source of many errors of assessment. A high-speed train can reach the same destination as quickly as a car, and the time involved can be used more efficiently. In the former Federal Republic of Germany, ten per cent of the trips made by car are no longer than one kilometre, fifty per cent are no more than three kilometres and most trips reach their destination after five minutes.

Thirdly, he said that the assumption that people's mentalities never change is unduly rigid. Some 70 per cent of city car trips can be made by alternative forms of travel and the present change in public attitudes may well be more far-reaching than the decision-makers think.

Lastly, Mr. Brög turned to pollution. Future generations will realise that the two generations existing today have exploited the environment in an irreparable way. Any policy reflecting this thinking would certainly lead to a reduction in motor traffic.

One aspect focused on in the general discussion was the fact that transport problems cannot be separated from those of towns. Since the Second World War, it has tended to be the policy to favour individual transport and individual houses, both of which require more space than traditional towns can offer, thus leading to changes in the urban system. In this connection, Mr. Bonnafous said that policymakers no longer have a real choice. There is a crisis in public transport in terms of both congestion and funding, so policymakers will have to take measures to regulate and manage the system. He thinks that the most reasonable solution will be through pricing (parking fees, urban tolls, etc.) to prevent cars from entering towns.

According to Mr. Brög, in order to solve this problem it is necessary to see mobility in an integrated way, incorporating all vehicles that can provide a substitute for the motor car (e.g. public transport, bicycle, etc.). In Germany, the view is that three groups of measures have to be envisaged:

i) "Push" measures, which make driving more difficult (speed limits, parking fees, etc.);

ii) "Pull" measures, which make other forms of transport more attractive;

iii) Measures to influence people's attitudes; providing information and incentives to change.

Only with these three groups of measures working in harmony is it possible to have soft policies. Such policies have to be focused not only on citizens, but essentially the decision-makers in towns and regions: politicians, planners and those shaping public opinion. In cities where such measures are taken, changes really do occur, even within a short time.

Mr. Banister said that the traditional role which governments have taken in decision-making has been through direct intervention (financing and fiscal policy, regulation, safety, etc.) and that there are two other areas where government intervention may also be crucially important:

-- Taking steps to convince people of the value of having different sets of attitudes, different sets of responsibilities towards the car, but also to convince the public of the acceptability of policies such as pricing and limitations on the freedom to use cars;

-- Giving clear signs to industry as to what they intend to do; this affects all industries and businesses -- not just the transport industry -- in terms of objectives such as reducing energy consumption and reducing levels of mobility.

Action along these two lines would allow sufficient lead time for the policies to be introduced effectively.

SECOND SESSION

ECONOMIC TRENDS AND TRANSPORT SPECIALISATION

Chairman:	P. Goodwin (GB)
Rapporteurs:	M. Turró (E),
	M. Nordström (S),
	C. Kaspar (CH)
Panel Members:	J.-C. Houtmeyers (B),
	A. Gaspar Rodrigues (P),

Opening the session, Mr. Goodwin, the Chairman, drew attention to one way in which this topic and the previous one interrelate in that the lesson to be drawn from the first session is that today's social behaviour cannot be used as a model for tomorrow's because the world is always changing. Changes are occurring in many other areas: in legal rights, in transport theory, in policy and, as regards the present topic, in the economic factors that influence all these behavioural and policy questions.

Mr. Turró, the first rapporteur, highlighted the major factors leading to the most dramatic changes within western Europe:

-- External migration, in the short term from eastern countries and in the longer term from less-developed countries in the Mediterranean area;

-- Internal migration towards the southern regions of the Community, where a higher quality of life can be expected;

-- The crisis of the megalopolis, the major urban areas which are unable to cope with congestion and social decay, and the consequent appearance of a "mesh" of intermediate cities, forming a new motor of economic development in the territory;

-- Technological breakthroughs are also to be expected -- more efficient vehicles will be developed which will curb the prospective negative impacts on energy conservation and the environment;

-- Automation and information technology will contribute to improved capacity utilisation and reduce accidents and pollution;

-- New construction techniques, especially in tunnelling, should help to curb the increase in infrastructure costs attributable to the shortage of space and environmental constraints;

-- Specialisation in intermodal co-ordination will make the transport system more efficient.

Nevertheless, many constraints prevent the establishment of a truly efficient European transport system, such as missing links (particularly in frontier regions where they clearly have a negative impact on market integration), congestion and severe market distortions (payment for infrastructure, costs, taxation, subsidies, etc.).

The funds needed to cope with the growing requirements of the system have been estimated at some 300 to 400 billion ECU over the next ten years within the Community alone.

Mr. Turró concluded by setting out the major steps that have to be taken in order to convert the present transport system:

-- There is an urgent need to frame pan-European transport policies;

-- Appropriate planning strategies have to be determined with clear-cut mechanisms for the European, national, regional and local levels;

-- The harmonization process has to be speeded up, mostly in technical, fiscal and administrative matters, due allowance being made for the proper use of liberalization measures;

-- Adequate funding mechanisms have to be established to cope with the foreseeable increase in investment in the system;

-- A substantial increase is called for in the resources allocated to planning, information and research in this sector.

Mr. Nordström focused on four points. As regards the first -- the process of economic growth -- he described the development of international trade from past to present times, saying that industrialism and the subsequent development of industrial enterprise is a function of intensive specialisation and that this last has moved from a local level to a regional, national and, today, global level.

The second point -- the growth of commerce and transport -- relates to the expansion of economic activity and transport. Gross National Product in Europe has risen by around two per cent per year, while trade and transport have increased by about four per cent per year.

Thirdly, Mr. Nordström indicated some parallels and differences between transport and industrial development. The industrial sector has become increasingly specialised, and this process is now to be found in the transport sector. However, industrial production has in many cases been market oriented on a global scale, while the transport sector has been local and regulated in many respects.

Lastly, as regards the immediate future and ways of learning from different sectors, Mr. Nordström said that the same patterns of thinking found in industry for the past two hundred years will now play a part in discussions on the transport sector. Transport will be more specialised and will have a global market. There will be ever more noticeable similarities between transport and industry. The transport sector will increasingly become one of the many businesses that are subject to global development and global competition. Government will exercise little control.

Mr. Kaspar, the last rapporteur of this session, said that the development of transport has accompanied that of the economy in four stages: integration, expansion, intensification and specialisation. The increase in competition and the spectacular results of technological development have led to improvements in the supply of transport services, which has called for high capital input.

This has also entailed the rationalisation of transportation processes (automatic coupling systems, etc.), improvements in road safety, higher speeds (supersonic aircraft, high-speed trains) and increases in transport capacity (supertankers, block trains) and supply.

Organisational measures taken by international and national transport enterprises as regards tariff levels, container transport pricing and differential legal bases (in line and charter services) have certainly benefited from these developments. New carriers, new transport techniques and a new and better organisation of transportation procedures have led to a better division of labour and specialisation of the economy. The just-in-time concept is an example that shows the possible rationalisation with a strong increase in time-sensitive and smaller shipments.

Mr. Houtmeyers, the first panel member, said that transport has become a victim of its own success, but that the maintenance of an acceptable supply of traffic is indispensable to our way of life. The great increase in road transport is the best response to the need for flexibility and comfort, even if people have slowly become aware of the social disadvantages entailed.

Freight transport has developed in a similar way. Concepts, such as just-in-time, mean that stock costs are reflected in transport, and a larger capacity is needed on the part of transport systems to respond to these requirements. Road transport has reacted rapidly in a very flexible way to this new type of industrial logistic.

The new response, in terms of challenge for mobility for the year 2000 will require action on the part of all politicians (at national, regional and local levels) and a co-ordinated approach at international level. Unduly radical measures can have perverse effects, and measures which are too limited will be inadequate. Balanced development is necessary and should be encouraged by the ECMT Ministers of Transport.

Commenting on the reports presented, Mr. Gaspar Rodrigues said that, while management was naturally concerned with reducing costs and guaranteeing quality, companies and individuals are increasingly attracted by what he called "offers of comfort". The interlinking of modes of transport will be needed not only by customers but also by companies to increase profits.

Mr. Gaspar Rodrigues agreed with Mr. Turró about harmonization leading to liberalization. He thought, however, that greater liberalization and greater deregulation are good, while fierce competition without any control cannot be allowed. Speaking of Mr. Nordström's presentation, he said that the connection between industry and transport can take two different forms:

-- Certain types of company can hand over the organisation of the transport to specialised firms;

-- Specific sectors of activity, which establish contract prices to place their goods with customers, do so by using their own transport fleet or by subcontracting transport managed by the producers.

These two types of systems will be maintained in the future.

Regarding Mr. Kaspar's statements, Mr. Gaspar Rodrigues emphasized some key aspects: the growing organisation of transport operations with the application of new information and communications technologies, and the logistics of transport which must be global. The actual customers of transport are not interested in the individual aspects of transport. They prefer global solutions, including all the different operations upstream and downstream. This is what Mr. Gaspar Rodrigues called the concept of comfort, and the concept of price being an important factor will have to respond to this new concept of comfort.

One of the main points brought up in the discussion was the question of transport prices. One participant said that a prerequisite for an improvement in the transport situation is the acceptance that all motorised transport is greatly under-priced and that extensive structural changes are required in order to move the current low level of transport prices to something more in line with the long-run marginal cost. This is where it is necessary to have international co-operation, in having targets for greatly increasing the cost of transport over a long period. This must be agreed at an international level, otherwise there is the danger of unfair competitive advantages among different countries.

Other participants have asked how to implement the social margin tariff, based on a true knowledge of costs which are very complex, and what the effect might be for the development of industry if transport prices rose.

The just-in-time system was the other main subject in the discussion. One participant pointed out that just-in-time is based on an economic system which can make good use of space with low costs and reliability and which allows enterprises to limit stocks as much as possible. With the congestion of transport infrastructures and the environmental aspects which imply added external costs, transport becomes more expensive and less reliable. Under these conditions, will those companies with logistic layouts based on just-in-time concepts keep their layouts and think about their location, their labour and consumer markets, or will they change their systems?

Mr. Kaspar thought that the future development of just-in-time has to remain open to question, since the system is very fragile, both for traffic and enterprises. He doubted whether the system would expand very much in the future.

Mr. Turró saw two different perspectives: micro and macro. At the microscopic level there are the just-in-time systems and firms interested in improving their efficiency, which means they will take the most that they can get from the system. There are also technologies and different types of systems that will improve the performance of the system for companies and private users. This micro approach to efficiency in the transport system, where the distortions are enormous, does not provide overall economic efficiency. What is needed at the political level is to have a new approach to transport. A harmonization process will have to be implemented to allow for liberalization. It is necessary to have a global planning approach.

The empty runs issue in road transport was approached by a participant when he asked how to reconcile the need to reduce these empty runs with the fact that transport had become increasingly specialised.

Mr. Nordström thought that we shall in future see a trend whereby industries move to new industrial regions, just as industries earlier moved from city centres to suburbs and other areas. This can reduce the number of empty runs, and if just-in-time will not function in certain regions, industries will move elsewhere.

THIRD SESSION

INFRASTRUCTURE CAPACITY AND NETWORK ACCESS

Chairman: J. M. Consiglieri Pedroso (P)
Rapporteurs: R. Izquierdo (E),
R. Marche (F),
H. Priemus (NL)
Panel Members: W. Winkelmans (B),
D. Bjørnland (N)

Accessibility was Mr. Izquierdo's topic. The concept of accessibility was introduced and developed in the transport sector at the end of the seventies and the beginning of the eighties, since when it has become a planning instrument for transport policy. Given the new socio-economic context and the new European economic space, it will become a very useful instrument for providing economic and social cohesion.

The policy adopted up to now for infrastructures has been based on gearing those that exist to demand. This gives rise to an important concentration of investment in certain areas or on specific axes in the emerging cities, which have now become diseconomies and have had a suction effect, producing very unbalanced centres.

Economic and social cohesion should be strengthened, which implies a very clear political will and greater solidarity in order to construct a more balanced area, thanks to better integration of the periphery. It is necessary to strengthen the Mediterranean axis which is now beginning to emerge spontaneously as an axis with a clear European "sun-belt" vocation. Accordingly, it is first necessary to define, in the Community or in Europe, a new territorial model where the network provided will allow good access to the peripheral regions.

Any infrastructure policy which aims to improve the interconnection of regions initially requires a clear knowledge of average accessibility by using pre-established indicators. This means that it will be necessary to establish accessibility indicators for the regions in relation to their degree of connection to the communications network and the level of service that exists. It will then be possible to analyse objectively the contribution of the transport system to the potential development of the regions.

The analyses conducted by Mr. Izquierdo on practical applications show that a large number of different methods have been used to measure accessibility, thus showing that there is no simple, generally accepted methodology. This lack of unity is obvious both from the theoretical and practical points of view, particularly in the case of planning where the indicators used have proved to be very basic and inadequate to carry out a precise analysis of the territorial system.

Mr. Izquierdo believes, however, that the application of these accessibility indicators should not be centred exclusively on territorial analysis, or on the possible implications in terms of action on infrastructures, but should serve as a basis for economic aid distribution policy, thus contributing towards the economic and social cohesion needed by the Internal Market.

Mr. Marche concentrated on generalised costs, saying that the economic and social evaluation of a project should be carried out on the basis of an overall view of the transport system, looking at it on a long-term basis but also with regard to land use. These generalised costs take account of factors such as the cost of time (statistical distribution), expenditure and other aspects.

In regulating demand through tariffs, it is important to take account of changes in demand and in spatial structure in the course of time, in this way tolls can be increased over time.

The paper by Messrs. Nijkamp and Priemus took the view that mobility problems will not be resolved in future by simply investing in conventional physical infrastructure but by making better use of the existing infrastructure.

Infrastructure capacity is conditioned by five factors:

-- Hardware (more advanced technological standards -- higher capacity);

-- Software (better traffic and information systems -- higher capacity);

-- Orgware (better management of freight transport -- higher capacity);

-- Finware (more economic efficiency -- higher capacity);

-- Ecoware (stronger environmental criteria -- lower capacity).

A distinction can therefore be made between different types of maximum capacities:

-- Technomax: The maximum volume of traffic that is possible in an infrastructure network, given the technical constraints;

-- Enviromax: The maximum volume that is allowable, given the sustainability constraints;

-- Orgmax: The maximum volume that is possible, given the management structures and the regulatory system of the infrastructure at hand;

-- Informax: The maximum volume, given the available information.

Mr. Priemus discussed the external costs of traffic and, like other participants, stressed that mobility is much too cheap.

As demand for transport is a derived demand, it is possible to use some non-transport policies to influence modal split, increase infrastructure capacity, curb the growth of mobility and reduce the external costs:

-- Use of public transport infrastructure by urban and regional planners as a crucial structuring and guiding element in physical planning;

-- Time policy: changing opening hours of shops, working hours, holiday periods, etc.;

-- Information policy: promoting multimodal freight transport; promoting the interconnections between different modes of public transport, etc.

Mr. Priemus and Mr. Nijkamp thought that a really European transport policy is urgently needed. In this respect, they advocate the following strategy:

-- The declaration of infrastructure as being of basic economic interest to Europe;

-- The definition of a priority plan for European infrastructure networks, in terms of network quality and performance;

-- Strategic policy analysis of how to implement such a European network;

-- Creation of efficient decision-making procedures for European infrastructure;

-- A clear strategy on setting priorities among European infrastructure projects, including sound transnational financing.

Mr. Winkelmans, the first panel member to have the floor, focused on the issue of implementation of transport integration, his first point being that international network infrastructure will play a key role in the internationalisation processes. The main issue is how to establish an interactive equilibrium between the current demand-driven transport policy and supply-driven transport policy. Both imply continuous efforts for upgrading and improving existing infrastructure networks.

Public intervention was the second point raised. Mr. Winkelmans thought it much better and effective not to use the transport sector for non-sector-related reasons, such as employment, income redistribution, mobility rights, etc. In Belgium more than 80 per cent of the subsidies are mainly income-redistributional and less than 20 per cent of them are more or less efficiency-motivated or for technological reasons.

The third point concerned transport users. Although everybody in society is, directly or indirectly, an interested party where transport and mobility are concerned, most of the main users of goods transport (shippers, importers, exporters, etc.) do not seem prepared to involve themselves in the essential transport issues in order to find feasible solutions.

Mr. Winkelmans' fourth and last point covered modal choice. Changes in modal split are influenced by sound information on the social cost of transport.

Mr. Bjørnland showed some concern about transport growth in the future, since it is difficult to see an end to that growth. Indeed, the Single Market will promote the growth of transport. Working with the Iron Curtain effect and the frontier effect in transport, a conservative estimate points to growth of at least 4 or 5 per cent per year.

The question of accessibility indicators was raised by participants. Mr. Izquierdo thought it necessary to incorporate accessibility as a variable that should influence decision-makers in Europe -- particularly when using multicriteria analysis -- and to reach a consensus on the definition of indicators that will be generally accepted by the scientific community. The majority of specific applications in transport planning have not, unfortunately, made full use of the potential of these indicators, as in some cases the domain is relatively small and in other cases there have not been enough variables to adequately describe the complex situation in the area in question.

The other way to consider the social aspects in the planning process is by means of cost-benefit analysis in the evaluation process. It is necessary to have a detailed description of the different modes and their quality of service instead of simply knowing where improvements can be made in certain circumstances. Participants, rapporteurs and panel members agreed that it is essential that a global integrated approach be adopted in terms of generalised costs to compare infrastructures in the European network.

The discussion of accessibility indicators led to an exchange of views on peripheral areas. To take indicators, it is obvious that the countries that can benefit from the Cohesion Fund created after the Maastricht Treaty (Ireland, Portugal, Greece and southern Spain) have a handicap in terms of both per capita income and land transport. But there are other types of transport. The situation is changing rapidly with high-speed networks which tend to shorten distances. It is not possible to isolate transport from economic development.

One participant mentioned the possibility of coastal navigation being used as a substitute for road transport. Mr. Priemus considers there are some opportunities for such substitution in the Mediterranean and Scandinavian areas. On the other hand, however, there are cases where coastal shipping will be replaced by road transport, as is the case of the Channel Tunnel.

Another participant said that it is not possible to talk about multimodal transport, because only one mode of transport is used at a time. Intermodal transport should be the correct term. In this connection, Mr. Winkelmans said that in modern transport policy it is necessary to use transmodal approaches. Transmodality is much more important than intermodality, because the final aim is mobility together with social welfare, so the transport mode itself is not so important.

Mr. Laconte, from the UITP, focused on the problem of mobility within large towns. There is no point in reducing journey times between large towns if time is then lost in the towns themselves. In large towns there is a huge rail infrastructure that is under-used but which should be reorganised so as to provide for more efficient operations between towns.

FOURTH SESSION

THE IMPACT OF NEW TECHNOLOGIES ON EFFICIENCY AND SAFETY

Chairman: G. Dobias (F)
Rapporteurs: J.-P. Baumgartner (CH), F. Crowley (IRL), K.-H. Lenz (D)
Panel Members: P. Ayoun (F), A. Ekström (S), P. Hills (GB)

Mr. Dobias, the session Chairman, introduced this topic and emphasized the fact that transport is a very specific type of industry from the technical point of view. It is, however, an industry and therefore has to make extensive use of technology. Many types of technology are involved, because a transport system needs infrastructure for vehicles, modes of operating, labour to make the whole system function and people to use it.

The technologies involved differ considerably and in the course of time have led to increases in infrastructure capacity, in reliability of services and in the quality of the services available, particularly in terms of higher speeds, greater capacity and more comfort. They have also reduced the consumption of energy and, to some extent, helped to protect the environment.

Many action programmes regard technical solutions as fulfilling two chief aims:

-- Managing the demand for transport more efficiently; and

-- Improving and increasing infrastructure capacity.

In this latter respect, major research programmes are being developed in Europe -- such as DRIVE and PROMETHEUS -- which are based on developing telematics and communications, and at the same time improving safety.

Mr. Baumgartner gave some examples of new technologies, the first being the "rolling road" through the Alps. Its aim was to carry all road transport (lorries, coupled combinations, articulated vehicles), together with their drivers, through the Alps by rail. This system has not been successful because it is some 50 per cent more expensive than the road transport that it replaces.

One quite successful example of new technology is the high-speed train travelling on dedicated infrastructure, e.g. the TGV, whereby passenger and freight services can be separated, thereby achieving the maximum capacity for each service.

The Maglev system is another technique proposed for land transport at high speed. Its main characteristics are:

-- An infrastructure consisting of a track in a T or U shape, usually as a viaduct;

-- Vehicles propelled by linear motors with magnetic levitation; the commercial speed and infrastructure investment are on the same scale as those for the TGV.

The Swissmetro is an extension of the Maglev technique. It uses magnetic levitation and is also driven by linear motors, but it differs from Maglev in two fundamental ways:

-- The infrastructure consists of two parallel underground tubes (one in each direction);

-- In the tubes a relative vacuum is established, reducing the aerodynamic drag.

The total width of the two tubes in the two directions is three times narrower than a double-track rail tunnel and the propulsion by vacuum saves energy (about 90 per cent at a speed of 500 km/h). This technique has no harmful effects: no noise, air pollution or visual intrusion.

Swissmetro promoters are suggesting a standard running time of twelve minutes for distances of 50 to 100 km (250 to 500 km/h average speed) between two successive stops.

Mr. Baumgartner concluded by saying that there is at present no new technology for passenger transport which poses a threat to the technical and economic advantages of the car over short distances and air travel over long distances.

Mr. Crowley took up the question of reducing accidents and identified five areas in which he thinks technology could make a useful contribution:

i) Factors associated with darkness;

ii) Factors associated with skid resistance;

iii) Problems associated with young drivers;

iv) Drivers not making a successful adaptation of speed in response to a change in road layout and conditions;

v) The failure of the road engineer to transmit sufficient information to drivers about the nature of the road ahead.

Mr. Lenz, the final rapporteur, discussed the framework conditions that we have to deal with. On our planet there are 5.3 billion people and 500 million cars, 400 million of them being privately owned. To talk about private cars is therefore like talking about a minority. However, the figures are not insignificant because car ownership is distributed in a very uneven way. In Germany, for instance, there is one car for every two people, but in Russia there is one car per hundred people.

Road traffic is a space and time problem. Since present capacities in some cities cannot be increased, it is necessary to manage their use, a process that can be carried out more intelligently in future by means of computers.

Mr. Ayoun gave some examples of new technologies in France. Paris has a tele-toll system to provide time-scale charges which can then change demand, and "corridors" have been provided in towns. However, insufficient account is taken of professional vehicles such as public transport, taxis and heavy vehicles for which the new technologies should be applied.

Rail systems can also be changed by using technology to manage safety and provide for the transmission of information between trains and stations in order to reduce the interval between trains. The SACEM system based on a mono-coded processor, which is in use on line A of the Parisian express network, has increased capacity by 20 per cent by using a minimum time interval of 2.5 minutes.

The ASTREE programme, for automatic monitoring of trains in real time, aims both to improve rail safety by eliminating all risk of collision and to increase capacity. The equipment is in the train rather than on the line and information is transmitted between trains by radio. The TGV's technological programmes are also being extended to respond to increased and diversified demand insofar as this train will be running on European networks with different electrical systems.

The COMMUTOR system is being developed in France in connection with combined transport. This is a rapid transfer system, which will improve combined transport operations by reducing both the transfer time and cost and increasing flows.

Mr. Ekström described a project to introduce as much new road traffic information technology as possible in the Gothenburg area so as to carry out full-scale trials. A simulation has been carried out with a view to ascertaining how the various technologies affect travel time. The conclusion reached is that the effects are marginal and that the application of a full price mechanism has the greatest impact.

This conclusion had prompted Mr. Ekström to ask certain questions:

-- Should we invest in conventional technology (more and better roads), or in more sophisticated technologies (transponder beacons, etc.)?

-- Should we invest in hardware and software, or in education, human resources and traffic standards?

He also stressed the need to examine the social acceptance of the new technologies in relation to their technical possibilities.

Mr. Hills had certain comments to make on the rapporteurs' papers. First, Table 1 of Mr. Baumgartner's paper served as a reminder that the continuing fall in the real cost of car use is constantly contributing to the growth of private car traffic. Secondly, the fall in the real price of new cars which is expected as a result of over-production in the late 1990s means that substantial future growth of traffic is highly likely in all EC countries. Mr. Hills takes the view that urban congestion arising from unrestrained car use is the main challenge to new technologies.

Mr. Crowley's paper stresses the importance of the human factor in traffic accidents, so Mr. Hills concludes that new technology does not perhaps have much to offer as regards making the roads safer because this will depend to such a large extent on changes in social attitudes and in individual human behaviour, a view that is reflected in the balance of effort in the DRIVE and PROMETHEUS programmes which are accordingly predominantly centred on improvements in efficiency.

Mr. Hills thought that the PROMETHEUS programme referred to in Mr. Lenz's paper had so far focused on vehicle technology and improvements from the drivers' point of view. He hoped this would change, as the real improvements needed in efficiency and safety are in the public domain of traffic congestion, accidents due to inadequate control of peak demands for traffic flow and the relative speeds and headway of free-flowing traffic.

Mr. Hills drew attention to two interesting findings in Mr. Lenz's paper:

-- Huge potential benefits can clearly be derived from incident detection and on-line route guidance in a congested network;

-- Unless and until Germany adopts comprehensive maximum speed limits on its *autobahns*, car manufacturers right across Europe will continue to build machines with performance specifications of the wrong kind for traffic conditions in the 21st century.

Mr. Hills concluded by pointing out that, on the best estimate, a comprehensive route guidance system would save about 12 per cent in vehicle-kilometres, i.e. in terms of potential traffic growth, some three or four years' growth in most urban areas. He therefore thought that, in urban areas at least, overall demand would have to be curbed. The only really effective way of doing this is through direct pricing of vehicle use by means of remote automated toll-collection systems.

The general discussion opened with a number of comments on the "rolling-road" system, a system that is more expensive than transport by lorries, although account does have to be taken of savings with respect to externalities, such as social, pollution, congestion and safety costs. Mr. Baumgartner knew of no means of calculating these costs. He considered the "rolling-road" a solution for the time being until combined transport became a standard technique in general use. The future will bring more economic techniques, some of which are now being studied, more particularly those relating to container transport and the use of semi-trailers on railway bogies.

Mr. Ayoun pointed out in this connection that combined transport is a complicated mode that calls for research with a view to standardization and harmonization.

One participant drew attention to the fact that different types of infrastructure are needed for the high-speed train, Maglev, Swissmetro and other similar projects. From a technical standpoint, the high-speed train is entirely compatible with the conventional technical use of existing traditional rail networks, while the Maglev and Swissmetro are not. Accordingly, until a large network (including interfaces) is built, total supply by means of these new techniques will remain very marginal. Despite the technical benefits they may offer, therefore, the introduction of such systems may in practice be very limited.

Mr. Crowley levelled some criticism at the DRIVE programme from the safety standpoint. He found the programme to be technology-led, saying that the projects concerned with safety were not based on an adequate critical analysis of road safety needs.

Bringing the session to a close, Mr. Dobias emphasized the need for greater co-operation in research and development programmes at national and international levels. In order to get results more quickly, all those concerned in the transport system would need to combine their efforts.

FIFTH SESSION

THE ENVIRONMENT, GLOBAL AND LOCAL EFFECTS

Chairman: W. Legat (D)
Rapporteurs: R. Kürer (D) represented by J. Schmölling,
F. Befahy (F),
J. Short (IRL)
Panel Members: G.P. Können (NL)

In the absence of Mr. R. Kürer, his paper was presented by Mr. J. Schmölling. This paper was based on an extensive measurement of pollution factors in Germany.

Mr. Schmölling first identified the substances polluting the environment, at both local (within cities) and regional (larger areas) levels and explained the effects of these substances on human beings and the environment. Most of these effects are not very well known and limits for pollution levels are also not yet well established.

Secondly, he dealt with traffic emissions, one of the most widely recognised being noise. Although the perception of noise is a highly subjective matter, endeavours are being made in Germany to measure not only noise levels but also the public's perception of them.

Thirdly, Mr. Schmölling examined environmental pollution caused by traffic, saying that measurements taken in Germany over the past twenty years show what contribution traffic makes to such pollution, a contribution that is in fact substantial and mainly attributable to road traffic. The manufacture and disposal of vehicles also makes a contribution to pollution but one that cannot be attributed directly to traffic.

Lastly, the actual trends in environmental pollution by traffic were reviewed and it was seen that they point to an increase in emissions, thus underlining the need for stringent measures. Technical measures applied to vehicles will not suffice to achieve target values, and it will be necessary to introduce other measures in addition:

-- to shift road transport output to more environmentally friendly modes;

-- to improve transport operation and organisation;

-- to reduce emissions from the road traffic that remains;

-- to reduce transport operations wherever they are not absolutely essential.

Mr. Befahy discussed the railways and their impact on the natural and human environment. Taking the example of the TGV Paris-London-Amsterdam link, he described how the Belgian railways conducted their study of this project, saying that two aspects were developed:

-- A comparative study of different modes of transport (train, aircraft, car and coach) in relation to: use of land space, energy consumption, atmospheric pollution, noise and safety. A similar comparative study of freight transport was also carried out;

-- An environmental impact study, dealing mainly with the location and technical alternatives of the project.

Mr. Befahy then illustrated the comparative study with some graphs. Its main conclusions were:

-- The railway is certainly more favourable to the environment than other modes of transport, except for the waterway which has similar characteristics but is only used for freight transport;

-- Bearing in mind current forecasts of an increase in mobility and higher demand for the carriage of freight, a policy of increasing rail supply wherever possible -- and where it caters for economic needs -- can only serve to protect the environment.

Despite rail's relative advantages in terms of the environment, experience now shows that any railway project meets with a very negative reaction from people living near the new infrastructure. The environmental impact study considered alternative locations for infrastructure and technical alternatives for the implementation of the project. Following the initial phase in which the route layout was determined, three different assessments were carried out:

i) The reference assessment -- the probable situation if the project were not carried out;

ii) The rudimentary assessment -- the result of carrying out the project without taking account of measures to protect the environment;

iii) The advanced assessment -- the situation arising if the project were carried out with corrective environmental measures.

In spite of the environmental impact study, the TGV project and the construction of new lines will certainly jeopardise certain areas without any direct benefit being felt. In order to promote the TGV system in Belgium, it was decided to establish a fund to be used to pay for work designed to give environmental protection to these areas.

The railways realise that they cannot cater for the growth in demand on their own. A multimodal approach is needed, and the role of railways will necessarily be increased in the following spheres:

-- Long-distance transport by TGV;

-- Suburban services;

-- Freight hauls between major economic centres, particularly by using combined transport to a greater extent.

Although rail is considered to be favourable to the environment, that is not a sufficient reason in itself for companies and individuals to use it more frequently: individual behaviour is prompted not only by the general interest, but also by the quality and reliability of the service offered. Accordingly, if rail traffic is to be increased, that quality must be improved.

Mr. Short began by examining the relationships between transport and economic growth.

Very strong statistical relationships exist between transport and economic growth, and they are important for two reasons:

-- Environmentally, because transport growth is generally bad for the environment;

-- Politically, because they make it very difficult to suggest that transport growth should be curbed.

He then went on to discuss the concept of sustainable development as introduced in the Brundtland Report -- development that meets the needs of today without compromising the ability of future generations to meet their own needs -- which is of limited use as a guide to action. This definition may be clarified by looking at it from two angles:

-- The economic approach, putting the accent on maintaining the productivity of the total capital base;

-- The ecological approach, focused more on maintaining the stock of natural assets.

One general principle that must be recognised is that further environmental degradation is not acceptable. The attainment of existing international goals for the reduction of emissions would therefore presumably be one component of sustainability. However, very few of the countries that are party to the international agreements have set transport sector targets to achieve these reductions and very important parts of the transport sector are growing in a non-sustainable way (urban traffic, freight transport by lorries).

Secondly, Mr. Short considered the measures that ECMT countries are taking to reduce environmental problems in transport and pointed out that a great deal is happening:

-- Norms for emission standards have been substantially tightened within the EEC;

-- Some countries are introducing regular checks on vehicles in use;

-- Fuel quality has improved;

-- Environmental investment appraisal procedures have improved and they are more integrated into the decision-making process;

-- Urban traffic management has improved;

-- Fiscal incentives have been provided.

A gradual change in transport ministers' attitudes can be seen:

-- Most are beginning to argue for the best possible technology;

-- There is a new emphasis on investment in public transport;

-- Some are beginning to say that private transport is too cheap;

-- Some countries have brought together the various ministers (transport, environment, land use, energy and finance) to produce comprehensive plans for the sector;

-- In several countries, transport ministers are beginning to realise the importance of land use in planning for mobility.

This led to the third issue -- the policy challenge. Developing a more environmentally friendly transport system requires the full integration of environmental factors in transport policy decision-making. This has many facets:

-- Better information: very few countries have good data on transport and the environment. An intensive effort is needed to collect and disseminate comparable, coherent data on environmental quality and transport's responsibility for it;

-- Acceptability: new measures need the support of those affected. The main element of such measures is pricing. Convincing the population that pricing measures can work efficiently requires courage, time and effort. On account of this, it is likely that such action will not be taken lightly or often. Therefore, the traditional solution -- queuing -- will continue to be used in most places;

-- Transport policy approach: for most countries the approach of transport policy to the environment is piecemeal and ad hoc. Some countries have comprehensive plans and numerical targets to reduce transport's harmful effects. What is needed is an approach that considers the environment as an integral part of all transport policymaking.

Mr. Short then concluded by saying that most countries have a relatively narrow view on what the challenge is and there is no convincing strategy to deal with the substantial traffic growth forecast for the next twenty years.

Mr. Können focused on the question of changes in climate. Climatic change is more serious than chemical pollution or noise, because it is a slow process. It comes from CO_2 and other greenhouse gases. CO_2 has no smell and is not a poison, but it affects the radiation balance of the earth. It is a slow, long-term but progressive process and partially irreversible. Public awareness of this effect has to be stimulated and maintained.

The current projection of the greenhouse effect attributable to human activities gives a temperature rise of about 4°C in the second half of the next century. It is not clear if we are better off in a warmer climate. At least, heating is better than cooling.

The real problem lies in the earth's rapid adaptation to changes in climate. Some impacts of the temperature rise can be:

-- An increase in sea levels;
-- A shift in agricultural and fishery zones;
-- Changes in hydrological cycles.

On the whole, for some regions the effects will be beneficial and for others they will be negative.

However, the major problem is that the equilibrium of the present climate is maintained by very subtle processes. If forecasts of climate fail, it is possible that these processes may be disturbed and we may experience an enormous redistribution of heat over the earth's surface. The consequences are unpredictable and strange things can happen. So, it is very dangerous to play with the climate. The risks involved are much higher than just "a few degrees".

During the discussion, the problem of externalities in the transport sector was broached. These externalities are not direct money costs, so techniques that take account of externalities have difficulty surviving in the transport market. The need to quantify externalities in terms of money is very important. It is the way to make techniques with environmental concerns more attractive.

The question of sustainable mobility was addressed by a representative of the European Commission. The European Community adopted a policy document on the impact of transport on the environment, where sustainable mobility was defined as a balance between certain conflicting areas:

-- The importance of the socio-economic role of transport;
-- The need to protect the environment;

-- The need to safeguard the freedom of choice for the user.

Because it is very difficult to define the term "sustainable mobility", as long as no quantitative targets are fixed, four main areas of action to achieve sustainable mobility were identified:

-- The technical area and the rapid implementation of the best available technology;

-- Market organisation measures in order to ensure that optimal use is made of the available capacity;

-- A better charging of the externalities to the different modes of transport;

-- In research and development, more emphasis should be put on the environmental aspect.

In closing the session, Mr. Legat emphasized that policy action must be taken.

ALSO AVAILABLE

Structural Changes in Population and Impact on Passenger Transport. Series ECMT – Round Table. 88th (1992)				
(75 92 04 1) ISBN 92-821-1164-4	FF135	£20.00	US$35.00	DM55
High-Speed Trains. Series ECMT – Round Table. 87th (1992)				
(75 92 02 1) ISBN 92-821-1161-X	FF110	£15.00	US$27.00	DM44
Evaluating Investment in Transport Infrastructure. Series ECMT – Round Table. 86th (1992)				
(75 92 01 1) ISBN 92-821-1160-1	FF110	£15.00	US$28.00	DM43
Transport and Spatial Distribution of Activities. Series ECMT – Round Table. 85th (1991)				
(75 91 10 1) ISBN 92-821-1159-8	FF120	£17.00	US$30.00	DM49

Prices charged at the OECD Bookshop.

THE OECD CATALOGUE OF PUBLICATIONS and supplements will be sent free of charge on request addressed either to OECD Publications Service, or to the OECD Distributor in your country.

MAIN SALES OUTLETS OF OECD PUBLICATIONS
PRINCIPAUX POINTS DE VENTE DES PUBLICATIONS DE L'OCDE

ARGENTINA – ARGENTINE
Carlos Hirsch S.R.L.
Galería Güemes, Florida 165, 4° Piso
1333 Buenos Aires Tel. (1) 331.1787 y 331.2391
Telefax: (1) 331.1787

AUSTRALIA – AUSTRALIE
D.A. Book (Aust.) Pty. Ltd.
648 Whitehorse Road, P.O.B 163
Mitcham, Victoria 3132 Tel. (03) 873.4411
Telefax: (03) 873.5679

AUSTRIA – AUTRICHE
Gerold & Co.
Graben 31
Wien I Tel. (0222) 533.50.14

BELGIUM – BELGIQUE
Jean De Lannoy
Avenue du Roi 202
B-1060 Bruxelles Tel. (02) 538.51.69/538.08.41
Telefax: (02) 538.08.41

CANADA
Renouf Publishing Company Ltd.
1294 Algoma Road
Ottawa, ON K1B 3W8 Tel. (613) 741.4333
Telefax: (613) 741.5439

Stores:
61 Sparks Street
Ottawa, ON K1P 5R1 Tel. (613) 238.8985
211 Yonge Street
Toronto, ON M5B 1M4 Tel. (416) 363.3171

Les Éditions La Liberté Inc.
3020 Chemin Sainte-Foy
Sainte-Foy, PQ G1X 3V6 Tel. (418) 658.3763
Telefax: (418) 658.3763

Federal Publications
165 University Avenue
Toronto, ON M5H 3B8 Tel. (416) 581.1552
Telefax: (416) 581.1743

CHINA – CHINE
China National Publications Import
Export Corporation (CNPIEC)
16 Gongti E. Road, Chaoyang District
P.O. Box 88 or 50
Beijing 100704 PR Tel. (01) 506.6688
Telefax: (01) 506.3101

DENMARK – DANEMARK
Munksgaard Export and Subscription Service
35, Nørre Søgade, P.O. Box 2148
DK-1016 København K Tel. (33) 12.85.70
Telefax: (33) 12.93.87

FINLAND – FINLANDE
Akateeminen Kirjakauppa
Keskuskatu 1, P.O. Box 128
00100 Helsinki Tel. (358 0) 12141
Telefax: (358 0) 121.4441

FRANCE
OECD/OCDE
Mail Orders/Commandes par correspondance:
2, rue André-Pascal
75775 Paris Cedex 16 Tel. (33-1) 45.24.82.00
Telefax: (33-1) 45.24.85.00 or (33-1) 45.24.81.76
Telex: 640048 OCDE

OECD Bookshop/Librairie de l'OCDE :
33, rue Octave-Feuillet
75016 Paris Tel. (33-1) 45.24.81.67
(33-1) 45.24.81.81

Documentation Française
29, quai Voltaire
75007 Paris Tel. 40.15.70.00

Gibert Jeune (Droit-Économie)
6, place Saint-Michel
75006 Paris Tel. 43.25.91.19

Librairie du Commerce International
10, avenue d'Iéna
75016 Paris Tel. 40.73.34.60

Librairie Dunod
Université Paris-Dauphine
Place du Maréchal de Lattre de Tassigny
75016 Paris Tel. 47.27.18.56

Librairie Lavoisier
11, rue Lavoisier
75008 Paris Tel. 42.65.39.95

Librairie L.G.D.J. - Montchrestien
20, rue Soufflot
75005 Paris Tel. 46.33.89.85

Librairie des Sciences Politiques
30, rue Saint-Guillaume
75007 Paris Tel. 45.48.36.02

P.U.F.
49, boulevard Saint-Michel
75005 Paris Tel. 43.25.83.40

Librairie de l'Université
12a, rue Nazareth
13100 Aix-en-Provence Tel. (16) 42.26.18.08

Documentation Française
165, rue Garibaldi
69003 Lyon Tel. (16) 78.63.32.23

Librairie Decitre
29, place Bellecour
69002 Lyon Tel. (16) 72.40.54.54

GERMANY – ALLEMAGNE
OECD Publications and Information Centre
Schedestrasse 7
D-W 5300 Bonn 1 Tel. (0228) 21.60.45
Telefax: (0228) 26.11.04

GREECE – GRÈCE
Librairie Kauffmann
Mavrokordatou 9
106 78 Athens Tel. 322.21.60
Telefax: 363.39.67

HONG-KONG
Swindon Book Co. Ltd.
13–15 Lock Road
Kowloon, Hong Kong Tel. 366.80.31
Telefax: 739.49.75

ICELAND – ISLANDE
Mál Mog Menning
Laugavegi 18, Pósthólf 392
121 Reykjavik Tel. 162.35.23

INDIA – INDE
Oxford Book and Stationery Co.
Scindia House
New Delhi 110001 Tel.(11) 331.5896/5308
Telefax: (11) 332.5993

17 Park Street
Calcutta 700016 Tel. 240832

INDONESIA – INDONÉSIE
Pdii-Lipi
P.O. Box 269/JKSMG/88
Jakarta 12790 Tel. 583467
Telex: 62 875

IRELAND – IRLANDE
TDC Publishers – Library Suppliers
12 North Frederick Street
Dublin 1 Tel. 74.48.35/74.96.77
Telefax: 74.84.16

ISRAEL
Electronic Publications only
Publications électroniques seulement
Sophist Systems Ltd.
71 Allenby Street
Tel-Aviv 65134 Tel. 3-29.00.21
Telefax: 3-29.92.39

ITALY – ITALIE
Libreria Commissionaria Sansoni
Via Duca di Calabria 1/1
50125 Firenze Tel. (055) 64.54.15
Telefax: (055) 64.12.57

Via Bartolini 29
20155 Milano Tel. (02) 36.50.83

Editrice e Libreria Herder
Piazza Montecitorio 120
00186 Roma Tel. 679.46.28
Telefax: 678.47.51

Libreria Hoepli
Via Hoepli 5
20121 Milano Tel. (02) 86.54.46
Telefax: (02) 805.28.86

Libreria Scientifica
Dott. Lucio de Biasio 'Aeiou'
Via Coronelli, 6
20146 Milano Tel. (02) 48.95.45.52
Telefax: (02) 48.95.45.48

JAPAN – JAPON
OECD Publications and Information Centre
Landic Akasaka Building
2-3-4 Akasaka, Minato-ku
Tokyo 107 Tel. (81.3) 3586.2016
Telefax: (81.3) 3584.7929

KOREA – CORÉE
Kyobo Book Centre Co. Ltd.
P.O. Box 1658, Kwang Hwa Moon
Seoul Tel. 730.78.91
Telefax: 735.00.30

MALAYSIA – MALAISIE
Co-operative Bookshop Ltd.
University of Malaya
P.O. Box 1127, Jalan Pantai Baru
59700 Kuala Lumpur
Malaysia Tel. 756.5000/756.5425
Telefax: 757.3661

NETHERLANDS – PAYS-BAS
SDU Uitgeverij
Christoffel Plantijnstraat 2
Postbus 20014
2500 EA's-Gravenhage Tel. (070 3) 78.99.11
Voor bestellingen: Tel. (070 3) 78.98.80
Telefax: (070 3) 47.63.51

NEW ZEALAND
NOUVELLE-ZÉLANDE
Legislation Services
P.O. Box 12418
Thorndon, Wellington Tel. (04) 496.5652
Telefax: (04) 496.5698

NORWAY – NORVÈGE
Narvesen Info Center – NIC
Bertrand Narvesens vei 2
P.O. Box 6125 Etterstad
0602 Oslo 6 Tel. (02) 57.33.00
Telefax: (02) 68.19.01

PAKISTAN
Mirza Book Agency
65 Shahrah Quaid-E-Azam
Lahore 3 Tel. 66.839
Telex: 44886 UBL PK. Attn: MIRZA BK

PORTUGAL
Livraria Portugal
Rua do Carmo 70-74
Apart. 2681
1117 Lisboa Codex Tel.: (01) 347.49.82/3/4/5
Telefax: (01) 347.02.64

SINGAPORE – SINGAPOUR
Information Publications Pte. Ltd.
41, Kallang Pudding, No. 04-03
Singapore 1334 Tel. 741.5166
Telefax: 742.9356

SPAIN – ESPAGNE
Mundi-Prensa Libros S.A.
Castelló 37, Apartado 1223
Madrid 28001 Tel. (91) 431.33.99
Telefax: (91) 575.39.98

Libreria Internacional AEDOS
Consejo de Ciento 391
08009 – Barcelona Tel. (93) 488.34.92
Telefax: (93) 487.76.59

Llibreria de la Generalitat
Palau Moja
Rambla dels Estudis, 118
08002 – Barcelona
(Subscripcions) Tel. (93) 318.80.12
(Publicacions) Tel. (93) 302.67.23
Telefax: (93) 412.18.54

SRI LANKA
Centre for Policy Research
c/o Colombo Agencies Ltd.
No. 300-304, Galle Road
Colombo 3 Tel. (1) 574240, 573551-2
Telefax: (1) 575394, 510711

SWEDEN – SUÈDE
Fritzes Fackboksföretaget
Box 16356
Regeringsgatan 12
103 27 Stockholm Tel. (08) 23.89.00
Telefax: (08) 20.50.21

Subscription Agency-Agence d'abonnements
Wennergren-Williams AB
Nordenflychtsvägen 74
Box 30004
104 25 Stockholm Tel. (08) 13.67.00
Telefax: (08) 618.62.36

SWITZERLAND – SUISSE
Maditec S.A. (Books and Periodicals - Livres et périodiques)
Chemin des Palettes 4
1020 Renens/Lausanne Tel. (021) 635.08.65
Telefax: (021) 635.07.80

Librairie Payot
Service des Publications Internationales
Case postale 3212
1002 Lausanne Tel. (021) 341.33.48
Telefax: (021) 341.33.45

Librairie Unilivres
6, rue de Candolle
1205 Genève Tel. (022) 320.26.23
Telefax: (022) 329.73.18

Subscription Agency - Agence d'abonnement
Naville S.A.
38 avenue Vibert
1227 Carouge Tél.: (022) 308.05.56/57
Telefax: (022) 308.05.88

See also – Voir aussi :
OECD Publications and Information Centre
Schedestrasse 7
D-W 5300 Bonn 1 (Germany)
Tel. (49.228) 21.60.45
Telefax: (49.228) 26.11.04

TAIWAN – FORMOSE
Good Faith Worldwide Int'l. Co. Ltd.
9th Floor, No. 118, Sec. 2
Chung Hsiao E. Road
Taipei Tel. (02) 391.7396/391.7397
Telefax: (02) 394.9176

THAILAND – THAÏLANDE
Suksit Siam Co. Ltd.
113, 115 Fuang Nakhon Rd.
Opp. Wat Rajbopith
Bangkok 10200 Tel. (662) 251.1630
Telefax: (662) 236.7783

TURKEY – TURQUIE
Kültur Yayinlari Is-Türk Ltd. Sti.
Atatürk Bulvari No. 191/Kat. 13
Kavaklidere/Ankara Tel. 428.11.40 Ext. 2458
Dolmabahce Cad. No. 29
Besiktas/Istanbul Tel. 160.71.88
Telex: 43482B

UNITED KINGDOM – ROYAUME-UNI
HMSO
Gen. enquiries Tel. (071) 873 0011
Postal orders only:
P.O. Box 276, London SW8 5DT
Personal Callers HMSO Bookshop
49 High Holborn, London WC1V 6HB
Telefax: (071) 873 8200
Branches at: Belfast, Birmingham, Bristol, Edinburgh, Manchester

UNITED STATES – ÉTATS-UNIS
OECD Publications and Information Centre
2001 L Street N.W., Suite 700
Washington, D.C. 20036-4910 Tel. (202) 785.6323
Telefax: (202) 785.0350

VENEZUELA
Libreria del Este
Avda F. Miranda 52, Aptdo. 60337
Edificio Galipán
Caracas 106 Tel. 951.1705/951.2307/951.1297
Telegram: Libreste Caracas

Subscription to OECD periodicals may also be placed through main subscription agencies.

Les abonnements aux publications périodiques de l'OCDE peuvent être souscrits auprès des principales agences d'abonnement.

Orders and inquiries from countries where Distributors have not yet been appointed should be sent to: OECD Publications Service, 2 rue André-Pascal, 75775 Paris Cedex 16, France.

Les commandes provenant de pays où l'OCDE n'a pas encore désigné de distributeur devraient être adressées à : OCDE, Service des Publications, 2, rue André-Pascal, 75775 Paris Cedex 16, France.

10-1992

OECD PUBLICATIONS, 2 rue André-Pascal, 75775 PARIS CEDEX 16
PRINTED IN FRANCE
(75 93 01 1) ISBN 92-821-1180-6 - No. 46239 1993